GEORGE DU MAURIER

George
Du Maurier

Leonée Ormond

1969

ROUTLEDGE & KEGAN PAUL

LONDON

First published in 1969
by Routledge and Kegan Paul Ltd
Broadway House, 68–74 Carter Lane
London EC4
Printed in Great Britain by
Westerham Press Limited
SBN 7100 6211 7

Introduction

MY MAIN PURPOSE in writing this introduction is to thank those people who have given me access to original letters and journals of George Du Maurier and his friends. The Victorian memoir writer is always an unreliable biographical source, and in the case of Du Maurier, who became famous late in his life, anecdotal reminiscences have to be treated with even more caution than usual. Wherever possible, I have relied on contemporary evidence.

Most of Du Maurier's letters are scattered, a great many in University libraries in the United States, from whose librarians I have always received the greatest consideration. I should particularly like to thank Mr Herbert Cahoon of the Pierpont Morgan Library, and Mrs Clara Sitter, of the Miriam Lutcher Stark Library in the University of Texas, for their assistance, and their libraries for permission to publish documents in their collections. I am much indebted to Messrs Harper and Row for allowing me to quote from papers in the Harper Collection of the Pierpont Morgan Library. I have also received help from the Armstrong Browning Library, Baylor University; Colby College Library; the Milton S. Eisenhower Library, Johns Hopkins University; the New York Times; Princeton University Library; University of Oklahoma Library; and the Free Library of Philadelphia. I am grateful for permission to publish from the Houghton Library, Harvard; Haverford College Library; the Huntingdon Library, San Marino, California; the Berg Collection of the New York Public Library; the Historical Society of Pennsylvania; University of Oklahoma Press; the University Library, Yale.

In Great Britain, I have been helped by the Bodleian Library; the manuscripts department of the British Museum; the Cambridge University Library; the Brotherton Library, Leeds; and the John Rylands Library, Manchester. I am especially grateful to Miss Elizabeth Bower and Mr Victor Caudery of *Punch*. Miss Bower's help was invaluable to me, and Mr Caudery has allowed me to publish extracts from the diaries of Henry Silver and Shirley Brooks, both in

v

the *Punch* collection. I am also fortunate enough to be allowed to quote material from the Whistler Collection in the University of Glasgow, and I should like to thank Mr W. R. Hardie and Professor Andrew Maclaran Young for their kindness. I am also grateful to Mr Denys Sutton, for allowing me to republish material on 'A Legend of Camelot' which first appeared in *Apollo Magazine* for January 1967.

The largest collection of Du Maurier manuscripts is in the possession of his grand-daughter, Lady Browning (Daphne Du Maurier). This book could scarcely have been written without her help. Her kindness in lending me many of the letters received and written by George Du Maurier, in particular his correspondence with Thomas Armstrong, has greatly increased the scope of my biography, and Lady Browning's letters, always full of helpful information, have been a constant source of pleasure.

Among the others who have helped to clarify my ideas on various aspects of the subject, I should like to express my gratitude to Mr Richard Price, the historian of *Punch*, whose freshness of approach gave me new insight into the Victorian sense of humour. I owe particular thanks to Professor Terence Spencer of Birmingham University, who first introduced me to the subject, and who has always taken a sympathetic and helpful interest in my work. Above all, I wish to thank my husband, who has suffered bravely from Du Maurier for four years, and who gave up much of his time to help me with the final corrections.

A great many others have helped me in various ways: the Art Gallery and Regional Museum, Aberdeen; the Walker Art Gallery, Liverpool; the National Portrait Gallery; Miss Sybil Beaumont; Mr and Mrs Ruthven Davies; Mr Kerry Downes; Miss Angela Du Maurier; Miss Jeanne Du Maurier; Mr N. Edwards and Mr A. C. R. Pope have allowed me to reproduce drawings and paintings in their collections. In my attempts to track down some particular part of the background to the period, or to see places and objects associated with the Du Mauriers, I have been assisted by Lord Baldwin of Bewdley; Mr Bird of the Hampstead Town Hall; Miss Janet Cowan; Mrs Gwendoline Du Maurier; Mrs Elsie Duncan Jones; Mrs Dora Footman; Miss Genevieve Hawkins; Mr Bevis Hillier; Miss Marie Isaacs; Mr Evelyn Joll; Mr Lionel Lambourne; Mrs Mary Links; Lady Mander; Mr Nicholas Llewellyn Davies; Mr Ian Lowe; Mr Oliver Millar; Mrs Rosalind Millar; Mr John Randle; Mr M. R. Schweitzer; Mrs Virginia Surtees; Miss Tedbury of the Registrar's Department, University College, London; Miss Maud Waddell; Miss M. A. Woods; and by Professor Cocking, Mrs Norma Rinsler, and Dr F. R. Smith, all of the French Department, Kings College, University of London.

The following publishers and copyright holders have given me permission to use quotations, which I gratefully acknowledge: Mr John James for letters written by Henry James; Mr Gerald Millar for *George Du Maurier and Others* by C. C. Hoyer Millar; Mr Martin Secker for *Thomas Armstrong C.B. A Memoir*; Ernest Benn Ltd for *Confessions of a Caricaturist* by Harry Furniss; Chatto and Windus Ltd for *George Du Maurier* by T. M. Wood; Constable and Co Ltd for *The Life and Letters of Alfred Ainger* by Edith Sichel; Hutchinson Publishing Group for *Art and Anecdote* by M. H. Stephen Smith; Methuen and Co Ltd for *The Life and Letters of J. E. Millais* by J. G. Millais; John Murray for 'George Du Maurier at Thirty Three' by E. V. Lucas; John Murray and the Public Trustee for *The Diary of a Journalist* and *Sixty Years in the Wilderness* by Sir Henry Lucy; University of Oklahoma Press for *R. R. Bowker, Militant Liberal* by E. McClung Fleming; Oxford University Press for *A Long Retrospect* by T. A. Guthrie; Sir Isaac Pitman and Sons Ltd for *A Great Punch Editor* by G. S. Layard; and Yale University Press for *The George Eliot Letters*, edited by G. H. S. Haight.

Highgate   L.O.

Contents

INTRODUCTION   *Page* v

ILLUSTRATIONS   *Page* xi

1 *The Early Years*   PAGE 1

2 *Paris*   PAGE 34

3 *Malines and Dusseldorf*   PAGE 64

4 *London*   PAGE 84

5 Punch   PAGE 142

6 *Hampstead I*   PAGE 204

7 *The Aesthetic Movement*   PAGE 243

8 *The Social Cartoonist*   PAGE 308

9 *Hampstead II*   PAGE 361

10 *Henry James*   PAGE 392

11 Peter Ibbetson   PAGE 416

12 Trilby   PAGE 431

13 '*Joe Sibley*'   PAGE 463

14 *Oxford Square*   PAGE 480

BIBLIOGRAPHY   *Page* 499

INDEX   *Page* 503

Abbreviations

ARMSTRONG – *Thomas Armstrong C.B. A Memoir*, edited by L. M. Lamont (1912)

BROOKS' DIARY – Manuscript diaries of Shirley Brooks for 1867, 1872, in the *Punch* offices

DIARY – 'George Du Maurier at Thirty-Three', edited by E. V. Lucas. *Cornhill Magazine*, CL (October 1934), 385–410

THE DU MAURIERS – D. Du Maurier, *The Du Mauriers* (1937)

GERALD – D. Du Maurier, *Gerald* (1934)

Harper's New Monthly Magazine – Henry James, 'George Du Maurier', *Harper's New Monthly Magazine*, XXV (September 1897), 594–609

HOYER MILLAR – C. Hoyer Millar, *George Du Maurier and Others* (1937)

ILLUSTRATION – G. Du Maurier, 'The Illustration of Books from the serious Artist's Point of View', *Magazine of Art* (August and September 1890), pp. 349–353 and 371–375

LETTERS – '*The Young George Du Maurier: A Selection of his Letter, 1860–67*, edited by Daphne Du Maurier (1951)

The Martian – G. Du Maurier, *The Martian* (1897)

MILLAIS – J. G. Millais, *The Life and Letters of Sir John Everett Millais*. 2 vols. (1899)

Peter Ibbetson – G. Du Maurier, *Peter Ibbetson*. One volume edition (1891)

SHERARD – R. H. Sherard, 'The Author of Trilby', *McClure's Magazine*, IV (October 1895), 391–400

SICHEL – E. Sichel, *The Life and Letters of Alfred Ainger* (1906)

SILVER – Manuscript diary of Henry Silver (1858–1870), in the *Punch* offices

S.P.S. – G. Du Maurier, *Social Pictorial Satire* (1898)

Trilby – G. Du Maurier, *Trilby*. One volume illustrated edition (1894)

WOOD – T. M. Wood, *George Du Maurier* (1913)

Illustrations

*Illustrations are reproduced the same size as they
originally appeared, except where a size is given*

1. La Mare d'Auteuil, *Peter Ibbetson* (1891)   17
2. A Little Christmas Dream, *Punch* (1868) [8 × 6¼ in.]   18
3. The Institution F. Brossard, *The Martian* (1896)   21
4. Recollections of an English Gold Mine, *Once a Week* (1861)   29
5. Wharton Street, Pentonville, *Peter Ibbetson*   33
6. The Latin Quarter, *Trilby*   35
7. Taffy à l'échelle, *Trilby*   39
8. The Fox and the Crow, *Trilby*   41
9. The Atelier Gleyre (1857)   42
10. The Happy Life, Barbizon, *Trilby*   45
11. My Sister Dear, *Trilby*   52
12. All as it used to be, *Trilby*   55
13. Ye Societie of our Ladye in the Fields (1857)   57
14. Cooking the Dinner (1857)   59
15. Self-portrait sketch, Moscheles, above, as the evil genius (1858)   64
16. Moscheles et moi si nous avions été de beau sexe (1857)   65
17. Sketch of Du Maurier's oil painting executed in Antwerp (1857)   67
18. Portrait of Picciola (1858)   71
19. Coffee and Brassin in Bobtail's Rooms (1858)   74
20. A mesmeric seance in Mrs L's back parlour (1858) [4 × 7 in.]   75
21. Meeting in Dusseldorf (1860)   79
22. Am Rhein, *The Martian*   80
23. At the Hofrath's door (1859)   81
24. Sketch – Malines to London (1860)   83
25. Emma Wightwick, *Punch* vignette (1862)   85
26. Du Maurier's programme for 'The Thumping Legacy (1861)   101
27. The artist's studio, *Punch* (1860)   110
28. Whistler as the letter 'Q', *Punch* (1860)   111
29. On her deathbed, *Once a Week* (1861)   112
30. Beatrix, *Henry Esmond* by W. M. Thackeray (1868)   115
31. Non Satis *Once a Week* (1860)   120
32. A Time to dance, *Good Words* (1861)   127
33. Santa, or a woman's tragedy, *Once a Week* (1862)   135
34. Santa, or a woman's tragedy, *Once a Week* (1862)   136
35. The Notting Hill Mystery, *Once a Week* (1862–3)   137
36. The Notting Hill Mystery, *Once a Week* (1862–3)   138
37. Sketch from letter (1861)   139

38. Initial letter 'O', *London Society* (1863)   142
39. The Cicilian Pirates, *Cornhill* (1863)   144
40. Hurlock Chase, *The Leisure Hour* (1865)   145
41. Hurlock Chase, *The Leisure Hour* (1865)   146
42. Mokeanna or the white witness, *Punch* (1863)   147
43. Wives and Daughters, *Cornhill* (1864–5)   149
44. Wives and Daughters, *Cornhill* (1864–5)   150
45. The Awdries, *The Leisure Hour* (1865)   151
46. The Awdries, *The Leisure Hour* (1865)   154
47. Emma and Guy Du Maurier   159
48. A Pre-Raphaelite Sketch (*c* 1861)   174
49. A Legend of Camelot, Part 1, *Punch* (1866) [$5\frac{1}{4} \times 7$ in.]   177
50. A Legend of Camelot, Part 2, *Punch* (1866) [$5\frac{1}{2} \times 7$ in.]   177
51. A Legend of Camelot, Part 3, *Punch* (1866) [5×7 in.]   178
52. A Legend of Camelot, Part 4, *Punch* (1866) [$8\frac{1}{2} \times 4\frac{1}{2}$ in.]   179
53. A Legend of Camelot, Part 5, *Punch* (1866) [$5\frac{1}{2} \times 7$ in.]   180
54. The Royal Academy Exhibition, *London Society* (1863)   185
55. The St. John's Wood Clique. Initial letter 'C' by Linley Sambourne, *Punch* (1873)   193
56. Scenes of Club Life, *Punch* (1873)   195
57. Sketch of the Du Maurier family and Tom Armstrong (1866) [$3\frac{1}{2} \times 6\frac{3}{4}$ in.]   200
58. To Sufferers from Nervous Depression, *Punch* (1869)   202
59. The *Punch* dinner card (1870)   203
60. Initial letter 'M', Wives and Daughters, *Cornhill* (1864–5)   204
61. One of a series of engravings of the Du Maurier family (*c* 1873)   211
62. The Benefit of the Doubt, *Punch* (1874)   215
63. Reading without Tears, *Punch* (1869)   217
64. Elements of Mischief in Hypocritical Repose, *Punch* (1875)   218
65. *Divine and Moral Songs for Children* by Isaac Watts (1865)   221
66. Delicate Consideration, *Punch* (1873)   223
67. Kind and Considerate, *Punch* (1874)   226
68. A Fact – (Free Translation), *Punch* (1877)   229
69. George Eliot (*c* 1878)   235
70. Hobson's Choice, *Punch* (1872)   238
71. Sketch for 'How we slept at the Chalet des Chevres', *Cornhill* (1863)   242
72. Fleur des Alpes, *Punch* (1880)   244
73. Maudle on the Choice of a Profession, *Punch* (1881)   252
74. Distinguished Amateurs: the Art Critic, *Punch* (1880)   255
75. The Appalling Diffusion of Taste, *Punch* (1881)   256
76. Prudence at the Grosvenor, *Prudence* (1882) [$6\frac{1}{2} \times 4\frac{1}{2}$ in.]   259
77. A Love Agony, *Punch* (1880)   260
78. The Diffusion of Aesthetic Taste, *Punch* (1881)   263
79. Nincompoopiana, *Punch* (1881)   265
80. The Rise and Fall of the Jack Spratts, *Punch* (1878)   270
81. Nincompoopiana – The Mutual Admiration Society, *Punch* (1880)   271

82. Modern Aesthetics, *Punch* (1878)   272
83. An Impartial Statement in Black and White, *Punch* (1881)   275
84. A Damper, *Punch* (1876)   276
85. The Rise and Fall of the Jack Spratts, *Punch* (1878)   279
86. Refinements of Modern Speech, *Punch* (1879)   282
87. Music and Aesthetics, *Punch* (1878)   286
88. The Cimabue Browns – (Train up a Child &c), *Punch* (1880)   288
89. The Passion for Old China, *Punch* (1874)   291
90. Acute Chinamania, *Punch* (1875)   292
91. The Six-Mark Tea-Pot, *Punch* (1880)   294
92. An Aesthetic Midday Meal, *Punch* (1880)   300
93. Vers de Société, *Punch* (1877)   303
94. Initial letter 'A' (*c* 1861)   309
95. Est Modus in Rebus, *Punch* (1879) [9 × 6½ in.]   310
96. True Humility, *Punch* (1895)   313
97. A Pathetic Appeal, *Punch* (1874)   316
98. Farewell to fair Normandy, *Punch* (1880) [9 × 6½ in.]   318
99. Love's Labours Lost, *Punch* (1884)   319
100. Distinguished Amateurs – The Reciter, *Punch* (1883)   320
101. Picture Sunday, *Punch* (1887)   322
102. Original drawing for 'Knowing one's Place', *Punch* (1875)
    [9½ × 6 in.]   324
103. Egoism, *Punch* (1882)   325
104. Lady Gatheremall at Home, *Punch* (1881)   332
105. Humility in Splendour, *Punch* (1878) [6½ × 9 in.]   337
106. Two Victims of the Turf, *Punch* (1888)   342
107. The Ruling Passion, *Punch* (1872)   345
108. Whitsuntide Humours, *Punch* (1877) [9 × 6½ in.]   347
109. Bad Grammar, but Good Pluck, *Punch* (1885) [6½ × 9 in.]   348
110. Terrible Result of Higher Education for Women, *Punch* (1874)   355
111. Fifty Years Hence, *Punch* (1890) [9 × 6¾ in.]   356
112. Old Nikotin stealing 'away the brains' of his Devotees,
    Punch (1869)   358
113. Mistress and Pupil, *Punch* (1883)   359
114. Vignette from *Punch* (1863)   361
115. Souvenir de Fontainbleau, *Punch* (1886)   364
116. *The Adventures of Harry Richmond* by George Meredith (1880)   371
117. *Misunderstood* by Florence Montgomery (1874)   372
118. Der Tod als Freund, *English Illustrated Magazine* (1884)   374
119. Original drawing for 'A Combination of Disagreeables', *Punch*
    (1888) [6¾ × 10½ in.]   378
120. At the R.A. – Triumph of Realistic Art, *Punch* (1879)   385
121. Aesthetics, *Punch* (1886)   388
122. Vignette for 'Washington Square', *Cornhill* (1880)   393
123. Cricketiana, *Punch* (1883)   408
124. A Good-bye to Jolly Whitby, *Punch* (1882)   411
125. Sketch for the title-page of *Peter Ibbetson*   415
126. Initial letter 'I' from *Peter Ibbetson*   416

127. The Big Drayman, *Peter Ibbetson*   419
128. Portrait Charmant, *Peter Ibbetson*   424
129. The Duchess of Towers, *Peter Ibbetson*   427
130. Vignette from *Peter Ibbetson*   430
131. Wistful and Sweet, *Trilby*   444
132. Cuisine bourgeouise en Bohème, *Trilby*   447
133. 'Svengali...Svengali...Svengali!', *Trilby*   450
134. An Incubus, *Trilby*   455
135. Vignette from *Trilby*   461
136. Initial letter 'F' from *The Story of a Feather* by Douglas Jerrold (1867)   463
137. The Two Apprentices, *Trilby* (*Harper's Monthly Magazine* version)   464
138. Sketch, *Magazine of Art* (1890)   481
139. A Little White Point of Interrogation, *The Martian*   486
140. Three Little Maids from School, *The Martian*   489
141. I'm a Philistine and not Ashamed, *The Martian*   490
142. Vignette from *Trilby*   498

Plates

Between pages 240 and 241

1. GEORGE DU MAURIER, self-portrait. Watercolour. From the collection of Miss Jeanne Du Maurier.
2. EDWARD JOHN POYNTER, as a student in Paris, from a drawing by an unknown contemporary.
3. GEORGE DU MAURIER, as a student, from a miniature by an unknown artist. From the collection of Lady Browning.
4. JAMES WHISTLER, in Paris, by Edward Poynter. Photograph of a lost drawing.
5. SELF-PORTRAIT in oils of George Du Maurier. Executed in Paris in 1856 or 1857. In the collection of Mr Ruthven Davies.
6. EMMA DU MAURIER. From an unfinished oil painting by George Du Maurier. In the collection of Mr Ruthven Davies.
7. COX AND BOX. A photograph of the staff taken in 1867 by the London Stereoscopic Company.
8. GEORGE, EMMA and MAY DU MAURIER. From a photograph by Julia Margaret Cameron, 1874.
9. MAY DU MAURIER, from a photograph by Julia Margaret Cameron, 1874.
10. SPONSA DE LIBANO, by Edward Burne-Jones, Walker Art Gallery, Liverpool.
11. THE PRIVATE VIEW OF THE ROYAL ACADEMY 1881, by W. P. Frith. In the collection of Mr A. C. R. Pope.
12. CANON ALFRED AINGER, by George Du Maurier. 1881. From a watercolour by George Du Maurier. National Portrait Gallery.
13. HENRY JAMES by Rudolph Lehmann. 1887. From a lithograph by Rudolph Lehmann.
14. GEORGE DU MAURIER, by J. E. Millais. 1882. Macdonald of Kepplestone Collection. The Art Gallery and Regional Museum, Aberdeen.
15. MAY DU MAURIER, by George Du Maurier. 1889. From a watercolour. Collection of Lady Browning.
16. SELF-PORTRAIT in oils of George Du Maurier probably painted in 1880. National Portrait Gallery.
17. THE 'PUNCH' STAFF AT THE PARIS EXHIBITION. 1887. Photograph.
18. GEORGE DU MAURIER, from a photograph taken in the 1890s.

Chapter 1

The Early Years

IN 1895, Robert Harborough Sherard, a young journalist and writer, was commissioned by *McClure's Magazine* to interview the author of the best-selling novel of the day, *Trilby*. The author in question, George Du Maurier, was something of an oddity, for he had only begun writing in middle age after thirty years as a *Punch* cartoonist. A Parisian by birth, his easy familiarity with French life, and more particularly with the student life of the Quartier Latin, helped to make the book wildly popular. In order to get his interview with the novelist, Sherard had to make his way up to Hampstead, where Du Maurier had lived since 1869. No cabman willingly undertook Haverstock Hill without substantial payment, as Du Maurier had found to his cost, so Sherard walked up through Hampstead Heath to New Grove House, the Du Mauriers' large and oddly constructed home. He was received kindly, and taken into a comfortable room, 'with thick carpets and inviting arm-chairs'.[1] There the experienced interviewer took stock of the quiet and diminutive Du Maurier, surrounded by his own drawings and watercolours, with the opening chapters of a new novel standing neatly on a desk beside him. Sherard was immediately impressed by his warmth and friendliness, but, with a perception lacking even in Du Maurier's closest friends, saw in him:

> a man who has suffered greatly, haunted by some evil dream or disturbing apprehension. His welcome is gentle and kindly, but he does not smile, even when he is saying a clever and smile-provoking thing.[2]

The interview began with Du Maurier's account of his background and origins:

> My full name is George Louis Palmella Busson du Maurier, but we were of very small nobility. . . . Our real family name is Busson; the 'Du

1. Sherard, p. 392.
2. Sherard, p. 392.

Maurier' comes from the Chateau le Maurier, built some time in the
fifteenth century, and still standing in Anjou or Maine, but a brewery
to-day.[3]

This château, Du Maurier went on to explain, had belonged to
cousins of the Busson Du Mauriers, the Auberys, with whom they
had intermarried for centuries. Warming to the subject, and clearly
proud of his ancestry, he referred to family papers in the bank, and to
a Busson tomb in Notre Dâme de Paris. From these he deduced that
the Busson genealogy went back to the twelfth century at least. More
recently, he told Sherard, his grandfather, Robert-Mathurin Du
Maurier, had been a gentleman glassblower, driven into exile in
England during the French Revolution, who, on returning to
France, had found his old estates lost for ever.

That this whole family history was complete fiction George Du
Maurier never knew. Throughout his life he remained pathetically
proud of his noble origins in France, introducing them, thinly disguised into his first novel, *Peter Ibbetson*. In his youth he had taken the
trouble to go to the British Museum reading room, and had traced
the history of the Du Mauriers and their château back through the
centuries. Shortly before he met Sherard, he had even sent his wife
and daughter to look at the ancient family home in the village of
Chenu on the Loir. He was not, therefore, being entirely truthful
when he told Sherard that the question of descent was not one to be
taken too seriously.

It is only recently that evidence has come to light which con-
clusively proves that the Busson Du Mauriers were a perfectly
ordinary artisan family, and not aristocrats at all. Even the name, Du
Maurier, was a late addition without any foundation in gentility.
Du Maurier's grand-daughter, Lady Browning (Daphne Du
Maurier), began to investigate the records of La Sarthe, the area of
France from which the family came, and discovered that the
Bussons were master glass-blowers, but no more, and that Robert-
Mathurin Du Maurier had no right to his title of 'Gentilhomme
verrier', or indeed to his surname.[4] It was he, with his delusions of
grandeur, who had invented the whole family history. It was not the
French Revolution, but a charge of fraud, which brought him to
England. The few known facts about Robert-Mathurin Busson all

3. Sherard, p. 392.
4. These facts are published in Daphne Du Maurier's novel, *The Glass Blowers*
(1963).

point to a man with a pathological obsession with social status. During his childhood, his father had rented a château in order to use the glass-works in the grounds. Possibly the pleasure of living in such a place stimulated Robert-Mathurin's imagination, while the fact that it belonged to someone else accentuated his sense of inferiority.

This particular combination of self-delusion and conscious deception is not uncommon, and is usually, as in Robert-Mathurin's case, allied with an amoral attitude to other people's money. In order to support the fiction of gentility, he had to keep up a show of substance; his financial incompetence was directly related to his obsessive pretensions. Thoroughly irresponsible, Robert-Mathurin was always hoping for some stroke of good fortune which would release him for ever from his worries. Early in life he was imprisoned in La Force for fraud, when one of his more ambitious plans came to grief. Fear of a second prison sentence drove him to London in 1789, with his young second wife, Marie-Françoise Bruaire.

Once in London, among the earliest émigrés, Robert-Mathurin Busson was able to invent a noble family; poverty was not exceptional among the French exiles in St Pancras, where several aristocrats lived in reduced circumstances. No-one was able to refute the claims which Robert-Mathurin made for himself, and by 1793 he was signing himself, Busson Du Maurier, when buying a house in Cleveland Street. This territorial distinction he took from the name of his birthplace, the farmhouse le Maurier. Unfortunately, there was a real château le Maurier, and a real Comte du Maurier in La Sarthe, and, although this fact later confirmed the story in George Du Maurier's mind, it may have given Robert-Mathurin a few uneasy moments. The story of the relationship between the Auberys, the genuine counts, and the Busson Du Mauriers, which George Du Maurier mentioned to Sherard in his interview, was clearly added by his grandfather to explain why the family had not recently lived in the château itself.

Robert-Mathurin, as a result of his simple origins, was better off than most of the émigrés, for the Whitefriars glass firm took him on as a skilled craftsman. He ought, by steady work, to have established himself more comfortably than most, had his flair for speculation not re-asserted itself. This time he spent seven months in the King's Bench prison, emerging in February 1799. By 1802, he was the father of six children; two boys, Robert and Jacques, were followed by a daughter Louise. George Du Maurier's father, Louis-Mathurin, was their fourth child, born in 1797, and a daughter and a son, Adelaide and Guillaume, completed the family. In 1802, the Treaty of Amiens granted an amnesty to returning exiles, and Robert-Mathurin decided to go back to France, ostensibly to settle his financial affairs, but in reality to escape from the responsibility of his wife and children. After Robert-Mathurin's departure his family continued to exist on a small pension from the British government until they too were able to return to France. No record of their life in London during these years is known, but Robert-Mathurin never returned to them, and they may well have imagined that he was dead. In fact, he lived in France alone for nine years, dying as a schoolmaster in Tours in 1811.

Marie-Françoise Du Maurier returned to France some time after 1815, and settled in Paris with her four youngest children; Robert had elected to stay in London, and Jacques soon departed for a job in Hamburg. Life was hard for the returning émigrés, but an application made by Louise to the government in 1816 produced a civil pension of two hundred francs a year, which was better than nothing. While Louise, the elder daughter, taught English in a school for young ladies, Louis-Mathurin, who had a fine singing voice, began to train at the Conservatoire, intending to become an opera singer. It was unfortunate that the family's pretensions soon forced him to give up a career which was considered unsuitable, but which was the only one in which he might have succeeded. His choice of science was very much a second best. Louis-Mathurin's science, like his father's financial speculation, was based on great optimism, and a feeling that the world owed him a living. His work was entirely concerned with inventions which never succeeded, but which precluded any kind of settled or remunerative work. As his son put it: 'He was a man of scientific tastes, and lost his money in inventions which never came to anything'.[5]

Possessed of great natural charm, Louis-Mathurin was very attractive to women. It is, therefore, surprising that he did not make a 'good match', which would have rendered the business of earning a living unnecessary. Instead, in 1831, at the age of thirty-four, he married a woman of his own age, not blessed with good looks or a sizeable fortune. Ellen Clarke had been an adult pupil under his sister at La Maison d'Education in the rue Neuve St Étienne, and lived with her mother, Mrs Mary-Anne Clarke, in Auteuil. If they

5. Sherard, p. 394.

were not wealthy, they had at least a settled income of six-hundred pounds a year, the result of a successful attempt to blackmail the English Royal Family.

Mary-Anne Clarke, Ellen's mother, was the step-daughter of a London compositor. Attracted by her precocious good looks, one of her step-father's employers sent her to school for two-and-a-half years at Ham in Essex, where she acquired a limited education. She left at the age of fifteen, and in the following year married Joseph Clarke, the delinquent son of a merchant. Early in their married life, Clarke became a drunkard, and his wife eventually left him to become one of the most famous Regency courtesans. Ellen Clarke, George Du Maurier's mother, was the youngest of her five children, and may well not have been Clarke's daughter. She was certainly not, however, the daughter of her mother's most famous lover, Frederick Duke of York, brother of George III, who set Mary-Anne up in Gloucester Place in 1803, when Ellen was already six years old. The Royal mistress stayed in Gloucester Place for three years, in such extravagant luxury that even the Duke's generous presents could not satisfy her creditors. It was to increase her income that she began to accept bribes from army officers, desperate for preferment, who knew her influence with the Duke, then Commander-in-Chief of the British Army.

It is not certain whether or not Mary-Anne Clarke did secure any commissions from her lover, for none of the instances cited at the subsequent enquiry was conclusive, but she certainly accepted bribes. When the Duke left her in 1806, and then cut off her allowance in 1808, Mary-Anne decided that the only satisfactory revenge was blackmail, or the downfall of the Duke. She threatened to publish his letters, and then offered to sell her story to a radical group of politicians, eager to discredit the Duke, the crown and the established government. In January 1809, the leader of this group, Gwilym Lloyd Wardle, proposed in the House of Commons that a Committee of Investigation be set up to enquire into the Duke's conduct. The Committee, made up of the whole House, began sitting on 12 February 1809, and Mary-Anne, who was the chief witness against the Duke, was called to the Bar of the House no less than twelve times, and subjected to penetrating and frequently offensive questions. Although the Duke was formally acquitted of any misconduct, his reputation was so damaged that he was forced to resign. Mary-Anne, who clearly knew more than she should about the internal affairs of the Army, was the heroine of the hour. Her

triumph was short-lived, for two years later the Duke was rein-
stated, and her group of friends discredited. She still had one last
card to play, the Duke's love letters, and she played it for all it was
worth. After suppressing publication of her memoirs at the last
moment, she sold the letters to the Duke in return for a lump sum of
ten-thousand pounds and an annuity of four-hundred pounds a year
for herself, and two-hundred for each of her daughters. It was on this
annuity that her grandson, George Du Maurier, trained as an art
student in Paris. Although Mary-Anne had been paid off by the
Royal Family, she did not retire from political intrigue. She wrote a
number of highly libellous and sensational pamphlets, chiefly
against her former allies, which brought her further notoriety. In
1814 she foolishly attacked William Fitzgerald, Chancellor of
Ireland, who successfully sued for libel. Nine months in prison
proved a salutary lesson, and Mary-Anne emerged chastened and
subdued. As she had already written in one of her pamphlets: 'When
deserted by my Royal friend, I submitted to a life of undeserved
seclusion with more fortitude than falls to the generality of my sex
under similar circumstances'.[6] Her restlessness now drove her to
travel, and she wandered between English and continental resorts,
pursued by those who wanted to hear her reminiscences, but no
longer in the limelight.

With her elder daughter married and living in London, and with
her son in the army, Mary-Anne could always rely on Ellen as a
constant companion. Plain and unengaging, the younger daughter
had little chance of escaping from the demands and taunts of her
mother. All hope of marriage must have seemed extinct by 1831,
when she was already thirty-three. The advent of the affable and
good-looking Louis-Mathurin Du Maurier, who professed to be in
love with her, and then proposed marriage, must have seemed
miraculous. The repressed and deprived Ellen fell desperately in love
with him and accepted his proposal at once, without considering his
prospects or his remarkably slender achievement.

They were married in April 1831, at the British Embassy in Paris,
and settled in 'a pretty apartment' at no. 80 Champs Elysees. The
marriage was not a success, although it was saved from complete
breakdown by the loyalty and determination of Ellen, who brought
up her children with a courage inherited from her mother. Had the
Du Mauriers been more fortunate, a secure routine of every-day life

6. *The Rival Princes* (1810), p. vii.

might have established a pattern of affection and dependence. The chief basis of security, however, is freedom from acute financial worry, and this the Du Mauriers never enjoyed. As irresponsible as his father, Louis-Mathurin rose above his family duties on a cloud of promises which he could not fulfil. During the twenty-five years of their married life, his financial incompetence, linked to a love of speculation, kept the family on the very verge of penury. Ellen, driven to desperation, nagged him endlessly, which only increased his evasiveness. Like her husband, she fed on an illusion of grandeur, which subtly affected her attitude to the ordinary processes of earning a living. In spite of their simple lodgings and generally reduced circumstances, they both lived in hope of a sudden windfall. Their eldest son, George, was born while their illusions were still fresh, and they communicated to him the dream-world which they inhabited. It found expression in the three remarkable novels he wrote in old age.

Ellen had several miscarriages before George, her first child, was born on 6 March 1834. Louis-Mathurin immediately wrote to his sister:

> Ellen gave birth to a son yesterday, the sixth of March. She stood the ordeal well, and the child is strong and beautiful. I have already dedicated him to science. May he live up to our expectations. Ellen's mother crossed over from England to be with her for the event, and is full of her grandchild, whom she declares to be the image of myself. We have all three been discussing his future, and realise the importance of a string of initials before his name. And so we intend to name him George, after Ellen's brother, Louis, after myself, and Palmella, as a mark of respect towards your amiable friend and protector.[7]

The choice of the child's names, George Louis Palmella Busson Du Maurier, was an indication of Louis-Mathurin's hopes. Ellen Clarke's brother, George, who was doing well in the army, was asked to be one of the baby's godfathers. Even greater results were expected from the compliment to the Duke of Palmella, a wealthy Portuguese noble, whose wife was an old friend of Louis-Mathurin's sister, Louise; Palmella's eldest son agreed to be the other godfather. In 1830, Louise had contracted an unfortunate marriage with a young man who imagined her to be a great heiress. After the wedding, he discovered his mistake, and left at once. The Duchess of

7. *The Du Mauriers*, p. 115.

Palmella then asked Louise to come to Lisbon, where she was employed as a governess and companion for many years. Immediate results from Louis-Mathurin's gracious gesture were disappointing, but Palmella did extend his patronage to the Du Maurier family a few years later.

The birth of a son did nothing whatever to steady Louis-Mathurin, who was still undecided about his future:

> What course I shall take after a short time I cannot yet fix as it will depend upon many circumstances. N'importe all for the best and I trust we shall in a very few years be enjoying peace and happiness and plenty of the good things of this world in some snug quarter and the Devil will then never tempt me to stroll when once I can do without it. [8]

The indecision of his parents affected George from his earliest days. He was weaned too early, when his first nurse suddenly departed, and was breast-fed again by two unsatisfactory replacements. Louis-Mathurin was irritated by the trouble with the wet-nurses, but he found adequate compensation in the baby's good looks, his 'fair skin' and 'bright sparkling eyes'. [9]

From the first, George Du Maurier was subject to a conflict between his two nationalities. He was not only half-French and half-English, but the grandchild of a Frenchman exiled in England, and of an Englishwoman exiled in France. The aching nostalgia, which characterized his personality, had its roots as much in this family history as in his own memories of childhood. His early years were happy, and he remained ignorant of the financial worries which always dogged his parents. His mother adored him: an attractive child, blue-eyed and brown-haired, with a vulnerable look that brought out protective instincts in others. This shy look remained with him throughout his life, and in portraits of him his eyes gaze out, open and unprotected, always a little tentative.

The first of George's many trips across the English Channel was undertaken with his mother, some time before Christmas 1834. They went to stay at Rotherfield in Sussex, where Mary-Anne Clarke had taken a house. George played there with his cousins, Alfred and Charles Bowles, the sons of Mary-Anne's other daughter, who was also staying. Mrs Bowles was the best-looking of the family, tall and stately, with a beauty which her nephew recalled fifty years later:

8. To Louise Wallace, 23 Sept. 1834.
9. To Louise Wallace, 23 Sept. 1834.

'she had a handsome face & a beautiful foot & was the tallest of our race – five foot six; which was not bad in the year forty'.[10] Ellen Du Maurier had another miscarriage during the winter in England, and took several weeks to recover from it. Her mother, however, had taken a fancy to George, and nursed him at night: 'which is very kind, is it not?',[11] Louis-Mathurin told his sister. At a year old, the boy was already becoming a charmer: 'They tell me my little fellow is getting a fine fellow and is very intelligent, good tempered and affectionate – so that he is rather a favourite with his smile and the rest'.[12] Louis-Mathurin joined his wife in Rotherfield in the middle of April, 1835, intent on persuading George Clarke to join him in 'a contract with any Government for clearing any seaport or River'.[13] This came to nothing, but Louis-Mathurin was present at the Christening of his son in May 1835: 'had my boy christened after the eldest [Palmella] son I should be happy to know from *himself* if this has been *agreeable* to *him*'.[14] Ellen's peaceful stay at Rotherfield came to an abrupt end soon after Louis-Mathurin's arrival. There was a monumental row between Mary-Anne and her son-in-law, probably over money, and Louis-Mathurin wrote to his sister in October that he could never hear Mrs Clarke's name mentioned 'but with horror or think of her but with disgust'.[15]

The Du Mauriers now settled in Laeken, near Brussels, awaiting developments in Lisbon, where their chief hopes were centred. Louis-Mathurin travelled about the continent in pursuit of some money he had lost in a foolish speculation, and angled for recommendations from the Duke of Palmella. He was finally successful, for the Duke found him a post as scientific adviser to the Portuguese embassy in Brussels in 1836. The details of this particular preferment are not clear from Louis-Mathurin's letters, and it is equally uncertain why the Portuguese embassy should have needed a scientific adviser at all, but the post carried with it a regular salary. This period in Brussels was one of the most settled of George's childhood. He acquired his nickname of Kicky there, a corruption of his Belgian nurse's term of endearment, 'manneken'.

The Du Mauriers' second son, Eugène, was born in Laeken on 9 February 1836. He was more honoured than Kicky, for the Duke and Duchess of Palmella were his godparents, and he was christened Alexander Eugène in a Catholic Church and brought up in the

10. To T. Armstrong, 26 Aug. 1895.
11. To Louise Wallace, 25 Dec. 1834.
12. To Louise Wallace, 13 March 1835.
13. To Louise Wallace, 25 Dec. 1834.
14. To Louise Wallace, May 1835
15. To Louise Wallace, 19 Oct. 1835.

Catholic faith, in order to please them. George, on the other hand, always remained a Protestant, though Louis-Mathurin would have brought him up as a Jew or a Moslem if the rewards had been great enough. George was his mother's favourite child, and little Eugène never received much love or attention from her. Kicky himself was devoted to his little brother, whom he nicknamed Gyggy. In later years, George envied Eugène for his audacity and popularity, at times even seeking to emulate him. While Eugène, who was intelligent, lazy and gay, inherited the family legacy of irresponsibility, George was quiet and introspective, liable to vivid dreams and hallucinations:

> I remember with peculiar vividness a Belgian man-servant of ours, called Francis. I used to ask him to take me in his arms and to carry me down-stairs to look at some beautiful birds. I used to think that these were real birds each time that I looked at them, although, in fact, they were but painted on the panes, and I had been told so. I remember another childish hallucination. I used to sleep in my parents' room, and when I turned my face to the wall, a door in the wall used to open, and a *charbonnier*, a coal-man, big and black, used to come and take me up and carry me down a long, winding staircase, into a kitchen, where his wife and children were, and treated me very kindly. In truth, there was neither door, nor *charbonnier*, nor kitchen. It was an hallucination; yet it possessed me again and again.[16]

It is not difficult to see a link, in this description, with the recurring dreams of Peter Ibbetson in Du Maurier's first novel. His imaginative response to the dream is dominated by the theme of the staircase, here an image of fear. After the first shock of the coalman's frightening appearance, the child's discovery of the family and their kindness to him, suggests either the hopeful mind of a small boy, or an innate sense of security which ultimately overrode his fears. What is remarkable about these dreams is not their imaginative quality, common enough in early childhood, but the memory which recalled them with such intensity sixty years later.

Wrapped up in himself, and in his own dreams, George was slow to establish contact with the outside world. For a long time he did not talk at all, and then spoke in fully-formed sentences, thoughtfully remarking: 'Papa est allé chez le boucher pour acheter de la viande pour maman'.[17] His role of observer was established early. After this

16. Sherard, pp. 393–4.
17. Sherard, p. 394.

slow start, George became fluent in English and French, 'and is fond of music, his memory is excellent so that I think he will be anything but a fool'.[18] The boy was not as attractive as he had been, although his white skin and rosy cheeks made him striking in appearance: 'his features are not handsome as you see – his skin is so fair that you can count his veins and those on his temples have a good effect . . . his eyes are much like my own with a little more blue than grey, his nose a little straiter [sic] than this sketch makes'.[19]

The secure and comfortable life in Brussels collapsed when George was three-and-a-half. The Duke of Palmella had become Portuguese Ambassador in Paris, and his power in Lisbon seems to have been eclipsed. Whatever the reason, Louis-Mathurin was removed from his post in Brussels. By the winter of 1837, the family were in London, where they first lived in a house called Dove Cottage, and then in 13, Alpha Road, Regents Park, which possessed a large garden. Their third home was an even grander one, 1, Devonshire Terrace, later the home of Charles Dickens. Louis-Mathurin, surprisingly prosperous for a change, had some kind of business to carry on in the city, to which he went every morning on an omnibus. He had made, he told Louise, 'some very interesting discoveries',[20] but his references to lawyers suggest that he was still trying to recover money from his disastrous speculation. George was already writing and drawing, although his progress was temporarily interrupted by a sore right hand incurred while at his 'gymnastics'. Eugène had fallen out of bed and hurt his head, but seemed to be recovering. The family stayed in Devonshire Terrace until the spring of 1839, when the Du Maurier's third and last child, Isabella Louise, was born.

Du Maurier's later recollections of his life in London were rather gloomy, and contrasted unfavourably with his early life in Paris: 'a dingy house in the heart of London, in a long street of desolating straightness, that led to a dreary square and back again, and nowhere else for me'.[21] This surprising memory of gloom in Devonshire Terrace may have been conditioned by his later experiences in Pentonville as a student.

The quarrel with Mary-Anne Clarke had evidently been patched up, for the Du Mauriers spent a long holiday with her in Dover, where George Clarke was stationed, in the summer of 1839. Du Maurier fell in love there with a girl many years his senior, Miss Ellen

18. To Louise Wallace, 14 Feb. 1836.   20. To Louise Wallace, 2 Nov. 1837.
19. To Louise Wallace, 14 Feb. 1836.   21. *Peter Ibbetson*, p. 8.

Glascock, the daughter of an Admiral: 'my first love' as he later informed Henry James. He met her on a little pier at the extreme end of the beach, and had 'sweet recollections of a delightful circle of parents, uncles, cousins, aunts & a grandmother'.[22] While George returned to London with his mother and the baby, Eugène was taken off to Margate by Mary-Anne Clarke, who fed him until he became as 'fat as butter of course and as impudent as ever'.[23] Eugène's grandmother was devoted to him, which must have done something to compensate for his mother's indifference.

The holiday with Mary-Anne had been a success, and when she moved to a large house in Boulogne, she invited her daughter and family to join her. Once again the Du Mauriers were able to live at someone else's expense, and the arrangement lasted for nearly three years. Du Maurier recalled Boulogne in a letter of 1871 to his great friend, Tom Armstrong:

> Boulogne is a lovely place, with a different stink for almost every house, and every stink full of subtle reminiscences for me. (I *did* happen to visit the last resting place of my sainted grandmother and prayed that I might be the means of transmitting to my offspring her manifold gifts, bar one.)[24]

Ellen stayed in Boulogne with her mother and sister and their children, while Louis-Mathurin returned to his scientific studies in the rue du faubourg Poissonnière in Paris. There he concocted his wild business schemes: 'I did intend to get my family up to Paris but I cannot do that immediately – we may perhaps pass the Winter here & perhaps go to London – I cannot fix yet – My English partners are begging me etc'.[25] In the early days of their marriage, Louis-Mathurin had complained about Ellen's suspicious jealousy whenever he was away from her, but she was now content to live apart, although life with her mother was never easy. Ellen made herself responsible for the education of her children:

> [George had] an Irish professor goes to the house every day to teach him Latin cyphering and writing – his Mama teaching him Geography, English and history in which he is rather advanced and he sometimes teaches his cousin who is two and a half years older than himself as to master Eugène his taste for learning has not yet shown itself he far prefers

22. 18 Sept. 1884. Houghton Library, Harvard.
23. To Louise Wallace, 21 Jan. 1839.
24. Sept. 1871.
25. To Louise Wallace, 14 July 1841.

riding a pony or a donkey than learning a column of spelling – but he seems inclined to learn drawing.[26]

Both of the Du Maurier boys had a natural talent for drawing, but Eugène was the more precocious:

> They still say the youngest has the greatest facility, from a natural *coup d'oeil* tho' he be too young to expect application from him. The Eldest works hard. They are now drawing skeletons, écorchés and from the bosse, and delight in what I should have thought would have discouraged them.[27]

Isabella too was developing a determined character:

> Mademoiselle is very impudent and scolds the servants either in French or English when they will not let her have her own way – She is sharp and imitative, and much inclined to use her little tongue either for talking or singing.[28]

While the family were in Boulogne, Mary-Anne Bowles died, after nine years of illness, and was buried in the Protestant cemetery. During the funeral George, Eugène and the two Bowles boys were taken to Pont de Brigue along the coast by George Clarke: 'while Alfred fished Charlie and I made sand pies near a little watermill and my uncle laid himself down and cried as I very well perceived but I could not understand why'.[29]

Louis-Mathurin's business arrangements collapsed once more in October 1841, and he temporarily returned to Boulogne to live with his mother-in-law. In 1842, he decided to move his family to Paris, for reasons which are not known. They settled in Passy, a quiet village on the outskirts of Paris, facing the Bois de Boulogne. Passy had been dominated by the Royal Château of la Muette, but the house had been pulled down by the time the Du Mauriers moved there. The gardens, however, were still preserved, and lay just behind the Du Maurier's second house. Passy was quiet and healthy, with a school opposite the house for the boys, but Ellen found it dull, although she 'put up with it with proper resignation'.[30] The Du Mauriers soon moved from their first home in the rue de la Tour to a house on the corner of the rue de la Pompe. They stayed here for three years, from 1842 to 1845, in what George Du Maurier later

26. To Louise Wallace, 10 Oct. 1841.   29. Letters, p. 192.
27. To Louise Wallace, undated.   30. To Louise Wallace, 6 March 1842.
28. To Louise Wallace, 10 Oct. 1841.

called 'the dearest of all these Passy dwellings'.[31] In 1845, they moved again, to number sixty-six in the rue de Passy, where they took an apartment in a house known as 'le cabinet de physique du roi' because Louis XV had once used it as a laboratory. The Du Mauriers never stayed anywhere for long, and in 1846 they moved into another house, this time in the rue Basse, closer to Paris.

The Duke of Palmella visited Paris in November 1843, and Louis-Mathurin took the opportunity to call with his three children, Isabella carrying a bouquet of flowers. Louis-Mathurin formally presented a brooch containing the hair of all three children, and a box of drawings by the two boys. Eugène was still thought to be the more gifted, although lazy:

> It is impossible to stimulate him by the ordinary means. What he does he does from natural inclination – The Eldest is different – besides some excellent qualities, he is bright quick and ambitious affectionate also, he is his mother's pride, and according to all appearance, likely to turn out a smart man. When you write always add a note for him, he is sensitive of such a mark of affection.[32]

The visit to the Duke did not lead to any further preferments. He was uninterested in Louis-Mathurin's latest invention, a patent lamp, which was being tried out in the Louvre. The inventor was anxious to see them in the streets of Lisbon, and then all over the world. At the same time he had an even more bizarre scheme of establishing his claim to the mysterious Mosquito lands, which he believed had been given to his father by the Pope. His family continued to live on a very reduced budget.

These years in Passy were extremely happy ones for George, and the source of a profound nostalgia for his childhood. The experience of this time is enshrined in the opening chapters of his first novel, *Peter Ibbetson*, written with an imaginative force lacking in the less autobiographical sections of his fiction. A preoccupation with the events of childhood is not uncommon in sensitive adults. Several nineteenth-century authors wrote compellingly on the subject. For some, like Wordsworth, childhood was a time of truth and vision, the 'Angell-infancy' of Henry Vaughan. For others, like Dickens and Samuel Butler, it held bitter memories of cruelty and repression, which were still agonisingly fresh when they came to write

31. Letters, p. 272.
32. To Louise Wallace, 5 Nov. 1843.

David Copperfield and *The Way of all Flesh*. Accounts of happy childhoods in Victorian novels are pitched in a lower key. Among the best
is Disraeli's description of his youth in his early novels. A secure and
happy home, however, was not always an advantage. Ruskin's
Praeterita is as terrible an indictment of a disastrous upbringing as
David Copperfield. Surrounded by claustrophobic affection, Ruskin
remained in a state of suspended adolescence, unable to decide
anything for himself, or to form mature relationships.

The aching nostalgia to which both Du Maurier and Ruskin were
prone might suggest other analogies between them. Du Maurier,
however, was forced out of the family fold early on, and never
developed the crippling dependence on his parents which characterized Ruskin. His experiences at school, and later as a student,
compelled him to come to terms with the world, and successful marriage completed the process. If his longing to return to an ideal childhood played a significant part in his imaginative development, it did
not affect his career, or his every-day life. Du Maurier enjoyed his
work and his family, and seemed to all his friends to be a contented
and fortunate man. When his novels were published, no-one was more
surprised than his children to discover the secret dreams which had
haunted him for so long. Du Maurier's power of memory, and the
illusions associated with it, had been a source of strength and
consolation to this apparently prosaic *Punch* cartoonist. They provided an escape from the limited circumstances of his life, and his
sense of frustrated ambition. Very little of his secret life emerges in his
letters, or in the recollections of him by his friends. It is only in his
novels that it erupts with such sustained and passionate force.

The account of Du Maurier's early childhood in the opening
section of *Peter Ibbetson* follows the pattern of real events very closely.
There are several romantic distortions, which are, however, easily
recognisable. Peter's mother and father are not the ageing and
impecunious parents of Du Maurier's own childhood, but a young
and gay couple, whose financial problems are a source of amusement rather than worry. Only the arrival of unpleasant letters from
Peter Ibbetson's uncle suggests that George did have some knowledge
of the threatening letters which regularly arrived from his father's
creditors. For the most part, however, the novel is entirely based on
Du Maurier's memories of his childhood. The 'old yellow house,
with green shutters and Mansard roofs',[33] on the corner of the rue de

33. *Peter Ibbetson*, p. 14

la Pompe, describes the Du Mauriers' second home in Passy exactly. Du Maurier himself was devoted to this house, and wrote to his wife, on a nostalgic visit in 1867, that 'in passing this corner which I have dreamt of distorted and exaggerated quite lately I thought I should go quite crazed – I was as one in a dream and yet awake'.[34] Two days later he persuaded the porter to let him see inside: 'upon my word the sensation was so powerful as almost to bring on diarrhoea'.[35] In *Peter Ibbetson*, Du Maurier recalled the back garden of this house, its much-loved apple tree, and the avenue which led from it to the deserted park of la Muette, where the children frequently played. In 1867, he found the apple tree had been cut down, and the park desecrated by the Passy Railway, and some stucco villas: 'I plucked a piece of ivy from the gate that used to open from the Avenue into it, and which has been shut for many years and walled in, but it is the same rusty gate, ni plus ni moins'.[36] Nothing could destroy the magic of his childhood, the rows of familiar houses, the names of the shopkeepers clearly remembered, and the mysterious figure of the lamplighter in the dusk. These are the most sacred and poignant memories enshrined in *Peter Ibbetson*, where the hero is, significantly enough, an only child. Du Maurier was not intent on painting an accurate picture of his childhood, and felt no necessity to preserve its less congenial aspects, the inevitable rainy days and scenes of jealousy. He sought only to recreate the essential happiness that had been his as a small boy.

From the evidence of the novel, it is apparent that several significant traits in Du Maurier's character were formed during his early years in Passy; one of these was his sensitivity to landscape. The image of the flowering shrub, glistening in sunlight, is common in *Peter Ibbetson*. The book recalls several expeditions to the old Bois de Boulogne, not yet the tamed and formal park modelled on the lines of Hyde Park by Napoleon III. The family frequently walked to the old town of Boulogne, from which the forest took its name, and from there to what Du Maurier later called 'that magical combination of river, bridge, palace, gardens, mountain, and forest, St Cloud'.[37] St Cloud was occupied by the Prussians in 1870 and 1871, and the Palace and many of the oldest buildings were destroyed, as well as George Du Maurier's beloved railway station, the 'grande gare' of the Paris-Versailles line. He was not wholly absorbed in natural beauty,

34. Letters, p. 269   36. Letters, p. 272.
35. Letters, p. 272.   37. *Peter Ibbetson*, p. 17.

LA MARE D'AUTEUIL !

The very name has a magic, from all the associations that gathered round it during that time, to cling for ever.

1. *Peter Ibbetson* (1891)

for, like other small boys, he enjoyed the novelty of railway trains, and the eating of ice creams in the Tête Noire Hotel, notorious and thrilling as the scene of a recent murder. Deep in the Bois de Boulogne was a small pond, the Mare d'Auteuil, surrounded on three sides by a dense forest and just hidden from the road by a line of trees; it is now covered by a race-course. The Du Maurier children rarely met anyone else there, except for the occasional lovers, and they came to regard it as their own, fishing for reptiles in his muddy waters. These reptiles obsessed George, particularly after his father had presented him with a book on pre-historic zoology. In bed at night he would think of the pond in the darkness, and, falling asleep, would imagine that the water was shrinking, leaving the reptiles crawling over and over each other in the slime at the bottom. These first nightmares were the result of an over-active mind running on over the picture of:

> huge fat salamanders, long-lost and forgotten tadpoles as large as rats, gigantic toads, enormous flat beetles, all kinds of hairy, scaly, spiny, blear-eyed, bulbous, shapeless monsters without name, mud-coloured offspring of the mire that had been sleeping there for hundreds of years, woke up, and crawled in and out, and wallowed, and inter-wriggled, and devoured each other.[38]

38. *Peter Ibbetson*, pp. 19–20.

A LITTLE CHRISTMAS DREAM.

Mr. L. Figuier, in the Thesis which precedes his interesting Work on the World before the Flood, condemns practice of awakening the Youthful Mind to Admiration by means of Fables and Fairy Tales, and recommends, in thereof, the Study of the Natural History of the World in which we live. Fired by this Advice, we have tried Experiment on our Eldest, an imaginative Boy of Six. We have cut off his "Cinderella" and his "Puss in Bc and introduced him to some of the more peaceful Fauna of the Preadamite World, as they appear Restored in Figuier's Book.

The poor Boy has not had a decent Night's Rest ever since!

2. *Punch* (1868)

Then he would awake in a cold sweat, chilled with fear, and longing for morning. Even as an adult, Du Maurier was still haunted by the remembrance of his panic, and produced several nightmare cartoons for *Punch*, which are frighteningly grotesque.

Another of Du Maurier's early characteristics was his love of music. In *Peter Ibbetson*, he describes how he lay in bed with the door ajar, listening to his mother playing the harp or the piano, and to his father's superb voice as he ran through his seemingly inexhaustible repertoire. Familiarity with these songs taught the child the basic patterns of music, and gave him a profound appreciation that he never lost. The power of his memory was so strong that he could recall his life at Passy whenever he sang or heard any of his father's songs, even fifty years later.

There is little sense of the passage of time in *Peter Ibbetson*, and the impression of his childhood years is a composite one. In his interview with Sherard, and in *The Martian*, Du Maurier implied that his first school had been the Pension Froussard, which he entered at the age of thirteen, but, in fact, he was at school in Passy from the age of eight. His first school was opposite his home:

> [they] only have to cross the street backwards and forwards and not exposed to dirty sights etc – which is continually the case in the beau pays de France. Of course they do not board and sleep at school, though it is a very good reputed school and great attention is paid to the morals and religion of the children still I would rather they never went to school at all than be at a French school entirely. [39]

The Du Maurier boys seem to have attended further schools in Passy. In 1867, Du Maurier told his wife that he had been in 'many schools . . . in one way or another', [40] and he specifically referred to a meeting with an old schoolfellow: 'He was 5 years old when I was externe at the pension Pelieu, now Charronat'. [41] At home George spent much of his time reading, his preference being all for romantic literature. Particular favourites were *The Swiss Family Robinson* and *Robinson Crusoe*, and later the novels of Dumas, Hugo, Scott and Eugène Sue, and the more adventurous poems of Lord Byron. Much of his reading was in French, for he was entirely bilingual. Illustrated books also attracted his attention, and, in attempting to copy their steel engravings, he developed a gift for drawing.

39. To Louise Wallace, 6 March 1842. 41. Letters, p. 272.
40. Letters, p. 269.

This fragmentary education was obviously inadequate for intelligent children, and Ellen Du Maurier decided that, at whatever cost, her two sons must go to a boarding-school. From 1847 to 1851, George and Eugène were educated at the Pension Froussard in the Avenue Bois de Boulogne, described by Du Maurier in *The Martian*:

> The Institution F. Brossard was a very expensive private school, just twice as expensive as the most expensive of the Parisian public schools. . . . These great colleges, which were good enough for the sons of Louis-Philippe were not thought good enough for me by my dear mother.[42]

The Pension Froussard catered for the sons of professional men, who preferred exclusiveness to academic quality. Since the Du Mauriers were exclusive, but not well-off, they had to give up their delightful apartment in Passy, and remove to a cheaper one in the rue du Bac, in order to pay the school fees. This new home was on the south bank between the Latin Quarter and St Germain.

The opening of *The Martian*, which begins with an account of Du Maurier's schooldays, presents a more complex problem than *Peter Ibbetson*. Barty Josselin's enormous popularity with his schoolfellows in *The Martian* strongly suggests that Du Maurier was deliberately disguising his own unhappiness at school, and identifying himself with his fictional hero. His autobiographical intention was, however, explicit in his statement to Sherard: 'I shall write my school life in my new novel "The Martians" '.[43] The school curriculum at the Pension Froussard was not an easy one for the new-comer. Away from home for the first time, Du Maurier was awakened at five o'clock in the morning (five-thirty in the winter), and spent the hours until breakfast in preparation for the day's work. Breakfast was at seven-thirty, and consisted of a hunk of dry bread and thick, dark vegetable soup which the boys called 'brouet noir des Lacédémoniens'. This soup was evidently not very appetising, for when it was replaced on Thursdays with a lump of butter, the boys thought it a red-letter-day. After breakfast came four hours in class: 'from eight till twelve, class – Latin, Greek, French, English, German – and mathematics and geometry – history, geography, chemistry, physics'.[44] Lunch was followed by a further four hours of work. As in England, the educational system was primarily based on the classics, which Du Maurier cordially loathed: 'How I disliked the

42. *The Martian*, p. 18.   44. *The Martian*, p. 20.
43. Sherard, p. 394.

3. The Institution
   F. Brossard,
The Martian (1896)

pious Aeneas! I couldn't have hated him worse if I'd been poor
Dido's favourite brother (not mentioned by Publius Virgilius Maro,
if I remember)'.[45]

There was, however, one compensation in the shape of a teacher of
French literature, who came for two hours on Saturday afternoon
and taught the boys

> all about Villon and Ronsard, and Marot and Charles d'Orléans
> (*exceptis excipiendis*, of course), and other pleasant people who didn't deal
> in Greek or Latin or mathematics, and knew better than to trouble
> themselves overmuch about formal French grammar and niggling
> French prosody.[46]

45. *The Martian*, p. 9.
46. *The Martian*, pp. 8–9.

At six o'clock the boys had dinner, and after this were left to their own devices until bedtime at nine o'clock. Thursday was a half holiday and Sunday a free day, when George and Eugène would visit their parents, or enjoy their freedom to wander in Paris.

As new boys, George and Eugène were an obvious butt for bullying, besides being 'English'. In 1865 Du Maurier was still smarting under the insult, as he informed his colleagues on the *Punch* staff: 'D.M. was bullied at school for being an Englishman – though he was born in Paris and came of French extraction. He says French boys can't bear pain'.[47] Armstrong, a life-long friend, recalled similar outbursts in Paris, when Du Maurier would 'express great dislike for French school-boys and their ways, both in class and in the playground, but I think his opinions were modified as he grew older'.[48] Barty Josselin, the hero of *The Martian*, is also bullied at school, but is more than a match for his tormentors. He is blessed with all the qualities which Du Maurier lacked, academic ability, and popularity with boys and masters. He clearly embodied all Du Maurier's youthful dream-wishes, for even his brother could keep the class amused, while Du Maurier was unable to impress anybody. He nevertheless surprised his school-fellows by his skill in 'la savate', boxing with the feet. Slight as he was, he worked hard at strenuous sports, particularly swimming, riding and fencing, which he kept up after he had left school. His remark that 'French boys can't bear pain' suggests that he had found a weak chink in the armour of his oppressors, which he learned to exploit. By the time he had finished *The Martian*, in 1896, he had largely forgotten his bitterness, and even spoke with pleasure of his companions at the Pension Froussard, favourably comparing their egalitarianism with the snobbery of the English public schools.

Du Maurier's unhappiness at school increased his nostalgia for Passy. The long account in *Peter Ibbetson* of the hero's desire to be back in Paris, while at school in London, is another reflection of this period of conflict. The Thursday half-holiday and the free Sunday were the best times of the week, when George and Eugène would visit their parents in the rue du Bac, or later at 108, Champs Elysées. Revisiting Paris in the 1880s, Du Maurier found his former home was now a café, and it saddened him to see waiters at the window instead of his mother's familiar face, anxiously watching

47. Silver, 29 March 1865.
48. Armstrong, p. 161.

out for him. Not all of his free time was spent at home, however, for it was during this period that he really came to know Paris well. His intimate knowledge of every quarter of the city is recalled again and again in all his novels. As a school-boy he enjoyed wandering through the narrow streets, imagining himself in the world of Hugo or Eugène Sue. With the keen eye which eventually made him such an excellent social cartoonist, he watched the life of the poorer citizens; a lower-class wedding, a pauper funeral, or the mass being carried through the streets to give extreme unction. Among the crowds he listened to the cries of the street vendors, to the crack of the whip and the rattle of cartwheels over the cobbles. He strolled through the residential areas, judging the status and habits of their inhabitants by the size of the buildings, and the sounds and smells which issued from them. On the other side of the river, near the rue du Bac, he would gaze at the mansions of the Faubourg St Germain, where every house belonged to a nobleman and had a name which 'read like a page of French history'.[49] Significantly enough he gave his own date of birth in *Trilby* to a Duc de Rochemartel, born in one of these palaces.

One of the more dramatic incidents in his school life was the revolution of 1848 which deposed Louis Philippe. On 23 February, fighting broke out in Paris which ended the following day with Louis Philippe's abdication. The Pension Froussard was near enough to the disorders to be in a state of 'quite heavenly demoralisation'[50] for a week. Ordinary routine was entirely disrupted, while boys and staff sat on the terrace, looking at Paris with mingled excitement and apprehension. There was a constant muffled sound of musketry and cannon from Montmartre and Montfaucon, and, in the evening, the watchers could see flames rising from the burning houses. The boys slept on the floor, to escape possible stray bullets, and were then sent home. Returning to his parents, Du Maurier was fascinated by the smell of gunpowder in the streets, and by the soldiers who searched his clothing for cartridges. Only the occasional sight of a dead soldier, or the sound of a firing squad at work behind the church of St Vincent de Paul, convinced him that there was more to the revolution than a few days' holiday from school.

The object of a French education was then, as now, to pass the leaving examination, or baccalauréat, without which many

49. *Peter Ibbetson*, pp. 56–7.
50. *The Martian*, p. 61.

professions were closed. Du Maurier took the exam in 1851. Only in his last year did he really attempt to work hard at the subjects in the curriculum, and not at the romantic novels which he read under his desk. His unexpected failure caused him a great deal of distress at this time, and for several years after. During the Latin paper, the cause of his failure, he was much disturbed by the constant surveillance of a professor who seemed to imagine that he had a crib. In *The Martian*, Barty Josselin also fails his baccalauréat, but, with a nonchalance which Du Maurier evidently lacked, he shrugs it off light-heartedly. To the average French schoolboy, however, failure was a major disaster, and suicides were not uncommon as a result.

At the time of the exam, both Du Maurier's parents were away, his mother at her brother's wedding in Boulogne, his father in London. When Ellen Du Maurier returned home she was, understandably, 'very vexed with me for my failure, for we were very poor at that time, and it was important that I should do well'.[51] In the meantime, nobody had dared to tell Louis-Mathurin what had happened, and when a letter arrived from him, summoning his son to London to begin his scientific career, there has no alternative but to go. After a wretched journey, the trembling Du Maurier arrived at London Bridge, expecting fearful recriminations. Instead, his father, realising from Du Maurier's glum face what had happened: 'burst out into a roar of laughter'.[52] Du Maurier recalled his overwhelming relief in his interview with Sherard: 'I think that this roar of laughter gave me the greatest pleasure I ever experienced in all my life'.[53] Louis-Mathurin Du Maurier never referred to his son's failure again, and it in no way upset the educational programme which he had planned for him. Du Maurier was entered as a pupil at the Birkbeck Chemical Laboratory of University College to study chemistry under Dr Williamson; George described his new existence in a letter to his Aunt Louise:

> As for myself I am from 9 till 2, in the laboratory, testing all the nastiest substances that were ever inclosed in glass bottles; just fancy me with an old coat, and a stained black apron down to my feet, scarcely visible among fumes and vapours of all colours and smells; in one hand a sandwich, in the other a bottle of sesquifferocyanide of potassium, or protosulphate of iron, or other substances with names no less euphonious. I am full of ardour in the pursuits of my profession; indeed I am

51. Sherard, p. 394.
52. Sherard, p. 394.   53. Sherard, p. 394.

quite forgetting the usual terms of common things, and instead of asking for salt, or water, etc. I ask for the chloride of sodium or the protoxide of nitrogen.[54]

His father had meanwhile taken a house for the family at 44, Wharton Street, in Pentonville, a grim contrast to the rural atmosphere of Passy, although Wharton Street today seems very charming: 'I disliked Pentonville, which, although clean, virtuous, and respectable, left much to be desired on the score of shape, colour, romantic tradition, and local charm'.[55] Ellen Du Maurier soon followed her husband with Isabella and Eugène, Betty the crow, and five cats. Away from his school-friends, the city he knew, and the language to which he was most accustomed, Du Maurier found London dreary and unfamiliar. Worst of all, he was embarking on a training which had no interest for him: 'I disliked my profession, for which I felt no particular aptitude, and would fain have followed another'.[56]

There is very little reliable information about Du Maurier's year as a student at University College. In *The Du Mauriers*, Daphne Du Maurier states that he found Birkbeck Laboratory uncongenial, 'the little work he did was monotonous and his fellow-students were loud-voiced and smutty-minded'.[57] This echoes the description of the architect's office in Pentonville in *Peter Ibbetson*:

> I disliked my brother apprentices, and did not get on well with them. . . .
> They thought I gave myself airs because I did not share in their dissipations; such dissipations as I could have afforded would have been cheap and nasty indeed.
> Yet such pothouse dissipation seemed to satisfy them, since they took not only a pleasure in it, but a pride.[58]

Like Peter Ibbetson, Du Maurier was very short of money, which made life even more difficult. Feeling acutely lonely, he became a regular visitor at the free galleries and museums, even sitting for hours in the British Museum Reading Room. Very occasionally he had enough money for a cheap seat at the opera or a concert, but usually he would walk dismally round the streets, or stand on London Bridge, gazing enviously at the steamers departing for Boulogne.

This picture of unhappiness is, however, startlingly challenged by

54. To Louise Wallace, undated.
55. *Peter Ibbetson*, p. 97.
56. *Peter Ibbetson*, p. 96.
57. pp. 194–5.
58. p. 97.

an anonymous fellow-student, who sent his reminiscences of Du Maurier at University College to Sir Henry Lucy, who later published them in his own autobiography. Du Maurier, it seems, was one of the leading spirits of the college, who impressed everybody with his French background and general savoir-faire. He exchanged quips with Monsieur Ragan, the French master, insisting on Ragan's using the suffix to his name, and scattering the poor man's papers with his feet. His skill at la savate was formidable:

> He would come close up to you, his eyelids rapidly blinking, his hands in his trousers' pockets (bad form in '50) and emphasise a torrent of questions by knocking off your cap with one foot, and sending your books flying with the other. Before you could get at him, 'Bewsong', as his name was pronounced, was ten yards off. All this was in perfect good humour. Sometimes he instructed us in 'Savate'. . . . In dividing the honours at these lessons there were no ha'pence for him, but unlimited kicks for us, which he delightedly administered with a perfectly calm face.[59]

This recollection seems incompatible with the story of Du Maurier's depression, but it was written when he was already famous, and is probably exaggerated. In any case, high spirits are often an expression of nervous excitement, which might conceal fundamental unhappiness. The description of the hero's period of apprenticeship in *Peter Ibbetson* probably embodies Du Maurier's real feelings about University College. Another student there, some years before Du Maurier, was Sir Henry Thompson, the famous surgeon, who has left an account of his experiences in his first novel, *Charley Kingston's Aunt* (1885).

If the University was uncongenial, Du Maurier's home was scarcely less so. His mother was continually worried, usually about Isabella's education, front teeth or marital prospects. She had managed to save enough money to send Isabella to school, but it was hard to pay the fees, and her daughter did not seem to derive much benefit. Isabella had one particular friend whom she was anxious to show off to her brother, Emma Wightwick, the daughter of a well-to-do Bond Street shop-keeper. One morning in 1853, George and his sister met Emma by the gates of the Foundling Hospital, and Du Maurier was immediately struck by her:

a fine, straight, bony child of twelve, with a flat back and square

59. Henry Lucy, *Sixty Years in the Wilderness* (1909), p. 387.

shoulders; she was very well dressed, and had nice brown boots with brown elastic sides on arched and straight-heeled slender feet, and white stockings on her long legs. . . . She also wore a thick plait of black hair all down her back . . . and she swung her books . . . with easy movements, like a strong boy.[60]

Emma soon became a great favourite with the Du Maurier family, and Louis-Mathurin encouraged Isabella to bring her home. One of Du Maurier's regrets was that his father did not live to see Emma Wightwick become his wife in 1863. Eugène's career at University College was even shorter than his brother's. He ran away to France, and put himself under the protection of his Aunt Louise. Intending to join the French army, he pestered his father for his birth certificate, and other documents, and then light-heartedly informed him that he was entering the army as a private, not an officer. His parents quietly washed their hands of him.

While George Du Maurier was wasting his time at the University, his father was pursuing his own erratic career. His financial prospects steadily declined as speculation followed speculation. When his brother, Jacques, died in Hamburg, Louis-Mathurin cheerfully offered to support the widow and her children. They arrived in London, discovered that there was no money to support them, and returned to Hamburg with justified annoyance. It was a typical episode, and one that wore down poor Ellen Du Maurier's nerves: 'We are all well, but Christmas is not an agreeable time for us, and Louis is very uncertain with his speculations'.[61] Nor did she believe that her son had any chance of becoming a good chemist: 'Kicky says that as soon as he makes any money from his chemistry he will make Eugène an allowance, but I very much doubt Kicky ever earning enough to keep himself, let alone his brother'.[62] Another gloomy letter described her son's indolence: 'He has no initiative, no energy. He sits about and dreams. Always a pencil in his hand – and I think of the money wasted on his education'.[63] In fact, Du Maurier's dreams were centred on opera rather than art. He did not ignore his pencil, for his caricatures of his fellow students and tutors were widely popular, and enhanced his reputation at the college, but it was not his chief interest. His wish to become an opera-singer was poorly received in the family circle. The Du Mauriers did not regard music as a 'legitimate career', and Du Maurier's voice was

60. *The Martian*, pp. 141–2.
61. *The Du Mauriers*, p. 194.
62. *The Du Mauriers*, p. 199.
63. *The Du Mauriers*, p. 200.

not even as good as his father's. Louis-Mathurin proved this dramatically one night when he and his son were walking home through Smithfield Market. George sang what he believed to be a perfect 'a', and was followed by his father: 'And then and there rang out a note of music, low and sweet at the outset, and swelling as it went, till it seemed to fill all Smithfield with divine melody'.[64] Eventually George was allowed to take singing lessons, drawing a caricature of himself bowing to the applause of fellow-students after an illicit song at the Birkbeck Laboratory.

The family's financial position improved considerably in June 1852, on the death of Mary-Anne Clarke, when her annuity of four-hundred pounds a year passed to Ellen Du Maurier. This comparative affluence enabled them to pay George's university fees for the Autumn term in a lump sum of ten guineas, instead of monthly instalments as they had done in the past. It was George's last term, for he left the college at Christmas in order to begin work as an analytical chemist in his own laboratory at Barge Yard, Bucklersbury. He was not much happier there, for he had no interest in the subject, and little work to do:

> I had a good deal of time on my hands, and read many novels and smoked many pipes, as I sat by my chemical stove and distilled water, and dried chlorate of potash to keep the damp out of my scales, and toasted cheese, and fried sausages, and mulled Burgundy, and brewed nice drinks.[65]

During his career as a scientist, George Du Maurier seems to have received only two commissions. The first came from Colonel Greville, a friend of George Clarke, who kindly sent soil samples for analysis. Then, in September 1854, he introduced Du Maurier to the chairman of the Victoria Gold and Copper Mine Company, which claimed to have uncovered deposits of gold at North Melton in Devon. After the initial discovery, no further ore had come to light, and the disgruntled shareholders wanted an explanation. The company board, therefore, decided on a scientific analysis of the mine, and Du Maurier was appointed to carry this out. In an amusing sketch, he described the days of 'golden peace and plenty' in that 'jolly month of September'.[66] It was perfectly obvious from the start, even to a scientist as incompetent as Du Maurier, that there

64. Sherard, p. 396.
65. *The Martian*, p. 152.

66. 'Recollections of an English Gold Mine', *Once A Week*, V, (21 Sept. 1861), 360.

4. Recollections of an English Gold Mine, *Once a Week* (1861)

was no gold, but neither he nor the workmen were much concerned
about it. With his great natural charm, Du Maurier soon became a
great favourite with the rough and illiterate miners:

> [I] used to tell them long stories about foreign lands, while they were
> distilling the pure mercury, or performing other innocent operations
> suggested by the board, and enlighten them on various subjects on which
> I felt their ignorance to be equal to, or greater, than my own.[67]

On one auspicious day, the directors came down to inspect opera-
tions, bringing with them their wives and daughters:

67. 'Recollections', p. 360.

they invited me to partake of lunch with them. The hampers were un-
packed, and delicious cold things were laid out on the grass, beneath the
combined shadows of a wide-spreading chestnut tree and one of the
huge water wheels; everybody was in the best of tempers, and we soon
got very happy indeed. There was a pastoral freshness about this way of
settling gold mines which had an inexpressible charm. [68]

This pleasantly unbusinesslike state of affairs did not continue
indefinitely, and Du Maurier was soon summoned to London to
deliver his report. The directors, no longer in a holiday mood,
severely censured him for not giving them the answer they wanted,
and then, rather ignominiously, dismissed him. No other employment followed on the goldmine, and Louis-Mathurin began to
consider sending his son to Paris to learn 'a new process of instant-
aneous photography whereby I think he could make a good bit of
money'.[69] Instead, George suffered a severe attack of measles, and
was sent out of London to convalesce. He spent Christmas at Milford
in Wales with his uncle, George Clarke, and his pretty young aunt,
Georgina. She was delighted at Du Maurier's arrival, for she found
life in the country very boring, and was already regretting her
marriage to a dull man much older than herself. The care she took
of Du Maurier, which much impressed his mother, was only partly
altruistic. She enjoyed flirting with her attractive and charming
nephew, and the romantic interest she aroused in Du Maurier
caused him some embarrassment later on. In one letter sent to his
mother, Du Maurier drew sketches of the intolerably dull local
residents with whom he went out to dinner, and who were delighted
by his singing. He felt considerable sympathy for his aunt, and the
thought of the tedium of her existence drew him closer to her.

Back in London, Du Maurier, longing to escape from his scientific
career, began to investigate other possibilities. His mother was
reasonably sympathetic:

It is hard to have a son, one and twenty and no profession. He, poor
fellow, is anything but happy, and I know would work hard if there was
anything like a certainty of success. . . . Since his return from Milford
he has been consulting his friends about studying painting, as he
certainly draws very well and has great taste. They tell him it is hard
work to make his way as an artist. I don't see what else he can do – as to
his ever being a man of business, he has no talent for it, and his father's
success that way anything but encouraging. [70]

68. 'Recollections', p. 361.   70. The Du Mauriers, p. 214.
69. To Louise Wallace, 12 Oct. 1854.

In 1852, with his mother's encouragement, Du Maurier had obtained a ticket to draw from the sculpture in the British Museum,
and it was there that he first acquired a taste for classical forms and
figures. As he drew the Elgin Marbles, he dreamt of becoming a
painter in his own right, like the other students around him. His
parents were not happy about him, but they recognized that he was
more stable and reliable than their delinquent younger son, who had
so obviously disgraced himself:

> Instead of feeling shame and disgrace at seeing what he puppishly called
> 'the sons of peasants' getting advancement in preference to the 'sons of
> Gentlemen' – he has sufficient absence of good sense and manly feeling
> to ask for a sacrifice of money to be made to indulge him in the treat of a
> pleasure trip – the only advantage of which would be to go and show your
> friends at Versailles that he, to our disgrace, is still a *'common soldier'*.[71]

George Du Maurier's scientific concerns were certainly not
flourishing, for at Easter 1855 he was in Milford again, and in May he
took another holiday, this time in Norfolk. He was the guest of the
young designer, Thomas Jeckyll, whose father was a nonconformist
minister. In spite of the cold meat on Sunday, Du Maurier found
Norfolk an exciting change from Pentonville, and thoroughly enjoyed rushing around the countryside in Jeckyll's gig, on their way to
visit 'the neighbourhood':

> The people are charming, and we spend the day riding, or boating, or
> drawing, and the evening in singing and dancing. Went over to Cam-
> bridge the other day, some seventy miles, by train of course, and met
> some of the Collegians – great dandies – and we spent the evening with
> them – supper, wine and singing.[72]

The 'great dandies' included Charles Stuart Calverley, the brilliant
parodist, then a fellow of Christ's College, and Walter Besant, who
knew Du Maurier much later in Hampstead, and who wrote an
account of this evening in Cambridge:

> One day Calverley, then a fellow, stopped me in the court and invited
> me into his rooms after hall. 'I've got a young Frenchman', he said. 'He's
> clever. Come and be amused'. I went. The young Frenchman spoke
> English as well as anybody; he told quantities of stories in a quiet,
> irresponsible way, as if he was an outsider looking on at the world. No

71. To Louise Wallace, 3 June 1854.
72. *The Du Mauriers*, pp. 218–9.

one went to chapel that evening. After the port, which went round with briskness for two or three hours, the young Frenchman went to the piano and began to sing in a sweet, flexible, high baritone or tenor. Presently somebody else took his place at the instrument, and he, with Calverley, and two or three dummies, performed a Royal Italian Opera in very fine style. The young Frenchman's name was George Du Maurier.[73]

Louis-Mathurin Du Maurier had been in poor health for some time, suffering from asthma and palpitations of the heart, but he still hopefully continued with his speculations. Early in 1856, however, he lost a law-suit, presumably about the patent for his lamp, and the strain of paying the costs finally broke his spirit. He now lay in bed all day, sinking into a depression from which he showed no desire to recover. His son frequently sat by his bedside, reading him stories, or trying to make him laugh, in an effort to raise his spirits. Louis-Mathurin refused to see a doctor, and his condition deteriorated. On the afternoon of 8 June, Du Maurier was startled to hear his father's tenor voice ringing through the house. Rushing upstairs, for his mother was away from home, he held his father in his arms, until he died, 'singing one of Count de Segur's drinking songs. He left this world almost with music on his lips.'[74]

The link between father and son had never been a close one, for Ellen Du Maurier had managed to alienate her elder son from his father. The only quality which Du Maurier appreciated in his father was his superb singing voice, and a love of music was his only positive inheritance from Louis-Mathurin. Strongly affected by his mother's frustration and unhappiness, Du Maurier reacted violently against his father's philosophy of life. His subsequent career was based upon hard work, and careful effort, not upon vague hopes, or impossible speculations. With his gay spirits and good humour, Louis-Mathurin should have been a liberalising force in his children's lives, but his pig-headed refusal to settle down, or to understand his children, antagonized them. His ruthless determination to force Du Maurier into an uncongenial career made his death a moment of release, not one of sorrow or deprivation.

Louis-Mathurin Du Maurier was buried in Abney Park Cemetery, Stoke Newington; once the funeral was over, the family immediately left Pentonville, without even making any arrangements to mark his grave. They decided to return to Paris, for which they had all longed

73. W. Besant, *Autobiography of Walter Besant* (1902), pp. 96–7.
74. Sherard, p. 396.

during the dispiriting years in London. Du Maurier had definitely decided that his future was in art, and intended to train at one of the great Parisian art-schools. While his mother and sister took a few months' holiday with George Clarke in Milford, he was sent across the Channel to find accommodation for himself and the family.

PENTONVILLE.

5. Wharton Street, Pentonville, *Peter Ibbetson*

Chapter 2

Paris

HAD GEORGE DU MAURIER BEEN TOLD, as he left London Bridge on the Boulogne steamer, that he was to spend the last thirty-six years of his life in England, he would have found it hard to accept. His one desire in the summer of 1856 was to get away from the frustration and loneliness which he associated with London: 'I stood by the man at the wheel, and saw St Paul's and London Bridge and the Tower fade out of sight; with what hope and joy I cannot describe. I almost forgot that I was me'.[1] As he walked through Paris on the day of his arrival, gazing at the streets and buildings which he had remembered so poignantly in Wharton Street, he remained in buoyant spirits. If the Champs Elysées and the Arc de Triomphe were still as memory had painted them, however, an unpleasant shock awaited him in the Bois de Boulogne, the scene of his happiest days:

> I made for the Bois de Boulogne, there to find, instead of the old rabbit-and-roebuck-haunted thickets and ferneries and impenetrable under-growth, a huge artificial lake, with row-boats and skiffs, and a rockery that would have held its own in Rosherville gardens.[2]

Since Du Maurier's departure in 1851, Napoleon III had given the Bois de Boulogne to the city of Paris, on condition that it was laid out like Hyde Park, in a planned and formal pattern. It was no longer the untamed and mysterious woodland of his memory.

This change in the Bois de Boulogne was symbolic of a change in himself. Paris was no longer the city of his childhood, bathed in a glow of nostalgic recollection, but the city where he must face the world and decide what his part in it was to be. He could not re-experience the happiness of the past, and his attempt to do so was a source of bitter disappointment. In *Peter Ibbetson* he later wrote of his emotion at this time:

1. *Peter Ibbetson*, p. 168.
2. *Peter Ibbetson*, p. 175.

6. The Latin Quarter,
Trilby

Oh, surely, surely, I cried to myself, we ought to find some means of possessing the past more fully and completely than we do. Life is not worth living for many of us if a want so desperate and yet so natural can never be satisfied. Memory is but a poor, rudimentary thing that we had better be without, if it can only lead us to the verge of consummation like this, and madden us with a desire it cannot slake.[3]

Continual backward looking was a central feature of Du Maurier's personality, the cause of much personal unhappiness, but also the source of his later creative power as a novelist.

He could not, however, dream for ever. The necessity of deciding on a career was imperative, and it was as an artist, where he had already shown some youthful talent, that he intended to make his mark. Du Maurier was probably more talented as a singer, but art seemed to offer a better avenue to success. A friend from University College had spoken highly of the atelier of Charles Gleyre, and it was there that he registered. In Paris, Du Maurier was one of a large number of English art students, drawn to the city by its reputation as a great art centre, and the freedom from restraint which they enjoyed there: 'Critical judgement of the character of the French school for students was challenged then as now, for the young naturally wished to study in the gay city'.[4] The picture of the respectable and middle-aged Queen Victoria driving through Paris with the vivacious Empress Eugénie in the summer of 1855, seemed to underline the difference between England and France. For a young man, Paris offered a carefree time of pleasure and camaraderie, before the serious business of establishing a reputation arose. Most English students were aware that it was only a temporary interlude, and they made the most of it before returning to the straitjacket of English life.

3. *Peter Ibbetson*, pp. 176–7.
4. W. Holman Hunt, *Pre-Raphaelitism and the Pre-Raphaelite Brotherhood* (1909), I, 190.

La vie Parisienne was not the only lure, however, and it was usually a secondary one. Most English art students were in Paris because they were genuinely dissatisfied with the system of art-teaching in England. Du Maurier himself had stepped onto the bottom rung of the well-trodden ladder to Academy success, when he began to draw from casts in the British Museum in 1852. Nearly ten years earlier, William Holman Hunt had set out on the same path, and it was beside the Elgin Marbles that he first met John Millais in 1844. Hunt's account of the system is damning:

> The British Museum, where I had commenced the special study of the human figure, was in many respects not the best drawing school for a tyro. The Pheidian marbles realise one type of perfect human form, but the mutilations they have suffered make few of them of instructive value for the copying practice of a novice who has not a connected knowledge of human proportions.[5]

Eventually, after submitting a satisfactory drawing from the antique, Hunt was admitted to the Royal Academy Schools. Du Maurier would presumably have done the same if he had stayed in London. After a year or more in the antique school, copying from classical casts, Hunt progressed to the life school and began to draw from the living model. The Academy made little attempt to teach the technique of painting, and its whole system of education was diffuse and unimaginative. A series of senior academicians, who changed each year, acted as visitors, and provided a contradictory and fragmentary tuition.

The Pre-Raphaelite Brotherhood, formed by Hunt, Millais and D. G. Rossetti in 1848, was in revolt against the Academy Schools, and the second-hand traditions which they perpetrated. Du Maurier was not involved in any way with the art world in the early 1850s, and there is no reason to suppose that he understood, or had even heard of, the Pre-Raphaelites. He had been assured that drawing from plaster-casts was the best training for an artist. His decision to go to Paris was not a rejection of English art-education, but a passionate longing to return to the place he regarded as home.

Drawing from the antique had no place in most Parisian ateliers. Students started drawing and painting from the model at once, and, in consequence, they acquired a much surer grasp of fundamentals than their English counterparts. This helps to explain why French

5. I, 39.

academic draughtsmanship was so much better than English throughout the nineteenth century. Art students in Paris did attend classes at the École des Beaux-Arts (not Du Maurier or his friends), but this was supplementary to their other work. The ateliers, run by successful and well-known painters, were the basis of the French system. These were quite separate from those in which the masters themselves painted. The teaching there was far less deadening and formal than in England. A model was provided, and the students worked from it by themselves, the younger students often receiving advice from the more experienced. The master would call occasionally, perhaps once or twice a week, to comment on the work of his students. A payment was usually levied for the use of the model and other facilities, a percentage of which most masters kept for themselves; as a result, the popular ateliers could be very lucrative. This method of teaching naturally appealed to the more adventurous art student, and the ateliers were attended by students from all over Europe, and, in increasing numbers, from the United States.

The advantages of the French method can be seen in the influence which a conscientious master could exert on a brilliant student – the influence of Carolus-Duran on John Singer Sargent, for example. With the lack of personal tuition at the Royal Academy Schools, a precocious talent was not given much scope to develop. Carolus-Duran, and even Gleyre, Du Maurier's master, taught their pupils the groundwork of painting with enormous thoroughness, but they did not impose on them a rigid style. Other artists were less scrupulous. The inherent danger in the French system was summed up by John Millais in an interview of 1884:

> You are evidently taken with the atelier system. . . . Now, if I had a dozen young men painting in this studio of mine, the chances are that they would imitate my faults, as a certain French set do those of their master, who himself, however, imitates nobody. You would have a number of young men painting alike, and turning out work of the Millais pattern of a kind of average quality. Who are the influential men? The very ones who have worked almost alone.[6]

Hunt also believed that originality was more important than technical competence. Writing on the baneful influence of the French system, Hunt drew particular attention to the school of Ary Scheffer, whose work he had seen in Paris in 1849: 'no one looking with

6. Millais, II, 359.

impartial eyes, who really knew the history of art, could fail to foresee that his work courted the fate of the feebly rooted and the sterility of the meretricious'.[7] Scheffer's influence was pervasive, and it is nowhere more evident than in the work of Du Maurier's great friend, Tom Armstrong, who studied in Scheffer's atelier from 1853 to 1855, and from 1856 to 1858.

Du Maurier himself attended the atelier of the Swiss painter, Charles Gleyre, in the Rue de Vaugirard. Gleyre, a disciple though not a pupil of Ingres, was a melancholy and in many ways a disillusioned man. The two most profound influences on his life were those of Rome, where he spent five years, and of the Orient, which he visited from 1834 to 1837. Dogged by financial worries, and on one occasion insulted by his idol, Ingres, Gleyre finally achieved recognition in the salon of 1840, with his *St John Inspired by the Apocalyptic Vision*, and more resoundingly in 1845 with his *Evening* or *Lost Illusions* (now in the Louvre, Paris). This last work shows a poet in contemplation before a barge-full of classical beauties, who are leaving the shore, and epitomizes Gleyre's sentimental style, his feeling for line rather than colour.

Gleyre had taken over the atelier of Paul Delaroche in 1843. Previously the atelier of David and Gros, it was one of the most profitable in Paris. Gleyre, however, never took any money himself, and his students paid only for the use of the studio. The principles of his atelier were entirely founded on the teachings of Jean-Dominique Ingres, the heir of David's classicism. When Du Maurier came to Paris, Ingres was nearing the end of his working life, and so was his revolutionary rival, Eugène Delacroix. The profound conflict between Ingres' frigid line, and the swirling baroque forms and romantic vision of Delacroix, was a subject of endless discussion among the art students of the time. In choosing the atelier of Gleyre, Du Maurier had committed himself to one side in this battle of styles, but it is unlikely that he had given the matter much thought. The atelier Gleyre was well-known and inexpensive, with a reputation for providing a thorough grounding in the essentials of artistic practice. Gleyre believed that skill in drawing was the basis of all art, and was never satisfied with superficial effects, like the sentimental school of Ary Scheffer. Gleyre was uninterested in colour, and his pupils had to make up their palettes beforehand, so that they could give their whole attention to line.

7. Hunt, I, 188.

7. Taffy à l'échelle, *Trilby*.
Whistler can be clearly seen on the left

Du Maurier's description of the atelier Gleyre in his second novel, *Trilby*, is idealised and romantic, but its basic outline is close to the truth. On arrival at the studio, Du Maurier was put through a series of initiation ceremonies, which he later described through his hero, Little Billee. The older students strap Little Billee to a ladder and carry him around in procession, intending to put him under the pump if he cries out. This seems to have been standard practice in all the ateliers, but the severity of the initiation ceremonies varied. Henry Stacy Marks, who studied at Picot's in 1852, remembered the savage method of crucifying the nouveau, then in vogue there:

> This consisted in tying him securely by his head and limbs to a ladder, and, preceded by one of their number blowing on an old hunting-horn, he was borne by four students along the suburb, the remainder following in solemn procession. Now and then ladder and *nouveau* would be placed against some convenient blank wall, and left there for a while, exposed to the jeers and laughter of the passers-by.[8]

According to Val Prinsep, Whistler was put 'à l'échelle', while he

8. *Pen and Pencil Sketches*, I, 40.

himself, who went to Gleyre's in 1859, was so tall and strong that no one dared to touch him. It seems unlikely that Whistler suffered any such indignity, and his testimony contradicts Prinsep's. Besides being physically mauled, every nouveau was expected to provide a feast of cakes and wine for the whole atelier, and to entertain them with a song or a speech. In *Trilby*, the song which Little Billee sings, is that performed by Edward Poynter, when he was a nouveau at Gleyre's:

> a song about a gay cavalier who went to serenade his mistress (and a ladder of ropes, and a pair of masculine gloves that didn't belong to the gay cavalier, but which he found in his lady's bower) – a poor sort of song, but it was the nearest approach to a comic song he knew.[9]

Little Billee's performance is appalling, but he is sarcastically applauded by the other students, who take up the refrain: 'ze-ese glâ-âves, zese glâ-âves, zey do not belong to me'.[10] They demand encores, and Little Billee becomes so absorbed in his song that he misses the food. There is no record of Du Maurier's performance as a nouveau, but it was probably he who missed the cakes and wine, as he had always been proud of his tenor voice.

The students at the atelier Gleyre were less vicious and crude than those in other Parisian studios. The Italian painter, Raffaelli, trained under Gêrome, and he was appalled by the atelier: 'the wretched young fellows, most of them coarse and vulgar, indulge in disgusting jokes. They sing stupid obscene songs. They make up shameful masquerades. . . . And never, never, in this assemblage of men called to be artists, is there a discussion about art, never a noble word, never a lofty idea. Over and over again, this dirty and sense-less humbug, always filth'.[11] Physical cruelty was as rife as ob-scenity, and the atelier Delaroche, which Gleyre took over, was 'actually closed in consequence of the death of one of the pupils through the stupid cruelty of his *confrères*. It was said that he was scorched to death by being held before the stove and "ironed down" with books. Most boys know the process, but it required the brutality of the French student to carry it to a deplorable end'.[12] During the 1850s, however, the atelier Gleyre seems to have been conducted on 'dignified principles', as Whistler informed the Pennells many years

9. *Trilby*, p. 82.
10. p. 83.
11. J. Rewald, *A History of Impressionism* (New York, 1946), p. 62.
12. V. C. Prinsep, 'An Artist's Life in Paris in 1859', *Magazine of Art*, (Feb. 1904), p. 338.

8. The Fox and the Crow, *Trilby*

later: 'There was not even the usual tormenting of the *nouveau*. If a man were a decent fellow, and would sing his song, and take a little chaff, he had no trouble'.[13] Whistler's visits were not frequent, but he could remember only one unpleasant incident, when a coffin was placed at one end of the room with the name of an unpopular student on it. The gesture was effective, for the student never returned.

If the students of the atelier Gleyre were not actively cruel, they often behaved like schoolboys:

> In those days it was somewhat a rough place, and the carefully and religiously brought-up lad was much shocked at the manners and customs of the students. . . . I have seen the whole atelier astride of their chairs, prancing around the model, shouting the *Marseillaise*, which during the Empire was a song forbidden by the police. Some wag would slip out of the room and coming back rap threateningly at the door, when the procession would stop, the song cease, and each student would at once pretend to be hard at work at the drawing or painting before him, no matter whose it was. When the man who had knocked appeared instead of the terrible police he was received with a yell of indignation, and sometimes the strange gallop was recommenced.[14]

13. J. and E. Pennell, *The Life of J. McNeill Whistler* (1908), I, 49.
14. Prinsep, pp. 338 and 340.

Du Maurier illustrated the gallop in *Trilby*, but he was more explicit about the incident at the *Punch* table in 1865: 'd. M. tells tales of Whistler and his vie de Boheme in Paris, and of the nude model fingering his fair friend while the students made hobby horses of their chairs . . . d. M. tells of students drinking champagne at a sou a bottle'.[15] Gleyre's was not always as decorous as Whistler implied. He himself was present at an atelier performance, where *Macbeth* was turned into a 'shameful masquerade'.

There is evidence that the standards of the atelier Gleyre declined. Monet and Renoir, who studied there in the 1860s, both described the difficulty of working in such an undisciplined atmosphere. Renoir told an interviewer: 'While the others shouted, broke the window panes, martyrized the model, disturbed the professor, I was always quiet in my corner, very attentive, very docile, studying the model, listening to the teacher . . . and it was I whom they called the revolutionary'.[16] Even in Du Maurier's day, the atelier was so crowded that concentration can scarcely have been easy, if his drawings in Felix Moscheles' book, *In Bohemia with Du Maurier* (1896) are accurate.

9. The Atelier Gleyre (1857)

15. Silver, 24 Dec. 1865.
16. Rewald, p. 64.

Du Maurier described the life of the atelier in *Trilby* in some detail:

> [They] drew and painted from the nude model every day but Sunday from eight till twelve, and for two hours in the afternoon, except on Saturdays, when the afternoon was devoted to much-needed Augean sweepings and cleanings.
>
> One week the model was male, the next female, and so on, alternating throughout the year.
>
> A stove, a model-throne, stools, boxes, some fifty strongly-built low chairs with backs, a couple of score easels and many drawing-boards, completed the *mobilier*.
>
> The bare walls were adorned with endless caricatures – *des charges* – in charcoal and white chalk; and also the scrapings of many palettes – a polychromous decoration not unpleasing.[17]

The students were of all kinds:

> Irresponsible boys, mere *rapins*, all laugh and chaff and mischief – *blague et bagout Parisien*; little lords of misrule – wits, butts, bullies; the idle and industrious apprentice, the good and the bad, the clean and the dirty (especially the latter) – all more or less animated by a certain *esprit de corps*, and working very happily and genially together, on the whole, and always willing to help each other with sincere artistic counsel if it was asked for seriously, though it was not always couched in terms very flattering to one's self-love.[18]

In the evenings, like many other students, Du Maurier attended the atelier of Suisse, an ex-model, who ran an evening-class. It was there that 'la petite Sara', the original of Mimi la Salope in *Trilby*, sang crude argot songs in a sweet and innocent voice, while she posed in the nude.

Du Maurier spent a year at the atelier Gleyre, and, throughout this period, he continued to live in lodgings with his mother and sister, first in the Faubourg Poissonière, and later in Passy. This was scarcely a bohemian life, and Du Maurier never endured the poverty and discomfort, which are described so graphically in Murger's *Scènes de la Vie de Bohème*. This novel, published in 1848, presented a romantic picture of student life in the Quartier Latin; it stressed the bonhomie and gaiety of young artists in the face of disease, hunger, and cold. French students in the Quartier Latin were generally poor,

17. *Trilby*, pp. 73–4.
18. *Trilby*, pp. 75–6.

and they lived in appalling conditions. Sometimes they were helped
by their mistresses, the grisettes as they were called, who earned a
little money by modelling, sewing or serving in shops. The heroine of
Du Maurier's famous novel, *Trilby*, is a grisette, and Du Maurier
must have known some of these girls, both as models, and as the
mistresses of his friends. He was, however, still living at home, and
still immature in many ways, and at first he probably preferred the
camaraderie of masculine friends, to the difficulties and fears of a
relationship with a woman. The excessive purity of the young men in
Trilby is not, however, an accurate picture of even the most respectable English art-students, nor of Du Maurier himself.

It is surprising that, having returned so thankfully to Paris, Du
Maurier now consistently chose to be in the company of Englishmen.
His first friends in Paris were not Frenchmen, but boisterous
English medical students from the much despised University
College. Through them he met three art students, Thomas Lamont,
Thomas Armstrong and Edward Poynter, who were to become his
close friends. It is worth asking how French Du Maurier really was,
when one considers how few French friends he made, and how
profoundly English in attitude he remained. Henry James, who later
attached so much importance to Du Maurier's dual nationality,
recognized how little influence his French background had on his
every-day life. He believed, however, that it had profoundly affected
the cast of his mind. By a curious paradox, Du Maurier's disenchantment with the French way of life and temperament, coincided
with his happy year as an art student in Paris. The memory of his
Passy childhood remained untarnished, but a marked dislike of the
French race soon became evident.

The English students in Paris formed a group of their own, drawn
together by a common language and background, but not by any
united artistic intention. Many of them never achieved distinction,
like Harris Butterfield, who wrote to Du Maurier in 1894 to say that
Trilby had awakened 'pleasant memories . . . of a happy time I
spent in Paris in '57, much of it in your society . . . I cannot forget the
days when you used to fetch me from my roost in the rue des Pères to
witness some of the scenes you so vividly describe'. Most of the
English students were comfortably off, and for them life entailed no
greater hardship than a few days on rice pudding while awaiting an
allowance from home. Even pawning their valuables was not taken
very seriously, for, as one of them put it, 'we were none of us real
Bohemians, for we had those behind us in England who would have

10. The Happy Life, Barbizon, *Trilby*

come to our help if we had been in dire necessity'.[19] Not in the least forward-looking, they sincerely believed that all that was necessary to become a good artist was the requisite number of attendances at the atelier, complemented by work of their own along the same lines. They would occasionally discuss the relative merits of the great modern masters, Ingres and Delacroix, but the naturalism of the Barbizon School, and Courbet's 'réalisme' were regarded as amusing aberrations, which the true artist should avoid. They did, on occasion, visit Barbizon for a restful weekend in the country, but Du Maurier's comic sketch of a Barbizon painter in *Trilby* is a reflection of their attitude to this school. Thomas Armstrong was the only one of the group to take any interest in their work, or in landscape painting at all; he had spent some time in Barbizon before Du Maurier arrived in Paris: 'Barbizon was then, to the eye of an untravelled Englishman, a mean and untidy-looking village; it had houses at intervals on both sides of one long street, many of them with

19. Armstrong, p. 121.

dunghills in front of them'.[20] Even Armstrong was not working in the Forest of Fontainebleu itself, but in the village, where he 'did a painting of the front of Vannier's inn, a building ugly and almost squalid in appearance'.[21]

While the English group were pursuing a conventional and academic art education, the Impressionists were already forging a revolutionary technique with which to express their individual vision of the world around them. The indifference of Du Maurier and his friends to avant-garde experiments in French painting is typical of the insularity of English art, and of the gulf which divided it from the continent. Most English artists regarded painting as the illustration of a pleasant story or myth, and were only worried that their subject might be stolen by a rival, never questioning the fundamental aims of narrative art. This attitude was basically philistine, and it is not surprising that the English group in Paris should miss the significance of Courbet, Millet and Manet. Even the expression 'English group' is misleading, for unlike their successors at Gleyre's, Renoir, Monet, Bazille and Sisley, they entirely lacked any revolutionary zeal. While the Impressionists rejected everything that Gleyre taught them, the English group were willing to accept his classical tradition without question. They lacked, therefore, any uniting sense of artistic struggle or rebellion, and were only drawn together by friendship and communal amusements. They were in Paris to learn the craft of painting, rather than to question its basic principles.

The English students all agreed that the atelier system was more progressive than the teaching of the Academy Schools. Nevertheless, it was austerely classical in bias. Monet told the story of a disagreement with Gleyre which epitomised their conflicting attitudes. Looking at Monet's drawing of a model, Gleyre informed him that it was not bad, but rather ugly – the feet were far too large and the figure too heavy. Monet tentatively replied that he was trying to paint what he saw in front of him, which provoked a characteristic lecture. Praxiteles had combined the best features of a hundred models to construct a masterpiece: 'Quand on fait quelque chose, il faut penser à l'antique!'.[22] Auguste Renoir, a fellow-student of Monet, fell out with Gleyre on the question of colour; he did not believe that it should be subsidiary to outline. D. G. Rossetti told

20. Armstrong, p. 122.   22. G. Geffroy, *Claude Monet* (Paris, 1922), p. 27.
21. p. 125.

Val Prinsep, 'that French colouring was bad, that it was heavy, and so on, and that any Englishman who learnt to paint there was ruined as an artist'.[23] As a result of this advice, Prinsep only practised drawing in Paris, and did no painting at all, which he lived to regret.

Thomas Armstrong was the chronicler of the English group, and his 'Reminiscences of Du Maurier', published posthumously in 1912, is of great importance biographically. The son of a Manchester cotton manufacturer, Armstrong was a student of Ary Scheffer. He first met Du Maurier in the summer of 1856, three years after his own arrival, at the Hotel Corneille, near the Odéon, through two Cornish medical students. Armstrong was immediately impressed by him:

> It is strange that my recollections of that first meeting with him should be so vivid, but I suppose his personality from the beginning attracted me. I can revive the picture of him in my mind's eye, sitting astride one of the dingy Utrecht velvet chairs, with his elbows on the back, pale almost to sallowness, square-shouldered, and very lean, with no hair on his face except a very slight moustache.[24]

Compared with Thomas Lamont, whom Armstrong met at roughly the same time, a red-faced and conventional Scotsman, with little imagination or artistic ability, Du Maurier appeared as a delightful and engrossing companion. Armstrong found 'frequent opportunities of seeing him'[25] after that first meeting. Released from the gloom of Pentonville and University College, Du Maurier was bubbling over with excitement and high spirits, back once more in a conducive and stimulating environment. He dazzled Armstrong and Lamont with his careless bonhomie, fluent French, ease and charm of manner, his delicate wit, fine singing voice, and even his surprising skill with boxing gloves. He had about him a certain panache, which enabled him to cut a dash among his English friends, who thought his 'Noah's Ark' coat the height of fashion. With James Whistler, however, he had to play second fiddle. Whistler, who had arrived in Paris from America in the summer of 1855, was another pupil at Gleyre's, and he became intimately acquainted with the English group. Intensely bohemian, and interested in the more avant-garde experiments of French art, he spent little time at Gleyre's, preferring to sit at café tables, discussing Courbet's theories

23. Prinsep, p. 338.
24. Armstrong, pp. 117–8.   25. Armstrong, p. 120.

with men like Carolus-Duran, Braquemond, Alphonse Legros and, later, Henri de Fantin-Latour. His views on art and life were profoundly antipathetical to his English friends, but he was a commanding and irresistible personality. Du Maurier, in particular, was exhilarated by Whistler's unconventional behaviour, and enjoyed meeting him and his fiery mistress Heloïse, or 'Fumette'. Armstrong, easily the most urbane and adult of the group, regarded Fumette with considerable understanding and sympathy:

> She was a remarkable person, not pretty in feature, and sallow in complexion, but with good eyes and a sympathetic sort of face. . . . She used to go about bareheaded and carrying a little basket containing the crochet work she was in the habit of doing, and a volume of Alfred de Musset's poems. This little pose added to the interest excited by her flowing locks and her large eyes. She was a chatterbox, and at times regaled us with songs, rather spoken than sung, for she had not much voice or power of musical expression.[26]

Whistler himself was also very conspicuous:

> he was clothed entirely in white duck (quite clean too!), and on his head he wore a straw hat of an American shape not yet well known in Europe, very low in the crown and stiff in the brim, bound with a black ribbon with long ends hanging down behind.[27]

It is not difficult to see why Whistler was attracted to Du Maurier and his friends; they were an audience whom he could impress, and they spoke the same language. In later life, Whistler and the Englishmen were to deny that their relations had ever been close, but contemporary evidence proves otherwise. Indeed, Poynter and Lamont had shared rooms with Whistler for some months before Du Maurier's arrival. Poynter was the exact opposite of Whistler in character and temperament, and he followed an entirely different artistic tradition. He had come to Paris because of his dissatisfaction with English art education (he had been at three schools in London, including the Academy), but he was in no sense a progressive. Once in Paris he followed the classical tradition of Ingres without question. The most intelligent of the English group, and the most dedicated and hard-working, he knew exactly where he was going.

The English group really came into being when Armstrong rented

26. Armstrong, pp. 191–2.
27. Armstrong, p. 174.

a studio at 53 rue Notre Dâme des Champs in the autumn of 1856, and suggested that he and his four friends should take it on as a joint venture. They had, in various combinations, become friendly during the summer of that year, but Armstrong's suggestion was the catalyst. The rent was reasonable, but the studio seemed rather large, and the scheme was carefully discussed and analysed. When they finally decided to take it, Whistler opted out, but he continued to call, and remained friendly. He had by now acquired more exciting friends than the English, his so-called no-shirt friends.

Before moving into the studio, the group organised a Christmas dinner, which was held in Lamont's lodgings. It was Armstrong's idea again, conceived while he was lying ill in a Paris nursing home. He had made an expedition to Barbizon in October, and he had contracted rheumatic fever there from working in the incessant rain. Seriously ill, his mind ran on food:

> even at this critical time I discussed with the greatest interest the very serious question of cooking the turkey, whether it should be boiled or roasted. A boiled turkey would be more English, to be sure, but we wanted to have a "plat" more English even than a boiled turkey, and that was a boiled leg of mutton, a dish never heard of in France.[28]

The turkey, the leg of mutton, a plum-pudding, two bottles of whisky and a stilton were ordered from London, while English beer and French liqueurs were bought in Paris, together with other delicacies:

> truffled galantines of turkey, tongues, hams, *rillettes de Tours, pâtés de foie gras, fromage d'Italie* (which has nothing to do with cheese), *saucissons d'Arles et de Lyon*, with and without garlic, cold jellies peppery and salt . . . sweet jellies, and cakes, and sweetmeats, and confections of all kinds, from the famous pastry-cook at the corner of the Rue Castiglione.[29]

The days before Christmas were spent in a delicious state of anticipation, but on Christmas Eve the hamper from England had still not arrived. Not too concerned, the English students walked through a moonlit and frosty Paris to the midnight service in the Madeleine, where the baritone from the Opéra Comique was to sing Adam's *Noël*. Protestants themselves, they listened to the service with 'mixed

28. Armstrong, p. 130.
29. *Trilby*, p. 154.

feelings',[30] but Du Maurier at least 'melted at the beautiful music'[31] like the hero of *Trilby*, Little Billee:

> whose way it was to magnify and exaggerate all things under the subtle stimulus of sound, and the singing human voice had especially strange power to penetrate into his inmost depths – even the voice of man.[32]

Throughout his life, Du Maurier experienced these spiritual sensations when listening to fine music. In a poem written in the 1880s, he explained that, while prayer or orthodox dogma meant nothing to him, he experienced deep religious emotion when inspired by music:

> Sick am I of idle words, past all reconciling –
> Words that weary and perplex, and pander and conceal;
> Wake the sounds that cannot lie, for all their sweet beguiling;
> The language one need fathom not, but only hear and feel.[33]

The events of that Christmas Day are described in some detail in Armstrong's 'Reminiscences', and also in *Trilby*, where Du Maurier made few alterations from the facts. Significantly, it was Lamont's concièrge, and not the beautiful Trilby, who did the cooking. It must have required a feat of imagination to replace Lamont's landlady, 'a very fat, good-natured woman, who took much interest in the Christmas meal of the crazy English',[34] with 'Trilby, tall, graceful, and stately, and also swift of action . . . like Juno or Diana'.[35] Lamont's lodgings were 'on the third storey and small', and the building itself was 'already condemned for demolition by the city authorities.'[36] The hamper had not yet arrived but it was still confidently expected. Only in the late afternoon did they become really worried, and call at the depot to see what had happened to it. There they found that the customs had refused to release it – because of the two bottles of whisky, which were confiscated. It was not until six o'clock that the hamper arrived in Lamont's studio, the bottles of whisky having been replaced, at considerable expense, from a shop in the Rue de Rivoli:

30. *Trilby*, p. 156.
31. *Trilby*, p. 156.
32. p. 158.
33. 'Music' (After Sully Prudhomme), *English Illustrated Magazine* (June, 1884), p. 542.

34. Armstrong, p. 132.
35. *Trilby*, p. 164.
36. Armstrong, p. 132.

And suddenly the studio, which had been so silent, dark, and dull, with Taffy and Little Billee sitting hopeless and despondent round the stove, became a scene of the noisiest, busiest, and cheerfullest animation. The three big lamps were lit, and all the Chinese lanterns . . . every one was pressed into the preparations for the banquet. There was plenty for idle hands to do. Sausages to be fried for the turkey, stuffing made, and sauces, salads mixed, and punch – holly hung in festoons all round and about – a thousand things.[37]

According to Du Maurier, the meal took three hours to prepare, but Armstrong's estimate of four was probably nearer the mark. No ladies were present at the real Christmas dinner, for, as the Laird in *Trilby* puts it: 'Them wimmen spiles the ball!'.[38] Armstrong recalled his delight in drinking English bottled beer with the food, and having whisky and water afterwards. The drinking and singing lasted into the early hours of the morning. Only at six o'clock did Armstrong, still far from well, fall asleep in Lamont's bed, and it was not until eight o'clock that Du Maurier set off towards Passy. No-one, said Armstrong, was 'much "over the line",'[39] but Du Maurier was far enough over to need a sleep in the Champs de Mars before completing his journey. A week later, on New Year's Eve, the four friends took possession of their studio, and Du Maurier's real student life began. Over thirty years later he described it in his second novel, *Trilby*, which is, like his other two books, part autobiography and part melodrama. It is the most robust of his novels, for his student memories were less poignant than those of his childhood. This one year of gaiety and irresponsibility became a symbol of his youth; companionship had been easy there, unhampered by the social barriers which later drove the group apart. *Trilby* is a tribute to masculine friendship, and the joys of bachelor life:

Oh, happy days and happy nights, sacred to art and friendship! oh, happy times of careless impecuniosity, and youth and hope and health and strength and freedom – with all Paris for a playground, and its dear old unregenerate Latin Quarter for a workshop and a home![40]

The account of the Latin Quarter in *Trilby* was of course much idealised, for the passage of time had blurred and softened some of Du Maurier's memories. Most of the characters of the novel were founded on his friends: Lamont became 'the Laird'; Whistler and

37. *Trilby*, pp. 162–3.
38. *Trilby*, p. 154.
39. Armstrong, p. 133.
40. *Trilby*, pp. 39–40.

11. My Sister Dear, *Trilby*. The Christmas Dinner –
Alecco Ionides is the fourth male figure from the right,
Poynter the fifth, Whistler the eighth, Du Maurier the
tenth and Lamont the eleventh

Poynter, Joe Sibley and Lorrimer respectively; and Alecco Ionides, 'the Greek'. There was much of Du Maurier himself in 'Little Billee', and of Armstrong in the affectionate and dependable Taffy. The novel begins with 'the three musketeers of the brush', Taffy, the Laird and Little Billee, moving into a studio in the Place St Anatole des Arts, which was of course the studio at 53 rue Notre Dâme des Champs. The studio is a central feature of the book, as it became the focal point of Du Maurier's student life. In 1856, the rue Notre Dâme des Champs was still unspoilt: 'About and behind the old houses in our street were gardens, and the trees which grew in them overtopped the high walls of our courtyard and gave quite a country-like appearance'.[41] The large houses were divided into apartments and studios; number 53 had a central courtyard with four separate staircases in each corner. A wooden gate opened onto the street, near which lived the concièrges, M. and Mme Vinot, the Vinards of *Trilby*. Other artists also lived in the house, including a sculptor whose model would come across the yard to talk to the Englishmen, dressed only in her shift, and a couple who passed as brother and sister 'about whose position we were much given to speculate'.[42] The girl, in particular, intrigued Du Maurier: 'He admired the lady very much as being of a highly-bred appearance, and she certainly was very good looking, thin and tall, with a great deal of black hair and large dark eyes, and with very finely shaped feet such as one does not often see'.[43] He never got beyond saying good-morning to her, but he gave her feet to Trilby, while Trilby's first appearance in the novel, hastily dressed after posing in the nude, was taken from the sculptor's model.

The studio itself had a large north window, and smaller windows to east and west. Lamont installed his few pieces of furniture there when his own apartment was condemned, and the group slowly decorated the room with plaster casts, copies of famous paintings, and works of their own:

> there were alcoves, recesses, irregularities, odd little nooks and corners, to be filled up as time wore on with endless personal nick-nacks, bibelots, private properties and acquisitions – things that make a place genial, homelike, and good to remember, and sweet to muse upon (with fond regret) in after years.[44]

41. Armstrong, p. 135.   43. Armstrong, p. 134.
42. Armstrong, pp. 133-4.   44. *Trilby*, p. 3.

Du Maurier drew a sketch of Whistler on the wall, 'then a fainter one, and then merely a note of interrogation – very clever it was and very like the original'.[45] In addition to the studio, there was a small bedroom in which Lamont slept; when Armstrong moved in, Lamont slept on the divan in the studio itself. Du Maurier still lived in Passy, and Poynter's lodgings were in the rue Jacob. The everyday life of the studio began in the afternoon, for in the morning Du Maurier continued to go with Poynter to Gleyre's. The four young men would settle down to their own work after lunch, trying to keep warm with the two inadequate stoves which 'had to be crammed' full of fuel 'before one's fingers could hold a brush or squeeze a bladder'.[46] Du Maurier's one achievement during the seven months in the studio was a small oil painting of *Osbaldistone and Di Vernon*, taken from the story of *Rob Roy* which was a favourite novel of his. Armstrong later managed to sell it to a Mr Edward Green for five pounds, and it was Du Maurier's first professional income. Armstrong was trying to finish two works begun in Barbizon, and Lamont's attention was taken up with his six foot high study of *Lorenzo and Isabella*, a subject already successfully executed by John Millais. One afternoon, during a fencing match, a foil accidentally pierced it, but nobody was much concerned. The 'masterpiece' was finally ruined after Du Maurier's departure for Antwerp, when the sculptor, Maître, who lived above, fell through it during a boxing match.

Poynter worked much harder than the other three, and Armstrong later remarked that 'if he had been older he might have had a wholesome influence in making us work more steadily'.[47] In his use of clear-cut outlines, and his uncompromising adherence to flat areas of colour, Poynter revealed the effect of his education at Gleyre's. During a lecture in 1871, he described his attempts to run the Slade School of Art on French lines:

> I shall impress but one lesson upon the students, that constant study from the life-model is the only means they have of arriving at a comprehension of the beauty in nature, and of avoiding its ugliness and deformity; which I take to be the whole aim and end of study.[48]

The four Englishmen devoted three hours' work to their own painting during the afternoon; at four o'clock the time came for recreation. Joseph Rowley, another art student and friend, who

45. Pennells, I, 51.   47. Armstrong, p. 137.
46. *Trilby*, p. 152.   48. Sir E. J. Poynter, *Ten Lectures on Art* (1879), p. 107.

12. All as it used to be, *Trilby*. Whistler is the sixth figure
from the right

often arrived before they had finished working, walked up and down
the room with a thirty-pound dumb-bell in each hand until they
'knocked off'. He then offered to box with anyone who would take
him on. Fencing and gymnastics were other favourite sports, for a
predecessor in the studio had put up a trapeze and a pair of ropes.
Val Prinsep, who arrived in Paris two years later, found the references to the trapeze in *Trilby* hard to believe: 'I do not imagine
any student in my time had a trapeze erected in his studio – indeed,
very few of them had any studio at all',[49] he wrote. Armstrong's
Memoir, however, proves that Du Maurier had invented nothing.
Whistler was greatly amused by these sports, but he never joined in.
He had other outlets for his surplus energy. The games were followed by baths, a practice which vastly amused the French, who
were unused to regular washing. Considering the cynical and bohemian attitude of most French art students, it is not surprising
that the English group remained closely united, and made few
friends outside.

Du Maurier often entertained the group with songs, accompanied
on a hired piano:

> Du Maurier . . . was the life and soul of the party that used to gather
> within its shabby walls to spend the evening after dinner. Amongst its
> rare and prized pieces of furniture was a piano, at which du Maurier was
> constantly playing when he ought to have been working. He had a
> beautiful tenor voice, and was always ready to oblige with a song.[50]

Du Maurier's favourite songs were the anti-imperialist 'Sieur de
Framboisy', Thackeray's 'Little Billee', Martini il Tedesco's
'Plaisir d'Amour', and the French folk-song, 'Le Vin à Quatre Sous':

> Fi! de ces vins d'Espagne,
> Ils ne sont pas faits pour nous.
> C'est le vin à quatre sous
> Qui nous sert de Champagne.[51]

Lamont also was famous for his Scottish folk-songs, 'Hie diddle dee
for the Lowlands low',[52] and Poynter would thunder out airs from
Il Trovatore and the *Hallelujah Chorus*. Whistler amused them with
Negro spirituals: 'He used to take a stick or an umbrella and,

49. Prinsep, p. 338.   51. Armstrong, p. 149.
50. H. Lucy, *Nearing Jordan* (1916), p. 106. 52. *Trilby*, p. 165.

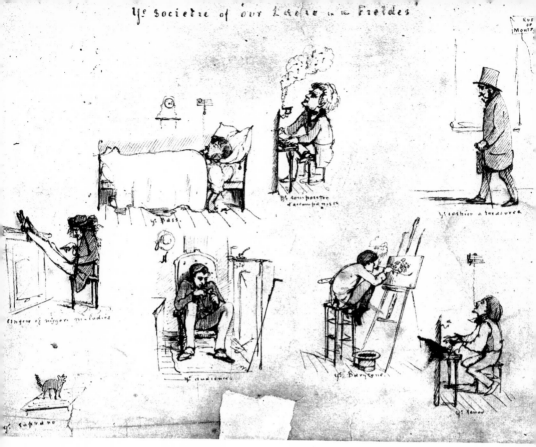

13. Ye Societie of our Ladye in the Fieldes (1857)

holding it in his left hand like a banjo, twiddled on it with the finger and thumb of the right hand while he pattered grotesque rhymes founded on the supposed adventures of Scripture characters'.[53] Occasionally the Greek composer, Sotiri, was present, and he could sometimes be persuaded to play part of his unfinished opera, or accompany Du Maurier's singing. Years afterwards, another friend, Luke Ionides, claimed that Sotiri was the original of Svengali, but Thomas Armstrong denied it emphatically. In Du Maurier's caricature sketch of this time, *Ye Societie of Our Ladye in the Fieldes*, Sotiri and Poynter can be seen playing the piano, Lamont is lying in bed, while Armstrong, still weak from his illness, is hobbling along with a stick. A curiously attenuated Whistler appears on the left of the design with his feet on the mantlepiece, and next to him is the seated figure of Alecco Ionides. Alecco (Alexander) and Luke Ionides were the sons of a wealthy Greek merchant in London, and were very friendly with the English group. Alecco was a student

53. Armstrong, pp. 183–4.

somewhere in Paris, but nobody ever found out exactly what he was
doing. He liked to drop in at the studio, and colour pipes or listen
quietly to the conversation. Luke's visits were rare, for he travelled
extensively all over Europe, but be became intimate with Whistler,
and his *Memories*, published in 1935, are, if unreliable, another source
of information about the group.

In the evenings, Lamont, Armstrong and Du Maurier would dine
together, with any other friends who happened to be there. They
would sometimes visit a restaurant run by le père Trin, who served
food so highly spiced that it was often impossible to tell whether it was
meat or fish. On other evenings they cooked their own supper, a
familiar diet of chops, fried potatoes, salad and cheap wine. These
meals are a distinctive feature of *Trilby*:

> Little Billee . . . would dive into back streets and buy a yard or so of
> crusty new bread, well burned on the flat side, a fillet of beef, a litre of
> wine, potatoes and onions, butter, a little cylindrical cheese called
> 'bondon de Neufchâtel', tender curly lettuce, with chervil, parsley,
> spring onions, and other fine herbs, and a pod of garlic.[54]

A drawing by Du Maurier, reproduced in Armstrong's 'Reminiscences', shows Armstrong, Lamont and Du Maurier preparing the
supper in extremely cramped surroundings. Armstrong is waiting to
peel the potatoes, which Du Maurier has forgotten to bring, while
Lamont sits crouched over the stove cooking chops. On one occasion
an English artist, Willie O'Connor, came to supper very smartly
dressed, and was sent out with Armstrong to fetch the chops and the
salad, which spoiled his pale grey kid gloves. O'Connor took this in
good part, and the story is told again in *Trilby*.

On Saturdays, the group made a pilgrimage to the English
restaurant in the rue Royale, which served roast beef and mutton,
English beer and gin. They enjoyed these evenings in the company of
'people in some way or other connected with horseflesh, swell
grooms, or men about horse-dealers' stables'.[55] After dinner they
went on to see the wild-boar in the Place St Sulpice. Their return
to the Quartier Latin was accompanied with boisterous songs:

> En revenant de Barbizon,
> Zon zon zainé zon zon,

54. *Trilby*, p. 38.
55. Armstrong, p. 140.

14. Cooking the Dinner (1857)

J'ai rencontre Mam'zelle Suzon,
Zon zon zainé zon zon.

J'aime l'oignon fait a l'huile,
J'aime oignon quand il est bon.
Au pas, Camarades, au pas!
Zing tra la la, &c., &c., &c.[56]

They were not habitués of the Moulin Rouge or the Moulin de la Galette, nor did they enjoy female society on these Saturday evening expeditions into Paris.

The English group were willing to make few concessions to another culture and way of life, sticking grimly to their national traditions. As Armstrong later put it: 'We were at that time like those wearing dog collars, about whom the old riddle was made, "Pourquoi porte-t-il des faux cols? Parce qu'il est fier d'étrangler

56. Armstrong, p. 141.

(d'être Anglais)".'[57] Their practical jokes were typical of the un-sophisticated background from which they came. On one occasion Lamont, who was then in his thirties, took a three-foot notice advertising 'mince pies' from an English Public House in the rue de Rivoli and carried it into an exclusive French cake shop, expecting to confuse the assistants. The joke misfired, however, when they not only understood it, but sold him some at a high price.

While the English group carried on a united social life, they had few definite artistic links, except their activity at Gleyre's, and the comments which they passed on each other's work. Whistler was responsible for one project, which deserves some mention. He had learned etching in the coastal survey office in Washington, and he suggested to the others that they might all earn some money by producing five etched plates and sending them to an author in England, who would write a book around them. They referred to this hypothetical gentleman as the 'literary bloke'. Calling themselves Plawd, a name made up from the first letters of their names, their enthusiasm did not last, and only three plates were ever produced, Whistler's, Poynter's and Du Maurier's. The subject of Du Maurier's plate shows that his mind was still running on his family's history; he appeared in it himself with a fictitious wife and son, and entitled it 'George Louis Palmella, Comte Busson du Maurier, with Madame la Comtesse and Monsieur le Viscomte'. Du Maurier had explained to his friends that his grandfather had been created a count by the Pope, and that the patent of nobility was at home in a box. The others teased him about this, and on one occasion offered to give him a bottle of gin in exchange for the patent. This document, presumably a forgery of Robert-Mathurin's, was eventually left behind in Malines, two years later. A print of the etching remained in Armstrong's possession until his death in 1911.

Before leaving Paris, it is worth discussing Whistler's relationship with the English group, and with Du Maurier in particular, in more detail. He appears in *Trilby* as Joe Sibley, but his characterization there incorporates events and developments which took place long after Paris:

> Then there was Joe Sibley, the idle apprentice, the king of bohemia, *le roi des truands*, to whom everything was forgiven, as to Francois Villon, 'à cause de ses gentillesses'.

57. Armstrong, p. 140.

Always in debt, like Svengali; like Svengali, vain witty, and a most
exquisite and original artist; and also eccentric in his attire (though
clean), so that people would stare at him as he walked along – which he
adored! But (unlike Svengali) he was genial, caressing, sympathetic,
charming; the most irresistible friend in the world as long as his friendship lasted – but that was not for-ever![58]

In contrast to the 'idle apprentice' Du Maurier portrayed Poynter as
Lorrimer, 'the industrious apprentice'. Where Lorrimer adored the
old masters, Sibley's favourite artist was himself: 'He was a mono-
theist, and had but one god, and was less tiresome in the expression
of his worship'.[59] In Paris, however, most of the English group were
prepared to acknowledge Whistler's talent, and to look at his paintings with an open and admiring eye. His qualities as a painter were
unmistakable, and even his early works have the stamp of an original
and powerful genius. This was not only true of him as a painter. His
set of Alsace etchings of 1856 show that he could master a specialized
and difficult medium. Most of the comments on his idleness and
eccentricity were the product of later years, when his old English
friends were entrenched in conventional and middle-class lives, and
could view his pictures and his personality from a safe distance.
Poynter alone had disapproved of Whistler almost from the start,
although he had briefly shared rooms with him. Poynter was the
most intransigent of the English friends, and he had already taken up
a stand to which he was to adhere for the rest of his life. He was not as
likely to fall victim to Whistler's charming but dominating personality as the more pliable Du Maurier. Poynter was not, however,
such an insensitive and unthinking reactionary, as one might
imagine from Du Maurier's description of him as Lorrimer in *Trilby*:

Tall, thin, red-haired, and well-favoured, he was a most eager, earnest,
and painstaking young enthusiast, of precocious culture, who read
improving books, and did not share in the amusements of the Quartier
Latin, but spent his evenings at home with Handel, Michael Angelo,
and Dante, on the respectable side of the river. Also, he went into good
society sometimes, with a dress-coat on, and a white tie, and his hair
parted in the middle!
But in spite of these blemishes on his otherwise exemplary record as an
art student, he was the most delightful companion – the most affectionate, helpful, and sympathetic of friends. May he live long and
prosper!

58. 'Trilby', *Harper's Monthly Magazine*, LXXXVIII (March 1894), p. 577.
59. *Harper's Monthly*, p. 578.

Enthusiast as he was, he could only worship one god at a time. It was either Michael Angelo, Phidias, Paul Veronese, Tintoret, Raphael, or Titian – never a modern – moderns didn't exist! And so thoroughgoing was he in his worship, and so persistent in voicing it, that he made those immortals quite unpopular in the Place St Anatole des Arts. We grew to dread their very names. Each of them would last him a couple of months or so; then he would give us a month's holiday, and take up another.[60]

Poynter later became president of the Royal Academy and director of the National Gallery. His work on the catalogue of paintings there is impressive, and this impression is confirmed by reading his *Ten Lectures on Art*. He expounded his views on art in a lucid prose style, which reinforces the uncompromising nature of his opinions. In one lecture, he advocated the introduction of the atelier system into England. In another, he extolled the values of classical art, stating that the one aim of his painting was 'the lofty one of trying to recall the glories of antique art'.[61] Poynter had some talent as an artist, but his work does not invite sympathy. Both he and Armstrong were later heads of the South Kensington School of Art, and they could have done something to introduce new ideas and techniques into English art education, had they been more flexible. Whistler and Poynter were too deeply divided on artistic and temperamental grounds ever to be able to like or respect each other. Shortly before Whistler died, Poynter was heard to remark at a private view of Whistler's work: 'A genius, but the devil wouldn't work!'.[62] He was even less generous when he was called upon to speak about Whistler at the Royal Academy dinner of 1904, shortly after Whistler's death. Recalling their time together as students in Paris, Poynter remarked: 'if he could be called a student, who, to my knowledge, during the two or three years when I was associated with him, devoted hardly as many weeks to study'.[63] The truth was, of course, that Whistler was anything but idle, and the time he spent in his own studio or in the cafés of Montparnasse was not wasted. He knew that Gleyre could tell him nothing, that academic drawing from the life was useless, and that a true creative vision must be forged elsewhere. Poynter's comment was not only untrue, but an irrelevant taunt to belittle the stature of his rival. It had been used

60. *Trilby*, pp. 140–1.
61. *Ten lectures on Art*, p. 118.
62. E. R. and J. Pennell, *The Whistler Journal* (Philadelphia, 1921), p. 50.
63. Pennells, *Life of Whistler*, I, 52.

before, at the *Whistler v. Ruskin* trial, and was then, as now, the despairing last shot of a reactionary. Armstrong, always more balanced in his judgments, in whatever direction his real sympathy lay, firmly contradicted Poynter:

> I may perhaps correct the impression, common among outsiders, that Whistler's pictures were done in a rapid and slap-dash manner. I have never seen or heard of any painter who took so much time in making up tints on his palette before applying them to the canvas, and he worked very slowly.[64]

Whistler, looking back in his turn, remembered Armstrong with affection, setting him apart from the other 'solemn Britons'.

Du Maurier left Paris for Antwerp in the summer of 1857, after only one year of what he later called 'my happy student life'. His place in the studio was taken by Joseph Rowley. There is no convincing reason to explain why Du Maurier suddenly left his congenial companions, a happy studio and a comfortable home to go to an unfamiliar city in a new country. He had, it is true, learned little about art at Gleyre's atelier, but it is difficult to believe that a sense of vocation alone drove him to Antwerp. There must have been more urgent reasons for his departure.

Although Du Maurier spent less than a year in Paris, it was a crucial period in his life. The English side of his personality became dominant, and set the pattern for the rest of his life. His new friends were very different from the coarse medical students at University College, and he responded to them eagerly. Not a profound person himself, he was uneasily contemptuous of Whistler's intellectual friends, and preferred to discuss such well-worn themes as the relative merits of Dickens and Thackeray, Greek and Roman, Delacroix and Ingres. The simplicity and warmth of his friendship with the members of the English group was the chief source of his happiness and well-being, but it was probably not the only one. His mother's casual advice in 1862 that he should take a mistress to relieve his mental tension does not suggest that she would have placed an embargo on his relations with the other sex in Paris. The guarded references to girl friends during his early years in London show that Du Maurier was not a virgin when he married, and there may have been relationships in Paris which it will never be possible to trace.

64. Armstrong, p. 197.

Chapter 3

Malines and Dusseldorf

IN THE EARLY SUMMER OF 1857, Du Maurier began his studies at the Antwerp Academy of Fine Arts, then under the direction of Nicaise de Keyser, a well-known historical painter. History painting was the dominant school in Belgium at this period, for the advent of political independence in 1830 had revived interest and pride in the national past. The leading exponent of the school was Gustav Wappers, with de Keyser and Jacob Van Lerius, professor of painting at Antwerp, among his foremost disciples. Their huge canvasses, often of battle scenes, are highly detailed, but curiously static, in spite of their intention of emulating the achievement of Rubens. Designed for imposing architectural settings, their work now seems ponderous and theatrical. It is difficult now to appreciate the fame and importance of the Antwerp Academy, then regarded as one of the leading European schools, and the spearhead of a new Belgian Renaissance. There was, therefore, nothing unusual in Du Maurier's choice, for Antwerp was already beginning to rival Paris as a centre for art students. Its methods of teaching differed too from those current in Paris, for its accent was on colour and tone, and not on line: 'in the atelier Gleyre you might have studied form and learnt to fill it with colour, but here you would be taught to manipulate colour, and to limit it by form'.[1] Its principles were otherwise broadly romantic, teaching the importance of chiaroscuro and dramatic effects.

Du Maurier arrived in Antwerp alone, for his mother had

15. Self-portrait sketch, Moscheles, above, as the evil genius (1858)

1. Moscheles, p. 22.

arranged to spend a few months with her brother in Wales, taking Isabella with her. Du Maurier settled down to hard work at the Academy, foregoing the social pleasures which he had enjoyed in Paris. He described his strict régime in *The Martian*:

> He rose before the dawn, and went for a swim more than a mile away – got to the academy at six – worked till eight – breakfasted on a little roll called a pistolet, and a cup of coffee; then the academy again from nine till twelve – when dinner, the cheapest he had ever known, but not the worst. Then work again all the afternoon, copying old masters at the Gallery. Then a cheap supper, a long walk along the quais or ramparts or outside, a game of dominoes, and a glass or two of 'Malines' or 'Louvain' – then bed.[2]

16. Moscheles et moi si nous avions
été de beau sexe (1857)

He made one good friend at the Academy, however, Felix Moscheles, a strange fellow-student of mixed descent. The son of a famous pianist and music teacher, Moscheles was a bohemian character, accustomed to mix with artists and musicians all over Europe. He was highly scornful of conventional behaviour, dressing in a bizarre over-blouse, covered in paint and cryptic messages, and a band of crochet work round his head to keep his hair out of his eyes. With his

2. pp. 190–1.

odd clothes and strong Jewish features, he became one of Du
Maurier's favourite subjects for caricature, many of which are
reproduced in Moscheles' delightful book, *In Bohemia with George Du
Maurier*, one of the few sources for this period of Du Maurier's life.
The story of their meeting is told both by Moscheles and by Du
Maurier in *The Martian*, providing further evidence of the autobiographical nature of Du Maurier's novels. Moscheles, eager for
news of his old friends at Gleyre's, where he had studied before
coming to Antwerp, approached Du Maurier, whom he knew had
recently been there. Soon the two were deep in conversation,
speaking in French, which they each imagined to be the other's
native tongue. Du Maurier even referred to 'un nommé Pointer',
pronouncing it in French, and was staggered when Moscheles
turned to an American and made a remark in perfect English.
' "What the D. are you – English?" broke in du Maurier. "And
what the D. are you?" '[3] replied Moscheles.

Du Maurier and Moscheles soon became intimate, and gathered a
small group of fellow spirits around them. One of these was the Dutch
painter, Jean Heyermans, a talented artist and linguist, who later
became a prosperous art teacher in London. Another was T. A. G.
Sprenk, a young English businessman, who did little except wait for
one of his commercial ventures to come to fruition. An unexacting
companion, he enjoyed cigars, girls and whisky, which he drank with
patriotic fervour in preference to local stimulants. He was nicknamed Tag, after his initials, while the other two called themselves
Bobtail and Rag. Du Maurier addressed a doggerel verse to Moscheles on the subject:

> For I walk slowly, and you walk fast,
> And Tag lies down (not to fall);
> *You* think of the Present, *I* think of the Past,
> And Tag thinks of nothing at all.[4]

Among Du Maurier's companions at the Academy were Lawrence
Alma-Tadema, future Royal Academician and leader of the 'Marble
School', Matthew Maris, one of a large family of famous Dutch
artists, and the armless painter, Charles Jelu, who made excellent
copies of the old masters with his feet. Du Maurier's major work at
the Academy was a life-size oil painting of an old woman with a

3. Moscheles, p. 19.
4. Moscheles, p. 73.

17. Sketch of Du
Maurier's oil painting
executed in Antwerp
(1857) CvB

young boy in her lap. Moscheles reproduces a pen-and-ink sketch of
it in his book, which, if it is accurate, shows that the figure of the
woman was competently done, but the boy was poorly proportioned,
with outsize arms. It is difficult to forecast on the evidence of this
single work what talent Du Maurier had as an oil painter, a largely
academic question in any case, but he himself felt happier about his
prospects than he had in Paris.

Three or four months after Du Maurier's arrival in Antwerp, an
event occurred which he could scarcely bear to speak of, even to
Sherard, nearly forty years later: 'The voice of Du Maurier, who till
then had been chatting with animation, suddenly fell, and over the
face came an indefinable expression of mingled terror and anger and
sorrow'.[5] On that morning in 1857, Du Maurier suddenly lost the

5. Sherard, p. 397.

sight of his left eye, and the whole course of his life was changed. Without warning, his hopes of becoming a painter were destroyed, and he was plunged into a despair which he later realized had 'poisoned all my existence'.[6] The actual loss of his eye, in comparison with its consequences, was a simple and horrifyingly rapid process:

> I was drawing from a model, when suddenly the girl's head seemed to me to dwindle to the size of a walnut. I clapped my hand over my left eye. Had I been mistaken? I could see as well as ever. But when in its turn I covered my right eye, I learned what had happened. My left eye had failed me; it might be altogether lost. It was so sudden a blow that I was as thunderstruck.[7]

Shocked and frightened, Du Maurier sat in front of his easel, until Van Lerius, seeing his dazed expression, came up and asked him what the matter was. As Du Maurier explained, Van Lerius tried to encourage him: 'he said that it was nothing, that he had had that himself, and so on'.[8] Scarcely realizing, even now, what had happened, Du Maurier clung desperately to the hope of recovery, and on Van Lerius' recommendation, visited a famous Jesuit oculist in the University town of Louvain. The priest looked at his eye, and confidently told him that the blindness was temporary, and could be cured by a few days' rest at Blankenberghe, on the coast, and some slight treatment. Unless the priest imagined that Du Maurier's trouble was psychosomatic, his treatment was extremely primitive, though he used an opthalmoscope, a new device, to look at the eye: 'he was to have a seton let into the back of his neck, dry-cup himself on the chest and thighs night and morning, and take a preparation of mercury three times a day'.[9] In fact, Du Maurier had almost certainly suffered a detachment of the retina, followed by a haemorrhage at the back of his eye; something which made all treatment useless. His visit to Blankenberghe, which lasted for five weeks, did his general health some good, but had no effect on his eyes. He tried to keep up his spirits by joining in the social life of the place:

> But when alone in his garret, with his seton-dressing and dry-cuppings, it was not so gay. He had to confess to himself that his eye was getting slowly worse instead of better; darkening day by day . . . He could still see with the left of it and at the bottom, but a veil had come over the middle and all the rest.[10]

6. Sherard, p. 398.
7. Sherard, pp. 397–8.
8. Sherard, p. 398.

9. *The Martian*, p. 195.
10. *The Martian*, p. 214.

Writing to Moscheles, he made light of the situation: 'very jolly; no end of pretty girls; sing duets',[11] but it was in reality the most wretched period of his life.

Ellen Du Maurier had been thoroughly alarmed by his letter, telling her what had happened, and she immediately rushed to Belgium. Together they took lodgings in the town of Malines (Mechelen), which lay on the railway line to Louvain, between Brussels and Antwerp. Today, Malines is a busy, commercial town, with one spectacular architectural feature, the huge, unfinished tower of the cathedral. When Du Maurier and his mother arrived there in 1857, it was, despite its air of quiet charm, one of the dullest towns in Northern Europe. The spiritual centre of Belgium, it was full of abbeys, seminaries and convents, which set the tone of pious tedium. In *The Martian*, Du Maurier described it as a 'most picturesque but dead-alive little town, where the grass grew so thick between the paving-stones here and there that the brewers' dray-horses might have browsed in the "Grand Brul" – a magnificent but generally deserted thoroughfare leading from the railway station to the Place d'Armes'.[12] One reason why the Du Mauriers chose Malines was because it was inexpensive, but Ellen Du Maurier and the oculist must also have felt that Du Maurier needed rest – the nineteenth century remedy for all ills. It was the one thing he did not need, for it allowed him to brood over his misfortunes. In the afternoons his only occupation was walking, either in the Botanical Gardens, or in the countryside around the town, with its low horizon, unvarying flatness and straight roads: 'the monotonous perspective of which is so desolating to heart and eye; backwards or forwards, it is always the same, with a flat sameness of outlook to right and left'.[13] The one bright event of the day came after dinner, when Ellen Du Maurier would read aloud from the Tauchnitz editions, sent by the circulating library in Brussels.

Du Maurier looked forward passionately to the weekends, when Moscheles or his other friends would come over from Antwerp. Moscheles in particular was a constant visitor, who regarded Malines as a 'haven of rest', and thoroughly enjoyed his weekends there. He seems scarcely to have been aware of Du Maurier's real feelings, for his only comment on the loss of the eye, admittedly written many years later, was callously prosaic: 'His eyesight sud-

11. Undated, University of Texas Library.   13. *The Martian*, p. 230.
12. *The Martian*, p. 224.

denly gave him trouble, and before long put a stop to his studies at
atelier or academy. He was not to become a painter'.[14] In the evenings, Moscheles entertained the Du Mauriers by mimicking famous
singers of both sexes, and he encouraged Du Maurier himself to sing,
accompanying him brilliantly on the piano. These musical evenings
became such an established event that Du Maurier began sending
doggerel verses to Antwerp, so that Moscheles could set them to
music before his next visit. The verses were usually love-songs, of a
rather banal kind:

> La fleur que sous ton pied tu blesses
> Baise ton pied – oh! tends les bras!
> Que valent toutes les caresses
> Si tu ne me caresses pas?[15]

A thorough egoist and a blatant exhibitionist, Moscheles was an ideal
companion at this time, and he certainly helped Du Maurier to forget himself and his troubles. Even in Malines, which he described as
'beating the record for dry-as-dustiness',[16] Moscheles was able to
find abundant distractions. He would walk round the streets in
search of pretty girls, and Du Maurier, in spite of his gloomy preoccupations, discovered a new pleasure in this sport:

> we considered it our duty to take special notice of these pretty girls
> wherever we came across them. It is probably the conscientious per-
> formance of his duty in that direction which enabled du Maurier to
> evolve those ever-attractive and sympathetic types of female beauty we
> are all so familiar with. Nor would it have been becoming in me, who
> had everything to learn, to lag behind, or to show less ardour in the
> pursuit of my studies.[17]

Their most successful find was Octavie, the seventeen-year-old
daughter of a recently deceased organist in Malines. When Moscheles and Du Maurier first saw her, she was selling tobacco in a shop
run by her mother, and both were enthralled by her 'very blue
inquisitive eyes . . . brown curly hair . . . and a figure of peculiar
elasticity'.[18] Half in jest, half in earnest, they set up as rivals for her
affection. Their letters of the time were full of schemes to carry her
off, illustrated with suitable caricature drawings. Together they went
and stood at her counter, gazing longingly at Carry, as they called
her:

14. Moscheles, p. 29.   17. Moscheles, p. 46.
15. Undated, University of Texas Library.   18. Moscheles, p. 47.
16. Moscheles, p. 45.

there was a subtle quality in Carry, well worthy of appreciation, a faculty of charming and being charmed, of giving and taking, of free and easiness, coupled with ladylike reserve. She seemed to be born with the intuitive knowledge that there was only one life worth living, that of the Bohemian, and to be at the same time well protected by a pretty reluctance to admit as much.[19]

18. Portrait of Picciola (1858)

Du Maurier had the advantage of being in Malines all the week, and he sang and danced with Carry in Moscheles' absence. She, however, preferred two admirers to one, as Du Maurier ruefully informed Moscheles: 'The fair performer was much pleased with ye darke Bobtaile, and considers him tout à fait charmant blast your b—y eyes coming and putting my nose out of joint'.[20] Du Maurier later told him that 'Carry & I expecting you', and boasted:

I gave her a 3 hours dancing lesson yesterday, great fun – fortunately for her Rag is an honourable Rag. Mind & come on Sunday, and thou shalt disdamage thyself on Monday & Tuesday when painting her. I would advise you to bring a domino. If not let me know & I will procure one here.[21]

19. Moscheles, p. 47.   21. Undated, University of Texas Library.
20. Undated, University of Texas Library.

Du Maurier read these letters in 1895, before Moscheles published
his book, and he erased several passages in one of the most revealing
of them. What remains of the letter begins with a reference to
Carry's cousin, and continues:

> all go to make it original & jolly and I hope it will terminate without too
> great a headache or a heartache to either person concerned; quant à toi
> je t'admire thou hast risen much in my esteem & a damned honest feller –
> you did quite right in not going on the fatal Monday as it would have
> been all up for certain.[22]

In another letter, Du Maurier described himself as a hunter seeking
Carry out through a dark primeval forest, and eventually finding her
sitting with Moscheles by a camp-fire. Du Maurier confessed to his
mother, a few years later, that she had been correct in calling it a
'morbid passion born in idleness'.[23] It seems likely that Carry had
become his mistress. He began a novel about her entitled *Les Noces
de Picciola*, and completed a series of illustrations showing himself,
Moscheles and Carry in a 'ménage à trois'. Thirty years later, Carry
was transformed into *Trilby*, the Parisian grisette, who became the
rage in England and America. She had undoubtedly helped to save
Du Maurier from suicide, or complete nervous prostration.

That he was in a state of very real despair is clear in a letter of
November 1857, written by Sprenk, then in Paris, to Moscheles:

> As du Maurier's eye, though better, will, most probably, not allow him to
> resume his profession as a painter, we have determined to try our fortune
> together in Australia, and mean to start from here early in February. He
> hopes to obtain employment by drawing sketches, caricatures, &c., for
> the Melbourne *Punch*, and other illustrated papers. You know how
> eminently suited he is for that kind of work, and we hear that an artist of
> talent of that description is much wanted out there, and would be sure
> to do exceedingly well.[24]

Christmas, however, found Du Maurier still in Malines, depressed
and lethargic, and quite unable to make plans for emigration or
anything else. He was, in any case, too cosmopolitan and ambitious
to regard Australia as anything but a haven of retreat and failure.
Looking back on this period, Du Maurier regarded the two Christ-
masses which he spent in Malines as 'the lowest pitch'.[25] The Lou-

22. Undated, University of Texas Library.   24. Moscheles, p. 74.
23. Letters, p. 45.   25. Letters, p. 28.

vain oculist continued to be optimistic about an eventual cure, but Ellen Du Maurier and her son were becoming sceptical about his expertise and his treatment. Writing to her sister-in-law, Mrs Du Maurier said:

> I shall go with him and protest against him taking all this medicine – better to lose his eye, I keep telling him, than to ruin his constitution, which he is steadily doing. As for his work, I have given up all idea of his ever painting again.[26]

The tone of this letter does not suggest that she was a very cheerful or encouraging companion for her son. Probably at her request, Du Maurier tried another doctor, this time a professor at the University of Ghent, who told him that the Louvain specialist was incompetent and that a rapid cure was still perfectly feasible. All Du Maurier's hopes were soon dashed, however, as the treatment had no effect whatever. Panicking now about his other eye, which was showing signs of strain, and fearing that he would soon be totally blind, Du Maurier returned to the Louvain oculist. He described his horrific last interview there in *The Martian*, and gave a similar account to G. H. Lewes, who was so shocked that he wrote it down in his diary for August 1878:

> Du Maurier when he lost the sight of one eye consulted a Belgian oculist – a cold, hard catholic, who although knowing he was a poor student, took the largest fee each time, and after some weeks examined the other eye, and said, patting an Italian greyhound as he spoke: 'You seem a courageous young man, and I may tell you that one day when I told a young man what I am going to tell you, he blew his brains out at my door. *Your other eye is going*, and I advise you to seek some employment in which eyesight will not be much needed'. He then made evident signs that the interview was ended, took his fee, and pulled off his skull cap to bow him out.[27]

Nearly suicidal, like the doctor's other patient, Du Maurier returned to the Professor at Ghent, who still claimed that he could at least save the right eye. The strain resulting from these conflicting medical opinions, and the doubts and fears of the previous years, were now beginning to tell on mother and son. Du Maurier remembered how dark rings appeared round his mother's eyes

---

26. *The Du Mauriers*, p. 269.
27. *The George Eliot Letters*, edited G. S. Haight (1956), VII, 60–1.

19. Coffee and Brassin in Bobtail's Rooms (1858)

whenever she was kept awake by her worries about his worsening eyesight.

Occasionally Du Maurier could escape from his own thoughts by visiting Moscheles in his large and untidy room in Antwerp, but he never stayed for long in case his mother should worry about him. A common love of music bound Moscheles and Du Maurier together, and their evenings in Antwerp were frequently spent at concerts. Sometimes well-known performers, like the pianist, Louis Brassin, would visit Moscheles in person, for his contacts in the musical world were wide. A sketch by Du Maurier shows Brassin hunched over the piano, while Du Maurier himself gazes rapturously at the ceiling. Writing to thank Moscheles after this particular visit, he said:

> may thy room be always as jolly, thy coffee be ever so sweet, as on that happy morning! May Brassin's fingers be ever so brilliant and inspired! May Tag be ever as lazy, and with equal inspiration to himself, and may I never be blinder![28]

Moscheles' other great interest was mesmerism, then in an early stage of development. He had learnt the art in Paris, and practised on any

28. Moscheles, p. 82.

willing victim. Du Maurier, fascinated by his friend's skill, eagerly
cross-examined Moscheles about his earlier experiments, and in
particular about a certain Mme Virginie Marsaudon who had been
Moscheles' best subject. Du Maurier became obsessed with the more
sinister aspects of mesmerism, especially when he lay awake at night
worrying about his eyes, as he informed Moscheles in a partly
humorous letter:

> it's all very well to ask a nervous fellow to Antwerp and amuse him and
> make him ever so jolly and comfortable – But why, when the bleak
> November wind sobs against the lattice and disturbs the dead ashes in the
> grate, when everything is damned queer and dark, and that sort of
> thing, you know – why should you make nervous fellows' flesh creep by
> talk about mesmerism, and dead fellows coming to see live fellows
> before dying, and the Lord knows what else?[29]

Although Moscheles never tried to mesmerize Carry, as Svengali
mesmerized Trilby, he did carry out experiments in the back
parlour of her mother's shop, which provided Du Maurier with the
basic theme of his novel. That he recognized this is clear from a letter
which he sent to Moscheles with a copy of *Trilby* in 1895: 'You'll see
that I've used up all your Mesmerism and a trifle more in my new
book'.[30]

29. Moscheles, pp. 59–60.
30. Moscheles, p. 9.

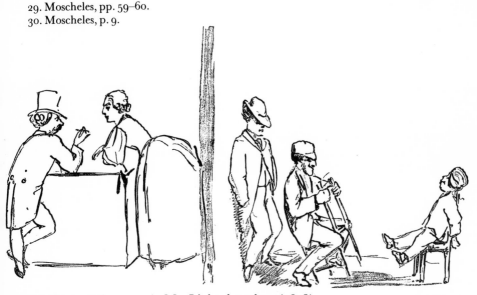

20. A mesmeric seance in Mrs L's back parlour (1858)

While Du Maurier and Moscheles were pursuing Carry, Du
Maurier himself had attracted the attention of a near neighbour, a
military surgeon called M. Gellens. The latter sent Du Maurier a
long letter expressing the hope that they would become friends, as he
longed to discuss art and literature. Would Du Maurier call? Du
Maurier was rather uneasy, but he did call; when, in course of conversation, he casually asked M. Gellens what sort of woman he would
like to marry, he received 'a detailed description so damnably like
moi Rag that I was ready to pounce on my patelot – after knocking
out the lamp until he said "Je voudrai qu'elle eut un nez légèrement
aquilin" '.[31] Du Maurier spent the rest of the evening in a less
'funked' state.

These excursions, excitements and pastimes were, however, only a
temporary alleviation to Du Maurier's continuous worry about his
eyes. In a sketch which he sent to Moscheles, he showed himself,
depressed and introspective, sitting next to a grinning Moscheles,
with the caption underneath: 'Rag thinking of his eyes, in a pair of
tight boots, with Bobtail whispering: "Say something clever, you
stupid muff!".[32] Moscheles did his best to provide his friend with
amusements, inviting him a wild and successful birthday party,
during which Moscheles, intoxicated on hot punch, gave an even
more brilliant series of impersonations than usual. Du Maurier sent
him an inevitable sketch of the party afterwards, depicting himself in
his now familiar spectacles, a wistful and pathetic figure. Another
party was held in Moscheles' rooms to celebrate a visit by the latter's
father and his sister, Clara. Du Maurier was happily performing
duets with her, when he suddenly stopped, sat down, and began to
describe his terrible doubts:

> No, I had better face the enemy and be prepared for the worst. If it
> comes, you see, my dear fellow, there is Nature's law of compensation,
> and I firmly believe that one cannot lose one faculty without being
> compensated by some great gain elsewhere. I suppose one gets to see more
> inside as things grow darker outside. If one can't paint, one must do
> something else – write perhaps; that is, as long as one can, and then, if the
> steam accumulates, and one wants a safety valve to let it off, dictate.[33]

Moscheles was too superficial to see that Du Maurier's apparent
equanimity was very brittle, and covered no real philosophic calm or

31. Undated, University of Texas Library.   33. Moscheles, p. 85.
32. Moscheles, p. 95.

resignation: 'I often wondered how quietly he took it, and how cheerfully he would tell me that he was "fearfully depressed" '.[34] Pride would not allow Du Maurier to disclose his real feelings, although he made bitter jokes about his approaching blindness. He was in fact terrified by the prospect of it. On the same evening that he talked to Moscheles so calmly, he made a drawing of Clara's lovely eyes for her album, and wrote underneath: 'Quand je les vois, j'oublie les miens. (Reflexion d'un futur aveugle)'.[35]

The period of desperation and langour at Malines came to an end in 1859, largely as the result of news contained in a letter from Isabella. She had spent Christmas 1858 with the family of her friend, Emma Wightwick, and Mrs Wightwick strongly recommended that Du Maurier should consult a famous German oculist, Hofrath de Leeuwe, who practised in Gräfrath, near Dusseldorf. After careful consideration, mother and son decided to go. Shortly before leaving Malines, Du Maurier's spirits were raised by another event, which was to be of crucial importance to him. At Christmas he was sent a copy of the *Punch* almanack, possibly by Lamont or Jeckyll, and he was profoundly impressed. Recalling his pleasure in a lecture, which he gave in 1891, he said: 'To be an apparently hopeless invalid at Christmas-time in some dreary, deserted, dismal little Flemish town, and to receive *Punch's Almanac* (for 1858, let us say) from some good-natured friend in England – that is a thing not to be forgotten!'.[36] Du Maurier had already considered a career as an illustrator a year before, when he had planned to emigrate to Australia, but he was now quite enthralled by the delicate and charming drawings of John Leech. He suddenly realized that illustration was not the hack work he had imagined, but an art requiring skill and imagination. He little thought that six years later he would take John Leech's place on the *Punch* staff.

After a brief holiday in Antwerp and Blankenberghe with Moscheles, Du Maurier finally left Malines in May 1859, having spent the best part of two unhappy years there. The whole course of his life had changed, not only in a material, but in an emotional sense. He had not become embittered or self-pitying, only more tentative, withdrawn and melancholy. He was to recover his gaiety and enthusiasm, but he could never regard the world with the unimpaired optimism of his Paris days. The threat of total blindness never left

34. Moscheles, p. 84.   36. S.P.S., p. 15.
35. Moscheles, p. 85.

him, nor a sense that illustration was a second best, however successful he might become. His dream of being a great painter was shattered, and if he appeared to his friends, and even to his family, as a
contented man who had come to terms with himself and his disability, this was not entirely so. His thwarted ambition, his grandiose
illusions, were to be finally fulfilled in the heroes of his fiction.

In 1859, however, the relief of escaping from Malines was a tonic
in itself. Du Maurier's spirits rose sharply in the more vigorous
atmosphere of Dusseldorf, which was a gay and social place, with the
summer season just beginning. He wrote gleefully to Moscheles:

> jolly place, lots of beauties, plenty of singing and sketching and that sort
> of thing, you know. Long walks in beautiful valleys, most delightful. The
> fact is, I'm so beastly merry since I've been here that I don't think I'm
> quite sane, and altogether only want your periodical visits and per-
> mission to have my fling on Saturday nights to be in heaven. Doctor says
> he'll do me good; have to go to Gräfrath once a week. Ça me bote
> joliment.[37]

This time the doctor really did do him some good, and eased his
more extreme fears. Authoritative and knowledgeable, he simply
told Du Maurier that he would never see again with his left eye, but
that with care, his right eye should last for the rest of his life. Comparatively happy after this straightforward verdict, Du Maurier
began to enjoy himself. Through other patients, and English visitors
in general, he collected a wide acquaintance, which even extended
to minor German princelings. Ellen Du Maurier took rooms in the
Schadowstrasse, and there Isabella joined them in the autumn,
intent on finding a husband. The prospects seemed good, as she was
popular and attractive, but it soon became clear that eligible
bachelors in Dusseldorf were there to enjoy the season, not to be
entrapped into marriage. The other member of the family, Eugène,
was doing moderately well in the French army, and his family could
forget him with an easy conscience. He had never been his mother's
favourite.

Du Maurier had arrived in Dusseldorf intending to write a novel
about Carry, to be called *Les Noces de Picciola*, but he was soon caught
up with an artistic set. There was a school of painting in Dusseldorf,
and Du Maurier started to paint again, though only for an hour or so
a day. He knew that his eye would never stand the strain of full-time

37. Moscheles, pp. 97–8.

painting, and he had no illusions about ever becoming a professional painter. By the end of the summer he was recovering his health and buoyancy, sharing a studio with a Swiss artist, Huniker, 'a touching and beautiful character'.[38] He met several other students, including

21. (1860)

Lionel Charles Henley ('Bill'), a boisterous and entertaining companion. Early in the following year, 1860, Du Maurier's old friend, Tom Armstrong, arrived in Dusseldorf on his way home from Algeria. Du Maurier, who had only seen him once since leaving Gleyre's, during a weekend in Malines, was overjoyed when his friend decided to stay on. Armstrong's decision seems to have been prompted more by his attraction to Isabella than by Du Maurier's entreaties. With an American, John Chandler Bancroft, and a young English aristocrat called Best, son of Lord Wynford, Du Maurier, Armstrong and Henley formed a gay group of artists, reminiscent

38. Letter to Clarence McIlvaine, 7 June 1894. Pierpont Morgan Library.

AM RHEIN

"LED WE NOT THERE A JOLLY LIFE
BETWIXT THE SUN AND SHADE?"

22. Left to right, 'Bill' Henley, Du Maurier, Barty Josselin
the fictional hero, Tom Armstrong, John Chandler
Bancroft, *The Martian*

of the Paris group. Moscheles noticed that Du Maurier's letters were becoming more English in tone, which he put down to Armstrong's influence, Du Maurier himself admitted to 'getting English again by degrees'.[39] Nevertheless, when Moscheles paid his long-promised visit, the two sat up late into the night, drinking Rhine wine, reminiscing about Carry and Malines, and discussing their future plans. They agreed to spend a week together in Antwerp, which occurred shortly before Du Maurier's departure for London in May 1860. They visited Malines, together, and found that Carry had become more vulgar in their absence, and no longer possessed her engaging innocence. Her later career is of some interest, as it parallels Trilby's to some extent. After a promiscuous life in Malines, Carry was won back to the path of virtue by a young doctor, who married her, and took her away to live in Paris. Several years later, Moscheles learnt that her husband had died, leaving her with a small baby, but he was unable to find any trace of her. He concluded that if she had ever

39. Moscheles, p. 119.

reappeared, it would not have been as a famous singer, like Trilby, but as a prostitute. Unlike Moscheles, who became obsessed with Carry and her fate, Du Maurier soon lost any personal interest in her. Writing to his mother in April 1861, he told her: 'I received a letter from Bobtail full of absurd romantic bosh about Picciola'.[40]

In Dusseldorf, Du Maurier's attentions to the fair sex were divided between two young ladies. One of these, nicknamed 'Damask', was dying of consumption, and seems to have aroused real affection in Du Maurier. She appears in his early *Punch* cartoon, entitled *A Dodge*, where she looks a frail and attractive figure. Her identity is otherwise a mystery. Moscheles, who was introduced to her, thought her very desirable, and executed a humorous drawing of himself and Du Maurier fighting a duel for her favours. Du Maurier's other flame

AT THE HOFRATH'S DOOR.

" SHE.   REALLY I DON'T SEE THE SLIGHTEST MOTE IN YOUR EYES."
" HE.   NO, BUT I CAN SEE THE BEAMS IN YOURS."

23. (1859)

was a Miss Louisa Lewis, a friend of Isabella, whose father was in Dusseldorf for his health. Du Maurier enjoyed flirting with her when the two families met, and their relationship deepened. Louisa seems to have taken the affair more seriously than Du Maurier, who, if he did not trifle with her affection, seems to have unwittingly encouraged it. Ellen Du Maurier commented on their relationship in a

40. Letters, p. 40.

later letter to her sister-in-law: 'he is as fickle as the wind. This time last year it was all Miss Lewis, I believe she still thinks of him'.[41] Another shadowy figure from Du Maurier's Dusseldorf days was a Mrs Fortescue, whom he continued to see in London. She seems to have been an older woman who took a fancy to the young man, and became a good friend of his. She was godmother to his third daughter, and the Du Mauriers occasionally visited her in Richmond. Dusseldorf was not the safest place for ladies. Du Maurier and Armstrong and their sisters were stopped by a group of soldiers: 'who wanted to kiss the girls. It seems that civilians there are always liable to be sabred and that there's no redress'.[42]

Du Maurier's various flirtations came to an end early in May 1860, when the Wightwicks arrived in Dusseldorf on holiday, bringing with them their beautiful daughter, Emma. Tall and graceful, with masses of plaited dark hair, and huge velvet eyes, her strength of character was clear in her pronounced jaw, a feature Du Maurier was fond of caricaturing. In *The Martian* there is an echo of their romantic reunion, and its attendant difficulties, when the affection of the handsome hero, Barty Josselin, is torn between two women, both of whom love him. One of them, the blonde and aristocratic Julia Royce, is capable of giving him the wealth and position which he lacks, but it is the quiet, dark-haired Jewess, Leah Gibson, who has really stolen his heart, and whom he finally marries. There was something of this clash in Du Maurier's life, for when he tried to extricate himself from his relationship with Miss Lewis, the situation became embarrassing both for himself and his family. There is no evidence that he had ever proposed to Miss Lewis, but it is clear that she had been led to expect an engagement. When they met later in London, Miss Lewis, who had at first pined for him, became vindictive, and Du Maurier assumed the air of a martyr, with what justification it is not known.

This situation encouraged Du Maurier to think seriously about his future career. His right eye was now much better, and he felt stronger in mind and body. As he still had to pay his oculist's bill, and as he had no hope of earning any money in Dusseldorf, he decided to try his luck as an illustrator in London, remembering Leech's drawings for *Punch*. He was encouraged by Armstrong, who was also returning home, and by Emma Wightwick, with whom he was already half in

41. *The Du Mauriers*, p. 305.
42. Silver, 21 Dec. 1864.

love. Mrs Du Maurier, relieved by the thought that he was not going to be a hopeless invalid, made no objections. She gave him ten pounds and a great deal of advice. Late in May 1860, Du Maurier set off for Rotterdam and the London boat, in company with Armstrong and the Wightwicks, who were returning from their short holiday. He left Dusseldorf on the Rhine steamer, dreaming with excitement of his future career and its fabulous success, while his mother and sister drearily trudged back to their lodgings in the rain.

24. Sketch – Malines to London (1860)

Chapter 4

London

AS DU MAURIER SET OUT on his decisive journey from Dusseldorf to London in May 1860, he may have recalled his journey of four years before from London to Paris. Released then from the misery and gloom associated with his home and chemistry studies, he had faced the undefined but expansive prospect of life as an art-student in a city which he knew well and adored. He was untried, but full of confidence in his own ability to become a great painter. Those dreams had been destroyed, and a more sober assessment of his future forced upon him by the loss of his eye. The immediate threat of complete blindness had disappeared during his stay in Dusseldorf, and it was with a relatively easy heart that he said goodbye to his family. His journey to London represented a deliberate cast of the die, a rejection of the dream-world associated with Paris and his youth in favour of a specific career. He had not as yet displayed any real talent as a draughtsman, he had no influential connections or friends, nor any specialised knowledge of the field he had selected, but he had made the decisive step of choosing a profession, and he had the optimism and courage to follow it through. In company with Armstrong and the Wightwicks, he sailed from Dusseldorf on a Rhine steamer, quickly discovering in Emma an exciting and sympathetic companion. After the journey down the river, they explored Rotterdam together in high spirits, clearly attracted and stimulated by each other, while their more prosaic companions had to consume a quantity of brandy before they too felt 'very jolly'. The crossing to London was rough, and it was in an excited and confused state that Du Maurier wrote to his mother from the Wightwicks' comfortable sitting-room in Grosvenor Street, on 28 May 1860, the day after his arrival: 'I hope you will not mope and be grumpy – I can't help feeling very happy and elated *now* . . . Oh, hang it, you know, to be in all this life, and to think of Malines, eh ?'[1]

1. Letters, pp. 2–3.

25. Emma Wightwick,
Punch vignette (1862)

The 'life' into which Du Maurier had arrived was the world of
high-Victorian England. Prince Albert was still alive, Palmerston
had been in power for a year, and the country was slowly recovering
from the profound economic depression of the 'fifties. Chartism, the
Crimean War and the Indian mutiny were all unpleasant facts of the
past. It was an age of peace, prosperity, and enormous material
progress, with little to disturb the complacency of English power and
pretension. Society was still dominated by an apparently rigid
hierarchy and a fixed standard of ethics, but it was becoming more
sophisticated and permissive, and would, under the influence of the
Prince of Wales, become more so. The art world, in which Du
Maurier would inevitably take his place, was dominated by the
Royal Academy. For successful painters, like Maclise, Landseer or
Frith, the rewards were enormous, but for those who lay outside the
pale of Academy patronage and approval there were, in the absence
of any alternative, few opportunities to earn a living or a reputation.
In contrast with Paris, or even Antwerp, where Du Maurier had
trained, English art was insular and unsophisticated. It had, in a
very real sense, succumbed to popular taste, and its insistence on
the importance of narrative qualities had led to a neglect of the more
essential problems of artistic creation. English painters lived as
English gentlemen. There was no real interchange of ideas or experience between them; on the contrary the fear that a good subject
might be stolen by a rival led to incredible secretiveness. This
essentially amateur approach to art, where talking about one's work
would have been regarded as 'bad form', was in marked contrast

to the attitude of certain groups of French artists, who heartily despised public opinion, and sought to forge a coherent artistic vision in terms that were painterly, original, and loudly blazoned forth. The only comparable movement in England was that of the Pre-Raphaelite Brotherhood, whose united endeavour, based more on friendship than unity of purpose, lasted for a relatively short period, from 1848 to 1852.

Du Maurier could never hope to become a painter or an Academician (he was to remain obsessed as a result with a sense of failure and inadequacy), but it is interesting to see how quickly he adapted himself to the attitudes and prejudices of the English art world, unlike his friend, James Whistler, who remained an incorrigible rebel. He never questioned the values of contemporary art, nor the position of the Academy as the sole arbiter of an artist's fate. His attitude to painters whom he did not know personally was strictly related to their current popularity. This was partly due to a lack of critical insight, but more to a lack of interest in the whole question of the fine arts, especially later when he was no longer directly concerned in their development, and had retired to Hampstead. In the days before his marriage, however, under the immediate influence of Whistler and other friends, he kept up the familiar studio talk of his student days, and his letters to his mother are full of comment on painters and paintings. As an unnoticed illustrator, on the fringes of the art world, he felt a profound need to stay up with those friends who were beginning to make reputations, and to remain attached, however tenuously, to their world and its concerns. His attitude to his own profession was ambivalent. If he was forced to come to terms with magazines and editors, he did so disdainfully, aware that he was of a superior mould, an artist primarily, who had only descended to illustration because he had to. In his social life, therefore, he did everything he could to compensate for this, spending much of his time in the company of artists, and always eager to meet the more famous of them. The equality he had enjoyed in Paris with the English group was still the standard by which he intended to live.

Du Maurier did not, however, pursue his career half-heartedly because of his personal doubts and frustrations. He knew that it was imperative for him to make a reputation and to earn money as quickly as he could, if he was to succeed in any context in London. Illustration was an art that was to achieve a new force and distinction in the 1860s, and the leading illustrators were often not painters doing hack work for easy money, as they had been in earlier decades,

but specialists in a difficult field. Du Maurier was aware of the possibilities which black-and-white art offered, and of the striking
results which had already been achieved. His hopes that he would
make his fortune overnight were, however, soon dispelled. He went
to see the water-colourist Samuel Read, his only real contact in
London, who gave him some encouragement, and, more important,
several introductions to magazine editors. Armed with these, Du
Maurier set out on his own to find employment as an illustrator in
the early summer of 1860: 'Clambering up the staircases and
knocking at the doors of editors who are always busy and always in a
bad temper. Sometimes treated rudely, sometimes put off with much
politeness and slight hopes of future employment etc'.[2] After a
fortnight of such activity, he was tentatively offered a contract by
the editor of a second-rate paper, *The Welcome Guest*, on the understanding that he would not work for the rival magazine, *Once A Week*.
Du Maurier was enormously heartened by this initial success, only to
discover later that he had been passed over in favour of another
artist. His first fee came from the *British Lion*, which accepted a
drawing from him, very much in the style of John Leech, but never
published it, as the magazine folded up almost at once. Du Maurier
did receive a guinea for this drawing, his first professional income. To
his chagrin, he found that it was customary to treat everyone to a
drink on such an occasion. Rather ungraciously explaining that he
was not allowed beer because of his eye, Du Maurier was let off, on
the understanding that he would present a gift to a friend. As a
result he bought a copy of the 1857 Moxon edition of Tennyson's
poems, illustrated by Millais, Holman Hunt, Rossetti, and others,
which he presented to Emma Wightwick, after studying the drawings carefully himself. They were to provide him with much of his
'copy' for his famous Pre-Raphaelite satire, 'A Legend of Camelot'
of 1866.

The need for illustrators had grown enormously in the middle of
the nineteenth century. The vast increase in the number of illustrated
books and magazines had opened up a new and lucrative field for
black-and-white artists. The founding of the *Illustrated London News* in
1842, a weekly magazine crammed with illustrations of current
events and personalities, or even of *Punch*, started in 1841, would have
been unthinkable ten years before. The famous fine-art-illustrated
magazines were not founded till the late 1850s or later, *Once A Week*

2. Letters, p. 5.

in 1859, *The Cornhill* and *Good Words* in 1860, and *London Society* in 1862, and it was these which enabled artists like Du Maurier to contemplate illustration as a serious career. Earlier magazines like *Blackwoods*, *The Quarterly*, and *Frazer's Magazine* had been mainly political, economic or philosophical in their bias, with long articles intended chiefly to teach, edify or reform. The growth of a large but less intellectual reading public, eager for pleasure and amusement, led to a totally different kind of magazine. The various annuals which at first catered for this demand were of a very low literary standard, and the illustrations, where they existed, were of the most banal and sentimental kind; Frank Stone's contributions to Heath's *Book of Beauty* during the 1830s, for which he was paid five shillings each, are a typical example. *Household Words*, of which Dickens was editor, was a new type of magazine, based primarily on the serialised novel and short story, for which there seemed to be an unlimited demand. Dickens himself had helped to establish fiction as the most popular literary form of his period, and it was novelists, rather than poets, who became best sellers. Dickens was a ruthless editor, altering or rejecting work that did not come up to his own high standards, and establishing a list of contributors which included Thackeray, George Eliot and Mrs Gaskell. Literary standards on other early Victorian magazines were necessarily much higher than they had been earlier, as competition for readers became more fierce, and the readers more discerning. The success of illustrated books had led directly to illustrated magazines (only the very best could afford not to be illustrated by 1860), where the standard of illustration was viewed by editors as critically as the stories themselves. Writers would frequently insist on a particular illustrator, which helped to establish partnerships, like Dickens and Hablôt Knight Browne (Phiz), Trollope and Millais, or Lewis Carroll and John Tenniel, a development which made it difficult for outsiders, like Du Maurier, to break in. Furthermore, *Punch* had established a regular staff of black-and-white as well as literary contributors, and other leading magazines like *Good Words* and *The Cornhill* tended to do the same. They would accept work from exceptionally talented newcomers, but on a piecemeal basis: the illustration of long serials, the most important and lucrative commissions, would invariably go to one of the regular illustrators. This 'closed shop' attitude forced Du Maurier to negotiate with second-rate magazines, and to send in odd contributions to the best ones, on the chance that they might include them, or commission more. It is not surprising that he was jubilant when his first drawing was accepted by the *Cornhill* in March 1863: 'You see I'm in devilish good company – Leighton and Millais'.[3] He was never secure, however, till he succeeded John Leech as a regular member of the *Punch* staff in the winter of 1864. He had achieved a considerable reputation by then, but the irregularity and uncertainty inevitably connected with free-lance work forced him to live very much from hand to mouth. Leighton and Millais were primarily painters, for whom illustration was a lucrative and pleasant side-line. It was Du Maurier's only source of income and reputation.

Du Maurier was not completely absorbed in his professional career. He pursued an active social life in several spheres of London society, and his comments on events and personalities in letters to his mother and sister in Dusseldorf, or to his friend, Tom Armstrong, in Manchester, are often pungent and witty. Published in 1951 by Daphne Du Maurier, these letters are almost the only source on Du Maurier's early life in London, besides being a valuable reference work for art and social historians in their own right. As the largest autobiographical comment in which Du Maurier ever indulged, their importance cannot be overestimated, but it must be remembered that most of them are letters from a favourite son to a doting mother, and that they present a picture which there is little other biographical material to corroborate or correct. Du Maurier was not brilliant or important enough to attract much attention from contemporary memoir-writers or diarists, and the recollections of his friends were written in retrospect, and are more concerned with his later success than with his first years as an illustrator.

Du Maurier's letters to his mother, and even to Armstrong, have enormous vitality and spontaneity, revealing an ambitious and high-spirited young man, who was anxious to prove how well he was doing, and to minimize the difficulties and depression which he undoubtedly experienced. He was very much on the fringes of the art world and fashionable society, but he continually stresses the prominent and central position which he did not really occupy. Famous people whom he did not know are denigrated, while those he did know or who noticed him, are lengthily and enthusiastically described and praised. His success with women, his entrée into the Ionides and Prinsep families, the enthusiasm which his singing and his conversation aroused, his friendly rivalry with James Whistler, his knowledge of artists and the art world, are all related in a spirit of

3. Letters, p. 201.

jocular and cynical familiarity. He is aggressive, boastful, and un-compromisingly ambitious. His style catches the current jargon of the young man about town, who knows the inside secrets of the artist's studio and the fashionable salon. He was out to amuse and impress his family, like that young literary prodigy, Vernon Lee, whose letters to her family in Italy provide a devastating picture of London literary and artistic circles in the 1880s. Du Maurier's letters home were a means of keeping his own spirits up, for his situation was at times extremely tenuous and depressing. Beneath the carefree and optimistic facade which he presented to his family and the world in general, there lurked a tense and uneasy personality, prone to ex-tremes of emotion, which later resulted in a nervous breakdown. During the early years in London, it is certainly true to say that Du Maurier lived on his nerves. This helps to explain the tenacity with which he clung to emotional and financial security after his marriage, and his retirement into a quiet and carefully regulated domestic shell in Hampstead. This complete volte-face from the gay and gre-garious existence he had led as a bachelor never ceased to surprise his old friends.

Du Maurier's letters to Tom Armstrong are more prosaic than those to his mother, but they are less interesting biographically. He could not inflate his social successes or relate those incidents which rebounded to his own credit, for Armstrong was too intelligent and knew him too well to accept such egoism at its face value. Armstrong was isolated in Manchester, and Du Maurier's concern in writing to him was to keep him in touch with the careers of mutual friends and with art gossip in general. This inevitably centred on the Royal Academy, the yard-stick by which success or failure was measured. Du Maurier wrote about the pictures Henley, Whistler, Poynter, and the rest of his friends were painting for the next Academy exhibition, their feverish efforts to finish in time for the submission day, their anxiety until they knew whether their pictures had been accepted or refused, the position which accepted works occupied in the exhibition, whether 'skied' or 'on the line', public and personal criticisms of exhibited paintings, the sales which resulted and the slow progress or decline of reputations. Du Maurier related to Armstrong in considerable detail the day-to-day activities, the hopes and fears, the work and plans, of himself and his fellow-artists, and this account is more accurate and factual than that which he sent to his mother.

Du Maurier's relationship to Whistler is a dominating topic in his letters, and has generally been exploited by Whistler scholars to Du Maurier's disadvantage. As students in Paris they had known each other well, but Whistler had not singled out Du Maurier from the rest of the English group for particular attention. In London their relationship became more intimate. Still under the spell of Paris, and the sophisticated and bohemian attitudes it had encouraged, they drew together in the philistine atmosphere of London, recognizing in each other fellow-spirits, who ridiculed the conventions and the taboos of the society they had come to conquer. Whistler was not yet the invulnerable 'enfant terrible' of legend, and, although he was flattered by Du Maurier's obvious adulation, their relationship was by no means that of master and disciple. Whistler still needed sympathetic companions, who would confirm the existence of his genius and pander to the demands of his relentless egoism. Du Maurier was proud to be the friend of an artist whose paintings were arousing intense interest and controversy, and whose dynamic personality and caustic wit were earning him an enviable reputation socially. He was under Whistler's spell, but he was not simply an admiring cypher; he had his own intelligence and youthful high spirits to contribute to their friendship. They stimulated each other, and if Du Maurier was a less exacting sounding-board, he did not bask contentedly in Whistler's reflected sunshine. The latter's successes were a spur to him, and his letters often compare his own achievements with those of his friend. Whistler had come to England in 1859, the year before Du Maurier, partly attracted by the possibility of commissions, but probably more by the prospect of being a big fish in a small pool. In 1865, when Du Maurier had tired of Whistler, he shrewdly remarked: 'I don't believe Jemmy *will* go to Paris, he will be less appreciated there than here. If he *does*, why, I don't suppose England will be exactly "brackish with the salt of human tears", and as for his pictures he will send them over here – trust me'.[4] In France, Whistler's painting was by no means in the forefront of the revolutionary movement, and his personality, overshadowed by artists and writers who were just as original and avant-garde, did not stand out in such sharp relief as it did in England. He preferred a field without rivals where he could occupy the centre of the stage, and become the undisputed spokesman for the ideas which he had brought with him from the continent. Like Sargent in the early 1860s, he had also discovered that it was almost

4. To T. Armstrong, 1865.

impossible for a foreigner to find a buyer for paintings in France.

Du Maurier got into contact with Whistler very soon after his arrival in London in the early summer of 1860. Whistler took him off to meet his half-sister, Joanna, and her husband, the surgeon and amateur etcher, Seymour Haden, who had provided Whistler with his first commissions and contacts. Du Maurier went to the Royal Academy to see Whistler's portrait of Joanna and her daughter, *At the Piano*, his first exhibited picture in England, which, as Whistler was careful to point out to him, had been much commented on and praised. Du Maurier sent a full account of the reunion to his mother in a letter of May 1860:

> You've no idea of the kind welcome from O'Connor and Whistler; the others I've not yet seen. I must tell you about Jemmy since there is not much more to say at present about your unappreciated Kycke. I have seen his picture, out and out the finest thing in the Academy. I have seen his etchings, which are the finest I *ever* saw. The other day at a party where there were swells of all sorts he was introduced to Millais, who said: 'What! Mr Whistler! I am very happy to know – I never flatter, but I will say that your picture is the finest piece of colour that has been on the walls of the Royal Academy for years'. What do you think of that old lady? And Sir Charles Eastlake took the Duchess of Sutherland up to it and said 'There Ma'am, that's the finest piece of painting in the Royal Academy'.
>
> But to hear Jemmy tell all about it beats anything I ever heard. A more enchanting vagabond cannot be conceived. He will introduce me to his brother-in-law etc and I shall not lack nice houses to go to.[5]

Although *At the Piano* was in no sense a revolutionary picture, it is interesting to notice that the Royal Academy was far less reactionary than the academically minded salon in Paris, which had rejected the same work in the previous year. Whistler's *The White Girl* was turned down there in 1862, and occupied a prominent place in the Salon des Refusés. The Royal Academy were not totally blind to the merits of advanced painting, for they accepted Whistler's works consistently and hung them well. Whistler's attack on the official art establishment became in time an article of faith, and it was he, rather than the Royal Academy, who broke off relations.

Du Maurier's reunion with Whistler was productive of more than good fellowship. Du Maurier, still staying with the Wightwicks, was looking for permanent lodgings, when Whistler suddenly offered him

5. Letters, p. 4.

his own room, optimistically described as a studio, at 70 Newman Street. Whistler had recently become excited by the Thames as a subject for his art, it was to remain a life-long passion, and he was staying temporarily at Rotherhithe. Du Maurier unhesitatingly took the room at ten shillings a week, with the owner's sheets, towels, bed, etchings and dress-suit (when not in use) included, and moved in a week after his arrival in London. He knew that he could have obtained a cheaper room, and one that was indisputably his own, but the prospect of Whistler's company in a lonely city was more than adequate compensation, or so he imagined. He was taken care of by a maternal landlady, who brought him gruel and a large breakfast for sixpence a week. Even so Du Maurier's doubts were not set at rest by his friend, Bill Henley, who described the room as a 'blasted apartment', an epithet confirmed by Armstrong:

> It was long and narrow, with a window at one end looking out to the back, and about the middle of it a string was fixed across from wall to wall. Over this hung a piece of silk drapery about the size of two pocket handkerchiefs. This was supposed to separate the parlour from the bedroom.[6]

Another visitor was Du Maurier's uncle, George Clarke, who gave him a much-needed dress suit of his own, but appeared quite out of place in the chaos and discomfort of his nephew's room. Whistler himself frequently called at Newman Street, and would sometimes stay the night. At first Du Maurier was delighted to see him:

> J. and I slept two nights here together and spent 48 hours during which he talked nearly the whole time. He is in my opinion the grandest genius I ever met, a giant – considered besides, as a 'wit', greater than either Hook or Sidney Smith, by those who have met those swells.[7]

That Whistler did most of the talking is evident from the reminiscences of William De Morgan, who had made an accurate assessment of their respective personalities without knowing either of them:

> I occupied a first-floor front studio in Newman Street. There I pretended to be a Painter. The back room was the den of a young artist who sang French songs all day. It was not, I believe, his own studio, but a friend's.

6. Armstrong, p. 151.
7. Letters, pp. 10–11.

When this friend turned up, which he generally did, the noise and laughter, the lulls for comic anecdotes and the outbursts that followed, the suggestions of capsized furniture and chases round the room – well! they were what I have heard described as a *caution*! When the actual occupant was alone, he made no more noise than went with the singing of an enjoyable selection of French songs; I think the *Sieur de Framboisy* was a favourite.

The young man in possession was du Maurier, and the visiting landlord was Whistler.[8]

At first Du Maurier did not understand Whistler's passion for the lower Thames, as he told his mother in October 1860:

> He *is* a wonder, and a darling – we are immense chums, though I see less of him now for he is working hard & in secret down in Rotherhithe, among a beastly set of cads and every possible annoyance and misery, doing one of the greatest chefs d'oeuvres – no difficulty discourages him.[9]

Later Du Maurier went down to Rotherhithe, and was surprised to find that he enjoyed spending an evening at the Thames-side 'free-and-easies', where the dockers drank and entertained themselves with songs and choruses. Du Maurier, who loved singing at any time, joined in cheerfully. He later described the scene in *Trilby*, where Little Billee joins a working-man's club in a dockland area. Du Maurier was impressed by the pictures Whistler was painting on the Thames, the most important of which was *Wapping*, a study of three figures against a background of Thames shipping. One of the models was Alphonse Legros, who had been persuaded by Whistler to come to London, and who eventually took British citizenship. Another was a red-haired Irish girl, whom Whistler had just met, Joanna Heffernan. Du Maurier thought the background 'perfectly gorgeous', and referred to the work as '*the* picture'. It must have been this painting which Whistler described to Fantin Latour as a 'chef d'oeuvre', and Du Maurier was probably echoing him when he used the same expression. At the same time Whistler was working on a series of Thames etchings, and on two other oils, *The Thames in Ice*, and *Old Westminster Bridge*. Du Maurier once told his mother that he was going down to Rotherhithe with Bill Henley, but Henley was not his only companion. Thirty-five years later, when *Trilby* had established Du Maurier as a famous author, Whistler received the

8. Armstrong, preface.
9. Letters, p. 16.

following letter from a workhouse in Edmonton: 'Dear Sir, Many years ago I accompanied you and a young woman (called Annie), Du Maurier – and a greek named Ionides to Rotherhithe to see a picture – a *nautical* one I think you were then about finishing'.[10] After explaining that she was Miriam Levy, sister of one of the artists at the Covent Garden Opera House, she went on: 'Dear Mr Whistler will you give this to George Du Maurier for *me* asking him for assistance to enable me to get from this institution and I hope as God has been merciful to and made him a successful man he will not deny this first *appeal* he never thought his fiancee would enter the union'.[11] Du Maurier was certainly never engaged to Miriam Levy, but she may have felt that the euphemism fiancée made her appeal more respectable. She had evidently tried to speak to Du Maurier in person, but 'he was too abrupt. My heart fell to my feet, he said he could not think of speaking to me now he was married'.[12] Nothing else is known of Miriam Levy, but she and others like her, account for the twinges of conscience from which Du Maurier suffered when he fell in love with Emma Wightwick.

Whistler's work at Rotherhithe impressed Du Maurier. His more informal oil sketches were showing an astounding simplicity and control of tone, which might well have placed him in the main impressionist tradition, had his attitude towards painting been less unpredictable and adventurous. Du Maurier had never doubted Whistler's enormous talent, but he was surprised by the quality of the work Whistler was producing. He had known him in Paris as a rather indolent and pleasure-seeking fellow, who never appeared to be doing much, and hardly ever turned up at Gleyre's; he was, therefore, amazed by the concentrated effort which Whistler was devoting to his Thames painting. It added more fuel to his growing friendship with the painter, which reached its climax at this period:

> I am beginning to be a little lion and the big lion Jemmy and I pull together capitally dans le monde – no rivality whatever, both being so different. Jemmy's bons mots which are plentiful are the finest thing I ever heard; and nothing that I ever read of in Dickens or anywhere can equal his *amazing* power of anecdote.[13]

Du Maurier's exaggerated admiration for his friend was something

10. 5 April 96. Glasgow University, History of Fine Art Department Library.
11. 5 April 96. Glasgow University, History of Fine Art Department Library.
12. 5 April 96. Glasgow University, History of Fine Art Department Library.
13. Letters, p. 16.

of a hot-house growth. Once the novelty of knowing such an unusual man had worn off, he began to see Whistler in a more objective light, and eventually became irritated by his colossal egoism and lack of consideration for others. Whistler was a demanding friend, who expected loyalty and adulation as his due. As Du Maurier began to make his own way in London, and as his social horizon broadened, he became more critical. Whistler was not in the least interested in Du Maurier's career or activities, except as they affected himself, and he made no attempt to understand or to sympathise with his friend. He was the 'big lion', Du Maurier the small lion, who soon wished to assert his own independence, or at least his equality. Once this happened, the intimacy inevitably collapsed.

In November 1860, Du Maurier moved to a studio of his own at 8A Berners Street. This was not the end of his friendship with Whistler, but it marked a turning point. Only when Du Maurier had become a staunch upholder of established values, and something of a 'blimp', would he describe Whistler's paintings as daubs, and the man himself as a poseur. In the early 1860s their paths had not divided so completely, and they continued to meet frequently, though not on an intimate basis. They both belonged to a loose group of impoverished bachelor artists, who were in the habit of dining at inexpensive restaurants, and spending the evening together. This included members of the English group in Paris, like Poynter and O'Connor; Du Maurier's friend from Dusseldorf, 'Bill' Henley; the architect, Thomas Jeckyll; Henry Stacy Marks; and the *Punch* artist, Charles Keene. Nearly all of them lived close together in the area between Oxford Street and the Middlesex Hospital, the great artists' settlement of Victorian England. After spending the day alone working over his drawings, Du Maurier enjoyed the relaxing, congenial company of fellow artists, and the conviviality and sense of comradeship to which it gave rise. The group had been in the habit of dining at a cheap and homely eating-house in Castle Street, near Cavendish Square, when Du Maurier joined them in 1860, but soon after his arrival the idea of a more refined and sophisticated restaurant was mooted. Charles Keene, in those days a noted epicure, was sent out to explore, and returned with the news that Pamphilon's in Argyle Street was comfortable, possessed of a reasonable cook, inexpensive, and had the added advantage of a coffee-room for smoking and conversation after dinner. Pamphilon's now became the favoured meeting place, and remained so until October 1862, when most of the group deserted it for the new school of cookery in Berners Street. A good meal at Pamphilon's cost less than two shillings, which was all that Du Maurier could afford, but he cheerfully left the waiter a penny, remarking, 'I know it isn't much, but I can't afford more'.[14] For a gregarious person like Du Maurier, Pamphilon's provided a counter-poise to the isolation he felt as a free-lance illustrator, and gave him a constant background of friendship and sympathy, which was essential to keep up his spirits in the struggle for survival. Felix Moscheles, who joined the group when he came to England in 1861, described it as a restaurant

> of the familar type that exhibits outside its door a bill of fare with prices appended, to be studied by those who count their shillings and pence as we did. We had got beyond the days when no wines are sour and when tough meat passes muster, if there is only plenty of it; we wanted a sound dinner, and we got it at the Pamphilon; to wind up we adjourned to the coffee-room and talked and read and smoked.[15]

As his affection for Whistler cooled, Du Maurier began to see more of his less exhausting friends. Poynter had arrived in England in 1860, and, like Du Maurier, he was struggling hard to make a living, receiving some of his first commissions from the architect, William Burges; these included ceiling decorations at Waltham Abbey, painted cupboard doors, and designs for stained glass windows. Soon after his arrival Du Maurier was invited to meet Poynter's sister, Mrs Bell, and he continued to see the painter regularly, chiefly at Pamphilon's. Du Maurier found the company of anyone in adversity congenial, particularly such a dedicated and ambitious artist as Poynter, but he could not bring himself to admire the latter's early works. His qualified praise of Poynter's 1862 Academy picture, *A Bunch of Blue Ribbons*, which he thought 'the best thing he has painted',[16] looks forward to the 'curate's egg' joke of 1895: 'Poynter painting a girl doing her hair in a looking glass which is devilish well painted in some parts'.[17] Poynter's other exhibit of that year was his *Dante's Angel* which the Academy had refused in 1860, and now 'skied', 'fortunately for it I think'[18] was Du Maurier's rather unkind comment. He seems to have liked *The Day Dream* of 1863 even less:

14. Moscheles, p. 126.
15. Moscheles, p. 126.
16. Letters, p. 139.

17. Letters, p. 118.
18. Letters, p. 139.

'Poynter's over the line in the big room, looks rather black & lacks interest – pretty girl with a book in her lap and her hand on a piano'.[19] Poynter was a reserved and austere personality, hardly likely to engender any warm enthusiasm, and his relationship with Du Maurier remained friendly but unemotional. Despite the fact that they had known each other so well in Paris, Du Maurier never called him Edward, although Whistler was always Jemmy or Jimmy. 'Bill' Henley, on the other hand, had all the high spirits and human weaknesses likely to endear himself to the volatile Du Maurier. A prodigious drinker and womanizer, he often spent his visits to Newman Street or Berners Street on Du Maurier's bed, sleeping off the effects of his previous night's debauch. He was gay and amusing, 'the dearest fellow that ever was',[20] and someone to whom Du Maurier could talk with perfect frankness. Unlike Whistler or Poynter, Henley was very good-natured, and very little trouble, but his mind was, in Du Maurier's words, 'an empty nutshell'.[21] Other close friends whom Du Maurier saw from time to time were Thomas Lamont and Thomas Armstrong, both of whom visited him on their infrequent journeys to London. Once he had become disillusioned with Whistler, Du Maurier threw himself whole-heartedly into the Pamphilon's set, and when, in May 1861, he sent home a list of his closest friends, it is noticeable that he omitted 'Jemmy' entirely: 'What a lucky beast I am in my friends. Great or little, they are each stunners – T.A., Poynter, Keene, Bancroft, Alecco, Henley'.[22]

Du Maurier's social orbit was not entirely confined to artists. He was anxious to establish a place for himself in the more general and fashionable world of London society, where his talents as a wit and conversationalist could be more effectively exploited than in the narrow company of other ambitious young men. One of the first homes to which he was invited was that of Alexander Ionides on Tulse Hill in south-west London, and it remained a favourite stamping-ground for many years. Ionides was a wealthy Greek merchant, a Victorian Onassis, and one of the most important members of the Anglo-Greek community in London, who had migrated there because it was the centre of world trade and world finance. The Ionides family were a huge clan, they were cosmopolitan, charming, hospitable, unconventional, intellectual and

19. Letters, p. 204.   21. Letters, p. 12.
20. M. H. Spielmann, 'Death of Mr. Du Maurier',   22. Letters, p. 46.
Daily Graphic (9 October 1896).

intensely interested in the arts. Alexander and his sons patronised many young and avant-garde artists, Rossetti, Edward Burne-Jones, G. F. Watts, Legros, Whistler, and Fantin Latour to mention the most important, and the collection of Constantine Alexander (the eldest son) now forms a large and significant section of the art department in the Victoria and Albert Museum. A full study of the houses owned by the Ionides family, always decorated in an advanced style, the extensive patronage which they exercised, and their innumerable links with artists and writers, would be enormously interesting and fruitful, for they were real pace-setters, in contact with all the significant movements of their period. Du Maurier had known Alecco Ionides (third son of Alexander, and younger brother of Constantine Alexander) in Paris, and they had become warm friends. Alecco and his family lost no time in inviting Du Maurier to visit them, and gave him the kindest of welcomes. Their home was luxurious and easy-going, quite different from the formality and starchiness of most big London houses, and they enjoyed entertaining young and impoverished artists. Their conversation was uninhibited, never trivial, though often light-hearted, aggressive and wide-ranging. On Sundays they held open house, and Du Maurier would often, in the days before his engagement, drive out to Tulse Hill in company with Henley, Whistler or Poynter. In an undated letter to Aglaia Coronio, Alecco's married sister, Du Maurier drew a sketch of himself and Bill Henley, with the smoke from their pipes forming the words 'Visions of Tulse Hill'. The doggerel verse below underlines Du Maurier's relationship with his informal hosts:

Kicky: Long time since we've been to Tulse Hill!
        I'm afraid they've forgotten us, Bill.
Bill: Then they must have forgotten us quick,
        Which is not at all like them, friend Kick.
Kicky: We might go on Sunday, no doubt.
Bill: What a sell it will be if they're out.[23]

On his first visit to Tulse Hill Du Maurier went in company with Whistler. The latter's success with the beautiful Ionides women made him envious, but he wrote to his mother with a touch of bravado: 'He talks women over to him, and I sing them back again

23. A. C. Ionides, *Ion: A Grandfather's Tale* (Dublin, 1927), II, 19.

to me.'[24] On their way home, Whistler daringly professed to be in love with Alexander's elder daughter, Aglaia Coronio, one of the most intelligent and witty women of the period, and the intimate friend of many artists, whose sharp tongue concealed an unhappy but immensely warm-hearted soul. The Ionides were all magnificent physical specimens, tall, dark, attractive and striking. In *Trilby*, Du Maurier described his first impression of Mrs Ionides:

> a Greek matron so beautiful and stately and magnificently attired that they felt inclined to sink them on their bended knees as in the presence of some overwhelming Eastern royalty – and were only prevented from doing so, perhaps, by the simple, sweet, and cordial graciousness of her welcome.[25]

She was an enormously kind and generous woman, who used to leave jam, marmalade and other luxuries at the lodgings of her indigent protégés, and provided maternal solicitude when required. The Ionides girls and their cousins, the Major sisters, would have stood out in company, but their beauty was surpassed by that of the stunning Spartalis, also relatives, who will be mentioned later. Du Maurier thought the Majors 'very pretty' and 'accomplished', particularly Rosa, who had published poems in *Once A Week*. When Whistler spat in her pork-pie hat, he was given it, and remarked: 'By jove, Miss Rosa, if that's the way things are to be obtained in your family I only regret I didn't spit in your hand!'[26] Du Maurier used this witticism as the subject for a *Punch* cartoon in 1873.

The Ionides girls provided Du Maurier with female companionship of a very desirable and disinterested kind, when relations between the sexes were generally so strained and artificial:

> The women will sometimes take one's hands in talking to one, or put their arm round the back of one's chair at dinner, and with all this ease and tutoiement, or perhaps on account of it, they are I do believe the most thoroughly well bred and perfect gentlefolks in all England.[27]

Such behaviour might appear to be loose, but Du Maurier felt they were all 'good' women, and described his feelings as very virtuous when he left their company. This suggests that there were other times when he did not feel virtuous: enforced chastity certainly contributed to his nervous breakdown in 1862. Dinner on Sunday was not the

24. Letters, p. 16.   26. Letters, p. 66.
25. p. 239.   27. Letters, p. 31.

26. Du Maurier's programme for 'The Thumping Legacy'
(1861). Du Maurier, Alecco Ionides and Whistler are
from left to right at the top, Luke Ionides and Algaia
Coronio are on either side of the cast list

only entertainment which the Ionides offered to their guests, though it must have been especially pleasurable for Du Maurier and his friends, used to cheap restaurants for the rest of the week. After dinner, music, singing and amateur theatricals were all freely indulged in. Du Maurier's tenor voice was a valuable social asset, which secured him more invitations than anything else. It especially endeared him to the Ionides circle, where special talents were eagerly seized on and employed. An early listener tried to express the quality of his voice:

> He would sit down to the piano, and in a moment the room would be full of divine melody, not loud, not declamatory, but music in the fullest sense of the word; a nightingale singing in an orchard full of pink apple-blossom was not as sweet, and I have heard a sudden hush come over a large assembly should he sing, albeit he liked best a small audience, and one he knew really loved to hear his tender *traînante* voice.[28]

Amateur dramatics were very popular at Tulse Hill, and both Du Maurier and Whistler were frequently drawn into this activity. These performances often formed the entertainment at the fancy-dress balls given by the Ionides family, which were sometimes attended by as many as two-hundred guests. Du Maurier designed the programme for *The Thumping Legacy* which was produced on 14 January 1861, and included sketches of the principal actors, Whistler, Madame Coronio, himself, Luke and Alecco Ionides. The piece was played in Greek costume provided by the Ionides, and was a great success. The actors nearly collapsed in giggles, when Du Maurier who was meant to say 'I would arrest you', accidentally changed it to 'I would eat you'. The quick-witted Whistler at once replied: 'Are you quite sure you wouldn't throw me up?',[29] which delighted the audience. They congratulated Whistler so profusely that he became over-excited, and very drunk. Among the audience was Lawrence Alma Tadema, the popular academic painter, who came clad, very suitably, as an ancient Roman, 'in toga and eye-glasses, crowned with flowers – "amazing", Whistler said, "with his bare feet and St John's Wooden eye!" '[30] The impact of Tulse Hill on Du Maurier cannot be overestimated. As he wrote many years later to Madame Coronio:

28. J. M. Panton, *Leaves from a Life* (1908), p. 196.
29. L. Ionides, *Memories* (Paris, 1925), p. 10.
30. E. R. and J. Pennell, *The Life of James McNeill Whistler* (1908), I, 79.

[I am] much touched that your mind should have gone back to the old Tulse Hill days of which I have such a pleasant recollection – when Poynter and Whistler and I . . . found so warm a welcome in that hospitable house, and had such a good time there. . . .[31]

Another cultural and intellectual circle with which Du Maurier came into contact was that of the Prinseps at Little Holland House, which he first visited in 1862. Val Prinsep, the second son, had gone to Paris to train at Gleyre's in 1859, two years after Du Maurier's departure, but they had many common friends, and inevitably met in London when they both returned there. Prinsep had his own rooms in London, and though he repeatedly asked Du Maurier to visit his parents' house, Du Maurier did not like to give up his evenings with Emma Wightwick, and only got round to going there after a year or more had elapsed. The Prinseps were more serious in their pursuit of art than the Ionides, more conventional in their attitudes, more impressed by success, and more comprehensive in their lionizing; they were, *par excellence*, cultural snobs. Their most complete success was the capture of G. F. Watts, who came to dinner in 1850 and stayed for twenty years, their official artist in residence. The Pattle sisters, Mrs Prinsep, Lady Somers, and Mrs Dalrymple, were the presiding genii of this exclusive and high-minded circle (another sister was Julia Cameron, the photographer), beautiful, aspiring, but at times a little ruthless and insincere. Nothing revealed the ambivalence of their attitude to the artists with whom they surrounded themselves more than their treatment of Watts' girl-bride, Ellen Terry. Their circle was extremely large by the time Du Maurier was invited, and included most of the literary and artistic lions of the period, whom he was so anxious to meet:

the nobilitee, the gentree, the litherathure, polithics and art of the counthree, by jasus! It's a nest of proeraphaelites, where Hunt, Millais, Rossetti, Watts, Leighton etc, Tennyson, the Brownings and Thackeray etc and tutti quanti receive dinners and incense, and cups of tea handed to them by these women almost kneeling.[32]

There were unfortunately few people of any importance present on Du Maurier's first visit, and he was disappointed in the company. He was uneasy too and suspicious, for he felt that the atmosphere was brittle, superficial and immoral, in contrast with Tulse Hill. He later

31. A. C. Ionides, II, 19.
32. Letters, p. 112.

did a grotesque drawing, in a letter to his mother, of a woman in a very décolleté dress, to illustrate his disgust at the fast and self-conscious behaviour which lay below the surface: 'all the women were décolletées in a beastly fashion – damn the aristocratic standard of fashion; nothing will ever make me think it right or decent that I should see a lady's armpit flesh folds when I am speaking to her'.[33] Possibly his own obsession with sexual morality distorted his vision of the Prinsep circle, but it seems probable that he had accurately assessed the mixture of pretension, vanity and social ambition, which animated it. Nor was he very impressed with Watts:

> Instead of dressing for dinner there, you undress; Watts without a shirt collar, and in long velvet painting jacket & list slippers; dines frugally on toast & butter; handsome romantic fellow, said to have been desperately in love with Mrs Prinsep's beautiful sister Countess Somers (probably does private soda waters besides his toast & butter).[34]

Watts had certainly wanted to marry Lady Somers in his early days, and his portrait of her, together with several of his allegorical pictures, still hangs at Eastnor Castle. Du Maurier did eventually meet several interesting and influential people at Little Holland House, but his attitude remained hostile, and he was not a frequent guest. A description of a dinner at the house of Lady Somers provides another glimpse of the society dominated by the Pattle sisters:

> Lots of swells, as you may fancy – damn their style, etc. I who feel so small at Lewises felt myself quietly & mildly big at the Somerses; as if it would be something too absurd for me to be patronised by people whose dinner conversation was such as I heard last night – not but what they were very flatteurs & charming in the extreme and nobody tried to be swell except an imperious old maid Miss Duff Gordon, who patronised my Gordigiani's rather, and was put down with irresistible tenderness and simplicity.[35]

Du Maurier's reaction to Val Prinsep's family did not in any way affect his friendship with the painter. A short man himself, Du Maurier always admired tall and commanding figures, and Val Prinsep, six feet two and over sixteen stone, was no exception. Prinsep was a jovial, self-confident, popular and intelligent man, whose history pictures, painted on a lavish scale to match his

33. Letters, p. 126.   35. Letters, p. 126.
34. Letters, p. 119.

personality, are now almost entirely forgotten. Like Du Maurier, he later turned to literature, and wrote a number of comedies, but he made his reputation as a painter, and was eventually a respected and prominent Royal Academician. As a young man, he belonged to the St John's Wood Clique, of which Du Maurier was an irregular associate, and which is discussed later. Du Maurier always hoped that Prinsep might marry his sister, Isabel, a brother-in-law of whom he could entirely approve. Prinsep, however, remained a bachelor until 1884, when he married the heiress, Florence Leyland, whose father had been one of Whistler's most important patrons.

One other cultural meeting-place which was important in Du Maurier's social life was the bachelor home of Arthur Lewis, in Jermyn Street. Lewis was a partner in the drapery firm of Lewis and Allenby in Regent Street, and held bachelor parties on Saturday evenings during the winter months. These parties were dominated by music, for which Lewis had a passion, and by the time Du Maurier was invited (probably through Charles Keene), during his first or second winter in London, they had already become famous. Lewis had organised his own choir, the backbone of all the musical entertainment, which was later named the Moray Minstrels, when he moved to Moray Lodge on Campden Hill in 1863, and which became in time a group of highly professional singers. Individual singers, pianists, and other musicians, were enthusiastically received, providing they were good, and Du Maurier was soon a regular visitor and performer, at least by the winter of 1861 to 1862:

> You can't fancy anything jollier than Lewises; as Marks says, the artists make a noble appearance there, & so they do; lots of professional glee singing & comic ditto (need I say that my Schuberts & Gordigianis meet with due appreciation?) [36]

Du Maurier met many artists at these parties, including his chief rivals as illustrators, Frederick Sandys, John Leech, and Frederick Walker, who designed all the invitation cards for Lewis. Leech was earning two thousand pounds a year as the social cartoonist for *Punch*, and Du Maurier was inevitably jealous of him. He was, however, disarmed by Leech's charm, good-nature, and 'great civility', and, more important, by his absence of superior airs: 'I remember feeling somewhat nervous lest he should take me for a

36. Letters, p. 99.

foreigner on account of my name, and rather unnecessarily went out of my way to assure him that I was rather more English than John Bull himself. It didn't matter in the least; . . . he was kindness and courtesy itself'.[37] Holman Hunt remembered seeing Du Maurier at Lewis' parties, usually talking to Frederick Walker, to whom he was devoted. Six years younger than Du Maurier, Walker had started work on *Once A Week* shortly before Du Maurier's arrival in London, and he had quickly developed into one of the most brilliant and original black-and-white draughtsmen of the century. Like Leech, he was among Du Maurier's most dangerous professional rivals, but he was so generous, so unworldly and delightful, that Du Maurier immediately fell under his spell. Other artists whom Du Maurier met at Lewis's were his friends, Stacy Marks and Keene, and such distinguished painters as Holman Hunt, Millais, Leighton and G. F. Watts, none of whom he got to know well at this period. He was not the only person to enjoy the parties, for the literature of the period is full of references to Lewis, and his 'evenings'. Even the serious Holman Hunt enjoyed them thoroughly:

> In summer, when garden parties were given, and on 'Moray Minstrel' nights, it was a merry crew that greeted one another as they drove up to the Lewis domain. The host always welcomed his guests with cheery greetings. . . . It was a strange mixture of company that might be found at these meetings in Lewis' house, for the entertainments became famous, and men of all classes were pleased to go into Bohemia for the night.[38]

The invitation was always the same, 'Music at 8.30. Oysters at 11'. Later on, Du Maurier took part in the famous production of *Cox and Box* at Moray Lodge, and he always enjoyed his evenings there. In *Trilby*, he created a figure called Sir Lewis Cornelys, an amalgamation of Lewis and Alexander Ionides, but the following passage evidently refers to Lewis:

> And what added so much to the charm of this delightful concert was that the guests were not packed together sardine-wise, as they are at most concerts; they were comparatively few and well chosen, and could get up and walk about and talk to their friends between the pieces, and wander off into other rooms and look at endless beautiful things, and stroll in the lovely grounds, by moon or star or Chinese-lantern light.[39]

37. S.P.S., pp. 16–7.   39. p. 241.
38. W. Holman Hunt, *Pre-Raphaelitism and the Pre-Raphaelite Brotherhood* (1905–6), II, 149 and 151.

After a time, however, the parties tended to become smarter and smarter, and were eventually visited by the Prince of Wales, which effectively ruined their informal and spontaneous character. Gone were the days when Stacy Marks could lead off into a comic sermon, or Whistler stand on a chair and sing low songs in argot French. Lewis' marriage to Kate Terry in 1867 killed the parties off altogether, for they had remained very much bachelor affairs. Shirley Brooks noted in his diary that many people, sad to lose their evenings at Moray Lodge, had predicted that the marriage would be a failure. Du Maurier was certainly not pleased about it, as he told his *Punch* colleagues: 'No more Moray Minstrelsy – D.M. regrets the marriage, for robbing us of a nice actress and some jolly meetings'.[40]

By the end of Du Maurier's first summer in London he had made several friends, and had spent fifteen pounds of his mother's money, but he had no drawing to his name in any periodical. Experience had soon taught him to ignore second-rate magazines and journals, which provided work irregularly, and paid badly. He realised that he could only succeed by establishing himself permanently or semi-permanently on one of the three leading illustrated magazines of the period, *Punch*, *Once A Week*, or *The Cornhill*. They all demanded a very much higher standard than Du Maurier had expected when he first arrived in London. In June 1860 he had written home: 'I find the first steps are the great difficulty, but once my footing is established I think I shall make money like dirt – The beast Gilbert makes 3,000£ a year'.[41] Ironically enough, John Gilbert later recorded in his diary, with some bitterness, the high price which Du Maurier had received for 'A Legend of Camelot' in *Punch* for March 1866. Gilbert, however, belonged to an earlier era, and something better was now demanded of a young black-and-white artist, striving to oust more established illustrators. Du Maurier had learnt little in Paris or Dusseldorf except competent draughtsmanship, and with the range and quality of talent available in the 1860s, he needed to develop his skill if he was to compete successfully. Illustration was now recognised as an art in itself, which demanded specialised talents. Earlier illustrators, like John Gilbert, Daniel Maclise, Richard Doyle, George Cruikshank and Hablôt Knight Browne (Phiz), had relied on a fairly sketchy and conventional technique, which attempted a straightforward visual accompaniment to the

40. Silver, 16 Oct. 1867.
41. Letters, p. 9.

story or poem. Their illustrations are often simple, vapid and man-
nered, using the medium of the woodblock to reproduce an ordinary
drawing. The Pre-Raphaelites, and Rossetti in particular, attempted
something quite different. Realising that they had to make their
drawings expressive in a very small area, they frequently distorted
the perspective and scale to compress the design, and bring it forward
to fill the space more effectively. In an oil painting the artist has size,
colour and atmosphere to hold the interest, and can afford to set his
figures well back into the picture space. The black-and-white artist
has none of these advantages. He must make his point simply and
directly. The Pre-Raphaelites not only brought a new realism and
clarity to the woodblock, but an imaginative and poetic sensibility,
which heralded a new movement. However archaic and stylised
Rossetti's designs may appear to be, his figures have a tangible and
concentrated presence, and his background and detail an intense
clarity, even where the setting itself is unrealistic. Millais, with his
dark, rich textures, his statuesque women, his evocative landscapes
and haunting night scenes, had a less highly-charged talent than
Rossetti's, but one which was just as original, and considerably more
productive. *The Music Master* by William Allingham, published in
1855, with illustrations by Hughes, Millais and Rossetti, was a
significant herald, followed by the more important Moxon edition of
Tennyson's *Poems*, published in 1857, illustrated by Millais, Hunt,
Rossetti and others. Frederick Walker, George Pinwell and John
North certainly owed a debt to Millais, but they were soon producing
designs of high quality, which owed nothing to outside example,
powerful, broadly-conceived, realistic, and emotional. Leighton and
Poynter worked in a more severe and restrained classical idiom, while
Sandys, perhaps the most brilliant of all, designed with a Durer-like
precision. Keene, Tenniel and Leech belonged essentially to an
older generation, and were, in any case, by the 1860s working in a
pattern dictated by the exigencies of the *Punch* cartoon. The achievements of black-and-white art in the sixties, are too numerous to be
listed here, but they do in many cases rival the best paintings of the
period. It is unfortunate that so many of the best illustrators should
have died so young, and that the movement which they initiated,
should not have lasted for more than a decade or so. Theirs was the
great age of the woodblock, before the days of photo-lithography,
when craftsmen like Joseph Swain and the Dalziel brothers achieved
an incredibly high standard of reproduction, which really made
possible the success of the artists. It would not have been possible in

the 1840s, but increasing demand had led to great advances in technique. Gleeson White described some of these factors in his *English Illustration, 'The Sixties'*:

> Hitherto, the engraver had only accepted as many blocks as he could engrave himself, with the help of a few assistants; but not very long before the date we are considering factories for the supply of wood-engravings had grown up. The heads of these, practical engravers, and in some cases artists of more than average ability, took all the responsibility for the work intrusted to them, and maintained a singularly high standard of excellence; but they did not pretend that they engraved each block themselves. Such a system not merely permitted commissions for a large quantity of blocks being accepted, but greatly increased speed in their production.[42]

It took Du Maurier some time to realise the importance of these changes, first made apparent in the Moxon Tennyson, the book which he had given to Emma Wightwick. His own early drawings, influenced by Leech and Phiz, were often perfunctory and sketchy, lacking any of the characteristic grace and elegance of his later designs, except when he drew from the living model. His first published drawings were illustrations for an Eastern story, 'Faristan and Fatima', which appeared in *Once A Week* on 29 September 1860. The model for one of the figures was Luke Ionides, but the drawings themselves were mediocre. Du Maurier's work now appeared at regular intervals in *Once A Week*, which was profusely illustrated (unlike the more selective *Cornhill*), but it was not till later that he was offered a whole serial to illustrate. Du Maurier had been recommended to *Once A Week* by Mark Lemon, the editor of *Punch*, whom he had approached for work, and who published a drawing of his on 6 October 1860. This was a cartoon showing himself, Whistler and Lamont entering a photographer's studio, and satirized the contemporary photographic craze:

> Photographer: 'No smoking here, sir!'
> Dick Tinto: 'Oh! A thousand pardons! I was not aware that –'
> Photographer (interrupting, with dignified severity): 'Please to remember gentlemen, that this is not a *Common Hartist's studio!*'

Until 1864, Du Maurier's relations with *Punch* were very unpredictable, for Mark Lemon was a shrewd editor who believed in keeping

---

42. *English Illustration: 'The Sixties'*, 1855–1870 (1897), pp. 11–12.

PHOTOGRAPHER. "*No Smoking here, Sir!*"

DICK TINTO. "*Oh! A thousand pardons! I was not aware that——*"

PHOTOGRAPHER (interrupting, with dignified severity). "*Please to remember, Gentlemen, that this is not a Common Hartist's Studio!*"——[N.B. Dick and his friends, who *are* Common Artists, feel shut up by this little aristocratic distinction, which had not yet occurred to them.]

27. The artist's studio, *Punch* (1860)

young artists on their toes. While *Once A Week* kept Du Maurier in more or less regular employment, Lemon frequently told him that he could dispense with his services for the time being. Many of Du Maurier's early designs for *Punch* were initial letters, for which he was paid fifteen shillings each. Quite the best of these was a letter 'Q', with Whistler sitting inside the letter, his leg negligently forming the tail, which appeared on 27 October 1860. Lemon was accurate in his criticism that much of Du Maurier's work was hurried and incompetent, for the quality of his drawing was directly related to the amount of time and effort he devoted to it. Like other young men anxious to get on quickly, he had to learn that there were no short-cuts. Only a few early drawings show him at his best, a study of Emma Wightwick, which he used in November 1860 to illustrate a poem entitled 'Non Satis' in *Once A Week*, and 'On Her Deathbed', which appeared in the same magazine in May 1861. These two drawings were the result of more time and thought than usual, and Whistler, who was a good judge of the arts, 'went on about them' a great deal. In both these drawings the influence of the Pre-Raphaelites was uppermost, particularly in the firm shading of the figures. In 'Non Satis' he drew Emma standing among some flowers and ivy, and rendered the detail precisely, in obvious imitation of the work of Millais. Of the two, 'On Her Deathbed' is considerably the better, and might be mistaken for the work of Matthew Lawless, an artist directly working in the Pre-Raphaelite tradition. The solidity of the old woman sitting by the bed, and the well-realised shape of the bed hangings, show Du Maurier progressing from the flimsy technique of his first published drawings.

Du Maurier had not been settled in Berners Street more than a few weeks, when he decided to move into Henley's lodgings in 85, Newman Street, where he took the second floor, probably because he was feeling lonely. The change of residence did not stretch Du Maurier's purse too much, for Alecco Ionides paid him six shillings a week for one of his two bedrooms, but rarely came to London to make use of it. The new house was a delightful change from the 'squalid discomfort' of his earlier rooms, and Henley was a much easier companion than Whistler. 'I don't think I could live without Henley – he's as good as a wife; and makes 85 Newman Street feel like a home'.[43] This

28. Whistler as the letter 'Q', *Punch* (1860)

43. Letters, p. 30.

29. On her deathbed, *Once a Week* (1861)

arrangement worked well till June 1861, when Henley, for reasons unknown, decided to live with his mother and step-father, who had recently come to London, while Du Maurier rather unwillingly moved to 91 Newman Street, which had once been the home of his cousin, Charles Bowles, and also of Peter Jeckyll (possibly the brother of Tom Jeckyll). Both his predecessors were dead, and Du Maurier found the rooms 'full of very blue recollections'.[44] Feeling lonely again, and missing the easy comradeship of Henley, Du Maurier decided that Felix Moscheles would enjoy the bohemian life of London, and wrote encouraging him to leave Paris, where Moscheles was doing moderately well as a portrait painter. Now that he was settled in London, Du Maurier had typically become a little patronising in his attitude to Paris: 'But I suppose Paris is just as jolly in its way. My ideas of Paris are all Bohème, quartier latin, &c.,

44. Letters, p. 51.

et si c' était à recommencer, ma foi je crois que je dirais "zut" '.[45]
Du Maurier insisted that Moscheles would have no trouble at all in
finding sitters in London, and that he would be very welcome among
the Pamphilon's group: 'a band of brothers . . . that dovetail beautifully'.[46] He had himself, he pointed out without modesty, settled
down particularly well:

> It was quite a freak of mine coming over here; I did it against every-
> body's advice – came over with a ten-pound note and made the rest. . . . I
> go knocking about as happily as possible, singing and smoking cigars
> everywhere.[47]

Du Maurier expressed similar self-satisfaction in a letter to his sister,
who was talking of following her brother to London: 'But you would
require a year's training my dear, to get on with these fellows . . . I
tumbled into it in about three *months*, mais tu sais, moi!'[48]

Perhaps encouraged by Du Maurier, Moscheles arrived in London
in May 1861, but Du Maurier soon wished that his old friend had remained in Paris. The man who had been so dear to him in the profound depression following the loss of his eye now seemed, 'a poor
little posing Frenchman among a lot of heroes'.[49] Since last meeting
Moscheles, Du Maurier had decided that 'a lack of humbug' was the
supreme human virtue, and on reconsideration he found that the
flamboyant Moscheles and his whole family no longer came up to his
expectations. The delightful Clara was now a 'conceited girl', for
whose singing he did not 'care a damn', although he had unwillingly
to admit that she was a good pianist. In the days of their intimacy,
Du Maurier had done innumerable sketches and drawings for the
amusement of the Moscheles family, many of which are reproduced
by Moscheles in his book of memoirs, *In Bohemia with Du Maurier*,
but Du Maurier now imagined that his friend only wanted them for
his own profit. It is true that Moscheles produced his book in the
wake of *Trilby*, and later sold the drawings, but it is difficult to
believe he was that far-sighted in 1861. Du Maurier's attitude to his
old friend is rather repellent, and reflects the snobbery and desire for
respectability and position which increasingly dominated his
thinking, and which alienated him from Whistler and other incorrigible bohemians. The chief source of annoyance, however, was

45. Moscheles, p. 124.
46. Moscheles, p. 125.
47. Moscheles, p. 125.

48. Letters, pp. 33–4.
49. Letters, p. 41.

Felix Moscheles' success at portrait painting, for Du Maurier's prognostication had proved only too accurate, and Moscheles' cheap portraits were selling very well. Du Maurier was scornful, but envious: 'Moscheles painting is not much, but he will get on by charlatanism at first and that's just what we fellows don't sympathise with'.[50] Such emotions are common among struggling artists, and Du Maurier in particular was irritated by all successful painters, especially by such prodigies as John Millais and Frederic Leighton, who were very near his own age, and whose pictures were the talking point of the Royal Academy exhibitions. When he caught sight of Leighton at a party, he acidly described his behaviour: 'very blasé and finikin, and quite spoilt – one of the world's little darlings, who won't make themselves agreeable to anything under a duchess'.[51] The effortlessly successful Leighton was anything but a snob, and Du Maurier's remark was only a sign of his own acute insecurity. In fact, as he found later, Leighton had so polished a personality, that it was difficult to find anything in him to dislike. Leighton, on the other hand, took an immediate liking to Du Maurier, and introduced him to Mrs Sartoris, who, as Adelaide Kemble, had been an opera singer, and with whom Leighton was said, by idle and malicious gossip, to have had a liaison. Du Maurier enjoyed her dinners, but was not impressed by her appearance:

> Mrs S. no longer fit for Norma; fat red face; Leighton looks so pretty & fresh by the side of her, and the contrast naturally suggests itself when one has heard all about them. Verb. sap. – Le monde me dégoûte, quoi. Mrs Prinsep & Mrs S. awful enemies I fancy but very loving to each other.[52]

It was at a party given by Mrs Sartoris in June 1862, that Du Maurier first saw his great idol, Thackeray. Knowing his passion, Mrs Sartoris offered to introduce them:

> I was too diffident. I was so little, and he was so great. But all that evening I remained as close to him as possible, greedily listening to his words. . . . And my admiration for Thackeray increased when, as it was getting late, he turned to his two daughters, Minnie and Annie, and said to them 'Allons, mesdemoiselles, il est temps de s'en aller', with the best French accent I have ever heard in an Englishman's mouth.[53]

50. Letters, p. 55.
51. Letters, p. 33.
52. Letters, p. 119.
53. Sherard, pp. 398–9.

30. Beatrix, *Henry Esmond* by W. M. Thackeray (1868)

Du Maurier never did meet Thackeray, although, years later, he became a good friend of Annie Thackeray Ritchie.

Du Maurier was not introduced to Millais until later, for in those early years of success, Millais was in the habit of accepting invitations and then not turning up. Du Maurier found such casual behaviour particularly galling, and, after a dinner-party given by Abraham Solomon, he told his mother: 'As usual at all great artist spreads, Millais *was* to have been there, and *wasn't*'.[54]

54. Letters, p. 54.

Du Maurier's first year in London was not significantly different from his year in Paris. Although he was not a student any longer, he felt no spur to work very hard, and rather expected success to drop into his lap as a birthright. Poynter thought he had 'a dangerous tendency towards laziness', and took a dim view of his failure to get drawings accepted by *Punch*: 'He had obtained a foothold on *Punch*, which, owing to this characteristic [laziness], he was in danger of losing. Mark Lemon, then editor, found it necessary to talk seriously to him on the subject'.[55] Du Maurier, who enjoyed the company of his friends and the bonhomie of Pamphilon's, set too much store by social success, and had not yet learnt the necessity of dividing work from pleasure, which was so pronounced a characteristic of James Whistler. A new development and distraction in his life, however, was his growing love for Emma Wightwick, which was to cause him a great deal of anxiety and unhappiness before he finally married her. He had always admired Emma, and he had found it pleasant to call on the hospitable Wightwicks during his early days in London. Emma was the only child of middle-class and conventional parents, totally lacking in any cultural awareness, although their daughter began to take a significant interest in paintings and artists. Mrs Wightwick, characterized as Mrs Gibson in *The Martian*, was rather a silly woman, quite unable to manage the simplest things for herself, and utterly dependent on her capable daughter. Her husband was, if anything, worse, a facetious and vulgar man, always cracking feeble jokes, or speaking in atrocious French at Du Maurier's expense. Du Maurier became profoundly irritated by both of them, but at first their way of life seemed a relaxing change from the more competitive atmosphere of Pamphilon's: 'I have two sets you see, the genuine kind-hearted unintellectual W. set, where I am cock of the walk, and the cultivated lot, where I shall be, if things go smoothly'.[56] On one occasion he even tried to mix the two sets, but with very limited success:

> I took Jimmy Whistler to the Wightwicks, he delighted mother and daughter but the old fellow couldn't stand him, tried to shut him up, failed and went to bed sulky and sick with a cigarette Jimmy made him smoke.[57]

Du Maurier probably saw the Wightwicks two or three times a week,

55. H. Lucy, *Nearing Jordan* (1916), p. 106.   57. Letters, p. 10.
56. Letters, p. 7.

and in his first letters home, he spoke of Emma as if she were a cousin or friend, an easy and jolly companion, but nothing more. After repeated enquiries from Dusseldorf, he soon had to admit that he was 'flirting a little' with her. The partial collapse of the Wightwick family business in October 1860 temporarily put a stop to any thoughts of marriage which Du Maurier may have entertained. The Wightwicks were not bankrupted, but they were forced to live on very limited means. When this situation occurs in *The Martian*, the hero brushes it lightly aside, and marries Leah Gibson without her money, but, in real life, Du Maurier was more cautious. He ceased to visit the Wightwicks for some weeks, and made no attempt to continue relations of any kind with Emma. When his mother callously wrote advising him to give her up, he replied tartly: 'You are mistaken when you think I want to flirt with Emma – it would be absurd now'.[58] The romantic overtones of Emma's impoverished state were entirely lost on him at the time, although late in 1862, when they were engaged, he wrote comparing her to Thackeray's Amelia in *Vanity Fair*, whom George Osborne at last decided to marry in spite of her father's financial crash. Du Maurier was certainly harrassed by the same doubts as Osborne, because money meant the position in society which he so ardently craved, and because he was haunted by financial insecurity all his life. The only row between Emma and himself, which his children could remember, followed the death of her father, when the expected legacy did not materialize. Du Maurier remained parsimonious all his life, till the success of *Trilby* lifted the threat of poverty, and left him dazed but incapable of spending.

During the period of coolness with the Wightwicks, Du Maurier met a cousin of the Ionides, Mary Cassavetti, one of the most striking beauties of the period. Tall and dark, her classical features are touched with melancholy in the portraits of her by Rossetti, and Burne-Jones, but she was also possessed of a self-willed and passionate streak, which made her formidable and exciting. Her fortune of eighty thousand pounds was an added attraction, and rendered her sufficiently independent to defy all her relations, and engage herself to a poor Greek doctor in Paris, Zambacco. Concerted family opposition to the proposed match had made her sulky and obstinate, and when Du Maurier met her at Tulse Hill in the autumn of 1860 she refused to speak to Poynter or Whistler. Much to everybody's

58. Letters, p. 20.

surprise, and to Du Maurier's own amusement and delight, she talked to him for over an hour, greatly adding to his own self-esteem. Realizing that such a prize could not be wooed by conventional means, he made her the subject of slanderous comment at Tulse Hill in the hope that she would hear his deprecatory remarks. Apparently she did so, for in November 1860, Mary Cassavetti broke away from a group of friends, and pursued Du Maurier round Kensington Gardens with only a little girl as a chaperone. Du Maurier was apparently too frightened to speak to her in such unconventional circumstances, and pretended not to recognise her behind her thick veil, but he was excited by the incident. He sent a full account to his mother, prefaced with the self-conscious 'funny rather'. His mother, equally intrigued by the financial incentive, wrote back at once urging him to make use of this advantage, but however 'significative' his meeting with Mary Cassavetti may have been, it did not lead any further. She married Zambacco, but lived an unhappy and stormy life, which included passionate affairs, with, among others, Burne-Jones.

In place of Mary Cassavetti, Mrs Du Maurier was soon writing to suggest another match, this time with his old Dusseldorf flame, Louisa Lewis, who was apparently pining for him, and to whom he was urged to write. Du Maurier replied guardedly:

> I am very sorry and, confess, conscience-stricken about L.L. If she is as bad as you say – Elle devrait avoir plus de bon sens. Does she think that I am realising a rapid fortune to come back and carry her off?[59]

He sent Miss Lewis a copy of *Once A Week*, significantly enough the number which contained a drawing of Emma Wightwick, 'Non Satis'.

It was Emma who continued to dominate his imagination, and, unless he found another girl friend of sufficient beauty and attraction to replace her, it seemed inevitable that he would eventually return to her. Absence was intensifying his emotion, and Emma sensibly made no effort to win him back, but remained quietly and sadly at home. Du Maurier did try to break away from her coils. In a letter to Armstrong he wrote: 'Your letter aroused me this morning from the arms of Somnus and dreams of the talented Angelina Levy with whom I spent the evening last night'.[60] Annie and Helen (Nellie) Levy were

59. Letters, p. 39.
60. Letters, p. 24.

the daughters of Joseph Levy, the successful Jewish printer, who founded the *Daily Telegraph*, and the younger sisters of Edward Lawson, later Lord Burnham. Angelina, who seems to have lived with them, may have been a cousin. Annie was described as an 'old playfellow', so the Levys must have been old family friends of the Du Mauriers, almost certainly from their Pentonville days. It is probable that the Levy girls had been school fellows of Emma Wightwick and Isabel Du Maurier. At this period the Levys lived in Lancaster Gate, but later they moved to Grosvenor Square, where Mrs E. M. Ward recalled their home:

> In an age when most people did not make their homes beautiful, the Levys gathered round them everything that was artistic and valuable. . . . The whole place fairly laughed with flowers, flowers of the loveliest and rarest description, whilst the atmosphere, impregnated with their sweet and delicate scent, conveyed with it a sense of joy and most innate refinement.[61]

If Du Maurier had married one of the Levy girls, it would have been a stroke of incredible financial acumen, for they became, by the end of the century, one of the richest families in England.

Another girl in whom Du Maurier became interested at this time and with whom he almost certainly had an affair was Polly, who used to call on him in Berners Street, unchaperoned, and dined alone with him in Leicester Square. He described one of her visits as 'innocent', which suggests that others were not. She may have been an artist's model, but she was not, in any case, a respectable young woman, or one whom he can have considered as a possible wife. He was proud enough of his relationship to write about her to Armstrong:

> I expect Polly here every minute – En v'là une qu'a l'air de tenir à moi depuis trois mois que j'ai pas l'sou, qu'elle vient m'épuiser avec une regularité. . . . Decidément j'ai le feu sacré pour taper dans l'oeil du sesque! un doux regard plein de feu, une voix enchanteresse, et un certain petit mouvement ondulé qui me fait regretter que je ne suis pas femme, afin de m'avoir pour ma que . . .[62]

Du Maurier's affection for Emma soon began to reassert itself, and he almost certainly began to see her again in the late winter of 1860, though he was cautious enough to avoid mentioning her to his

61. E. M. Ward, *Memories of Ninety Years* (1926), p. 162, and *Reminiscences* (1911), pp. 151–2.

62. Letters, p. 27.

family. His mother continued to urge marriage with an heiress, and showed no understanding or sympathy for the real dilemma which faced her son. When Isabel wrote to Du Maurier demanding to know the truth, he replied ambiguously:

31. Non Satis, *Once a Week* (1860)

You ask me about the state of my fickle mind. Well, I adore Emma, who sat for my block, but what's the use, you know, *pas le sou, hein?* and then her relatives – what?! I wonder how much she likes me, the dear prude. She is quite converted to all the pictures and books and music that I admire.[63]

63. *The Du Mauriers* (1937), p. 301.

Du Maurier asked Armstrong for his advice, and was sensibly told to propose, and to think less about money. In May 1861, Du Maurier's love for Emma triumphed over worldly considerations, and he asked for her hand on the way back from an afternoon performance of *Ruy Blas* at the Princess's Theatre. She accepted him calmly enough, only asking him if he was sure he would not change his mind. Her parents, suddenly alarmed at the prospect of losing the chief prop of their household, were more depressed than pleased, and demanded that Du Maurier should establish himself financially before the marriage took place. Du Maurier rashly suggested one thousand pounds in the bank as a suitable figure on which to set up house with Emma. Once engaged to his 'good angel', who was only a 'prude' in so far as she constituted an inevitable break with Du Maurier's bohemian past, he felt that he had escaped for ever from the possibility of falling into evil ways:

> her influence on me is wholesome; good in every way; had it not been for her I should have yielded to the seduction of society and other seductions very much more dangerous (in Society) – perfect ruin to an artist like me.[64]

Du Maurier was not sure how to divulge the enagement to his mother, and did his best to conceal the news among other family gossip. Opening his letter of May 1861 with the announcement that he had 'several things to tell', he first mentioned his aunt Georgina, and then his brother's latest escapade: 'Thirdly the mutual affection of the angelic Emma and talented Kick has grown to such an extent that it was absurd to go on any longer without speaking'.[65] In this manner he contrived to deprive the announcement of any element of surprise, and then spent the rest of the letter in an attempt to prove that it was all for the best. Mrs Du Maurier, who had tried to break off the relationship at long range, must have been horrified by her son's letter, for, only a few weeks before, she had told her sister-in-law, Louise Du Maurier:

> She is an excellent girl, but I can't say I should like such a connection, and now her family have lost so much money they could not do much for her, so it would not suit at all.[66]

64. Letters, pp. 44–5.
65. Letters, p. 44.

66. *The Du Mauriers*, p. 305.

Faced with a fait accompli from London, however, Mrs Du Maurier
evidently decided that it was best to accept the situation gracefully,
and she therefore wrote to Emma to congratulate her: 'I know no one
so well calculated to make him happy as yourself, and who has such
influence over him'.[67]

Emma's 'influence', to which Du Maurier's mother refers with
perhaps a touch of sarcasm, soon began to affect Du Maurier's
whole way of life. He had told Emma that he had been 'a great
vagabond and all that sort of thing',[68] and Emma was anxious that
there should be no further lapses from virtue or from conventional
behaviour. She did not like Whistler or Tom Jeckyll, and thought
they were most unsuitable companions for her fiancé, described by
Du Maurier as 'a few restrictions towards Jimmy & a slight exception
in favour of T. Jeckell'.[69] This hostility on Emma's part was not just a
zealous desire for respectability, although this certainly existed, but a
feeling, probably correct, that close male friendships were incompatible with an intimate and equal relationship between herself and
Du Maurier. His unsuitable friends would lead him on, and seduce
him away from all that she represented and wanted. Emma did not
have to fight a battle against Du Maurier's friends, for he was
already tired of them, and anxious to change his way of life. His
engagement was a symbol of his desire to become part of the establishment, and to accept the conventional values of society. Whistler
had long since ceased to excite his admiration, and Jeckyll was now
described in his letters home as 'a tuft hunter', 'a liar' and 'a snob'.
He was aware that these two friends would disapprove of his marriage, and particularly to 'a linen draper's daughter, unless I make a
great name like Leech, in which case il me léchera les pieds'.[70] He
was defensive and hostile, unsure himself if he was doing the right
thing by marrying the impoverished daughter of a tradesman. Emma
was delighted to meet and encourage Du Maurier's other friends like
Prinsep, Lamont, Keene, Poynter, Marks and Armstrong. She
especially liked Armstrong, whom she regarded as a good and
steadying influence on Du Maurier, and who had of course encouraged him to marry her. Armstrong was still living comfortably
with his family in Manchester, where he was doing very little painting. From time to time he would visit London and join the group at
Pamphilon's, but Du Maurier was convinced that Armstrong's

67. Letters, p. 46.   69. Letters, p. 81.
68. Letters, p. 45.   70. Letters, p. 56.

work would only improve if he settled in London, and really applied himself to the task, something he was always encouraging his friend to do.

Du Maurier wisely decided to visit his family in Dusseldorf after dropping the bombshell of his engagement on them. He had hoped to take a holiday there in the summer of 1860, but lack of funds had effectively prevented him. In April 1861, Du Maurier's uncle, George Clarke, had died, and his not inconsolable widow, Georgina, with whom Du Maurier had flirted in earlier days, decided to join Mrs Du Maurier and Isobel in Dusseldorf. Before the engagement was announced in May 1861, Georgina had asked Du Maurier to accompany her, and offered to pay his fare, an arrangement which he gratefully accepted. When the news of Du Maurier's engagement reached her, she decided to continue with the plan, indeed it would have been very difficult for her not to have done so, and she sent a charming note of congratulation to Emma. Du Maurier was naive enough to imagine that his aunt and his ageing mother might settle down happily together, and, in wilder moments, even envisaged a household of Emma and his female relatives all together in London, with himself as the centre of admiration. Mrs Du Maurier harboured no such comfortable illusions, and obstinately refused to consider any idea of living under her son's roof. She and Isabel far preferred to remain independent in Dusseldorf, and had anything but happy memories of London. Isabel was hoping that a gentleman, by the name of Sam Perrot, who had been paying her court, would eventually propose, and, in any case, enjoyed her position as a belle of Dusseldorf society, which included many dashing military men and wealthy foreigners. Both she and her mother had a suspicion that they would be superfluous additions in the young couple's household, once they were married, and had no desire to pursue a conventional existence on Wightwick lines. In this, they showed considerably more perception than the excited Du Maurier, who was eager to please everybody.

Any hopes which Georgina may have entertained of dallying pleasantly with Du Maurier on the journey were quickly dashed when he produced a photograph of his fiancée, and announced his intention of 'showing' her the countries through which they were going to travel. Du Maurier set out at the end of July with Mrs Clarke and her son, Bobby, crossing the channel on a calm night in the wake of a superb sunset. Sitting alone on deck, for Georgina had retired below feeling ill, Du Maurier thought of the future and of

travelling with Emma: 'I hope we shall have many trips and
journeys some day',[71] he told her. He had brought with him all the
letters which he had received from his old Dusseldorf flame, the
mysterious 'Damask', now living in Antwerp, which he intended to
return to her on his way back. It was a great relief to him that his
other girl-friend, Louisa Lewis, had left Dusseldorf with her family
only a few days before his arrival. He and his aunt reached Dusseldorf late in the evening, where there was a joyful reunion of the
family. Du Maurier and his mother were so delighted to see each
other that they sat up until three in the morning, talking about Du
Maurier's work, his friends, his engagement, and also about Isabel's
chances of marriage. Du Maurier only stayed for a week in Dusseldorf, much to his mother's disappointment, pleading work as an
excuse for his return, though Emma was probably a more powerful
stimulus, as his mother had already surmised. Du Maurier's hopes
that his mother and Georgina would get on well together were at first
high, but he quickly became more doubtful: 'I don't know how
they'll all agree when I'm gone – doocid problematic I should say'.[72]
From later letters, it is clear that Georgina's unwanted and delinquent son was the prime cause of the disagreement between herself
and Mrs Du Maurier. This is not surprising for he seems to have been
a difficult and unattractive child. Georgina was neither interested
in him, nor fond of him, and much preferred flirting with the German princelings and army officers, to looking after him. Mrs Du
Maurier was incensed by Georgina's treatment of Bobby, conveniently forgetting how entirely she had rejected her own son,
Eugène, still struggling to make a career in the French army. Du
Maurier, like his mother, had no affection for Eugène, and regarded
him as thoroughly disreputable:

> Yesterday I received a letter from G. asking me to pay his debts and
> saying that otherwise he will be broke; whether that is true or not I don't
> know, but I wrote him 8 pages by return of post, saying it was out of my
> power and blowing him up but in a very kind manner.[73]

His condemnations of Eugène became more cruel and arrogant as he
began to establish himself in London, revealing in him a characteristic habit of judging people by a rigid moral code. He had seen
very little of Eugène since they had grown up, for Mrs Du Maurier

71. Letters, p. 59.   73. Letters, p. 109.
72. Letters, p. 59.

had done all she could to discourage her younger son from coming
home. He had visited Du Maurier in Paris, bringing with him an
aristocratic fellow-officer and friend, the Prince de Ligne. They
appear in *Trilby* as Dodor and L'Zouzou, who are repeatedly reduced
to the ranks for practical joking and insubordination. Eugène was
popular with his army friends, but found it difficult to keep up with
them on his army pay, and continually wrote to his mother asking
for money, and threatening to arrive on their doorstep if it was not
forthcoming. He also asked Du Maurier for help, who, as he was
equally impoverished, sent letters of advice encouraging his brother
to reform his morals. He lived in constant fear of Eugène's arriving in
London and disgracing him. Eugène was an amiable scoundrel, who
hardly deserved the unkindness and moral censure which his family
bestowed on him. Later in life he reformed and came to England,
where Du Maurier felt a return of the old affection of their childhood.
Georgina Clarke and her son remained in Dusseldorf for a year, but
in an atmosphere of growing irritation, and, when they finally left,
they disappeared for good from Du Maurier's life. Bobby became in
time a respectable professional man, while, as Daphne Du Maurier
discovered, Georgina eventually joined the Salvation Army.

On his return from Dusseldorf in the first week of August 1861,
Du Maurier settled down to hard work, for his chances of marrying
Emma depended entirely on his earning enough money to satisfy
her parents. He organised his time very carefully, working hard all
day, eating very little, and spending the evenings in Grosvenor
Square with Emma:

> I live the quietest and most wholesome life, no racketing whatever;
> leave the W's at 11, straight to bed, and breakfast at 8. In spite of my
> great anxiety, and little pecuniary deficiencies, I am happy as I have
> never been before, so full of hope and conscious of the power of fulfilling
> it in the end.[74]

During his first frenetic efforts to find employment he had been too
nervous to work slowly and carefully, but, as he looked through the
past numbers of contemporary magazines, he realised that the slap-
dash methods of the old school must be discarded:

> a day is coming when illustrating for the million (swinish multitude) à
> la Phiz and à la Gilbert will give place to real art, more expensive to

74. Letters, p. 57.

print and engrave and therefore only within the means of more educated classes, who will appreciate more.[75]

Just before his visit to Dusseldorf, *Once A Week* had rejected his illustration to Fred H. Whymper's poem 'From My Window' on the grounds that he had not accurately represented a muslin dress. Du Maurier was furious, and quarrelled with the editor about the rejection, but Lucas was adamant, and commissioned another artist, Frederick Sandys, to do the work. Sandys' drawings, much influenced by German artists, were among the finest of the period, and Du Maurier generously acknowledged the superb technique of his illustration to 'From My Window': 'Wasn't Fred Sandys's drawing exquisite? That was the poem that I illustrated, and which they refused'.[76] Inspired by his example, Du Maurier began to copy the drawings of the German draughtsmen whom Sandys so much admired. Tom Armstrong remembered his attempts to improve his technique:

> Du Maurier used to practise methods of execution about this time with pen and brush, and I remember his careful copy of a portion of one of Rethel's famous woodcuts, *Death the Friend*, and also portions of Menzel's work in the life of Frederick the Great. This book, of which Charles Keene was the first among us to own a copy, impressed English draughtsmen on wood very much.[77]

An immediate result was the drawing 'A Time to Dance', which appeared in *Good Words* for October 1861. The left hand side of the design is entirely taken up by the figure of a crouching girl, seen in steep perspective in the immediate foreground, from whose hands a pennant streams out into the wind, while behind and below her are a great crowd of people. The whole effect is extremely dramatic, with a clarity and dislocation typical of German art. 'A Time to Dance' is a remarkable drawing, but it is not typical, and was produced under the immediate influence of Sandys. As mentioned earlier, Du Maurier had met Sandys at a party given by Arthur Lewis in the early winter of 1861, and went round the next day to Sandys' studio, where he received some valuable advice:

> Sandys . . . told me never to let a block go out of my hands unless I was well satisfied that all that patience, time and model could do for it had

75. Letters, p. 36.
76. Letters, p. 65.
77. Armstrong, pp. 159–60.

32. A Time to dance, *Good Words* (1861)

been done. It does not pay one so well at first as quick drawing from chic but in the end one can command any amount of work and any price one likes.[78]

Sandys always drew from nature for his landscape backgrounds, as well as from the model for his figures, and Du Maurier slowly learnt that this was the secret of his success:

He showed me two crayon portraits he is doing, the finest things of the

78. Letters, p. 86.

sort I ever saw, and as for his studies they are wonderful. If he has a patch
of grass to do in a cut, an inch square, he makes a large and highly
finished study from nature for it first; tu conçois qu'un gaillard pareil ira
loin; he has work on hand for 2 years.[79]

Du Maurier gave up the use of a lay figure, and in the summer of
1862, he even went down to Hampton Court to draw a landscape
'en plein air', an idea which would certainly not have occurred to
him a year earlier. He enjoyed the experience, and the relief from
poring over woodblocks in his own studio. Sandys continued to pass
salutary comments on Du Maurier's work, asking him, in February
1862, why he still could not draw any better.

This particular period, during which he was trying to improve his
work by laborious and time-consuming efforts, was very difficult for
Du Maurier. In December and January 1861–2, he had illustrated a
three part serial, 'The Admiral's Daughters' for *Once A Week*, but the
author disapproved of them, and he was soon back to illustrating
individual poems and stories. During the spring of 1862, he executed
a great many initial letters for *Punch*, but few half-page cartoons,
probably because one member of the *Punch* staff was actively hostile
to him. Du Maurier imagined that this was Shirley Brooks, but he
later discovered that it had been Tom Taylor, who disliked this
genteel and perky upstart. Henry Silver, whose unpublished diary is
an invaluable source of information on Du Maurier and his colleagues, did his best to help the young man, by sending him the initial
letters for his own dramatic column, and by supporting his case at
the weekly dinners. The initial letters did not pay very well, and Du
Maurier had difficulty in extracting from Mark Lemon the little
money which he earned, and which was so vital to him. Fresh hope
came when a new magazine, *London Society*, started publication in
February 1862, and seemed disposed to give Du Maurier a good deal
of work. He designed the first cover for them, but his drawing of
London Bridge in the rush hour was sent back as a 'shocking
failure', and it was only after he had submitted other versions that
the drawing was finally published in 1863.

Despite his hard work and regular hours, Du Maurier was still
not doing as well as he had hoped, and, on his return from Dusseldorf in August 1861, he decided to try his hand as a writer, hoping
in this way to supplement his meagre income. He began with an
autobiographical short-story, based on his experiences at the

79. Letters, p. 99.

North Molton Gold Mine, which was published in *Once A Week* in
September 1861. If it is not the most exciting of stories, it is readable
and competent, and received favourable comment. *Once A Week* had
paid him eleven guineas for his story, but if he could get another
accepted by *The Cornhill*, still under the editorship of W. M. Thackeray, he would receive twenty-five guineas. The autobiographical
vein attracted him, as it did when he became a novelist in the 1890s,
and he spent the autumn working on a story about his days in the
Quartier Latin, which he described in a letter to Armstrong:

> Lamont is there as the wise and facetious Jerry, you as the bullnecked &
> sagacious Tim; the street is our Lady of the Bohemians. I shall idealise
> in the illustrations (if I get them to do), make us all bigger, and develop
> you into strong muscularity; having insisted on our physical prowess &
> muscular development – the natural antidotes to morbid Quartier-latin
> Romance.[80]

This early version of *Trilby*, which has still to be discovered, did not
find favour with *The Cornhill*, nor with *Once A Week*, and Du Maurier,
disheartened by his failure turned back to illustration. Had his story
been accepted, he might have become a novelist then, rather than
waiting another thirty years. He was himself aware of this, for the
hero of *The Martian* gives up illustration for writing at exactly the
same point in his career when Du Maurier was himself producing his
early short stories.

Despite all his attempts to establish himself in a secure financial
position, Du Maurier's tendency to idleness needed little encouragement. When the Wightwicks went down to Ramsgate for three
weeks in the summer of 1861, he found it only too easy to slip back
into his old pursuits. Feeling lonely without his 'good angel', he went
off to Pamphilon's and found Poynter there with Charles Keene, and
another old friend, Chapman. After dinner Poynter invited them to
his rooms where they drank six bottles of Maçon between them.
Du Maurier excused himself to Emma, by remarking that 'Nothing
else could cure me of the fidgets'.[81] Not surprisingly he found it hard
to work next day, and again spent the evening with Poynter, this time
at the Alhambra, watching Léotard, the tight-rope walker. On their
way home they noticed a fire in the city, and were out until long after
midnight, watching the flames and the engines from Waterloo

80. Letters, p. 92.
81. Letters, p. 67.

Bridge and Ludgate Hill. The usually restrained Poynter, who was the instigator of most of the wildness, was ecstatic at the sight of the fire, and insisted on another meal after the excitement was over, and a further walk to the Haymarket. Du Maurier arrived home very late and very damp, with the natural consequence that he felt considerably worse in the morning:

> I awoke with seedy eyes and weary back and parched mouth; doocid familiar sensation, yet seems quite forgotten; brought back all sorts of recollections which I hate with the whole strength of my affection for you, recollections of so many nights with Whistler and Tom A, and Tom J. and lots of fellows, years ago and even lately; and in which a great deal too much wine and smoke have been taken in, and too much wild talk let out, for happiness. So Miss Salvation . . . you had better *not* lose your nose or your life in a collision.[82]

The strain of this absence from Emma gave Du Maurier a horrifying sense of his dependence on her. That she might die, or leave him to fall back into his old way of life, was a thought which obsessed him, and to which he gave expression in his letters to her and to his mother.

The nervous strain of this period had its effect on Emma, who grew thin from worry, resentful at the success of Fred Walker, and insistent that Du Maurier was a better artist. Her fiancé was less confident:

> in the estimation of all here, I am nothing to little Walker, and by Jove I don't wonder at it for his execution is discouragingly perfect. Yet I feel somehow that if I could ever get to that perfection of pencilling, and exquisite rendering of texture, I have more go in me than he has, and a larger field of fancy. I needn't say that I work very hard, and as much from nature as I can.[83]

Their marriage seemed farther away than ever, and Emma wanted to take a practical hand instead of sitting at home and hoping that something would happen. She decided to learn to engrave Du Maurier's drawings herself, perhaps in order to sell them separately, certainly to support his efforts. Through Val Prinsep, Du Maurier and Emma were introduced to Edward and Georgiana Burne-Jones, and it was arranged that Mrs Burne-Jones should teach Emma whatever she could about engraving. Du Maurier enjoyed visiting

82. Letters, p. 69.
83. Letters, p. 99.

Burne-Jones' studio, thought him 'an angel and *what* a colourist'[84] and was enchanted by the informal atmosphere of his family life. Emma persevered with the engraving for some time, producing a few tolerable results, but, after she had driven a graver into her hand, she was dissuaded from continuing the experiment. The only result was a warm friendship, broken by one long period of coolness, between Du Maurier and Burne-Jones. Du Maurier had always intended to send some part of his earnings to his mother and sister, who were not very comfortably off in Dusseldorf. Very little ever reached them, however, for Du Maurier was having difficulty in earning enough to live on himself, and he was forced to make excuses and future promises to his family. As early as July 1861 he told them that nervousness made it hard for him to concentrate, which his mother realised was the result of frustration generated by his long wait for Emma, with no certain end in sight. The buoyant spirits in which he had at first faced the prospect of a long engagement were slowly sapped away, as, like many other young men of the time, he found the position intolerable. Mrs Du Maurier, who was a practical woman, and not a rigid moralist, suggested that he should take a temporary mistress: 'Your advice, Madam, won't do, I simply can't follow it. It is in the nature and constitution of your firstborn to be passionate and exclusive, and every woman but one is a gorilla'.[85]

Sitting alone at his work, feverishly trying to earn the necessary thousand pounds, without even the release of sex, it is not surprising that Du Maurier's health became affected. In September 1861, he had the first of a long bout of violent stomach upsets, and by December he was taking doses of quinine as a general tonic. As a result of his financial crisis, he had sold his great coat to a Jewish pedlar for a pound, and was only eating one cheap meal a day, together with a glass of stout. Underfed, and over-wrought, he became really ill in February 1862, when his stomach trouble struck him with renewed violence. Mrs Wightwick took care of him, and gave him hot fomentations, which seemed to improve his condition, but headaches and a general feeling of ill health persisted, and made it impossible for him to concentrate on his work. In March he had what was clearly a nervous breakdown, violent indigestion and headaches, together with a complete deadening of emotion, and a tendency to tears at the least provocation. He tried to describe his terrifying state

84. Letters, p. 120.
85. Letters, p. 102.

of mind in *Trilby*, but the letters which he wrote at the time give a more powerful impression of his experience: 'I awoke early to the same fearful state, feeling myself utterly lost for ever and ever, dead to all natural affection, and resolving hard to lead henceforth a life of martyrdom to duty'.[86] Du Maurier's later statement to his *Punch* colleagues that before he was married he had been 'tempted to suicide'[87] must refer to this period. In desperation he turned for help to Whistler's brother-in-law, Seymour Haden, and remembered grovelling on the floor and crying incessantly. Haden assured him that the trouble was purely physical, and prescribed some very strong medicines, which merely accentuated his symptoms. The faithful Emma did all in her power to comfort Du Maurier, but he remained 'as hard to her and as insensible as a flint'.[88] After two days of complete wretchedness, he wept uncontrollably in her arms, which provided a temporary release from his appalling depression. He was morbidly sensitive to criticism. When a provincial newspaper wrote of his drawings in *London Society*, 'We have no doubt Mr du Maurier has his admirers – but we have never had the pleasure of meeting with any of them',[89] Du Maurier, in a letter to Armstrong, affected to be unconcerned. He told the truth to his sister, however: 'The seven small demons enter my soul – I rush to my Pem [his nickname for Emma] and bury my head in her faithful bosom'.[90] Haden's assistant, Traer, who took over Du Maurier's case, believed that his main trouble was jaundice, but recognised that there were strong psychological complications. He advised Du Maurier to marry quickly, and in the meantime to take a holiday immediately. Du Maurier went down to Brighton alone, where large and regular meals, constant exercise and fresh air, did much to restore his health and spirits. He wrote to his mother, rationalizing what had happened to him:

It suddenly came across me that I was a thoroughly bad man who had by a marvel been sustained by good example until now, and that the original badness of my nature was just going to break out at last like a regular conflagration, and that the last year's virtue had been the crowning point of my goodness on the earth – a temptation suddenly to break loose and indulge in every riotous excess, drink, opium, and the most shameless intrigues, for I felt that come over me (*as it seemed* you know) that no woman in the world could resist – and that when I felt downright mad-

86. Letters, p. 124.
87. Silver, 17 May 1865.
88. Letters, p. 124.

89. Letters, p. 185.
90. Letters, p. 188.

ness reach me, as it would inevitably have done according to my theory at the time, I would kill myself and escape the asylum.[91]

The letters in which Du Maurier's mental agonies are minutely described provide a fascinating insight into the possible effects of a rigid Victorian sexual code on a high-spirited young man. Like Arthur Hughes' famous painting, *The Long Engagement* (City of Birmingham Museum and Art Gallery) they recall the over-intense atmosphere only possible in such a restrictive society.

Du Maurier's psychological tension was not lessened by a visit in February 1862 from Whistler, who had just returned from a holiday at Trouville in company with Courbet, and could not stop talking about his latest masterpieces, *The White Girl* and *The Coast of Brittany*. Flaunting his immorality before the tantalised Du Maurier, he arrived with his mistress, Joanna Heffernan: 'got up like a duchess, without crinoline – the mere *making up* of her bonnet by Madame somebody or other in Paris had cost 50 fr'.[92] This seems an appropriate point to finish off the story of Du Maurier's relations with Whistler. Du Maurier continued to see him occasionally during 1862, and in December commented that Whistler was thinking of retiring from the world altogether and concentrating on his work. 'As a beginning', Du Maurier cynically noticed, 'he is getting up some private theatricals at the Greeks'.[93] By February 1863, when Whistler came to congratulate the Du Mauriers on their marriage, he was less enthusiastic about the quiet life, though he was still busily painting:

> Jimmy is also working – got 300 lbs. of orders from the Greeks. His tone is rather changed lately – he has become more modest about his own performances... peculiarly modest about his etchings.[94]

In spite of his modesty, Whistler was beginning to embrace public unpopularity with enthusiasm, and to devote himself exclusively to the new techniques which excited him. After painting *The White Girl* in 1862, his style became increasingly impressionist, a search for harmonies of tone and colour. *The Last of Old Westminster*, exhibited at the Royal Academy in 1863, was still just within the limits of acceptable subject painting. His later river pictures, the nocturnes,

91. Letters, p. 143
92. Letters, p. 105.
93. Letters, p. 185.
94. Letters, p. 197.

were quite undescriptive, conveying to the Victorians a mood which was alien and disturbing.

Du Maurier saw *The Last of Old Westminster* 'down on the ground' at the Academy, but sent Armstrong no description of it. He continued to admire Whistler's work, even when it became more experimental:

> On the other hand, there is Jimmy, almost the greatest genius of the day, with scarcely anybody big enough here to rank by him, who isn't making a sou, and borrowed a shilling of me yesterday.[95]

Towards the end of 1863, Whistler became increasingly involved with Rossetti and the circle which gravitated round the Queen's House in Cheyne Walk, and this finished the process of Du Maurier's disenchantment:

> Jimmy doesn't seem to be doing much. He has bought some very fine china; has about sixty pounds worth, and his anxiety about it during dinner was great fun. He, Legros, Fantin & Rossetti are going to open an exhibition together. Jimmy & the Rossetti lot, i.e., Swinburne, George Meredith, & Sandys, are as thick as thieves;
> > Ces animaux vivent entre eux comme cousins;
> > Cette union si douce et presque fraternelle
> > > Enveloppe tous les voisins.
> Their noble contempt for everybody but themselves envelops me I know. Je ne dis pas qu'ils ont tort, but I think they are best left to themselves like all Societies for mutual admiration of which one is not a member.[96]

Du Maurier found the permissive and amoral atmosphere which the Rossetti circle generated rather distasteful, and his criticism of it is priggish and half-envious. His relationship with this group is described in a later chapter, but it is no coincidence that Whistler's connection with them heightened Du Maurier's distaste for both. Whistler, with new friends and new interests, and probably aware of Du Maurier's hostility, rarely called in on his old friend. In the letters to his mother, Du Maurier now referred to Whistler by his surname, no longer used the familiar 'Jimmy'. In November 1863, he was writing rather delightedly to Armstrong to tell him about Whistler's break-up with Legros: 'Jimmy & Legros are going to part company, on account (I believe) of the exceeding hatred with which

95. Letters, p. 150.   97. Letters, pp. 218–9.
96. Letters, p. 216.

33. Santa, or a woman's tragedy, *Once a Week* (1862)

the latter has managed to inspire the fiery Joe: one never sees anything of Jimmy now'.[97] Even more dramatic was Whistler's quarrel
with Seymour Haden:

> Jimmy and Haden à couteaux tirés; quarrel about Joe, in which Haden
> seems to have behaved with even unusual inconsistency and violence;
> for he turned Jimmy out of doors vi et armis, literally, without his hat;
> Jimmy came in again, got his hat and went and said goodbye to his
> mother and sister. It appears he had told Haden that he (Haden) was no
> better than him (Jim)![98]

This is Du Maurier's last important reference to Whistler in his early
letters, and, apart from the most superficial social meetings, it was
not until the row over *Trilby* that he had any further dealings with
the painter.

98. Letters, p. 227.

34. Santa, or a woman's tragedy, *Once a Week* (1862)

Because of his illness, Du Maurier did very little illustration in the spring of 1862, but once he began to feel stronger, he found it far easier to work than before. The more modest figure of two hundred pounds in the bank had now been suggested by the Wightwicks as a financial guarantee, and Du Maurier began to hope that he might reach it by the winter. In July *The Illustrated Times* published one of his drawings, and the *Punch* initial letters continued to come in regularly, with an occasional cartoon to supplement his income. *London Society* decided to take him on again, and gave him nine illustrations between August and Christmas. Best of all was the offer of a five-part serial from *Once A Week*, for 'Santa, or a Woman's

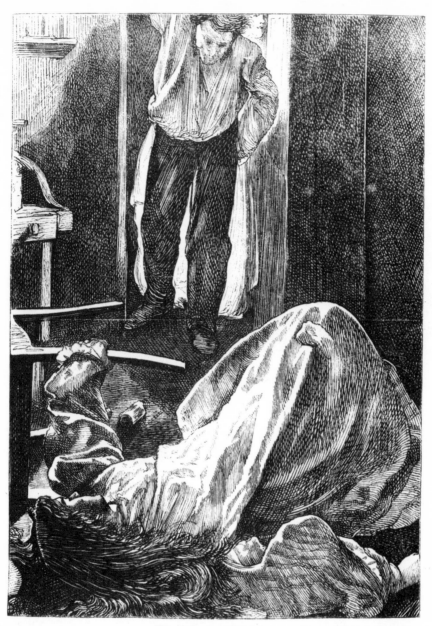

35. The Notting Hill Mystery, *Once a Week* (1862–3)

Tragedy', by the author of 'Agnes Tremorne', which appeared between August and September. Du Maurier worked on the last two drawings for this serial at Hampton Court, and both of them show his new-found confidence in the treatment of landscape, which was such a characteristic of his best work. Du Maurier rarely worked

36. The Notting Hill Mystery, *Once a Week* (1862–3)

without a model now, although it was an expensive extra, which was not always covered by his payment for the drawings. He was well aware, however, that without models he could not keep up with his rivals, and that only the most careful and thoughtful work could keep him in the same class as Walker. Efforts to break into *The Cornhill* had failed, but *Once A Week* were now sufficiently confident to offer him another serial, 'The Notting Hill Mystery' which ran from November 1862 to January 1863 in seven parts. For this serial he produced two of his finest drawings. The first, of a girl swooning beside a lake, shows Du Maurier's style at its most elegant and assured, while the second, of a strange figure in a white nightdress, about to take poison under the influence of hypnotism, is more powerful and haunting. As an artist Du Maurier was just reaching his prime, and for the next few years his work was of a standard to match the best illustration of the period. He had set himself a task in life, which, for a time at least, was to be his guiding principle: 'I want to reach the utmost perfection that my talent is susceptible of, and get to that point that everything I attempt should turn out a complete and perfect work of art'.[99]

Although his work was going well, Du Maurier still had other troubles to worry him. One afternoon in May 1862, when he and Emma were walking around the International Exhibition, Emma recognised Louisa Lewis, who, on the spur of the moment, cut Emma dead. Very annoyed, but rather guilty, Du Maurier pretended not to see the Lewis sisters next time they passed, and so began a series of misunderstandings and affronts which only ended with Louisa's marriage in 1863. Then, in June 1862, Eugène threatened to sell his commission and set up in business with friends. Du Maurier and his mother were both appalled at the idea. Ellen Du Maurier feared that he would arrive in Dusseldorf expecting her to support him, while Du Maurier imagined Eugène arriving in London and disgracing himself there, to the detriment of Du Maurier's own reputation. Isabel was despatched to France to dissuade Eugène from either course, a mission which was successful for the time being. Du Maurier paid another visit to Dusseldorf in the summer of 1862, and had the rather alarming experience of seeing Carry in Malines station. He very prudently moved to another carriage, out of sight. More insular and respectable than ever, he thoroughly disliked Dusseldorf, and thought that his mother and sister were living in

37. Sketch from letter (1861)

99. Letters, p. 163.

'such a funny Bohemian manner and when my Aunt and Isabel are there, the conversation is such, I am sorry to say, that Maman Bellemère would be in the seventh heaven of delight, and I should not like Poynter to be listening behind the door'.[100] On his return to London, Du Maurier decided that he could not live without Emma, and, pointing out that his prospects had now vastly improved, he asked her father's permission to marry in January. The permission was grudgingly given, for the Wightwicks had probably begun to hope that the marriage would never materialize. Du Maurier's evenings in Grosvenor Street became very tense and uncomfortable, and Emma began to find life at home intolerable. Despite all parental protests, they began to make their plans, and took a small apartment at 46 Great Russell Street, close to the British Museum and over Pears' soap shop. For twenty-five shillings a week they had three rooms on the second floor, and for twenty-five pounds a year, Du Maurier took a studio on the ground floor. After all the worries and delays, the autumn of 1862, with the wedding at last in sight, was a comfortable and mellow period for Du Maurier. He began to enjoy visiting Little Holland House, where he had at last met John Millais, whom he thought: 'awfully big . . . such a spoilt child of nature and society and everything – and much of it owing no doubt to his astonishing beauty and naïf impudence'.[101] He did not, however, think very much of Millais' conversation which was 'not awfully wise', nor of Mrs Millais, '(the late Mrs Ruskin, you know). She is quite passée'.[102] Later, he made the more scandalous suggestion that Ruskin had a 'sneaking gratitude' to Millais for taking her away, and in consequence praised Millais' pictures warmly in all his reviews.

Du Maurier and Emma were finally married in Marylebone Parish Church on 3 January 1863. Armstrong, who was to have been best man, was ill, and a cousin of Emma's took his place. Du Maurier appeared in 'grey bags and a sweet thing in neckties, blue', but he could only remember that Emma was 'beautifully got up'.[103] 'Mrs W. crying dreadfully, Emma as white as a sheet; and I in an awful state of seriousness for it is an impressive performance'.[104] After the wedding the newly married couple drove round Regent's Park before returning for the wedding-breakfast which was 'very merry'

100. Letters, p. 169.
101. Letters, p. 158.
102. Letters, p. 158.

103. Letters, p. 191.
104. Letters, p. 191.

in spite of Mrs Wightwick's unhappy frame of mind. Among the guests were Jeckyll, Poynter and all the Levys, but not Henley, who had just shocked everybody by marrying his ex-mistress, an unpardonable sin in mid-Victorian society, which put him beyond the pale. Du Maurier was upset to see Henley's mother and step-father as he returned from the altar after the ceremony. They had visited Du Maurier on the previous day to break the news of their son's disgrace, which Du Maurier passed on to Armstrong:

> you will be very much shocked to hear that he has married his woman – the same he lived with in London years ago. . . . From what Morgan says, (& Morgan approves of it) Henley married this woman to '*do her proper justice before the world*', '*feeling that he owed her no less*' as if he didn't owe 50 times as much to his father & mother. I think his conduct has been as heartless as it is stupid, that such a nice fellow should be pumpernickled away from us all in this fashion![105]

These words reflect Victorian morality it is true, but Du Maurier was an artist, the grandson of Mary Anne Clarke, and had once been a close and sympathetic friend of Henley and knew all about his love affair. It was the idea of marriage with a fallen woman which appalled him, and made him so unrelenting, even as he attained his own happiness.

105. Letters, pp. 194–5.

Chapter 5

Punch

'ONCE MARRIED I AM SAFE', had been Du Maurier's own words to Tom Armstrong, and his expectations were amply fulfilled. Emma was the most devoted and unassertive of companions:

one of the wives of that period, the women who lived for their homes and their husbands, and there was not a load Mrs Du Maurier did not take from his shoulders when she could, not a thing she would not do to help him, and see that no small worries stood between him and his work.[1]

38. Initial letter 'O', *London Society* (1863)

Another description of her was written by her son-in-law, Charles Hoyer Millar:

an unfailing companion, always at hand and with no interests outside her home life. Placid in temperament, nothing ever seemed to move her strongly or excite her. She literally waited on her 'Kiki' hand and foot, each and every day, and lived only for him and her children.[2]

During their brief honeymoon in Boulogne, and the months that followed, Du Maurier found a new peace in life, and a happiness he could scarcely comprehend. If in the long run, domesticity sapped his talent and vitality, it was not entirely the fault of his 'guardian angel', but of the choice he had made in marrying her. He himself recognized that without Emma he might never have achieved

1. J. M. Panton, *Leaves from a Life* (1908), p. 195.
2. Hoyer Millar, p. 33.

anything, and shortly before his death he paid tribute to her in his last novel, *The Martian*. Acknowledging her occasional fits of jealousy and her inflexibility, he wrote:

> How on earth Barty would have ever managed to get through existence without her is not to be conceived. . . . It was quite amusing to watch the way his wife managed him without ever letting him suspect what she was doing, and how, after his raging and fuming and storming and stamping . . . she would gradually make him work his way round . . . to complete concession all along the line, and take great credit to himself in consequence.[3]

Only the kindness of the Levy family, who paid for their tickets, enabled the Du Mauriers to get away at all after the wedding, and they were then trapped in Folkestone for three days by bad weather. They stayed in Boulogne at the Hotel de Paris, on the Quay, where they were the only guests. The port had many memories for Du Maurier, who felt 'quite an old Thackeray' as he took Emma round the scenes of his childhood, becoming excited and nostalgic as he did so. Memory always had this power to move him. To his mother and sister he sent rather a morbid reminder of the place, moss and grass from the graves of Mary-Anne Clarke and Aunt Mary-Anne Bowles. He and Emma could only afford five days in Boulogne, and they returned to 46 Great Russell Street (now no 91) on 11 January 1863:

> Though in reality the great struggle is to begin (let us say to-morrow or the day after) it feels as if all my struggles were over and I had got into port at last, and though I have tasted so little of married life I almost wonder how I could have existed unmarried.[4]

Their simple lodgings were largely furnished with wedding-presents, which Mrs Wightwick had carefully arranged during their absence, so that the return would not be too bleak.

The Du Mauriers had little chance to settle down quietly, for circumstances forced Du Maurier to work at top pressure, sometimes for as much as twelve hours a day, which he found almost pleasant with Emma beside him. For a time, his drawings were of better quality than they had ever been. He began work on a design for *The Cornhill*, to illustrate a poem by W. Frank Smith entitled 'The

3. pp. 357–8.
4. Letters, p. 192.

39. The Cicilian Pirates, *Cornhill* (1863)

Cicilian Pirates'. The magazine was not satisfied with the first version, and Du Maurier, who was extremely anxious to establish himself there, was forced to start the block again without complaint. The final drawing has a classical restraint more typical of Poynter's work than his own, but it is, nevertheless, one of the finest illustrations of the period, and the beginning of Du Maurier's long and regular association with *The Cornhill*:

> What I have learnt by it is immense, but it's been hard labour I can tell you. 20 guineas won't pay me, and yet I doubt if they will give me even that, but I hope it will repay me in another way.[5]

Another magazine from which Du Maurier received an important commission was *The Leisure Hour*, to which he contributed twenty-seven superb drawings in 1864, for 'Hurlock Chase' by G. E. Sargent, brilliantly economic in technique and enormously evocative and effective as illustrations.

5. Letters, p. 198.

At the same time he achieved another success, when *Once A Week* commissioned him to illustrate a long serial, seventeen drawings for Miss Braddon's 'Eleanor's Victory'. These were not in any way exceptional, probably because Du Maurier became bored with the subject, though he persevered to the end. As became obvious later, he rarely produced his best work in conditions of comparative security. To *London Society* he contributed ten competent but not outstanding drawings in 1863, but his best single work for the year was for *Punch*, illustrating F. C. Burnand's 'Mokeanna or the White Witness'. This clever parody of a sensation tale was written in the style of the *London Journal*, where many of the originals had been published. *Punch* invited the best artists of the day to contribute pastiches of their original illustrations, among them John Millais and Sir John Gilbert. Du Maurier's cartoon, of a long-haired girl in a

40. Hurlock Chase, *The Leisure Hour* (1865)

41. Hurlock Chase, *The Leisure Hour* (1865)

42. Mokeanna or the white witness, *Punch* (1863)

white dress standing by an open window in a thunderstorm, is partly a 'send up' of his own sensational designs for the 'Notting Hill Mystery', published in *Once A Week* in 1862. On the left of the design is the small figure of a dwarf, a grotesque and sinister distortion worthy of Du Maurier's later nightmare subjects for *Punch*, which convey an authentic horror. After Du Maurier's success with this cartoon, there were rumours that he was to be offered a permanent appointment on the *Punch* staff, but the offer, if it was ever contemplated, did not materialize. One other important commission must be mentioned here, Du Maurier's illustrations to the novels of Mrs Gaskell, after Thackeray, his favourite contemporary novelist. Between 1863 and 1867, he worked on eight volumes of an edition of her novels published by Smith and Elder, beginning with *Sylvia's Lovers* (he named one of his daughters Sylvia), illustrated from photographs of Whitby, which Du Maurier had not yet visited. Mrs Gaskell's *Wives and Daughters* ran from 1864 to 1865 in *The Cornhill* and Du Maurier's eighteen accompanying illustrations are possibly his best work. Elegant and sophisticated, they clearly show his awareness of the evolution which had taken place in black-and-white technique; his graceful figures, perfectly related to their setting, strongly recall the work of Millais.

For all his hard-won success, Du Maurier was still cherishing hopes of being 'something more than a draughtsman on wood', and hoped eventually to find time to write or paint. For the moment, however, financial insecurity kept him hard at work. He was anxious to own more furniture, and eventually, a house of his own, where he could establish his mother and sister. As yet, no gulf had divided him from his old friends who had chosen the harder path, and were trying to establish themselves as painters. Poynter had received little recognition, and was keeping himself largely by book illustration, furniture painting, and church frescoes, while his oil paintings were regularly rejected at the Royal Academy. Whistler, after a brief period of initial success, was frequently abroad, and increasingly concerned with avant-garde experiments, which were not likely to bring him popular acclaim. Lamont was working in Spain, and discovering the hard way, like the Laird in *Trilby*, that Spanish pictures are better painted in the imagination than in their authentic setting. Still in Manchester, Armstrong was pursuing a dilatory and unproductive way of life. Du Maurier had to lend him a five pound note on one occasion, and was constantly exhorting him to come to London and work harder. Bill Henley, with his unsuitable wife, was probably

43. Wives and Daughters, *Cornhill* (1864–5)

44. Wives and Daughters, *Cornhill* (1864–5)

worse off than anyone, already in deep water financially, and rarely getting his pictures accepted by the Royal Academy. Only two of Du Maurier's old friends were making any progress; Moscheles, back in London from Leipzig, was still doing well with his sycophantic portraits, and had also embarked on profitable, sentimental genre scenes; Val Prinsep, with all the right connections, was beginning to make a name for himself, and had received high praise for his 1863 Academy picture *Whispering Tongues Can Poison Truth*: 'Val Prinsep's right on the line, and I must say it deserves its position. . . . One of Leighton's best was kicked out, Salome dancing'.[6] With so much painting going on around him, it is not surprising that Du Maurier felt envious, and began to do a little work in oils in the summer of

6. Letters, p. 204.

45. The Awdries, *The Leisure Hour* (1865)

1863. He must have been relieved that he was not dependent on it, for Emma was expecting a baby in the winter.

The change for Du Maurier from bachelorhood to married life was quite considerable. One of the first of his group to marry, he was largely cut off from the easy converse of the Pamphilon's set, and was more dependent for social contacts on formal invitations and appointments. He could now take Emma to Little Holland House and to the Ionides at Tulse Hill, but she was unused to such smart and sophisticated company, and felt awkward and ill at ease. She would perhaps have preferred to stay at home, detecting an attitude of patronage to her in her husband's friends. She was to some extent saved from social oblivion by her striking good looks, and by Du Maurier's refusal to go out without her. Unlike Dickens, and other celebrities, who pandered to the snobbery of fashionable society by leaving their dreary wives behind, it is to Du Maurier's credit that he refused to accept the inequality implied by such an arrangement. Once, when the subject of Watts and Ellen Terry came up at the *Punch* dinner table, Du Maurier took the opportunity to express his opinion about those people who left the young actress out of their invitations: 'Kicky is savage against Snobs in High Life inviting a husband without his wife'.[7] Closely knit together, the Du Mauriers began to see more of other young married couples, particularly the Burne-Jones, just down the road at no 62 Great Russell Street, and the Courtney Bells in Tavistock Square, the sister and brother-in-law of Poynter. Edward and Georgiana Burne-Jones led a rather unconventional and informal life, centred round the studio. Although he had few sympathies with 'the clique', as he described the Rossetti group, Du Maurier was glad to record meeting them at one of Burne-Jones' parties:

> Also had a delightful Evening at Burne Jones's, who's got the jolliest wife & sisters-in-law imaginable (Poynter head over years). Met lots of jolly fellows there – William Rossetti & his two sisters etc.[8]

Burne-Jones, who was still very much under the influence of D. G. Rossetti, seems to have kept the two sides of his life apart, for Du Maurier never met Dante Gabriel Rossetti or William Morris in Great Russell Street. Clara Bell and her husband were very hospitable, and often entertained the Burne-Jones and Du Mauriers

7. Silver, 12 June 1867.
8. Letters, p. 138.

together. Clara was a fine singer and a great musical enthusiast, and would often arrive at Du Maurier's house in the morning to arrange duets and trios with Emma, and her own sister, Miss Poynter. Emma was not quite so enthusiastic about the music, but enjoyed the company of sympathetic friends during her often lonely days. Poynter himself was a frequent guest at the Bells, and one evening gave an uproarious and rather tipsy party at his bachelor digs, an event difficult to imagine in his stuffy and conventional later years. Nothing showed the change which marriage had wrought in Du Maurier more than his annoyance when the Arts Club, of which he had been an original proposer, was finally established in Hanover Square. Enthusiastic enough about the idea when it was first mooted, and when it promised pleasant and convivial company, Du Maurier now grudged the ten guinea subscription for an amenity which he no longer wanted. He much preferred to spend his evenings quietly at home, with Emma reading aloud to him to save his eyesight. When the Bells moved to Kew, and the Burne-Jones to Kensington, their life became even quieter, and he was not entirely regretful.

One break in his routine was the long-promised trip to Germany, which finally took place in June 1863. Ellen and Isabel Du Maurier were now living in Bonn, which was even gayer and smarter than Dusseldorf. Du Maurier, who had bought a new suit to 'crush & utterly annihilate my mother and sister with our respectability',[9] found himself looking like a country cousin in the brilliant throng. The weather was hot, the food meagre and unappetising, and Ellen Du Maurier's bohemian household rather too irregular for her very proper son and daughter-in-law. They were not very sorry to return to London after only a week.

The idea of being a parent had always attracted Du Maurier, although he realised the increased financial burden involved, and he awaited the arrival of Emma's first child with considerable excitement. He was overjoyed when a daughter was born in January 1864, and named her Beatrix after his favourite Thackeray heroine, and Isabel after his sister. Not at all a conventional Victorian paterfamilias, Du Maurier loved his children with a generous and easy affection. Unlike other artists and writers, he made no attempt to keep them in the nursery while he was working, but preferred them to come and go as they liked, even at the risk of disturbing him. One frequent visitor to the Du Maurier household remarked that: 'It was

9. Letters, p. 207.

46. The Awdries, *The Leisure Hour* (1865)

always a delight to me to climb the stairs and watch Du Maurier
draw, while Mrs Du Maurier sat and sewed, and the children played
about the room unchecked'.[10] Until she married, 'Trixy' (Beatrix's
nickname), remained his favourite child, and his pride is unmistakable in his first description of her:

> She is of stupendous size and power of lung and appetite. In colour &
> feature she favours the type of her Bussonian ancestors, such of them at
> least as may have possessed extraordinary beauty; for everybody who
> has seen it agrees that it is a beautiful babe.[11]

10. *Leaves from a Life*, p. 195.
11. Letters, pp. 220–1.

In February 1864, Isabel Du Maurier arrived in London, ostensibly to help Emma, but probably in search of adventure and new suitors. She found life in Great Russell Street very tedious, and preferred paying visits to her friends to looking after the new baby. As soon as Armstrong heard of her arrival, he rushed to London from Manchester (a step he had been contemplating for some time), and took rooms in Great Russell Street. Isabel's feelings towards him had not changed in the least, and she had no intention of marrying such a penniless suitor. She quickly tired of London, and returned to Bonn in April 1864.

During Armstrong's visit, he accompanied Du Maurier on a Sunday afternoon visit to Tulse Hill. A cab load of young artists, set out:

> Whistler, Rossetti, du Maurier, Legros, Ridley, and myself were in or on it. It seems to me that there were others in that four-wheeler, Poynter perhaps, but I am not sure, and I want to be accurate. The occasion was a memorable one. Then for the first time was revealed to this artistic circle the beauty of two girls, relations or connections of the Ionides family, and daughters of the Consul-General for Greece in London, Mr Spartali. We were all à genoux before them, and of course every one of us burned with a desire to try and paint them.[12]

The two girls were Christine and Marie. Whistler painted Christine in his *Princesse du Pays de la Porcelaine* (Freer Gallery, Washington), and Marie, later Mrs Stillman, was the subject of a painting and some drawings by Rossetti. She herself became a painter, working in a derivative Pre-Raphaelite style. She was one of the most beautiful women of her generation. Armstrong remembered her 'as if it were yesterday, coming out on the lawn of her father's house on Clapham Common when there was a large garden party, and Swinburne, who was with us, saying, "She is so beautiful I feel as if I could sit down and cry" '.[13] Du Maurier could not understand why she had married W. J. Stillman, an American journalist, as he told Henry James in 1884: 'I . . . was much interested to see what kind of man it was who as a poor and middleaged widower married the most beautiful woman I ever saw against her parents' consent, and still keeps her apparently, in a state of adoration'.[14]

Very shortly after this visit to Tulse Hill, Du Maurier and Emma took their baby on her first holiday, to Clovelly in North Devon. The

12. Armstrong, pp. 195–6.   14. 18 Sept. 1884. Houghton Library, Harvard.
13. Armstrong, p. 196.

seaside holiday, undertaken in an earlier age for health reasons, was becoming an established event for the Victorian family. The Du Mauriers adopted the custom enthusiastically, and always looked forward to leaving London. The indifferent food and uncomfortable seaside boarding houses, a frequent theme in Du Maurier's cartoons for *Punch*, did not discourage them, but rather emphasized the break with the normal routine of London life. For Du Maurier himself, the holiday was not a complete rest, as he still had to produce his weekly *Punch* cartoons, or finish book illustrations, but he always benefited from the change.

In 1864, the Du Mauriers took two holidays, a short one in Devon, and then a longer visit to Whitby in August and September. Du Maurier had just finished illustrating *Sylvia's Lovers*, and had been impressed by its description of Whitby and surroundings, The 'Monkshaven' of the novel. It was not as fashionable as the south-coast resorts, but the Du Mauriers were not disappointed by their choice, and were able to find cheap lodgings on the quay. This was the first of many visits, and, by the end of his life, Whitby had joined Passy and old Paris as part of Du Maurier's private mythology. Shortly before his death, he included a description of 'the best place on earth' in his last novel, *The Martian*, where the narrator, looking down on the town from a hill, describes the scene:

> the wide North Sea . . . the two stone piers, with each its lighthouse . . . the busy harbour full of life and animation; under our feet the red roofs of the old town and the little clock tower of the market-place; across the stream the long quay with its ale-houses and emporiums and jet shops and lively traffic; its old gabled dwellings and their rotting wooden balconies. And rising out of all this, tier upon tier, up the opposite cliff, the Whitby of the visitors, dominated by a gigantic windmill that is – or was – almost as important a landmark as the old abbey itself.[15]

The Du Mauriers were enchanted by Whitby, once they had got used to it, and Du Maurier realized at once that it would be a superb place to do water-colours; he began one which he never finished. They stayed in Whitby until the end of their holiday, although Emma caught cold in the sharp wind, and Du Maurier himself retired to bed with a boil over his left ear. They did not go to Whitby merely in search of fresh air and solitude. Reunion with old friends was an important feature of the holiday calendar, and Whitby

15. p. 456.

eventually became the focus for a whole circle of holidaying families. On their first visit, Du Maurier persuaded Tom Armstrong to come over from Manchester for a few weeks in late August to keep them company. Together they made the acquaintance of the *Punch* cartoonist, John Leech, who had just returned from Bad Homburg after a fruitless attempt to regain his health. It was in Whitby, during the last weeks of Leech's life, that Du Maurier really began to appreciate the struggle and tragedy of the older man's existence. As a young man, Leech had witnessed the collapse of his family's fortunes, and he remained obsessed with the idea of regaining his social status. His compulsion to make a parade of the gentility to which he felt entitled over-straitened his *Punch* salary, and he was forced to sell sets of hunting-prints and water-colour versions of his cartoons as a financial expedient. His hunting expeditions, in company with fashionable friends, the smart dinners he held in his beautiful house in The Terrace, Kensington, the increasing social pretensions of his feather-brained wife, who encouraged rather than restrained his financial irresponsibility, all added to his growing debts. Worse still were the constant demands for money from his own family, especially from his father, who sponged unmercifully on his well-to-do son. Physically frail and highly-strung, John Leech had already worn himself out, and faced only the prospect of increasing drudgery and anxiety. His work for *Punch*, to which he had been an early contributor, perfectly illustrated his qualities and weaknesses. The famous Leech girl, who appeared in so many cartoons, was, in fact, Mrs Leech herself. After years of married life, her girlish charm must have begun to pall, but in the pages of *Punch*, her esprit never declined. Du Maurier called her:

> 'just a daisy', as the Americans say. She was the love of my salad days . . . what a darling she was! She played croquet, and rode to hounds, and was a great archer, and screamed when the crackers were let off, and did not make an unseemly fuss when her soldier cousin with the waxed moustachios kissed her under the mistletoe; and *didn't* she enjoy her holiday at the sea-side![16]

The 'pretty girl' was the best and most charming part of Leech's work, the ideal medium for his delicate humour. As an artist, he was not outstanding, though always delightful, and he made no concessions to the contemporary revolution in style and technique.

16. Illustration, p. 372.

Today his political and social cartoons are out of favour because of his persistent and rather cruel jokes at the expense of the lower classes, and the cockney sportsman in particular. On the other hand, his extraordinary cartoon on prostitution, 'The Great Social Evil', which shows two girls in the Haymarket at night, one asking the other: 'Ah, Fanny, how long have you been gay?' has an honesty rare among contemporary artists and writers.

That Leech, sick, nervous and depressed, could still captivate Du Maurier and Armstrong, is some measure of the man's personal attraction. Du Maurier and Leech took long walks together in the surrounding countryside, and Du Maurier thought him: 'one of the grandest and most delightful men I ever met; not at all funny as you would fancy him to be, though, but the most simple hearted modest fellow in the world'.[17] His opinion of Mrs Leech was 'Silliest I ever met',[18] but the two Leech children were general favourites, and Armstrong soon became very much attached to the ten-year-old daughter, Ada. In fact, Armstrong was so popular with the Leech family that he stayed on for some time after the Du Mauriers had returned to London. Through Leech, Du Maurier met several other visitors in Whitby, among them the surgeon Henry Thompson, and his wife, a well-known concert pianist. Thompson, who had risen from humble origins, was now one of the most famous surgeons of the time; he had just gained enormous prestige after his successful operation on King Leopold of the Belgians. Du Maurier liked Thompson, and was encouraged by the discovery that the surgeon had only begun his training at twenty-eight, proving that a late start was not necessarily fatal. The *Punch* writer, Shirley Brooks, was also in Whitby, having come specially to keep Leech company, and cheer him up. Later during the Du Maurier's stay in Whitby, W. P. Frith, the painter, arrived with his family on a similar errand of kindness. The Du Mauriers returned to London in September, so impressed by Whitby that they planned to spend three or four months there the following summer. Du Maurier hoped to paint water-colour landscapes, for he had been impressed by Fred. Walker's success in this direction, and needed to supplement his income. The autumn was rather an uneasy time for the Du Mauriers. No large commissions were offered to Du Maurier, and he had to content himself with occasional illustrations for the smaller magazines. Emma was

17. Letters, pp. 241–2.
18. Silver, 18 March 1868.

. Emma and Guy Du
Maurier

expecting another baby, and they would have to find a larger apartment. Du Maurier had expressed a rather forlorn hope to his mother that there would not be a baby every year, aware of the precarious nature of his profession. Guy Louis Du Maurier was born in the following year, on 13 May.

Late in October, however, the most severe of his worries came to an end. The Leechs had returned to London, where John Leech's condition was deteriorating. Most of his friends, including Du Maurier, imagined that his mental depression was the cause of his illness: 'I think that if he does not take great care of himself he will go mad'.[19] On Friday 29 October, Du Maurier visited Leech and found him wracked by worry and ill-health, and quite unable to work on the current *Punch* almanack: 'these last three nights he got quite funked, his sufferings were so great. I have a presentiment that he will not be able to do the almanac or that if he does it will nearly

19. Letters, p. 242.

kill him'.[20] In spite of her husband's failing health, Mrs Leech
decided to go ahead the next day, a Saturday, with a long-planned
birthday party for one of her children. 'Sissie' Frith, the painter's
daughter, who was present on this occasion, remembered a sudden
hush falling, and then being hustled into her coat and taken home.
Leech, who had experienced several agonising spasms of angina
pectoris during the day, had finally died at seven o'clock. The news
soon spread to his friends and *Punch* colleagues. The gaiety of
Arthur Lewis' Saturday evening party was cut short by the dramatic
appearance of John Millais, shattered by the death of his close
friend, and unable to conceal his grief. Du Maurier was not present
at Jermyn Street, but Charles Keene took the news to him in Great
Russell Street early on Sunday morning. Du Maurier's feelings must
have been very mixed. He had admired Leech's work in Malines,
but he had become understandably jealous of him in London, and
blatantly referred to him as the man in the way. In Whitby, under
Leech's personal spell, Du Maurier's attitude changed dramatically,
and he found the older man's charm irresistible. Now suddenly, the
new friend was dead, and the rival's position vacant. Since Mark
Lemon was a well-known opponent of new appointments to the
Punch staff, unless absolutely necessary, and since Tenniel and Keene,
at forty-four and forty-one, were unlikely to retire for many years,
Leech's death gave Du Maurier his great opportunity. The mingled
feelings of guilt and exhilaration inevitable in such a situation must
have made the next few days extremely tense for him. It was almost
certain that he would be appointed to replace Leech, for there were
no other serious rivals, and he had made it quite clear to Henry
Silver, and probably to Keene, that he wished to join *Punch*. The
suspense did not last long, for the almanack, on which Leech had
been engaged, was barely started, and Lemon needed another man
at once. He called a meeting on 1 November 1864, at the Bedford
Hotel, Russell Square, where the question of a successor to Leech
followed the funeral arrangements on the agenda. Keene and
Tenniel proposed Du Maurier, and Silver added that he was
'anxious to join us'. Du Maurier thus achieved security three days
before Leech's burial, which took place on 4 November, at Kensal
Green. Du Maurier sent a harrowing account of it to Armstrong,
who was unable to attend:

You never saw such an affecting sight as when they put him into his

20. Letters, p. 244.

grave. Millais suddenly burst out crying convulsively, and several others sobbed out loud, while the parson . . . read in a trembling voice and could hardly help breaking down too. Poor old Mark Lemon, as well; really it was quite awful, and I was so demoralized that my nervous system is hardly steady yet.[21]

Punch was probably the most successful of all nineteenth-century magazines. By the time Du Maurier joined the staff, *Punch* had been flourishing for twenty-three years, and had assumed the status of a national institution. In the minds of its staff and readers, there was never any doubt that it would continue to survive, and to direct its ponderous humour at current events and attitudes. This confidence was well-founded, but it is, nevertheless, a surprising indication of faith in something as ephemeral as a comic magazine. Its rivals faded away, *Joe Miller*, *The Man in the Moon*, *The Tomahawk*, *The Arrow*, *Lika Joka*, but *Punch* went on from strength to strength, and continued to amuse generations of Englishmen. *Punch*, however, had not sprung fully-armed into the magazine world, and the establishment of its characteristic form, was only achieved after a period of experiment and internal discussion. The idea of combining political humour with social comment, which led to the founding of *Punch* in 1841, was an original one, but it was not without precedent. *Frazer's Magazine*, started in 1830, under the editorship of the gifted but erratic Irishman, William Maginn, brought a new vigour and sparkle into contemporary journalism which shocked its more serious rivals. Preaching a brand of radical Toryism, it attacked humbug and pretension in both political parties, and demanded active social legislation. Lampooning its enemies with impassioned and devastating satire, it set out to reform, to amuse and to shock. *Frazer's* was often tasteless and vulgar in its criticism, but with a dazzling list of contributors, including Carlyle, Thackeray, Coleridge, Father Prout, and William Jerdan, it produced some of the most brilliant journalism of the decade. Thackeray and Douglas Jerrold, who joined the *Punch* staff, had both worked for *Frazer's*, and they continued its traditions, together with Henry Mayhew. The battle on the *Punch* staff between the *Frazer's* element, who wanted *Punch* to be hard-hitting, controversial and deeply committed, and their opponents, Mark Lemon, Shirley Brooks, and later John Leech, who wished to placate their middle-class public,

21. Armstrong, p. 14.

continued throughout the early 1840s, and only ended with the
resignation of Mayhew in 1845. The forces of respectability, which
gathered during the early Victorian period, were irresistible, and
even if *Punch* had stood for a real freedom of expression in the manner of *Frazer's*, it would probably not have survived. It might, on the
other hand, have exercised a conscience, and in its humour cham-
pioned the cause of the poor and oppressed, but it chose not to do so.
Punch, in its final form, expressed the comfortable, middle-class
attitudes of Victorian England, and if its humour was sometimes
sharp and to the point, it never seriously questioned the values of the
society to which it pandered. *Punch* owed its success to the quality
of its humour and illustrations, its pursuit of a consistent policy, and a
series of first-class editors. Mark Lemon, for instance, was not an
outstanding comic writer, but he was shrewd and incisive as an
editor, and able to get the best out of his staff. He did not perform this
by magic, but by visiting the homes of his contributors during the
week to see how they were progressing, and by refusing anything
which did not come up to his own exacting standards. His treatment
of Du Maurier as a young man is an excellent illustration of this.

In 1864, *Punch* was not only a successful magazine, but an exclusive
social club. Every Wednesday, publication day, the regular staff
met for the famous weekly dinner, ostensibly to discuss the subject
of the large political cartoon for the next issue, but more to enjoy a
pleasant and amusing evening together. Bradbury and Evans, who
bought the paper from Ebenezer Landells in 1842, had instituted
the dinners, and always paid for them. In the early days, they had
been informal affairs in various city pubs, but by 1864, the dinner
was an established ritual which took place at 11 Bouverie Street,
with the whole staff seated at the round table, 'The Mahogany Tree'
as Thackeray called it. The diary of these dinners which the writer,
Henry Silver, kept from 1848 to 1870, is a fascinating document, and
allows the historian to reconstruct the atmosphere and gaiety of these
occasions. The ribaldry and bawdiness which characterized the
later events of the evening reveal how very much funnier *Punch*
might have been if it had been published in a less emasculated age.
The quarrels and arguments, the wit and good humour, the personal
troubles and triumphs, are all related by Silver in a detached and
impartial spirit. A whole world is summoned up, and the personalities who contributed their humour and art to *Punch* are vividly
brought to life. A few examples of their conversation give an idea
of the quality of their repartee:

Arthur Lewis had a daughter on the 6th – 'Born with spectacles and grey hair like Tom Taylor's says D.M.

D.M. says boys have big bums – F.C.B. doubts – '*You* had at any rate' says Kiki. F.C.B. retorts something about Christopher Columbus – Apropos de quoi? Shirley cuts in with 'Christopher would look a long while round this table before he discovered the Continent!' Good![22]

Du Maurier first dined with the *Punch* staff at the Bedford Hotel, kept by Mark Lemon's sister-in-law and often used by *Punch* contributors for informal parties, on the Monday after Leech's death. According to Silver, he was a little too garrulous and bumptious for a newcomer, and rather offended his colleagues. He immediately made a suggestion for the cartoon subject, not accepted, as if he were an old hand, and then chattered on about Rossetti, Whistler, and their craze for blue-and-white china. Silver wryly noted, 'Du Maurier talks of French novels fluently enough!' At his first official *Punch* dinner on Wednesday, also at The Bedford for some reason, Du Maurier was called upon to make a little speech:

> he made the Staff a little uncomfortable by referring to his blindness. After complaining that people were for ever calling him '*de* Maurier', and expressing the hope that the *Punch* men would give the devil his 'du', he went on to remind them that he was blind of one eye, and begged them to pardon him if he failed at any time to 'see' a subject that might be suggested for his pencil.[23]

The embarrassment caused by this rather self-conscious remark was eased by a reply from Lemon's second in command, Shirley Brooks:

> But . . . Tenniel has only one eye left, and it really *is* the left, for he lost his right while fencing, whilst you have your right eye left. So you see you two fellows have two good eyes between you, and a pair of good eyes are far better than a score of bad ones. In the country of the blind, you know, the one-eyed man is king, and here we're blind as bats – to one another's failings. So I drink to your good health, you two one-eyed royal Majesties.[24]

After this incident, with its implied snub, Du Maurier was a little quieter, but his powers as a conversationalist soon rallied, and he began to indulge in repartee with Shirley Brooks and Horace

23 and 24. G. S. Layard, *A Great 'Punch' Leader: Life, Letters and Diaries of Shirley Brooks* (1907), p. 223.

Mayhew. Silver did not quite approve of his calling the others by their nicknames and Christian names so soon: 'How familiar seems his "Mark" and "Shirley" and "Ponny" – moi, que je suis modeste!'

At these *Punch* dinners, Du Maurier made the inevitable discovery that his colleagues were not so brilliant and witty as they had appeared to be from outside. The atmosphere of the dinners was rather quieter and more pedestrian than he had imagined: 'it would be a most mistaken idea to judge of these fellows from the letter-press of Punch, et voilà ce que je ne puis pas comprendre'.[26] It was not until 7 December 1864, that Du Maurier first dined in the *Punch* offices at 11 Bouverie Street. 'Pater' Evans, the proprietor, formally welcomed him and proposed his health. He then turned back the table-cloth on the famous round table to reveal the initials of John Leech, beside which Du Maurier chose to carve his own some days later. In a lecture of 1890, Du Maurier remarked: 'I flatter myself that convivially, at least, my small D.M., carved in impenetrable oak, will go down to posterity in rather distinguished company!'.[27] He was right, for the table still exists, and is still used by the *Punch* staff. After meeting his new colleagues, Du Maurier was soon writing to Armstrong to tell him his first impressions, a remarkably perceptive account:

> Old Mark I like immensely, the most genial old fellow that ever lived; Shirley Brooks is a deuced amusing fellow, but rather snarling & sarcastic; Sir Tom de Taylor, very jolly too, but so beastly well informed that he rather imbeasts one at times; the nicest of all is Percival Leigh I think, and old Evans whom we call Pater, next to whom I sit . . . Tenniel is a delightful fellow though very quiet – Burnand very amusing, Horace Mayhew often very drunk; bon enfant mais bête. Silver rarely opens his lips, at which I wonder for he's got lots to say for himself. Our dear old stiffnecked Keene doesn't get quite in tune with the others, and I think these dinners haven't as much charm for him as for this child.[28]

His first days on *Punch* were not all a question of dinners, and good fellowship. Du Maurier's first official task was to complete nine cartoons for the annual *Punch* almanack, a calendar with pages of illustrations and quips, which Leech had been engaged on when he died. Working at top speed, Du Maurier completed eight cartoons before the almanack went to press on 21 December. Although Keene,

25. Silver, 26 Sept. 1866.   27. S.P.S., p. 31.
26. Letters, p. 248.   28. Letters, pp. 247–8.

Millais and Fred Walker contributed designs, the success of the almanack was largely due to Du Maurier's work, particularly his two full-page cartoons, 'Probable Results of the Acclimatisation Society'. Both show huge, terrifying and quite imaginary pre-historic animals in London street and park scenes, and perfectly combine Du Maurier's realism with his talent for the grotesque. Lemon was most relieved to get the almanack published in time, and the whole staff drank to its success, some of them with one foot on the table. At later almanack dinners, lark and kidney pudding was traditional, but there is no record of what was eaten on this occasion. As a result of his work for the almanack, Du Maurier's reputation took a sharp turn upwards, and he received several letters of congratulation. His pleasure in his own success led to boastfulness at the expense of Leech: 'To believe some of them poor dear Leech was all very well in his way but nothing like the great man I'm expected to turn out'.[29] As Du Maurier fell into the depths of gloom when things went wrong, so when he was successful, he could not restrain his enthusiasm. For all his pose of being an English gentleman, his volatile nature clearly revealed his Gallic origin:

> I've no doubt that when I get into the reins, in a few months or so, they will find DM a very useful person, and pay him accordingly . . . The Wednesday dinners are very jolly and I think I am rather a favourite, being the juvenile of the lot; besides which they think me still juveniler.[30]

Du Maurier wisely did not communicate his own high opinion of himself to Lemon, who would have given him short shrift. After Lemon's death, Shirley Brooks recalled a private conversation with him on the subject of Du Maurier:

> I remember, before he regularly joined, M.L. gave him something of mine to illustrate, a 'relic clock', some Papist tomfoolery of the Q. of of Spain, I think, and I thought the idea frittered in the picture, and had some of the detail cut out. M.L. said he was 'cocky'. As a *young* fellow with brain should be. I hate your Blifils.[31]

The writers on *Punch* had, in the early days of the magazine's existence, always been considered more important than the artists.

29. Letters, p. 251.   31. Layard, p. 536.
30. Letters, p. 252.

Lemon's famous remark about the successful draughtsman, John Gilbert, 'we don't want a Rubens on our staff', was typical of the early attitude towards illustration. The popularity of John Leech, however, had vastly improved the standard of the cartoons, and Lemon himself had become much more discerning and critical. In 1850, when Dicky Doyle resigned from *Punch* as a protest against its anti-catholic bias, Lemon invited a promising young artist, John Tenniel, to join the paper. Tenniel was hesitant, as he did not want to give up his career as a painter, and become a mere illustrator on a comic magazine; this was in the days before illustration had become respectable. He accepted, however, and slowly began to establish himself as the 'first, one might say the only cartoonist upon *Punch*'.[32] With the death of John Leech, who had always executed some of the large political cartoons, Tenniel acquired a monopoly in this sphere. With his strong, bold outlines, his gift for the grotesque, and the memorable image, Tenniel never drew from life, and really enjoyed the large allegorical figures, which appear so often in the political cartoons, quite as much as the personal caricatures. It is for his drawings, more than for anything else, that Victorian *Punch* will be remembered. Taking over from Leech, Du Maurier might well have expected to be allowed to do some of the political work: 'Shouldn't I like to do political cuts for *Punch* some day; ça viendra j'espère without any damage to that jolly fellow Tenniel'.[33] In fact, Du Maurier had not the slightest interest in politics, a colleague once referred to his 'dilettante radicalism', and he soon gave up any idea of trying to 'muscle in' on Tenniel's field. Later on, he did not even take any interest in the subject for the political cartoon, though he occasionally commented on general issues, replying to Shirley Brooks' remark that the poor were all scoundrels, that 'it makes his blood boil to hear such bosh'.[34] Tenniel himself, who was not a talkative man, rarely produced ideas for the subject of his cartoon, although he would sometimes suggest an alteration on technical grounds. If it was his work which gave *Punch* so much of its conservative and respectable character, it is hardly surprising when the man himself is considered: 'He was tall, slim, and upright, clean-shaven, except for long and drooping moustaches, quietly courteous and dignified, with a peculiarly distinguished voice'.[35]

32. C. Monkhouse, 'The Life and Work of John Tenniel' *Art Journal* (Easter Annual, 1901) p. 22.
33. Letters, pp. 252–3.
34. Silver, 12 April 1865.
35. T. A. Guthrie, *A long Retrospect* (1936), p. 159.

Tenniel was an ideal acquisition for *Punch*, but it is rather more difficult to see why Lemon appointed Charles Keene. He was the greatest artist ever to work for *Punch*, but he was not really a humorist, or even a gifted cartoonist. He drew much of his inspiration from others, most noticeably Joseph Crowhall, who provided him with at least two hundred and fifty jokes, and even an occasional idea for the drawing itself. Keene had no real sense of humour, and often repeated his favourite jokes, but his sketches of low life are usually outstanding as drawings. Du Maurier had known Keene well when they both belonged to the Pamphilon's set, but he never became intimate with this lonely and eccentric man. He did not really appreciate his colleague's gifts, accepting his relative lack of popularity as the sign of an inferior talent. Though Du Maurier can have had no interest in drawing cabmen, urchins, and private soldiers week after week, he liked to imagine that he could equally well have tackled these subjects, remarking to Henry Lucy: 'I have generally stuck to the "classes" because C.K. seems to have monopolized the "masses" '.[36] It was really an arrangement which suited them both equally well. Keene (Carlo to his friends), was even quieter than Tenniel and less talkative at the *Punch* dinners, sitting over his pipe, and taking little interest in the food and wine or the conversation. He would occasionally tell jokes of excruciating dullness, and obscurity, at which his confrères laughed heartily in their embarrassment. Stories of his eccentricities have often been told, the actor, John Jeaffreson, describing him as 'the most peculiar and strikingly unusual person' he had ever met.[37] Lemon understood the talents of his three artists, and Du Maurier later explained his first instructions:

> I was particularly told not to try to be broadly funny, but to undertake the light and graceful business, like a *jeune premier*. I was, in short, to be the tenor, or rather the tenorino, of that little company for which Mr Punch beats time with his immortal bâton, and to warble in black and white such melodies as I could evolve from my contemplations of the gentler aspect of English life, while Keene, with his magnificent, highly trained basso, sang the comic songs.[38]

Most of the atmosphere and conversation at the *Punch* table was provided by the writers. They were divided, quite sharply, into two

36. H. Lucy, *Sixty Years in the Wilderness* (1909), p. 391.
37. J. C. Jeaffreson, *A Book of Recollections* (1894), II, 122.
38. S.P.S., pp. 117–8.

groups, the old faithfuls, who had helped to establish the magazine, and the new men, who were in fact of the same generation as the artists. Mark Lemon himself was part of a largely bohemian group of writers, who had been loosely connected with the Dickens circle, and with the famous amateur theatricals which the novelist organized. Lemon, Shirley Brooks and Tom Taylor were all dramatists, and so was Francis Burnand in the younger generation. Lemon and Brooks, with the other old stagers, Percival Leigh, known as the 'Professor' because he was a qualified doctor, and Horace Mayhew, brother of the founder, all believed that alcohol, and plenty of it, was a necessary preliminary and conclusion to every function. Burnand was typical of the younger *Punch* generation in preferring to think of himself as a gentleman, and in finding the behaviour of his older colleagues rather vulgar and distasteful:

> They were not drunkards: they were not Teetotallers: they were simply Boozers. Occasionally fuddled and muddled, but rarely so far as to find Mr Bob Sawyer's remedy essential to the regaining of their ordinary common sense.[39]

Burnand's criticism is both snobbish and innaccurate. Lemon was an outstanding editor, who managed to control the discordant personalities on his staff with great tact and firmness, particularly when tempers began to rise. The handsome and genial Shirley Brooks was easily the most witty member of the staff, and the most naturally gifted comic writer, a master of puns and epigrams and deft repartee. One of the greatest gossips in London, his forthright diaries, from which only the most innocuous passages have been published, provide a fascinating glimpse of those scandals and relationships which the Victorians so desperately tried to conceal. Unlike Lemon, Brooks was unhappily married, and he liked to surround himself with beautiful and talented young women, Louise Romer (Mrs Jopling), Sissie Frith, and the part-time *Punch* artist, Georgina Bowers, for whom he was both a father-figure and a devoted sugar daddy. The dirtiest jokes at the *Punch* table always originated with him, but he was not really a cynical roué, only a frustrated and unhappy man. The 'Professor', Percival Leigh, and 'Ponny', as Mayhew was known from his habit of doing the pony work, were much more typical 'Boozers' than Lemon and Brooks. On

39. Layard, p. 251.

one occasion they fell down the stairs on top of one another, in a drunken stupor, and then solemnly picked themselves up and shook hands. Leigh wrote the dog Latin verses for *Punch*, and was much concerned with mysticism and Swedenborgianism, about which he loved to indulge in long discussions. His taste for strong-smelling, edible fungi was well-known to his colleagues, who always did their best to avoid meeting him in the street, when he was carrying his prize finds. Horace Mayhew, with his handsome, Jewish face, was something of a dandy, and had a reputation for womanising. Du Maurier used to claim that all his best-looking models had been fathered by Mayhew, and teased him unmercifully at the *Punch* dinners, though he was the first to help when Mayhew was in any real trouble. Edmund Yates summed Mayhew up well:

> He was not largely endowed with native wit, but treated what he had on the gold-beater's principle, and made it go a long way. He was a cheery, lighthearted, good-natured creature, with some power of drawing, a knowledge of French, a good bass voice, and unfailing power of emitting jokelets.[40]

Another writer of the older generation was Tom Taylor, who was neither a bohemian nor a drunkard. He lacked the sparkle and verve of Lemon and Brooks, and his writing tends to be heavy. Despite assertions to the contrary in later memoirs, he seems to have been a difficult man to work with, 'impatient', 'vacillating', and 'fidgety', as Yates described him, but also kind-hearted, charitable and punctual. Henry Silver, from whose diary so much of the history of *Punch* (at this period) is derived, was a quiet man, who methodically wrote down his impressions on his return from the dinners. Not a brilliant writer, his dramatic reviews are very sound. Francis Burnand was the most forceful personality of the younger generation, a Cambridge man, and a founder of the A.D.C. (Amateur Dramatic Club), who was both a clever dramatist and wit, but who preferred the attractions of high society to the bohemian circle of his colleagues of whom he was often scornful:

> A stout stick, thick boots, overcoat, and wallet, these were all the outfit necessary in Charles Keene's or Percival Leigh's opinion for a 'brother brush' or brother penman, with an occasional ride on a 'bus.[41]

40. *Recollections and Experiences* (1884). II, 152–3.
41. F. C. Burnand, *Records and Reminiscences* (1904), II, 4.

Burnand was a conceited man, who tended to dominate conversation at the *Punch* table, but his intelligence was considerable.

The *Punch* dinner itself was usually excellent, and not simply a 'working-meal'. References to 'first asparagus' or 'first strawberries' show that the proprietors took great care to feed their staff well. The menu for one of the earliest *Punch* dinners which Du Maurier attended read as follows: 'Whitebait and cyder cup – pickled salmon, soles, chickens, cold lamb and the "London" Pudding'.[42] At first champagne had been the usual drink, but later port and sherry became popular. Coffee was always introduced with the cigars and cigarettes, but Du Maurier, who was not allowed coffee because of his eye, would fidget uneasily until his large cup of tea arrived. A chain smoker for most of his life (at this point he smoked forty cigarettes a day), he would consume cigars and cigarettes for the rest of the evening. He rarely drank to excess, although Henry Silver found him at home with a 'Punch headache' after his third dinner. During his first years on the staff, Du Maurier attended the Wednesday dinner regularly. With Burnand and Brooks, he soon became one of the more vocal members of the staff, and an adept at the bons mots and puns then so much in favour. Most of those recorded by Silver certainly never found their way into *Punch*, for Ruskin's impotence, Swinburne's relationship with Adah Isaacs Menken, G. F. Watts' marriage to Ellen Terry, were all the subjects of obscene jokes. The *Punch* feud against Dickens had once resulted in scandalous gossip at his expense, but by 1864, *Punch* was involved in few vendettas of this kind. Gossip was aimed more at artistic circles like that surrounding Rossetti, and concerned their sexual eccentricities or aberrations. Du Maurier's French background stood him in good stead, for he was always a good talker, nimble and quick-witted:

> Kicky and Burnard are younger at the board, but are older hands at chaff. Still I remember the talk of Thackeray and Leech, and don't envy their successors their inferior gift of gab.[43]

During the summer, the *Punch* dinner was often held in the country, usually on the river, in one of the good hotels or restaurants favoured by the fashionable Londoner. The Trafalgar at Greenwich was a great favourite. The staff would catch the train from London in

42. Silver, 24 May 1865.
43. Silver, 29 Dec. 1868.

the middle of the afternoon, eat in the early evening, and then come back on the late train in hilarious spirits. The other great meeting time for the staff was Saturday afternoon when the magazine went to press, and everyone gathered in Whitefriars to make corrections and additions with the aid of the inevitable drinks and cigars.

Although one may regret Du Maurier's decision to join the *Punch* staff, as far as the quality of his work is concerned, his desire to do so was overwhelming. At last he was assured of a regular income, and the financial worries, which had dogged his footsteps, and certainly contributed to his nervous breakdown in 1862, were at last over. His growing family, and his fears that his mother and Isabel would eventually become dependent on him, made financial security essential for his peace of mind. He was not, however, assured of a pension, should he go blind, nor was his income exceptional, as he wrote to tell his mother: 'It is not the highest unfortunately, but a paying one I suppose, and leads the way to immense popularity if one is lucky and does one best'.[44] While it is possible to discover how much Leech earned, because he was quite open about it, the gentle-manly cult which became so pronounced a feature of the younger generation, makes it impossible to discover how much they were paid, and in what form, as they refused to discuss the matter, even among themselves. Leech and Tenniel do seem to have been paid a regular salary, but Keene apparently demanded to be paid for what he produced. Du Maurier's attempts to extract more money out of *Punch* for his drawings, suggest that he was paid on a piecemeal basis:

> I have recently struck for higher wages with Punch; I used to charge 4 and 3 guineas, and asked in an imperial manner for 6 and 4, saying that I could not work for them at a lower wage (*what* a lie!).[45]

No accurate assessment of the sums earned by *Punch* contributors can be made from the available evidence, as the records relating to salaries have been lost. If Leech really did earn two-thousand pounds a year, which is not absolutely certain, and may have included money from other sources, Du Maurier must have received a similar sum. However, he normally contributed two cartoons a week, a large and a small, for which, having obtained the rise

44. Letters, p. 264.
45. Letters, p. 264.

requested above in June 1865, he was receiving just over five hundred pounds a year. The insoluble question is whether he was also paid a retaining salary over and above what he earned for the individual drawings.

Du Maurier did not like to regard *Punch* as a life-sentence. He still harboured the illusion that it was only a temporary measure, a stepping-off point for some really dramatic achievement. He expressed this idea with some arrogance to his *Punch* colleagues:

> Du Maurier wishes for £500 a year to enable him to follow his own fancies in his work – and not to do drudgery; and be obliged to think of *Punch* when his inclination is to the Sunday Magazine. H.S. [Henry Silver] thinks living for mere amusement vastly tiresome.[46]

Such an idea was idle day-dreaming, for illustration is by its very nature a field where the artist cannot follow his own fancies. Du Maurier was really only expressing his frustration that he was not a free-lance painter. Had he possessed a private income of five hundred pounds a year, he would probably have produced no illustrations at all.

In his early days on the magazine, Du Maurier did, however, make some attempt to break away from the single cartoon, and to produce more ambitious work. In January 1865, he contributed his first piece of written work to *Punch*, a pseudo-French ballad 'L'Onglay à Paris', which was moderately successful. The following year he undertook two vastly larger and more important projects, his satires on contemporary art and literature, 'A Legend of Camelot', and 'A Ballad of Blunders', which are perhaps his most sustained and interesting comment on contemporary culture. In 'A Legend of Camelot', his aim was not to ridicule the original Pre-Raphaelite Brotherhood, which had long since fallen apart, but to attack the romantic cult which centred on Rossetti and his circle. This aspect of Pre-Raphaelitism, so different from the realist tendencies of Hunt and Millais which Florence Claxton had parodied in her *The Choice of Paris: An Idyll* of 1857, had increasingly come to be regarded as the true Pre-Raphaelite ideal. With its pseudo-medieval subject-matter, highly-wrought imagery and over-stated love symbolism, it was an ideal target for a satirist such as Du Maurier, spokesman for the prejudices and common sense of the English middle-classes. Unlike

46. Silver, 15 March 1865.

many of the earlier satires, 'A Legend of Camelot' is a sophisticated and effective piece of work by an artist who thoroughly understood Pre-Raphaelitism and knew several of its exponents. It was a prelude to his subtle pastiche of Swinburne's poetry, 'A Ballad of Blunders', and to the long series of cartoons in which he mercilessly attacked the affectations and pretensions of the aesthetes, through such familiar figures as Postlethwaite, Maudle and Mrs Cimabue Brown. When he first came to England, Du Maurier had been eager to know the leading artists of the day, and he had hoped to meet the *avant-garde* Pre-Raphaelites as a group, little realising that they had long since ceased to collaborate. By 1866, he was friendly with Millais and Burne-Jones, and knew the full history of the Pre-Raphaelite break-up. In a letter to his mother, written in April 1864, he gave his own version of it:

> Rossetti is the head of proe [sic]raphaelites, for Millais and Hunt have seceded; spoilt so to speak by their immense popularity; whereas Rossetti never exhibits and is comparatively unknown; this strange contempt for fame is rather grand.[47]

In conceiving 'A Legend of Camelot', it was chiefly Rossetti and William Morris whom Du Maurier wished to ridicule, as well as the group around them, whom he had once described, half enviously, as a 'society for mutual admiration'.[48] He had first met Rossetti in 1864 at a bachelor party given in Simeon Solomon's studio in Howland Street. Du Maurier felt uneasy in such company, where status meant nothing, and his suspicion that they had capacities which he lacked certainly provided one stimulus for 'A Legend of Camelot'. Both Du Maurier and Tom Armstrong left full accounts of Swinburne's extraordinary behaviour on this occasion, and Du Maurier's, given in a letter to his mother, exactly indicated his equivocal attitude:

> As for Swinburne, he is without exception the most extraordinary man not that I ever met only, but that I ever read or heard of; for three hours he spouted his poetry to us, and it was of a power, beauty and originality unequalled. Everything after seems tame, but the little beast will never I think be acknowledged for he has an utterly perverted moral sense, and ranks Lucrezia Borgia with Jesus Christ; indeed says she's far greater, and very little of his poetry is fit for publication.[49]

47. Letters, p. 235.
48. Letters, p. 216.

49. Letters, p. 235.

Among the poems which Swinburne recited was Rossetti's translation of Villon's 'Ballade des Dames du Temps Jadis', the original of
which Rossetti had placed in the coffin of his wife, Elizabeth Siddal:
'It was said that Swinburne had seen and read the manuscript once
only, and it must have been several years earlier, for Mrs Rossetti
had died in 1862'.[50] Neither Du Maurier nor Armstrong was quite
sure what to make of this display:

> Tom and I felt like two such bourgeois that night, so healthy and human;
> didn't get home till three, and wasn't it jolly just after this strange but
> gorgeous nightmare of an evening, to wake up and find a healthy
> innocent little baby weighing over 20 pounds.[51]

48. A Pre-Raphaelite Sketch (c 1861)

Du Maurier's choice of an Arthurian subject for 'A Legend of
Camelot' is a clear indication of the date and object of his attack. The
attraction of the Middle Ages as a golden age of permanence,
religious faith, chivalry and ideal love was a profound motive for
much nineteenth century romantic art and poetry. Rossetti first
illustrated a subject from Malory's *Morte d'Arthur* in 1854, and it was
he who suggested the Arthurian cycle as the theme for the Oxford
Union murals of 1857. Edward Burne-Jones and William Morris,
who collaborated with Rossetti in this project, continued to be
fascinated by the *Morte d' Arthur*, and the pictures of the former, and

50. Armstrong, p. 164.
51. Letters, p. 236.

the poetry of the latter are often concerned with it. Two other members of the Rossetti group, Frederick Sandys and Ford Madox Brown, had also completed works on the subject in 1864, after Rossetti himself had tired of it. As Du Maurier connected all these painters with Rossetti, and as most of them had been present at Simeon Solomon's soirée, it is not surprising that he selected an Arthurian theme for his satire.

'A Legend of Camelot' appeared in *Punch* during March 1866 in five instalments, each one covering a full page of the magazine, and combining a drawing with a doggerel verse below. Du Maurier's combination of verse and drawing enabled him to satirize both the visual imagery of Pre-Raphaelitism, and its highly distinctive verse structure. The story of 'A Legend of Camelot' is an elaborate parody of an Arthurian story. The heroine, Braunighrindas, who arrives in Camelot unclothed, is persuaded by Sir Gawaine and Sir Lancelot to have her hair woven into a more permanent garment. A Jewish pedlar who foolishly offers five shekels for the hair is immediately felled by Sir Gawaine. Braunighrindas, for reasons unexplained, then shoulders the apparently lifeless Jew and wanders off. In course of her travels he meets another maiden, Fidèle-Strynges-le-Fay, who, she discovers to her horror, is also secretly married to Sir Gawaine. In despair at this revelation, the two girls sink into a marsh, finally losing their hair to the revivified Jew; in the last part they are mourned by Camelot in a Gilbert and Sullivan scene of comic grief. Within the framework of this absurd story, Du Maurier displays surprising verbal agility in parodying the more obvious aspects of Morris's verse – his archaic terminology, simple rhythms, banal refrains ('O Miserie'), unnecessary obscurity and over-indulgent use of alliteration ('Hard by his wares a weaver wove / And weaving with a will, he throve'). Nor was Morris the only target for Du Maurier's pen. The outline of his parody and the character of his heroine lean heavily on Tennyson's *The Lady of Shalott*. Instances of more precise borrowings abound. Du Maurier's

> The bold Sir Lancelot mused a bit,
> And smole a bitter smile at it,

echoes Tennyson's

> But Lancelot mused a little space;
> He said, 'She has a lovely face'.

Tennyson's preoccupations were often strikingly similar to those of the Pre-Raphaelites, and it was no coincidence that Du Maurier should link his work with theirs.

At first sight Du Maurier's illustrations for 'A Legend of Camelot' appear only as a general parody of Pre-Raphaelite subject and style. The first drawing, with its steep perspective, stylized treatment and archaic details, recalls many aspects of Pre-Raphaelite design. Closer examination, however, reveals that several details were directly borrowed from the Moxon edition of Tennyson's poems. The figure of Sir Galahad, on the left in Du Maurier's drawing, is a careful copy of Rossetti's illustration to Tennyson's poem, 'Sir Galahad', with the question mark motif as the only overt piece of satire. Du Maurier's skill lies in the slight innuendoes which turn heroism into farce. For his Sir Lancelot, he turned to Rossetti's illustration to 'The Lady of Shalott', and reduced the figure to absurdity by the introduction of check trousers. The effeminate appearance of the two knights, and of Sir Gawaine, who walks behind with his thumb in his mouth, expresses a popular prejudice against the Pre-Raphaelites, who were thought affected, if not actually homosexual. For Sir Gawaine's helmet, Du Maurier copied another design from the Moxon Tennyson, Holman Hunt's 'Ballad of Oriana', while the figure of Braunighrindas, with her flowing tresses disappearing off the edge of the design, is similar to Hunt's drawing for 'The Lady of Shalott'. The cramped building with the desperate figure of a weaver (surely meant for Morris), accurately conveys the impression of compressed space found in many Pre-Raphaelite book illustrations.

In the second illustration Du Maurier shows Camelot gone mad on a larger scale. The profusion of towers in the background echoes Tennyson's 'many tower'd Camelot', while the detailed landscape is a more general comment on Pre-Raphaelite technique. The figures in the landscape, the abbot, damsels, page, knights, square tower, winding river and funeral barge are all mentioned in Tennyson's poem, and once again there are precise borrowings from Rossetti, this time the details of the arch and the decorated woodwork, taken from his 'Lady of Shalott'. The dominating figure of Braunighrindas, with her pronounced chin and soulful expression, is an excellent rendering of the Pre-Raphaelite ideal of beauty:

O Moshesh! vat a precioush lot
Of beautiful red hair they've got!...

49. A Legend of Camelot, Part 1, *Punch* (1866)

50. A Legend of Camelot, Part 2, *Punch* (1866)

51. A Legend of Camelot, Part 3, *Punch* (1866)

How much their upper lipsh do pout!
How very much their chins shtick out!

How dreadful shtrange they shtare! they sheem
Half to be dead, and half to dream!

The Camelot peoplesh alvaysh try
To look like that, I vonder vy?

Du Maurier evidently decided after his first two designs that he
could take no more from Moxon, and his third and fourth illustrations rely on a more general and disappointing parody of Pre-
Raphaelite technique and subject-matter. In the third illustration,
the dark forest and the over-wrought symbolism of raven and skull
evoke the usual gloomy preoccupations of Rossetti and, to a lesser
extent, of Burne-Jones, while the spiral staircase is a recurring *motif*
in the work of both painters. The extraordinary precision of flowers
and foliage round the comically small castle suggests some of the more
surrealist aspects of Pre-Raphaelite art, but the design as a whole
lacks incisiveness. The fourth illustration is the weakest of all. The
placing of the standing figure, with the hedge behind his head and
the reflections in the water, suggest a parallel with Charles Collins'
Convent Thoughts (Ashmolean Museum, Oxford). The substitution of

52. A Legend of Camelot, Part 4, *Punch* (1866)

a Jew for the nun is the kind of oblique and ironic twist which Du Maurier would have enjoyed, but the similarity may be coincidence.

The illustration to Part Five again suggests a parallel with a Pre-Raphaelite picture. The repeated groups of three figures seem an obvious reference to Rossetti's *Rosa Triplex*, the earliest known version of which is dated 1867. Tangled rose briars were a common

53. A Legend of Camelot, Part 5, *Punch* (1866)

motif in the work of Burne-Jones, but the roses in Sir Gawaine's lap prove conclusively that *Rosa Triplex* was Du Maurier's immediate source. For a comic artist to parody a picture unknown to the public, and presumably unfinished, is unusual, and confirms the fact that Du Maurier had a double audience in mind. 'A Legend of Camelot' is, like the later 'Ballad of Blunders', partly an 'in joke', although there was, of course, plenty of material which would have been immediately recognisable to the general public.

The largely philistine *Punch* staff were delighted with the parody, and applauded what they described as 'a take off of the Rossetti school. Tennyson gone mad style'.[52] Du Maurier himself, however, continued to defend the Pre-Raphaelites at the *Punch* table, where he stated in February 1870 that he ranked 'Millais A.1 – then Rossetti; Burne Jones; and Albert Moore'.[53] The only unpleasant result of the 'Legend of Camelot' was a disagreement between Du Maurier and William Bradbury about payment. Du Maurier had already received a rise in pay the previous August, when his earnings for the two social cartoons was increased from seven to ten guineas, Bradbury amiably remarking that he had only asked for his due. During March 1866, the full page instalments of 'A Legend of Camelot'

52. Silver, 28 Feb. 1866.
53. Silver, 9 Feb. 1870.

had been Du Maurier's sole contributions to *Punch*, and he argued
that he should receive ten guineas for each one, as they cost him at
least as much effort as his two ordinary cartoons. Bradbury, who
probably felt that Du Maurier should have been satisfied with his
original pay-rise, refused his demand. Du Maurier was justifiably
angry, for the series had involved him in a great deal of concentrated
and complex work, and had also been very successful. A long struggle
now ensued between the staff, who backed Du Maurier, and the
proprietors, who refused to give in. It was not until 20 June that
Lemon, Bradbury, and Du Maurier finally met to try and reach
agreement, and that Bradbury eventually offered the ten guineas
when he realised how embittered his staff had become over his
parsimony. The incident cast rather a shadow over the outing to
celebrate the *Punch* silver jubilee which took place on 27 June. The
staff travelled down to Slough by train, visited Gray's grave at
Stoke Poges, and then enjoyed a picnic lunch at Burnham Beeches.
As they settled on the grass with their cold meat, lobster, veal and
ham pie, salad and champagne, Du Maurier tactlessly remarked that
'Bradbury looks the most uncomfortable man here', referring to his
uneasy posture on the ground. Silver, however, commented: 'I
apply it to his position on *Punch* [Bradbury's], after the row about
D.M.'s pay and seeing our good feeling towards Mark'.[54] The staff's
support for Lemon was obvious. After lunch, Shirley Brooks made a
speech in honour of his editor, and then presented him with a watch
and a chain with eleven links, one for each of the staff. Lemon was
moved to tears by the gift, and spoke of the need for everyone to work
together for the good of the paper. Before the toasts, a set of testi-
monials, one from each contributor, was presented to him, Du
Maurier's being noticeably the longest, Charles Keene's the shortest.
They enjoyed the afternoon in the country before going on to dine at
Skindles in Maidenhead, where there were more toasts, more
speeches, and the presentation of a silver cup to Lemon. In the course
of his speech of thanks, Lemon spoke of each member of the staff in
turn, referring again to Du Maurier's recent work: 'Then I come to
Du Maurier whose Legend of Camelot is an honour to Punch – and
I hardly know which to praise most, his pencil or his pen'.[55]

  The success of 'A Legend of Camelot' encouraged Du Maurier to
try another satire at the expense of 'the mutual admiration society',

54. Silver, 27 June 1866.
55. Silver, 27 June 1866.

this time an attack on the poet, Algernon Swinburne. 1866 was the year when his *Poems and Ballads* was first published, in which several of the poems deal more or less specifically with flagellation in an erotic context. In 'Anactoria', for example, Swinburne had written:

> Yea, though she scourge thee, sweetest, for my sake,
> Blossom not thorns, and flowers not blood shall break.
> Ah that my lips were tuneless lips, but pressed
> To the bruised blossom of thy scourged white breast.

Swinburne's peccadillos were well-known to the *Punch* staff, and provided them with an endless target for obscene and hostile comment. Du Maurier, remembering Simeon Solomon's soirée, was probably responsible for the following remark, recorded by Silver, but not attributed: 'A nasty conceited drunken impotent beast who recits poetry with a St. Vitus' dance'.[56] Du Maurier's sense of something unhealthy and repellent in Swinburne's work, did not, however, entirely blind him to its merits. Years afterwards, he said of *Poems and Ballads*: 'Swinburne was a revelation to me. When his "Poems and Ballads" appeared, I was literally frantic about him, but that has worn off'.[57] That Du Maurier was extremely familar with the book is evident in his parody of 'A Ballad of Burdens', which appeared in *Punch* on 1 December 1866. He signed it 'Chatouillard', to echo the title of Swinburne's play, *Chastelard*, and gave it the title 'A Ballad of Blunders'; these two hints were, however, an almost unnecessary aid to identification. Du Maurier aimed to attack the most prominent aspects of Swinburne's style, his alliteration, pointless repetition, eroticism, forced melancholy and lack of concrete meaning. Swinburne's work was full of obscure references to perversions, and hints of mysterious excesses, and it was in this luxuriant atmosphere that Du Maurier conceived his satire. In the second stanza, for instance, Du Maurier refers, obliquely and wittily, to flagellation:

> Strange delight;
> Thy seething garb shall cleave to thee, and cling;
> Thy red wet palm shall reek beneath the white;
> And fierce black shining leather bite and sting,
> A future of sore troubles gathering.

56. Silver, 1 Aug. 1866.
57. Sherard, p. 395.

In a later stanza, Du Maurier parodies actual lines from 'A Ballad of Burdens', twisting them, with considerable ingenuity, into a direct attack on Swinburne himself:

> If thou write
> That once again that should be once for all,
> These market men will buy thy black and white
> Till thy keen swift full fervent ways shall fall
> On sated ears; thy stinging sweetness pall;
> And barren memories of bright success
> Shall burst in thee the bladder of thy gall.

Du Maurier's parody was extremely clever, exactly underlining Swinburne's faults as a poet, and indulging in sly references to the poet's own vices, his taste for flagellation, and his habit of coming home intoxicated in the early hours of the morning. On the whole, however, his parody was too subtle for *Punch*, and its significance was lost on the general reader, who did not realise how superior it was to the usual run of satirical poems. Its real significance can only have been understood by a small group in London who knew Swinburne well. It is probably the only published work by Du Maurier which shows a keen intellectual grasp, and it is as such a rather sad reminder of what he might have achieved had he disciplined himself earlier in life. Even Swinburne recognised its excellence, for, some time afterwards, he wrote to Du Maurier 'Your *Ballad of Blunders* I read when it appeared. I am certain no one enjoyed or appreciated it more – if so much. It was perfect'.[58] In the same way that Du Maurier had defended the Pre-Raphaelites at the *Punch* table, after 'A Legend of Camelot', so he defended Swinburne after 'A Ballad of Blunders', feeling perhaps that by satirizing him, he had established a proprietorial relationship: 'D.M. sticks up for Swinburne as the writer of lovely verses, the weaver of words – the rhymer of rhymes. More musical than Tennyson'.[59]

After 1866, the quality of Du Maurier's drawings undoubtedly declined, not only in his work for *Punch*, but in other magazines to which he occasionally contributed. Having achieved a consistent standard of high quality by dint of concentrated endeavour and experiment, he now slowly abandoned all that was most original in his style in favour of a stereotyped technique. It is easy to blame

---

58. D. P. Whiteley, *George Du Maurier* (1948), pp. 26–7.
59. Silver, 18 March 1868.

his regular employment on *Punch* for this deterioration, and Du Maurier himself often suggested that the strain of monotonously producing two cartoons week after week had stultified his talent. It may have been difficult for him to think up cartoon captions, but Keene, who found it even more difficult, did not allow his draughtsmanship to suffer in the same disastrous way. By twentieth-century standards, Du Maurier's load of work, two weekly cartoons and a gradually decreasing number of designs for other magazines, was scarcely an arduous one, especially when a loving wife relieved him of all other burdens. After careful consideration, the critic is forced to conclude that it was his own inertia which ruined Du Maurier's talent. References to his hard work, continuous struggle, and fear of eyestrain, are monotonously repeated in the memoirs of his contemporaries, but they were probably a reflection of Du Maurier's own vocal complaints, rather than an accurate assessment of his difficulties. All his life he tended to work unevenly, long bouts of idleness alternating with sudden bursts of activity. It is significant that Du Maurier's outstanding designs belong to the period immediately before and after his marriage, when he was working consistently for several hours a day. If he became enthusiastic, as he did with his great series of aesthete cartoons, his work immediately improved in quality, but enthusiasms were unfortunately rare in his later years. He did not possess the discipline to tide him over. *Trilby*, written under the pressure of intense excitement, was followed by *The Martian*, where his failure of inspiration is only too apparent.

The deterioration of Du Maurier's style is paralleled by the general decline in the quality of illustration during the 1870s and 1880s. The reasons why the achievement of the 1860s was not sustained are various and complex. New technical developments, and the failure of the succeeding generation of illustrators, were certainly prominent causes. Older artists, like Millais, Leighton and Poynter, no longer needed to supplement their incomes, and began to concentrate solely on painting. Even Frederick Walker and Frederick Sandys were turning to water-colours, pastels and oils, though their black-and-white work, when they produced it, showed no signs of weakening inspiration and skill, as did Du Maurier's. It was not until the 1890s, with the exception of a few isolated and original illustrators, that artists like Beardsley and Shannon revived and rediverted black-and-white art.

Like other ambitious illustrators, Du Maurier was irritated by the gulf which separated him from successful academicians. Du Maurier

contributed a few drawings to the Royal Academy exhibitions, but
no *Punch* artist became even an A.R.A. during his lifetime, nor was
one considered. It was felt, quite rightly, that the gulf which
divided the best illustrators from the more minor painters, was an
invidious and artificial one, based on snobbery. Du Maurier was
furious when he was asked by a society 'grande dame' if the *Punch*
dinner was in payment for his 'little drawings', as if he were an

54. The Royal Academy Exhibition, *London Society* (1863).
The four girls bear a striking resemblance to Emma

amateur idly sketching for his own amusement. In many cases, the
best illustrations of the 1860s were of a very much higher standard
than the usual run of Academy pictures, and the illustrators were not
unnaturally resentful at their exclusion from official recognition. It
may be asked why they were so concerned with the Royal Academy,
and why they wanted a position there. The Royal Academy was the
centre of Victorian patronage, where reputations were made, and
the values of contemporary art established. The illustrators wished

their work to be recognised as a legitimate form of artistic expression, as the water-colourists had done long before, and their only means of doing this was to gain a foothold in the official hierarchy. Du Maurier constantly preached the virtues of illustration, and if he was forced to give up his ambition to be more than a contributor to *Punch*, he continued to brood on his failure. He gave up his experiments with water-colour, to return to them later only spasmodically, chiefly because he was lazy. His status as a gentleman was quite secure, and he was able to mix in the best society. But, with the publication of *Trilby* and *The Martian*, his secret frustration and jealousy burst out as an impassioned regret that his life had not developed differently.

Without being in possession of the full facts, it is impossible to estimate how far the trouble which Du Maurier experienced with his remaining eye was of psychological or physical origin. It can never have been easy to work on detailed drawings with only one eye, but Tenniel seems to have managed adequately and with much less fuss, though it is only fair to remember that he had not lost his other eye through disease. Du Maurier's letters to his mother during his early years in London make light of his eye trouble, probably in order to reassure her, perhaps to reassure himself. By the end of the 1860s, it is clear from his own diary and Silver's *Punch* diary that he was becoming increasingly worried that his good eye was diseased. Like most Englishmen, Silver disliked any reference to personal disability, and found Du Maurier's moans embarrassing and cowardly. On 15 November 1865, he noted tersely: 'D.M. funky about his eye', and suggested that he should give up smoking. During the next winter Du Maurier's eye seems to have been stronger, although the slightest cold was liable to frighten him. In March 1867, he again became seriously worried, and wrote in his diary: 'Lots of stupid eye worry', and 'much eye worry'.[60] Temporary panic, and the thought of possible blindness, drove him to think about writing:

> I've found out that I can't be improving much in my art, *mes petits bons hommes & bonnes femmes*, that I'm paid so well for – two hours a day to work is not much, and the eye worry distracts me from much thought on Art, and encourages me to think of other possible fields for bread winning in which the eye is not an indispensable implement.[61]

60. Diary, p. 387.
61. Diary, p. 389.

Silver was just as unsympathetic: 'D.M. . . . has the blue devils
because of his eyes. And I because . . . But we all have our troubles . . .
and every one fancies his the worst'.[62] Nothing would have induced
Silver to mention his marital difficulties at the *Punch* table. English as
Du Maurier was in many respects, his resort to vocal self-pity at the
slightest provocation revealed the Gallic strain in his personality. In
April 1868, his eye was troubling him again: 'Du Maurier low and
nervous for his eye. H.S. all serene. Advises "give up smoke" . . .
Kiki's way of inhaling cigarette smoke must be killing'.[63] The eye
remained troublesome all summer, and in November Du Maurier
decided to take a daily ride, 'live frugally', and cut his cigarettes to
five a day. Although he had occasionally been hunting, Du Maurier
was not a good horseman, and it was probably at this time that he
took what proved to be his last ride, on a hired hack in Richmond
Park. After passing a windmill, he began to ride down the slope on
the other side, when, wondering how much good the outing was
doing him, he began to examine his tongue in his watch-case mirror.
He was so engrossed in this activity, typical of such an inveterate
hypochondriac, that he forgot about his mount entirely, and fell
ignominiously to the ground. By December he had cut his cigarettes
to four, but he never managed to give up the habit altogether. The
Punch staff were not the only people who heard about his eye. The
poet, William Allingham, noted in his diary that he had dined with
Du Maurier and that 'D.M. on his fear of blindness'[64] had been one
of the conversational topics. Sissie Frith, who knew him before she
married and left London in 1869, remembered that that he was 'in
daily terror of losing his sight':

> He was never a robust man, but had immense virility, and was one of
> those charming natures which give out hope, life, and amusement to all
> who come in contact with them, and I should essentially sum him up in
> one word – joyous. Naturally he had his dark days and times, but these
> he never showed to the public.[65]

It was some years before the Du Mauriers returned to Whitby for
their annual summer holiday. After Du Maurier had joined the

62. 13 March 1867.   65. *Leaves from a Life*, p. 195.
63. Silver, 22 April 1868.
64. W. Allingham, *A Diary*, edited H. Allingham and D. Radford (1907), p. 196.

Punch staff, he tended to spend holidays in the company of his colleagues, at places suggested by them. 1865 was an exception, for that
year Du Maurier decided to go to Felixstowe for reasons of health,
he had heard that it was cheap and bracing. Even there, however, the
Du Mauriers soon collected a group around them, and spent their
time at picnics, and dinner-parties, as well as croquet, yachting and
swimming. In the following year, he and Emma accompanied
Shirley Brooks and his family to Boulogne. An epidemic, described as
English Cholera, broke out, and Du Maurier had a mild attack of it.
The weather was bad, and the noise made sleeping extremely
difficult. Shirley Brooks described their activities: 'we did not much
enjoy Boulogne. We went to several balls, at two of which our party,
5, formed the majority of the revellers. We ate many shrimps. We
looked out at the window a great deal. These were out chief excitements, but a contented mind is a continual feast'.[66] In 1867, Du
Maurier and Emma made several outings from London. One was to
Lyndhurst in the New Forest, where they stayed with the writer,
artist and dilettante, Hamilton Aïdé, one of those personalities, well-
known in their own day, who are now largely forgotten. Exquisite in
appearance, Aïdé was something of a celebrity between 1870 and
1890: 'He was slightly below the average height, neat in figure, and
always perfectly turned out; he knew everybody and went everywhere, and his musical parties in his Hanover Square flat were
always crowded in the Season'.[67] Aïdé, who liked Du Maurier, had
given him a certain amount of help in making contacts and finding
commissions in his early days as an illustrator. On this visit to
Lyndhurst, Du Maurier met the Irish poet, William Allingham,
who noted in his diary for Saturday, 4 May: 'Sit under the Big
Oak. . . . Then through forest glades appears a carriage with Aïdé,
George du Maurier and his wife, and Miss Middlecoat'.[68] Du
Maurier's own diary states: 'Then drove to Queen's Bower, lovely
place, to find Allingham reading under an oak *As You Like It*'.[69]
Hamilton Aïdé's mother was the model for many of Du Maurier's
aristocratic old ladies, but Aïdé's own importance in Du Maurier's
life came some years later when he introduced him to Henry James.

Another expedition was undertaken by Du Maurier in August,
this time without Emma. 1867 was the year of the famous Paris
exposition, which Du Maurier decided he must see. He had tried,

66. Layard, p. 290.   68. Allingham, p. 152.
67. Guthrie, p. 150.   69. Diary, p. 399.

unsuccessfully, to persuade Tenniel to accompany him, but in the end he set off with Oscar Deutsch, an assistant librarian in the British Museum, and a well-known Semitic scholar. They arrived in Paris on 23 August, in blazing hot weather. In a comic story which he wrote for *Punch*, Du Maurier recreated his experiences in Paris. Mr Titwillow, the hero of the story, is the father of intolerable twins on holiday in Ramsgate, who suddenly decides to desert them for a jaunt to Paris with his friend, Mr Pip. Du Maurier had, in fact, left Emma to take the children to Ramsgate by herself. In his skit, Du Maurier makes light of his feelings on arriving in Paris: 'Mr T. was in a highly excited state, treading as he did again the *pavé* of his dear familiar Paris (where he had once spent a fortnight five years ago)'.[70] In reality, Du Maurier found the heat excessive after a tiring journey, and

> couldn't get into the proper key for enjoying the familar drive. We went into the Exposition and chiefly confined ourselves to the outer buildings which are most delightful; especially the Algerian and Japanese women so like the pictures we know. After paying demi francs here and there and doing absinthes and beers now and then we went twice round and inspected the restaurants of all parts of the world. Spiers and Pond's young ladies I am sorry to say did not come up to my expectations. Deutsch and I got on very well; his amiability is irresistible; but funnily enough we didn't get to talk with anything like geniality until we got into an argument about Jesus Christ going to visit the leper, of all things in the world – and that we would have done just as comfortably in Great Russell Street. At 6 we dined at the Diner Européire as we were very hungry and casually minded – so our dinner, which was excellent, cost us five francs a head.[71]

After dinner, described in *Punch* as 'pleasant, piquant and witty, as only dinners in Paris can be', Deutsch and Du Maurier wandered about the outer courts of the exhibition, taking their coffee at the Algerian cafe, and drinking bad beer at a 'café chantant'. Du Maurier evidently enjoyed the exotic girls, for in *Punch* he referred to the Arab maiden who sang 'I would I were a bird', accompanied on a native concertina, and the picturesque Neapolitan girl, who spoke 'with a lurid flash of her dark Italian eyes'. After all the excitement, Deutsch began to feel tired, but Du Maurier, who had suddenly

70. *Punch*, 28 Sept. 1867.
71. Letters, pp. 267–8.

caught sight of the lights of Passy down the river, insisted on dragging his wilting companion to the scene of his childhood. Deutsch ate an ice-cream to keep himself awake, but on the return journey fell asleep with the motion of the 'bus. Du Maurier tried unsuccessfully to show him his old school as they drove past, 'the dear little chap didn't say damn it, or anything of the kind, but fell asleep again like a baby'.[72] They finally arrived back in their hotel, after a further stroll on the boulevards, and Du Maurier sat down to compose a long letter to Emma, which he continued throughout their stay as a diary of his activities. On Saturday morning, Deutsch was treated to another sentimental journey, this time to Du Maurier's old studio in the rue Notre Dame des Champs in the Quartier Latin. Madame Vinot and her husband greeted him with delight:. 'They felt my biceps and mourned over my lost eye like a mother'.[73] From there, Du Maurier went on to his ageing aunt Louise in the rue de Bayeux for his first visit in nine years. Deutsch was not subjected to any other relatives or old friends, but was allowed to cool off in the Pont Royal baths: 'Deutsch is great fun in a state of nature, so white and plump, like a little white Hercules'.[74] After dinner in the Palais Royal, they went on to the theatre, which they found rather sentimental and maudlin in comparison with the English stage. It contributed to their thirst, and they consumed several pints of beer before retiring to bed. The hot weather continued, and on Sunday morning, Du Maurier took Deutsch for another bathe, this time in the baths at Pont de Grenelle, where he had himself learnt to swim: 'You can fancy my delight in plunging in, knowing what a crazy chap I am about these things',[75] he told Emma. The rest of the morning was spent revisiting Passy, particularly the old family houses in the rue de la Pompe and the Grand Rue. The faithful Deutsch must have found these nostalgic expeditions rather tedious, with a companion who was 'no longer quite myself',[76] but he apparently made no complaint, nor had any alternative suggestions to offer. The Bois de Boulogne was a great disappointment to Du Maurier, for the alterations effected by Napoleon III had quite destroyed its wild and natural character. The Tête Noire, however, was still standing in St Cloud, and they ate a very pleasant dinner there, Deutsch confiding his most secret hopes to a sympathetic Du Maurier. Perhaps in furtherance of

72. Letters, p. 269.
73. Letters, p. 271.   75. Letters, p. 271.
74. Letters, p. 271.   76. Letters, p. 272.

Deutsch's desire to marry soon, or at least to enjoy female company, they went to a six sou ball, 'which was very dreary', and prompted them to return to their hotel comparatively early. The ostensible reason for coming to Paris had been to see the exhibition, but Du Maurier showed little enthusiasm for it, and was only excited by the two giants, Chang and Chung (the picture galleries he found 'very fatiguing'). His own small stature partly explains his passion for huge men and women, but his ability to turn the huge into the monstrous in his cartoons suggests that his fascination was rotted in fear. On Tuesday, Deutsch went to the exhibition by himself, because Du Maurier could not keep away from his old haunts, or the poignant memories they evoked:

> I took a turn for the last time all over Passy, as the sensations I get by doing so are priceless and worth all the exhibitions in the world, including pictures. Explored well every street or nearly so, and almost every porte-cochère, corner, pillar, post and what not brought back a souvenir. It seemed so funny to think of my having a merry English wife and kids all the while at an English watering place, while all the former part of me which I evoked was so French.[77]

The visit came to an end the next day, for Du Maurier was thoroughly exhausted from his intensive sight-seeing. He preferred to leave his French half behind, and return to his English 'wife and kids' in Ramsgate, in the same spirit as Mr Titwillow, who awakes to find, with some relief, that he has dreamed his whole visit.

Du Maurier returned to Ramsgate with Deutsch, to find the resort packed with his friends, Shirley Brooks, the Friths, Edmund Yates and his beautiful wife, the Philip Calderons, G. A. Storey, and the Twisses. It was an infinitely more successful holiday than Felixstowe had been in 1865, or Boulogne the year before. Sissie Frith recalled, in suitably purple language, an evening when Du Maurier entertained the gathering with his superb tenor:

> 'Den lieben lange Tag' wailed out across the night, and I was gazing at the moon on the sea, listening to the mingled ripple of the waves on the shore and the lovely voice in the drawing-room, my eyes filling with tears, I do not quite know why, and my heart beating as sentimentally as that of any love-sick maiden in her teens. Never did any moon shine before or since as that moon did, or any sea and voice mingle as did those.

77. Letters, p. 274.

Then the tune would change; dainty little ripples ran along the keys of
the piano; we were in France; despite the very obvious moonlight on the
sea, the sun shone, soldiers clanked along the Boulevards, girls came out
and beckoned and smiled, the leaves rustled on the trees, and all was
spring, and gaiety, and pleasure.

One never had to ask him to continue; one little song after the other
would make the evening memorable; he knew his audience, knew that
we could never have enough, and he played upon us all with his voice,
another Orpheus with his lute, until we travelled miles into the 'Country
of Make-Believe', and wandered with him along his myriad roads of
fancy. How I wish I could reproduce that *voix d'or!*[78]

Storey and Calderon were both members of the St John's Wood
Clique, to which Du Maurier was loosely affiliated, and with which
he had close personal connections before he moved to Hampstead.
Following in the tradition of The Sketching Society, founded by
Francis Stonor and the Chalon brothers in 1808, the St John's
Wood Clique was a group of young artists living in St John's Wood,
who were in the habit of meeting on Saturdays to compare and
criticize each other's sketches on a set subject. More than other
similar sketching clubs, they formed a coherent social group who
were constantly in one another's company. Founded by David
Wynfield, who is best known now for his photographs, the group
included G. D. Leslie, W. F. Yeames, J. E. Hodgson, Phillip
Calderon, Adolphus ('Dolly') Storey, and Du Maurier's friends,
Henry Stacy Marks and Frederick Walker; Val Prinsep and
Frederic Leighton were both honorary members. Most of the group
became accomplished and successful history or genre painters in a
conventional Victorian idiom, but there were few real artistic
links between them. Essentially the St John's Wood Clique was a
merry group of young artists who happened to live close together.
Du Maurier's connection with the clique was purely social. He did
not join in their Saturday 'grillings' (their badge was a gridiron
with the motto 'Ever on thee'), but came to the after-dinner entertainments, bringing Emma, who was a great favourite. Again it was
his singing voice which was remembered:

He had a very pretty sympathetic voice in which he would sing delightful
little French songs, for he was one of those nice people who, although a
master of his craft, was always ready to contribute to the success of an
evening by his efforts, whether by singing or acting, or any other way.

78. *Leaves from a Life*, pp. 196–7.

55. The St. John's Wood Clique. Initial letter 'C' by
Linley Sambourne, *Punch* (1873). Notes added by
Shirley Brooks

. . . The songs in his repertoire, in which the Clique used to delight most, were 'Pourquoi, Margot?' 'Bon jour, Suzanne, ma fleur de bois', and 'Je suis triste' . . . And of course there was 'Vin a quat' sous', a drinking song hailing from the Latin Quarter. It had a rousing chorus with a hiccup in the refrain, in which all joined with great gusto. To have had the privilege of hearing the members of the Clique lifting up their voices and hiccuping gloriously together must have been most edifying.[79]

It is noticeable that Du Maurier chose his songs to suit his audience. When he first came to London, he felt the need to aim high with 'Svegliaté la mia mia' by Pergolese, and Gordigiani's 'il nome de mia madre', which would frequently reduce the more susceptible members of his audience to tears. Later on, he realised that his lighter French songs, like the anti-imperial 'Sieur de Framboisy' which William De Morgan heard in Newman Street, were more original, and he began to develop his performance of these.

79. M. H. Stephen Smith, *Art and Anecdote* (1927), pp. 138–9.

Dolly Storey remembered the expressive use of his eyes, and the gestures with which he indicated the appearance of new characters. The clique obviously liked his risqué, comic songs, which alternated with Storey's Italian and Spanish ballads, Calderon's rather ineffective rendering of Mephistopheles' aria from *Faust*, and Marks's songs about 'Betsy Waring, who went a-charing', and 'your 'umble servant, Crewe'. The comic sermons of Hodgson and Marks were well-known, one of Marks's best beginning:

> 'The wilderness, where the wangdoodel roameth and the mastodon mourneth for its first-born'. From the moment he gave out the text to the last sad sentence which explained why the mastodon mourned its son and heir, we were in fits of laughter, while Marks was absolutely solemn, and would end by gazing at us mournfully and closing his book with an air that intimated to us without words where we might expect to find ourselves on the last day.[80]

Marks was Du Maurier's closest friend in the Clique, a rather bumptious and noisy man, who became Guy Du Maurier's god-father. He achieved the greatest popular success among the clique, with his historical fancy-dress pictures, and his appealing studies of birds in mock-human situations.

Du Maurier was still a frequent guest at Arthur Lewis' bachelor musical parties, where his voice was much appreciated. He was an honorary member of the Moray Minstrels, which he regarded as the finest choir in London, but his greatest successes were his solos and duets. In 1865, he and Harold Power, son of the famous Irish comedian, Tyrone Power, performed Offenbach's comic duologue, *Les Deux Aveugles*; blindness was a sensitive subject with Du Maurier, but he does not seem to have interpreted his part as the blind soldier, Stanislas Giraffier, on a personal level. The duologue was revived several times in succeeding years, but Du Maurier never minded performing it again: 'H.P. got his face up hideously, and a roar of laughter greeted his appearance; I did nothing to my face, but wore the blouse, white bags & father-in-law hat'.[81] His audience was often distinguished, and on one occasion Du Maurier was expecting to perform before the Prince of Wales (it is not known if he did so). Arthur Sullivan, then in his thirties, was so impressed by *Les Deux Aveugles* when he heard it in March 1867, that he decided to try and

80. *Leaves from a Life*, p. 131.
81. Diary, p. 390.

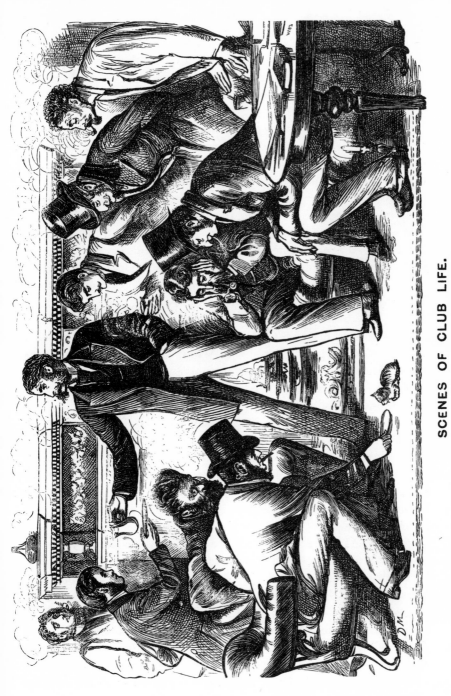

56. *Punch* (1873). The Arts Club – third from the left is
Calderon, sixth from the left is T. R. Lamont, and the
three standing figures on the right are Walker, Leighton
and Keene

compose a similar work, which eventually resulted in the famous comic operetta, *Cox and Box*.

Cox and Box was performed as a benefit performance for the *Punch* artist, Charles Bennett, who had died in April 1867, only two years after his appointment to the staff, leaving a widow and nine children. In the days before national insurance and pension schemes, artists and writers who died young left their families totally unprovided for. Charity performances, like the amateur theatricals organised by Dickens, and subscription funds, were of regular occurrence during the Victorian period. On *Punch*, both Mark Lemon and John Leech died relatively poor, and the staff did their best to help the surviving families. The programme of the benefit performance for Bennett's widow was to include *Les Deux Aveugles*, Tom Taylor's short play, *A Wolf in Sheep's Clothing* and John Oxenford's farce, *A Family Failing*. The last two plays were performed by Tenniel, Silver, Burnand, Taylor, Mayhew, Shirley Brooks, and the three Terry sisters, Kate, Ellen and Florence, who were already making theatrical history; one result of the performance was Arthur Lewis' marriage to Kate Terry. The fourth item in the programme was *Cox and Box*, adapted by Frank Burnand from the popular farce by Madison Morton, and set to music by Sullivan.

There has in the past been considerable confusion as to exactly when and where the first performance of *Cox and Box* occurred, but it has usually been assumed that it was in aid of the Bennett benefit. In fact the operetta had been played some time before Bennett's death, on Wednesday 23 May 1866, at Burnand's house in Belgrave Road. The cast on this occasion is given in a dated programme, now in the possession of Lady Browning: Cox, Harold Power; Box, George Du Maurier; Bouncer, John Foster. As far as can be ascertained this was the very first performance, a fact which is confirmed by the later statements of Du Maurier, Armstrong and Burnand himself. After Bennett's death, Sullivan agreed to produce the operetta again for his widow. On 28 March 1867, Du Maurier had written in his diary, 'Arthur Sullivan came and asked if I would do *Cox and Box* for charity. I said yes'.[82] They began rehearsing the play with a new cast, Quentin Twiss played Cox, and Arthur Blunt played Bouncer. The next known performance was on 27 April 1867 at Moray Lodge, during one of Arthur Lewis' Saturday evenings. Many years later, Burnand heard it said that *Cox and Box* had first

82. Diary, p. 390.

been performed at Moray Lodge, and went to great pains to prove that this was not so, writing to *Punch* and *The World* about the matter. When Lewis went to Du Maurier in 1890, asking him to support the Moray Lodge claim, Du Maurier claimed to have forgotten whether the performance held at Burnand's house was a rehearsal or a formal occasion. The fact that there was a printed programme for it seems, however, to be conclusive. Du Maurier went on to pay tribute to Lewis' generosity: 'of course I have always associated Cox & Box with your hospitable house & the Moray Minstrels, of which Power & I were "honorary members" – and if asked, should certainly have said that had there been no Moray Lodge there would have probably have been no Cox & Box – no Foster, no Power (no du Maurier !!!!!!!!)'.[83] Du Maurier mentions Foster and Power who had performed at Burnand's house, but not at Moray Lodge in April 1867. This may have been a confusion in his memory, but it also implies that there may have been an earlier performance at Moray Lodge.

The first public performance of *Cox and Box* took place at the Adelphi on the afternoon of 11 May 1867, with Blunt as Bouncer, Twiss as Cox and Du Maurier as Box. Du Maurier was extremely worried by the thought of appearing on a public stage for the first time in his life, and went to bed the night before with a cold compress, and gargled ginger essence in the morning. Before the curtain went up, he fidgeted uneasily in the side-wings, drinking stout and smoking furiously, and nearly missed his first entrance. After his opening conversation with Bouncer, he was left on the stage alone to sing 'Hush a bye Bacon', one of the most successful songs in the piece:

> much applause – all the theatre was of course a mist as I did not wear my glasses, but recognized E. Levy's bald head in the front row, and thought of it during the second verse (suppose I'd said 'Hushaby, Levy!').
>
> Then Twiss sang his song very well – then I flung his chop out of window and we managed the duet 'Who are you, sir', very well – recovered all my self-possession. The second duet got an encore – The grand scena went off all right & so did 'Sixes'; I watching Arthur Sullivan for my cues – Triumphant finish. Blunt was splendid in 'rataplan' – Twiss a regular old stager.[84]

After the performance, Du Maurier went to the boxes, where he was

83. 22 July 1890. Pierpont Morgan Library.
84. Diary, pp. 400–1.

heartily congratulated by his family, Emma, his sister, his mother, and Mrs Wightwick, and by Hamilton Aïdé and the publisher, George Smith. Du Maurier's desire for praise had clearly overcome his musical taste, for, during the compliments, he noted: 'all this time Moray Minstrels singing'.[85] *A Wolf in Sheep's Clothing* and *Les Deux Aveugles* were next performed, and the afternoon ended with *A Family Failing*. A public appeal for funds, in verse, was made by Shirley Brooks:

> You did not know, except some friendly few,
> That he was earnest, gentle, patient, true.
> A better soldier doth Life's battle lack,
> And he has died with harness on his back.[86]

The appeal evidently went home, for the whole entertainment raised six-hundred guineas for Bennett's widow, who wrote to thank Brooks for his help: 'Your efforts on behalf of my family and myself have been such that I do not know how to acknowledge them'.[87]

Another performance of *Cox and Box* was given in Manchester on 29 July 1867, at the Theatre Royal, with the same cast, and part of the same programme. The actors travelled from London on the afternoon of Sunday 28 July, singing loudly for the first three hours of the five hour journey: 'Of the row made . . . no idea can be given'.[88] In Manchester they stayed with different members of the Agnew family, who owned several large houses on the outskirts. In the morning a full rehearsal of *Cox and Box* was held, and then in the evening a special dinner was laid on by Tom Agnew at Summerhill. They played games on his lawns, where Ellen Terry charmed the whole group by her capering about. The performance took place in the evening before a vast crowd, and raised a thousand pounds, which one *Punch* article claimed was a record for any charity entertainment; it certainly bettered the proceeds of Dickens' theatricals. Brooks again delivered a rhymed address, adding a special stanza for the citizens of Manchester:

> In this great town, – a glory of our land, –
> Where enterprise the richest guerdon meets,

85. Diary, p. 401.
86. Shirley Brooks, *Diary for* 1867, unpublished. In the *Punch* offices. Appendix.

87. Brooks' Diary, 4 June 1867.
88. Brooks' Diary, 28 July 1867.

And the great heart of commerce proudest beats,
Now own that heart, which nobly speaks in you,
'Keeps a warm corner' for the artist too.[89]

After the last play had finished, Du Maurier, imagining that the
curtain calls would be taken in front of the curtain, began to dance
about behind it. Burnand then signalled to the curtain raiser, 'and up
the curtain went, and I was nearly solo . . . dressed in a flannel shirt
and dirty pair of white ducks'.[90] Du Maurier had one further
triumph, for he won a bet with Arthur Blunt that he and not Blunt
would be the man to escort Ellen Terry to her carriage. He defeated
his rival by leaving a piece of pastry outside his dressing room, which
the greedy Blunt could not resist, and Du Maurier carried off Ellen
Terry without a struggle. Shirley Brooks described the rest of the
evening in his diary:

> By this time we were all ready to gag & chaff, & did. Finally got back into
> black, & we all went off to a grand supper, given us by the magnates at
> the Queen's. Would have greatly preferred to go to bed, but was on the
> left of the chair, Ashton, (M.L. on R.) and made lots of speeches. Was
> asked to give the Terrys, & did it pretty well. Smoke. About 4 we got
> away, & T.A.'s pretty garden looked very fresh in the dawn. That was
> the end of *the* day.[91]

Ellen and Isabel Du Maurier, who both attended the Bennett
charity performance, had moved to London in 1865, but had wisely
refused to live under the same roof as Du Maurier. Isabel's romance
with Sam Perrot had apparently ended, and she had resigned herself
to life in London, probably at her mother's request, who felt the need
to be near her son. Du Maurier was still optimistic about finding a
husband for Isabel among his friends. Armstrong had his last chance
on Boxing-Day 1865, when an accident took place in 91 Great
Russell Street:

> Girl dressing in the shop for the Hairdressers' Ball. Turned on 2 burners
> and lit one and left it burning! D.M. and wife dressing on the top-floor.
> bang! like a 100 pounder and then rattle-smash-crash 'O the children' . . .
> Dn. it! they're all right! first time he ever swore before his wife. Sister

89. Brooks' Diary, 29 July 1867.   91. 29 July 1867.
90. Diary, p. 408.

"Harivler" 16 Dec. 1866 — This sketche includeth the dowager D M. The present countesse of that ilke — The lady Isabelle — ye sheep Healin Thomasse de Armstronge — and ye famous hartyfse, D M hymselfe.

57. Sketch of the Du Maurier family and Tom Armstrong
(1866)

tried to jump from window but Armstrong held her back. Baby crowing in his arms at the fun as he came downstairs. The nursemaids had run away of course. Lucky no one on the stairs or they'd have been killed.[92]

The Du Mauriers had a rather disturbed Christmas, for on Christmas Eve, Du Maurier had found two burglars on the roof. Fortunately they ran away.

Armstrong's masterful gesture passed unrewarded. Isabel's character is hard to assess from the available evidence, but she seems to have inherited her mother's caustic wit and sharp tongue. When she did eventually find a husband, it was not one of Du Maurier's friends, but a member of the London literary world. Clement William Scott was a part-time dramatic critic of the *Weekly Dispatch*, and a full-time war office clerk, a vivid personality with a hard shell and a soft heart. His hopes that Isabel would provide warm and adoring female companionship were rudely shattered, and the marriage was an unqualified disaster, as Shirley Brooks had suspected: 'I hope it is a hopeful match, it can't be more'.[93] They were

92. Silver, 17 Jan. 1866.
93. Brooks' Diary, 14 August 1867.

married at Brompton Oratory on 30 April 1868, and Du Maurier probably breathed a sigh of relief at having one responsibility off his hands. After having four children, Isabel and Clement Scott eventually separated with a great deal of bitterness. Ellen Du Maurier, as plaintive as ever, continued to criticize the conduct of her son's life, particularly the way he and Emma spoiled the children. One of the few accounts of her is to be found in Shirley Brooks' diary for 1867: 'The dowager Mrs du M. Very intelligent old lady, keen, quick, & a linguist'.[94] She died in February 1870. Eugène Du Maurier went out to Mexico with the army, to his family's relief, but he was soon back in France. In 1867, he married an exemplary French wife, Marie, and settled down to an eminently respectable career as a commercial traveller, in England and France.

George and Emma Du Maurier had been contemplating a move from their lodgings in Great Russell Street to a house of their own for some time. Shortly before Guy Louis was born in 1865, they were seriously contemplating this step, but then the landlord offered them another floor, and they stayed. When Sylvia Jocelyn appeared in November 1866, they decided that their quarters really were too cramped, but it was not until March 1868 that they moved to 12 Earl's Terrace, Kensington, where they occupied the whole house. The Silvers were living very near them in Leech's old home, which may have influenced the Du Maurier's choice of a new residence. Du Maurier was excited by the thought of his new home, and visited it on 6 March 1868, his thirty-fourth birthday: 'Went with T.A. [Armstrong] and a colour box to our new house in Earl's Terrace to settle the paint for the drawing rooms'.[95] Some of the walls were hung with William Morris papers, probably those which Du Maurier had chosen a year before: 'the Pomegranate & the yellow. Morris quite civil in spite of the Legend of Camelot'.[96] He was appalled when the tenants to whom he assigned the lease of Earl's Terrace in 1869 drove nails into the paper:

> Altho' we spoke her fair and never made any remark about it we are boiling over with indignation nailing pictures on to the bard's paper without consulting us seems a great liberty.[97]

They moved to Kensington on 25 March 1868, but it was not a successful experiment, although Du Maurier described the house as

94. 14 Aug. 1867.   96. Diary, p. 394.
95. Diary, p. 409.   97. To T. Armstrong, 1870.

TO SUFFERERS FROM NERVOUS DEPRESSION.

58. *Punch* (1869)

'a palace after 91 Great Russell Street'.[98] He thought that the Kensington air did not suit his family, and was himself several times unwell during their time there. Marie-Louise was born in Earl's Terrace in August 1868, and in the spring of 1869 Du Maurier moved all four down to Ifield House in Crawley for a holiday, in the hope that the country air would benefit his eye, and prove healthy for his children. In the event, Emma and Guy became seriously unwell and they all returned to Kensington in rather a sorry state. Du Maurier was now determined to move, and remembering his love of Hampstead Heath as a boy, decided to try and rent a house up there. They had difficulty in finding anyone to take up the lease in Earl's Terrace, but eventually managed to do so in the early summer of 1869. By 24 June they were installed in Hampstead.

59. The *Punch* dinner card (1870). From left to right, the heads are those of Shirley Brooks, Tom Taylor, Charles Keene, Horace Mayhew (pulling Du Maurier behind), R. F. Sketchley, Percival Leigh, F. C. Burnand, and John Tenniel

Chapter 6

Hampstead I

60. Initial letter 'M', Wives and Daughters, *Cornhill* (1864–5)

'HAMPSTEAD WAS MY PASSY – the Leg-of-Mutton Pond my Mare d'Auteuil',[1] Du Maurier wrote in *Peter Ibbetson*, and the comparison was an apposite one. Relatively close to the centre of London, Hampstead still retained the atmosphere of a country village, facing the Heath as Passy still faces the Bois de Boulogne. Du Maurier must have hoped that his children, growing up in similar surroundings to his own, would re-create the magic he had known as a child, and allow him to revive those feelings which lay so deeply hidden in his past. In this he was perhaps disappointed, for all his children showed a healthy preoccupation with the world around them, which did not encourage that strain of self-indulgent daydreaming, characteristic of their father.

The village of Hampstead, high up on the northern side of the Thames Valley had long been popular with artists, both as a subject for painting, and as a desirable place to live. Shortly before Du Maurier moved there, it still stood, like the neighbouring village of Highgate, isolated in the middle of open country, a small group of houses around a Georgian church. Before suburban development choked the surrounding area, Hampstead was rural enough to attract a landscape painter of Constable's quality, and other artists

1. p. 108.

like John Linnell, John Varley, and William Collins, have left an enduring record of its past and unspoilt beauty. One of the finest landscapes ever painted in Hampstead was Ford Madox Brown's *An English Autumn Afternoon* (City Museum and Art Gallery, Birmingham). Brown painted the view from his own lodgings in the Vale of Health, looking across the East Heath to London below. Executed with all the meticulous precision of Pre-Raphaelite art, it still has an all-embracing unity of space and atmosphere, a richness and warmth of colour, which make it one of the most satisfying and evocative of all nineteenth-century English landscapes. It explains why Hampstead, overlooking London as Grinzing overlooks Vienna, or Montmartre overlooks Paris, was so attractive to artists and writers, desirous of breathing fresh air, and escaping from the noise and confined space of London's gloomy streets.

The scene which Brown painted in 1852 had altered very little by the time the Du Mauriers came to Hampstead in 1869. The population, however, had almost trebled in the intervening years, and continued to rise steeply until the end of the century. Most of the building developments took place on the west side of the village, where open country had once stretched to Golders Green and Harrow-on-the-Hill. Suburban homes were springing up along the Finchley Road, constructed in 1830, which now formed the natural centre of the new Hampstead conglomeration. Wilkie Collins' haunting description of Walter Hartright's first meeting with the woman in white, near Frognal Lane, must have seemed out-of-date soon after it was written in 1859. Although Hampstead village was soon deprived of its rural environs, part of the Heath was saved from building schemes by successful public protests, and generous benefactions. The largest surviving section of the Heath was bought in 1871 for £47,000, and the rest was acquired in separate transactions between then and 1907. These purchases were not made solely for the benefit of the inhabitants of Hampstead, but to maintain an open space which had become a popular play-ground for Londoners in general, and particularly for the poorer classes. On Sundays, and bank-holidays, the Heath was crowded with pleasure-seekers. There were fairs, and steam organs, country-dancing and popular games, besides the benefit of fresh air. Thirty thousand people might be found there on a warm bank holiday afternoon towards the end of the century. The poet, James Thomson (B.V.), expressed the feelings of the Cockney visitors:

This is the Heath of Hampstead,
There is the dome of St Paul's;
Beneath, on the serried house-tops,
A chequered lustre falls:

Here we will sit, my darling,
And dream an hour away:
The donkeys are hurried and worried,
But we are not donkeys to-day.[2]

Visitors to Hampstead today may find the expression 'heath' an inappropriate description of the East Heath, with its rolling hills, smooth grass, and carefully planned clumps of trees. It is a more accurate description of the West Heath on the other side of Spaniard's Road, beyond the Spaniards' Inn and Jack Straw's Castle. In James Reid's painting, *Hampstead Heath in 1860*, this area, around the Leg of Mutton Pond, can be seen as it once was, much wilder in appearance than the East Heath, with broken, sandy ground, and scrubbly vegetation. The West Heath is still rough and unparklike, but a description of it in the 1860s, shows that it was then indistinguishable from open country:

> Hampstead, remember, as it was then, undefiled by demon builders, a real wild heath of acres and acres of sand, bracken, and gorse-covered country, real country ... Leaving the knife-board of the old Atlas 'bus at the Swiss Cottage, these gay young men would tramp up the muddy meadow (now Fitzjohn's Avenue) to the stile at the top, past the old church ... through the little lane along the wood fence, and from thence to the Pond. Here with a feeling of exhilaration, they would look back over the smoky roof-tops of the London they had left behind, and would then start tramping off through country lanes, sweet scented with the first breath of spring, stopping to admire a quaint cottage here, 'a nice little bit' there.[3]

This was the Hampstead to which the Du Mauriers came, but it was fast-changing as modern amenities made it a more convenient place to live in. In the late 1840s a Hampstead schoolboy, Basil Field, could remember water-carriers with yokes on their shoulders, carrying buckets of water to Hampstead village from the nearest well, in what is now Fitzjohn's Avenue. A direct water-supply was laid on in 1856, and 1855 saw the extension of the railway to the foot of Haverstock

2. 'Sunday afternoon on Hampstead Heath' (1865).
3. M. H. Stephen Smith, *Art and Anecdote* (1927), pp. 145–6.

Hill. It was not until 1907, ten years after Du Maurier's death, that the long threatened tube reached Hampstead, and completed the annexation of the former village to the greater London metropolis.

Hampstead's popularity rested primarily on its high position, semi-rural character, and bracing air, an important consideration for such persistent hypochondriacs as George and Emma. They found many friends and fellow-spirits there, for it had always possessed a colony of writers and artists. It was an ideal situation for those who did not have to work in London every day, but who did not wish to cut themselves off altogether from the city. Although often compared with Montmartre, Hampstead was not in the least bohemian (property has never been cheap there), and it had always cultivated an air of gentility and prosperity. People who had their own carriages regularly spent the evenings in town, but those who had to hire a cab to take them down the hill preferred to stay at home or dine out in the village. In the days before the tube, Hampstead had a self-contained society like that of a country-town, but it was saved from parochialism by the proximity of London, and the high incidence of intellectual and artistic inhabitants.

Many of the buildings in Hampstead dated from the first half of the eighteenth century, like the Du Maurier's first home there in Holly Mount, a narrow street of terraced houses. They rented no. 4 in June 1869, but moved on 18 September to a more permanent residence at Gangmoor House, on the summit of Heath Street, still one of the finest Georgian houses in the village. Du Maurier wrote to Armstrong about it:

> Here we are since Saturday, 'than which' a lovelier situation, a more genial old house, and pleasanter state of things altogether, if it could only last could not be found anywhere. There is a spare bedroom facing the west with the most beautiful view in Middlesex, so mind your eyes: you will want to live here altogether.[4]

They stayed at Gangmoor for only one winter, perhaps because of the unprotected position of the house, which is open to the elements on all sides – a bitter prospect in those days of inadequate heating. By Michaelmas 1870 the Du Mauriers were living in their third Hampstead home, 27, Church Row, where they remained for four years. The rent, originally fixed at fifty pounds a year, was soon increased

4. To T. Armstrong, 21 September 1869.

to seventy, while the rateable value went up from forty to sixty pounds, a good indication of Hampstead's rising status. Church Row, which leads from Heath Street to the Parish Church of St John, is still one of the finest eighteenth-century terraces in London, although marred by an unfortunate block of flats on the north side. In the 1860s, the street was quite unspoilt, and beyond the church stretched open country. The Du Mauriers lived on the south side in a superb Queen Anne house, their front door shaded by lime trees. In fine weather they had an uninterrupted view of central London and the North Downs from their upper windows. Du Maurier was delighted by the eighteenth-century elegance of Church Row, and, in 1874, he helped to save the Georgian church tower at the end of the street, threatened by an insensitive scheme for rebuilding. The committee formed to save the tower included three architects, G. F. Bodley, who lived at no. 24, Basil Champneys, and Richard Norman Shaw, as well as other distinguished men, J. Talbot Airey, Sidney Colvin and Henry Holiday. Closely connected with them was George Gilbert Scott, who lived at 26, Church Row, and whose scheme of saving the tower, and of moving the altar to the west end was eventually adopted. Du Maurier got up a petition signed by three-hundred supporters of the original tower, and it was eventually saved from its neo-Gothic fate.

On their first Monday at Gangmoor, Du Maurier was sent off down the hill, with a carpet bag, to buy groceries at the Civil Service Stores:

> who should I meet straddling up heath street with a Shapeless Bullcock hat on his valuable head but Topsy [William] Morris, looking out for lodgings for his wife & kids. We greeted each other with distant courtesy, and I led him to some lodgings, which he straightaway took. We then clomb the buss' & went to town together; during this journey the idle singer of an empty day came out in such a delightfully genial style that I in my heart swore him eternal friendship; he must have understood my sentiments, for he proposed we should go to maiden lane and eat together, which we did, with stout, and had a jolly good time of it. Then he took me to his publishers and made me a present of the Earthly Paradise, having written my name on the flyleaf. He is going to bring Mrs Topsy here on Saturday.[5]

Morris and his family had returned from a visit to Ems on the Rhine

5. To T. Armstrong, 21 September 1869.

the previous week, and Janey Morris was still suffering from the journey. It was hoped that Hampstead would be beneficial for her health. If the Morrises did move to Hampstead it was not for long, and Du Maurier's obvious desire to 'get on with the Topsys' was never fulfilled. Du Maurier, who was not a great admirer of Mrs Morris' looks, wrote in 1885: 'was depressed by Mrs Morris, Rossetti's famous model, sitting opposite in an old Florentine costume and her old Florentine face above it'.[6]

The Du Mauriers made frequent expeditions to the West End to shop, see people, and look in on Earls Terrace, for which they were still responsible. Du Maurier prided himself on being *au fait* with the art world, and at first he had no intention of allowing Hampstead to cut him off from it. He was a regular habitué of the few art exhibitions that occurred, and watched the career of Edward Burne-Jones with particular interest and delight. In July 1869, he had been ecstatic about *The Wine of Circe* at the Old Watercolour Society:

> Oh my! *isn't* the Circe a stunner . . . It pleases me more than any Jones I've ever seen & more than any picture I have seen this year. I was also much delighted with Pinwell's pictures . . . I think he's got the better of Walker in the W.C. . . . I don't think any other of E.B.J. to compare with Circe. The dragon is a very duffing animal for a man in armour to take so much trouble about. I heard a lady say that was *not* drawn from nature.[7]

In the same letter, Du Maurier made a surprising admission, though one that was not entirely true: 'Going to Exhibitions excites & unsettles me; that's why I go so seldom (That's why I prefer the Zoo to the National Gallery)'. In spite of the excitement, Du Maurier did go to a great number of exhibitions, and always enjoyed retailing gossip about painters and their activities to Armstrong:

> Agnew has also taken to buying Rossettis. Gives 80£ for any scrap of paper Rossetti has stamped in any way with the idiosyncrasy of his genius – so at least the Greeks tell me. – (Even an old bit of *Telegraph* or *Pall Mall Gazette*); but perhaps that's an exaggeration.[8]

6. Hoyer Millar, p. 47.
7. To T. Armstrong.
8. To T. Armstrong, July 1869.

In 1873, Du Maurier made a special expedition to the Dudley
Gallery

> to see the Burne Joneses. Love amongst the ruins is very stunning – almost
> the best thing he's done I think, altho' the lovers are not quite to the taste
> of your humble servant – The colour is exquisite. The faces are beautiful
> also, especially the man's – The woman is badly drawn the length of the
> thighs being out of all reason & she has neither hips nor belly, and is as
> bottomless as the everlasting pit, and the insufferable grief expressed in
> both their faces is owing to the fact that these physical peculiarities of
> hers preclude the possibility of any but platonic love (her medical man
> indeed having forbidden all other). The other picture of Jones's is a
> bogy – I cannot discover any redeeming point; perhaps you know it, the
> Garden of the Hesperides – The B.J. face carried to excess – bloodless
> illshapen leather feet – and a tone of sentiment which is quite aperient.[9]

By 1873, Du Maurier's interest in the art world was as much for
Armstrong's benefit as his own. He and Emma were slowly becoming
absorbed in Hampstead society, withdrawing from the circle of their
old friends, and their old haunts. Writing to Armstrong during their
first week at Gangmoor, Du Maurier made a humorous play on the
name of their new Hampstead friends, the Gilbert Scotts: 'We are
going to dine at the Scotts to meet the Gilberts. The Scotts and ourselves are getting that thick that we shall find ourselves living
together like a happy family'.[10]

The Gilbert Scotts did not stay long, at 26, Church Row, but other
Hampstead inhabitants soon became intimate with the Du Maurier
family circle. In 1873, they entertained 'the George Leslies, Hen-
nessys & Basil Champneys at a simple but elegant repast. G.L. very
amusing as usual – so much so that B.C. went to sleep after dinner!'[11]
Basil Champneys, a fellow member of the tower preservation committee, was then only twenty-nine. A late Gothic revival architect,
he was best known for his many collegiate buildings and churches in
Oxford, which included Mansfield College, the Somerville College
Library, the church of St Peter le Bailey, and the Indian Institute.
In 1870, Champneys, who was then twenty-eight, had just completed his first important work, St Luke, Kentish Town, and was
already establishing a reputation as a traditionalist. His own house,
Hall Oak, was built in Frognal in 1881, and is aptly described by

9. To T. Armstrong, 1873.   11. To T. Armstrong, 1873.
10. To T. Armstrong, 21 September 1869.

BEFORE DINNER.—THE MARCH PAST.

61. One of a series of engravings of the Du Maurier
family (*c* 1873)

Professor Pevsner as 'red brick, very snug and solid'.[12] Champneys
is now largely forgotten, probably rightly, as he was not very
inspired, but he had other interests besides architecture, in the
polymath tradition of the Victorian period. He was a close friend of
Robert Louis Stevenson, wrote a *Memoir of Coventry Patmore*, and a
guide to Romney Marsh, *A Quiet Corner of England*. It was probably
because of his literary links that Du Maurier gave Champneys the
first draft of *Peter Ibbetson* to criticize, but little else is known of the
relationship between the two men. Du Maurier's choice of Champneys as an executor of his will suggests that they were close friends,
but there is little supporting evidence.

Next door to the Du Mauriers, who had moved by this time, lived
the elderly portraitist and miniaturist, Margaret Gillies, at no. 25,
Church Row, a popular figure in the village, whose tea-parties were
an established fixture on the social calendar. Her lodgers were
Charles and Gertrude Lee Lewes, and it was through them that Du
Maurier came to know George Eliot and G. H. Lewes (the father of
Charles Lewes) who lived at The Priory, in Regents Park. Another
family with whom the Du Mauriers became very friendly at this time
were the Fields at Squire's Mount. Edwin Wilkins Field was a
lawyer and reformer, who died in 1871 from a heart attack after
saving a drowning man from the Thames. Du Maurier knew three of
his children particularly well, the artist Walter, Emily, who later
became Honorary Secretary of the Hampstead Heath Protection
Society, and the solicitor, Basil, one of Du Maurier's rivals at
Hampstead-after-dinner entertainments. In a humorous letter to
Miss Field, Du Maurier told her that if he met her brother alone on a
dark night he would not answer for the consequences; he had also
found a splendid song, with which to defeat Basil at their next
encounter.

The Du Mauriers were not entirely dependent on new acquaintances in Hampstead. The poet, William Allingham, lived in Eldon
House, and one of the most delightful Victorian publishers, George
Smith, of *Smith, Elder*, was at Oak Lodge, Frognal, until 1872. Smith,
who was responsible for the complete edition of Mrs Gaskell's work
which Du Maurier had illustrated, was very kindly disposed towards
him, and once bought some shares on Du Maurier's behalf, allowing
repayment over an extended period. Later, Smith commissioned Du
Maurier to design a label for Apollinaris Water, of which he was

12. *The Buildings of England: London except the cities of London and Westminster* (1952),
p. 199.

part-owner. Together they decided on a design with a delightful but indecent nymph rising from a fountain, which proved a little *risqué* for the other members of the board. The final label showed 'a spring bubbling up among some reeds & a lovely evening sky'.[13] Du Maurier complained bitterly at having to leave out 'Venus Apollinaris' as they had named her: 'If I might only replace Venus by some comic gnome, sexless and hideous, but genial!'[14] According to Harry Furniss, Du Maurier received fifty guineas for this commission, and Charles Hoyer Millar considered it his best-known drawing.

Sir Walter Besant, the novelist, whom Du Maurier had first met at Cambridge in 1855, now lived in Frognal End, and the two men clearly saw much of each other in Hampstead society. As in the case of Champneys, few facts have come to light about their friendship. It was Besant who first introduced Du Maurier to the Rabelais Club, founded in 1879 as a dining club for Rabelais enthusiasts. Virility was a pre-requisite for membership, but Mrs Hardy's story that Henry James was rejected for lack of this quality was a calculated untruth, designed to belittle her husband's rival. The dinners took place six or seven times a year and each member was supposed to submit some form of literary contribution to the club's magazine, *Recreations of the Rabelais Club*. Three volumes appeared between 1881 and 1889, and Du Maurier published a poem in French, 'Aux poètes de la France' (volume two) and a doggerel verse in English (volume three). The subject of the French poem was inspired by an argument with Henry James, and concerned the differences between English and French prosody. It was a rather loose and pointless exercise on an abstruse subject, and one not suited to Du Maurier's gift for light and satirical verse. It ended by praising the English poets:

> Laissez donc tous vos Boileau, Racine, et Corneille :
> Lisez Milton, Pope, Burns – Shelley, Keats, Byron !
> Shakspere !!! ... et parmi les vifs, rimant à merveille,
> Browning, Swinburne et surtout ... milord Tennyson !
>
> Quand vous les saurez-par coeur, si vous êtes sages,
> Je vous permettrai Musset, et le grand Victor.
> Pour que vous puissiez comprendre, en lisant leur pages,
> Ce qui nous déshérita de la harpe d'or.

13. To George Smith, University of Texas Library.
14. To George Smith, University of Texas Library.

The English poem, 'A Lost Illusion', rephrased an idea already expressed in a *Punch* cartoon. It was a take-off of a popular sensation novel, written in the style of the lady authoresses whom Du Maurier so detested, and concerned a certain Barbara Blakeshepe. After murdering three husbands, she is looking for a new occupation:

> Then she suddenly found that she couldn't control
> The yearning for love of her ardent young soul,
> So – (this is the cream of the story – prepare)
> She took a large house in the midst of Mayfair:
>
> Where she started a kind of a sort of a – eh?
> Well, a sort of a kind of a – what shall I say!
> Like *Turkey*, you know – only just the reverse;
> Which, if possible, makes it a little bit worse!

Among other members of the Rabelais Club were Thomas Hardy, Oliver Wendell Holmes, Henry James, John Millais, Alma Tadema, Thomas Woolner, Bret Harte and Edwin Abbey. Until its demise in 1889, it was one of the more lively and amusing societies of its kind.

Du Maurier's favourite fellow-artist in Hampstead was Kate Greenaway, who moved to a house built for her by Norman Shaw in Frognal, where she lived with her parents and her brother. Norman Shaw was often employed by successful artists who wished to live in discreet and distinctive style, like the clique in Melbury Road, where he built two of his best houses. Kate Greenaway's drawings of children, fruits of a delicate if limited talent, had delighted Ruskin, with whom she carried on a long and intimate correspondence. Du Maurier often went to take tea with her, seated in a deep basket chair, and surrounded by blue china and brightly coloured pottery. Their conversation rarely concerned illustration, and usually centred on Miss Greenaway's garden, or the general interests of the village community. After Du Maurier's death, Kate Greenaway finally read *Peter Ibbetson*, and was surprised how little she had understood the man she saw so often. Thinking back, she could only recall that she had always liked him, and that 'he was such a nice man'.[15]

In spite of his new interests and friends, the pleasant afternoon teas, and the occasional dinner-parties, Du Maurier sometimes complained that Hampstead was 'healthy but dull'. He was willing,

15. M. H. Spielmann and L. S. Layard, *Kate Greenaway* (1905), p. 205.

THE BENEFIT OF THE DOUBT.

Ethel. " AND, O MAMMA, DO YOU KNOW AS WE WERE COMING ALONG WE SAW A HORRID, HORRID WOMAN WITH A RED, STRIPED SHAWL, DRINK SOMETHING OUT OF A BOTTLE, AND THEN HAND IT TO SOME MEN. I'M SURE SHE WAS TIPSY."

Beatrice (who always looks on the best side of things). "PERHAPS IT WAS ONLY *CASTOR OIL*, AFTER ALL !"

62. *Punch* (1874). One of many cartoons drawn of the family at Hampstead

however, to put up with the dullness for reasons of economy and health, and because his family so obviously enjoyed it. There had been four children in four years, but the fifth, Gerald, born in Church Row on 26 March 1873, was the last. Emma was more content in Hampstead than her husband, for she had never enjoyed smart social occasions, and soon became absorbed by her children. Hampstead was an ideal environment for them, and they all established themselves at the centre of village life and society. As they grew older they played tennis and badminton in the summer, skated on the Hampstead ponds in the winter, rushed out to parties, and frequently indulged in what their father called 'juvenile dissipation'. Du Maurier himself found his health slowly improving, and he became more relaxed away from the frenzied rush of London dinners and soirées. In time, he began to regret his isolation, but, while his children were still young, he threw himself wholeheartedly into family-life, allowing his patient wife to undertake most of the accompanying burdens. It is probably true to say that if Du Maurier had stayed in London, he would have experienced further nervous disorders, possibly resulting in blindness. A Hampstead friend, Canon Alfred Ainger, accurately evaluated the sacrifice and its rewards:

> Hampstead was moreover a real foster-mother to George du Maurier, not only in what it brought him, but in what it saved him from. He was by nature and by practice one of the most generous and hospitable of men. He loved to entertain his friends from town, and to take them afterwards his favourite walks. But he disliked dinners and evening parties in London, not because he was unsociable, but because good dinners and long journeys 'took it out of him', and endangered the task of the following morning. The distance from town and the long hills made late hours inevitable. To listen to some new book read aloud in the studio, which was also the common sitting-room of wife and children, made the chief happiness of his evenings.[16]

The truth of this assessment is proved by Du Maurier himself, who wrote to Armstrong in 1879: 'Plenty of gaieties, to very few of which we can go on account of distances. Nothing but Henschel and Sarasate can compensate for the corvée of going all the way to London'.[17] That the Du Mauriers did occasionally dine in London is borne out

16. 'George Du Maurier in Hampstead', *Hampstead Annual* (1897), pp. 18–9.
17. To T. Armstrong, 25 May 1879.

"READING WITHOUT TEARS."

Teacher. " And what Comes after S, Jack ? " | *Teacher.* " And what Comes after T ? "
Pupil. " T ! " | *Pupil.* " For all that we have Received," &c. &c.

63. *Punch* (1869)

ELEMENTS OF MISCHIEF IN HYPOCRITICAL REPOSE.

64. *Punch* (1875)

by the few surviving letters of this period. In 1873 Du Maurier
wrote: 'The other day we dined at the George Smiths in Queens
Gate – the Anthony Trollopes, Matthew Arnolds & Locker &c. –
very jolly – 10/6 there & back'.[18] He continued to meet many of
the leading literary and artistic lions of the period, for all his apparent seclusion in Hampstead. In 1878, he went to dinners given by
Alma Tadema and the Courtney Bells in one week and in the next to
the Friths,

> to Moscheles & afterwards to Comyns Carr's, where Jemmy seemed in
> great spirits & louder than ever . . . Moscheles' parties are delightful –
> amusants *et* honnêtes – so are Tadema's – so are Lehmanns – Willingly
> would I be a Hebrew of the Hebrews, to get oh such oh heavenly
> fiddlers & singers![19]

Life at Church Row, and later at New Grove House, soon began to
fall into those familiar patterns common to large families. Du
Maurier would breakfast in his bedroom, and then work in the studio
for two hours, from ten to twelve, carefully settling himself with his
back to the north light. While he was drawing, the children played
around him, and, if his *Punch* cartoons are to be believed, occasionally perched on his shoulders. Du Maurier joined in their chatter, or
listened to Emma reading aloud from the latest library book, completely eschewing the traditional concentration of the artist at work.
He now almost always drew from models, who had to be hired unless
Emma or the children would stand in. Throughout the 1870s the
Du Maurier children appeared again and again in *Punch*, to the
delight of the public, and it is to be supposed, of their economically
minded father. Even the household staff were sometimes recruited,
or the children's teachers.

At twelve o'clock either with a friend, or with Emma and the older
children, Du Maurier would set out for his daily walk on the Heath.
In the early days he often walked widely, noting the behaviour of
interesting passers-by, whom he sometimes used in his cartoons,
walking along familiar paths which can still be recognised. Henry
James recalled the quality of those walks,

> of old square houses in old high-walled gardens, of great trees and great
> views, of objects consecrated by every kind of repetition, that of the

18. To T. Armstrong, 1873.
19. To T. Armstrong, 25 May 1879.

recurrent pilgrimage and of my companion's inexhaustible use of them. The Hampstead scenery made, in *Punch*, his mountains and valleys, his backgrounds and foregrounds, a surprising deal, at all times, of his variously local color.[20]

Du Maurier usually went out accompanied by a dog. The most famous of these was Chang the giant St Bernard, named after the Chinese Giant whom Du Maurier had so enjoyed at the Paris Exhibition of 1867. Chang lived from 1875 to 1883, and became a popular feature in Du Maurier's cartoons. The children loved him, and would often go out protected only by this huge and amiable animal, whose massive bulk completely satisfied Du Maurier's yearning for the outsize. Rumours of an illness would bring in letters of sympathy from local residents and *Punch* readers, but St Bernards are often short lived, and Chang died of old age in 1883, aged only eight-and-a-half years.

The family usually walked on the West Heath, going first to the Whitestone Pond, which stands near 'Jack Straw's Castle' at the summit of Heath Street, and from which a wide panorama extends, to Hendon and Harrow on one side, and to the East End and the Thames Estuary on the other:

> Harrow-on-the-Hill, with its pointed spire, rises blue in the distance; and distant ridges, like receding waves, rise into blueness, one after the other, out of the low-lying mist; the last ridge bluely melting into space. In the midst of it all gleams the Welsh Harp Lake, like a piece of sky that has become unstuck and tumbled into the landscape with its shiny side up.
>
> On the other side, all London, with nothing but the gilded cross of St Paul's on a level with the eye; it lies at our feet, as Paris used to do from the heights of Passy, a sight to make true dreamers gaze and think and dream the more.[21]

After a pause to enjoy the view, there were two possible routes, either down to the Leg-of-Mutton pond, and then up towards the fir trees above the Bull and Bush public house, or along the Spaniard's Road, where Du Maurier would always tap the last tree 'at the end with his stick, and so back again the way they had come'.[22] Chang usually decided the choice of path, by wandering off lethargically on his own to be followed by Du Maurier, whose 'walking-pace was

20. *Harper's New Monthly Magazine*, p. 598.   22. *Gerald*, p. 31.
21. *Peter Ibbetson*, pp. 293–4.

65. *Divine and Moral Songs for Children* by Isaac Watts.
Landscape of Hampstead Heath (1865)

always of the slowest'.[23] One day, an event took place on the familiar walk, which became part of family legend. It occurred on a Sunday afternoon in Winter, when the whole family were returning home past the Whitestone Pond, which was almost entirely frozen. A bystander had apparently encouraged his dog to go under the ice, by throwing sticks there, and the dog had eventually become trapped. An ardent dog-lover, Du Maurier at once took off his coat and dived into the water, which was only a few feet deep. When he emerged triumphantly with the dog, he was cheered by the bystanders, much to the embarrassment of his family. A worse humiliation followed, however, when the dog's owner came up and offered Du Maurier half-a-crown for his feat. When this was refused, the owner increased the sum to five shillings, whereupon the gallant rescuer lost his temper. 'I beg your pardon, sir', said the enlightened owner, 'I didn't know you were a gentleman'.[24] Even this was not the end of the story, for the next morning a letter arrived, beginning with the words: 'Little did I know who it was that saved my canine pet from a watery grave'.[24a] Today, Du Maurier would surely have been awarded a medal by the R.S.P.C.A.

On weekdays the main meal of the day came after the walk, but on Sundays it came before. Everyone was always late. The patient Emma would sit alone at the table until a ritual peal on the piano announced her husband's arrival. He would eat simply, drinking only claret, and never taking coffee for fear of exciting the nerves of his retina. The rest of the afternoon and evening were usually spent in the studio, where Du Maurier continued drawing while Emma went on with the current book. Some idea of her staying power is given by the fact that she read Hawthorne's *The Scarlet Letter* in three days. When a dinner engagement or a musical evening took them out, they always complained, but usually enjoyed themselves. Music was still an important element in Du Maurier's life, although, as his fine tenor deepened, he no longer volunteered for after-dinner singing. He had given it up some time before 1883, when Charles Hoyer Millar met him for the first time. He was full of hopes that the children would be musical, and insisted that Beatrix should learn to play the piano, and Guy the violin. All the children sang well, and they were encouraged to amuse themselves with amateur theatricals and concerts. Guy was particularly talented on

23. Hoyer Millar, p. 22.   24a. *Gerald*, p. 33.
24. *Gerald*, p.33.

DELICATE CONSIDERATION.

Mamma. "What a Din you're making, Chicks! What *are* you Playing at?"

Tricy. "O, Mamma, we're Playing at Railway Trains. I'm the Engine, and Guy's a First-Class Carriage, and Sylvia's a Second-Class Carriage, and May's a Third-Class Carriage, and Gerald, he's a Third-Class Carriage, too— that is, he's really only a Truck, you know, only you mustn't Tell him so, as it would Offend him!"

66. Delicate Consideration, *Punch* (1873)

the theatrical side, and usually acted as stage manager or producer. Organised games and card games were forbidden indoors, and even reading was not encouraged. A visitor to the family in the 1880s noted how few books there were in the house; the circulating library was their only source of reading matter. Conversation was indulged in with a vigour and freedom rare in most Victorian family circles, and was perhaps their greatest collective talent. All the children were uninhibited and outgoing, able to express themselves fluently, and adept in banter and repartee.

On the whole the children were very lucky in their parents, for many Victorians repressed or ignored their children. The little Du Mauriers were seen and heard a great deal of the time. They became their father's deepest interest in life, and 'he was never happier than when listening to this conversation or the account of their daily doings'.[25] As a result of this attitude they were all refreshingly spontaneous, if a little spoilt. Beatrix was a tough, determined and very high-spirited child, while Guy was quieter and more reliable. In the 70s the other two girls were a little disappointing, for Sylvia was distressingly plain by her father's high standards, and even May (Marie-Louise) who had been a bewitching baby, was 'rather passée', at four, although 'still extremely presentable with her hair crimped'.[26] Later on she developed a violent temper, which her parents kindly put down to her frail constitution, for she and the baby, Gerald, were both liable to coughs and colds. In fact, with two hypochondriacs for parents, the five children must have spent a good deal of their time in bed, and could always use ill-health to escape anything disagreeable.

The climax of family life during the early 1870s was the annual summer holiday, which was usually taken in England. The summer of 1871 was very wet, and the Du Mauriers spent an uncomfortable September in Folkestone:

> we manage to get on thro' knowing so many people. Dr Smith & Howard have just arrived; and the Rudolf Lehmanns are here, so we shall make music & be as merry as circumstances will permit. . . . Then there is Elmore & the Friths & Polands & other people too numerous to enumerate. The three Miss Friths have been sitting to me.[27]

25. Hoyer Millar, p. 21.
26. To Mrs Fortescue, 10 April 1873. Historical Society of Pennsylvania Library.
27. To T. Armstrong, September 1871.

Du Maurier spent one day on a sentimental journey to Boulogne:
Pellew, an illegitimate son of Lord Exmouth, happened to be crossing on the same boat:

> we fraternised & I found him one of the most delightful companions I
> ever met. Half French, musical, Balsacky, everything – so we break-
> fasted & coffeed together & then I went off to the scenes of my childhood,
> but not till past one o'clock. Déjeuner à la fourchette is fatal to the recol-
> lections & it was not till past two o'clock that I began to luxuriate, when
> my boots got so tight I absolutely had to leave off recollecting & go & buy
> another pair.[28]

Even this desperate measure failed to put Du Maurier into a nostalgic
mood so he rejoined Pellew. Together they went to a concert, dined
with two bottles of beaune and caught the boat back at seven o'clock.
Folkestone did not become a favourite Du Maurier resort, in spite of
the proximity of Boulogne, of 'prettier girls & women here than I
have ever seen together before, except at an Eton & Harrow
match'.[29] One of these was a famous Victorian courtesan: 'Skittles
is here, but has not called on us; she goes about in a bath chair and
spectacles, not to be identified'.[30]

Between 1870 and 1873, the Du Mauriers went alternately to
Ramsgate and Folkestone, usually with the Friths and Brooks, but
the death of Shirley Brooks in 1874 broke this holiday pattern, and
left them free to explore new places. In 1874, they were encouraged
to go to the Isle of Wight by the Prinseps, who were there in force
with all their relatives and attendants. Mrs Prinsep's sister, Julia
Cameron, pursued her subjects, camera in hand, and the Du
Mauriers could not escape her attentions:

> Val was here painting in a box near the beacon – we used to go up there
> of an afternoon & be very jolly. He has done a very good thing there –
> downs and sheep. Watts' House is very jolly and he seems very well &
> happy – Mrs Cameron is without exception the greatest character I ever
> met; I find her delightful but don't think she would suit as a permanent
> next door neighbour for the next 30 years or so unless one could now &
> then get away. She is going to photograph May – also the Missus – also
> me. She says I have a fine head – (I had always suspected this.)[31]

Mrs Cameron's photographs of May (plate 9) are enchanting

28. To T. Armstrong, September 1871.   30. To T. Armstrong, September 1871.
29. To T. Armstrong, September 1871.   31. To T. Armstrong, September 1874.

KIND AND CONSIDERATE.

Maud (who, with Ethel, has just been invited to go for a Cruise in a friend's Yacht). "NOW, THE QUESTION IS, WHOM SHALL WE ASK TO CHAPERONE US?—OLD MRS. BUSBEE, OR OLD MISS MAJORIBANKS?"   *Maud.* "MRS. BUSBEE."
Jack (who is to be of the Party). "WHICH IS THE WORST SAILOR?"   *Maud.* "MRS. BUSBEE."
Jack. "O, THEN ASK HER! FOR THE SOONER SHE GOES DOWN BELOW THE BETTER, YOU KNOW."

67. Kind and Considerate, *Punch* (1874). In the centre
Mary Prinsep and Andrew Hichens

and much more successful than the Du Maurier family group (plate 8), but the latter does allow one to see exactly what Du Maurier and Emma looked like at this period. The photograph clearly does not flatter Emma, but it proves how much Du Maurier idealised her in his cartoons. The Du Mauriers enjoyed the Isle of Wight (they always liked to spend their holidays with friends), staying at Lorne Villa, Freshwater, spending their days on the beach (Beatrix had a passion for donkeys), or walking in the interior. The Prinsep's beautiful daughter, May, was in Freshwater, and Du Maurier noticed that Andrew Hichens, the future author of *The Green Carnation*, had 'quite lost his heart' to her: 'A.K.H. is a very good looking chap of 40 with loads of tin – He has hired a yacht of 64 tons & is going to take us cruising about the island'.[32] Du Maurier drew at least three *Punch* cartoons from May Prinsep, and two actually show her with Hichens, whom she later married. Another old acquaintance in Freshwater was G. F. Watts:

> Watts and I resumed our conversation here just where we left it off in Earls Terrace – it was about the beauty of the Elgin Marbles and the desirability of growing as like them as possible ... Tennyson coming back in a fortnight. He & I are to become bosom friends and spend the rest of our lives together – He does not know this.[33]

Holidays for the rest of the decade can only be roughly traced from the evidence of Du Maurier's *Punch* cartoons. In 1875, 1877, and 1880 they were abroad, first at Dieppe, then Le Havre and finally Étretat. With one exception, their visits to France were always to the channel ports. Until 1877, Du Maurier seems to have had no desire to plunge deeper into his native land, not at least when he had his family with him. The one exception, and the happiest of all these holidays, was taken in September 1877. The Du Mauriers went first to Ste Adresse, near Le Havre, for a seaside holiday. Beatrix was then fourteen and Gerald four, the ideal age limits for a family holiday. Du Maurier described it all in *The Martian*:

> It was very good fun to see those rosy boys and girls taking their 'hussardes' neatly without a splash from the little platform at the top of the pole, and solemnly performing 'la coupe' in the wake of their papa; one on his back.[34]

32. To T. Armstrong, September 1874.   34. pp. 430–1.
33. To T. Armstrong, September 1874.

On other days they went to Trouville and Deauville by sea, or up the Seine to Rouen:

> In the afternoons and evenings we took long country walks and caught moths, or went to Hâvre by tramway, and cleared out all the pastry-cooks in the Rue de Paris, and watched the transatlantic steamers, out or home, from that gay pier which so happily combines business with pleasure.[35]

The only trouble with Ste Adresse was that it produced in Du Maurier a disinclination to work. He remedied this state of affairs by moving the whole family to Auteuil, near Passy, and installing them in one of the Villas Montmorency at a rent of 1,200 francs a month. There he found it easier to concentrate, and the resulting cartoons all exploit traditional differences between the English and French, a subject which intrigued Du Maurier, which accounts for their success. The holiday was an enjoyable experiment and proved that Du Maurier could continue working satisfactorily abroad for long periods, three months in all. The only real drawback was the St Bernard, Chang, whom they had unwisely decided to take with them. Du Maurier derived enormous satisfaction from exhibiting such a large dog to the French. Chang seemed to be a triumphant symbol of his Englishness, but the triumph was dearly bought as he informed Tom Armstrong:

> I cannot describe all the trouble Chang has been ... what fiend induced me to tie such a millstone round my neck! We cannot sit outside a café, or stop at a shop window without a crowd collecting & I have to go thro' all the history of him; at hotels I have to take a bedroom à part, for him to sleep with me; he alternately drinks & snores all night & every time I move he comes & licks me in the dark; at every new place he howls the whole of the first night if alone & the railway journeys are too fearful! ... If I talk of parting with him there's a general howl all round, let alone my own fondness for the beast & his tyrannical affection for me, which would perhaps kill him if we were to separate.[36]

One day in Ste Adresse, three policemen called at the Du Mauriers' lodgings to see if they had paid the eight francs tax for Chang, but 'when they saw the dog, they preferred not meddling in the matter, as it is their duty to walk off the untaxed dog straight to the Mairie, & they didn't like the job'.[36]

35. p. 431.
36. To T. Armstrong, September 1877.

A FACT.—(FREE TRANSLATION.)

Custom-House Officer. "HAS YOUR DOG BEEN VERIFIED?"   *Brown.* "WHAT DO YOU MEAN?"

Custom-House Officer. "HAS HE BEEN PASSED BY THE VERIFICATOR, LIKE THE REST OF YOUR 'BAGAGES'?"   *Brown.* "MY DOG'S NOT A 'BAGAGE'!"

Custom-House Officer. "HE IS VERY *LARGE* FOR A DOG! HOW WOULD YOU THAT WE SHOULD KNOW IF HE DOES NOT CONTAIN OBJECTS OF CONTRABAND, *PARBLEU!*"

68. *Punch* (1877)

The villas Montmorency were in the Avenue de Tilleuls on the site of the old Villa near the Bois de Boulogne, and Du Maurier made it a starting point for yet another exploration of his childhood topography. It was his first visit to Paris since the Franco-Prussian war of 1870, when the Prussians had bombarded St Cloud, cut down much of the Bois de Boulogne and actually invaded Paris. Du Maurier was shocked by what he saw:

To tell you what a disappointment Paris is to me is impossible – as everything is changed so terribly since the war – All round here is the berceau of my enfance, and I had been accumulating tears to drop at every corner & under every tree – but all the corners are gone, and the beautiful trees, cut down during the war & the commune & replaced by a quite young growth. I am quite convinced that *nobody* can feel these things with the acuteness I do thro' peculiarities of circumstance & temperament.

Anything more painfully shorn of its glories than the Champs Elysées I defy you to show – all the trees gone; all the houses rebuilt except one fine old one and a few shabby ones. Our career 35 years ago being a wandering one from house to house all about here, there are still some houses left we have inhabited, but the ground floors turned into esta-minets or agencys & what not, and new streets destroying all the old landmarks.[37]

There were some less dispiriting moments. The Pension Froussard had long since been pulled down, but the gardens, attached to another house, were still there:

Nothing remained of our old school – not even the outer walls; nothing but the big trees and the absolute ground they grew out of. Beautiful lawns, flower-beds, conservatories, summer-houses, ferns, and evergreen shrubs made the place seem even larger than it had once been – the very reverse of what usually happens – and softened . . . the disenchantment of the change.[38]

On later visits to Passy, Du Maurier found even this garden dese-crated by new buildings, and he was eventually unable to tell where the site of his old school had been.

Perhaps because of the expense of their French holiday, the Du Mauriers were relatively unadventurous in 1878, when they spent their summer holiday at Witley in Surrey. They took the Manor House close to G. H. Lewes and George Eliot at 'The Heights'. When Thomas Trollope and his wife paid a two day visit to 'The Heights' from 21st to 23rd August, Lewes and George Eliot, both of whom were far from well, were afraid of boring them and invited the Du Mauriers to dinner: 'which went off very pleasantly, D.M. making himself extremely agreeable, singing and telling stories till 11 at night'.[39]

Early in 1874 the Du Mauriers had moved to New Grove House, their home for the next twenty years, and the Hampstead house generally associated with them. It had been built originally in the late eighteenth century, rather unfeelingly tacked onto the back of the much earlier Old Grove House, facing Grove Place. Around

37. To T. Armstrong, September 1877.   39. *George Eliot Letters*, VII, 64.
38. *The Martian*, p. 435.

1840, it was in Professor Pevsner's words, 'stuccoed and Tudor-ized',[40] and has, as a result, a rather gauche Victorian appearance. Today ivy covers most of the dark red brickwork, and the plaque executed to Du Maurier's memory is only just visible. Planned haphazardly on a variety of levels, it cannot have been the easiest house to run, or live in. It did, however, possess an extraordinarily light and spacious studio, which was its chief attraction for Du Maurier. There was also more room than the Du Mauriers had enjoyed in their earlier houses. 'This is a regular house for children', he said, 'a kindergarten for all ages'.[41] Du Maurier found it healthier than Church Row, a distinction difficult to appreciate, and several times informed his friends that the move definitely resulted in an improvement to his eyesight. If this was really so, the light studio may have been the cause, or more probably, a calmer family atmosphere as the children grew older.

A certain restlessness with his quiet life becomes evident in Du Maurier's letters from the late 'seventies. In 1893, writing to John Millais, and looking back over the last twenty-four years, he bitterly recalled that Val Prinsep, Guy's godfather, had never once come up the hill to visit them: 'So much for living in Hampstead!'[42] Hampstead was not the only reason for this neglect. Prinsep and Poynter were both settling down to high society life, Prinsep relying on family connections, Poynter making his way through his success as a painter. Poynter's career was the more spectacular, and must have aroused Du Maurier's jealousy. His old friend, who had married Agnes Macdonald, Georgiana Burne-Jones' sister, in 1866, became an A.R.A. in 1869, from then on his path led straight to the heights. In 1871 he was appointed Slade Professor of Art at University College, then in 1875 he became director and principal of the South Kensington Art School. In the following year he was elected a full Academician, and in the year of Du Maurier's death he succeeded John Millais as President; he was also director of the National Gallery from 1894 to 1904. Such a career was no more than Poynter deserved. If he was not a good painter, he was a first-rate administrator, and his National Gallery Catalogue is a work of considerable scholarship. Nevertheless, it was galling for Du Maurier to be cold-shouldered because he was less successful. By the 1880s they were no

---

40. *London except the cities of London and Westminster*, p. 193.   42. Millais, II, 278.
41. *Gerald*, p. 26.

more than nodding acquaintances, although there was a brief re-
sumption of friendship in the Isle of Wight in 1884. Du Maurier's
description of this encounter, written in a letter to Henry James,
shows how cynical he had become:

> One day walking we came across the Poynters who were at Bonchurch
> close by, & renewed our old intimacy, dined with each other & & & – You
> know them, I believe – when his stomach is in order, and he has got out of
> bed the right way, and the wind is in the proper quarter, & there are no
> dukes nor duchesses within hail, he can be one of the most delightful
> companions in the world –.[43]

Prinsep remained a bachelor until 1884, when he married the
heiress, Florence Leyland. Du Maurier found him easier to talk to
than Poynter, perhaps because Prinsep was less conscious of his
dignity and importance.

Of the old group only Armstrong and Lamont remained intimate
with Du Maurier, perhaps because their achievement as artists was
not very great. Lamont ceased to exhibit at the Royal Academy after
1880, and lived a quiet life in St John's Wood and on his estates in
Scotland, continuing with his watercolours. Like Lamont, Armstrong never became A.R.A., and his career was nearly as un-
distinguished until 1881 when he followed Poynter as director of the
South Kensington Museum. He remained very fond of the Du
Maurier family, but he did not often visit them in Hampstead, and
felt that newer friends were supplanting him in Du Maurier's
affections. He also married late, in 1881. After his death his wife
remembered having a

> general impression of their enjoyment of family life & the fun to be got
> out of it. Our visits, on Sunday evenings, were not so frequent after my
> husband's appointment as Director for Art at the South Kensington
> Museum, for Hampstead Heath was not so easy to reach then as it is
> now.[44]

In the light of Du Maurier's alienation from his oldest friends, it
is surprising his closest new friend was the most successful artist of the
day, John Millais. From the guarded distrust and envy of their early
meetings, Du Maurier had been won to warm affection, largely

43. 18 September 1884, Houghton Library, Harvard.
44. 10 May 1934.

because of Millais' behaviour at the time of John Leech's death. Much of their correspondence survives and provides an interesting contrast to the letters between Henry James and Du Maurier. Millais' letters are light, skittish, and humorous, typical of a warm friendship between men at this period. Millais was not very intelligent, and the topics covered in their letters reflect this limitation. One of their common passions was a love of huge men and women, and they had a flutter of excitement when a Canadian giantess arrived in London in 1869. She proved a bitter disappointment, however, chinless and all but brainless. Millais who was ill at the time, replied to Du Maurier's letter in verse:

> Dear du Maurier, you can't be sorrier –
> In lower spirits than I'm in
> As you express, the giantess'
> Failure is a *want of chin*.
>
> And oh! That goitre, as I loiter,
> Haunts me on the sad sea sand,
> It seems to mingle with the shingle
> That drowns the Hastings German band.[45]

Millais and Du Maurier would sometimes wander on Hampstead Heath, talking of their work and their respective families, telling atrocious stories, and cracking bad jokes. Less ambitious than Poynter, though far more successful, Millais appreciated Du Maurier's charm as a companion, and never demanded that his friends should be as successful as himself. Possibly Effie Millais, who did much to push her husband into society, thought differently, for she is rarely mentioned in their letters. The Millais children adored Du Maurier, and were delighted by his visits, especially when he brought the St Bernard, Chang, with him. They took the greatest interest in the dog's health, and it was with sadness that one day early in 1883, they informed a visitor, Beatrix Potter, that 'his big dog was dying'.[46]

Occasionally, Du Maurier would make the effort and go down to London for the evening, sometimes he went with Emma to dine with friends like the Millais or the Brooks, or on his own to attend the Wednesday *Punch* dinner, or Sir Henry Thompson's famous octave

45. J. G. Millais, *Life and Letters of J. G. Millais* (1899), II, 266.
46. Linder L., *The Journal of Beatrix Potter* (1966), p. 54.

dinners, restricted to eight men at eight o'clock for eight courses. Du Maurier always ordered the local cab for these evenings, unless it had already been reserved by Samuel Jealous, the editor of *Hampstead and Highgate Express*. Jealous was a friend of the Du Mauriers, and their rivalry for the one means of transport was a source of good-natured banter. Du Maurier argued that since Jealous lived below in the Vale of Health, he should give way to those who lived above him in the village itself. Neither of them could afford their own carriage, so, at the end of an evening in society, they invented preposterous names for themselves to conceal their humble conveyance. As the Hampstead cabman came to the door to collect Du Maurier, he would be told to announce: 'Sir Hampstead Landau's Carriage' or 'The Duke of Montmorency's carriage stops the way'; Du Maurier still remembered that the palace of Auteuil had belonged to the Duke of Montmorency; Jealous, less flamboyant, preferring the simpler 'Mr Montmorency's Cab'. In his cartoons, which were usually based on his own experiences in society, Du Maurier several times explored the theme of the carriageless snob, anxious to disguise his hired cab. He himself seems to have suffered from no sense of deprivation or social inferiority on that score, but regarded the matter with a certain wry amusement.

On Sunday afternoons Du Maurier often visited George Eliot and G. H. Lewes, who were then 'at home' at The Priory, Regent's Park. Unfortunately he left no written account of these occasions, although he drew at least one unflattering sketch of George Eliot, which Armstrong later reproduced in his memoir of Du Maurier. It is hard to imagine Du Maurier at 'The Priory', where intellectual prowess, and an accompanying high seriousness, resulted in a rather gloomy atmosphere, but his characteristic blend of sophistication and charm soon won the hearts of this strange couple. Writing to his son, Charles Lee Lewes, in 1872, G. H. Lewes asked after 'that dear fellow? I wish I could see his sweet smile and hear his delicious voice occasionally'.[47] Tom Armstrong, who had been at 'The Priory' some years earlier was frankly amazed at reports of Du Maurier's singing little French songs in such a setting:

> it seems to me that the tone must have altered very much in a few years, and . . . become 'joliment dégourdi' to call for and relish so frivolous an

47. *The George Eliot Letters*, V, 278.

entertainment. I wish I had kept up my visits and had been witness of the process of demoralisation.[48]

Frederick Locker Lampson, who was a witness, found the recitals a great relief:

for unless Du Maurier sang, or W. K. Clifford talked, or Vivier, the horn-blower, gave one of his impersonations, her *réunions* had somewhat of the solemnity of religious functions, with the religion cut out.[49]

Both G. H. Lewes and George Eliot so far descended from their Olympian heights as to send Du Maurier jokes for *Punch*, and their

69. George Eliot (*c* 1878)

'demoralisation' even extended to 'The Priory' dinner parties, as George Eliot explained in January 1872:

Next Saturday we are going to have a party – six to dine, and a small rush of people after dinner, for the sake of music. I think it is four years at least since we undertook anything of that kind.[50]

48. Armstrong, p. 30.
49. *My Confidences* (1896) p. 310.
50. *The George Eliot Letters*, edited
G. S. Haight (Yale, 1956), V, 238.

Du Maurier, Emma, Charles Lewes and Miss Gillies were among 'the small rush' after dinner, but it is not known whether Du Maurier sang or not.

Probably not, for he was passing through a period of intense depression. The threat of blindness, quiescent for many years, had suddenly become a terrifying possibility again, when his good eye began to cloud over in the New Year of 1872. On New Year's Eve Du Maurier was at Shirley Brooks' annual party in Kent Terrace, and Brooks noted in his diary: 'Kiki sang excellently'. On 3 January, however, Brooks received a 'sad' note from his cartoonist, who had been ordered to give up work for a time in order to save his failing eyesight. Two cartoons, already submitted, appeared on 6 January 1872, but the next six issues contained none by Du Maurier. A certain amount of doubt exists about the actual method by which the *Punch* staff were paid, but Du Maurier seems to have calculated his own income in terms of the number of cartoons actually published. Even if he did receive a regular retainer, he could not expect the paper to continue to support a blind and useless artist for any length of time. In this frightful extremity, Du Maurier's scarcely submerged fears flooded to the surface, and he panicked. He was thirty-seven, the father of four little children, and he had saved nothing. Memories of the hand-to-mouth existence of his own childhood came into his mind, and mingled with the realization that he had led Emma into the same position. The doctors, whom he frantically consulted, were reasonably hopeful, but could not give him the definite assurance necessary to his mental equilibrium. Shirley Brooks' diary as usual contains the most honest account of what Du Maurier was really feeling:

> Dear old Kiki called. He came up to my den. At first he was hysterical, but soon rallied. I think he chiefly wanted to talk to a friend, but his desire was to know whether, if he ceased to be able to draw, his writing could be available, on which I gave him the strongest assurance that it could and should. But I did not gather that Bowman, the great oculist, has given him reason to despond – rather the contrary, but K. declares he knows himself & his constitution best. It is very sad to see him, so full of life, & esprit, & affection, mournful for such a cause.[51]

It was not until 14 January that Du Maurier's oculists could give him a favourable report on his eye. This soothed his more extreme

51. Brooks' Diary, 4 January 1872.

fears, but the effects of those eleven days of agonising suspense lasted until the end of his life. Since Malines he had been moderately hopeful that his sight would never seriously fail, now he knew that it might go at any moment without warning. This encouraged his latent parsimony, and made him conscious of every penny which he earned. He had always tried to keep his original drawings, but now he made it a rule, and his tin box full of them became a familiar article of family furniture. 'These will make you a rich widow' he told Emma, an inaccurate but consoling reflection. He never again escaped from the spectre of poverty and even in his last years, when the success of *Trilby* had made him a rich man, he continued to resent any unnecessary expenditure. For his children, brought up in an atmosphere of cheese-paring, this was particularly galling.

The threat of blindness gave Du Maurier a severe shock, but more serious than its effect on his personality, was its effect on his work. Since his marriage, he had been drawing fluently and successfully, only his *Punch* cartoons showing signs of inevitable repetition in design and technique. When the doctors allowed him to resume work in February 1872, it was with the proviso that he should draw on a much larger scale in order to avoid eye-strain. His finished drawings were now as much as twice as large as the published cartoons, and had to be reduced by photographic process before the blocks were made. Du Maurier found it extremely difficult to adapt to the increased scale and his first cartoon published after his eye trouble 'Hobson's Choice', is ungainly and out of perspective. Trained to work on a small and intimate scale he could not simplify or broaden his style, and his drawings lose their assurance and clarity. Writing to the engraver Swain, who was taking so much trouble on his behalf, Du Maurier hoped that he would soon 'get into the way of drawing less elaborately'.[52] He never did, and his period of creative achievement was over. Relapsing into stereotyped formulas, he took less trouble with his work, content to exploit a large but not unlimited stock of themes and motifs. The demands which new subjects and new editors had made upon his draughtsmanship in the 1860s had led to some extraordinarily powerful designs. *Punch* ceased to make such demands, and whether or not he recognised it, Du Maurier had thrown up the creative sponge. Though he was the first person to insist that illustrators were artists and not hacks, his own example did not lend very eloquent support to his argument.

52. University of Texas Library.

HOBSON'S CHOICE.

Ethel. "Isn't it Sad, Arthur? There's the Drawing-Room cleared for a Dance, and all the Dolls ready to Begin, only they've got no Partners!"

Arthur. "Well, Ethel! There's the Four Gentlemen in my Noah's Ark; but they don't Look as if they cared very much about *Dancing*, you know!"

70. *Punch* (1872)

As in the case of his friend, John Millais, public approval was a more comfortable and complacent method of measuring success than searching self-analysis.

Du Maurier's return to work was a relief to his friends, who had been disturbed and often embarrassed by his despair and lack of control. Noticing how gloomy Du Maurier was at his evening party in late January, G. H. Lewes asked him the reason, and was appalled to discover the abyss over which he was poised. More practical than Du Maurier's other friends, he at once decided to help, and acting on a suggestion of Frederick Locker Lampson's, began to collect signatures from people willing to give money if Du Maurier should go blind. The signatories included Dean Stanley, G. F. Watts, George Howard and Sir Frederic Burton. It is not known if Du Maurier was aware of the efforts made on his behalf, but his gift of a drawing to Lewes in the summer 'as a mark of affectionate regard' suggests that he did. When Lewes died in December 1878, Du Maurier wrote to his son: 'I like to think how much he has been in my thought lately, and I realise in great distress of mind that I have lost a good friend whom I shall always remember with warm gratitude and affection'.[53]

Du Maurier was too mercurial a character to be cast down by his misfortune for long, although the memory always remained at the back of his mind. Writing to his old Dusseldorf friend, Mrs Fortescue, he remarked philosophically: 'I have suffered much from my sight, but it has not affected my spirits in the way it used to do'.[54] Shirley Brooks, editor of *Punch* since Mark Lemon's death in 1870, was impressed by his determination not to allow his work to be affected, writing to him on his thirty-ninth birthday in 1873:

> I think you have every reason to be glad – specially, your artistic repute has been greatly advanced this year, and what seemed a discouragement has actually assisted you with higher excellence of execution.[55]

As Brooks wrote a similar note in his diary, he was presumably sincere, and, with Du Maurier's other contemporaries, felt that there had been no decline in the quality of his work. Du Maurier was grateful for Brooks' appreciation, and replied with a sketch of himself 'holding the said letter, and pointing to a likeness of me [Brooks] in his heart, inscribed "*Cor Cordium*" and below "Enshrined"'.[56]

53. *The George Eliot Letters*, VII, 84.
54. 10 April 1873, Historical Society of Pennsylvania Library.
55. 6 March 1873.
56. G. S. Layard, *Life, Letters & Diaries of Shirley Brooks of 'Punch'* (1907), p. 536.

Du Maurier's happiest years on *Punch* were those under the editor-ship of Mark Lemon and Shirley Brooks. Both were men whom he respected, and both were considerably older than himself. Brooks' death on 23 February 1874 was a tragedy for the paper, and a source of personal sorrow to Du Maurier. Emma and he had gone to the Brooks' New Year's Eve Party as usual, with W. P. Frith and his wife and Frank Burnand. Another guest, Mark Twain, proposed the toast to host and hostess. Writing to Percival Leigh, Brooks said: 'Kiki sang French songs *exquisitely*. I wish you could hear some of his *chansons*'.[57] At the end of January, Brooks, who had already been warned that his heart was not strong, was seized with another attack of gout, and developed a hacking cough. He soon became seriously ill, but continued working in bed until his death, a great profes-sional to the last:

> On the morning of the 23rd he looks over the forthcoming number of *Punch*, and makes some suggestions. A boy is waiting below for 'copy'. Shirley writes a small make-up paragraph, asks for a cigar, takes a couple of whiffs, '*looks very surprised*', and falls back dead.[58]

Du Maurier's first ten years on *Punch*, under Mark Lemon and Shirley Brooks, saw few changes either in the paper or the staff. Henry Silver left at the time of Lemon's death to become a successful lawyer, and his unique record of *Punch* activities, written up in the *Punch* diary, came to an end. Shirley Brooks' diary, although less directly concerned with the Wednesday dinners, does show, however, that the atmosphere of boisterous communal effort was maintained until his death in February 1874. Believing, like Lemon, that changes were bound to have an adverse effect on the magazine, Brooks made only one significant appointment, promoting an outside contributor, Linley Sambourne, to full membership in 1871. 'Sammy', as he was called, was one of the liveliest members of the staff, a constant source of amusement with his naïve jokes, spoonerisms and mixed metaphors. An original and subtle artist, he possessed a sophistica-tion far in advance of his time and provides a link between the 1860s and Aubrey Beardsley, although his elaborate studies of ladies dressed as birds seem curiously out of place in the solid mid-Victorian *Punch* of Tom Taylor and Frank Burnand. Taylor was an obvious choice to succeed Brooks and he was duly appointed editor. He had

57. Layard, p. 581.
58. Layard, p. 586.

1. George Du Maurier, self-portrait in watercolour

Fontainebleau
March. 58.

Sketch of E. J. Poynter by

2. Edward John Poynter, as
a student in Paris 1858.
From a drawing by an
unknown contemporary

3. Miniature of George Du
Maurier as a young man, by
an unknown artist

4. James Abbott McNeil Whistler in Paris 1856.
From a lost drawing by Edward John Poynter

5. George Du Maurier in Paris. From a self-portrait
in oils, executed in Paris in 1856 or 1857

6. Emma Du Maurier, from an unfinished oil
painting by George Du Maurier

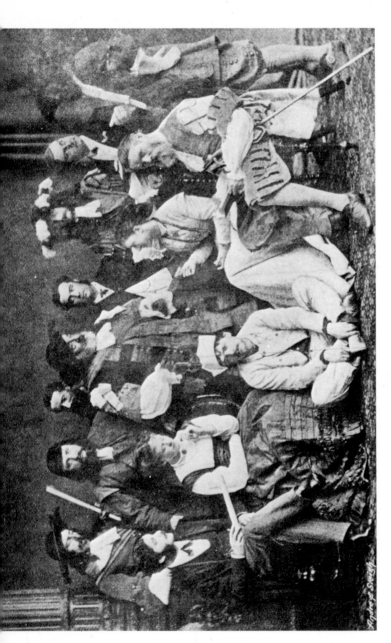

7. *Cox and Box*, 1867. The cast were photographed in their costumes by the London Stereoscopic Company. From left to right, standing: R. T. Pritchett, Shirley Brooks, Arthur Lewis, Mark Lemon, Quentin Twiss, John Tenniel, Arthur Blunt (later Arthur Cecil), Henry Silver. Seated: Arthur Sullivan, Ellen Terry, George Du Maurier, Kate Terry, Tom Taylor

8. [*opposite*] George and Emma Du Maurier with their third daughter Marie Louise (May). This photograph was taken by Julia Margaret Cameron at Freshwater, Isle of Wight in September 1874

9. [*opposite*] May Du Maurier, from a photograph taken by Julia Margaret Cameron in 1874

10. *Sponsa de Libano* by Edward Burne-Jones, 1891, with its clusters of lilies and swirling draperies, this painting illustrates the qualities which made Burne-Jones so popular with the aesthetes

11. *The Private View of the Royal Academy*, 1881 by W. P. Frith. Sir John Millais is the second figure from the right, and Henry Stacy Marks the fourth. Oscar Wilde is prominent among a group of aesthetic admirers on the right of the picture

The heads of John Tenniel and George Du Maurier can be seen between the two aesthetic ladies on the left

12. Canon Alfred Ainger, from the
watercolour by George Du Maurier, 1881

13. Henry James, from the lithograph by
Rudolph Lehmann 1887

14. George Du Maurier, from the portrait in oils by
J. E. Millais, 1882

15. May Du Maurier, from the watercolour by
George Du Maurier, 1889

17. The *Punch* staff at the Paris Exhibition, 1887.
They are, from left to right: Sir Henry Lucy,
Harry Furniss, W. H. Bradbury, Sir William
Agnew, Frank Burnand, Arthur À. Beckett,
John Tenniel, E. J. Milliken, George Du Maurier

16. [*opposite*] George Du Maurier, from a self-
portrait in oils in the National Portrait Gallery.
The Gallery tentatively attributes the work to Du
Maurier himself, but it is almost certainly by his
hand. Thomas Armstrong refers to an unfinished
oil self-portrait executed many years after Du
Maurier left Paris, and this portrait, which belonged
to his family is apparently the one in question

18. George Du Maurier, from a photograph taken
in the last years of his life. The desk at which he is
working now belongs to Miss Jeanne Du Maurier

been with the paper since 1844, and commanded considerable respect outside as a playwright and critic. The son of a self-educated labourer, who had risen to be head of a brewery firm, Taylor was thought to be something of a social climber. He was also one of the finest scholars ever to work on *Punch*, having been Professor of English Language and Literature at London University for two years, as well as a barrister, and an official on the board of health. He was also the regular art critic of *The Times* and *The Graphic*, and wrote a long series of popular and successful plays.

In spite of his varied talents, Taylor was not an inspired editor of *Punch*:

> It cannot be said that his editorship was a success. His fun was too scholarly and well-ordered, too veiled, deliberate, and ponderous; and under him *Punch* touched its lowest point of popularity.[59]

Although the paper continued with what remained of the old team (Horace Mayhew had died in 1872), the loss of Brooks was nearly catastrophic, for he had not only been a first-rate comic writer, but a superb co-ordinator. Edwin J. Milliken was appointed to replace him in 1877, and together with Burnand, he eventually helped to rescue the paper from its humourless pomposity. A rival magazine published a cartoon during this era, entitled 'An Editor Abroad', which showed Burnand and Du Maurier trying to push Taylor and his *Punch* show out of the mud. There is no reason to suppose that Du Maurier disliked Taylor personally, for he often referred to him by affectionate nicknames, like 'Old Cockalorum', but it was during his editorship that Du Maurier began to cut himself off from the society of his *Punch* colleagues. Like the others he found it hard to behave calmly when illegible and dictatorial instructions were sent to him in Hampstead. Brooks had left Du Maurier alone, unless he thought interference absolutely necessary, as he did in April 1872:

> Wrote Kiki that I had altered the legend to one of his pictures. I seldom alter the legends, but of course hold the right to do so, if I see aught objectionable, or if a print can be mended. Both were the case here.[60]

But, where Brooks was the soul of discretion, Taylor continually sent unwanted letters of advice and instruction. Towards the end of

---

59. M. H. Spielmann, *The History of Punch* (1895), p. 340.
60. Brooks' Diary, 7 April 1872.

Taylor's reign, Du Maurier began to inject new life into the magazine
with his great series of aesthetic cartoons. He was understandably
angry when Taylor told him to shorten the caption of some of his
cartoons, and take out a reference to Darwin, for fear of antagonizing
public opinion. His reply expresses scarcely concealed sarcasm:

> The temptation is sometimes great to give Prigsby's language, for in-
> stance, which is as characteristic as his appearance – But you know best,
> having the best means of knowing, and I will avoid subjects requiring
> long legends – also the breeding subject; which I regret, as I had many
> more notions – I of course did not feel the subject coarsely – It is in the
> air, & an important one, but perhaps *Punch* is not the place to treat it –
> altho' it was treated pretty openly in a *Times* leader. Times are changed
> since Mark Lemon – but still . . .[61]

If Du Maurier had justification for this letter, he was perhaps on
less certain ground when he asked for more money in 1880. He had
become a better social commentator by then, but he had sadly declined as an artist. Was he entirely unaware of this when he wrote the
following letter to William Bradbury, Manager of *Punch*?

> The time has come when I think I may fairly ask you to make an increase
> in my salary.
>   The quality of my work has greatly improved of late years and my
> popularity has grown in proportion, and these results have been ob-
> tained at great expense of thought and labour, and I find as a rule that
> the more time I devote to each production, the more favour it meets
> with from the public.[62]

Du Maurier was given his rise, but the amount is not recorded.

61. 1880, Charles Roberts Autograph Collection of the Haverford College Library.
62. Wood, p. 153.

71. Sketch for 'How we
slept at the Chalet des
Chevres', *Cornhill*
(1863)

Chapter 7

The Aesthetic Movement

IT WAS UNDER TOM TAYLOR's pedantic and unimaginative rule that Du Maurier began his sustained and brilliant cartoon series on the aesthetes. During the mid-1870s he became increasingly aware of their existence, and their indulgence in an elaborate cult of beauty. They were to be an important feature of the London scene until the exposure and fall of Oscar Wilde in 1895. Du Maurier was fascinated by the outward signs of changing taste, and he very soon noticed that certain ladies had taken to wearing loose and unconventional dresses, and flat shoes. At the same time the craze for blue-and-white china started, and Du Maurier was soon launched on a major satirical attack on the new movement.

A certain confusion is evident in contemporary and later comment on the aesthetic movement of the 'seventies and 'eighties. Contemporary commentators were unable to dissociate it from the later activities of the Pre-Raphaelite Brotherhood, while few recent critics have attempted to distinguish it from the succeeding, but not synonymous, fin-de-siècle movement of the 'nineties. That Du Maurier was not concerned with the last movement is made clear when we remember that Aubrey Beardsley, in some ways the most characteristic figure of that era, published his first illustrations for the Dent *Morte d'Arthur* in 1893, eleven years after Du Maurier's last aesthetic cartoon. The *Yellow Book*, of which he was art editor, did not come out till 1894, two years before the cartoonist's death.

The origins of the aesthetic movement are open to wide speculation, and difficult to define with any certainty. The term 'aesthetic' was first applied to the criticism of taste by the German philosophers of the eighteenth century, and gradually became current in England in the early nineteenth century. It was Paris, however, and not Germany, which provided the main stimulus for the English aesthetes. Among the first important events there was the publication, in 1835, of Théophile Gautier's novel, *Mlle. de Maupin*. In the character of D'Albert, the hero, Gautier portrays a man who is externally beautiful, but rotten within, and his preface to the novel is an important document in the history of 'art for art's sake'. Discussing the different functions of the 'useful' and the 'beautiful', he writes:

> There is nothing truly beautiful but that which can never be of any use whatsoever; everything useful is ugly, for it is the expression of some need, and man's needs are vile and disgusting like his own poor and infirm nature. The most useful place in a house is the water-closet.[1]

His concept of beauty is not restricted to the visual, for he continues:

> I would willingly consent, so far as I am concerned, to the return of the anthropophagous Charles X, if he brought me back a hamper of Tokay or Johannisberger from his Bohemian castle.[2]

Gautier is the most eloquent of those early French writers usually considered as the forerunners of the aesthetic movement. This was not because he was the best, but because he summarized his views succinctly in one place. Baudelaire's influence cannot be shown from any definite statement of his position; rather it is implicit in his poetry. In 1857, he published *Les Fleurs du Mal*, which, with their

1. T. Gautier, *Mlle. de Maupin* (1835), translated by A. C. Bessie (New York, 1930), p. 413.
2. Gautier, p. 414.

72. Fleur des Alpes,
    Punch (1880)

distilled fragrance and strange, mysterious sensuality, opened up a new field of poetic sensibility. At the time they were first published, and for the rest of the century, they raised a storm of protest, because of their perversity, amorality and eroticism. Baudelaire's poems were to become a byword for the 'decadence' of the 'nineties, but in the 'seventies and 'eighties they were still relatively unknown in England.

The French writers of the 'thirties and 'forties, Gerard de Nerval, Gautier and Baudelaire, had been activated by something more than a love of beauty or a craving for sensation. They were anxious to 'épater le bourgeois', and to flaunt the values of a hypocritical and conventional society. This desire to shock was nothing new. It had provided a stimulus to the romantic movement, and informed some of the more eccentric activities of poets like Byron and Shelley.

John Keats was a major influence on the English aesthetic movement. It is possible to see in his medieval poems, 'The Eve of Saint Agnes', 'Isabella', and 'La Belle Dame Sans Merci', an attempt to escape from the tedium of everyday existence. In the more idyllic 'Endymion', the escape is into a world of dreams. To see Keats in this light is a little limiting, but it was certainly the reason why the Pre-Raphaelites admired him so much; they were largely responsible for popularizing his poetry after a period of neglect. It was the romantic narrative, the lusciousness and colour of Keats' poetry, that particularly attracted them, and led to their illustrating so many incidents from his poems in their early pictures. They did not, perhaps, appreciate the intellectual strength that underlay his writing. The looseness and emptiness of much of Rossetti's and Swinburne's verse contrasts strongly with Keats' essential control, the way he is able to link his thought with his words, and to make every adjective add to the whole, rather than merely providing local colour.

Ruskin had defended the Pre-Raphaelites in their early days, and his reputation as an art critic was very great from the 1850s onwards. His importance here lies in the new outlook to the visual arts which he succeeded in introducing to the British public. His quarrel with Whistler, and his dislike of 'art for art's sake', implicit in his lifelong fight for a true morality in art, tend to disguise his very real link with the aesthetic credo. By imparting his pleasure in art and nature, he did much to revive a sense of beauty in an age of increasing industrialization and materialism. Ruskin was not always able to reconcile his essentially sensuous nature with the demands of morality,

but his enthusiasm, his richly jewelled prose, his intense love of the
early Italian painters, attracted the attention and admiration of the
aesthetes.

The most important single influence on the English aesthetic
movement was, however, Walter Pater. Like Ruskin he wrote about
Italian painters, but from a very different standpoint. In the
'Conclusion' to his book of essays, *The Renaissance*, first published in
1873, Pater outlined his philosophy of beauty. Life, he says, should
be an attempt to experience as many moments of exquisite awareness as possible: 'To burn always with this hard gem-like flame, to
maintain this ecstacy, is success in life'. A man should spend his days
in 'high passions', and the best are those of 'art and song'.[3] Pater did
not live according to his philosophy. He was rather shocked by
Oscar Wilde, and withdrew his 'Conclusion' from the 1877 edition of
The Renaissance, because it might lead young men astray. Pater was
the complete antithesis of the aesthetes satirized by Du Maurier, and
there are no direct references to him in Du Maurier's cartoons.

Deriving as it did from the ideas and attitudes of various writers,
painters and thinkers, what we now call the aesthetic movement
began to affect social behaviour and the arts in widely differing
ways. If we find it difficult to make the necessary, if apparently
artificial, step of dividing it from the decadent movement of the
'nineties, contemporary commentators failed to see any difference
between the aesthetes and the Pre-Raphaelites. An example of the
prevailing muddle is found in the memoirs of Mrs J. Comyns Carr,
wife of one of the directors of the Grosvenor Gallery. Talking of the
popularity of Oscar Wilde in the years between Oxford and America
(1878–1881), she describes him as a type of the Pre-Raphaelite
movement, something which Wilde, born six years after the Brotherhood was founded, most certainly was not.[4] Another contemporary
writer, and a staunch defender of the aesthetes, Walter Hamilton,
talks in his book, *The Æsthetic Movement in England*, of those painters,
'who are known either as Pre-Raphaelites, Impressionists, or
Æsthetes'.[5]

It appeared at the time that the Pre-Raphaelites were connected
with the latest aesthetic trends in house decoration, language and

---

3. W. Pater, 'Conclusion', *Studies in The History of The Renaissance* (1873).
4. *Reminiscences of Mrs J. Comyns Carr*, edited by Eve Adam (1926), p. 86.
5. W. Hamilton, *The Aesthetic Movement in England* (1882), 3rd revised edition
(1882), p. 31.

dress, which were later adopted as 'a craze' by people quite un-connected with them. The influence of certain personalities gave rise to this confusion. Dante Gabriel Rossetti, with his romantic poetry, his interest in the medieval, and his paintings of strange, unearthly women, appeared to be at the centre of an aesthetic cult, and a leader of the aesthetic movement. This was even more true of Morris and Burne-Jones, who, though not aesthetes in any sense, were closely identified with the movement in the public mind. It was Rossetti again, who, with Whistler, began the craze for collecting blue-and-white china. Whistler, one of the painters associated with aesthetic tendencies in art, was frequently seen with Rossetti, and Algernon Swinburne, the great aesthetic poet, lived for a time in Rossetti's house in Cheyne Walk, Chelsea. Rossetti seemed to be involved in both the aesthetic and the Pre-Raphaelite movements, and it was assumed, quite erroneously, that the movements themselves were the same. One difference is immediately apparent. The Pre-Raphaelites, although they quickly disintegrated as a group, were in theory moving together towards a common end. There never was an aesthete group, nor were there any real leaders. Pater was shocked by Wilde, Burne-Jones spoke against Whistler at the famous 'Whistler v. Ruskin trial', William Morris was wholly out of sympathy with the refined clients who bought his furnishings. Always a set of individuals, those who influenced the aesthetic movement never indulged in the excesses of their undiscerning disciples, whom Du Maurier found both amusing and disgraceful. There was nothing affected or effete about Burne-Jones, Morris, Rossetti or Whistler, all of whom were masculine and positive personalities.

It is, nevertheless, untrue to say, like Hesketh Pearson, that 'there was no such thing as the aesthetic Movement',[6] if 'movement' is thought of, not as a coherent group, but as a mood affecting large numbers of people. Perhaps it is best compared to the beat move-ment of today, which has few strict adherents and no central body of leaders, but has affected students and young people everywhere; people who, like the aesthetic disciples, wear the clothes and adopt what suits them of the philosophy. The similar spread of beat culture, to those among whom social revolt is particularly prevalent, makes easier an understanding of the real relations between Pre-Raphael-itism and aestheticism. Both movements were rebelling against a popular ethos and an established way of life, and, set in a Victorian

6. H. Pearson, *The Life of Oscar Wilde* (1946), p. 43.

context, both stood out in startling clarity from conventional patterns. No modern critic could write about trends in contemporary art and literature with the burning moral indignation found in the critics of the Pre-Raphaelites. One has only to cite Buchanan's attack on the 'Fleshly School of Poetry',[7] which was aimed at Rossetti and Swinburne, to see how savage those critics could be. The Pre-Raphaelite rebellion sufficiently undermined established values in art and literature to allow for a wider mood of revolt. The succeeding aesthetic movement was not just an ineffective, social rebellion by a minority, but a formative influence on culture and fashion. Taste in clothes, and to a large extent in house decoration, is nearer to aesthetic standards today, than to those of the mid-Victorians.

The early aesthetes were a butt for many satirists. James Laver describes the position of *Punch* in his life of Whistler:

> During this period *Punch*, than which there is no more accurate reflection of the opinions and prejudices of the more philistine of the British upper middle classes, devoted a considerable portion of its space every week to ridicule of the Aesthetes. The master of the revels was Du Maurier.[8]

Du Maurier's aesthetic cartoons, apparently humorous and light-hearted, really concealed his bitter distrust of Whistler and Rossetti, which the quiet years in Hampstead had done nothing to ameliorate. Whistler had remained loyal to the bohemian and unconventional precepts of his youth, which Du Maurier had abandoned for middle-class family life and social standing. That Du Maurier, who had already satirized the Pre-Raphaelites and Swinburne, should attack the aesthetes is readily understandable. Disliking affectation of any kind, he was eager to find subjects which were amusing in themselves and also required deflating. Du Maurier's aesthete cartoons must also be seen in the wider context of his comments on social behaviour in general. His treatment of the rise of the professional classes and the nouveaux riches, as typified by Mrs Ponsonby de Tomkyns and Sir Gorgius Midas, reveals his essential snobbery, conservatism and loathing of change. Henry James was entirely in agreement with Du Maurier about the aesthetes. He attributed

7. Thomas Maitland (pseud. R. W. Buchanan), 'The Fleshly School of Poetry: Mr D. G. Rossetti', *Contemporary Review*, XVIII (October 1871), pp. 334–50.
8. J. Laver, *Whistler* (1930), 2nd (revised) edition (1951), pp. 138–9.

their excessive enthusiasm for certain types of art and literature to a lack of real aesthetic discrimination, typical of the English, and felt that Du Maurier's correct evaluation of them was due to his French blood, and to the irony of the 'thorough-going artist'.[9]

James and Du Maurier were not the only critics of a movement, which, like all intense enthusiasms, laid itself open to parody. W. H. Mallock had given a satirical portrait of Pater as Mr Rose in *The New Republic*, published in 1877. Rose's conversation is essentially vacuous and sensuous, a clever parody of Pater's own highly subjective prose, but entirely lacking its serious meaning and intention. Like Du Maurier's cartoon characters, Rose is yearning for exquisite sensations, and, in this sense, he represents an attack on Pater's followers, rather than on Pater himself.

Gilbert's libretto for *Patience* is the best known satire on the aesthetes. It was produced at the Opéra Comique in London on 23 April 1881, and ridicules two aesthetes, Bunthorne and Grosvenor. Much of the comedy of the piece is provided by the three officers, who dress up as aesthetes in order to win back their girl-friends from Bunthorne. The script is an extensive satire on aesthetic language, colour, poetry and admiration for the medieval. The characters were dressed in full aesthetic costume.

A more serious satire on aestheticism is Vernon Lee's first novel, *Miss Brown*, published in 1884. Walter Hamlin, a fleshly poet, finds a young and beautiful servant-girl, Anne Brown, whom he educates with a view to marrying her later. Much of the book is concerned with her impressions of the aesthetic circle in London, with which her natural common-sense is contrasted. Hamlin is partly drawn from D. G. Rossetti, and much of the satire is directed against the Pre-Raphaelites. In comparison with Du Maurier's cartoons, *Miss Brown* suffers from an unsettled viewpoint. At the opening of the book Hamlin is appalled by the excellently described 'lank, limp, lantern-jawed . . . Sapphic profile'[10] of Mrs Perry, yet it later transpires that Hamlin himself is an arch-aesthete. Although the book is now largely forgotten, it is a witty and caustic comment on the London of the period.

The aesthetes, on the other hand, were less eloquent in their own defence. Walter Hamilton, a fellow of the Royal Geographical Society, is the most interesting of their advocates, and the best

9. Henry James, 'George Du Maurier', *Partial Portraits* (1888), pp. 370–1.
10. V. Lee, *Miss Brown* (1884), I, 9.

contemporary writer on the subject. Although not an aesthete himself, he was greatly in sympathy with their aims. Hamilton attacked Gilbert's *Patience*, and Frank Burnand's *The Colonel* in particular, but he believed that they had

> taken hints from a journal which had, at one time, some claim to the title of a *comic* paper.
>
> But supposing a small percentage of the theatre-goers to have traced a resemblance between the dramatic characters and the Maudles, Postlethwaites and Company, of the aforesaid comic paper, the question would still arise, as to whether Maudle, Postlethwaite and Company were purely imaginary individuals, or were living and walking in our midst, and so grossly deceiving the world with sham Art, Poetry, and Criticism, as to deserve to be subjected to the scorn and derision of all people of intellect and education, and to find their pictures, poems, and essays laughed out of the market, and themselves reduced to living in the unromantic humdrum manner of ordinary civilized beings.
>
> But the fact is, that Maudle and Company, as portrayed, were not altogether imaginary individuals, but belonged to a comparatively new school, which has done, and is still doing, an immense amount of good towards the advancement of Art in this country and in America. That there are persons of Aesthetic tastes who carry them to the borders of absurdity goes without saying; every movement in intellectual, or political, life has its over-enthusiastic apostles, who damage the cause they have at heart; but that there must be *some* good in the movement is clearly shown by its having earned the abuse of a journal which never has a generous word to say for any one beyond its own immediate and narrow circle.[11]

There is no detailed criticism by Hamilton of the actual aesthetic cartoons, and he concludes by saying that Du Maurier's cartoons if 'somewhat impersonal', were not 'unkindly' in their approach.[12] Hamilton's most pungent criticism is reserved for F. C. Burnand's play, *The Colonel* (1881), which he dismisses as 'Plagiarism'. His complaint that the audience of the play, and the readers of *Punch*, knew nothing 'about Æstheticism before it was made the target of our sneering satirists',[13] is undoubtedly a sound one. Hamilton's little book maintains a fairly objective view-point, examines in detail the actual development of the movement, and does much to redress the balance of ridicule. He is not a profound or philosophical writer, and he ignores the wider issues of aestheticism. When he describes the

11. Hamilton, pp. v–vi.   13. Hamilton, p. 93.
12. Hamilton, p. 91.

colony at Turnham Green, for instance, he conveys an accurate impression of the neighbourhood, without labouring his conclusions. Muddled as he is about the Pre-Raphaelite connection, he is a useful guide to the events and atmosphere of the period.

Du Maurier's aesthete cartoons are widely scattered in *Punch* over the nine years during which they appeared (1873–82). Until the advent of Mrs Cimabue Brown in 1877, and Maudle and Postle-thwaite in 1880, the only effective unity is provided by the 'china-mania' series, which are linked by theme and not by personalities. These eleven cartoons on the blue-and-white china craze appeared at wide intervals between May 1874 and December 1877, with one later example in 1880. Du Maurier's cartoons give considerable insight into the way that the aesthetic movement snowballed, and help to establish the pattern of events, as they appealed to the eye of the cartoonist.

Mrs Cimabue Brown is the figure usually remembered in con-nection with the aesthete cartoons, but in fact she only appears on ten occasions. The choice of her name reveals the cartoonist's very considerable gifts in this direction. Du Maurier not only makes use of the artistic significance of Cimabue, but allies those four syllables, so redolent of early Florence, with the most prosaic English surname. A parallel use was made by Max Beerbohm in his short-story, 'Savon-arola Brown', published in *Seven Men* in 1919. The lady herself, with her haggard appearance, is the leader of a similar circle of friends. Mrs J. Comyns Carr wrote in her memoirs:

> when George Du Maurier's Mrs Cimabue Brown appeared in *Punch* as the companion-figure to Postlethwaite its origin was commonly attri-buted to the wife of the director of the Grosvenor Gallery [i.e. herself].[14]

Mrs Comyns Carr, a friend of the Du Mauriers, based her claim on her clothes, which seem to fit the part (she was a theatrical costume designer with advanced taste). Vernon Lee described her as a ghoul, and wrote that she was considered by some to be '*the* artistic siren'.[15] Mrs Cimabue Brown seems, however, to have been a synthesis of the more extreme aesthetic women whom Du Maurier had met, rather than a particular individual.

Jellaby Postlethwaite, who first appeared in 1880, is an aesthete

---

14. Comyns Carr, pp. 84–5.
15. *Vernon Lee's Letters*, edited Miss I. Cooper-Willis (1937), p. 123.

MAUDLE ON THE CHOICE OF A PROFESSION.

Maudle. "How CONSUMMATELY LOVELY YOUR SON IS, MRS. BROWN!"

Mrs. Brown (a Philistine from the country). "WHAT? HE'S A NICE, MANLY BOY, IF YOU MEAN THAT, MR. MAUDLE. HE HAS JUST LEFT SCHOOL, YOU KNOW, AND WISHES TO BE AN ARTIST."

Maudle. "WHY SHOULD HE BE AN ARTIST?"

Mrs. Brown. "WELL, HE MUST BE SOMETHING!"

Maudle. "WHY SHOULD HE BE ANYTHING? WHY NOT LET HIM REMAIN FOR EVER CONTENT TO EXIST BEAUTIFULLY?"

[*Mrs. Brown determines that at all events her Son shall not study Art under Maudle.*

73. *Punch* (1881)

poet and the epitome of extreme aesthete behaviour. Many people thought he was a caricature of Oscar Wilde, but Du Maurier emphatically denied it. In an interview with the *Pall Mall Gazette* in 1894, he described Postlethwaite as:

the aesthetic character out of whom I got some fun. Postlethwaite was said to be Mr Oscar Wilde, but the character was founded not on one person at all, but a whole school.[16]

Postlethwaite's death's-head appearance does not, in any case, favour the identification. With his skin drawn tightly across his cheek-bones, and his bush of black hair sticking out behind, he carries no suggestion of Wilde's fleshiness and lank locks. Maudle's claim to be Wilde is equally unconvincing. His is necessarily a supporting role, and when he first appears, in 'Nincompoopiana – The Mutual Admiration Society' (14 February 1880, p. 271), he has a weak, receding chin, and a tiny mouth. Only on one occasion does Maudle look and sound like Wilde. This is in the cartoon, 'Maudle on the Choice of a Profession' (12 February 1881), where he is lounging back in a chair, with a heavy face and figure. Two other cartoon characters also suggest Wilde in appearance. Algernon in 'A Discussion on Woman's Rights' (31 December 1881) is uttering a Wildean epigram to his sisters, cousins and aunts:

> If you want equality among the sexes, you must learn to be independent of us, as we are of you. Now we men live chiefly to please ourselves first, and then each other; whereas you women live entirely to please *us*!

Again there is the large corpulent figure, basking in the glow of feminine admiration. The third and least definite of these caricatures occurs in 'The Six-Mark Tea-Pot' (30 October 1880, p. 294), where the aesthetic groom bears a physical resemblance to Wilde. The Colonel's comment on Postlethwaite in his first appearance in *Punch*: 'Who's this young hero they're all swarming over now?' (14 February 1880, p. 271) does recall Wilde's success in London between 1878 and 1882. In the autumn of 1878, Wilde had left Oxford with a certain reputation for poetry, witty remarks and unconventional behaviour. Most of his plays and other writings belong to the 1890s, when Du Maurier had ceased to ridicule the aesthetes, but during his early years he was an easy target. Wilde did not start aestheticism, nor did he initiate any of its most distinctive characteristics. If a study of Du Maurier's cartoons establishes nothing else, it does prove the lack of any true originality in Wilde's outrageous behaviour. Whistler actually challenged Wilde with taking his ideas from Du Maurier:

16. 19 May 1894.

Mr Du Maurier and Mr Wilde happening to meet in the rooms where Mr Whistler was holding his first exhibition of Venice etchings, the latter brought the two face to face, and taking each by the arm, inquired:
'I say, which one of you two invented the other, eh?'[17]

Whistler's etchings appeared at the Fine Art Society in December 1880, shortly before the two most likely caricatures of Wilde were executed by Du Maurier in *Punch*.

Prigsby, the hanger-on, is decidedly more ridiculous than Postlethwaite or Maudle, and lacks something of their charm. It is he who sings nursery rhymes, and talks rapturously about the head of the headless Ilyssus torso. This last cartoon, 'Distinguished Amateurs, the Art Critic' (13 March 1880), is a particularly fascinating example of Du Maurier's ambivalent viewpoint. It was because he himself admired beautiful things so much, that he detested the excessive and affected enthusiasm of the aesthetes:

> The head of Alexis is distinctly divine! Nor can *I*, in the whole range of ancient, medieval or modern art, recall anything quite so fair and precious; unless it be, perhaps, the head of that supremest masterpiece of Greek Sculptchah, *The Ilyssus*, whereof indeed, in a certain gracious modelling of the lovely neck, and in the subtly delectable curves of the cheek and chin, it faintly, yet most exquisitely, reminds me!

In a letter written to Armstrong soon after the appearance of this cartoon, Du Maurier expressed a very similar appreciation for this piece of sculpture:

> Illyssus is *distinctly* divine in all the three dimensions – But to find out *how* divine one must be forty-six and try to draw him, even from a photograph, and of all the creatures who ever wasted their sweetness on the desert air, Ilyssus (and the rest of the Parthenon stuff) are the most pathetic. I haven't got over him yet. I hope his anatomy is all right & believe it *must* be – but for his beauty there is no name.

It was the manner and not the substance of aesthetic admiration that antagonized Du Maurier.

Another cartoon figure is Peter Pilcox, the sculptor, who was once a chemist's assistant, but has given up that profession for art. He is mentioned at some length in 'Fleur des Alpes' (25 December

---

17. J. Mc N. Whistler, *The Gentle Art of Making Enemies*, edited Sheridan Ford, New York (1890), p. 241.

DISTINGUISHED AMATEURS.—2. THE ART-CRITIC.

Prigsby (contemplating his friend Maudle's last Picture). "The head of Alexis is distinctly divine! Nor can I, in the whole range of Ancient, Mediæval, or Modern Art, recall anything quite so fair and precious; unless it be, perhaps, the Head of that supremest Masterpiece of Greek Sculptchah, the Ilyssus, whereof indeed, in a certain gracious Modelling of the lovely Neck, and in the subtly delectable Curves of the Cheek and Chin, it faintly, yet most exquisitely, reminds me!"

Chorus of Fair Enthusiasts (who still believe in Prigsby). "Oh, yes—yes!—of course!—the Ilyssus!!—in the Elgin Marbles, you know!!! How true!!!!"

Always ready to Learn, and deeply impressed by the extent of Prigsby's information, our Gallant Friend the Colonel takes an early opportunity of visiting the British Museum, in order to study the Head and Neck of the Ilyssus.

74. *Punch* (1880)

THE APPALLING DIFFUSION OF TASTE.

Much as he hates a joke, Sir Pompey Bedell has a still greater loathing for Nature, Poetry and Art, which he chooses to identify with Postlethwaite, Maudle, & Co. ; and Grigsby's lifelike imitations of those gentlemen—whom, by the bye, Sir Pompey has never seen—have so gratified him, that he honours our funny friend with a call.

Sir Pompey (aghast). "What, Mr. Grigsby, can this Room really be yours?—with a Dado!—and Artistic Wall-Paper!!—and a Brass Fender!!!—and, gracious Heavens, a Bunch of Lilies in a Blue Pot!!!!"

Grigsby. "They're not for Luncheon, Sir Pompey ; they're only to smell, and to look at, I assure you! Let me offer you one!"

Sir Pompey. "Not for the world, Mr. Grigsby!"   [*Beats a solemn retreat.*

75. *Punch* (1881)

1880) as a close rival of Postlethwaite's for public popularity. Milkington Sopley is also mentioned in this article, and with his name Du Maurier satirizes the effeminate aesthete male. The female disciples of the movement include Miss Mariana Bilderbogie, and her sisters, who first appear in 1873, before the series of aesthete cartoons have really started. Mariana later marries Peter Pilcox, thus establishing a continued connection between Du Maurier's creations. There are other figures in the cartoons, who are not named as anything more than 'ineffable youth' or 'fair intense one'.

One of the most interesting characters to appear is Grigsby, who is also found in cartoons outside the aesthete series. He is the plain man, affected, as many were, by a transient fashion, which he tries to copy. He is seen at the Cimabue Browns playing a pseudo Florentine canzonet, which he is asked to repeat, but is unable to do so because he has only just made it up ('Flippancy Punished', 14 April 1877). Finally he goes so far as to buy the trappings of the aesthetic home, and horrifies Sir Pompey Bedell ('The Appalling Diffusion of Taste', 19 March 1881). Grigsby, on his rare appearances, is one of the most amusing characters, because he does not really understand aesthetic principles, but only apes the more obvious manifestations of the cult.

Du Maurier frequently solves the question of his own view-point in these cartoons by the introduction of the rude and hearty voice of common sense. This cold-water, which is thrown on aesthetic enthusiasm, establishes for the spectator exactly what he ought to be thinking, and rather heavily underlines the joke. The most amusing of these 'cold-water' figures is 'our friend the colonel', because he is the least self-confident and prejudiced. He actually goes to the bother of looking at the headless Ilyssus, on the strength of Prigsby's eulogy of the head. Less gullible, and cruder in consequence, is the 'Matter-of-Fact Party' in 'Modern Aesthetics' (10 February 1877), and the 'Ruddy Philistine' visiting the 'chinamaniac' in 'Chronic China-mania' (*Almanack*, 1875). These figures, who appear frequently, are bluff and uncomprehending, and represent *Punch's*, and hence the popular, view of the aesthetic movement.

The actual reign of Postlethwaite and Maudle is a short one. They first appear in February, 1880, and make their last appearance with Mrs Cimabue Brown in May 1881. In the last cartoon they are all in the throes of discovering that they are no more than a figment of Mr Punch's imagination, and perhaps it was this shock which removed them for ever from his pages ('Frustrated Social Ambition',

21 May 1881). Du Maurier may well have felt that the production of *Patience*, in April 1881, made further comment superfluous, or he may simply have become bored with the subject. Vernon Lee, who went to see *Patience* in 1881, wrote: 'It takes off aesthetic high art people, but aestheticism it seems . . . has wellnigh died out in London'.[18]

In his cartoons, Du Maurier attacks most aspects of the aesthetic movement. He implies that it is only an excuse for a rather silly kind of conceit and narcissism, and that it is not a defensible philosophy of life. The drooping of the lily, the unhealthy preoccupation with self, reflect the later mood of the 'nineties. Du Maurier tells us nothing of this, nor of the strain of perversity and unnaturalness, inherited from Edgar Allen Poe and Baudelaire, which was latent in aestheticism. Rarely bitingly satirical, he is never profound. The real implications of the Wilde story would always have escaped him.

The modern painter most admired by the aesthetes was undoubtedly Burne-Jones, whose swirling draperies, reminiscent of the Florentine quattrocento, and sexless faces, provided them with an ideal of beauty. Aesthetic gowns were modelled on those worn by the Burne-Jones maidens, which were neither truly medieval, nor in the least modern. Rossetti, less well-known than Burne-Jones, because he refused to exhibit his work, also came into vogue, and the Rossetti face, modelled on Mrs Jane Morris, had its part in the aesthetic concept of beauty. It too was other-worldly, with a characteristic columnar neck, long bushy hair, and large curved lips. E. F. Benson, who was not an enthusiast, described this type in his reminiscences, *As We Were*:

> For whether these new types were statuesque or diaphanous, whether they were well nourished or highly anaemic, they all wore an air of remote inhuman melancholy . . . No gleam of intelligence, no spark of humour, no hint of joy or healthy animalism ever lit those brooding or downcast countenances: they seemed completely taken up with the task of being beautiful and sad, each sundered from her companions (for there were very few men among them) in a cell of her own, where she fed on her own world-weariness and perfect features.[19]

Benson approximated these women to 'Rossetti's Junos and Burne-Jones's wan women (the latter in swiftly increasing numbers)'.[20]

---

18. *Vernon Lee's Letters*, p. 77.   20. Benson, p. 259.
19. E. F. Benson, *As We Were. A Victorian Peep-Show* (1930), pp. 258-9.

PRUDENCE AT THE GROSVENOR.

76. Prudence at the Grosvenor, *Prudence* (1882)

Mrs Cimabue Brown has a haggard yearning face, and the long bushy hair associated with Rossetti, and so do her friends. It was succinctly described by another *Punch* cartoonist as, 'frizzled, flamboyant hair'.[21]

The Burne-Jones boom began in 1877 with the founding of the Grosvenor Gallery by Sir Coutts Lindsay. Intended as an alternative to the Royal Academy for advanced, but talented artists, it had an avant-garde reputation, which was only partially justified. The most famous painters who exhibited there were Burne-Jones, Albert Moore, Walter Crane and James Whistler. Du Maurier only includes Burne-Jones' name in one aesthete cartoon, at the bottom of a picture frame in 'The Appalling Diffusion of Taste' (19 March 1881). He is referred to again in the 'Rise and Fall of the Jack Spratts' (7 September 1878), as the 'gifted leader' of the Grosvenor Gallery disciples. For the Spratts and their purist friends, however, he is 'a base apostate, who, having once known the better way, had chosen to depart from it, and had been branded in consequence with the indelible Hall Mark of ineffaceable popular renown'. The Jack Spratts are the great enemies of the Royal Academy:

21. 'The Two Ideals' *Punch*, LXXVII, 120.

A LOVE-AGONY. DESIGN BY MAUDLE.

(With Verses by Jellaby Postlethwaite, who is also said to have sat for the Picture.)

RONDEL.

So an thou be, that faintest in such wise,
With love-wan eyelids on love-wanton eyes,
Fain of thyself! I faint, adoring thee,
Fain of thy kisses, fainer of thy sighs,

Yea, lo! for veriest fainness faint I, Sweet,
Of thy spare bosom, where no shadows meet,
And small strait hip, and weak delicious knee!
For joy thereof I swoon, and my pulse-beat

Shepherd art thou, or nymph, that ailest there?
Lily of Love, or Rose? Search they, who care,
Thy likeness for a sign! For, verily,
Naught reck I, Fairest, so an thou be but Fair!

77. *Punch* (1880)

they held it in merely passive contempt, and were satisfied with never having heard the names of its most celebrated members. Their especial scorn was reserved for that school of Art which finds its home on the walls of the Grosvenor Gallery.

This is only a case of 'sour grapes', as the Jack Spratts and their friends have never been asked to exhibit there.

Only one of Maudle's paintings is represented in the cartoons, and although it is very crude, it is a recognizable parody of a Burne-Jones' mythical subject. Entitled, 'A Love-Agony' (5 June 1880), it shows the reclining form of Postlethwaite, in a swathe of cloth, surrounded by lilies, and a butterfly chased by a swallow. Maudle's dreadful pictures are always excessively praised by his friends, a form of mutual and exclusive admiration, which Du Maurier detested. In 'Nincompoopiana' (24 April 1880), the model is deputed to show round an 'august foreign visitor', and has to explain that his master has not come 'down to exhibitin' his pictures in public!' Only his closest friends are allowed to see and admire them. When asked who buys the pictures, the model is forced to confess, 'Mrs 'Arris' ... and 'Mr Brooks, of Sheffield'. This cartoon may have been aimed at Rossetti, who rarely exhibited his work.

Among the other artists, who had exhibited at the first Grosvenor Gallery Exhibition of 1877, was Whistler. It was on this occasion that Ruskin, who had praised Burne-Jones, and been unpleasantly patronizing about the founder, described Whistler's *Nocturne in Black and Gold: The Falling Rocket*, as 'a pot of paint in the public's face'.[22] The resulting law-case for libel in 1878, became a battle-ground for and against 'art for art's sake'. Ruskin's contention that the critic was there to save the public from charlatan painters, and that a work of art should be judged by the amount of work put into it, was challenged by Whistler, who believed that the artist was a law unto himself, responsible neither to the critics nor the public. Asked whether he had seriously demanded two hundred guineas for two days' work, he replied that he asked it 'for the knowledge he had gained in the work of a life-time'.[23]

Whistler's choice of musical titles for his paintings appealed to the aesthetes and again linked his name to the movement. The relation of music to art was under discussion at this period. Whistler sought to

22. J. Ruskin, *Works*, edited by T. Cook and A. Wedderburn (1903–1912), XXIX, 160.
23. 'Whistler v. Ruskin', *Times* (26 November 1878), p. 9.

harmonize colours as the composer harmonizes tones, but, at the trial he denied any intention of establishing 'a kind of connection between the two arts', and explained that ' "An arrangement" was an arrangement of light, form, and colour', and that 'Among his pictures were some night views, and he chose the word "Nocturne" because it generalized and simplified them all'. The whole case was enlivened by Whistler's relentless wit and intelligence. He seemed to be undermining the comfortable Victorian view of art with new and disturbing ideas. The farthing damages reflect how little the Victorians wished to know about those ideas.

Punch found Whistler, as it found anyone who behaved unconventionally, a source of amusement. Du Maurier's view of *The Falling Rocket* is found two years after the case in a cartoon called 'The Diffusion of Aesthetic Taste' (22 January 1881). The couple, who discuss the meaning of a nocturne, provide a rather crude vehicle for Du Maurier's satire: 'Then you may depend upon it that mysterious black-and-yellow smudge we couldn't make head or tail of meant the *waits*'. Du Maurier's reference to Whistler's *Falling Rocket* was not the only comment on the titles of his pictures. The caption for a cartoon called 'Reciprocity' (16 January 1875) reads:

> The Arts are borrowing each other's vocabulary – painting has its 'harmonies' and 'symphonies': music is beginning to return the compliment.

A musical virtuoso, having finished his performance on the piano, is receiving the adulation of his female admirers, who comment on the 'colour' in his 'fortissimoes', the 'roundness of modelling' in his 'pianissimoes', the 'perspective' in his 'crescendoes', the 'chiaroscuro' in the 'diminuendoes' and the 'anatomy' in his 'legatoes'. Du Maurier was not alone in thinking that Whistler's titles were pretentious. Even Hamilton felt that Whistler's works had been noted principally 'for the affected titles bestowed upon them'.[24]

Burne-Jones' and Rossetti's paintings were not only popular on aesthetic grounds, but also because their idealized, medieval atmosphere suggested a pleasant means of escape from contemporary materialism. Du Maurier's most prolonged comment on this

24. Hamilton, pp. 23–4.

THE DIFFUSION OF ÆSTHETIC TASTE.

Mrs. B. (*after Visit to Picture-Gallery*). "WHAT IS A NOCTURNE, MR. B. ? "
Mr. B. (*vaguely*). "A NOCTURNE IS—AHEM !—A—A SORT OF NIGHT MUSIC, I BELIEVE, MY DEAR."
Mrs. B. "THEN YOU MAY DEPEND UPON IT THAT MYSTERIOUS BLACK-AND-YELLOW SMUDGE WE COULDN'T MAKE HEAD OR TAIL OF MEANT *THE WAITS !*"

78. *Punch* (1881)

desire to go back in time to a more colourful and romantic age, is found in the early sections of the 'Rise and Fall of the Jack Spratts', which began to appear in *Punch* on 7 September 1878. This prose narrative deals with the Spratts' attempt to live a simple life. They play old games like cat's cradle, 'battledore and shuttlecock, and hunt the slipper, and puss in the corner, and hide-and-seek'. They sing early French and Italian songs; English, not being old enough, is only allowed in their own sad measures. The Spratts dress in medieval clothes, eat 'frugal' and simple meals, and surround themselves with old furniture. The climax of the story comes when Mr Spratt's picture is accepted by the Royal Academy, and he and his wife are fêted by society. Their whole mode of life changes dramatically, and Mrs Spratt becomes a society belle. This underlines Du Maurier's contention that most of the aesthetes were nonentities, who had no other way of attracting attention. That the Spratts, and for that matter, the Cimabue Browns, were not wholly without prototypes is clear from Vernon Lee's description of a party at the house of Henry Holiday the painter:

> full of weird people, women in cotton frocks of faded hues, made wide at the hips & tight at the feet like Turkish trowsers [sic] – and lank draperies of all sorts... Miss Holiday fiddled, and a youth with anaemic face & hair played the piano, & someone, in a nasal voice, sang a long, long pseudo mediæval ballad about a King's daughter & a swineherd, with an idiotic & melancholy refrain. It felt so completely high art.[25]

The aesthetes were also attracted by older schools of art, particularly the Italian Quattrocento where Botticelli aroused their admiration, Ruskin had lectured on Botticelli in his series, 'The Æsthetic and Mathematic Schools of Art in Florence', which he delivered at Oxford in 1874:

> And as I told you that all the delight of Angelico in material things became sacred in its intensity, so the material workmanship of this greater master becomes sacred in its completion. Of this falling golden rain he has burnished every separate ray into enduring perfectness; it is not gilding, but beaten gold, wrought with the inherited Etruscan skill of a thousand years, and able to stand for a thousand years to come.[26]

Such superlative criticism fanned the aesthetes' adulation of Botticelli, to which Pater contributed with his essay on the painter in *The Renaissance*. Rossetti, who had inspired several of the aesthetes' enthusiasms, was in the forefront of the Botticelli craze, as William Michael Rossetti was careful to point out:

> Botticelli was little or not at all in demand at that now remote date. If my brother had not something to do with the vogue which soon afterwards began to attach to that fascinating master, I am under a misapprehension.[27]

Du Maurier only mentions Botticelli once, in a cartoon for the 1881 *Punch Almanack*, 'Nincompoopiana'. Prigsby stands with 'the

25. *Vernon Lee's Letters*, p. 124.
26. *Works*, XXIII, 274.
27. *D. G. Rossetti: his family letters*, edited with a memoir by W. M. Rossetti (1895), I, 264.

NINCOMPOOPIANA.

(*A Test.*)

The Squire. "I BELIEVE IT'S A BOTTICELLI."
Prigsby. "OH, NO! PARDON ME! IT IS *NOT* A BOTTICELLI. BEFORE A
BOTTICELLI I AM MUTE!" [*The Squire wishes it was.*

squire' in front of a picture (not shown), which the squire imagines
to be by Botticelli. Not so Prigsby: 'Oh, no! Pardon me! It is *not* a
Botticelli. Before a Botticelli I am mute!' A footnote adds: 'The
squire wishes it was'. Du Maurier's lack of respect for, and one
suspects lack of interest in, other early Italian artists is shown in his
cartoon, 'A Damper' (2 September 1876, p. 276). On seeing Boniface
Brasenose's fifteenth-century 'Madonna and Child', a fashionable
lady remarks: 'I should have thought it earlier!', and when asked
why, replies: 'Oh, I should have thought they could paint better than
that, so late as the fifteenth-century!'. Most of the cartoons concerned
with early Italian art, occur at the beginning of the aesthete series,
although the reference to Botticelli comes as late as 1881. Du Maurier
had a considerable flair for inventing fictitious names for Italian

painters. In 'Modern Æsthetics' (10 February 1877), we can just see a work by 'an extremely Old Master – say, Fra Porcinello Baba-ragianno, A.D. 1266–1281 ?'. The 'matter-of-fact party' remarks that the subject is 'repulsive', the drawing 'vile', the colour 'beastly', and that the picture is 'out of *perspective* and *untrue to nature*'. The young aesthete dismisses these criticisms as trivial, because subject is unimportant, drawing incomprehensible, and, in any case, he is 'cullah-blind'. His reiteration of the picture's beauty leads his companion to exclaim, 'Where the *dickens* is the *beauty*, then ?', which receives the appropriate answer, 'In the picktchah!'. This reveals a typical aesthete attitude of superiority in the face of philistine criticism, and the use of paradox to mystify and outrage.

A group of even more remarkable names than 'Fra Porcinello Barbaragianno', was derived by Du Maurier from Italian words for food, and interior decoration. They were invented as the favourite painters of the Jack Spratts. Spratt himself muses regretfully on

> grand old sunsets, by the grand Old Masters, in the National Gallery, and the quaint old children and mothers by Bogofogo, Antima Cassaro, Vecchio Coccoloro, Fra Stoggiato di Vermicelli, Saraparillo dello Strando, and other painters of that ante-prae-Raphaelite school.

He regrets that his paintings are not like theirs, for he could 'already draw, colour, compose, and put into perspective quite as badly as they did'. The Spratts' 'trusty friends' are constantly sad,

> for the death of the early Italian Masters still weighed on their souls with all the force of some recent domestic bereavement, and they always be-haved with the solemnity that befitted them as chief mourners, speaking of the dead in hushed and reverential whispers (7 Sept. 1878).

Another painter, who was excessively praised by the aesthetes, was Luca Signorelli. Mr and Mrs Spratt make a point of going to see his 'Martyrdom of Cupid' in the National Gallery. The nymphs in this picture

> are of a beauty so overpowering that J. Spratt and the trusty friends would always feel faint, and weak in their backs and legs, through sheer excess of sensuous pleasure when they gazed at it (21 Sept. 1878).

Mrs Spratt's great regret, at this stage of her life, is that she does not resemble the nymphs. Jack Spratt has tried, without success, to turn her into one of those 'singularly seductive types of female loveliness which the early Italian masters have made so especially their own', but unable to change her 'form, features, and complexion, he had endeavoured to teach her most of the early Italian attitudes' (21 Sept. 1878).

The most obvious and distinguishing feature of the aesthetes was their costume. Any change in fashion in general was noted by *Punch*, which is the source for much study of nineteenth-century costume. The ridiculous and artificial crinoline was a constant butt for John Leech, while Du Maurier indulged himself at the expense of the bustle; he was delighted to turn his attention to aesthetic costume. The aesthete ladies wore no corsets, and although their dresses emphasized the waist, they were comparatively loose. As a style it never became widely popular, but it seems to have contributed to the fall of the high bustle. The aesthete ladies considered the main influence on their choice of dress to be medieval, but their garments were not strictly of medieval pattern. Their high waists were really closer to the 'Empire line', while their sleeves were usually of the sixteenth-century leg-of-mutton variety. The aesthetic style was also influenced by the vogue for the oriental, their long, pale-coloured garments suggesting a Japanese source.

The aesthetes themselves did try to popularize their ideas on costume. Books like Mrs Oliphant's *Dress* (1878) and Mrs Haweis' *The Art of Dress* (1879) embodied aesthetic concepts: 'Now, dress *ought* to be beautiful, useful and comfortable'.[28] Oscar Wilde entered the lists in 1884, describing female costume that already existed, and had even appeared in *Punch*:

> The over-tunic should be made full and moderately loose; it may, if desired, be shaped more or less to the figure, but in no case should it be confined at the waist by any straight band or belt; on the contrary, it should fall from the shoulder to the knee, or below it, in fine curves and vertical lines, giving more freedom and consequently more grace.[29]

The Rational Dress Society, of which Oscar Wilde and Lady Haberton were leading members, and the Healthy and Artistic Dress Union, were inspired by a new concept of beauty, and by a hatred of existing fashion, which seemed to them not only ugly but

28. Mrs Haweis, *The Art of Dress* (1879), p. 25.
29. *Pall Mall Gazette*, 11 Nov. 1884.

positively harmful. The Journal of the Healthy and Artistic Dress Union, explained its purpose: 'We propose to inculcate sound principles such as may guide us in the devising and executing of beautiful and healthy garments'.[30] They brought heavy medical guns to bear on the effects of tight corseting – lateral curvature of the spine, failure of the supporting muscles, gallstones, deformities of the liver, perforating ulcer of the stomach, and chronic constipation. Their positive ideas were less practical, G. F. Watts helpfully remarking, 'That lines are beautiful in proportion to their capacity for variety, and the interest greater by the display of light and shade'.[31] This useless advice was echoed by Walter Crane and Henry Holiday, who invoked the example of classical art. Lady Haberton was more practical:

> Lady Haberton is well known as practising what she preaches, and at her lecture wore Turkish trousers of black satin merveilleux with a sash round the hips, and a black velvet jacket trimmed with jet passementerie, caught together at the waist with a buckle over a full waistcoat of white satin and lace. This rather bizarre costume suited her exceeding well, although the riding-whip with which she emphasised her periods gave her a somewhat mannish appearance.[32]

Lady Haberton belongs to the great revolt against women's position in society, which led to the suffragette movement. Conventional fashion was to them a sign of female bondage. The early aesthete women were less concerned with the practical and medical side of costume, and were intent only on looking beautiful. The same is true of Du Maurier's satire, which belongs to the late 1870s and early 1880s, before the social implications of aesthetic costume had become apparent.

Although Du Maurier's first obvious reference to aesthetic fashion is in the 1875 *Almanack*, an earlier hint is found in the appearance of the Misses Bilderbogie, in the cartoon 'A Happy Man' (25 Jan. 1873). These ladies, who were later to become part of the established aesthetic personnel, are not shown in full aesthetic dress, but they are not wearing bustles. It is the comparative simplicity of their costume and their yearning expressions which suggest the

30. *Aglaia: The Journal of the Healthy and Artistic Dress Union*, no. I (July 1893), 3.
31. G. F. Watts, 'Women's Dress', *Aglaia*, no. I (Spring 1894), 25.
32. 'Viscountess Haberton on Ladies' Dress', *Pictorial World*, New Series X (10 Feb. 1887), p. 144.

aesthetes, for they stand out sharply from their over-dressed companions. Two aesthetically dressed women are particularly noticeable in the early cartoons. In 'Acute Chinamania' (*Almanack*, 1875,
p. 292), the mother, who has just broken a precious blue-and-white
pot, is seen leaning forward on a chair, in long, loose garment. It falls
fully from a high waist, and seems to be bustleless. In 'Chronic Chinamania' (*Almanack*, 1875), the woman is seen in a long, straight dress,
again without a bustle, although with a marked waist. More interesting is the actual patterning of her dress, which is Japanese in flavour,
with a pagoda and horseman running down one side, while the rest
of the dress is covered in swirling, floral patterns. The other women in
the room are shown with coats, full bustles and tight waists.

Aesthete women did not really distinguish between the medieval
and the renaissance, but borrowed from both at will. This was not
because they were unaware of the nature of real medieval styles. In
several cartoons, dealing with fancy dress parties, which were very
popular at this time, Du Maurier details authentic medieval dress.
In 'A Faithful Guardian' (17 June 1876), the woman is dressed in full
medieval costume, with a high wimple, tight inner sleeves, and a flat
oversleeve. The wearing of real medieval dress by the aesthetes, is
best seen in Du Maurier's 'Rise and Fall of the Jack Spratts'. The first
illustration (7 Sept. 1878) shows Mrs Spratt in a long fur-trimmed
garment with narrow sleeves, and Mr Spratt in tights, a jerkin with
enormous sleeves, and long, pointed shoes. The 'trusty friends', who
are gathered round, are dressed less accurately. The man on the right
is wearing a flat, Tudor hat, and his sleeves are also Elizabethan. The
other friends wear hats of assumed medieval appearance, one with a
spray of peacock feathers. The whole effect is of a jumble of periods.
This is in keeping with the general ideas of the aesthetes, who borrowed fashion styles from any period which seemed suitably distant
and romantic. In the second illustration (14 Sept. 1878), Mrs Spratt
is seen posing in full medieval outfit:

> Mr Punch forgets what Mrs Spratt's very best consisted of at this particu-
> lar period of her career; but rather thinks it must have been a broidered
> wimple, surcinctured with a golden liripe over a welted chaisel-smock of
> watchet sergedusoy, lined with shalloon and edged with vair, or possibly
> ermine.

Mrs Cimabue Brown and her friends always appear in aesthetic
costume, and their long drooping dresses are easily recognizable from

THE RISE AND FALL OF THE JACK SPRATTS.
A Tale of Modern Art and Fashion.

80. *Punch* (1878)

NINCOMPOOPIANA.—THE MUTUAL ADMIRATION SOCIETY.

Our Gallant Colonel (who is not a Member thereof, to Mrs. Cimabue Brown, who is). "AND WHO'S THIS YOUNG HERO THEY'RE ALL SWARMING OVER NOW?"

Mrs. Cimabue Brown. "JELLABY POSTLETHWAITE, THE GREAT POET, YOU KNOW, WHO SAT FOR MAUDLE'S 'DEAD NARCISSUS'! HE HAS JUST DEDICATED HIS *LATTER-DAY SAPPHICS* TO ME. *Is NOT HE BEAUTIFUL?*"

Our Gallant Colonel. "WHY, WHAT'S THERE *BEAUTIFUL* ABOUT HIM?"

Mrs. Cimabue Brown. "OH, LOOK AT HIS GRAND HEAD AND POETIC FACE, WITH THOSE FLOWERLIKE EYES, AND THAT EXQUISITE SAD SMILE! LOOK AT HIS SLENDER WILLOWY FRAME, AS YIELDING AND FRAGILE AS A WOMAN'S! THAT'S YOUNG MAUDLE, STANDING JUST BEHIND HIM—THE GREAT PAINTER, YOU KNOW. HE HAS JUST PAINTED ME AS 'HÉLOÏSE,' AND MY HUSBAND AS 'ABÉLARD.' *Is NOT HE DIVINE?*"

[*The Colonel hooks it.*

N.B.—Postlethwaite and Maudle are quite unknown to fame.

81. *Punch* (1880)

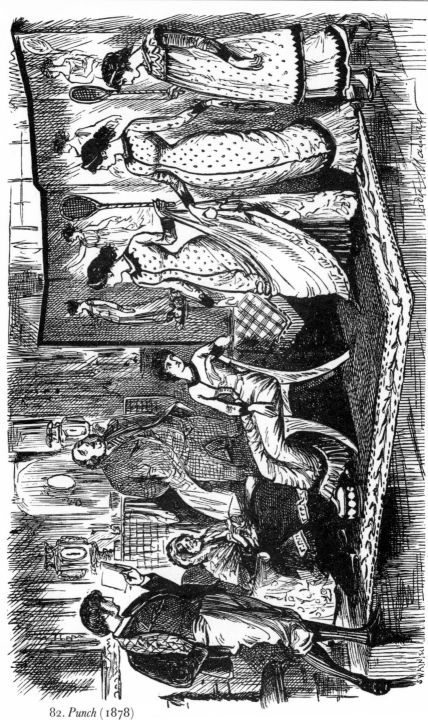

MODERN ÆSTHETICS.

Materfamilias. "WHERE HAVE YOU BEEN ALL THE MORNING, GIRLS?"   *Sophronia Cassandra.* "WE'VE BEEN PRACTISING OLD GREEK ATTITUDES AT LAWN-TENNIS, MAMMA?"   *Papa (who is not æsthetic).* "AH! HOPE YOU LIKE IT, I'M SURE!"   *Sophronia Cassandra.* "VERY MUCH, PAPA—ONLY WE NEVER HIT THE BALL!"

82. *Punch* (1878)

currently fashionable clothes. Two good examples are 'Nincompoop-iana – The Mutual Admiration Society' and 'Distinguished Ama-teurs – The Art Critic' (14 Feb. and 13 March 1880, pp. 271 and 255).

The influence of classical costume on aesthete fashion is seen in the *Almanack* for 1878, in a cartoon entitled 'Modern Æsthetics'. This shows three young ladies in pseudo-Grecian dress against a classical screen. All three have long, tight dresses and fillet bands in their hair. The costumes are obviously unsuitable for tennis, although the girls are holding rackets, and are only practical for striking 'atti-tudes'. It is not surprising that Greek costume should have been copied, for the Greeks had indirectly fostered the aesthetic cult of beauty. Oscar Wilde wrote: 'from a combination of the Greek principles of beauty with the German principles of health will come, I feel certain, the costume of the future'.[33] Another classical cartoon, very different from the one above, appeared on 25 Jan. 1879, entitled 'Where Ignorance is Bliss'. The caption begins,

'Some aesthetic person has suggested that a familiarity with the splen-dours of Greek art should be fostered in the young, by means of plaster casts from the antique and so forth'.

In the cartoon Du Maurier wonders what would become of the 'Opéra Bouffe', or the 'Modern Burlesque', if female loveliness in the future were to be judged by the 'Elgin Marbles' and the 'Venus de Milo'. His answer is to show a group of fat chorus-girls with buskins on their well-developed legs, short, full skirts, curious bodices and peacock feather hats. The result is quite ludicrous. The ladies are almost indecent, and the clothes which they wear are neither classical nor aesthetic, but a confusion of the two.

Du Maurier is not always an unthinking critic. In 'An Impartial Statement in Black and White' (9 April 1881), he shows the two worlds of fashion. On the left is an ugly aesthete female contrasted with an attractive, well-dressed woman of fashion. On the right the same ladies appear again, with their roles reversed. The aesthete woman is now in fashionable costume, but she still looks ugly, while her companion reveals the attractive possibilities of aesthete dress. Du Maurier could forgive a beautiful woman anything.

How far Du Maurier is an accurate guide to real aesthete fashions it is difficult to say. Mrs Comyns Carr wrote:

33. *Pall Mall Gazette*, 14 Oct. 1884.

I had long been accustomed to supporting a certain amount of ridicule in the matter of clothes, because in the days when bustles and skin tight dresses were the fashion, and a twenty-inch waist the aim of every self-respecting woman, my frocks followed the simple, straight line as waist-less as those of to-day.[34]

The *Patience* costumes resemble those in Du Maurier's cartoons, and were in fact made out of Liberty prints, bought by Gilbert himself.

Perhaps the most important of all aesthete influences on dress, and certainly their most lasting one, was their attempt to introduce less garish colour schemes; they preferred lighter shades and more subtle harmonies, as described by Mrs Haweis:

> But when you see a colour which is moderately dull in tone, and so far indescribable that you question whether it is blue or green, green or brown, red or yellow, grapple it to your soul with hooks of steel: it is an artistic colour, and will mix with almost any other artistic colour.[35]

In 'True Aesthetic Refinement' (17 Feb. 1877), a male aesthete refuses to go into dinner with a girl who has 'mauve twimmings in her skirt, and magenta wibbons in her hair'. 'She affects aniline dyes' he remarks as a final condemnation. These garish aniline dyes first came on sale around 1856, and soon replaced the softer vegetable dyes. In Du Maurier's cartoons, all of which are in black and white, it is impossible to convey any real sense of the more sophisticated colours introduced by the aesthetes, except in the captions underneath. The aesthete dresses depicted in the cartoons do seem to be lighter in tone, however, than ordinary fashionable dress; they are less worked over with pen lines, and often have sketchy, floral patterns which give the same impression. Except in cartoons like 'Too Literal by Half' (6 Oct. 1877), where an aesthetic husband and wife are trying to buy a peacock-blue fabric in France, one has to look elsewhere for evidence of colour.

We can gauge something from Du Maurier's cartoons of the effect which aesthete fashion had on those outside the immediate circle of devotees. From the summer of 1879, it is possible to trace the spread of aesthete ideas on fashion to upper-middle-class society in London. In 'Hygienic Excesses' (18 Oct. 1879), the O'Farrall-Mackenzie

34. Comyns Carr, p. 85.
35. Mrs H. R. Haweis, *The Art of Dress* (1879), p. 110.

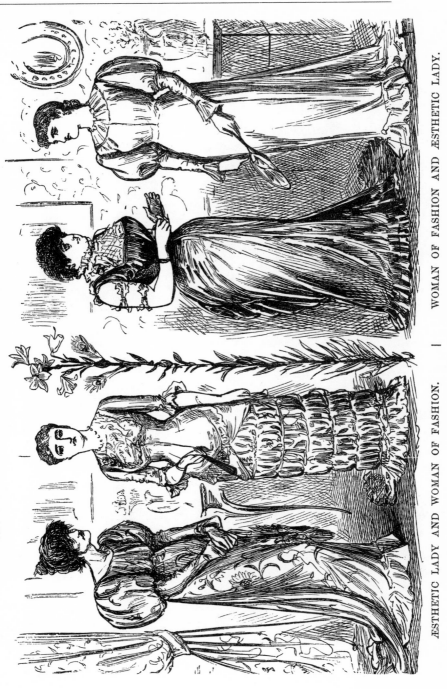

83. *Punch* (1881)

A DAMPER.

Boniface Brasenose (an amiable but æsthetic youth, exhibiting his Art-treasures). "THAT'S—A—A—MOTHER AND CHILD, A—A—FIFTEENTH CENTURY——."

Fashionable Lady. "I SHOULD HAVE THOUGHT IT EARLIER!"   *Boniface Brasenose.* "A—MAY I ASK WHY?"

Fashionable Lady. "OH, I SHOULD HAVE THOUGHT THEY COULD PAINT BETTER THAN THAT, SO LATE AS THE FIFTEENTH CENTURY!"

84. *Punch* (1876)

girls are said to have given up stays, and are trying to model themselves on Greek statues. Mr Punch 'fears they will set the fashion' with their exercises and healthy living, for they are all engaged to dukes. The pinafore style, popular in the summer of 1879, also seems to have derived from the plainer, aesthete style.

Du Maurier's aesthete cartoons finish in 1882, but from other sources we can see that the style continued to survive, even beyond the confines of London. An American girl, Maud Du Puy, later Mrs George Darwin, wrote home to her family in Philadelphia in 1883 about a garden party in Newnham, Cambridge:

> There were quite a number of aesthetic or ascetic [sic] costumes, at a Newnham Garden Party . . . Aunt C. has a simply perfect tea-gown; not aesthetic, but so graceful and lovely.[36]

The male aesthete dress was, as James Laver put it, 'a polite modification of the French artist costume of 1830'.[37] With its knee breeches, loose floppy tie, and wideawake hat, it is still well-known from *Patience*, the original costumes for which are very similar to Du Maurier's drawings in *Punch*. The fully-dressed aesthete male was to make an earlier appearance in *Punch* than his female counterpart. The dilettante De Tomkyns is an early example, ('Intellectual Epicures', 5 Feb. 1876), with his knickerbockers, dark, knee-length socks, and casual jacket. In other respects, however, De Tomkyns falls short of the ideal found in Postlethwaite. His face is healthy and not haggard, and his general stance is by no means willowy enough.

The true aesthete appears as Boniface Brasenose in 'A Damper' (2 Sept. 1876). This gentleman, presumably an undergraduate at Oxford, has rooms decorated in the latest aesthetic style, with clothes to match. He is dressed in knee-breeches, waistcoat, and a smoking jacket with quilted lapels, and he has long hair and an emaciated face. This cartoon above all others, shows that Wilde did not invent aesthete dress, but borrowed it from a style already in existence. A complete group of similarly dressed aesthete men is shown in the 'Rise and Fall of the Jack Spratts' (21 Sept. 1878), where they are labelled as 'Ye Aesthetic Young Geniuses'. These are the frequently mentioned 'trusty friends' of Mr and Mrs Spratt. Most of the group

---

36. G. Raverat, *Period Piece* (1952), p. 26.
37. J. Laver, *Taste and Fashion from the French Revolution to the Present Day* (1937), new and revised edition (1945), p. 66.

are dressed for outdoors, but the central figure is wearing normal aesthete fashion, an open jacket, broad-brimmed hat, and floppy tie. As a contrast to these drooping figures, Du Maurier illustrates three 'Gorgeous Young Swells' below, whom Mrs Spratt finds much more attractive. They are dressed in pin-striped trousers, top-hats, stiff, high collars, and neatly pinned cravats. The fashionable style of coat which they are wearing is exactly the same as that of the aesthetes, except that it is buttoned tightly at the waist, instead of flapping open. One development in aesthete male garb, more in line with the loud checks worn by Wilde, is found in 'Nincompoopiana' (14 June 1879), where the young man is wearing a check suit with knicker-bocker trousers, and a wide jacket with a high fastening, cut wide over the waist. The last of Du Maurier's knickerbockered aesthetes appears in 'The Line of Beauty' (6 Dec. 1879). From this time on aesthete men are dressed in more conventional clothes. Mr Cimabue Brown had already appeared in white trousers and his quilted smoking jacket, in 'Flippancy Punished' (14 April 1877), and it is in this style that the cartoonist introduces Maudle and Postlethwaite in 1880. The appearance of the male aesthetes in *Patience* (1881) suggests, however, that the original style had not entirely died out. One last point in regard to male aesthete dress is their frequent use of a monocle, which Du Maurier may have intended as a parody of Whistler.

The Oriental influence, and that of William Morris, on interior decoration in the late 1870s and early 1880s can be dealt with separately, although the distinction is in some ways a little artificial. There was little real distinction in the minds of those who were decorating their homes, or indeed in Du Maurier's comments on them. The cluttered sitting-room of the Victorian home could well acquire an occasional blue-and-white china pot, or a Sussex chair, without its owner being aware of any incongruity. Du Maurier described such a muddled interior in a letter of 28 July 1880 to Frank Burnand, who wanted to devise a set for his aesthetic play, *The Colonel*. It makes a fascinating supplement to his cartoons:

> Try & have a room papered with Morris' green daisy, with a dado six feet high of green-blue serge in folds – and a matting with rugs for floor (Indian red matting if possible) – spider-legged black tables & side board – black rush bottom chairs & armchairs: blue china plates on the wall with plenty of space between – here & there a blue china vase with an enormous hawthorn or almond blossom sprig . . . also on mantle piece

Yᵉ ÆSTHETIC YOUNG GENIUSES!...

85. The Rise and Fall
of the Jack Spratts,
Punch (1878)

Yᵉ GORGEOUS YOUNG SWELLS!

pots with lillies & peacock feathers – plain dull yellow curtains lined with dull blue for windows if wanted. Japanese sixpenny fans now & then on the walls in this picturesque unexpectedness. [38]

If styles were muddled in the average home, distinctions between the chief figures involved are much clearer. William Morris never dabbled in the oriental, and Whistler had no connection with Morris and Co. furniture. Among their followers the distinction became blurred. The plates of William de Morgan, who was himself closely associated with Morris and his circle, are often influenced by Medieval Persian pottery, and show a progressive use of flat design derived from the East.

In fact, both Morris and Whistler were rebelling against the same attitude to interior decoration, the attitude that empty spaces were there to be filled, the hopeless mixing of misunderstood styles, the over-alaborateness and heaviness of so much furniture and the cluttered effect of most Victorian rooms. The application of orna-mental details to buildings with no regard to their function or general effect, was matched by a lack of thought for essential pattern, or a sense of over-all design, in the home. Confusion, bad taste and mass-production were the order of the day.

William Morris was one of the first to launch an effective protest against this established and ingrained lack of taste. In 1856, wishing to furnish the rooms which he shared with Burne-Jones in Red Lion Square, he found the standard of furniture and furnishings so appall-ing, that he decided to design his own. This led directly to the found-ing of Morris, Marshall, Faulkner and Co. in 1861, later to become Morris & Co. To Morris the great enemy was the machine, which was destroying the individual craftsman, and producing goods not only badly made, but badly designed. Morris had a Utopian idea of returning to the medieval guild system, which would not only help to undermine the evil effects of materialism in Victorian England, but possibly create the right economic conditions for a new golden age, where everyone would have his allotted place, and the miseries of poverty and unemployment would be banished for ever. It was rather an individual theory of socialism, but it informed all Morris' activi-ties. It gave him a respect for simple, unpretentious designs and materials, solidly-made furniture, consistently designed fabrics and

38. Yale University Library.

so on. For Morris the workman's pride in his work was an essential part of good craftsmanship, and he surrounded himself with a company of craftsmen. By working himself with raw materials, stone, wood, glass, dyes, wool, he came to have a respect for the materials he used, which the machine manufacturers wholly lacked. Morris himself did not design or make furniture, though he is credited with having made a table to prove to a friend that he could. The so-called 'Morris chair' was derived from an old Sussex type, as was the equally famous sliding chair. Morris is famous as a designer of wall-papers and textiles. His work has a clarity and consistency that few Victorians possessed. His designs, based on simple motifs, like birds, flowers, or foliage, have an uncompromising adherence to the flat surface, which mark the true draughtsman, and are superbly decorative. Coupled with this sense of design was an unerring eye for colour, and it is interesting to note that recent reprints of his designs rarely have the intensity or subtlety of colour that he was able to achieve. Morris was deeply influenced by the middle ages. Not only is his poetry devoted to medieval subjects, but his designs have a sinuous quality of line, and a pleasure in pattern for its own sake, that recall the medieval limners. A love of the medieval period, with suitable romantic overtones, was a current part of Victorian escapism, but in Morris' case it was linked to a positive economic idea, which he believed, however mistakenly, could be adapted to modern conditions.

Morris was not alone in his attack on accepted decorative schemes. In 1868 Charles Eastlake published his *Hints on Household Taste*, a book which contains designs for comparatively plain furniture. His main criticism of contemporary styles was its unnecessary curves, but his own designs tend to be rather cumbersome, and lack the charm of Morris and Co.'s sophisticated productions. It is indeed the shadow of Morris and Co., which is in many ways the most dominant one on aesthete interior decoration.

As a black-and-white cartoonist, Du Maurier can only give a limited idea of the furniture of the period, and no sense of the colour scehemes. Occasionally he depicts a room in some detail, but in the smaller cartoons, he only has space for a chair or table, a patch of wall or a few ornaments. One of the most recognizable pieces of furniture is the famous Sussex chair, which appears, for instance, in 'Refinements of Modern Speech' (14 June 1879). It occurs infrequently in the cartoons, and almost always in aesthete circles, but Morris wall-papers seem to have reached a wider circle. It is hard, of course, to

REFINEMENTS OF MODERN SPEECH.

SCENE—*A Drawing-room in " Passionate Brompton."*

Fair Æsthetic (suddenly, and in deepest tones, to Smith, who has just been introduced to take her in to Dinner). "ARE YOU INTENSE?"

86. *Punch* (1879)

tell certainly whether the fugitive and sketchy wall-paper patterns, which we find in the background of Du Maurier's cartoons, are by Morris and Co., or not. Most of the examples which Du Maurier illustrates at this period are of similar floral pattern, but it is significant that the wall-paper is more detailed in the aesthete cartoons, than elsewhere. One paper is clearly recognisable; the pattern which was brought out by Morris in 1862, entitled 'Fruit' or 'Pomegranate', appears twice, in the autumn and winter of 1876, first in the cartoon 'Pet and Hobby' and then in 'A Vocation'. (26 Aug. and 11 Nov. 1876). Du Maurier himself must have known this pattern well as he had bought it for his own house in Kensington. Du Maurier not only uses Morris or similar wall-papers, as a background in the aesthete cartoons, but in the homes of ordinary fashionable society. The fact that he himself chose a Morris design as early as 1867 shows how quickly they had become popular.

The spread of Morris papers, like that of other new vogues in interior decoration, was hastened by the publication of little books, like Mrs Lucy Orrinsmith's *The Drawing Room*. Published in 1878, it sold six thousand copies in its first year, and clearly had some influence on interior decoration. Mrs Orrinsmith was the sister of Charles Faulkner, one of the founders of Morris, Marshall, Faulkner and Co., and she was inevitably influenced by the ideas of Morris, for whom she actually painted plates and tiles. She attacks the brilliant and strident colours of most popular wall-papers, which she divides into the purely ornamental and meaningless, and the pseudo-realistic, and she advises the purchase of Morris wall-papers.

While the diffusion of Morris papers in London at this period seems, from the evidence of the cartoons, to have been fairly wide, at least one discrepancy arises in Du Maurier's actual comments about them. De Tomkyns in 'Intellectual Epicures' (5 Feb. 1876) is considered aesthetic because, among other things, he has artistic wall-papers, which Du Maurier does not detail. Two years later in 1878, on the other hand, the Spratts are considered to be sane again because they have Morris papers in Acacia Lodge (26 Oct. 1878). Finally Du Maurier adds two exclamation marks to Sir Pompey Bedell's cry of 'Artistic Wallpapers' in the 'Appalling Diffusion of Taste' (19 March 1881, p. 256).

Fabrics in the Morris style also appear in the cartoons, as often as the wall-papers. Not all these floral fabrics were necessarily the products of Morris and Co., but even where they fall short of his very high standard, they represented a great improvement on the earlier and more garish furniture covers. New materials, such as cretonne and flowered chintz, were slowly being introduced into the drawing room, and were no longer confined to the bedroom. Unfortunately, in the seventies and early eighties, crudely coloured velvets, and dark green and brown plush, still held sway in many homes. In the cartoons, floral fabrics frequently hang as curtains, dividing one part of the room from another, or as covers for armchairs and tables. Settees covered in this type of fabric appear in 'A Pleasant Prospect' (3 March 1877), and in the Jack Spratts' house, where the floral motif is the sunflower.

The diffusion of Morris & Co., products was confined to the upper classes. Being hand-made, they were necessarily expensive, and Morris' hope that he could improve design in general was unrealized. Madox Brown did design some working men's furniture, but the venture was not apparently a success. In fact, Morris and Co. furnishings led to an aesthetic and upper-class snobbery, which Morris must have detested.

For the socialist and reforming views of Morris and his friends, Du Maurier can have had little respect. He uses one of the opening lines of Morris' *The Earthly Paradise* (1868–70) in the caption to 'Old Times' (31 Jan. 1880), which shows a stage coach in a thick fog:

> Not know what to do in a black fog? Why take a seat on the stage-coach now running to St Albans and back, of course! The state of the atmosphere will prevent you from seeing the railways and the telegraph-poles, and enable you to 'forget the spreading of the hideous town', as Mr Morris has it in *The Earthly Paradise* – and you can play at being your own grandfather (or your grandmother, if you like), just as comfortably as if you were sitting at home in your best Chippendale arm-chair, with your feet on the brass fender, in the wainscoted back parlour of that dear little red-brick house of yours, taking snuff, and reading the *Gentleman's Magazine* for the year One by the light of a tallow candle! (N.B. Mr Punch means to try it himself.)

Du Maurier's reference to Chippendale chairs, brass fenders, and tallow candles make it clear that he is ridiculing the aesthetes, as well as Morris' poem, which had begun:

> Forget six counties overhung with smoke,
> Forget the snorting steam and piston stroke,
> Forget the spreading of the hideous town.

The idea, certainly prevalent in aesthete circles, that age necessarily confers quality, is attacked by Du Maurier in a cartoon
entitled 'A Bargain' (31 March 1877). Two young ladies are inspect-
ing a carpet in an antique shop, and are persuaded that it really is
old, when the dealer shows them that it is falling to pieces. Among
the other 'really old' things collected by the aesthetes were brass
fender and the round mirror. In 'Music and Æsthetics' (16 Feb.
1878) one of these round mirrors distorts the image of the beautiful
female pianist, and similar examples appear in 'A Damper' and
'Dilettantism' (2 Sept. and 3 June 1876). Lucy Orrinsmith includes
one of these mirrors in her design for the ideal fireplace arrangement,[39] and their frequent appearance in these cartoons suggests
that they were very popular. It is worth quoting Rossetti's biographer, Marillier, on the vogue for old objects generally:

> Bric-à-brac was not of much account in England when Rossetti first began
> rummaging the dealers' shops for old and battered cabinets, Chippen-
> dale chairs, carved oak panels, 'hawthorn' jars (the name was his
> invention), and an infinite variety of brass implements, chandeliers,
> sconces, mirrors, and vases of antique and comparatively neglected
> types.[40]

Du Maurier does not deal much with architectural styles, but he
does refer to the aesthetes' preference for Queen Anne style houses.
The Jack Spratts live in a house of red brick, smothered in ivy, and
'built about Queen Anne's time, or before, and never repaired since,
nor meddled with in any way whatever' (7 Sept. 1878). The best
example of the Queen Anne style, so favoured by the aesthetes, is
Bedford Park, Chiswick, probably the 'beautiful old suburb' of
London, through which the Thames 'would still meander occasionally', mentioned in the first paragraph of the 'Rise and Fall of the
Jack Spratts', (7 Sept. 1878), as the site of the Spratt home. The
estate, bought by Jonathan Carr as a colony for intellectuals, was
begun in the late 1870s, with houses designed by Norman Shaw in a
mixture of Queen Anne and Dutch 17th century styles. Where
possible the trees were left standing, and the one inn, 'The Tabard',
was decorated with tiles by William De Morgan. Hamilton described the estate:

39. Orrinsmith, p. 36.
40. H. C. Marillier: *Dante Gabriel Rossetti: An Illustrated Memorial of his art and life*
(1899), p. 121.

MUSIC AND ÆSTHETICS.

THE LOVELY AND ACCOMPLISHED (BUT EXTREMELY SHORT-SIGHTED) MADAME GELASMA, YIELDING TO THE IMPORTUNITY OF HER MANY ADMIRERS, BENDS GRACEFULLY OVER THE PIANO, AND, AFTER STRIKING A FEW CHORDS, WARBLES ONE OF SCHUMANN'S SADDEST MELODIES IN HER OWN INIMITABLE MANNER. UNFORTUNATELY, HER HOST IS "ÆSTHETIC," AND, MORE MINDFUL OF MURAL DECORA- TION THAN BEAUTIFUL MUSIC, HAS FIXED ONE OF THOSE DELIGHTFUL OLD-FASHIONED ROUND MIRRORS JUST OVER THE PIANO.—

87. *Punch* (1878)

As one wanders along the avenues, under the gently rustling trees, the sunlight wavers and flickers on the red brick fronts of the houses; many of the doors are open, and the near halls are visible with their clean cool Indian matting, square old-fashioned brass lamps; comfort and elegance everywhere, lightness and grace abound. Even the names on the door-posts have a touch of poetry and quaintness about them: – Plesaunce, Elm-Dene, Kirk Lees, Ye Denne, for example.[41]

It is unfortunate that Du Maurier does not comment on this estate: his only geographical references are to 'Passionate Brompton', and to South Kensington. (14 June 1879, p. 282 and 19 Feb. 1881).

Another aspect of aesthete interior decoration was the 'Art' furniture movement of the 1870s, which must not be confused with Morris and Co. According to Elizabeth Aslin, the essential characteristics of 'Art' furniture, were the frequent use of:

black or ebonized baywood or basswood and black walnut. Legs, supports, balusters and other uprights were usually slender and turned, sometimes picked out in gold, and carving was limited to formal designs outlined in thin incised lines, also emphasized in gold.[42]

This ebonized phase lasted during the main aesthetic period, 1871–85. The furniture was fairly lightweight and often stained green or painted. Actual examples of this furniture in Du Maurier's cartoons are rare; its fine workmanship would have been hard to show on a small scale. In 1873 two young men are weighing up the possibilities of two young women, with a view to marriage. The cartoon is called 'Aesthetic with a Vengeance' (and one of the young men decides that the smaller girl would suit him better because she would go so well with his buhl and marquetrie furniture). In 'Frustrated Social Ambition' (21 May 1881), a very light table is shown, and perhaps, since this is a cartoon with Mrs Cimabue Brown, Postlethwaite and Maudle, we can assume that this is another example of 'Art' furniture. The unusually painted dado is also associated with the aesthetes in the cartoons, like the 'high blue dado' in 'Oil and Water' (21 Feb. 1880).

The other great influence on aesthetic interior decoration was the vogue for the oriental. Chinoiserie had provided a wealth of motifs and forms for every kind of decoration in the seventeenth and

41. Hamilton, p. 131.
42. E. Aslin, *Nineteenth Century English Furniture* (1962), p. 60.

THE CIMABUE BROWNS. ("TRAIN UP A CHILD," &c.)

Antiquated Grandpapa (fresh from Ceylon). "Now, my Darlings, we're going to make a regular day of it. First we'll go to the Zoo. Then we'll have a jolly good blow-out at the Langham Hotel. And then we'll go and see the Pantomime at Drury Lane!"

Master Cimabue. "Thanks awfully, Grandpapa! But we prefer the National Gallery to the Zoological Gardens!"

88. *Punch* (1880)

eighteenth centuries, but it was not this idyllic and decorative view of China, so pleasantly unreal and exotic, that appealed to the aesthetes. The first important event in the nineteenth-century vogue for Eastern art was the discovery of Japanese colour prints, particularly those by Hokusai, Hiroshiga and the whole Ukiyoye school. In 1856, or thereabouts, the printer Delatre found a volume of Hokusai prints which had been wrapped round some china. Delatre sold this volume to the painter and etcher Braquemond, who popularized it with his friends. Around 1862, Mme. Desoye opened an oriental shop in the Rue de Rivoli where Manet, Fantin-Latour, Tissot, Jacquemart, Solon, Baudelaire and the De Goncourts were customers. This vogue for oriental objects soon came to England, where blue-and-white china was particularly admired and collected. The blue-and-white china imported into England, known in the nineteenth century as 'Old Nanking', was usually that of the Chinese Kang Hsi period (1662–1722), or Japanese imitations of the work of that time (few Victorians were discriminating enough to know the difference). Kang Hsi is important in the history of this ware, because it was during his reign that the cobalt blue was refined to a brilliant and pure sapphire with no trace of purple or grey; the white at this stage was slightly tinged with blue and thus appears whiter than at any earlier or later period. Flower and plant patterns were popular motifs, particularly the prunus blossom. Other patterns are often of figures in a landscape, or the so-called 'lange lyzen', the tall figure of a woman.

Whistler, when he returned to London in 1859, brought blue-and-white china, and a host of other objects, 'sketch-books, colour-prints, lacquers, kakemonos, embroideries, screens'.[43] He told Rossetti of his enthusiasm, and Rossetti almost immediately bought two pieces of blue-and-white from Murray Marks. The craze was under way. Marks went to Holland to replenish his stocks of blue-and-white, where it was still quite cheap, and offered a large collection to Rossetti for 50 pounds: Rossetti himself could not afford it all, but shared it with a Mr Huth and Sir Henry Thompson, who both became enthusiastic collectors. Rossetti and Whistler were to remain rival collectors until they sold their porcelain back to Marks in the early 1870s. Du Maurier told Armstrong about Whistler's new passion in 1863: 'he has bought some very fine china;

43. E. R. and J. Pennell, *The Life of James McNeill Whistler* (5th Edition, 1911), p. 84.

has about sixty pounds worth, and his anxiety about it during dinner was great fun'.[44] On 7 November 1864, he mentioned Whistler's rivalry with Rossetti at the *Punch* table:

> Du M. tells of Whistler and Rossetti's rage for old china – and how R. once left his guests at dinner and rushed off to buy a piece for fear W. should forestall him.[45]

Whistler and Rossetti were both customers at a shop in the Strand, and at one near London Bridge, where a print was given away with every pound of tea. In Regent Street, Farmer and Rogers had an oriental warehouse, in charge of Mr Lazenby Liberty, soon to start his own specialized business in oriental objects. In May 1878, Sir Henry Thompson held a sensational exhibition of his china in Oxford Street, where, at the private view, supper was served by Scotts on blue-and-white china. It is said that on this occasion Rossetti tipped the contents off a plate in order to examine the mark underneath. The dinner and exhibition created an immense popular interest in blue-and-white, and helped to foster the craze, which Du Maurier found such a profitable subject.

Blue-and-white was already fetching large prices before Du Maurier's first cartoon in 1874. There was a large Christie's sale in 1867, and two years later Marks returned to Holland to buy enough china to meet the increasing rage. The first of the 'chinamania' cartoons appeared on 2 May 1874, entitled 'The Passion for Old China'. It was the beginning of Du Maurier's concentrated attack on the aesthetes. There are ten 'chinamania' cartoons over a period of six and a half years, the last appearing on 30 Oct. 1880. In 'The Passion for Old China' a wife is sitting with a blue-and-white teapot clasped to her bosom; behind her are various other pieces of porcelain. Her husband, who wears a velveteen jacket, is begging her to give him back the teapot which she has been holding all morning in apparent ecstasy. 'Incipient Chinamania' appears six months later, on 26 Dec. 1874. A little girl is standing before her mother in tears, because her nurse has given her cod-liver-oil in a plain white mug. The room itself has a high dado, and a characteristic display of blue-and-white china. In 'Chronic Chinamania Incurable' (*Almanack*, 1875), the collector is holding a much rivetted piece of English,

44. Letters, p. 216.
45. Silver, 7 Nov. 1864.

89. *Punch* (1874)

THE PASSION FOR OLD CHINA.

Husband. "I think you might *let me* Nurse that Teapot a little *now*, Margery! You've had it to yourself all the *Morning*, you know!"

not oriental, pottery, which he says, took three years to make, and was the only one 'made by the Fallowbrook pottery that was started in 1870', possibly a dig at William de Morgan. 'Acute Chinamania' appeared in the same *Almanack*. A mother with dishevelled hair is weeping over the broken pieces of a favourite pot, while one of her daughters tries to comfort her:

'Mamma! Mamma! *Don't* go on like this, pray!'
'What have I got left to live for?'
'Haven't you got me, Mamma?'
'You, child! You're not unique!! There are six of you – a complete set!!'

ACUTE CHINAMANIA.

May. "MAMMA! MAMMA! *DON'T GO ON LIKE THIS, PRAY!*"
Mamma (who has smashed a favourite pot). "WHAT HAVE I GOT LEFT TO LIVE FOR?"
May. "HAVEN'T YOU GOT ME, MAMMA?"
Mamma. "YOU, CHILD! YOU'RE NOT UNIQUE!! THERE ARE SIX OF YOU—A COMPLETE SET!!"

90. *Punch* (1875)

Eighteen months later came 'A Disenchantment' (29 July 1876), which shows the effect of blue-and-white china collecting on ordinary society. The Duke has invited a group of collectors to breakfast to discuss porcelain, most prominent of whom is Swellington Spiff, who collects it 'because it's the thing to do'. The collectors, expecting to be closeted with the Duke alone, are appalled to discover their rivals there. The last of Du Maurier's China cartoons, 'The Six-Mark Tea-Pot' (30 Oct. 1880), is separated from the rest by three years, and is really a comment on the affectations of aesthetic language and on Oscar Wilde in particular. The title may be a backward glance at Whistler's picture *Purple and Rose: The Lange Lijzen of the Six Marks* of 1864. The cartoon stands apart from the other china cartoons because the characters are conceived of as aesthetes rather than 'chinamaniacs'. It is their determination to 'live up to' the tea-pot, rather than the teapot itself, which is important. The 'china-mania' cartoons deal with the extremists who were the most obvious devotees of the cult. Other cartoons, ('Art in Excelsis', 5 Dec. 1874), show its dissemination to the fashionable world. A great many of Du Maurier's social cartoons, between 1876 and 1882, illustrate pieces of blue-and-white china in the conventional home, and such pieces were still appearing in the 1890s.

Blue-and-white china, however, was not the only aspect of the oriental phase. Whistler painted several Japanese subjects between 1864 and 1870, most famous of which are the *Lange Lijzen of the Six Marks*, *The Golden Screen*, *The Balcony* and *La Princesse du Pays de la Porcelaine*. Although these works have something of the linear qualities and flat composition associated with the Japanese print, they are essentially subtle evocations of various Japanese elements, painted in a European tradition. Whistler was one of the first to put Japanese fans on his plain-painted walls. Walter Greaves described Whistler's dining room, with its blue walls, darker blue dado and Japanese fans on the walls and ceiling.[46] The difference between Whistler's white or pale-coloured walls, and Morris' wall-paper, is paralleled in the contrast between Godwin's 'Butterfly Suite' and a piece of solid Morris and Co. furniture. Whistler and Godwin painted their furniture in various tones of yellow, a colour scheme never considered by other furniture decorators. The plain walls in 'Acute Chinamania' (*Almanack*, 1875, p. 292) may be an indirect reference to Whistler's influence, as it contrasts with most cluttered,

46. Pennells, p. 97.

THE SIX-MARK TEA-POT.

Æsthetic Bridegroom. "It is quite consummate, is it not?"
Intense Bride. "It is, indeed! Oh, Algernon, let us live up to it!"

91. *Punch* (1880)

Victorian interiors. The Japanese fan is, however, the only direct comment on his theories of interior decoration. Whistler had created a considerable stir with his highly original redecoration of F. L. Leyland's 'Peacock Room', now in the Freer collection, Washington, but Du Maurier did not comment on it. Leyland, a wealthy Liverpool merchant, had bought Whistler's *La Princesse du Pays de la Porcelaine*, as a centrepiece for his dining room, hung with Spanish leather and blue-and-white china. Whistler, deciding that the leather and carpet detracted from his painting, cut off the border of the carpet and painted peacocks over the leather, without Leyland's permission. The result is magnificent. Leyland, however, was furious, and Jekyll, the original decorator, is said to have gone home, painted his floor gold, and died soon afterwards in an asylum.

The public adapted the vogue for oriental objects in a typically inconsistent way. Depicted in the cartoons are Japanese pots, fans and screens, mixed up with ordinary furniture in the muddle of the Victorian home. Lazenby Liberty in Regent Street did extensive business in imported oriental objects, particularly the cheaper kind of blue-and-white china. Du Maurier often uses a Japanese screen in the cartoons to block off the main part of a room, and concentrate attention on a small area. The Japanese screen is not in any way restricted to aesthete homes. 'Our Artist' (10 Nov. 1877) has a screen behind his model, painted with prunus blossom, water-lilies and a rather indefinite flower, and a similar screen appears behind Sylvia and Daisy in 'Induction' (24 Aug. 1878). The Japanese fan, although occasionally carried in the hand in Du Maurier's cartoons, is usually found as a wall decoration. In 'Feline Amenities' (27 Feb. 1875), two young ladies are sitting in arm-chairs, and one of them is holding a Japanese fan. Mrs Ponsonby de Tomkyns carries a fan while talking to her husband in 'A Dilemma' (25 Oct. 1879), and they continue to appear till the late 1880s.

An early reference to the popularity of Japanese objects in general is found in the cartoon 'A Smart Youth' (5 April 1873), where Cousin Robert is given Millicent's favourite piece of Japanese enamel because he has desecrated it with cigarette ash. As late as 1889 Du Maurier is suggesting Japanese Sun Shades as a protection against electric light. An interesting description of a house, where a variety of motifs were employed, is L. F. Day's account of the Ionides home in Holland Park, which Du Maurier himself must have known well. Designed by Philip Webb, the interior decoration was carried out by Morris and Co., Walter Crane and Thomas Jekyll. Plain walls were contrasted with stucco, Morris paper with oak panelling, Japanese lacquer and pots with 18th century English furniture, Burne-Jones' pictures with Persian pottery.[47]

The oriental aspects of the aesthete movement reflect the wider issues of the 'cult of beauty', which they established. This is already apparent in the worship of the blue-and-white pot, and it becomes even more apparent in the worship of the flower. The flowers particularly associated with the aesthetes were the sunflower and the lily. Closely connected with these two flowers was the peacock feather, which could be carried, or used for decoration, in much the same way. Walter Hamilton does not analyse the reasons why the aesthetes chose these three symbols, but he describes their importance:

> But why the sunflower, the lily, and the peacock's feather have become so closely identified with the movement it is not easy to explain; certain it is they appear to be as distinctively the badges of the true Æsthete as the green turban is amongst Mahommedans the sign that the wearer has accomplished a pilgrimage to the holy place. In these minor details, I believe the examples of D. G. Rossetti, and more recently of Oscar Wilde, have had considerable influence.[48]

Flower worship was an important part of the extreme aesthete's affectation. They tended to carry or wear one conspicuous flower, too large to escape notice. The sunflower was the first aesthete motif, and it was followed by the lily, and eventually by the green carnation. This change of flower represents a gradual movement away from the 'natural', although its importance is hard to estimate. Whistler's 'One flower in Japanese pot', which the Italian landscape painter, Martini, thought such an inadequate breakfast,[49] was an early example of the flower vogue. Wilde's floral affectation was later, but better advertised.

The reasons for the popularity of the sunflower are difficult to understand. The sunflower certainly appears in some Pre-Raphaelite pictures, but not as frequently as the lily, a later aesthetic favourite, which has a better known symbolic history. The sunflower was prominent in Morris' mural in the Oxford Union of 1857, 'Sir Tristram and La Belle Iseult', which has now faded, but may have

47. 'A Kensington Interior', Art Journal (May, 1893), pp. 139–44.
48. Hamilton, p. 35.
49. Comyns Carr, p. 104.

influenced Wilde in his choice of the flower. One of the Morris wall-papers, introduced in 1879, is actually called 'Sunflower', and it may have added to the popularity of the cult. Among Morris fabrics there are several where the sunflower forms part of the pattern, for example in the 1878 woven-wool tissue, 'Bird'. The sunflower also appears in Burne-Jones' *The Wine of Circe* where its effect is both decorative and symbolic.

The popularity of the sunflower seems to have been unrelated to its classical significance, as a symbol of gratitude and affectionate re-membrance, derived from the story of Apollo and Clytie. It was probably adopted on purely 'aesthetic' grounds; for its size, colour and starkness. Wilde himself in America said that he loved the sun-flower, not 'for any vegetable fashion at all', but because its 'gaudy leonine beauty' was 'naturally adapted for decorative art', and gave to 'the artist the most entire and perfect joy'.[50] The sunflower became a popular decorative motif in the late 19th century, and could be seen in the decoration of the now-demolished Birmingham Reference Library, and in other public buildings. A pair of curtains at Windsor Castle, designed for Queen Victoria, had the same motif.

The sunflower is restricted to the aesthete homes in the early cartoons; its earliest appearance is in 'Intellectual Epicures' (5 Feb. 1876), where De Tomkyns has a single example in a blue china vase on the mantelpiece. One of the most valuable examples is in 'Music and Æsthetics (16 Feb. 1878, p. 286) where a painted sunflower grows up one side of the aesthetic host's piano. Four large blooms appear at the side and a fifth is growing along the outside edge of the keyboard. This illustration shows how quickly the motif was catch-ing on, even before the arrival of Oscar Wilde in London in 1878. Mrs Spratt's arm-chair is patterned in sunflowers, and real sun-flowers grow in her garden (28 and 7 Sept. 1878, p. 270). By the end of 1878, Du Maurier is showing the motif in the decoration of ordinary homes. In 'What we may come to in Time' (9 Nov. 1878), the mantel-piece is covered by a long piece of cloth embroidered with trailing sunflowers. Sunflowers also appear on several dresses in the cartoons. Mrs Robinson's medieval fancy-dress is decorated with them in 'A Faithful Guardian' (17 June 1876); the medieval sunflower was in fact the marigold, the true sunflower first being imported from America.

50. O. Wilde, 'The English Renaissance of Art' *Miscellanies,* edited R. Ross (1908), p. 276.

The lily seems to have succeeded the sunflower as the chief aesthetic motif around 1880. It does not appear in Du Maurier's cartoons until April 1880, by which time the sunflower is on its way out, only making three more appearances. Mrs J. Comyns Carr inaccurately chronicles the change: '[Du Maurier] drew Wilde as Mr Postlethwaite, with a huge sunflower in his buttonhole. In subsequent drawings he was usually depicted carrying a fine Madonna lily'.[51] In Postlethwaite's first appearance (14 Feb. 1880, p. 271), the flower is neither large nor a sunflower, and he does not carry one on any subsequent occasion, though Mrs Cimabue Brown is frequently shown with a lily. While the sunflower is associated with the bright sunlight, the lily is symbolically the flower of purity. In the early renaissance pictures so admired by the aesthetes, it is almost an essential part of any annunciation scene. It was also a common motif with Rossetti and the later Pre-Raphaelite disciples. Rossetti uses it in its old symbolic meaning in two of his early works dealing with the life of the Virgin Mary, *Ecce Ancilla Domini* and *The Girlhood of St Mary Virgin* (both in the Tate Gallery, London). Lilies appear in *The Blessed Damozel*, completed in 1876, which illustrates his own poem, first published in *The Germ* in 1850, and later revised:

> The blessed damozel leaned out
> From the gold bar of Heaven;
> Her eyes were deeper than the depth
> Of waters stilled at even;
> She had three lilies in her hand,
> And the stars in her hair were seven.

The clash of the rose and the lily, the white flower of Hera and the red rose of Aphrodite, is frequently touched on by the poets and painters of the time. It is very clear in J. F. Lewis' picture *Lilium Aratum* (City Museum and Art Gallery, Birmingham), where the two flowers grow together. Most famous of all is Swinburne's use of the contrast in 'Dolores':

> Change in a trice
> The lilies and languors of virtue
> For the raptures and roses of vice.

The frequent use of the lily by Burne-Jones certainly appealed to the

51. Comyns Carr, p. 85.

aesthetes; it echoes the drooping form of the maidens who carry it. Often it is purely decorative, as in the *Heart of the Rose Tree* and the *Sponsa de Libano* (plate 10), but in the *Flower of God* and *The Prioress Tale* it is used as a symbol of purity.

It is possible to exaggerate the symbolic overtones of the lily as adopted by the aesthetes. It is typical of the perverse delight which the later decadent movement in the 1890s took in corrupted purity, that this flower should become so popular with them. Perhaps its waxen quality, and its artificiality, played a part in their choice. The theme of the lily is a recurring one in the cartoons. It is significant that, in 'The Appalling Diffusion of Taste' (19 March 1881, p. 256), Mr Grigsby has placed his blue pot of lilies next to a vague painting clearly labelled 'Burne-Jones'. The lilies, in fact, are the final blow to Sir Pompey, and he reserves four exclamation marks for them. In 'An Æsthetic Midday Meal' (17 July 1880), Jellaby Postlethwaite is sitting in a pastry-cooks' shop with a lily in a glass of water, as a substitute for a midday meal. In 'A Love Agony' (5 June 1880, p. 260), Postlethwaite reclines half-dressed under clumps of drooping lilies, in Maudle's painting; the poem below refers to the 'lily of love'. The lily seems to have been less popular, as a decorative motif, than the sunflower, if we can take the evidence of the cartoons, where it appears only in aesthete homes, as in 'Nincompoopiana' and 'Frustrated Social Ambition' (24 April 1880 and 21 May 1881). The carrying of lilies was another aspect of the aesthetic flower cult. The Victorian memoir writer, R. E. Francillon, describes a 'youth . . . carrying throughout a whole evening, in melancholy silence, a tall white lily, with whose droop he was evidently doing his best to bring his own figure into imitation'.[52] In *Patience*, Bunthorne confesses that he is a sham, and that, 'A languid love for lilies does *not* blight me'.

Du Maurier's prose romp for Christmas 1880 is another attack on the flower vogue. Called 'Fleur des Alpes', or 'Postlethwaite's Last Love' (25 Dec. 1880), it is told in the first person by Postlethwaite. After an opening, full of 'aesthetic' exaggerations, he begins his story:

> One evening, for want of anything better to say, I told Mrs Cimabue Brown, in the strictest confidence, that I could sit up all night with a *lily*. She was holding one in her hand, as usual. She was deeply moved. Her

52. R. E. Francillon, *Mid-Victorian Memoirs* p. 212.

AN ÆSTHETIC MIDDAY MEAL.

At the Luncheon hour, Jellaby Postlethwaite enters a Pastrycook's and calls for a glass of Water, into which he puts a freshly-cut Lily, and loses himself in contemplation thereof.

Waiter. "SHALL I BRING YOU ANYTHING ELSE, SIR?"
Jellaby Postlethwaite. "THANKS, NO! I HAVE ALL I REQUIRE, AND SHALL SOON HAVE DONE!"

92. *Punch* (1880)

eye moistened. She said, 'Quite so!' and wrung my fingers. And it struck her as such a beautiful thought.

This story is an attack on Oscar Wilde, referring directly to stories told about him, for Wilde, frequently appeared in public 'carrying in his hand a lily or a sunflower, which he used to contemplate with an expression of the greatest admiration'.[53] Wilde once came down to breakfast at a country house, looking haggard and weary, because,

53. R. H. Sherard, *The Life of Oscar Wilde* (1906), p. 161.

he said, he had been sitting up all night with a primrose which looked rather ill. Du Maurier actually scribbled this story down for Frank Burnand. *Patience*, as usual, had its own comment to make:

> If you walk down Piccadilly with a poppy or a
>   lily in your medieval hand,
> And everyone will say,
> As you walk your flowery way,
> 'If he's content with a vegetable love which
>   would certainly not suit *me*,
> Why, what a particularly pure young man this
>   pure young man must be!'

Another popular motif with the aesthetes was the peacock, which again originated with the Pre-Raphaelites and their followers. A large peacock stands beside the seated figure of King David in the right hand panel of Rossetti's tryptich in Llandaff Cathedral, and another appears in *Silver and Gold* by Arthur Hughes. 'Peacock and Dragon' was one of the woven-wool tissues designed by Morris in 1878. For the early Christians, the peacock was a symbol of immortality and is often found on tombs in early Italian churches. It later became the symbol of pride. The aesthetes, however, were attracted solely by its magnificent colours.

In the Du Maurier cartoons, the peacock feather usually appears as a hat decoration. The young Cimabue Brown girls wear it as such ('The Height of Æsthetic Exclusiveness', 1 Nov. 1879), and so do the 'trusty friends' of the Spratts (7 Sept. 1878). The latter even try to eat a peacock, but are very sick. In consequence, they stick peacock feathers into some more edible bird, and so salve their aesthetic consciences. (7 Sept. 1878). Two references to peacock feathers are more interesting than their appearance as decoration in hats and fans. In 'A Scare' (5 Feb. 1881), two polar bears have disrupted the skating on a frozen pond, and the departing skaters leave behind their effects, including a lily and peacock's feather. Two weeks later we find Miss Bilderbogie telling Mrs Cimabue Brown about her love for Peter Pilcox, and of their decision to live in South Kensington where things are cheap: 'Peacock feathers only a *penny* a-piece!' ('Æsthetic Love in a Cottage' 19 Feb. 1881).

The captions under his *Punch* drawings provide Du Maurier with an excellent opportunity to satirize the affected language of the aesthetes. Wilde's imitators, of whom there must have been many in

London at the time, probably gave Du Maurier his 'copy'. Whistler was a different kind of conversationalist, more intelligent and malicious than Wilde, as revealed in *The Gentle Art of Making Enemies* (1890). The language of aestheticism was full of over-enthusiasm and wildly exaggerated rapture; it also affected flippancy in the face of conventional wisdom. As the century progressed, aesthete language grew more and more languorous, 'utterly utter' seems to have marked a kind of naïve enthusiasm not found in *Dorian Gray* (1891) where the attitude has become cynical, and blasé.

The actual words found in the cartoons, and the forms of expression used there, show how terms originally intended to intensify only, 'quite', 'utter', 'too', are frequently employed either to qualify other strings of adjectives, or even to qualify themselves ('utterly utter'), and so become the most distinctive features of the style. The use of these normally subordinate words in prominent positions is always startling in its effect. In Du Maurier's cartoons most of the unusual words are adjectival. The plain superlative is felt to be inadequate to describe the qualities of an object or person, and an intensive is added. The most popular of these are the variants of 'How quite too lovely'. This expression is first heard in 'Picture Sunday' (29 March 1873), where the young lady, flattering the painter, describes his pictures as *'quite-too-more than lovely'*. 'Quite' is found again, as an adjective meaning 'superb' or 'wonderful', in the expression 'really *most* quite', used to describe a successful ball ('Refinements of Modern Speech' 7 Feb. 1874). The 'Old Masters' at Burlington House are referred to as 'quite *too Too*' by a female aesthete in one of the cartoons, entitled 'Refinements of Modern Speech' (26 March 1881). Perhaps Du Maurier's most absurd superlative phrase is 'How really quite too far more than most awfully delicious!!!', with which the admiring chorus of ladies greet the poem 'To a Fair Archeress' by the Hon. Fitz-Lavender Belairs (13 Jan. 1877). The first use of 'awfully' as a slang intensive is given by the *New English Dictionary* as 1830, and it is still heard as a form of superlative today. Du Maurier uses it in another of the series, 'Refinements of Modern Speech' (15 Jan. 1876), where it appears as 'Ta! Awf'lly Ta!!', revealing the ludicrous conjunction of affectation and slang. 'Far' is found with a favourite aesthete word, in 'how far lovelier', used of Mrs Spratt's clothes (14 Sept. 1878).

The superlative adjectives used by the aesthetes in the cartoons seem to have been quarried from various sources. 'Blessed', taken from the Catholic ritual, is used by Bellamy Brown to describe a

VERS DE SOCIÉTÉ.

THAT PLAYFUL BUT TENDER YOUNG BARD, THE HON. FITZ-LAVENDER BELAIRS, ENJOYS THE ALMOST PERFECT BLISS OF READING A LITTLE THING OF HIS OWN TO A CIRCLE OF WEAK-MINDED BUT INTENSELY SYMPATHETIC WOMEN :—

"TO A FAIR ARCHERESS.

"Glad lady mine, that glitterest
  In shimmah of summah athwart the lawn,
Canst tell me which is bitterest—
  The glamaw of Eve, or the glimmah of dawn,

"To those with whose hearts thou litterest
  The field where they fall at thy feet to fawn ?
As a buttahfly dost thou fluttah by !
  How, whence, and oh ! whither, art come and gone ?"

Chorus, "HOW EXQUISITE ! HOW REFINED ! ! HOW REALLY QUITE TOO FAR MORE THAN MOST AWFULLY DELICIOUS ! ! !"
  [As the Poem is not of equal merit throughout we only quote the first Stanza.

93. Punch (1877)

picture in 'Artistic Amenities' (26 July 1879). Bellamy describes the picture as, 'a Poem', 'Precious', 'Blessed', 'Subtile', 'Significant' and 'Supreme', while Postlethwaite talks of the lily as, 'Consummate', 'Perfect', 'Supreme', 'Precious', and 'Blessèd' (25 Dec. 1880). 'Precious' has acquired a new shade of meaning in the English language, largely due to the aesthetes; from meaning costly and valuable, it now means 'over-nice and over-refined'. Muffington, a friend of Prigsby, uses the word to describe the tune of 'Little Bo-Peep' in 'Nincompoopiana' (20 Dec. 1879), and Prigsby himself uses it of a painting in 'Distinguished Amateurs. The Art Critic' (13 March 1880, p. 255).

'Supreme' is a word much used by both Bellamy and Postlethwaite. Like 'blessed' and 'precious', it is first used in 'Artistic Amenities' (26 July 1879), and then appears as part of the chorus of admiration for 'Little Bo-Peep' (20 Dec. 1880). Prigsby in 'Distinguished Amateurs' (13 March 1880, p. 255), calls the Ilyssus, 'that supremest masterpiece of Greek sculptchah'. Postlethwaite in 'Fleur des Alpes' (25 Dec. 1880) makes frequent use of it, and describes Maudle and Mrs Cimabue Brown in this fashion: 'For *she* is Supremely Consummate', whereas he is, 'Consummately Supreme'. He himself is a combination of 'Supreme Consummateness' and 'Consummate Supremacy'. 'Consummate' does not often appear in the cartoons, but was clearly popular with the aesthetes. At the end of 'Fleur des Alpes' Du Maurier gives the Philistine's view of this particular word. ' "Don't twig this lingo about ' Consummate ' "', said 'Arry. Robert the waiter thought it had something to do with soup'.

A very common adjective in the cartoons is 'exquisite'. Du Maurier describes the affected young people in a 'Refinements of Modern Speech' (7 Feb. 1874), as 'Female Exquisite' and 'Male Ditto'. In 'Vers de Société' (13 Jan. 1877, p. 303), an aesthete poem is greeted with cries of 'How Exquisite!'

Other popular words in the cartoons are 'beautiful' and 'divine'. Maudle considers that Mrs Cimabue Brown's son should be content to merely 'exist beautifully', a remark which anticipates Dorian Gray and the 'nineties (12 Feb. 1881, p. 252). For Prigsby 'the *Pictchah* is beautiful', even 'most Beautiful'; it has nothing else to recommend it, but it has beauty (10 Feb. 1877). Mrs Cimabue Brown uses the word to describe Postlethwaite, '*Is* not he *beautiful*?' (14 Feb. 1880, p. 271), and his sitting up all night with a lily strikes her as 'a beautiful thought' (25 Dec. 1880).

Among the words which illustrate the forced melancholy and seriousness which Du Maurier found so easy to satirise is 'intense'. In 'Passionate Brompton' (14 June 1879, p. 282), the aesthetic lady inquires of her stolid companion, '*Are you intense?*' It is perhaps surprising that Du Maurier does not use this word again, for it admirably expresses the drooping and melancholy spirit of the extreme aesthete. The influence of unnaturally gloomy subjects is found in the repetition of words like 'sad', and 'strange'. The Spratts' songs are 'sad', and the gloom of their friends is broken only occasionally by 'a sad strange merriment' (7 Sept. 1878).

Another interesting use of language is found in Du Maurier's adjectives, expressing simplicity, 'innocent', 'simple', 'pure'. Jack Spratt is a 'simple-minded young painter', his twins gambol with a 'lamb-like innocence', the family amusements are of the 'simplest, healthiest and most delightful kind' (7 Sept. 1878). Verbal inversion and unnecessary repetition are both used to express enthusiasm and wonder. An early example is 'On a broken egg shell' (7 Feb. 1874), where the 'Inspired Being', opens with the words, 'Whence, O Whence, ladies, whence, oh whence came the marvellous instinct . . .'; at the end of his speech, the admiring ladies take up the refrain, 'Whence, O whence, indeed?'. Postlethwaite's rondel in 'A Love Agony' (5 June 1880, p. 260) is made absurd by its constant repetition of the word 'fain' in various forms, and its juxtaposition with 'faint':

> Fain of thyself! I faint, adoring thee,
> Fain of thy kisses, fainer of thy sighs,
> Yet fainest, love! an thou wert fain of me.

The use of archaic language by the aesthetes is parodied in 'The Rise and Fall of the Jack Spratts'. William Morris, whose verse Du Maurier had already satirized in 'A Legend of Camelot', was an important source for archaic terminology. In the course of the first chapter of the 'Rise and Fall of the Jack Spratts' (7 Sept. 1878), Du Maurier brings a 'quaint' note into the story with a large number of archaisms:

> In a beautiful old suburb of London, undesecrated, as yet, by steam or telegraph-wires, and surrounded by low-lying flowery meads, through which the Thames would still meander occasionally, as it had been wont to do in days long gone by, dwelt Jack Spratt, a handsome, genial, and simple-minded young painter. He had a girl-wife of lofty stature, and truly transcending loveliness, a gift of which she seemed as yet unconscious.

The use of 'wont' is the only obvious archaism, but the whole tone of the passage is established by the use of such words as 'meads', 'meander', 'flowery'. The opening paragraphs are full of such examples. They 'were unto each other even as the apple of the eye'. The lay-figures have 'curiously-wrought' limbs, the meal is 'frugal', Mrs Spratt is 'embroidering some quaint device', the Spratts 'hie them to the flowery mead', they visit the 'leech' and do not draw, but 'limn'. There is even an echo of Milton in 'What time Sally the cook is dishing up a cold roast capon'. The erroneous 'ye', which the Victorians fondly imagined was the Old English for 'the', also appears in the story. It is used in the captions to the illustrations, 'Ye Gorgeous Young Swells', and 'Ye Aesthetic Young Geniuses' (21 Sept. 1878). The use of shortened verb forms is found in other cartoons. The aesthete poem, 'To a Fair Archeress' (13 Jan. 1877, p. 303), has 'canst', 'art', and 'dost', as well as the old form, 'that glitterest', and 'thou litterest'.

Another habit of the aesthetes, which Du Maurier frequently ridicules, is their drawled 'ah', ending on a word which normally ends with an 'er' or 'ure'. An 'Ineffable Youth' in 'Modern Aesthetics' (10 Feb. 1877) calls a picture a 'picktchah', says that he is 'cullahblind', and that he doesn't care for 'Naytchah'. The best example is the poem delivered by Hon. Fitz Lavender Belairs (13 Jan. 1877, p. 303):

> Glad lady mine, that glitterest
> In shimmah of summah athwart the lawn,
> Canst tell me which is bitterest,
> The glamaw of Eve, or the glimmah of dawn.

There are very few examples of aesthetic poetry in the cartoons; one is 'To a Fair Archeress', another 'A Love Agony' by Postlethwaite (5 June 1880, p. 260). The language of these poems has already been discussed. Their style is only noticeable for its extraordinary vacuity, recalling 'A Ballad of Blunders', but it is less pointed in the use of satire. Swinburne, Rossetti and Oscar Wilde were the chief sources, but Du Maurier's comic poems are not aimed at any particular poet. A good example of the poetry is the second stanza of *A Love Agony*:

> Yea, lo! for veriest fainness faint I, Sweet,
> Of thy spare bosom, where no shadows meet,

And limp straight hip, and weak delicious knee!
For joy thereof I swoon, and my pulse-beat,
Is as of one that wasteth amorously,
So an thou be!

As a social cartoonist, Du Maurier was interested in the way in which aestheticism was being used in the 'climbing' game. Swellington Spiff hopes that his china collection will bring him into contact with a Duke. Postlethwaite, in 'Fleur Des Alpes' (25 Dec. 1880), has his eye on social success as the outcome of his flower-worship:

> the Lily had carried me through my first season, the Primrose through my second. The question arose: what Flower of Flowers is to carry me through my next?

Wilde was open to censure on this score, but he was, after all, good value for money. Du Maurier had less time for the smaller fry:

> Of course since then [1878], the aesthetes have come more into society, especially Society – which has reacted upon them – Mrs Cimabue Brown, who can't endure Grigsby's admirable comic songs, listens complacently to the vulgar trash of Lord Plantagenet Cadbury. – The duchess comes to see her quite informally, takes tea out of the pretty handle-less china cups (& burns her fingers); praises all the pretty things, & takes precious care not to ask her to her great garden party, until she changes her attire – sage green coalscuttle bonnet, yellow sack blouse with gigot sleeves, tied round the waist &c. &c. &c.[54]

One lady aesthete, who had climbed successfully into society, appears in W. P. Frith's *The Private View of The Royal Academy* 1881 (plate 11) where she stands gazing at Oscar Wilde. The picture was painted to present a series of portraits of famous people, Ellen Terry, Lily Langtry, Irving, Gladstone, Browning and Huxley are included, and to satirize aesthete fashions in dress, and the folly of listening to self-elected critics in matters of taste. Du Maurier appears on the left in his role of perpetual observer, the great cartoonist of aestheticism.

---

54. Letter to F. C. Burnand, July 1880, University Library, Yale.

Chapter 8

The Social Cartoonist

IF GEORGE DU MAURIER had died in 1890, rather than in 1896, he would never have written *Trilby*, and his reputation would entirely rest on his *Punch* cartoons. To his friends he was always the cartoonist, thinking up captions and executing his meticulous cartoons week after week, year after year, in an unvarying round. The greater part of his life, over thirty years, was spent in this ephemeral activity, and he must be judged ultimately on his success or failure in his chosen profession. For a man who had studied art in the hope of becoming a great painter, his career as an illustrator often seemed a dispiriting endeavour: 'Alas for the draughtsman! the pleasure of his picture only lasts a few minutes',[1] he once told Henry James. While the paintings of Whistler or Poynter were the subject of sustained interest and comment, Du Maurier's vast output of drawings lay forgotten in the back-numbers of a comic magazine. In more optimistic moments, Du Maurier cherished the hope that black-and-white art would one day rival painting and literature:

> I can suggest ideas – not about me in particular, or anybody else, but about the noble craft still in its infancy of which we petits dessinateurs sur bois are the humble pioneers. . . . The mind of a Thackeray – the pencil of a Menzel – & two pages weekly in *Punch* for say 40 years! Tademas, Leightons, Burne Joneses, hide your diminished heads – Wattses, take a back seat – Poynters & Albert Moores, put your heads in a bag! You will never near Phidias & Titian & Raphael & if you did, you wouldn't be popular. Portrait painters & landscapists & seascapists, we still admit you & drink your health![2]

In a lecture of 1890 on the craft of the *Punch* artist, Du Maurier developed his theories about the supreme social cartoonist, who would express pictorially a world as complex as that of the novelist.

Posterity has done nothing to compensate Du Maurier for the

---

1. 1 May 1883, Houghton Library, Harvard.
2. To Henry James, 27 Sept. 1888. Houghton Library, Harvard.

frustrations of his lifetime. The critics of black-and-white art have dismissed his later work as stereotyped and disappointing, while the historians of humour have castigated him as a cartoonist without a true comic sense. Only the social historians have blindly and thankfully seized on his drawings as contemporary visual evidence, illustrating them without giving his name, and making no attempt to understand his viewpoint. For Du Maurier was a very personal

94. Initial letter 'A' (c 1861). Charles Keene and Du Maurier drawing portraits of each other.

social critic, with his own unconcealed likes and dislikes, and not an objective commentator or a camera. It is true that he had comparatively few axes to grind, and rarely revealed any violent partisanship. One outstanding weakness in judgement was, however, succinctly summarized by Henry James: 'The world was, very simply, divided for him into what was beautiful and what was ugly, and especially into what *looked* so'.[3] This fundamental prejudice had its effect on all Du Maurier's work as a cartoonist, for the world was conveniently divided into the 'haves' and 'have-nots', who were visibly distinguished into the beautiful and the ugly. Society women in the cartoons are tall, slender, and enormously dignified.

3. *Harper's New Monthly Magazine*, p. 594.

95. *Punch* (1879)

In an article on his own work, Du Maurier confessed to having added a few extra inches to their skirts, because he found stately women so much more attractive.[4] He may well have helped to bring the tall woman into fashion, and some frivolous commentators have even suggested that he permanently raised the height of the average English girl by several inches. Governesses and servant girls, when on duty, are also characterized by good looks and upright carriage, but the common 'arriet is usually round and small, with coarse features and no poise. The distinction between upper-class beauty and lower-class vulgarity is nowhere more tellingly made than in 'Est Modus in Rebus' (6 Dec. 1879), where the subtle alteration of line and silhouette suggests an absolute gulf. Similarly gentlemen in the cartoons are always tall and elegant, handsome in youth, dignified in old age, while their inferiors are short, stubby, and graceless. Small men were usually the object of ridicule, for, although Du Maurier was himself short, he cherished a familiar penchant for huge people and animals: 'It is noticeable throughout his work . . . that it is almost only the ugly people who are small and the small people who are ugly'.[5] Other prejudices are more openly expressed. He was anti-clerical, but not anti-episcopal (bishops are pillars of the establishment), and he disliked sanctimoniousness and cant of any kind, as he revealed so pungently in the famous 'curate's egg' cartoon ('True Humility', 9 Nov. 1895). His distaste for affectation explains the bitterness with which he attacked the 'aesthetes', whom he pursued with an almost personal animosity. The rising 'nouveau riches' were another object of savage attack, but the criticism that Du Maurier was rampantly anti-semitic cannot be fully substantiated. He produced less than a dozen cartoons directly mocking the Jews, and his attitude must, to some extent, be seen in the context of of contemporary prejudice. Du Maurier was not always on the side of reaction. Jokes at the expense of Frenchmen in *Punch* were replaced by cartoons which ridiculed the attempts of the English to speak French, and their insular behaviour abroad.

After his permanent appointment to the *Punch* staff in 1864, in place of John Leech, Du Maurier worked there almost without a break for the next thirty-two years, contributing the 'social cuts', in which he satirized the follies and excesses of fashionable society. Politics he never attempted, as he had no interest in the subject, and

4. Illustration, p. 372.
5. *Harper's New Monthly Magazine*, p. 597.

cartoons about the lower classes were usually outside his range, and left for Charles Keene: 'I have generally stuck to the 'classes' because C.K. seems to have monopolized the 'masses' – Division of labour',[6] Du Maurier told Henry Lucy, but there can be no real doubt that the division was as satisfactory to him as it was to Keene. For nearly thirty years, until Keene's death in 1891, the regular artists of the *Punch* staff, Keene, Tenniel and Du Maurier, divided the three major topics between them. The statement which Henry James made in 1883: '*Punch*, for the last fifteen years, has been, artistically speaking, George du Maurier',[7] may well have expressed a more general opinion than is ever admitted, though it has often been criticicized. Most of the public were no more capable than James of appreciating the genius of Charles Keene, which has only become recognized in the present century, while Tenniel's political cuts were so stereotyped and familiar that is must have been hard to think of them as 'art' at all. Du Maurier was undoubtedly one of the main attractions of the magazine, not only because of his social satire, but because his drawings never fell below a certain standard of competence and professional finish. A glance at *Punch* in the late 1880s and early 1890s will show how far he carried the paper over one of the dullest and tattiest periods, although he was one of the oldest contributors, who was no longer producing his best work.

Du Maurier was a born observer and recorder of other people's foibles. His own position in society, together with his French background and education, gave him an outside point of comparison. His choice of Hampstead as a home, with London spread out in perspective below, underlined his detachment from the social scene. Before he began renting a house in the centre, he had always to descend into 'Vanity Fair' to attend those functions at which he found most of his subjects. In no way caught up in the whirlpool of fashionable life, he would return up Haverstock Hill to Hampstead to cogitate on the events and personalities of his evening. In the secure and easy-going atmosphere of his family, he would in the morning communicate his own wry amusement to the readers of *Punch*. His keen awareness of social nuance was backed by a considerable intelligence, which must often have helped him to overcome his poor eyesight. Indeed, his limited vision, by forcing him to

---

6. H. Lucy, *Sixty Years in the Wilderness* (1909), p. 391.
7. H. James, *Partial Portraits* (1888), p. 340.

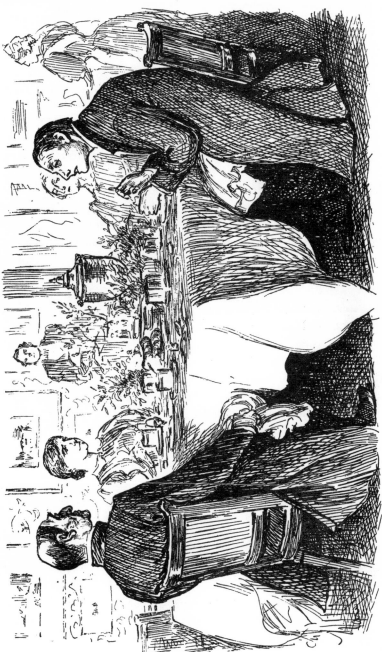

TRUE HUMILITY.

Right Reverend Host. "I'm afraid you've got a bad Egg, Mr. Jones!"
The Curate. "Oh no, my Lord, I assure you! Parts of it are excellent!"

96. *Punch* (1895)

look and analyse more carefully than other people, may actually have sharpened his perception.

He was not naurally gifted as a writer of jokes, and his laboured captions often reveal the struggle which they cost him. Both he and Keene relied to a certain extent on friends, who told or sent them good jokes which they had heard, or amusing situations which they had seen. One of Keene's 'ghosts' even submitted possible outlines for the actual drawings, which were frequently adopted. Tenniel was more fortunate in this respect, for the theme and even the caption of the political cartoons was a matter of general policy decided on by the whole *Punch* staff at their weekly dinners. Du Maurier's main collaborator was Canon Alfred Ainger, who had a real aptitude for witty dialogue, with which he generously supplied the cartoonist during their long walks on Hampstead Heath. Even with this help, Du Maurier still had to find a good many jokes out of his own head, and he increasingly complained of *Punch's* gaping mouth, which became more and more difficult to fill. He preferred to exaggerate and twist a situation he had himself observed rather than trying to conjure a joke out of his head, for which, like most people, he had no natural aptitude. In his early days, Du Maurier had regaled the *Punch* dinner table with some riotously bawdy jokes, which certainly never found their way into the magazine. His sense of humour became quieter and less ebullient as he grew older, and many of his friends later recalled the quality of his conversation: 'He was a delightful conversationalist, his talk lambent with fancy and humour',[8] was Henry Lucy's comment, and this is echoed by Anstey Guthrie: 'He was a fascinating talker, often with a wistful melancholy that was always relieved by humour'.[9] Du Maurier's personal letters, those to his mother and to Henry James, reveal occasional flashes of wit, but the general tone is one of detached and humorous observation. It was this trait which gave his novels their characteristic charm, particularly *Trilby*, from which this passage comes:

> Taffy would lay the cloth English-wise, and also make the salad, for which, like everybody else I ever met, he had a special receipt of his own (putting in the oil first and the vinegar after); and indeed his salads were quite as good as everybody else's.[10]

8. Lucy, p. 392.   10. p. 38.
9. T. A. Guthrie, *A Long Retrospect* (1936), p. 170.

This light and affectionate tone is unfortunately of rare occurrence in the cartoons. An outstanding exception is the early cartoon 'A Pathetic Appeal', which is a delicate and remarkable piece of understatement: a mother and daughter are talking together in the garden:

> 'Mamma, shall you let me go to the Wilkinsons' ball, if they give one, this winter?'
> 'No, darling!' (A pause.)
> '*You've* been to a great many balls, haven't you, Mamma?'
> 'Yes, darling – and I've seen the *folly* of them all.' (Another pause.)
> 'Mightn't I just see the folly of *one*, Mamma?' (A very long pause.)
> (17 October 1874)

The same delicacy is true of those very occasional cartoons in which Du Maurier made real use of his genius as a draughtsman, and abolished the caption entirely. In one such cartoon he drew some girls rowing a boat, in another a group of fisherwomen at Whitby, and in a third his own children walking up the beach on the last day of the holiday. ('Not fond of steering', 9 September 1882; 'The Viqueens of Whitby', 29 September 1883; 'Farewell to Fair Normandy', 2 Oct. 1880). Freed from the tyranny of the caption, Du Maurier's work becomes fresh and spontaneous, and loses entirely the label of 'stereotyped'. He could rarely allow himself the luxury of illustration purely for its own sake in a comic magazine, though it would be interesting to know if the average *Punch* reader was pleased or otherwise to be presented with a fine drawing instead of a joke.

The titles of the cartoons have rarely been singled out for mention, but they are often apt and witty. A number were taken from literature, or recalled Du Maurier's own classical education. His was an age which appreciated Latin puns, and Du Maurier's erudite allusion to the Whitestone Pond in Hampstead, with donkeys galloping round the outside, as the 'pons asinorum', would have made its point. So also would titles based on famous Latin maxims, 'Nos et Mutamur in illis', or 'Illi Robur, et Aes Triplex'. Other titles were often derived from famous works of literature: 'North and South', 'Hard' or 'Soft times', 'The Girl' or 'The Child of the Period', 'Love's Labour's Lost' or 'Won', 'Much Ado about Nothing'; from well-known lines of poetry: 'The Old Order Changeth', 'Those Yellow Sands', 'The Sad Sea Waves'; or from

A PATHETIC APPEAL.

"Mamma, shall you let me go to the Wilkinsons' Ball, if they give one, this Winter?"   "No, Darling!"

(A pause.)

"You've been to a great many Balls, haven't you, Mamma?"

"Yes, Darling,—and I've seen the folly of them all."

(Another pause.)

97. *Punch* (1874)

common maxims or sayings: 'We all expect a soft answer', 'Nothing like a Change', 'Town Mouse and Country Mouse'. Such titles are usually apposite and intelligently chosen, a welcome change from the repetitive 'Things One Might Have Expressed Otherwise'.

In the tradition of Ben Jonson, Fielding and Dickens, Du Maurier had a gift for selecting names which expressed the essential quality of his characters. Some of the more extravagant examples like Lady Godiva Rougepott, Sir Slangsby Jaunter and Mr Warbleton Peacocke were used only once for a particular situation. Du Maurier was more careful in his choice of names for those characters who reappear continually, and round whom he created a mythical existence: Sir Gorgius Midas (quite as good as Jonson's Sir Epicure Mammon), Mrs Lyon Hunter, Todeson, Mrs Cimabue Brown, Lady Clara Robinson née Vere de Vere (adapted from Tennyson), and Lady Snobbington née Shoddy. More subtle are those names which suggest rather than explain personality and qualities: Sir Pompey Bedell (of Bedell, Flunke & Co.), Grigsby, Mrs Ponsonby de Tomkyns, Lady Gwendoline Beaumanoir, The Duke of Haut-castle, and the Duchess of Stilton. On several occasions Du Maurier borrowed a name from Trollope's *Barchester Towers*, Mr Quiverful, perhaps the most charming example of the genre ever invented.

The lengthy captions to Du Maurier's cartoons have often been commented on and criticized. There are basically two kinds of caption, the conversational passage, which is the most common, and the pompous third-person statement by the cartoonist himself. A good example of the second category is 'Love's Labour's Lost; or Autumn Manoeuvres at Midas Towers' (23 Aug. 1884):

(The Stalking of Gorgius Midas Junior)
Lady Matcham de Ryde and her Diana patiently drive the quarry into the discreet little sage-green satin boudoir, whence, as they fondly anticipate, there will be no escape. Unfortunately, who should be lying in wait for him there but Lady Catchem de Wyde and her Constantia!

The use of pedantic language, the involved grammatical construction, and the unnecessary length of the explanation, repel most modern readers, but it must be remembered that the Victorian Age revelled in long-windedness. Novelists, poets, philosophers, theologians, historians and critics all wrote on an impressively large and turgid scale. Ponderous as the following caption appears to be, it

FAREWELL TO FAIR NORMANDY.

On their way back from their last Shrimping Expedition, the Browns sadly reflect that To-morrow they return to Bloomsbury and—Lessons !

98. *Punch* (1880)

conjures up most effectively the atmosphere of Victorian social entertainment, and its attendant horrors:

> Study of a group of people, who have been specially invited to an afternoon tea, to hear Herr Boguluboffski, the great pianist, and Signor Jenkini, the famous tenor. Somehow or other, however, neither of these gentlemen happen to turn up, and to compensate for their unaccountable absence, Little Binks, the host (who, by the way, tries to cultivate a personal resemblance to Mr Irving, and flatters himself he succeeds) manages to recite the 'Dream of Eugene Aram', (to very slow music on the piano by Mrs Binks), before anybody can manage to get away. ('Distinguished Amateurs – The Reciter', 4 Aug. 1883)

The other category of cartoon caption is arranged as a dialogue in dramatic style, with the names of the speakers and their remarks, and an occasional interpolation from the narrator. When Du Maurier began to write novels, several friends suggested that his work on

LOVE'S LABOUR'S LOST; OR, AUTUMN MANŒUVRES AT MIDAS TOWERS.

(The Stalking of Gorgius Midas Junior.)

LADY MATCHAM DE RYDE AND HER DIANA PATIENTLY DRIVE THE QUARRY INTO THE DISCREET LITTLE SAGE-GREEN SATIN BOU-
DOIR, WHENCE, AS THEY FONDLY ANTICIPATE, THERE WILL BE NO ESCAPE. UNFORTUNATELY, WHO SHOULD BE LYING IN WAIT FOR
HIM THERE BUT LADY CATCHAM DE WYDE AND HER CONSTANTIA!

99. *Punch* (1884)

DISTINGUISHED AMATEURS.—THE RECITER.

Study of a Group of People, who have been specially invited to an Afternoon Tea, to hear Herr Bogoluboffski, the great Pianist, and Signor Jenkini, the famous Tenor. Somehow or other, however, neither of these Gentlemen happen to turn up, and to compensate for their unaccountable absence, little Binks, the Host (who, by the way, tries to cultivate a personal resemblance to Mr Irving, and flatters himself he succeeds) manages to recite the "Dream of Eugene Aram," (to very slow music on the Piano by Mrs. Binks), before anybody can manage to get away.

100. *Punch* (1883)

cartoon captions must have given him valuable experience. The
dialogue in the captions is usually well-handled and realistic,
especially in examples like 'A Pathetic Appeal', but word-play is
out of favour today, and Du Maurier's delicate punning is often
tedious and sometimes embarrassing. T. M. Wood thought his
worst joke was the cartoon where the schoolboy decides his mother is
called 'mater' because of her efforts to marry off her daughters,[11]
and another gruesome example concerns a gentleman who has to
take four ladies down to dinner, and who predictably announces,
'forewarned is four armed'. Many of these captions are concerned
with slips of the tongue, which give a quite different meaning to the
one intended, like the long series entitled 'Things one Would Wish to
Have Expressed Otherwise'. The faux-pas committed by the
painter's wife in 'Picture Sunday' (9 April 1887) is a typical example:

> Artist: You'll come and see my pictures before they go?
> Influential Critic: My dear fellow, I never go and see pictures in fellows'
> studios – its such a bore, you know. Everybody saying the pictures are
> too charming and too delightful, and all that!
> Artist's Wife (Nervously): Oh, there's never anything of that sort in *our*
> house—A—! (wishes she hadn't spoken).

All three captions illustrate Du Maurier's technique as a cartoonist.
The joke, such as it is, lies entirely in the caption, which may be
more or less amusing, but is rarely side-splitting. The illustrations
on the other hand are not in the least intrinsically comic. Two of
them (figs. 99 and 101) are merely sketches of social scenes at which
anything could be happening. The expressions on the faces in the
hundredth cartoon do suggest boredom, but the caption is still entirely
necessary as an explanation. This contrasts sharply with the methods
of cartoonists today, where humour is expressed in the drawing
itself, either by the distortion of a well-known shape or face, or by an
easily assimilated chain of events. This is not an entirely modern
development, for Du Maurier's predecessor, John Leech, had a
strong grasp of the visually comic, and often submitted cartoons in
which the actual position or expression of the characters was as
effective as the caption, or made the caption unnecessary. Early in his
career, Du Maurier himself contributed a few cartoons without
captions, usually showing animals or birds in comic situations, but,
after the early 1870s, he settled into his characteristic pattern.

11. Wood, pp. 36–7.

PICTURE SUNDAY.

'You'll come and see my Pictures before they go?"

al Critic. "My dear Fellow, I never go and see Pictures in
3tudios—it's such a Bore, you know. Everybody saying they
.re too Charming, and too Delightful, and all that!"

Wife (nervously). "Oh, there's never anything of that sort in
—a——!"   [*Wishes she hadn't spoken.*

The late Victorian *Punch* of Du Maurier, Keene and Tenniel,
had almost no visual humour, with the exception of Tenniel's
caricatures of political figures like Gladstone and Disraeli. The
cartoonist's approach, like that of the artist, was essentially literary.
Du Maurier would think up a caption and then illustrate it, and it
would not be entirely unfair to suggest that he could easily have
interchanged his designs without anyone noticing what had happened. Year after year, Du Maurier produced beautiful, detailed
drawings, which infuriated the engravers, and provoked no cor-
respondingly detailed response in the reader. He never forgot that

he was primarily an artist, not a humourist, and the word 'un-professional' is still applied to him today among the *Punch* staff, who have inherited an enduring legend.

Du Maurier's *Punch* cartoons can roughly be divided into two groups. The larger and more important group contains the true social cartoons, which cover the whole field of social relationships, and provide such a goldmine for the social historian. The smaller group, which delighted his own public and still has a sentimental appeal, are the drawings of his family, largely based on the actual doings and sayings of his own children. The accompanying captions represent his conversational technique at its most charming. These cartoons about childhood are rarely critical or satirical. They reflect an unstudied delight in children as physical beings, in their spon-taneous reaction to the world around them, and in the combination of deviousness and innocence in their mental processes. He had a particular gift for drawing little girls, with short dresses, laced boots, flowing hair, and thin legs in black stockings. Their intrinsic vanity never escaped Du Maurier, especially when out-of-doors, their heads held high, and hands complacently hidden in large fur muffs. Their open, snub-nosed faces are difficult to resist, and so are their precocious, demanding and disturbing questions. While a compari-son with Millais' late paintings of children is not inapposite, Du Maurier's little girls avoid being sentimental through a certain toughness and vitality, which Du Maurier clearly knew at first hand. His devastating and high-spirited daughters allowed him to harbour no comfortable illusions about the innocence, purity and sweetness of childhood. Children of course do not change as much as social customs, which explains why Du Maurier's dialogue is still so familiar:

> Effie: 'Georgy and I have been down-stairs in the dining-room, Mr Mitcham. We've been playing husband and wife!'
> Mr Mitcham: 'How did you do that, my dear?'
> Effie: 'Why, Georgy sat one end of the table, and I sat at the other; and Georgy said, "This food isn't fit to eat!" And I said, "It's all you'll get!" And Georgy said, "Dam!" and I got up and left the room!'
> ('Awkward Revelations', 25 Aug. 1888)

Most realistic of all are those cartoons where one child tries to get the better of another, like that entitled 'Egoism', which contains one of Du Maurier's shortest captions (see p. 325).

103. *(right) Punch* (1882)

EGOISM.

" COME HERE, DORA ! I WANTS YOU ! "
" THANK YOU, ERIC ; BUT I WANTS MYSELF ! "

A good example of the fallacious reasoning which children some-times employ to get someone else to do something unpleasant occurs in 'A Clincher', where two little girls are lying in bed :

'Get up, and see the time, Eva. I don't know how to tell it.'
'No more do I.'
'O, you horrid story-teller, I taught you myself!'
(21 Feb. 1874)

While children provided Du Maurier with his least demanding subject-matter, it was far more tedious to descend to the West End in order to observe his fellow-guests at a dinner-party. It is hard to tell how far he regarded these excursions into society as a necessary part of his career. His close friend, Canon Ainger, believed that he detested evening parties and dinners in London, not because he was unsociable, but because the late hours and long journeys ' "took it out of him", and endangered the task of the following morning'.[12] Nevertheless evening functions were his chief means of gauging changes in dress and custom, and of observing human behaviour in a formal setting. By a curious paradox, the 'social' drawings of the years he was living in Hampstead contain far more detailed distinctions in fashion and interior decoration than those of his last years when he took a house in the centre of London for the winter, and was able to observe society more consistently. This was partly due to increasing ill-health in his later years, but it may also suggest that he made greater use of his opportunities, when his social life was more limited, and when he regarded it less as a pleasure than an exercise.

During his thirty-six years on *Punch*, few important changes took place in the style or content of Du Maurier's cartoons, though many features subtly altered. In the early 1860s, he frequently made jokes at the expense of the middle-classes, the world of the Wightwicks and his parents' friends in London. It was not long, however, before his own circle had changed and expanded, and by the end of the decade his cartoons were almost exclusively concerned with the upper and upper-middle classes. The increase in titled characters in the cartoons of the 'eighties and 'nineties might suggest that he continued the process into the realms of the aristocracy, but this reflected changes in society rather than in his choice of friends. Certain subjects became more frequent or dropped away during Du Maurier's long career, but the regular topics – the unfortunate remarks, social climbing and husband hunting – altered only in tone and detail, and were never discarded. In the same way the 'dandy' becomes the 'masher' or the effete 'dancer of the period', changing his clothes and gestures, but remaining part of the same generic type. Many of the changes are barely perceptible, unless seen at long range over a period of years. In his early days, Du Maurier's satire was generally aimed at subjects of little social importance, and it tended to be relatively gentle in its effect. As his survey came to include the aesthetic movement, the emancipation of women and the rise of the 'nouveaux riches', Du Maurier became increasingly analytical in his approach, closely in step with the changing mood of the century. It is the same change which divides Dickens from

12. A. Ainger, 'George Du Maurier', *Hampstead Annual* (1897) p. 19.

George Meredith, or the love poems of Elizabeth Barrett Browning from those of Ernest Dowson. Du Maurier, however, differed from his contemporaries in one important respect. One of the main causes of the darkening mood which became evident towards the end of the 19th century was the increase in religious doubt and scepticism. Du Maurier had never been a Christian, and his cartoons on the subject of Darwin and evolution give a most inaccurate picture of the furore which followed the publication of *On the Origin of Species* (1859). Du Maurier could light-heartedly discourse on the fun of being descended from a monkey, or trace the development of Mr Punch's huge nose, because he was an early disciple of Darwin, whose ideas tended to confirm his own. Most Victorians were profoundly disturbed by Darwin, which emphasizes the dangers of ever accepting an individual writer or cartoonist as the mirror of his age.

The basic format of the cartoons remained constant throughout Du Maurier's life, though the captions tended to grow longer, and the drawings less meticulous. His best work was produced in the 1870s and 1880s, when he had learned his trade thoroughly, and was still interested in the subjects of his survey. By the 1890s, a certain boredom is evident in his work, partly explained by the energy he was then devoting to his novels, but more through a failure of invention; the quality of his drawing becomes more summary and slap-dash. The most significant change in the content of the cartoons concerns the continuity of subject and character. In the late 1870s, Du Maurier created his famous and clever social-climber, Mrs Ponsonby de Tomkyns, who appears for the next six or seven years in a great number of the 'social' cartoons. Other figures who first appeared at the same time were Sir Gorgius Midas, Sir Pompey Bedell and Grigsby, and later on the famous aesthete characters, Mrs Cimabue Brown, Maudle and Postlethwaite. The recurrence of familiar figures helped to extend the range of the cartoons by allowing simple and effective contrasts to be made, and stories to be continued. They also caught on in the public mind as representatives of particular types, and greatly increased Du Maurier's popularity. In the 1890s, however, these characters disappeared, and Du Maurier returned to single cartoons with no connecting links, again revealing a failure of inspiration in his last years.

Any social cartoonist inevitably works within a narrow compass, dictated by the social milieu he chooses to depict, and by the limited number of situations which give scope for humorous comment. Du Maurier's world was primarily that of the London upper classes, and covered an area from Westminster in the south-east to Hampstead in the north and to Kensington in the west, including Mayfair, Belgravia, Knightsbridge, Regent's Park, and other fashionable areas – the region in which he himself might expect to be invited out for the evening. Although he did execute a few drawings of Rotten Row, Hampstead Heath, and the seaside, he was primarily an indoor artist. At home he could work comfortably from a model or one of his family, but drawing outside was more of a strain on his already weak eyesight. The number of outside functions in any case was strictly limited in an urban society. Du Maurier showed no interest in traditional rural pursuits, and though he once visited John Millais in Scotland for the fishing, he showed no inclination to leave London once the Season was over. Nor, unlike John Leech, did he frequent house parties, or join the fashionable hunting set, which at once cut him off from many aristocratic pursuits, and helps to explain the reserve with which he treated the aristocracy in his cartoons. His society was bounded at one end by professional families like Galsworthy's Forsytes, who had a gift for making money and keeping it, who lived in large and well-staffed houses, educated their sons at the best public schools and behaved with perfect decorum in society, without attempting to emulate the manners or customs of the aristocracy; and at the other end of the scale by old established families like that of Sir Pitt Crawley in *Vanity Fair*, managing unprofitable estates, and trying to maintain their standards in a competitive, modern world. It is easy to see how the two groups were forced together by social pretension and financial expediency, so that they became in time thoroughly intermarried, and indistinguishable from each other. Du Maurier was always careful to differentiate their relationship from that which developed between the higher aristocracy, with their heavily encumbered estates, and the new millionaire industrialists, who did not, like the Forsytes, behave with decorum and had no need to do so. Visiting duchesses are a feature of Du Maurier's cartoons, fought over by aspiring hostesses, but not an integral part of his social charade. Similarly artists and painters, with whom Du Maurier inevitably mixed, are nearly always shown in a social context, and rarely in their own studios or cliques. He always preferred the mixed social scene, where he could himself observe people. He did occasionally attempt scenes in which women are engaged in their own pursuits, at the dressmaker or the hairdresser, but never any form of male employment or business. Social entertainment was his perennial background, a dance or soirée, afternoon tea, a tennis party or private view, interspersed with domestic scenes in a lower key, or even a view below stairs (servants were an integral part of his world). The most notable lacuna from the list of fashionable entertainments is the theatre, which he rarely visited, and which is scarcely ever used as a setting for a cartoon. His favourite themes were after-dinner musicales, about which he was well-informed, and the endless manoeuvres in the marriage game. Even the inevitable 'clanger' was usually related to some form of social entertainment, for the essential feature of all his cartoons is a private confrontation in a social situation.

Before considering in some detail certain features of society as seen through Du Maurier's eyes, it is important to remember that he thought of himself primarily as an artist, then as a cartoonist, but never as a social historian or a social reformer. It was not at any time his intention to leave behind a permanent record of his own times, (though in his article of 1890 on illustration he did recognize that he had done so),[13] but to turn out two weekly jokes which would amuse the public and earn him his daily bread. Because he was highly observant, and meticulous as a draughtsman, Du Maurier did make a valuable contribution to our understanding of social habits and etiquette in the second half of the nineteenth-century. Who has caught so accurately the ponderous and claustrophobic atmosphere of a Victorian dinner-party? – the limited topics of conversation, the formality, the agony of sitting next to an uncongenial neighbour or a bore, the awful hazards which might occur in opening a conversation, the silent waiters, the endless courses, the absence of any relaxation or light relief? He viewed the after-dinner entertainments with an even sharper eye, the concerts which never seemed to end, the recitations and amateur theatricals, which might provide a welcome relief from tedious conversation, or merely an excuse to sleep. Below the surface of this fashionable world, with its brightly lit and airless rooms, its whiskered gentlemen and bustled ladies, and its air of complacent success, Du Maurier analysed the emotions which gave it life – the social jockeying, the carefully delivered snub, the misery experienced by the nervous and the misfits, the gaffes committed by the parvenu, the status which birth conferred and to which all paid court, the advantage enjoyed by wit and beauty, the callousness and superficiality which are the result of a rigidly organized and conventional society. In many ways, Du Maurier's

13. Illustration, p. 374.

cartoons provide a contrast, on a lower and less dramatic plane, to the novels of the period. He is rarely concerned with the private emotions of his characters, only with the more mundane hopes and fears which motivate them as social animals. It is in this clash or misunderstanding of motives that his humour has its roots. His drawings admirably suggest the cluttered and over-furnished effect of the Victorian drawing-room, without themselves becoming over-elaborate. He can equally well evoke the simple and 'arty' interior of the aesthete home with the deft arrangement of a Morris chair, a Chinese pot, and a boldly-patterned piece of floral material. His characters are so closely related to their backgrounds, that it is difficult to think of them apart.

After-dinner entertainments provided Du Maurier with his largest single subject for satirical comment. It was the ideal interruption to the normal pattern of an evening party, which focussed social tensions and behaviour, and was rich in humorous possibilities. The theme also had a personal attraction, which accounts, in part, for its continual recurrence. Du Maurier was a good amateur tenor, who was much sought after as an entertainer, and who had gained an entrée into several circles because of his talent. He never forgot the annoyance which he felt when people continued to talk during his performance, and several cartoons deal bitterly with the paradox of conversation lagging till the start of the music. Other cartoons are fairer to the audience, echoing Oscar Wilde's bon mot, 'Musical people . . . always want one to be perfectly dumb at the very moment when one is longing to be absolutely deaf'.[14] The quality of musical entertainment was often execrable, and Du Maurier once depicted a cat rushing for the door in a panic as the voice of a tenor wailed across the room. The complex situation engendered by after-dinner entertainment must have been appreciated by Du Maurier's readers, for the habit had spread right through the social scale. The majority of guests were not invited to dinner, which was only for a select few (Du Maurier's cartoons rarely show more than fourteen at the dinner table), but came to the evening party which followed it. The entertainment provided by the hostess usually took the form of a violin or piano solo, together with songs, which were performed by the more talented of her guests. In the very highest circles of society, musical performers were often professionals of the first quality, and invitations were accepted or refused on the merits of the entertainer.

14. *An Ideal Husband* (1895).

Such a situation allowed Du Maurier to pin-point one of the more obvious methods of social-climbing. Those hostesses, who were determined to entertain the very best society, could achieve this through the excellence of their parties, celebrities and entertainments. No-one was more tenacious or ruthless in her pursuit of this aim than Du Maurier's classic parvenu, Mrs Ponsonby De Tomkyns, a woman of great wit, beauty and boundless ambition, married to a dull and impoverished husband. She first appeared in *Punch* in 1878 as Mrs Peter De Tomkyns, but adopted the more aristocratic name of Ponsonby in the following year. She fascinated Du Maurier, as Becky Sharp had fascinated Thackeray, and it is no coincidence that *Vanity Fair* was one of the cartoonist's favourite novels. Like Becky, Mrs Ponsonby De Tomkyns is clever enough to work a way around her limited financial position, and she is also possessed of a cool judgement and iron nerve. In 'Mistress and Pupil', she reveals her methods in a conversation with Lady Midas, the vulgar and stupid wife of a millionaire sausage manufacturer:

> Mrs Ponsonby de Tomkyns: 'And how about your dinner-party, Lady Midas? Who's coming?'
> Lady Midas: 'Well it's *small*, but precious *select*, I can tell you. The Marquis and Marchioness of Chepe, Viscount and Viscountess Silverlacke, the Hon. Oleo and Lady Margarine Delarde, Sir Pullman and Lady Carr, and the Cholmondeley-Mainwaring Carshaltons'.
> Mrs P. de T.: 'My *dear* Lady Midas, you don't mean to say you've asked all these fine people to meet nobody but *each other?* Why, they'll be bored to death, and never forgive you! It's not as if you were already *one of themselves*, you know! You must wire to Grigsby at once to come and dine and bring his banjo, and I'll get you Nellie Micklemash and her husband from the Jollity. She's not acting now'.
> Lady M.: 'But my dear, she's not respectable, I'm told!'
> Mrs P. de T.: 'No, but she's amusing, and that's *everything*. And look here, I'll throw over the Botherby Joneses, and come *myself*!'
>
> (7 July 1883)

Mrs Ponsonby De Tomkyns is always, as one cartoon character remarked, 'clever enough to get the right people'. The key to her success is her after-dinner performers, who, by a variety of balancing tricks, she contrives to capture without paying them any fee. She entices Signor Jenkini to sing at one of her parties by the promise that the influential Duchess of Stilton will be present, and flatters

LADY GATHEREMALL AT HOME.

(Informal Introductions are best—especially when formal ones are not forthcoming.)

Ponsonby de Tomkyns (to Mrs. P. de T., who is artfully protruding a tiny foot). "WHAT'S THE GOOD? HIS ALL SERENITY'S AS BLIND AS A BAT. HE'LL ONLY TREAD ON IT!" *Mrs. Ponsonby de Tomkyns.* "I MEAN HIM TO!" *Ponsonby de Tomkyns.* "WHAT FOR?" *Mrs. Ponsonby de Tomkyns.* "WHY, HE'LL HAVE TO APOLOGISE, YOU GOOSE, AND THEN——BUT THERE, LEAVE IT ALL TO ME,

104. *Punch* (1881)

the Duchess, who would not normally stoop to such low society, with the prospect of Signor Jenkini's enormous talent. On another occasion she arranges for a simple French girl to give a performance before the Duchess, and by refraining to thank or pay her is herself cordially thanked for providing such an opportunity – a perfect example of Victorian one-upmanship. The balancing trick does not always work. Mme Gaminot marches off just before she is about to sing, and not even Mrs Ponsonby De Tomkyns can balance the see-saw: 'Exit also, alas! Her Grace, in a very bad temper!' ('One of Mrs Ponsonby De Tomkyns' Failures', 29 July 1882). Nor is Mrs Ponsonby De Tomkyns, in her endeavour to converse wittily and pungently, always as tactful or careful as she should be. In an un-guarded moment, she remarks to Lord Charles that the lady with the slit eyes looks just like a Chinese, only to discover that the lady in question is his sister – a faux-pas which she recovers magnificently with 'She struck me as having such *exquisitely* small feet!' ('Ready! Aye Ready!', 25 March 1882). Even an intelligence as fast as hers is defeated when she informs a noble peer that his books are old friends, only to be faced with an uncut copy of his latest volume in her book-shelves ('Catching a Weasel Asleep', 3 Nov. 1883). Eventually she achieves all that she has fought for; the Duchess becomes a 'dear' friend, and Royalty visit her house to pay tribute to her outstanding performers. By the late 1880s, she had lost her novelty and fascina-tion for Du Maurier, and she quietly disappears, one of the most sharply characterized, endearing and successful of all his cartoon characters. She was, however, spared the resounding crash which Du Maurier had prepared for her. Kate Greenaway remembered a conversation with him on the subject: 'He told me he got so fond of her in the end, he could not let the retribution fall upon her that he intended to finish her up with'.[15]

It was her beauty and wit which saved Mrs De Tomkyns from the final catastrophe. Much as Du Maurier disliked social 'pushers', he had created a woman of great vitality and charm, and he found himself caught in her snares, as Thackeray had been caught by Becky Sharp. The fate intended for Mrs Ponsonby De Tomkyns was to some extent inherited by her rival, Mrs Lyon Hunter, another recurring figure in the cartoons of the 1880s. Mrs Hunter is less subtle and intelligent, and in consequence much less amusing and success-ful. When she invites her friends to hear a special performer, or to

15. M. H. Spielmann and L. S. Layard, *Kate Greenaway* (1905), p. 205.

meet the social 'giant' of the season, the guests of honour nearly always fail to turn up, or refuse to do what is expected of them. She asks the great pianist, Herr Bogulboffski, to come and spend a quiet evening in her family circle, and then invites over a hundred guests with the lure that the great musician will be performing. When Herr Bogulboffski insists on sticking to the original arrangement, Mrs Hunter is left in a quandary from which Du Maurier offers her no escape. The audience are waiting, the lid on the grand piano has been raised, but the musician obstinately refuses to play ('Frustrated Social Ambition', 8 Nov. 1879). Like most of Mrs Hunter's strategems, it is based on calculated deceit, which, once exposed, has no power to move. The more intelligent Mrs Ponsonby De Tomkyns prefers to put her trust in the dominant principle of self-interest, trying to please herself and everyone else – an aim in which she often succeeds. Indeed, Du Maurier seems to have felt that Mrs Ponsonby De Tomkyns, by turning the evils inherent in society to her own account, was clever rather than culpable. It is also true that he could forgive a beautiful woman almost anything.

The subject of social advancement obviously exercised Du Maurier's mind a good deal, and its frequent treatment in *Punch* suggests that it was a common topic of conversation in his circle. The English upper classes have always survived by absorbtion, not exclusion. Brilliant and rising outsiders, who cannot be ignored, are simply swallowed into a class and atmosphere whose advantages are obvious, and which tends to lull into complacency even the most belligerent of reformers. The newest and wealthiest outsiders are, however, often difficult to assimilate, because they can afford to set their own standards. Where success has been sudden, the 'nouveau riche' emerges into society like a bull in a china shop. Women like Mrs Ponsonby De Tomkyns and Mrs Lyon Hunter operated with a certain finesse, because they were anxious to prove that they had absorbed the cultural manners of their social superiors, but men like Sir Gorgius Midas felt no compunction to do so. On the contrary they were positively proud of their bluffness, vulgarity and philistinism. Like the railway king, George Hudson, Sir Gorgius has crashed his way into the highest society, because he has a vast fortune which the impoverished aristocracy cannot ignore. Such a situation, dictated by greed and snobbery, did not reflect well on either side, but the industrialists usually appeared in a more honest and sympathetic light than the scheming and sneering aristocrats. Disraeli had analysed this relationship between nobility and trade thirty years before in his penetrating novel, *Coningsby*, where the sterling qualities of Oswald Millbank are at first ignored because of his low birth. It is also worth remembering that many Northern businessmen were not as untutored or uncultivated as popular prejudice, and Du Maurier in particular, seemed to imagine. Liverpool provided the Pre-Raphaelites with their first patrons, and cultural life generally in the provinces was in a very much more healthy state than it is today. On the other hand, it is possible to feel some sympathy for those who found the new arrivals repellent. There is nothing more galling for the liberal humanist, anxious to forgive a fellow for his faults, than to discover that the fellow in question is actually proud of them. Du Maurier was not the only sensitive man to be shocked into a reactionary attitude by the excesses of the new industrialists (it must be admitted that they were rarely the most attractive products of their class). In 1874, Anthony Trollope had published a long and bitter novel on social conditions, in marked contrast to the gentle sagas of Barsetshire, it was fittingly entitled *The Way We Live Now*, a title adopted by Du Maurier for a cartoon of 1882. Trollope's theme concerned the way in which London society could be swept by enthusiasm for a speculating financier. Auguste Melmotte, the dominating personality of the book, creates a mirage of wealth out of nothing, and bases his whole career on an enormous confidence trick. When confidence in him eventually fails, his position collapses at once, revealing the hollow financial juggling in which he had indulged. Melmotte was partly based on Albert Grant, but he was also an example of a particular type which came into prominence at the end of the century. Underlying *The Way We Live Now* is Trollope's fear that the old world was being shattered by financial greed, and that moral standards were disappearing in the worship of Mammon. This is most clearly illustrated by the intrigues for the hand of Marie Melmotte, who, paradoxically, is clever, courageous, and one of the few sympathetic characters in a very sordid story. The aristocratic young men who pay her court are quite unconcerned by her possible illegitimacy, lack of beauty and savoir-faire; they will accept her as long as the money is 'all right'. Trollope is more ambiguous in his attitude to the position of the aristocracy, and does not draw the obvious conclusion that the worthless young men who inhabit the 'Beargarden' should not be allowed to lead such indolent and wasteful lives.

The Way We Live Now provides an excellent background to many of Du Maurier's cartoons. Both he and Trollope were essentially kind-hearted, liberal and fair-minded traditionalists whose faith in the old order was being undermined by social upheaval. Trollope's Melmotte and Du Maurier's Midas are creatures of the same kind, born out of a common fear of change for the worst:

> Melmotte himself was a large man, with bushy whiskers and rough thick hair, with heavy eyebrows, and a wonderful look of power about his mouth and chin. This was so strong as to redeem his face from vulgarity; but the countenance and appearance of the man were on the whole unpleasant, and, I may say, untrustworthy. He looked as though he were purse-proud and a bully.

The features of Sir Gorgius Midas have nothing to redeem them from vulgarity, but the general outlines of Trollope's description could equally well be applied to him. He must have resembled actual individuals closely enough to be recognized as a clearly-defined type, with a set of attributes and habits which needed little exaggeration to create an effective caricature. The same is true of Lady Midas and Mme. Melmotte, coarse, fat, and entirely out of their depth in a sophisticated society, they vainly attempt to keep pace with the success of their husbands. But similarities should not be overstressed, for Trollope was writing a long and profound novel, while Du Maurier could only make a simple and direct point in the limited context of the cartoon. Sir Gorgius Midas is obviously a Northern businessman, blunt, ruthless, but still very English, whereas Melmotte is a financier who glides out of an obscure European past. It was the growth of a vast and complex financial pyramid, far more than industrial expansion, which dictated the enormous changes in the second half of the nineteenth century. In this sense, Melmotte is a more penetrating example of the new men than Midas, whose days of glory belonged to the early Victorian period. Du Maurier must, however, have realized that Midas, out of date as he might be, would be a more recognizable and effective character for a popular cartoon. It was the vulgar ostentation and the boasting of this corpulent millionaire at which Du Maurier aimed his most savage and frequent blows. Midas, informing a guest that the silver on the table is worth all of £20,000 ('Pleasant', 24 Feb. 1883), or telling his son to drink up his champagne and 'thank God you are English and can afford it' ('Sir Gorgius on the "Continong" ', 20 Aug. 1881), is satirized with a bitterness that is almost personal. The most cynical example of all is 'Humility in Splendour', where Midas, just back from a journey to America, is

HUMILITY IN SPLENDOUR.

The Rev. Lazarus Jones (who has been honoured by an invitation to lunch with that great man, Sir Gorgius Midas, just returned from America). "I SUPPOSE YOU ARE GLAD TO GET BACK TO YOUR COMFORTABLE HOME AGAIN, SIR GORGIUS?"
Sir Gorgius Midas (who perhaps does not like his palatial residence to be called a "comfortable house"). "YES, JONES! BE IT EVER SO 'UMBLE, THERE'S NO PLACE LIKE 'OME!"

105. *Punch* (1878)

irritated by the Rev. Jones, who foolishly asks if he is glad to be back in his 'comfortable' home: ' "Yes Jones! Be it ever so 'umble, Jones, there's no place like '*ome!*" ' (9 Feb. 1878). The seven waiters who stand round the vast table in the palatial interior lend eloquent support to his statement.

The excesses of Sir Gorgius and his family are thrown into sharp relief by the perfect manners of the aristocracy with whom they mix, and whose behaviour always suggests a contemptuous disdain for the outward forms of wealth and position. While Sir Gorgius travels first class on the railways, and his servants second, the third class compartment is occupied by the Duke of Hautcastle and his entourage ('Waiting for the Express', 11 Oct. 1890). In Du Maurier's predictable scale of social values, the aristocracy invariably succeed in crushing the upstarts. When Sir Gorgius informs Lady Gwendoline Beaumanoir that his wife always has to avert her eyes when passing an omnibus in her carriage, for fear of recognizing and having to acknowledge somebody on top, he is duly snubbed: ' "I'm afraid she'll often see *Papa* there; but never *me*, you know! Mamma and I always go inside!" ' (Almanack, 1885). In a similar vein, Lady Midas, criticizing the young man who had dared to show her to her carriage as 'most forward and pushing', collapses when she discovers he is Lord Bayard of Grandison, merely performing a social duty, and not out to cultivate her acquaintance (Almanack, 1885). Du Maurier's recurrent jokes at these easy and defenceless targets is at times repellent, and reflects a snobbery and social insecurity which demanded a victim. The sin of Sir Gorgius was not only ostentation. Like other self-made men, he is frequently cruel to his social inferiors, from whose ranks he has himself only recently risen. In one excellent cartoon, Du Maurier showed him entering his door at two o'clock in the morning to discover that only four flunkeys are there to greet him, the rest having retired: ' "A pretty state of things, indeed! So that if I'd a' 'appened to brought 'ome a friend, there'd a' only been you four to let us hin, hay!" ' ('The Height of Magnificence', 7 Feb. 1880).

As Trollope recognized in *The Way We Live Now*, one group rising in the social scale implies another group descending. During the 1880s, Du Maurier treated, in an extravagant form, the change of attitude forced upon the hereditary aristocracy. In a cartoon of 1888, a duke is shown on his knees in his own shoe-shop, fitting his Jewish son-in-law with a pair of pumps – a startling reversal of roles, which results, as it always does, in a classic joke ('Hard Times',

Almanack, 1888). Other cartoons about the aristocracy 'in trade' are less extreme, like Lord Plantagenet completing a large grocery order for a female customer. Pin-pointing their anomalous position is her request for an invitation to his sister's garden party, rather as a modern customer might ask for trading stamps ('What We May Look Forward To', 22 April 1876). An even more absurd example of such preferential treatment is found in 'The Old Order Changeth' (9 June 1888):

'By the bye, I wish you would get me a card for the Duchess of Beau-morris's Dance?'
'I'll try. But you'll have to get a costume from her, or a bonnet, or *something*, – as she only asks her *customers*!'

It would have been difficult to find any aristocrat behind a counter in the 1880s, but younger members of certain families were begin-ning to exploit the retail market. This gave the comic artist a unique opportunity to ridicule the hangers-on, who suddenly found them-selves out of step with social convention. The odious Todeson makes the fatal mistake of asking a duchess what society is coming to, when you may find yourself rubbing shoulders with a shopkeeper. Her snub is as crushing as that delivered to Sir Gorgius by Lady Gwendolen:

'Oh, dear me! Why my *husband's* a shopkeeper, Mr Todeson. He keeps that great bric-à-brac warehouse in Conduit Street! – and the Toy-Shop at the corner, that's mine! – And the confectioner over the way, that's my mother, the Duchess of Hautcastel!'.
('The Old Order Changeth', 12 May 1888)

There was a personal irony in this caption, for Du Maurier had himself felt uneasy over twenty years earlier on account of his father-in-law's warehouse in Conduit Street.

Trade was only an extreme example of those professions which were at last becoming respectable, art, the theatre and journalism for example, and which were all being invaded by members of the upper classes.

According to 'A Jubilee Private View' (18 June 1887), aristo-cratic ladies were coining an honest penny by becoming social, fashion, and art columnists, admittedly only one remove from the already respectable occupation of writing novels. The change in the status of the theatre was much more dramatic, and accounts for the large number of cartoons which Du Maurier devoted to the subject, though he continued to show little interest in the theatre itself. The rage for amateur theatricals, considered so disgraceful in Jane Austen's *Mansfield Park,* had slowly eroded the stigma attached to the stage. Having tasted success in private theatricals, many young men and women wished to take the next logical step and join the professional stage. The new enthusiasm provided Du Maurier with several good jokes, which again depended on incongruity for their effect. As early as 1870, he showed a bishop encouraging his favourite son to go into the theatre by telling him that 'Lord Ronald Beaumanoir, who's a year younger then yourself, is already getting *sixteen guineas a week* for low comedy parts at the Criterion!' ('Tempora Mutantur', Almanack, 1880). Lord Algernon puts the respectable professions to shame by proclaiming that he is carrying a banner in *The King and the Cockchafer* at the Parthenon Theatre, while, in another cartoon, a viscount and a baronet are complaining that they only receive six guineas a week after ten years in the theatre, whereas the duke is earning twenty after six months ('The New Craze', 23 May, and 9 June 1883). These cartoons which deal with the changing times are sympathetic rather than accurate. Du Maurier was partly aware of this, for he put into the mouth of Walter Lissom the revealing words: ' "I ask you all, ladies, has an actor ever yet been made a Knight of the Garter, or ever had the refusal of a Peerage! Never!" ' ('The Social Position of the Actor Has Improved of Late Years', 21 July 1883). The theatre was not invaded by the aristocracy, and it retained its own rather loose and cavalier conventions apart from society. Lily Langtry managed to go on the stage without becoming hopelessly declassé, but she was more of an exception than might be imagined. Leading actors and actresses were lionized by society, but the relationship was not between equals. It is significant that in the 'nineties Du Maurier was himself very unwilling to allow his son, Gerald, to take up a theatrical career, and to appear in repertory theatres all over the country.

The revolution in attitudes to unconventional professions promised a healthy result for the upper classes generally. The old idea that younger sons should live on inherited capital, or go into the church, the bar, diplomacy, politics or the army, had deprived the new industries of the best talents in the country. As younger sons began to break away from old established patterns, the dilution of the aristocracy, which Trollope and Du Maurier feared, gradually took place, and led to a greater levelling of society. The grandsons of Sir Gorgius Midas and the Duke of Stilton were not only indistinguishable, they were very often the same people. The aristocracy had often provided England with Imperial leaders, from Governor-Generals down, but the four titled men and women in 'Colonizing in Iowa U.S.' (subtitled 'A Hint to the Younger Sons of Our aristocracy, and Daughters Thereof', 12 Nov. 1881) were a new phenomenon, which was not a complete invention by the cartoonist. In a letter of 1888 to Henry James, he recorded a conversation with Lady Airlie, who had just been visiting her daughter on a ranch in Colorado. The last extreme example of the change in attitude to employment is 'Victims of the Turf' (5 May 1888), where Lord Charles and the Hon. Jack are recouping their gambling losses by working as pavement artists, 'better', as one of them remarks, 'than starving in the Coldstreams, eh?'

Du Maurier's attitude to the aristocracy was generally respectful, and his jokes at their expense mild and uncritical. They are drawn as impressive physical specimens, the natural magnets and leaders of society, who can crush a 'pusher' or an 'upstart' by the mere effect of their rank. Du Maurier was less tolerant of the sycophancy to which nobility gave rise:

> Interlocutor: 'Who's that showy woman who talks and laughs so loud, and digs people in the ribs?'
> Interlocutrix: 'Oh, that's the Duchess of Bayswater. She was Lady Gwendolen Beaumanoir, you know!'
> Interlocutor (with warmth): 'Ah, to be sure! That accounts for her high-bred ease, her aristocratic simplicity of manner, her natural and straightforward –'
> Interlocutrix (putting up her eye-glass): 'By the bye, pardon me! I have unintentionally misinformed you; it's Mrs Judkins. She's the widow of an Alderman, and her father was a cheesemonger in the New Cut!'
> Interlocutor: 'Dear me! – Ah! – Hum! – Er – Hum! – Ha! That quite alters the case! She is very vulgar, I must say – awful!' (N.B. It was the duchess, after all.)
>
> ('Noblesse Oblige', 8 April 1876)

Du Maurier was not entirely under the spell of aristocratic dignity. The Duchess of Stilton's behaviour is not always exemplary. In 'The Reward of Merit' (18 Jan. 1879), she is being introduced to a famous writer for the ninth time of the season, complacently conscious of giving pleasure, but quite unconcerned with her failure

TWO VICTIMS OF THE TURF.

Lord Charles. "WELL, JACK, HOW'VE YOU GOT ON TO-DAY? I'VE TAKEN NEARLY TEN POUNDS—MOSTLY IN SIXPENCES AND SHILLINGS—AND YOU?"

The Hon. Jack. "OH, ABOUT THE SAME! AND THREE HALF-SOVEREIGNS! BETTER THAN STARVING IN THE COLDSTREAMS, EH?"

106. *Punch* (1888)

to recognize him. Another cartoon shows her congratulating a pianist, and asking him to find someone to introduce them ('Drawing-Room Minstrels', 13 July 1812). The absurdity of the whole introduction system is stressed in 'Modern Social Problems' (1 May 1886), where a hostess agrees to introduce two young people as long as she is told their names. A further grudge to which Du Maurier gave expression was the habit in upper-class circles of inviting famous artists, scholars or writers without their wives. Coming often from a lower social milieu, the husbands were desirable additions to fashionable society, but their wives would merely have been a nuisance and an embarrassment. Du Maurier had himself experienced this treatment, and always refused to go to any social function without Emma. Many others, most notably Charles Dickens, were less scrupulous, and encouraged a system which was based on pernicious snobbery. Du Maurier's cartoons on the subject often concerned Lady Snobbington (née Shoddy), here seen 'At her Old Tricks Again' (7 Aug. 1886):

> Lady Snobbington (née Shoddy): 'Oh, by the way, Mr Löwe, do you ever dine out without your wife? I've a nice little Bohemian dinner-party on Sunday – nice clever people you will like. Come and dine, and bring your banjo, if Mrs Löwe will spare you, just for once!
> Mr Löwe (the Eminent Banjoist): 'Ach! You are ferry goot, Lady Schnoppington! If it is ferry Pohemian inteet, and de laties are coing to schmoke, and de chendlemen are going to tine in deir schirt-schleefs, I do not mind pringing my pancho, and leafing my vife at home, choost for vunce!'

If Du Maurier showed a natural aversion from treating subjects of lower class life, he found many of his best jokes below stairs. Domestic staff were an integral part of the upper-class world, and presented no brutal contrast, as their counterparts in the factories might have done, to Du Maurier's safe and self-satisfied view of society. Like John Leech and others of the *Punch* staff, Du Maurier created a whole world of humour out of the relations between master and servant. In a formal society, the domestic servant was one of the few people who could express himself freely and succinctly, and the mistakes and misunderstandings which might result with a reticent and genteel employer provided a humorous topic of endless variety. Du Maurier's attitude to his own servants was reasonably open-minded and egalitarian by the standards of the day. He resented the cruelty and lack of understanding with which many servants were treated by

boorish masters. The page-boy who could not resist a crack at Sir
Gorgy Guzzles clearly had his sympathy:

> Sir Gorgy Guzzles: 'Got a pain, have you? Well serve you right! I can-
> not understand why you and the other servants should think it neces-
> sary to make pigs of yourselves on one particular day of the year, just
> because it happens to be the 25th of December!'
> The Page: 'O, Sir, please Sir! Christmas makes no difference to you, sir.
> You and her ladyship can perform that hoperation hevery blessed
> day of your lives, sir!'
> A month's notice.
>
> ('All the Year Round', 10 Jan. 1874)

So too did another page-boy who was sacked for giving Sir Pompey
Bedell an empty up-turned egg for breakfast as an innocent April
Fool's joke. ('The Wrong Boy in the Wrong Place', 10 April 1880)
Ladies' maids, even more intimately involved in the affairs of their
employers, were often treated in the same summary fashion. In one
of his earliest cartoons, Du Maurier depicted an interview between a
lady and a new servant, the former explaining that the maid's
predecessor was sacked because of her treatment of the boy:

> '[He] has such animal spirits, you know; throwing everything about,
> or kicking his football through the window – perhaps he'll kick you, too –
> but you must not mind it, for he's a *lion-hearted, sensitive little fellow*!!'
>
> ('Missusism, 1 Feb. 1862)

Such examples are rare in the cartoons. Du Maurier's attitude to
the servant class is essentially patronizing, for while he was amused
by their naïve and ingenuous qualities, he regarded their position as
fixed in a social status quo. Jokes about hierarchy and snobbery
below stairs are common. The cook who decides not to leave because
she has discovered that 'kerridge people 'ad used to live in this very
street' ('The Ruling Passion', Almanack 1872), is rivalled by the
maid who turns down a job because she is not satisfied with the status
of her prospective employers:

> 'Why, when I got there, blest if there wasn't the two young ladies of the
> 'ouse both a-usin' of one piano at the same time! "Well" thinks I, "This
> *his* a comin' down in the world!" So I thought I was best say good
> mornin'!'
>
> ('Self Respect', 20 June 1874)

THE RULING PASSION.

Cook (condescendingly). "Please, 'M, if you ain't Suited, I've Changed my Mind, and would rather Stop!"

Missus. "O, I thought you said you Objected to the Neighbourhood, Cook?"

Cook. "Yes, 'M, so I did; but the Milkman, he Tell me this Morning as 'ow once Kerridge People 'ad used to Live in this very Street."

107. *Punch* (1872)

The final expression of servant pretension is 'The Ornamental v.
The Useful' (16 Oct. 1875):

> Servant: 'I suppose, Ma'am, I shall not have to wait at table?'
> Lady: 'Oh, no! I want a housemaid.'
> Servant: 'I suppose, Ma'am; I shall not have to make the beds?'
> Lady (suprised, but composedly): 'Certainly not!'
> Servant (thinking the place will suit): 'And I suppose, Ma'am, I shall
> not be expected to answer the door?'
> Lady: 'Of course not! The fact is, I want a servant to *look at, and I don't
> think you will do!*'

Despite the reforming principles of its founders, *Punch* had never
shown a great interest in the situation of the very poor. A comic
paper has to amuse to survive, and the public did not want to be
lectured weekly about social responsibility. The subject did not, in
any case, fall within Du Maurier's strict range, and it is unlikely
that he ever gave it much thought. Hampstead was a settled middle-
class area, and the building developments which took place around
him in North London were strictly suburban. From the cartoons it
would appear that Du Maurier only came into contact with the
lower-classes on bank-holidays, when they disported themselves on
the Heath or at the sea-side, and disturbed his peace and quiet. The
words of the sea-side hotel waiter in a cartoon of 1888, 'Out of Town
– Unfashionable Intelligence' (15 Sept. 1888), capture the mood
exactly:

> Visitor: 'What a roaring trade the hotels will be doing, with all these
> holiday folk!'
> Head Waiter at the George: 'Lor bless yer, sir, no! They all bring their
> nosebags with 'em!'

The drawing illustrates a band of peculiarly repellent people, with
dark moronic faces, advancing in a formidable and menacing mass.
It is a cruel joke. Even in those cartoons with less vicious captions,
the solid ranks of the populace always have something dour and
hostile about them. Drawing a scene on Hampstead Heath on Whit
Monday, Du Maurier carefully observed a group of lower-class
types and salvationists, and then added himself, a small figure
protected by his St Bernard, Chang, ill at ease in such an atmosphere

WHITSUNTIDE HUMOURS.

Holiday Maker (to Open-Air Preacher). "I SAY, GUV'NOR, JUST KETCH 'OLD O' THIS YER DOG, WIL YER, WHILE ME AN' MY MATE GETS A DROP O' BEER? 'OLD HIM TIGHT, AN' IF HE ...."

108. *Punch* (1877)

BAD GRAMMAR, BUT GOOD PLUCK.

" Now, THEN, FATHER, JUST LET ME KETCH YER A 'ITTIN' O' MOTHER, THAT'S ALL!"
" I AIN'T A 'ITTIN' OF HER, DRAT YER!"
" NO; BUT YER WAS JUST AGOIN' TO!   LET ME KETCH YER, THAT'S ALL!"

[Seen and heard by ye Artist.

109. Punch (1875)

('Whitsuntide Humours', 9 June 1877). But, as John Leech, whose fear and hatred of the masses was far more pronounced, could sometimes draw an appealing street arab, so Du Maurier occasionally took the part of the poor, usually when children were concerned, or some obnoxious philanthropist. Lady Clara Vere de Vere was his classic do-gooder, but her gestures towards equality are always abortive. When, as Lady Clara Robinson, she graciously allows her daughters to play with a group of 'deprived' (in fact middle-class) children, she is gravely informed that they never play with strangers ('The Tables Turned', 3 May 1879). The reply of a simple cottage girl to Lady Clara's offer of a wedding-present is too embarrassingly honest for that haughty lady, whose face assumes an expression of well-bred horror: 'Really, my lady, I can't 'ardly say. I 'aven't got nothing. But *you'd* know best, my lady – Anything just what *you'd* want, my lady, if *you* was in the same position.' ('Equality', 23 Oct. 1875.) Another sharply satirized benefactor appears in 'What Next Indeed!' (3 Sept. 1870):

> Grateful recipient: 'Bless you, my lady! May we meet in heaven!'
> Haughty donor: 'Good Gracious!! Drive on Jarvis!!!'

Other cartoons show a genuine concern with the hardship endured by pauper children. 'Those Yellow Sands', where a group of little urchins wistfully surround the carriage which is taking their more fortunate neighbours to the sea-side, is one of the most moving. Another recorded a scene which he had actually witnessed. A little girl, emerging from a cottage at North End, near Hampstead, in pursuit of her drunken father, yelled at him: 'Just let me *ketch* yer a 'ittin o' mother, that's all!' ('Bad Grammar, but Good Pluck', 3 July 1875.)

The position of women was the dominating feature of many late Victorian novels, and the whole subject of the relationship between the sexes was being publicly discussed. Unlike Dickens or Thackeray, who pandered to public taste by creating insipid heroines, younger novelists like George Meredith were attacking a society which allowed a woman to be subjected to a marriage which she had not fully understood, and then bound her by a set of inescapable rules to a life of total uselessness. Du Maurier's close friend, Henry James, was also concerned with this problem, but his attitude was more ambivalent, combining a repugnance for sexual immorality with an instinctive affection and sympathy for innocent young women, poised on the edge of a life which would inevitably disappoint them.

Du Maurier's own standpoint was fairly typical of his generation. A rigid upholder of female virtue at thirty, he was creating and apologizing for the 'fallen' Trilby in his early sixties. The cartoons reflect nothing of this personal change, for sex was an unmentionable subject in *Punch*, but they do show that his attitude to female emancipation, in any other field but love, remained entirely hostile to the last.

As an intelligent commentator, he could not entirely miss the incongruities and inconsistencies apparent in the position of women. They were usually given an inadequate and inferior education – a pale reflection of that enjoyed by their brothers, with the same classical bias. In 'The School-Room as it ought to be', Du Maurier suggested that girls should only be taught to cook, and not troubled with more demanding subjects. Such an attitude was horrifyingly reactionary, but it was more logical than the view which argued in favour of female education without a corresponding emancipation to allow them to benefit from it. Young women came out into society in their late 'teens, and passed a few seasons in London, preferably only one, with the specific aim of attracting a mate. Within a rigid social milieu, young girls were inevitably influenced by the brittle, romantic conventions of the day, which did not allow either sex much knowledge or understanding of the other. They descended straight from the nursery, or at any rate from upstairs, into the rapacious and knowing arms of society, with no preparation or initiation. 'Pray, is she out, or is she not out?' asks Mary Crawford in Jane Austen's *Mansfield Park*, anxious to know exactly how she should treat Fanny Price. This fascinating subject did not receive much attention from writers and cartoonists during the nineteenth century. It was Henry James who finally exposed the whole system in his brilliant novel, *The Awkward Age*, where a 'flourishing mother' is constrained to keep her daughter upstairs for as long as possible, putting off the 'sometimes dreaded, often delayed, but never fully arrested coming to the forefront of some vague slip of a daughter'. Du Maurier had already noticed the jealousy which pretty daughters sometimes aroused, and he wrote several captions at the expense of selfish mothers. 'Where the shoe pinches' (14 Dec. 1880), states, in a rather crude form, the case which James was to develop so subtly in his penetrating study of an utterly opposed mother and daughter:

Eldest Daughter: 'I think you might let me come out, Mamma! I'm twenty, you know, and surely I've finished my education!'

Festive Mamma (by no means prepared to act the part of chaperone and wallflower): 'Not yet, my love. Society is so hollow! I really must preserve that sweet girlish freshness of yours a little while longer!'

By the end of the century, with the general loosening of standards and behaviour, the idea of keeping a girl entirely innocent until she married became an obvious anachronism. But a society which allowed immorality as long as it was discreet, also demanded that young girls should not confess openly to reading risquée novels, or to understanding advanced adult conversation. When Nanda Brookenham in *The Awkward Age* is discovered to have read an immoral French novel, the young man she loves is profoundly shocked, and comes to regard her as something tainted. In a quite different tone, Du Maurier made fun of this in a cartoon called 'Emancipation', where a young bride stands at the railway book-stall, just off on her honeymoon, saying: 'Oh, Edwin dear! Here's "Tom Jones". Papa told me I wasn't to read it till I was married! The day has come. . . . At last! Buy it for me, Edwin dear.' (5 Dec. 1891).

Once the girls were 'out' it became the aim of every self-respecting mother to get them married as quickly as possible. The comedy of the husband-hunting game kept *Punch* in jokes throughout the Victorian period, and never lost its power to amuse through constant repetition. Du Maurier most enjoyed the spectacle of parents who were unfortunate enough to have only produced girls, and who became quite desperate in their attempts to place them. Typical examples are a mother who encourages a Moslem in the hope that he will take all four daughters, and the father who buys a tennis-court to attract young men. Du Maurier's sympathies were usually with the bachelors, hounded by match-making mothers, and often cornered by sheer persistence. Three bachelors pursued by a virago with 'three lovely daughters' book for a cruise as a last resort, only to find that the indefatigable woman has followed them ('Outward Bound' 29 Oct. 1881). In a situation where marriage was dictated by wit, beauty or money, the plight of a girl who had none of these things was very real. As the season came to an end, the unsuccessful girls settled down to the winter, their hopes of marriage decreasing with each succeeding year. In 'A Forlorn Hope' the last unmarried daughter of a noble family has clearly missed her opportunities; when her father suggests that a ball or a garden party might be efficacious, her mother crushes the suggestion: 'Oh, poor Maria's not worth a ball – nor even a garden party. We might give an *afternoon tea!*' (1 July 1876).

The influx of American heiresses in the last part of the nineteenth-century did not improve the temper of the native product. Not all of them were intent on securing English titles, but many, like Consuelo, Duchess of Marlborough and Lady Randolph Churchill succeeded in doing so. If the American girl often lacked sophistication, she had, like Henry James' Daisy Miller, a freshness and spontaneity which more than compensated for her lack of refinement. Du Maurier's bevy of American girls intently studying Debrett for eligible European aristocrats, or Miss Van Tromp replying to a query about her father; 'Pa's much too vulgar! It's as much as we can do to stand ma!', are typical examples of the trans-Atlantic phenomenon. ('What a Pity!' Almanack 1881; 'Yankee Exclusiveness', 20 Sept. 1890). His most pointed cartoon on the subject was 'The New Society Craze', in which an English mother is hiring a governess to teach her daughters to speak with an American accent, so that they too can marry dukes. A delightful passage in Oscar Wilde's *A Woman of No Importance* shows how far the English mother felt herself in an inferior position. Lady Caroline tells Lord Illingworth that 'These American girls carry off all the good matches. Why can't they stay in their own country? They are always telling us it is the Paradise of women'. His reply is to the point: 'It is, Lady Caroline. That is why, like Eve, they are so extremely anxious to get out of it'.

Du Maurier's treatment of the unmarried woman is probably the most unpleasant feature of his cartoons. Sympathetic in general, he had many friends among the old maids of Hampstead, but even this did not deter him from making fun of elderly and unattractive spinsters. Sometimes the captions have a certain wit, as in 'A Nuisance' (8 Oct. 1892), a cartoon about two spinster ladies who live on the coast:

> Miss Priscilla: 'Yes, it's a beautiful view. But tourists are in the habit of bathing on the opposite shore, and that's rather a drawback.'
> Fair Visitor: 'Dear me! But at such a distance as that – surely –'
> Miss Priscilla: 'Ah, but with a *telescope*, you know!'

Many other cartoons, however, are cruel stock-jokes at the expense of the most ill-used part of the Victorian upper and middle-class community. In 'Thought is Free' (11 Nov. 1871), two attractive young girls stand on either side of a hideous and elderly lady, who is saying:

> 'Honour and Obey! Indeed! Ha! Ha! I should *just* like to see a man ask *me* to "Honour and Obey" him!'
> (I've no doubt you'd like to see him *very much indeed!* thought the two Miss Marigolds – but they didn't say so).

The tragedy of the situation seems never to have occurred to Du Maurier, who, like most of his contemporaries, male and female, made fun of those shadowy and dependant figures to be found in every Victorian home. Even that most feminist of novelists, Meredith, amuses himself at the expense of Willoughby Patterne's maiden aunts in *The Egoist*, while Trollope's only attractive examples of the type are those with wealth and position, like Miss Dunstable in *Framley Parsonage*.

It is not surprising that female emancipation should strike an equally unsympathetic chord in the cartoonist. He assumed that 'the new woman' must be either too hideous to get a husband, or infatuated with a passing fad. There are several jokes about young wives who don't understand the gas-meter or the stock-exchange, for he liked women to be decorative, charming, and incompetent in practical matters, and felt uneasy if they exceeded their own proper province. The growing agitation for women's rights was difficult to ignore, so Du Maurier comforted himself by making facile jokes about small and feminine husbands with huge and dominating wives, or about daughters large enough to knock their fathers down. It never occurred to him that Mrs Ponsonby De Tomkyns might have used her energy and intelligence more profitably than in social intrigues. Du Maurier enjoyed meeting clever and high-spirited women, but the thought that they might compete professionally with men filled him with horror. His real bête noire was the sensational woman novelist (not serious writers like George Eliot and Annie Thackeray Ritchie), whose effusions filled the periodical publications of the period. He countenanced the proverbial cliche that women who wrote passionate love stories must themselves be frustrated, like the ugly authoress of *Passionate Pauline*, who sits in front of a mirror, and fondly imagines that she is describing what she sees there:

I see a pair of laughing, *espiègle* forget-me-not blue eyes, saucy and defiant; a *mutine* little rose-bud of a mouth, with its ever-mocking *moue*; a tiny shell-like ear, trying to play hide-and-seek in a tangled maze of rebellious russet gold.

('The Secrets of Literary Composition', 24 Jan. 1891)

In an earlier cartoon, of 1874, Du Maurier took up an idea which he later expanded into a poem for the *Recreations of the Rabelais Club*. In 'Realizing The Ideal' (11 April 1874) he describes the shock which a young man sustains when he discovers that the authoress of ' "Heart-Throbs: A Life's Earthquake, and other poems"; "The Siren: a Tale of Passion"; "Dalilah: A Story of the Day"; and a large family of sensations in three volumes, under equally suggestive titles', is a small and glowering woman, without the least trace of the unrestrained and unconventional beauty he had imagined. One of the best cartoons on the subject shows the 'Fair authoress of Cavalry Mustaches Etc' sitting at a dinner-table, next to a colonel, 'who has just been made a grandfather, and can talk of nothing else'. He therefore asks her: 'Do you take any interest in very young children, Miss Crauncher?' 'I loathe *all* children!' is her reply ('Breaking the Ice', 10 Jan. 1880). Most Victorian men tried to defeat the movements for women's rights by ridicule, and, where this failed, resorted to bluster. Du Maurier was the spokesman of this viewpoint, although he did make one very gallant tribute, in a cartoon of 2 July 1887, to Miss Agneta Frances Ramsay, the earliest woman to take a 'first' at Cambridge. In a few of his cartoons, like 'The Terrible Result of the Higher Education of Women' (24 Jan. 1874), he struck a note of amused sympathy, and managed to avoid an obvious display of prejudice. The caption read:

Miss Hypatia Jones, spinster of arts (on her way to refreshment), informs Professor Parallax, F.R.S., that 'young men do very well to look at, or to dance with, or even to marry, and all that kind of thing!' But that 'as to enjoying any rational conversation with any man under fifty, *that* is *completely* out of the question!'

Du Maurier was always enthralled by scientific discoveries, an interest presumably inherited from his father, and he included a few fascinating examples of his own theories in *Punch*. In one cartoon he suggested that, in the future, there would be a bridge from England to France, or, at least a tunnel, and, in another, he foresaw that the

TERRIBLE RESULT OF THE HIGHER EDUCATION OF WOMEN!

MISS HYPATIA JONES, SPINSTER OF ARTS (ON HER WAY TO REFRESHMENT), INFORMS PROFESSOR PARALLAX, F.R.S., THAT "YOUNG MEN DO VERY WELL TO LOOK AT, OR TO DANCE WITH, OR EVEN TO MARRY, AND ALL THAT KIND OF THING!", BUT THAT "AS TO ENJOYING ANY RATIONAL CONVERSATION WITH ANY MAN UNDER FIFTY, THAT IS COMPLETELY OUT OF THE QUESTION!"

110. *Punch* (1874)

FIFTY YEARS HENCE.

FROM LONDON TO PARIS IN—JUST TIME ENOUGH TO ALLOW OF A COMFORTABLE LUNCH AND A QUIET CIGAR ON BOARD THE ELEC
PLATE-GLASS CLUB EXPRESS.

111. *Punch* (1890)

voices of famous singers would be conserved in carefully labelled
boxes, to be taken out when required. The most progressive of all his
ideas concerned telephonic communication, then in its infancy,
where he envisaged telephones with a television link. His ideas are
surprising, perhaps a throw-back to the period when he was himself
working as a scientist. In his novels, Du Maurier often devoted his
scientific knowledge to the workings of the mind, particularly
during dreams. Only a few cartoons exploit this topic, but those
which do are quite unique in the history of *Punch*. A series of four
cartoons, published in February 1868, are concerned with the
experiences of a 'Mr Jenkins', who is pitched out of a horse-cab when
the horse collapses, and who subsequently suffers nightmares. He
dreams of a huge and terrifying cab-horse, which prances down a
narrow London alley, so that 'he cannot quite make out whether he
is riding in the cab, or whether it is he who stands, powerless to move,
right in front of the infuriated animal' (15 February 1868). Du
Maurier had an outstanding ability to depict the horrifyingly
grotesque, which he exploits to the full in the first of Jenkins' dreams.

In the second dream, the horse is whirling round in a fury, but in the third, Jenkins dreams that he is about to kill the creature which is now reduced to a pitiful condition.

An even better nightmare drawing is 'A Little Christmas Dream' (p. 18), in which a two-headed prehistoric monster, is slowly following a little boy down the street. The sense of inescapable horror is underlined by the two huge lumps of snow on the boy's feet, which effectively prevent his escape. The caption explains that the little boy had been given the book on prehistoric monsters for Christmas in accordance with the theories of M. Figier, who believes that natural history is more efficacious for children than fairy stories. 'The poor boy has not had a decent night's rest ever since!' The cartoon was based on Du Maurier's own childhood experience, still vivid to him thirty years later. One other grotesque cartoon deserves mention, 'Old Nickotin stealing away the brains of his devotees', which shows a group of men smoking pipes in the shape of long snakes, which, curling round to the back of their heads, are slowly sucking out their brains. The scene is that of an orgy, with the bizarre figure of a fiendish violinist playing on, while the heads of the smokers are consumed in flame. The picture has a quality reminiscent of Bosch, and is quite terrifying.

This study of Du Maurier's cartoons has been almost entirely concerned with their social implications. This is partly because their artistic qualities are strictly limited, and have, in any case, been discussed at length by other critics. Du Maurier was a gifted draughtsman, but the necessity of preparing his designs for the woodcut, imposed on him a meticulous and narrow technique. His sketches and studies often have a freedom and vitality, which he was unable to retain in his finished cartoons. Perhaps his most considerable gift was his ability to group his figures effectively, and to relate them perfectly to their setting. His compositions are always balanced and satisfying, the chief participants of his story clearly distinguished from the general melée and decorative accessories. His accent always falls in the right place. Millais once remarked that when he was in difficulties with a group picture, he often turned to Du Maurier's cartoons for help. Like Millais, Du Maurier had a real gift for statuesque and stately figures, and understood the fall of a dress, and texture of its material. His quality as an illustrator is ultimately proved by the way in which he has conditioned our view of Victorian society, so that we think of the period visually in terms of his images. This explains their familiarity, even for those who have not thumbed

OLD NICK-OTIN STEALING "AWAY THE BRAINS" OF HIS DEVOTEES.

GAUDEAMŬS IGITUR, JUVENES DUM SUMUS ;
IN JUCUNDÂ JUVENTUTE, NOS HABEBIT *FUMUS !*

112. *Punch* (1869)

MISTRESS AND PUPIL.

Mrs. Ponsonby de Tomkyns. "AND HOW ABOUT YOUR DINNER-PARTY, LADY MIDAS? WHO'S COMING?"

Lady Midas. "WELL, IT'S *SMALL*, BUT PRECIOUS *SELECT*, I CAN TELL YOU. THE MARQUIS AND MARCHIONESS OF CHEPE, VISCOUNT AND VISCOUNTESS SILVERLACKE THE HON. OLEO AND LADY MARGARINE DELARDE, SIR PULLMAN AND LADY CARR, AND THE CHOLMONDELEY-MAINWARING-CARSHALTONS."

Mrs. P. de T. "MY *DEAR* LADY MIDAS, YOU DON'T MEAN TO SAY YOU'VE ASKED ALL THESE FINE PEOPLE TO MEET NOBODY BUT *EACH OTHER*? WHY, THEY'LL BE BORED TO DEATH, AND NEVER FORGIVE YOU! IT'S NOT AS IF YOU WERE ALREADY *ONE OF THEM-SELVES*. YOU KNOW! YOU MUST WIRE TO GRIGSBY AT ONCE TO COME AND DINE AND BRING HIS BANJO, AND I'LL GET YOU NELLIE MICKLEMASH AND HER HUSBAND FROM THE JOLLITY. SHE'S NOT ACTING NOW."

Lady M. "BUT, MY DEAR, SHE'S NOT RESPECTABLE, I'M TOLD!"

Mrs. P. de T. "NO, BUT SHE'S AMUSING, AND THAT'S *EVERYTHING*! AND LOOK HERE, I'LL THROW OVER THE BOTHERBY JONESES, AND COME *MYSELF*!"

113. *Punch* (1883)

through old copies of *Punch*. Any social commentator looking for
visual material falls on his work with relief to illustrate anything from
upper-class snobbery to the habits of servants. Perhaps the most
surprising eulogy of his work comes from that strange and unpredictable critic, John Ruskin in his lecture *The Art of England*:

> I have therefore had enlarged by photography . . . the heads of two of
> Mr Du Maurier's chief heroines, Mrs Ponsonby de Tomkyns, and Lady
> Midas, in the great scene where Mrs Ponsonby takes on herself the
> administration of Lady Midas's at home.
> You see at once the effect in both depends on the coagulation and
> concretion of the black touches into masses relieved only by inter-
> spersed sparkling grains of incised light, presenting the realistic and vital
> portraiture of both ladies with no more labour than would occupy the
> draughtsman but a few minutes, and the engraver perhaps an hour or
> two. It is true that the features of the elder of the two friends might be
> supposed to yield themselves without difficulty to the effect of the
> irregular and blunt lines which are employed to reproduce them; but it is
> a matter of no small wonderment to see the delicate profile and softly
> rounded features of the younger lady suggested by an outline which must
> have been drawn in the course of a few seconds, and by some eight or ten
> firmly swept parallel penstrokes right across the cheek.[16]

16. J. Ruskin, *The Art of England* (2nd Edition 1887), pp. 174–5.

Chapter 9

Hampstead II

T HE 1880s WAS A DISPIRITING decade for Du Maurier, increasingly conscious that life had passed him by. He entertained hopes of becoming editor of *Punch* when Taylor resigned, although no artist had ever occupied the position. Predictably enough, the appointment went to Frank Burnand on Taylor's death in July 1880. More than anyone else, Burnand had kept

114. Vignette from *Punch* (1863)

the magazine alive under his dull and ponderous predecessor, and, with his forceful personality, he was the obvious choice. Du Maurier preferred to think otherwise. Henry Harper, who, with Thomas Hardy, went to lunch at New Grove House on the day of the election, 21 July, to discuss the illustrations of Hardy's *A Laodicean* in Harper's Monthly Magazine, asked Du Maurier about Burnand's chances: 'None at all, for he is a Roman Catholic, and every one is aware of the emphatic stand *Punch* has always taken against Romanism'.[1] Du Maurier himself appeared nervous on this occasion, undoubtedly because he felt that he was in the running. In fact, the only people summoned by the owners that afternoon were Burnand, Arthur À Beckett, Percival Leigh and Tenniel – the leading writers and the political cartoonist. Shortly after Taylor's death, Du Maurier had written to Burnand: 'who will be boss now, I wonder. Sans doute

1. J. Henry Harper, *The House of Harper* (1912), p. 534.

quelqu'un qui ne sera $\begin{cases} \text{ni-cathol} \\ \text{ni-agnost} \end{cases}$ ique!'.[2] Punch's attitude had changed radically since Dicky Doyle's resignation in 1850 as a protest against the magazine's anti-papal and anti-catholic bias, and Burnand was chosen unanimously by the selection board. He remained in the post till 1906, when he was gracefully forced to retire, having allowed the magazine to slide downhill once more.

Du Maurier concealed his disappointment, and settled down to work under Burnand, who wisely did not interfere with him as Taylor had done. Du Maurier did not really have the qualities of leadership, or the breadth of ideas, necessary for an editor, but he might have risen to the occasion had he been appointed. *Punch* would certainly have been more sophisticated and culturally minded under his control, and readers might have been spared the long and laborious comic verses which became such a feature of the magazine. Du Maurier's interest in the affairs of *Punch* declined after Burnand's appointment, and he rarely attended the Wednesday dinners. Harry Furniss, who was a member of the staff from 1880 to 1894, did not have an official seat at the round table, but he often took the place of the absent cartoonist. When Du Maurier did attend, he was conscious of being one of the elder statesmen, and no longer indulged in the high spirits and salacious jokes so characteristic of him in the past. Among the young men who now looked up to him was T. A. Guthrie (Fred Anstey), the author of the best-selling *Vice-Versa*, who worked for *Punch* from 1887 to 1897, for three guineas a week. More talented than Guthrie was Henry Lucy ('Toby' of *Punch*), an intelligent and witty political commentator, who really knew the House of Commons from the inside. He joined *Punch* in 1881, and was always delighted when Du Maurier attended the dinner, though his place was too far away to allow for intimate conversation. Lucy's chance came when William Bradbury, whose chair was next to Du Maurier's, departed at about ten o'clock, and he could then drop into the empty seat: 'and listened whilst du Maurier, mellowed by his claret, soothed by his cigarette, delightfully chatted'.[3] Harry Furniss makes a similar comment: 'It was always a treat to have du Maurier at "the table". He was by far and away the cleverest conversationalist of his time I ever met, his delightful repartees were so neat and effective, and his

2. July, 1880. University Library, Yale.
3. H. Lucy, *Nearing Jordan* (1916), p. 104.

daring chaff and his criticisms so bright and refreshing'.[4] Such appreciation explains the attraction which Du Maurier had for Henry James, and makes their friendship less surprising.

Now that he was so well established, Du Maurier did not even pretend to take any interest in the discussion about the following week's political cartoon. Henry Lucy could only remember a very few occasions on which Du Maurier made any suggestion with regard to the subject at the *Punch* dinner; when he did, it was usually accepted. The political situation only once profoundly upset him, and this was in 1870, when the Prussians were advancing on his beloved Paris. Harry Furniss states that Du Maurier suggested the Tenniel cartoon in which Napoleon I warned Napoleon III against a rash assault. His usual behaviour, however, is summed up by the following description:

> George du Maurier . . . , I learned, had been in the habit, directly the discussion set in, of drawing up another chair for his legs, placing a handkerchief over his face and going to sleep. He woke up once with a start and inquired if the company were still talking about Gladstone and Disraeli, and on hearing that this was the dismal truth, 'Good Heavens!' he exclaimed, 'why don't you talk about something sensible? Why don't you talk about the beauty of women?' and again passed into oblivion.[5]

During the first decade of Burnand's rule, the *Punch* staff worked well together, although the community spirit of the early days had largely disappeared. The staff now regarded themselves as professional men and gentlemen, rather than journalists or humourists, an attitude which Burnand was careful to impress on newcomers. Du Maurier gradually became irritated by Burnand, but they remained friendly during the 1880s. In May 1886, they went across to Paris for three days, together with Harry Furniss, to unearth some French material for *Punch*. They stayed at the Grand Hotel in the Boulevard des Capucines, where Du Maurier's bedroom looked out onto the Place de l'Opéra. He enjoyed staying at a good hotel, 'such a gay scene, all lighted up with electric light',[6] but he found Burnand rather tedious and conventional in a Parisian setting: 'Frank is such a 5 thousand a yearer in his habits'.[7]

Much more enjoyable for Du Maurier was his second expedition

4. H. Furniss, *Confessions of a Caricaturist* (1901), I, 223.
5. E. V. Lucas, *Reading, Writing and Remembering* (1932), p. 317.
6. To Emma Du Maurier, May 1886.
7. To Emma Du Maurier, May 1886.

SOUVENIR DE FONTAINEBLEAU.

Smith, Brown, Jones, and Robinson manage to enjoy themselves in La Belle France, in spite of the Anglophobia that prevails just now in that charming but misguided Country. They drive in her beautiful Forests, visit her historical Châteaux and Palaces, and Dine al fresco in her moonlit Hotel Gardens, where the Cuisine and Wines are unexceptionable. They are actually callous and unpatriotic enough to drink to her Prosperity, and, without prejudice to the absent Wives of their Bosoms, they couple the Toast with the Name of the "fascinating Daughters of Gaul!"

115. *Punch* (1886)

to France in September, again in company with Burnand and Furniss. They had been invited to spend three days in the Forest of Fontainebleau by a wealthy American, James Staat Forbes, who paid for their fares, and their rooms at the Hotel de Londres in Fontainebleau. The invitation was the result of a conversation at a dinner given by Burnand, when all three had expressed great interest in Forbes' description of the Forest of Fontainebleau and the Barbizon school. Du Maurier was delighted to be back in France, and rhapsodized about the accommodation in a letter to Emma: 'To stop at this perfect hotel is a little dream by itself'.[8] Their 'bedrooms looked out on to the hotel garden, and the windows could be kept open all night without fear of wasps, buzzing flies, or gnats'.[9] They 'did not take one single meal indoors, but the table was laid on a small lawn enclosed within four walls of high hedges, in one of which there was an open space serving as the doorway'.[10] Du Maurier illustrated this dinner table in one of his best *Punch* drawings, 'Souvenir de Fontainebleau', naming his companions, Smith (Forbes), Brown (Furniss), Jones (Du Maurier) and Robinson (Burnand). Every morning they rose at six, and breakfasted on a cup of tea, coffee or chocolate, before driving into the forest in a carriage 'drawn by a pair of sturdy horses'.[11] The forest itself was a surprise to them. Du Maurier told Emma: 'It is more wonderful than anything I ever dreamt of',[12] and Burnand remembered that: 'None of us, however light-hearted we may have been at starting, felt inclined to utter a word, or if we did it was whispered, as we were driven slowly and wonderingly about the forest'.[13] Even their driver was silent as they drove between the huge trees, every now and then coming out into the sunlight in an odd clearing, whereupon they would all laugh with relief. Du Maurier chatted to the coachman in the Parisian 'argot', of which he was such a master, describing his days as a student, and discussing the members of the Barbizon school, whom the coachman had known well. After a fork lunch at their hotel, they took a short siesta, driving out again in the late afternoon, and ending the day with dinner 'en plein air'. One afternoon they went to Barbizon itself, and saw Millet's cottage still in a mess, just as Millet had left it, and spoke a few words to Madame Millet. They preferred the forest to anything else, and one moonlit evening they

8. September 1886.
9. F. C. Burnand, *Records and Reminiscences* (1904), II, 251.
10. F. C. Burnand, *Records and Reminiscences* (1904), II, 251.
11. Burnand, II, 252.
12. September 1886.
13. Burnand, II, 252.

took a late drive there, glimpsing the occasional glow-worm, and revelling in the rich darkness under the trees. They returned to drink old cognac in the garden before going to bed. On the fourth morning of their visit they went into Paris, and returned from there to London. It had been a perfect holiday, and for Du Maurier, in particular, it was an oasis in a period of failing health and increasing depression.

Another *Punch* visit to France followed in May 1889, when ten members of the staff crossed the channel for the Paris Exhibition, Burnand, Guthrie, Arthur À Beckett, Linley Sambourne, Harry Furniss, E. J. Milliken, Henry Lucy, William Agnew, William Bradbury and Du Maurier. They all (except Guthrie) appear in the group photograph taken on the boat (plate 17). The party left London in the early morning, and lunched on the train between Calais and Paris, the subject of a caricature drawing by Harry Furniss. During this trip Du Maurier got to know Guthrie well. The latter had been in Whitby in 1883, and was much attracted by Du Maurier's charm, entitling him the Marquis d'Hampstead. In Paris they shared a room together at Durand's Hotel, overlooking the Madeleine. As usual on a staff outing, the organised activities did not please the participants. Du Maurier cut the dinner arranged at the Ambassadeurs, and took Guthrie on a long walk through the streets of Paris, which provided 'local colour', but no food. The central feature of the exhibition was the new Eiffel Tower, which Du Maurier and Guthrie conscientiously went up: 'only "two on a tower" out of the lot – Guthrie & I. The rest funked'.[14] Du Maurier could not help boring his companions with his past:

> How interesting it was to watch him in Paris, the place of his birth, standing, the ideal type of Frenchman himself, smiling and as amused as a boy at his own countrymen and women. 'So very un-English, you know!' Then, as we drove about Paris, he stood up in the carriage, excitedly showing us places familiar in his young days.[15]

Later, during this same drive, Du Maurier pointed out his birthplace to the rest of the staff:

> He started with the selection of a small but attractive suburban residence, afterwards correcting himself and pointing to a house much more

14. To Henry James, 20 July 1889. Houghton Library, Harvard.
15. Furniss, I, 224.

attractive-looking than the first. Soon, however, the puzzled expression which his companions had noticed in him before, returned to his face, and he called a halt for the third time, pointing to a large house in an extensive garden with a fountain. 'No', he exclaimed with conviction, 'I was wrong. This is where I was born. There's the fountain, there are the green shutters! and in *that* room!' The party descended again and poured out libations. After the sleepy stage of a long drive had been reached, du Maurier awoke, and, as if soliloquising, muttered, 'No, no, I was wrong, absurdly wrong. But I see my mistake.' And he roused his companions to view a fine mansion approached by a drive.[16]

At this point William Bradbury took a firm hand, and told Du Maurier that four birthplaces was quite enough for anyone. In spite of Du Maurier's pleas, 'You bring us out for a holiday, you take us about everywhere, and you won't let a chap be born where he likes',[17] Bradbury had the others on his side, and the drive continued. It is not surprising that, in *Trilby*, Du Maurier gave his own birth-date, 6 March 1834, to an aristocrat, Gontran Xavier François Marie Joseph d'Amaury de Brissac de Roncesvaulx de la Rochemartel-Boisségur, born in the Hotel de la Rochemartel in the Faubourg St Germain. Like his ancestor, he suffered from a touch of 'folie de grandeur'.

Du Maurier was present at a famous *Punch* dinner on 7 May 1889, when Gladstone was the guest of honour. Many of the staff wrote about this occasion in their memoirs, remembering Gladstone saying that he did not think about politics in bed, that he always slept for seven or eight hours a night, and that he disliked getting up in the morning. The conversation later turned to politics, Gladstone amusing the company with anecdotes about his political colleagues and opponents. Du Maurier's response to the dinner is not recorded, but he was probably bored, as he usually was by any political discussion.

Du Maurier's financial difficulties forced him to work for other illustrated magazines besides *Punch*. His enthusiasm for his craft was almost extinct, and his attitude towards authors became increasingly casual. He showed no desire to work out new creative designs, but relied almost entirely on his stereotyped cartoon technique. This worked very well in the case of Mrs L. C. Lillie's *Prudence: a story of Aesthetic London*, where he was able to adapt his Cimabue Brown

16. Wood, pp. 125–6.
17. Wood, p. 127.

drawings, but it was disastrous with serious authors like Hardy. In 1875, Du Maurier illustrated one of Hardy's inferior novels, *The Hand of Ethelberta*, in *The Cornhill*, and Hardy was impressed by the results. He became friendly with Du Maurier at the Rabelais Club in 1880, and suggested to his publishers, Harper's, that Du Maurier should illustrate his next novel. This was to be serialized in the first European edition of *Harper's Monthly*, and their London agent, R. R. Bowker, was keen that it should be a success: 'The firm was anxious that the engravings for Hardy's *A Laodicean* should be better than the usual work of the kind in the English magazines, and asked Hardy to suggest a first-class artist. He selected Du Maurier'.[18] It was Du Maurier's first commission for *Harper's Monthly*, and he too was anxious to do well. The first drawings seemed to be satisfactory, Bowker commenting on them in his journal for 30 July 1880:

> Saw some drawings of Du Maurier's at the engraver's. Hardy had told us he knew nothing of dress, but left that to his wife, who drapes all his models. This would surprise those who see his strength at toilettes. The children of his pictures are his own children. He *does* notice faces and is fond of bric-a-brac. I find he draws altogether in pen and ink, having the sight of but one eye, his engraver tells me, so that he cannot use a brush, scarcely seeing accurately where its point touches the paper.[19]

By December, Bowker had become thoroughly dissatisfied with the drawings, and a surviving letter from Du Maurier to Hardy shows how matters were progressing. In June, Hardy had sent Du Maurier two photographs 'for the chief characters', and suggested that he should call on him 'with the MS in my hand, read it over to you, & finish our talk about the first picture'.[20] Hardy sent another photograph as a guide to the landscape in a later episode, feeling that Du Maurier's illustrations were too vague and generalized for his precise topographical descriptions. Du Maurier was less concerned:

> Many thanks for the photograph – but I have done, as well as I could, the scene by the tumuli . . . Think of the poor artist, please, and give me a scene in every number if you can. When you have a notion for a picture, & feel inclined to move, come & lunch with me – we will talk of the next illustration & after luncheon I will paint your portrait.[21]

18. E. McClung Fleming, *R. R. Bowker* (Norman, Oklahoma, 1952), p. 155.
19. McClung Fleming, pp. 155–6.
20. T. Hardy to Du Maurier, June 1880.
21. To T. Hardy, 1880. Berg Collection, New York Public Library.

In October, Hardy took to his bed for six months, dictating the remainder of the novel to his wife, and showing little interest in the remaining illustrations. Not so Bowker. By 10 December, he was so concerned about the quality of the drawings that he decided to visit Du Maurier in Hampstead:

> I was ushered into his studio, where he was sitting by the open fire, the great dog, Chang . . . asleep in the window recess . . . . Du Maurier is really a Frenchman, born near Paris, a good, genial fellow, rather stout and jolly looking, and exceedingly agreeable . . . . I finally told him out and out that we were disappointed in his drawings for the Hardy story, whereupon he rather owned up that he was better at working his own will in social satire than under the limitations of other people's stories – though his Thackeray illustrations were among his best work. He said Hardy came up and gave him the points minutely and of course he felt constrained within these limits.[22]

It was common practice in America for the art editor to pass outspoken criticisms on the illustrations, and to get work redone:

> One of the illustrations for the 'Laodicean' was a picture of country folk dancing in a tent at night. As originally drawn, the opening of the tent into the outer darkness was shown as absolutely black, so that it stood out as a positive object – as would not be the case when one looked toward the outer blackness from a lighted room. There was also an amusing contretemps, quite accidental, by which two of the dancers seemed to be brandishing their fists in each other's eyes. Du Maurier took these suggested criticisms in good part, confounding good-naturedly his editor's 'microscopic eyes', and this episode illustrated thoroughly his wholesome tone and even temper.[23]

Du Maurier's even temper might have been construed as complacence.

After *A Laodicean*, Du Maurier, surprisingly enough, was asked to illustrate the more successful *Prudence* by Mrs Lillie, for *Harper's* but he did not work for the magazine again until May 1886, when Bowker's vigorous successor, James Ripley Osgood, arrived in London and persuaded him to contribute regular cartoons, like those in *Punch*. It was Osgood who accepted *Peter Ibbetson* for the magazine in 1889, but he had the sense not to ask Du Maurier to

22. McClung Fleming, p. 156.
23. R. R. Bowker, 'Recollections of Du Maurier', *The New York Times Supplement* (25 October 1896) p. 11.

illustrate Hardy's *The Woodlanders*, which appeared in 1886 and 1887. Possibly Bowker had warned him that Du Maurier 'did not in later years feel quite at home out of his own "society" world until he came to the illustration of his own stories'.[24]

Most of Du Maurier's other drawings appeared in *The Cornhill*, to which he continued to contribute until the magazine dispensed with illustrations in 1886. It had come down in the world since the 1850s, when Trollope's *Framley Parsonage* and *The Small House at Allington* were illustrated by Millais, George Eliot's *Romola* by Frederic Leighton, and Thackeray's *Adventures of Philip* by Frederick Walker. Du Maurier's long serials in the 1870s and 1880s included such inferior work as 'Zelda's Fortune' by R. E. Francillon, 'Three Feathers' by W. Black, and 'Carità' by Mrs Oliphant. Apart from Hardy's *The Hand of Ethelberta*, a novel of doubtful merit, he illustrated only two works by outstanding novelists, *The Adventures of Harry Richmond* by George Meredith in 1871, and *Washington Square* by Henry James in 1880. His most popular series of drawings were those for a book, Florence Montgomery's tear-jerker, *Misunderstood*, and it is comforting to hear that he had to draw the little hero, Humphrey, with a pipe in his mouth and a mug of beer beside him, to prevent himself from weeping over the illustrations. Needless to say, he rubbed them out afterwards. In his *Illustrators of the Sixties*, Forrest Reid complained of the sentimentality of the drawings, which are, however, the ideal accompaniment to the story.

Apart from his cartoons and illustrations, Du Maurier was turning his hand to other creative activities. He took up water-colour painting once more, possibly in emulation of Frederick Walker and George Pinwell, but he was not very successful. His watercolours show an inadequate colour sense, and an obsessive attention to line, which renders them little more than elaborate tinted drawings. The same criticism could be made of Leech's water-colours, the result, even more than Du Maurier's, of financial expediency. Du Maurier never made much money out of his water-colours. One of his first efforts was a portrait of his old friend, Alfred Ainger, which is surprisingly successful – a good likeness and a characteristic attitude. (National Portrait Gallery, London. plate 12). Later water-colours were mainly of his children. A portrait of Beatrix was exhibited at the Royal Society of Painters in Water-Colour in 1882, and two excellent portraits of Sylvia and May (plate 15) were completed in 1889. Lady

24. 'Recollections of Du Maurier', p. 11.

116. *The Adventures of Harry Richmond* by George Meredith
(1870)

Browning owns a study of an interior in New Grove House, which shows a more painterly and atmospheric approach, but is rather garish and crude in its effect. He was commissioned to paint the daughter of George Faudel Phillips, whose wife, Helen, was one of the Levy Lawson girls Du Maurier had known so well as a young man. He and Emma had attended their opulent wedding in 1867. Two other water-colours were based on *Punch* drawings. *Two Thrones*, a re-working of a cartoon of the same name, contained portraits of Henry James, Charles Hoyer Millar and Alfred Ainger, but it is now unfortunately missing; it was sold by Messrs. Agnew to Mr H. P. Grafton M.P. in 1884 for 250 guineas. Two years later, Du Maurier sold a similar water-colour, *Time's Revenge*. He was not happy about these productions, feeling the need to apologise for reworking *Punch* drawings to Armstrong, who disapproved of such mercenary habits. Harry Quilter, in an otherwise tasteless obituary, hit the nail on the head with regard to the water-colours: 'As I understand his work, Du Maurier, though a colourist – at all events at his best – in black-and-white, was absolutely deficient in the colour sense when he came to deal as a water-colour painter with the various hues of the prism'.[25]

25. 'Some Memories and a Moral', *Royal Society of Painters in Water Colours Catalogue* (Winter 1896–7).

117. *Misunderstood* by Florence Montgomery (1874)

Water-colours were a natural extension of Du Maurier's work as a cartoonist: poems were not. Du Maurier had no real gift as a poet, in spite of his brilliant parodies of Morris and Swinburne, and, left to himself, he merely produced doggerel verse, like his two contributions to the Rabelais Club. He sent one poem to Henry James for comment; James advised him to cut it very severely: 'You will think me very merciless – when you ask by the suppression of how *many* stanzas I think it would gain. But there remain 14 – a goodly enough number. I wd. omit *all* the tournament part'.[26] Du Maurier published twelve stanzas of this poem in *Peter Ibbetson*, under the title 'The Chime':

> There is an old French air,
> A little song of loneliness and grief –
> Simple as nature, sweet beyond compare –
> And sad – past all belief!
>
> Nameless is he that wrote
> The melody – but this much I opine:
> Whoever made the words was some remote
> French ancestor of mine.
>
> I know the dungeon deep
> Where long he lay – and why he lay therein;
> And all his anguish, that he could not sleep
> For conscience of a sin.[27]

He had some facility as a translator, and his English version of Sully Prudhomme's 'L'Agonie' was later chosen for *The Oxford Book of Victorian Verse* under the title 'Music'. Du Maurier originally published it in the *English Illustrated Magazine* for June 1884, without a title, accompanied by a drawing of a death-bed scene. The first, third, and fourth stanzas of the original more or less correspond to Du Maurier's, but he has taken general themes from the whole French lyric. The stanzas of the original which he translates most closely are these:

> Vous qui m'aiderez dans mon agonie,
> Ne me dites rien;
> Faites que j'entende un peu d'harmonie,
> Et mourrai bien.

26. H. James to Du Maurier, 1889. Houghton Library, Harvard.
27. pp. 139–40.

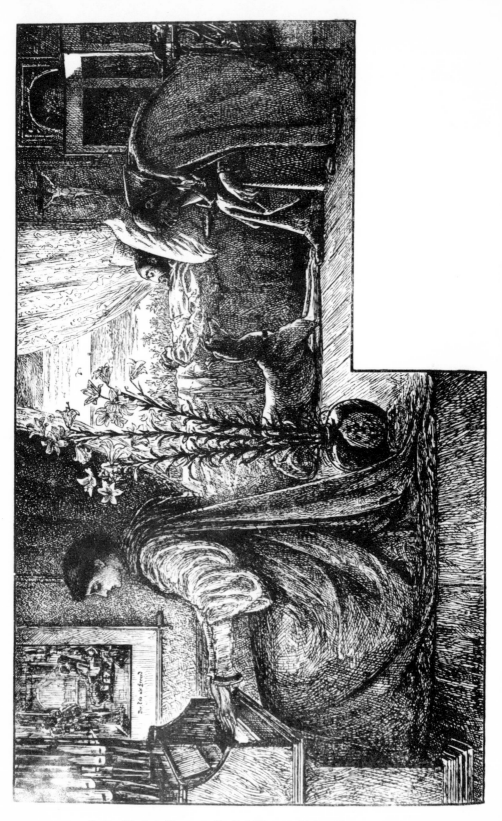

118. Der Tod als Freund, *English Illustrated Magazine*

Je suis las des mots, je suis las d'entendre
    Ce qui peut mentir ;
J'aime mieux les sons qu'au lieu de comprendre
    Je n'ai qu'à sentir ;

Une mélodie où l'âme se plonge
    Et qui, sans effort,
Me fera passer du délire au songe,
    Du songe à la mort.[28]

Du Maurier's version is more romantic and sentimental:

Kindly watcher by my bed, lift no voice in prayer,
Waste not any words on me when the hour is nigh –
Let a stream of melody but flow from one sweet player,
And meekly will I lay my head and fold my hands to die.

Sick am I of idle words, past all reconciling –
Words that weary and perplex, and pander, and conceal ;
Wake the sounds that cannot lie, for all their sweet beguiling ;
The language one need fathom not, but only hear and feel.

Let them roll once more to me, and ripple in my hearing,
Like waves upon a lonely beach where no craft anchoreth,
That I may steep my soul therein, and craving nought, nor fearing,
Drift on through slumber to a dream, and through a dream to death.

Du Maurier published another translation from Sully Prudhomme in *The Martian*, where the hero's daughter writes an English version of 'Prière'. This was far closer to the French, but without the personal intensity of 'L'Agonie'. His translation into French was less satisfactory because less idiomatic, like his 'Nocturne' based on Byron's 'Sun of the Sleepless, Melancholy Star', published in the *English Illustrated Magazine* for December 1886:

Salut ! mélancholique étoile !
Le ciel se fonce, le jour fuit,
Et ta splendeur tremblante luit
Comme une larme sous un voile,
Sans force à dissiper la nuit.

These attempts to extend his range had a double motive. He was anxious to secure himself and his family financially should his sight

28. *Les Solitudes : Poésies 1868–1878.*

fail altogether, and he wished to give fuller expression to the creative gifts which he felt he possessed. It is in this light that one must consider the extraordinary story told about him by Harry Furniss in his *Confessions of a Caricaturist*. Before quoting a tale which reflects so badly on Du Maurier, it must be stated that Furniss was mentally unstable, that he had a grudge against *Punch*, and that he was jealous of Du Maurier's success with *Trilby*: 'Du Maurier had a little of the green-eyed monster in his bosom, although he lived to laugh at all when he himself became the greatest success of any man in his sphere'.[29] According to Furniss, Du Maurier took a cab back to Hampstead with him soon after the opening of an exhibition of Furniss' comic drawings after old master paintings at the Grosvenor Gallery in 1887:

'My dear Furniss, I must be honest with you – I hate you, I loathe you, I detest you!'

'Thanks, awfully, my dear fellow! But why?'

'Ah!' he said, 'your success is too great. When I get the return you send me in the morning, showing me the number of people that have been to your Exhibition, the tremendous takings at the turnstiles, the number of albums subscribed for, the number of pictures you have sold, I cannot work. I go on to Hampstead Heath to walk off my jealousy; when I come in to lunch I find your first telegram, telling me you have made £80 that morning. I walk out again, and looking down upon London, although I shake my fist at the whole place, my wrath is for you alone. I come in to tea to find another telegram – you have made £100! How can I sit down and scratch away on a piece of paper when you are making a fortune in a week?'

This nearly took my breath away.

'My dear du Maurier,' I replied,' I feel hurt – seriously, irrevocably... Of course you are the victim of a practical joke.'

Du Maurier pulled out from his pocket my supposed returns. It was an imitation of printing, with the amounts filled in. 'This is the kind of thing I get every morning.'

'Why, of course, it is written, not printed. That is the work of the irrepressible practical joker. But it makes no difference, du Maurier; if you thought that I would be such a cad as to send you these returns, I cannot see how we can ever be great friends.'[30]

The story does not ring true, but it may have been an exaggeration of a real incident. Furniss and Du Maurier were not intimates, so

29. I, 225.
30. I, 225–6.

why should Du Maurier have expected to receive telegrams from him (he did not apparently find this circumstance surprising), and who would have gone to the trouble of sending them? Du Maurier's early letters contain many envious references to the wealth of others, but he would hardly have let his hair down to someone who was not a particular friend. Nevertheless, occurring as it did two years before the inception of *Peter Ibbetson*, the story cannot be entirely ignored.

Another of Du Maurier's persistent worries during the 1880s was his health. His neurotic obsession with his eyesight increased rather than otherwise, and every chill or upset seemed to worsen it. He had been treated for a colonic disorder in the 1870s, and he put many of his later illnesses down to this trouble. Dr Squire considered that his colon was causing 'my anxious heart's unrest',[31] and Dr Kidd gave him tonics to cure the condition. References to ill-health in his letters are frequent but tend to be cryptic. In April 1886, he was more explicit in a note to Henry James: 'Something busted in my throat last night & greatly relieved me. If only the same thing would take place in my eye, I should be a happy man'.[32] In September of the same year he went with his family to the Faudel Phillips in Hertford and sent the following account to James:

> We had a very pleasant time at Balls Park . . . unfortunately it ended badly – sore throats & faceaches & fevers & we have come back loving our hosts but more or less crippled; and I am sorry to say, our hosts are crippled too – a sudden throat seems to have come over Hertford with the hot weather. I had, not a throat, but a faceache which ended with an abscess, which gave me 48 hours of agony, which has left me a washed out rag – whether it was the drains or the heat, or 2 books of Guy de Maupassant . . . I can't say.[33]

Then, in March 1887, he was complaining of ' "peripheral neuralgia", which came on quite suddenly, in a minute, & has never left me – & a kind of numbness in my left & right hand, & sometimes in my leg, with pins & needles & sensitiveness to cold'.[34] A year later he was writing to James from 7 Pelham Place, Hastings, where the family had fled with sore throats from their London lodgings in

31. To Frederick Locker-Lampson, undated. Henry E. Huntingdon Library, San Marino, California.
32. Houghton Library, Harvard.
33. 1 September 1886. Houghton Library, Harvard.
34. 7 March 1887. Houghton Library Harvard.

Sussex Gardens. At the end of that year, Du Maurier became deaf in one ear, a terrible affliction for a man whose sight was bad. This condition passed, but at Easter 1889, Du Maurier wrote to Alfred Ainger that he was 'seedy' from too much dining out. Never strong, Du Maurier was easily tired, and when, in the late 1880s, he took a house in Bayswater for the winter months, he was out late most evenings. He was subject to the same strain that had induced him to move to Hampstead twenty years earlier, and he was much frailer now.

The decision to take a house in London for the winter was a direct result of the break-up of his family, beginning with Beatrix's marriage in 1883. As they grew older, the Du Maurier children became well-known for their animated conversation and humour, which seemed to illustrate the success of their unconventional upbringing. They all absorbed from their father the idea that physical beauty was of paramount importance, and they evaluated everyone they met by this stern criterion. Their mother was unable to keep up with their spirited discussions, which flowed round her, leaving her passive and uncomprehending. The children were all devoted to 'Mummie', who was a reliable and reassuring figure, but she lacked the intelligence and quickness of her family. To her father's delight, Beatrix grew up into a tall and stately beauty (she posed for the Duchess of Towers in *Peter Ibbetson*), and even the family ugly-duckling, Sylvia, became one of the most admired and attractive women of her time. When Beatrix 'came out' in 1881, Du Maurier experienced the delightful sensation of being the father of a socially successful young woman. Unlike Du Maurier, Beatrix remained cool and unimpressed:

> The gay world seems as yet to exert little fascination over Trixy, however, who thinks nothing so festive as a small dance in Bourgeouis respectable Hampstead, where she calls her partners by their Christian names, or even worse.[35]

Beatrix had already met the young man she eventually married, Charles Hoyer Millar, at a Hampstead dance. They became engaged in July 1883, when she was nineteen and Hoyer Millar twenty-three. It was an excellent match. Millar was well-to-do, six feet tall, and, what was more satisfactory to Du Maurier, extraordinarily handsome. Du Maurier was aware, however, that the marriage marked

35. To T. Armstrong, 16 June 1881.

. Original drawing for 'A Combination of
agreeables', *Punch* (1888). From the collection of
s S. Beaumont

the end of family life, and he was sad. Writing to Tom Armstrong, Beatrix' godfather, he sketched himself head in hand, sitting on Hampstead Heath:

> One's feelings are very mixed about one's daughter's settlement in life, however nice the son-in-law. I should have been content to go on just as we are for another 20 or 30 years. [36]

Beatrix and Charles Hoyer Millar were married in St George's, Hanover Square in July 1884, according to Henry James, they were quite the best-looking couple of that year. On the way to the church, Beatrix asked her father a difficult question: 'if one marries a good-looking man, does it necessarily mean one will have good-looking children?' [37] Fortunately, in the event, they were. Du Maurier went through the ceremony, which was taken by Ainger (Millais, Russell Lowell and Browning signed the register), in a dazed dream, and then, after seeing the couple off, returned to Hampstead to pack up the presents, 'a fond and bereaved father', [38] not knowing whether to laugh or cry.

After the honeymoon, Beatrix and her husband went to Canada and the United States for a year. At the same time, Guy Du Maurier received his commission in the Royal Fusiliers, and left England for Cannanore in Madras. After leaving Marlborough in 1881, he had gone to an army coach in Hampstead, and then to Sandhurst. Du Maurier was delighted at his son's success, but worried about the possibility of war. Du Maurier felt the break-up of his family keenly. New Grove House, with all its memories, was becoming un-bearable to him, and, in April 1886, he took a furnished house in Bayswater (27 Gloucester Gardens) for three months. This was to become a regular pattern of his life: 'Hampstead is really a place of exile, and now Guy & Trixy are gone, & Gerald soon going to school, the home is getting big & seems dreary'. [39] The loss of the two elder children made Du Maurier closer to May, his favourite child and the chief solace of his last years. May was the original of the delightful Marty in *The Martian*. Not as gay and dashing as her sisters, she was devoted to him, and possessed a wit and spirit which never failed to amuse him. On two occasions at least, she performed songs with a banjo accompaniment in Whitby, and, at a cricket match between

36. 24 July 1883.
37. *Gerald*, p. 40.
38. To T. Armstrong, 28 July 1884.
39. To T. Armstrong, Feb. 1886.

Whitby visitors and a team of clowns, she turned to Du Maurier with great seriousness: ' "Father, do you see *that*?" "Yes, what about it?" "Why", said May, with hushed reverence, "that's *the Wagonette the Clowns came in!*" '.[40] Besides his own family, Du Maurier also kept open house for Isobel Scott's four children. Her marriage had never gone well, and she returned more and more frequently to Dusseldorf, the only place where she had ever been happy. It was not until nearly the end of her life, in the late 1880s, that she finally left Scott and his succession of mistresses, and began to travel with her youngest daughter, Dora. Eugène's children were also frequent guests, all of them devoted to 'Uncle Kiki', and the ever-kind Aunt Emma.

During the winter months, the Du Mauriers let off New Grove House. One tenant was a Scottish lady, who did not mind the cold, and another was the famous actress, Mary Anderson, who complained that it was slow work getting down the stairs with all the *Punch* drawings there to distract her. The house was hard to let in the summer because there was no garden. In December, therefore, the Du Mauriers descended to Bayswater; 27 Gloucester Gardens in 1886, Bayswater Terrace in 1887 and 1890, Sussex Gardens in 1888, Porchester Terrace in 1889, Stanhope Terrace in 1893. Sitting in the front room of 15, Bayswater Terrace, Du Maurier would feast his eyes on the passers-by, informing Henry James that the shapes of buses gliding through the fog delighted him. Haverstock Hill became 'the hill of difficulty', and New Grove House 'the eyree', in this reorientation. Du Maurier, who, in the old days, had enjoyed quiet suppers and evenings at home, became a passionate diner-out. Between 1885 and 1890, the list of dinner engagements was formidable, including such diverse hosts as the Smalleys, Ritchies, Alfred Parsons, Burnand, the Alma Tademas, the Blake Richmonds, the Douglas Freshfields, the Edward Lawsons, the Boughtons and Lady Brett. Du Maurier was a popular guest, and he seemed to revel in the social life he had once rejected. He flirted with Lady Randolph Churchill, conversed animatedly with Lady Airlie, and was asked to Haddo House by Lord and Lady Aberdeen in 1885:

> Mummie succeeded in getting him up for early morning prayers, but before their conclusion he had managed to get his head entangled in the back of his chair and had to be helped to his feet before he could be extricated.[41]

40. T. A. Guthrie, *A Long Retrospect* (1936), p. 167.
41. Hoyer Millar, p. 170.

This high life had its effect on Du Maurier and his family, who were left pale and exhausted at the end of their Bayswater season. They continued remorselessly, however, Du Maurier informing James in February 1889: 'Next week we are dining out Monday, Tuesday, Wednesday, & Friday – most likely at home Thursday & Saturday'.[42] Fortnights at the seaside became a familiar feature of the spring, when the Du Mauriers and their sore throats left Bayswater for Brighton, Hastings, or some other resort. Letters to Millais and James are full of family illnesses, but there was no question of returning to the solitude of Hampstead.

Du Maurier had never entirely lost his argumentativeness, and in London society it revived. Stories of his blunders in the 1880s reveal that the bumptious and opinionated young man had not been entirely extinguished. One such tale, told by Clement Scott's second wife, Margaret, reflects badly on Du Maurier. He was dining with Scott at the house of George Wardle, the original manager of Morris & Co, when the discussion turned to the trial of the beautiful Madeline Smith, some years before charged with murdering her Italian lover under threat of blackmail. The Scottish court had acquitted her, though the evidence against her was very strong, and the case had roused enormous popular interest. After listening to the discussion, Du Maurier dogmatically maintained that Madeline Smith, beautiful or not, should have been hanged. His voice carried right round the table, and a deadly silence followed. It was only later that Du Maurier discovered his gaffe; his hostess, Mrs Wardle, was Madeline Smith.

The 1880s show Du Maurier divided within himself, and the friendships of this period reflect his internal conflict. Tom Armstrong was appointed director of the South Kensington School of Art (now the Royal College) in 1881, succeeding Poynter who wanted more time for his painting. Both men were committed to French methods of art training, and it was Poynter who introduced the life model to the school. Poynter had also begun to establish a museum of casts, now a period piece in the Victoria and Albert Museum, so that students could appreciate the great European achievements in sculpture and architecture. Armstrong continued with this scheme, and also bought a number of original works of art for the gallery. His appointment was a good one, for he was firm and sympathetic. His own painting, chiefly carried out in schemes of mural decoration,

42. 15 February 1889. Houghton Library, Harvard.

was not outstanding, and his talents were better used in the manage-
ment of the art-school.

In the year of his appointment, Armstrong, now forty-nine,
married Alice Mary Brine, the twenty-three year old daughter of a
close friend. Mrs Armstrong remembered that they often visited New
Grove House on Sunday evenings, but that after they moved to
Abbott's Langley in Hertfordshire in 1890, they saw far less of the Du
Mauriers. Their only child, Ambrose George, was born in 1883.
Armstrong and Du Maurier were bound by many old ties of affection, but they often irritated one another. Armstrong was jealous of
Du Maurier's new friends and interests, and disapproved profoundly
of his novels, which he felt were pandering to popular taste, the easy
road to success. In Armstrong's view, Du Maurier was an artist, who
could have made a reasonable income out of his water-colour portraits and maintained his integrity:

> It was, then, because I thought he was neglecting opportunities of
> success in a new kind of work, which would bring him more fame and
> considerable profit, if his sight grew worse, that I looked with a 'mauvais
> oeil' on the distraction of story-writing; for his energy, it was evident, to
> my regret, was being more and more directed into the channel of his
> new work.
>   It was natural therefore that he should not confide much in a person so
> little sympathetic. I think his Hampstead neighbours, Canon Ainger and
> Mr Basil Champneys, knew more of his literary plans than I did or any
> of his old friends, but he did tell Lamont and me, now and then, some-
> thing about the story he was composing.[43]

Armstrong might have added Henry James, a much stronger influence than Champneys or Ainger, but he does not seem to have been
aware how close James was to Du Maurier. Indeed, Du Maurier
kept his old and new friends very much apart, as if aware they would
not mix.

Armstrong and Lamont were old friends, closely linked to Du
Maurier's family life, and John Millais could perhaps be added to
the same group. The two men continued to meet in Hampstead, and
in Millais' house in Palace Gate, where Du Maurier was called upon
to criticize the paintings for which Millais received £30,000 a year:

> I shall . . . say: 'this nose might be a little broader on the left side of the

43. Armstrong, pp. 165–6.

tip': or 'you might make the northwest corner of that eye a little longer' –
and I shall be awfully flattered, because you will believe me.[44]

Their letters to each other are full of fun and high-spirits, quite unlike the more intense and thoughtful correspondence with Henry
James. One group of letters concerns the Royal Academy Exhibition
of 1879, when a Hampstead sculptor, Samuel Fry, submitted a bust
of Du Maurier. Millais was not impressed by the work, but he made
sure that it was included:

> My Dear George, I spotted you amongst the decapitations, and for the
> love of the original will do my best to place it, and myself add a wreath of
> bays around the unconscious temples, in token of my appreciation of the
> artist – *which* I leave you to guess. . . .[45]

Du Maurier made a sketch of the bust for *Punch*, which he included in
the background of a cartoon with imaginary busts of Lamont and
Armstrong – a good study of the three in middle-age. Later in 1882,
Millais was asked to contribute a portrait of Du Maurier to the
Macdonald collection of artists' portraits, now in the Aberdeen Art
Gallery. It was a particular pleasure for both of them, and they
looked forward to the sittings with keen anticipation. Du Maurier
sent Millais a small sketch of a portrait of himself in the style of
Whistler, complete with butterfly monogram, with an accompany-
ing verse:

> My dear John Everett Millais
> Macdonald writes to beg me pray
> That you will kindly fix a day
> Pour peindre mon petit portrait!
> Will any Tuesday suit you, say?
> Or even any Wed-nes-day?
> Hoping you're jolly, bright & gay,
> I'm ever yours, du Morriay.[46]

The reply, dated 25 November 1882, was in kind:

> Sunday week will suit me best,
> Because it is a day of rest.

44. 8 Nov. 1888. Pierpont Morgan Library, New York.
45. Millais, II, 267.
46. 23 November 1882. Pierpont Morgan Library.

AT THE R.A.—TRIUMPH OF REALISTIC ART.

Blenkinsop (complacently gazing at a Bust of himself by a fashionable Sculptor). "IT'S NOT SO
MUCH AS A *WORK OF ART* THAT I VALUE IT, BROWN; BUT THE *LIKENESS* IS SO WONDERFUL,
YOU KNOW!"

120. *Punch* (1879)

As painting you will be a pleasure,
I count the operation leisure;
So come to me at half-past ten,
And I'll begin your portrait then.[47]

Millais, on the make for a knighthood or baronetcy, could not resist
a dig at the soldiers:

47. Millais, II, 268.

> It would appear, a country's good,
> Is only gained by shedding blood.[48]

Du Maurier, who rather admired military heroes, now that Guy was going into the army, pointed out that Charles Darwin had already been honoured, and that the army needed these toys as a reward for devotion to a hard task:

> How would you like to march all night
> And, on an empty stomach, fight,
> Just about half-past five, A.M.[49]

Millais, replying by return, conceded Du Maurier this point, but insisted:

> It only did occur to me –
> If Shakespeare were still living,
> He wouldn't dine with Majesty,
> Apart from medal-giving.[50]

Millais' portrait of Du Maurier is, like the drawings for James' *Washington Square*, a disappointing relic of a great friendship. All their gay Sunday morning sittings only produced a dull and competent likeness, revealing even less of Du Maurier than his self-portrait sketches in *Punch*. The accuracy of Millais' work, however, is confirmed by Frith's study of Du Maurier in his *Private View of the Royal Academy, 1881*, painted in the same year, which shows a bland and uninspired public exterior.

Most of the correspondence is concerned with their health problems and with their respective families. It soon began to fall into an established pattern. Every May, Du Maurier would congratulate Millais on his Academy pictures, and every November he would thank him for a present of game, sent from Millais' estate in Scotland. Both were the fathers of pretty daughters, and both took an interest in the marriage market. It was on 28 November 1879, at the wedding of Millais' eldest daughter, Effie to Major William James, that Du Maurier first saw Lily Langtry.

48. Millais, II, 268.   50. Millais, II, 269.
49. 27 November 1882, Pierpont Morgan Library.

Such a crowd in the church today! . . . The bride looked very pretty, marching up with her papa, who looked very grey and much moved – Mrs M. as self possessed as if it were a luncheon party. I had a good study of Mrs Langtry, back, front & both profils – neither Poynter nor Millais have done her justice. Si Madame L. était Eve, et moi Adam, je n'aurais pas attendre qu'elle m'offre la pomme –[51]

In the autumn of 1885, Du Maurier at last visited Scotland, taking lodgings in St Andrews, and going on from there to visit Millais at Birnam Hall. He took Sylvia with him, by now a striking girl of twenty, leaving Emma, who was suffering from rheumatism, at St Andrews with May and Gerald. The visit was a huge success, the witty Sylvia delighted Millais, who subsequently took a great interest in her welfare. When his own daughter announced her engagement later in the year, he told Du Maurier: 'Love to Sylvia who I hope to see soon in a similar position although it will be a heavy blow to me'.[52] Like all sportsmen, Millais was boringly enthusiastic about his hobby, and insisted on showing Du Maurier all the ins and outs of shooting and fishing. He imagined that all *Punch* cartoonists must be as sportive as Leech:

I am going out to see the duck shooting, dear J.E.M. will have me see every blessed thing & learn all the small details – yesterday I spent all the morning watching him fish & learn all the business, not to be a fisherman, but to know all about it as Leech did – which now I do. Its horribly cruel but very exciting.[53]

Writing to thank Millais, Du Maurier wished him: 'More power to thy mighty elbow, J.E.M., both with rod and brush, and may the fifty-nine pounder, for which thy soul lusteth, soon be thine!'[54]

Du Maurier never indulged in violent exercise:

The walking-pace was always of the slowest and it was the only exercise my father-in-law ever took, except when once or twice he bathed with us at Shanklin and did the French over-arm stroke *la coupe* for twenty or thirty yards. In spite of this lack of exercise each calf and fore-arm was as hard as iron and very muscular, and this continued up to the last.[55]

He could, however, walk a considerable distance at his own funereal

51. To T. Armstrong, 28 Nov. 1885.   54. Millais, II, 272.
52. 28 Sept. 1885.   55. Hoyer Millar, pp. 22–3.
53. To Emma Du Maurier, 8 Sept. 1885.

ÆSTHETICS.

Indiscreet Sister. "WHY, HARRY, YOUR LEGS ARE GETTING MORE *CHIPPENDALE* THAN EVER!"

121. *Punch* (1886)

and contemplative pace. Whenever possible, either at Hampstead or on holiday, he liked to walk with a friend, deep in conversation. Anyone who called at New Grove House was liable to find himself out on the Heath, but, from the 1880s, the most frequent and oddest of Du Maurier's companions was Alfred Ainger, Canon of St Pauls, and Reader at the Temple. Ainger, who lived at 2 Upper Terrace, Hampstead, was on hand for a weekday, while Sundays were Henry James' preserve. This cox and box arrangement must account for the fact that neither Ainger nor James seems to have been acquainted with the other, indeed they were usually invited separately. It is surprising that Du Maurier ever became friendly with Ainger, for his anti-clerical feeling had in no way abated, and the mere sight of clergyman's collar was liable to antagonise him. Ainger was, however, a great friend of Margaret Gillies, and of several other Hampstead spinsters, including a Miss Coates and a Miss James, who were all known to Du Maurier. It was probably at their delicate afternoon teas that Du Maurier finally conquered his aversion sufficiently to accept the fact that Ainger was a delightful and loveable companion.

Canon Ainger was, like so many Victorian churchmen, an original and eccentric figure, a man of the world, witty and amusing, and at the same time a profound scholar and ecclesiologist. He was educated at King's College, London, and Trinity Hall, Cambridge, where Leslie Stephen was his tutor. Financial difficulties forced him to give up his original ambition of becoming a lawyer, and he went into the church instead. A low-church clergyman with evangelical leanings, Ainger was little affected by the problems of the mid-Victorian church. Faith was a matter of intuition, not reason. After various duties in the provinces, Ainger had become reader of the Temple in 1866, and was an entertaining and popular preacher. He would probably never have moved to Hampstead or taken a house, but for the death of his widowed sister, who left four children to his care, two of whom lived with him in Upper Terrace.

When Du Maurier and he finally became friends, they discovered that they had a remarkable amount in common. Not only was Ainger of Huguenot stock himself, but he traced his name back to the town of Angers on the edge of La Sarthe, the district from which the Du Mauriers came. He also shared Du Maurier's passion for music, and the words used by his niece, Edith Sichel, in her biography of him might equally apply to Du Maurier: 'Music-haunted he had been since his birth. From first to last beautiful music moved him to a kind of ecstacy; he lived as if on some Prospero's island, surrounded by "music in the air" '.[56] Ainger was not a grim-faced parson. Highly-strung and exciteable, he had a streak of exhibitionism and self-dramatization, fostered by acting with Dickens, which explains his powers as a preacher. Coupled with this was an oddity which Du Maurier might well have disliked in a fellow artist, but always tolerated in his 'caro Alfreddo'. The Canon had an ungovernable temper, which his niece tactfully alluded to in her adulatory biography:

> This wayward moodiness of his, which those who loved him later knew so well, acted from the first like a spell which he himself seemed powerless to break. Even as a boy at school his silences were alarming and his dislikes were apparently unaccountable, dependent on some habit, some gesture, or chance word that offended his fastidious taste; and if he once took objection to a person he did not get over it . . . There was an element of freakishness about him which always made him unique, but which, as the years went on, became softened and mellowed by the sympathies which grew with experience and by the judgment which they brought him.[57]

His walks on the Heath with Du Maurier began in the early 1880s, and soon developed into a regular habit on two or three afternoons a week. Both were small men, Ainger the more striking with his snow-white hair, pale face, and keen-eyed expression. Accompanied by Chang, or his successors, and by Ainger's Irish terrier, they soon became a well-known pair. Ainger did not have Henry James' intellectual interests, and it is far more difficult to trace the general lines of their conversation. After Du Maurier's death Ainger said he had heard every detail of Du Maurier's childhood and his student days on those afternoon walks, and recognised a good many of the anecdotes when the three novels were published. Du Maurier seems to have done most of the talking, Ainger adding occasional asides, or commenting on the peculiarities of passers-by. He had a natural gift for comic dialogue, and supplied Du Maurier with a great many of his cartoon subjects and captions, though the exact number is not known. Their correspondence is full of Ainger's suggestions, and Du Maurier's thanks, for the cartoonist found it increasingly difficult to invent ideas and situations for *Punch*. Most of Ainger's known contributions are clerical or scholarly in flavour, like the sketch of the

56. Sichel, p. 23.
57. Sichel, p. 25.

proud mother who intends to call her eighth child Octopus, or the bishop's daughter who refuses to waltz because she will not perform round dances in her father's diocese. The most famous of all Du Maurier's cartoons 'the curate's egg', actually came from Ainger, although the drawing in this case is as important as the caption. Christianity was a rare topic between them, for they both realised that in matters of faith they were intransigently opposed. In spite of Ainger's narrow-minded and formal attitude to salvation, he made no attempt to convert his friend. His affection for Du Maurier probably helped to widen his outlook, and his decision to conduct his old friend's burial service illustrates the 'mellowing' in his character, to which Miss Sichel alludes. Du Maurier's attitude was, in any case, anti-clerical rather than anti-Christian:

> It must not, however, be supposed for one instant that du Maurier was in any sense an irreligious man. True, he never went to church with the rest of his family, but on the other hand he was never heard to say a word against religion as such, or to make any remark of even a semi-blasphemous character. What he could not tolerate was narrow-mindedness of any sort, whether in religion or in any other direction. He once said to me that there was only one sin in the world – cruelty.[58]

In ordinary life their positions as clergyman and cartoonist were reversed. Ainger was conventional and respectable, but he was also an unselfconscious clown, quite prepared to make a fool of himself. It was the high-spirited canon who lay on the sofa in Du Maurier's studio 'with a donkey's countenance, rolling over and over and rubbing his back in great ease.'[59] As a mimic he was very popular with the children, who roared with laughter at his tricks, which included pretending to be fly or a parrot drawing a cork. The prim Charles Hoyer Millar, then a boy of sixteen, never forgot his amazement at finding the Du Maurier children standing on the Heath near Jack Straw's Castle, watching with delight as Ainger swung round and round a railing, 'with his hat on the ground and his coat tails flying in the air as he revolved'.[60]

58. Hoyer Millar, pp. 20–1.
59. Sichel, p. 134.

60. Hoyer Millar, p. 2.

Chapter 10

Henry James

AMONG THE SORROWS AND DISRUPTIONS of later middle-age, Du
Maurier was slowly working towards his new adventure as a novelist.
Although much of the impetus behind this startling change of
occupation came from a sense of overwhelming frustration with his
own life, and a desire to relive the past, his friendship with Henry
James provided an immediate incentive. They originally became
intimate when Du Maurier was chosen to illustrate one of James'
novels, *Washington Square*, in 1880. It was an unsuccessful venture,
which James remembered tactfully in his obituary essay on Du
Maurier:

> I am . . . fondly and confusedly conscious that we first met on the
> ground of the happy accident of an injury received on either side in
> connection with his having consented to make drawings for a short
> novel that I had constructed in a crude defiance of the illustrator. He had
> everything, in that way, to forgive me, and I had to forgive him a series of
> monthly moments of which nothing would induce me at this time to
> supply the dates.[1]

The twelve drawings, reproduced in *The Cornhill*, and the first
American edition of the book, are sadly uninteresting, and give no
hint of the later intimacy between novelist and artist. They are
competent, but dull; the novel was not lacking in material for the
illustrator, had Du Maurier felt any great enthusiasm for the
subject. James was particularly disappointed by the illustrations
because he had a high opinion of Du Maurier's abilities. He had
first heard of the artist in 1862, when John Chandler Bancroft had
taken lodgings in the same boarding house as himself in Cambridge,
Massachusetts. During meal-times, Bancroft would tell his confrères about his years as a student in Dusseldorf, and the English
friends he had made there. James, after fifty years, could vividly

---

1. *Harper's New Monthly Magazine*, p. 595.

remember the occasion when Bancroft showed him some of Du Maurier's early drawings for *Once A Week*:

> They glimmer upon me, darkly and richly. . . . Not to be rendered . . . our little thrilled awareness, William's and mine, though mine indeed but panting after his, of such peeping phenomena of the European day as the outbreak of a 'new man' upon our yearning view of the field of letters and of the arts. . . . More touching to me now than I can say, at all events, this recapture of the hour at which Du Maurier, consecrated to much later, to then still far-off intimate affection, became the new man so significantly as to make a great importance of John Bancroft's news of him, which already bore, among many marvels, upon the supreme wonder of his working, as he was all his life bravely to work, under impaired and gravely menaced eyesight.[2]

As a child, James had been a staunch admirer of *Punch* and of John Leech:

> *Punch* was England; *Punch* was London; and England and London were at that time words of multifarious suggestion to this small American child.[3]

He always regarded the magazine as a valuable guide to London life, and looked upon Du Maurier as the guardian of its high standards. The aesthetic cartoons particularly delighted him, not for any outstanding artistic merit, but because he recognized in Du Maurier another perceptive critic of the London scene:

122. Vignette for 'Washington Square', *Cornhill* (1880)

2. *Notes of A Son and Brother* (1914), pp. 313–4.
3. 'George Du Maurier', *Partial Portraits* (1886), p. 328.

he has made 'society' completely his own – he has sounded its depths, explored its mysteries, discovered and divulged its secrets. His observation of these things is extraordinarily acute, and his illustrations, taken together, form a complete comedy of manners, in which the same personages constantly reappear, so that we have the sense, indispensable to keenness of interest, of tracing their adventures to a climax. So many of the conditions of English life are spectacular (and to American eyes even romantic) that Du Maurier has never been at a loss for subjects.[4]

James was interested to see the artist in person, when he met him for the first time in the late 1870s, at a soirée given by Hamilton Aïdé. Although James thought him 'a delightful little fellow',[5] it was some time before they became friendly. Paradoxically, it was their clash over *Washington Square* which brought them together: 'our mutual confidence sprang, full-armed, from this small disaster'.[6] The understanding between the two men, arising from such an unpropitious incident, brought a new and profound influence to bear on the last years of Du Maurier's life. James was not only a good friend, he liberated Du Maurier's long-unused intellect. The climax of their friendship came in March 1889, when James pushed Du Maurier into his astonishing late career as a novelist.

In 1880, Henry James was thirty-seven, and Du Maurier nine years his senior, but, in everything but age, James was the more mature. In comparison with the conventional and domesticated Du Maurier, James was a man of the world, and the most sophisticated of all observers of later nineteenth-century society. He was not yet the 'master', and Du Maurier did not live to see James become the 'old pretender', living at Rye among a circle of admiring disciples. James had finally settled in England in 1876, having spent several years wandering between Europe and America. Never a successful novelist commercially, he had first won critical acclaim with the short novel, *Daisy Miller*, published in 1878. The immediate effect of this significant success had been to launch James into the best London society, and the years immediately before his meeting with Du Maurier were those in which he claimed to have dined out every evening during the winter. Living in his rooms in Bolton Street, James cherished his social reputation carefully, enjoying the glitter of a society so different from Boston, and using his experiences as material for novels and stories. When Du Maurier

4. *Partial Portraits*, pp. 357–8.   6. *Harper's New Monthly Magazine*, p. 595.
5. L. Edel, *Henry James: The Conquest of London*, 1870–1883 (1962), p. 333.

first met James, the latter had published only three novels, *Roderick Hudson*, a story of artistic circles in Rome, *The American*, set in Paris, and *The Europeans*, set in New England. *The Portrait of a Lady* of 1881 had several English scenes, but it was not until *The Princess Casamassima* of 1886 that James really began to draw on his observation of London for a major work. Du Maurier never had the chance to read those of James' novels which most closely parallel his own vision as a social commentator, the studies of nouveau riche society in *The Spoils of Poynton* and *The Wings of a Dove*, or the subtle social awareness of *The Awkward Age*. The sensitive treatment of a young girl's predicament in this last novel parallels several of Du Maurier's cartoons, where the mother is too selfish to let her daughter come out into society. In the novel, the mother is unwilling to sacrifice either her daughter's innocence or her immoral friends, so attempts to have her cake and eat it by keeping the daughter in the nursery. When the daughter finally descends, she is forced into the intolerable situation of mixing with her mother's circle, while pretending not to see their vices. Both James and Du Maurier had profound sympathy with the restrictions and double standards forced upon young girls in a highly artificial social situation.

In July 1882, James visited New Grove House for the first time, and spent the afternoon walking on the Heath with Du Maurier. He had conceived the idea of writing an article on Du Maurier's *Punch* cartoons, which eventually appeared as 'George Du Maurier and London Society' in *The Century Magazine* for May 1883; it was reprinted in a collection of essays, *Partial Portraits*, of 1888. James visited Du Maurier to collect some ideas for his article, but found himself captivated by the charm of his host. Shortly afterwards, James was forced to return to the United States on the death of his father. In April 1883, he wrote to Du Maurier from New York, enclosing the proofs of the article, and regretting his exile:

> after that very delightful walk and talk we had together last July – an episode of which I have the happiest, tenderest memory. Romantic Hampstead seems very far away from East 25th St.[7]

James returned to London in September, and during the following summers he was a frequent guest at New Grove House. It was soon his established practice to call on Sundays, the only day on which he

---

7. *The Letters of Henry James*, edited by Percy Lubbock (1920), I, 99.

would accept invitations in the afternoon. On fine days, he walked up from Piccadilly, or later from Kensington, and then joined Du Maurier on his slow walk round the Heath with the dog. Chang died in October 1883 (his vast skeleton was given to the museum of the Royal College of Surgeons), and he was replaced by a tiny terrier, Don. The frequency of James' visits to Hampstead is hard to estimate. In the middle and late 1880s he seems to have spent as many as eight or ten Sundays a year there. In the 1890s, when he rationed himself more stringently, his attendance was more erratic.

Writing to a friend in 1888, James described the usual pattern of those Sundays (he was accompanied on this particular visit by Jules Jusserand, the French chargé d'affaires):

> having scaled the long hill, which used to be so rural and pretty, and now is all red brick and cockney prose, we go and see du Maurier and he comes out and takes a longish walk with us – usually, or sometimes, with his pretty daughters (one of them is very pretty indeed) and his two little dogs. Then we go home and dine with him *à la bonne braquette* and walk back to London at 10 o'clock. Du Maurier is an old and good friend of mine and has a charming Anglo-French mind and temper.[8]

These walks on the Heath were the setting for the intimacy which grew up between Du Maurier and James, but they also met at dinner-parties, soirées and private views in London. They had many friends in common, among them the Edmund Gosses, the Joseph Comyns Carrs and the Richmond Ritchies.

Considering the importance of James in these last years, Du Maurier had remarkably little to say about their relationship in his writings. Unlike most of his friends, James never appeared, even thinly disguised, in Du Maurier's novels, and he is rarely mentioned in surviving letters, even in those to Tom Armstrong, which are normally such a good indication of Du Maurier's activities. All that survives is his correspondence with James, now in the Houghton Library at Harvard, which expresses in every line the depth and quality of his affection for the American novelist. With these letters, and with a knowledge of Du Maurier's life, it is not hard to appreciate the nature of his feelings. Throughout the 'eighties, Du Maurier was becoming bitterly conscious of the narrowness and dullness of his life, while at the same time clinging more tenaciously to the security of his home. In 1880, Tom Armstrong had written to

8. L. Edel, *Henry James: The Middle Years* 1884–1894 (1963), p. 206.

suggest that he should leave Hampstead, and return to London. Replying, Du Maurier reminded Armstrong that he had spent the 'six happiest years of his life' in New Grove House, and that:

> if there were only a few congenial spirits to play with, it would not be amiss (for altho' Chang never palls, one cannot confide to him one's aspirations vers l'infini; or quote to him the choice passages from Zola's Nana, for instance).[9]

Henry James was exactly such a congenial spirit, and Du Maurier suddenly found himself introduced into a wide and fascinating world from which he had previously felt himself excluded. The stories of his friend's travels in Italy (James was always trying to tempt him there) made him envious at times, but excited him:

> I hope you have been having a good time – Florence – Venice – to me these words are just magical – But I do not see much chance of my ever seeing what they represent. Yours seems a delightful existence enough – to winter in such places with a delightful occupation that depends on no skill of hand or eye, precarious organs![10]

Du Maurier himself rarely travelled abroad for more than a few weeks, preferring to spend his time with his family in anglicized resorts like Dieppe and Boulogne, but his generosity was quite large enough to overcome any moments of understandable jealousy. James brought with him a touch of the great world, with so little feeling of superiority, that Du Maurier was not made conscious of his own limitations. Like Du Maurier, James lived by his work, and his single-minded pursuit of his craft commanded Du Maurier's respect. Accounts of James at this time, show him as a serious, formal, yet humorous man, with a large and sombre beard. Edmund Gosse described him in 1882, more or less at the time Du Maurier became intimate with him:

> I recall his appearance, seen then for the first time by daylight; there was something shadowy about it, the face framed in dark brown hair cut short in the Paris fashion, and in equally dark beard, rather loose and 'fluffy'. . . . His manner was grave, extremely courteous, but a little formal and frightened.[11]

9. 1880.

10. 7 March 1887. Houghton Library, Harvard.

11. *Aspects and Impressions* (1922), p. 27.

Another, and slightly later, description is provided by Du Maurier's son-in-law, Charles Hoyer Millar, who met James in the later 1880s:

> He was always well dressed; perhaps even a little more than that, for he gave the impression – with his rather conspicuous spats and extra shiny boots – of having just come from an ultra-smart wedding ceremony.[12]

It is more difficult to decide why James, who had so much more to offer, became so fond of Du Maurier, but there can be no doubt that his affection for the cartoonist was genuine and profound. Nothing illustrates this more clearly than his refusal to burn Du Maurier's letters in the celebrated bonfire of his personal papers. The correspondence is almost the only one which survives intact on both sides, which may be fortuitous, but was probably deliberate. The letters of both men are at Harvard, illustrating fully the nature of their friendship between 1883 and 1895. As James' letters to his friends all tend to be effusively affectionate, the frequent expressions of passionate attachment to Du Maurier cannot be taken too seriously. One letter, describing his move to 13, De Vere Gardens in March 1886, ends: 'My dear du Maurier, how this little ghostly talk with you warms the heart of yours to the remotest ages, Henry James'.[13] Another, written in 1895, begins: 'Carissimo Kikaccio Mio! It is a mingled pleasure & pain for me to get your news – for it makes me aware that I shall just have missed you in town'.[14] Possibly the most amusing effusion of all is the following, written to sympathize with him on the horrors of the dramatic version of *Trilby*: 'my sympathetic bosom expands to you'.[15] Nevertheless, there is in James' letters, a genuine sincerity and warmth. His enquiries about Du Maurier's family were not formal and perfunctory, for he found the daughters enormously amusing and attractive, especially Beatrix, to whose son he later became godfather. Like Canon Ainger, he joined in their family romps like a benevolent uncle, on one occasion finding himself 'suddenly arrested in the narrow aperture by his *embonpoint*'.[16] James' feeling for the family suggests that the

12. Hoyer Millar, p. 90.   16. L. Edel, *The Middle Years*, p. 20.
13. 14 March 1886. Houghton Library, Harvard.
14. Aug. 1895. Houghton Library, Harvard.
15. Aug. 1895. Houghton Library, Harvard.

free atmosphere of New Grove House was nearer to that of a New England home than was usual in London at the time.

James wrote four separate essays on Du Maurier. The first, in the *Century Magazine*, concerned Du Maurier's work for *Punch*, a subject which he again tackled in the exhibition catalogue of Du Maurier's drawings at the Fine Art Society in 1884. Writing of Du Maurier's social world, James might almost have been describing one of his own novels:

> English society makes scenes all round him, and he has only to look to see the most charming combinations, which at the same time have the merit that you can always take the satirical view of them. He sees, for instance, the people in the Park; the crowd that gathers under the trees on June afternoons to watch the spectacle of the Row, with the slow, solemn jostle of the drive going on behind it. Such a spectacle as this may be vain and unprofitable to a mind bent on higher business, but it is full of material for the artist.[17]

A short article on the first chapters of *Trilby* appeared in *Harper's Weekly Magazine* on 14 April 1894, but it was, as James admitted, a hurried piece of work. His best commentary on Du Maurier was a long obituary notice in *Harper's Monthly Magazine* for September 1897. This essay, in James' tortuous late style, can have pleased few readers, but a close analysis of it reveals some astonishing insights into Du Maurier's personality. His death, like that of James Russell Lowell in 1891, left James with an agonizing sense of loss. He never forgot Du Maurier nor lost the consciousness that his had been a tragic and unsatisfied life. When the 'New York Edition' of James' novels was published in 1907, with photographs by Alvin Coburn, volume fifteen contained a photograph of the bench in Hampstead on which Du Maurier and James had so often sat. It was the Heath, and this bench in particular, which most recalled Du Maurier to the novelist's mind:

> I see it mainly in the light of Sunday afternoons, a friendly glow that sinks to a rosy west and draws out long shadows of walkers on the Heath. It is a jumble of recollections of old talkative wanderings, of old square houses in old high-walled gardens, of great trees and great views, of objects consecrated by every kind of repetition, that of the recurrent pilgrimage and of my companion's inexhaustible use of them.[18]

17. *Partial Portraits* (1888), p. 358
18. *Harper's New Monthly Magazine*, p. 598.

Du Maurier's reference to Zola in his 1880 letter to Armstrong, 'altho' Chang never palls, one cannot . . . quote to him the choice passages from Zola's Nana',[19] is an important key to his relationship with James. It was their common interest in, and their love of, the French language and nation which had first drawn them together. James had visited Paris as a very small child, but his earliest memories dated from 1855, when he and William had eagerly explored it on foot. In his later European wanderings, James had often visited the city, and was quite as familiar with it as Du Maurier; he had even considered settling there permanently. Possibly it was Paris which helped to cement the friendship between the two men as they wandered round Hampstead Heath on their first walk together in July 1882. James must have been delighted with his bilingual friend, for he had written shortly before: 'I am tired of the "common run" of the London world and of the British upper middle class'.[20] In Du Maurier he had a companion with a light and sophisticated touch, with whom he felt in sympathy. Du Maurier was ironical, detached and open-minded, and he poked fun at all the things which James found so regrettable in the English character. If he was not profoundly intellectual, he had a sharp and enquiring mind, and was quite prepared to follow James into a world of abstruse and esoteric ideas.

One of their chief topics of mutual interest was French literature. James had met Turgenev in Paris, and, through him, the whole realist circle of Zola, Maupassant, Flaubert and Daudet. James must have appeared a little prim and incongruous in such a cynical and amoral company, but he recognized that these writers were achieving something important, and revolutionary in literature. James might be repelled by Zola's savage treatment of human passion, and of the sexual element in particular, but he had to acknowledge Zola's enormous power as a creative artist. Returning to London, James was acutely conscious of the insularity and banality of much English literature. Few people knew or cared about French writers, or recognized the implications of their attitude to life and art. Similarly, the impressionists were ignored or treated as madmen. Du Maurier had read the French classics, and he was genuinely interested in French literature as a whole, which must have been a refreshing change for James. William Allingham, later noticed

19. 1880.
20. L. Edel, *The Conquest of London*, p. 339

serious lacunae in Du Maurier's knowledge of the English classics:
'He is better read, I imagine, in French than in English literature. . . .
He regretted he could not now read Shakespeare, the time was
past'.[21] Left to himself, Du Maurier would probably never have
extended his reading of Zola, or have begun on Maupassant or
Flaubert, but he responded to James' enthusiasm with excitement. A
new and unfamiliar world was suddenly opened up to him, where
taboo subjects were discussed with startling freshness and originality.
Du Maurier's attitude to such avant-garde literature might well have
been flippant and philistine, but he could not escape so easily with a
mind of James' calibre. He had to analyse and evaluate what he
read, because James approached it with such seriousness, and with a
critical power and penetration which he was forced to respect. Du
Maurier's mind, so long stagnant, began to sharpen itself on creative
literature of a very stimulating kind. Its effect on his literary ambi-
tions cannot be overestimated.

Du Maurier scrupulously read the novels which James sent him,
though he probably did not ask Emma to read them aloud. He took a
batch to Brighton for his Easter holiday in 1886, writing to James
about two of Zola's novels as soon as he had finished them:

> I have been wanting you very much, because – Ecco, I have been in hell –
> which means I have been in Zola – 'La joie de vivre' d'abord, and
> 'L'oeuvre', which I have just finished. How nice to sit on Benches in
> Parades and talk with you about 'l'oeuvre', which is very stupendous.
> The depressing aftertaste, the 'préoccupation douleureuse' when left
> is second only to my convalescence after 'l'assommoir' from which I
> conclude that it is really the greatest but one of the Rougon-Maquart
> series. Given the pitch (a very black one . . .) there is not one false note –
> not a single jarring gleam of hope or comfort on one hand, and nothing
> revolting on the other (like the accouchement in 'La joie de vivre', and
> the horrid 'filet de sang' on the lady's thigh as she surveys herself in the
> glass!) (or the horrid consummation of love of the two moribunds in
> 'Germinal').[22]

Believing that entertainment was an essential ingredient of literature,
Du Maurier did not really enjoy the novels very much. He told James
that he had no desire to read any more Zola for some time, though he
appreciated his merits. Prophetically, he added: 'If I belonged to the
craft, it would be otherwise; I should study him with passion'.[23]

21. *William Allingham: A Diary*, edited by H. Allingham and D. Radford (1907),
p. 386.
22. 23 April 1886. Houghton Library, Harvard.
23. 23 April 1886. Houghton Library, Harvard.

Maupassant he thought a cynic, after reading 'La Maison Tellier' and other stories: 'I really don't think I ever read such a bleeding piece of satire as la Maison Tellier which you related to me in the Finchley Road. It's too funny to laugh at even'.[24] James himself was not a great admirer of Maupassant's works, and thought the erotic element overdone. Although James defended the French novelists from the charge of obscenity, he was curiously inhibited about sex in his own novels, even when, as in *The Wings of a Dove*, it forms the central theme of the story. Du Maurier, on his side, rather enjoyed the sex, but was repelled by Maupassant's dark vision of life. He felt the greatest indignation at the 'vileness and baseness' of 'Mlle. Fifi' and 'Les Soeurs Nordoli', but enjoyed the honeymoon scene in 'Une Vie', 'which is either charming or revolting – I blush to say I found it the former'.[25] James' reply is unfortunately missing.

James' reading programme for Du Maurier was one side of their common interest in France. They also enjoyed discussing the differences between the English and French temperaments, a subject which obsessed them both at the time. James had become disillusioned with the French when he lived in Paris, and in 1876 he had decided to settle in England. He was still acutely conscious, however, of what he had left behind, and continued to indulge in comparisons between France and his adopted country. The French seemed natural, intelligent and sophisticated, even if they were difficult to meet, while the English lived behind a brittle facade of social obligations and unspoken rules. James was the outsider, the observant American, in this objective comparison of two very different cultures, which co-existed in Du Maurier. Although hardly an expatriate, Du Maurier had dragged up many of his roots by choosing to live in London, and James tried to analyse the result:

> This was nothing less than the rare chance of meeting a temperament in which the French strain was intermixed with the English in a manner so capricious and so curious and yet so calculated to keep its savor to the end. I say the French with the English as I might say the English with the French: there was at any rate as much in the case of mystification as of refreshment.[26]

France was a close bond between them. Several of their letters are

24. 23 April 1886. Houghton Library, Harvard.
25. 1 Sept. 1886 and 7 March 1887. Houghton Library, Harvard.
26. *Harper's New Monthly Magazine*, p. 596.

entirely in French, and almost all of them have passages or phrases in that language. James, who prided himself on his knowledge of the French character, must have been flattered by this compliment paid to him by Du Maurier:

> I feel the want to sit on Hampstead benches, weather-permitting, & talk with you about your books as we had so often talked about other books (mostly French!) You are very French, with a Frenchness beneficially checked & restrained by your Americanism & your Englishness – I think you will admit that coming from me that is not meant as a mortal insult.[27]

Their intimacy would have been impossible had Du Maurier not possessed 'the window that looked over the Channel, the French initiation, the French side to the mind and the French habit to the tongue'.[28] Torn between his own New England background, and his English way of life, James understood the insecurity which lay behind Du Maurier's passionate praise of all things English. He realized that the bad French accent, which Du Maurier occasionally affected, was 'the result of an almost passionate acceptance of the insular. To be mild with him I used to tell him he could afford that; and to be severe I used to tell him he had sacrificed his birthright'.[29] Du Maurier took refuge in a vigorous denunciation of the French, asserting that their physique was frail and meagre, whereas the English were a people of superior beauty and prowess. This was a trivial attitude, the significance of which James understood, but could not share. The idea of the international situation, usually that of the American in Europe, appears in most of James' novels, and there can be no doubt that Du Maurier's particular position as a man with a French education and background, employed to criticize the social life of England in *Punch*, fascinated James. Both of them were outsiders, but James saw himself gathering layers and accretions, whereas Du Maurier was split in two.

James sometimes felt that he had never really understood Du Maurier:

> I have never known, I think – and in these days we know many – an international mixture less susceptible of analysis save on some basis of

27. 1 Nov. 1886. Houghton Library, Harvard.
28. *Harper's New Monthly Magazine*, p. 596.
29. *Harper's New Monthly Magazine*, p. 596.
30. *Harper's New Monthly Magazine*, p. 596.

saying, in summary fashion, that all impulse, in him, was of one race, and all reflection of another.[30]

But, as James goes on to say, which was which? He compared Du Maurier's French half to the lodger occasionally met on the stairs, and briefly greeted:

> Better still for this, perhaps, the image – as it would have amused him – of an apple presented by the little French boy (with the characteristic courtesy, say, of his race,) to the little English boy for the first bite. The little English boy, with those large, strong, English teeth to which the author of *Trilby* appears on the whole in that work to yield a preference, achieves a bite so big that the little French boy is left with but an insignificant fraction of the fruit; left also, however, perhaps, with the not less characteristic ingenuity of his nation; so that he may possibly decide that his residuary morsel makes up in intensity of savor for what it lacks in magnitude.[31]

It was not, perhaps, entirely by chance that James' novel, *The Princess Casamassima*, written shortly after his meeting with Du Maurier, and published in 1886, had for its hero a man of mixed English and French descent, the child of a liaison between a French seamstress and a peer of the realm. If Hyacinthe Robinson has nothing else in common with Du Maurier than his small stature, and noble background, the passages in which he contemplates the clash between his English and French halves must reflect some of the conclusions reached during those Sunday afternoon walks on Hampstead Heath.

James listened attentively to the stories and anecdotes of Du Maurier's childhood, even when a whole walk was taken up with such recollections. He was fascinated by the way in which Du Maurier separated his French childhood from his ordinary existence: 'The far-off French years remained for him the romantic time, the treasure of memory, the inexhaustible "grab-bag" into which he could always thrust a hand for a pleasure or a pang'.[32] This was an essential difference between them, for James only twice called upon his youth in New England as the subject of a novel, while all Du Maurier's fiction recalls his long-distant past. When he tried to write about society his work became laboured and flat.

31. *Harper's New Monthly Magazine*, p. 597.
32. *Harper's New Monthly Magazine*, p. 596.

In the early years of their friendship, it was James who sent his work to Du Maurier for comment and consideration. The earliest examples were his two essays on Du Maurier, written for the *Century Magazine* and The Fine Art Society Catalogue. James was highly complimentary in both, and he elicited a warm letter of thanks from his subject, who suggested that he had been dealt with too kindly. There is no evidence that Du Maurier read *The Portrait of a Lady*, but James sent him a copy of *The Princess Casamassima*, his own attempt at a realist novel. Du Maurier made 'truth to life' the starting point for his long critique of the novel which he sent to James, praising especially the 'low life' passages, and the character of the cockney girl, Millicent Henning. He did not care for James' favourite, the Princess herself:

> The princess is an extreme type, for which no doubt you have chapter & verse in your experience & so is Lady Aurora – But these two (H & M) in their relation to each other make a touching & beautiful cockney idyll, if I may use such a term, and I could have wished you had even more elaborated it.[33]

In his criticisms of James, as of other fiction, Du Maurier had two basic critical criteria. He liked a novel to have a good story, and to be credible. He cannot have appreciated the involved convolutions of James' style, and he felt, like some later and more reprehensible critics, that James' glimpses of high life were outside his own experience, and, therefore, not valid for him. He did try, while reading *The Reverberator*, to escape from this limitation: 'I have read the reverberator with the greatest interest & lived in Paris at Hotels with your people & am great friends with them; altho' they belong to a kind which strictly speaking I have never met, I know them well & feel them to be very much alive'.[34] Du Maurier enjoyed James' essays far more than his novels. He read *Portraits of Places* and *Partial Portraits* with more pleasure than the novels, and explained his preference to James as tactfully as he could:

> Your work is never more delightful to me than when you are dealing with real people, or places – and this is no disparagement to your other work, for I may say at once that in dealing with people & places your work is more delightful than that of anyone else I can think of. – Where the

---

33. 1 Nov. 1886. Houghton Library, Harvard.
34. 3 April 1888. Houghton Library, Harvard.

special charm lies I can't say – but suspect that it is because you inter-weave a great deal more of yourself in such studies than when you are writing fiction.[35]

James did not merely introduce Du Maurier to modern French literature, but to the writers themselves. One of these was Alphonse Daudet, who came to England in 1895. Du Maurier and James dined with Daudet and his son at the Reform Club on 9 May, and Du Maurier told Jules Jusserand: 'it will be most interesting for me, as I admire him very much and owe him pleasant hours'.[36] Mau-passant was in London for a few days in August 1886, and James invited Du Maurier and Edmund Gosse to dinner at Greenwich to meet him, along with Count Napoleon Primoli. Although not a Bonapartist sympathizer, Du Maurier was delighted by the charm-ing and cultured count, a descendant of one of Napoleon I's two brothers. Du Maurier did not have much to say to Maupassant, and his subsequent attacks on the Frenchman's novels in letters to James suggest that he disliked him personally. For Maupassant, who had come to London in search of women and excitement, his dinner at Greenwich must have been a boring and formal interlude. Although Maupassant and Daudet were famous writers, Du Maurier took far more pleasure in the company of a young French diplomat and historian, Jules Jusserand. His *English Wayfaring Life in the Middle Ages, Fourteenth Century*, published in 1884, is still a classic work on the subject. Du Maurier so much enjoyed conversing in French with Jusserand that he several times asked James to bring him to New Grove House, or even to Whitby and Brighton. Charles Hoyer Millar remembered that he, James, Jusserand and Du Maurier would walk down to the common at Golder's Green and cross the bridge over the Brent: 'There we would change partners for the return journey'.[37] Like James, Jusserand enjoyed the easy atmosphere of New Grove House, and he left an account of the Du Maurier's Sunday evening 'at homes':

> Du Maurier's intimates could go and sup with him on Sundays, at Hampstead, unasked. We would stroll with him on the Heath and then repair to his house and up the staircase lined with some of his famous pen-and-ink sketches, drawn with a bold hand, on a much larger scale than they appeared in the paper. A classical English joint, which he himself

35. 14 May 1888. Houghton Library, Harvard.   37. Hoyer Millar, p. 90.
36. J. Jusserand, *What Me Befell* (1933), p. 104.

carved in masterly fashion, and some good claret, were the staples of the meal. James and Du Maurier offered a lively contrast. That best delineator of British foibles, whims and fads, a sharp-eyed critic but with no bitterness in his criticism, was of French origin, Paris born and a papal count. Like Moliere, this judge of manners who, every week, exhilarated countless people, was of a melancholy disposition, his smile was tinged with sadness.[38]

At the supper-table, Jusserand often tried to turn the conversation to English literature, for which he had an insatiable appetite. He was working on a history of English Literature in the eighteenth and nineteenth centuries and wished to pick everyone's brains. Unfortunately, Du Maurier was quite unable to cope with such heavy intellectual cross-examination, and only James saved the company from embarrassment. At the end of the evening, Du Maurier and Hoyer Millar walked down Fitzjohn's Avenue to Swiss Cottage with their guests, and caught the bus with them to Baker Street, from where Du Maurier would begin his long climb home.

Although he had chosen to live in Europe, Henry James did not turn his back on America. He had many friends in the burgeoning American community in London, and he did his duty by old friends who passed through England on their European tours. James' attitude to the American in Europe was not as unsympathetic as his novels might sometimes suggest. His closest friend was the poet and man of letters, James Russell Lowell, who was the American minister in London from 1880 to 1885. A man of intelligence and great integrity, Lowell was one of the most eminent and highly respected figures of the American literary scene. More simple and moralistic in his attitude to life and literature than James, and considerably older, Lowell remained rooted in New England, and looked upon the expatriation of his friend, however kindly, as the betrayal of a great American ideal. Lowell felt the attractions of the European way of life almost as keenly as James, and continued to visit Europe for his summer holidays after he had ceased to be the minister. His return to his own country was, in the final analysis, a profound act of faith. James introduced Lowell to Du Maurier, and the two became warmly attached to one another. Both were humorists in their own way, and established an easy and affectionate familiarity, which was only partly dependent on their mutual

38. Jusserand, p. 101.

CRICKETIANA.

Lucy Mildmay (who is fond of technical terms). "BY THE WAY—A—ARE THEY PLAYING '*RUGBY*' OR '*ASSOCIATION*'?"

123. *Punch* (1883). Drawn at a cricket match at Whitby. Second from the left is Beatrix Du Maurier, Charles Hoyer Millar standing

devotion to James. The great meeting-place for Lowell and Du Maurier, where their intimacy really developed, was Whitby.

The rediscovery of Whitby by the Du Mauriers in 1882, after an interval of eighteen years, was a propitious event. Surrounded by friends, their summer holidays there were stimulating and successful. Lowell had clearly known Whitby before 1882, and his example may well have encouraged Du Maurier to revisit his old haunt. Lowell came up in company with George Smalley, the correspondent of the *New York Herald Tribune*, a boisterous character, and a notorious social-climber and snob. Lowell's interest in Mrs Smalley was perhaps the cornerstone of the friendship; his own wife remained very much in the background. The Lowells and the Du Mauriers were both in Whitby by August 1882. On the twenty-seventh of that month, Lowell described an expedition to a gorge and waterfall thirty miles from Whitby, where the Du Mauriers laid on a picnic for twenty-one people, an indication of the number of friends they had gathered round them. The following year, the Du Mauriers entertained Thomas Anstey Guthrie, who became a *Punch* writer; Charles Hoyer Millar, Beatrix' fiancé; Walter Frith, son of the artist; and Alfred Scott Gatty of the College of Heralds. It was the last holiday which all the Du Mauriers spent together before Beatrix' marriage in 1884, and Guy's entry into the army, and it signalled the end of family life. If the gaiety and enthusiasm of that August and September had a bitter tinge for Du Maurier, it was only because the holiday was such a success. There were frequent walks and picnics, sometimes to the village of Sleights on the Esk above Whitby, or to Rigg Mill or Cock Mill, both of which stood by waterfalls south of the port on the Cock Mill Beck:

> walk to Cock Mill; there are 3 or 4 ways – one by the old town, one by Bagdale, one through the meadows over the wooden railway bridge, from the top of St Hilda's Terrace. Tell them to walk from Cock Mill to Rig Mill, and take tea at the latter place (and have a fly ready to take them back).[39]

Dreaming of those summer days with his children, Du Maurier described an alternative walk to Cock Mill in his last novel, *The Martian*, recalling sadly: 'which is the most delightful of those three ways has never been decided yet'.[40] On one Cock Mill picnic,

39. Sichel, p. 279–80.
40. p. 457.

Lowell, incongruously dressed in grey top hat and frock coat began
'dancing "the Lancers" with dignified accuracy on the lawn by the
creek'.[41] Lowell's youthful enthusiasm at sixty-four amazed the
younger members of the group. On another occasion he was
thoroughly drenched on an outing to the market town of Pickering,
twenty-one miles away, and appeared at Whitby in the evening, still
dressed in the same clothes, which he had allowed to dry on him.
True to their tradition of hypochondria, the Du Mauriers feared the
worst, but Lowell's sturdy New England constitution showed no ill
effects whatever. He refused even to acknowledge the dangers.

Du Maurier's favourite walk, south along the cliffs, to Upgang
and Sand End, was something of a sentimental pilgrimage. There
stood the small farmhouse which Mrs Gaskell had described in her
novel, *Sylvia's Lovers*, illustrated by Du Maurier, where the heroine,
Sylvia Robson, had lived; it subsequently disappeared in a landslide. Compared with other outings, this was only a short morning
walk, over the stiles and along the fields. Du Maurier was sometimes
accompanied by Lowell and Charles Hoyer Millar, who once recited
Horace odes in unison. When the tide was right, the Du Mauriers
and their friends often took a boat and rowed up the Esk to Ruswarp:

> and there we take another boat on a lovely little secluded river, which is
> quite independent of tides, and where for a mile or more the trees bend
> over us from either side as we leisurely paddle along and watch the leap-
> ing salmon-trout.[42]

Chang was always taken on these expeditions, carefully placing his
bulk in the centre of the boat, and never allowing it to tip over. At
five o'clock, the party took tea up the small river, either at Sleights,
'where the scones are good',[43] or at Cock Mill where the home-made
raspberry jam was the chief attraction. These rowing afternoons
often included impromptu concerts, as the audience lay in the boats
moored under the bank. Charles Hoyer Millar remembered the
Scott Gattys singing negro songs and duets, which Gatty had com-
posed, while Walter Frith would render the 'Burial of the Sea King'
in a deep base voice. Occasionally, Du Maurier himself, who had
long since given up after-dinner solos, would consent to sing "Little

41. Guthrie, p. 145.
42. *The Martian*, p. 457.
43. *The Martian*, p. 457.

A GOOD-BYE TO JOLLY WHITBY.

The Browns and their Family drag their Luncheon-Baskets over the Dam on the Esk for the last time, Alas! And for the last time, Brown Senior attempts a feeble French Joke, beginning "Esker la Dam——" and, as usual, falls down on the slippery Stones before he can finish it!

124. *Punch* (1882)

Billee", "A Wight went walking up and down", and "Mimi Pinson est une blonde". The best of all these expeditions was that to the little port of Staithes, tucked into a tiny secluded bay, north of Whitby. In the late afternoon, the Du Mauriers and their group helped to push the fishing boats into the water, and then stood gazing out to sea as 'the boats all sailed westward, in a cluster, and lost themselves in the golden haze'.[44] The visit to Staithes became a ritual, and one which Henry James poignantly remembered: 'I see Du Maurier still on the big, bleak breakwater that he loved, the long, wide sea-wall, with its twinkling light-house at the end, which, late in the afternoon, offered so attaching a view of a drama never over-done'.[45] Du Maurier revealed his admiration for the fishing com-munity in *The Martian*, the 'sturdy mariners . . . with their hands in their pockets and their pipes in their mouths', and the 'stalwart, scaly fisherwomen'[46] with baskets on their heads.

James certainly stayed in Whitby with Lowell, but the actual dates of his visits are hard to trace. He seems to have been there in August 1889, when the Du Mauriers were in Dieppe, but had evidently paid at least one earlier visit. In his essay on Du Maurier, he recalled that he was in Whitby during Lowell's 'liveliest and easiest rustications', and he remembered dinners there with both Lowell and Du Maurier 'on windy September nights'.[47] In 1905, when he was writing about Lowell in California, the image of Whitby stirred his memory again: 'I don't know why, but there rises from it, with a rush that is like a sob, a sudden vividness of the old *Whitby* days, Whitby walks and lounges and evenings, with George Du M. – bathed, bathed in a bitter-sweet of ghostliness too'.[48]

Lowell was recalled to the United States in 1885, and he could find no reason to justify a longer sojourn. Emma and George Du Maurier dined with the Smalleys in May 'to say farewell . . . which we forgot to do'.[49] Du Maurier, therefore, wrote him a letter of fare-well, expressing his admiration for Lowell's books, and advising him to watch *Punch* for news of the Du Maurier family. Lowell's letters to Du Maurier had always been complimentary about his cartoons, and now he replied, with touching sincerity: 'Watch for your pictures. . . . They are the main consolation of my old age. I strain

44. *The Martian*, p. 460.
45. *Harper's New Monthly Magazine*, p. 602.
46. *The Martian*, p. 455.
47. *Harper's New Monthly Magazine*, p. 602.

48. *The Notebooks of Henry James*, edited F. O. Matthiessen and K. B. Murdock (1947), p. 321.
49. Hoyer Millar, p. 48.

my eyes for them as men on a raft for a sail. Never mind my books, I had rather you should like *me*. God bless you & yours & love to all of 'em'.[50] Lowell returned to England for holidays in the summers of 1886, 1887 and 1889. In 1890, he was talking about another visit to Whitby that year, but he was prevented from going through ill-health. He wrote to Henry James: 'If you see du Maurier give him my love and tell him that my chief solace (since I have been well enough) has been in looking over Old Punches and enjoying him in them'.[51] Lowell died on 12 August 1891. The news reached Du Maurier in Whitby where he had hoped that Lowell might join them. James, more profoundly moved than Du Maurier by Lowell's death, found it difficult to return to Whitby. In September 1893, however, he did visit the Du Mauriers there and stayed in Lowell's old rooms. For him, Whitby would always be full of sad and ghostly memories, only intensified by Du Maurier's own death in 1896.

James wrote about Lowell in his unfinished novel, *The Sense of the Past*, but he does not seem to have included a description of Du Maurier in any of his fiction: *The Princess Casamassima* is only an oblique reference to Du Maurier's background. Du Maurier, however, did provide James with the idea for one of his short-stories, 'The Real Thing'. W. P. Frith had once sent 'an oldish, faded ruined pair'[52] to New Grove House, as possible models. The couple had once been members of 'society', but had come down in the world, and were seeking work. They were useless as models, because they had no idea how to pose, and were ignorant of the purpose for which they were employed. James made use of this situation to point the distinction between art and life; the old pair were inevitably doomed to failure, just because they were 'the real thing'. It is well known that Du Maurier offered James several other ideas for his stories and novels. One of these was the plot of *Trilby*, which James declined, but strongly urged Du Maurier himself to make use of. Their conversation occurred in Bayswater on 24 March 1889, a Sunday evening with 'a blessed sense of spring in the air'.[53] Du Maurier returned home in a state of excitement, sat down at his desk, and wrote the first quarter of *Peter Ibbetson*, not *Trilby* which they had been discussing, during the ensuing night. When questioned about

50. 14 June 1885.
51. *New Letters of James Russell Lowell*, edited by M. A. DeWolfe Howe (New York, 1932), p. 336.

52. James' Notebooks, p. 102.
53. James' Notebooks, p. 97.

his decision to become a novelist by friends and journalists, Du Maurier duly trotted out the story of his conversation with James, which avoided embarrassing questions about inspiration and motive, and allowed the whole matter to pass off lightly and easily: 'Plots!' I exclaimed, 'I am full of plots'; and I went on to tell him the plot of 'Trilby'. 'But you ought to write that story', cried James'.[54] The talk with James was not the first of its kind, however, nor was James the only person who had advised him to use his ideas for a novel. Du Maurier happened to reach a state of creative inspiration during that particular evening which demanded a release in the written word. It is impossible to believe that he was wholly dependent on James' advice, and that without it, his creative talents would have remained bottled up for ever. The desire to write had clearly been on his mind for several years. It was stimulated by his friendship with James, and its liberating effects, but it was not confined to a single occasion. The story of that dramatic evening in March 1889 is not known solely through Du Maurier's later interviews and conversations; he had outlined the plot of *Trilby* to James, who recorded it in great detail in one of his notebooks, where he kept ideas for stories and characters. Although he had encouraged Du Maurier to write the story, which differs in several important respects from the published version, James had clearly contemplated making use of it himself if Du Maurier did not:

> Last night it struck me as curious, picturesque and distinctly usable: though the want of musical knowledge would hinder *me* somewhat in handling it. I can't set it forth in detail here, now; I haven't the time – but I must do it later.[55]

In view of Du Maurier's precise description of *Trilby*, it is extremely surprising that he went home and wrote *Peter Ibbetson* immediately afterwards. His own explanation is not very revealing:

> But that night after going home it occurred to me that it would be worth while trying to write, after all. So on the impulse I sat down and began to work. It was not on 'Trilby', however, but on 'Peter Ibbetson'.[56]

54. Sherard, p. 399.
55. James' Notebooks, p. 97.
56. J. B. and J. L. Gilder, *Trilbyana* (New York, 1895), p. 12.

During the night Du Maurier wrote about his own childhood years in Passy. Although he had probably decided already on the main theme of the novel, the lovers 'separated by force of circumstance', he did not have to work out the plot in detail until he had described the background and upbringing of his hero. It was his unbounded pleasure in being able to bring alive his years in Passy once again, in a concrete and precise form, which carried him triumphantly over the stumbling-block of the novice, where and how to begin?

125. Sketch for the title-page of *Peter Ibbetson*

Chapter 11

Peter Ibbetson

126. Initial letter 'I' from *Peter Ibbetson*

THE DISCOVERY THAT DU MAURIER could write a romantic novel came as a great surprise to most of his friends. They scarcely knew what to make of *Peter Ibbetson*, published in *Harper's Monthly* in 1891. Kate Greenaway's reaction was characteristic: 'I have always liked Mr du Maurier, but to think there was all *this*, and one didn't know it. I feel as if I had all this time been doing him a great injustice – not to know'.[1] It was the age at which Du Maurier had decided to write that caused the most amazement. When he began writing *Peter Ibbetson* he was fifty-five. Although his health was still reasonable, he was becoming weaker and more frail, and he was finding it increasingly difficult to supply his two weekly *Punch* cartoons. Over the years, his eyesight had become more troublesome, and several critics have assumed that it was the fear of losing his post on *Punch* which stimulated him to write. Certainly the financial motive was of paramount importance. The Victorians were less precious in their attitude to literature than we are today, and Trollope could calmly detail his profits from his novels in his *Autobiography*, as if he were drawing up a company balance sheet. Du Maurier, like Trollope, was neurotically anxious to play down the creative side of his work, and probably stressed the financial aspect for this reason. The long delay between the book's inception and its publication shows that

1. M. H. Spielmann and L. S. Layard, *Kate Greenaway* (1905), p. 205.

his original impulse was by no means entirely practical. He began *Peter Ibbetson* in March 1889, when the fear of blindness and poverty was of little moment.

Du Maurier's advanced age as a novelist was not exceptional. Most novelists begin writing considerably later than lyric poets. Among Victorian novelists, George Eliot and Thackeray both started in their late thirties, while William De Morgan was already in his sixties when he wrote his fine autobiographical novel, *Joseph Vance*. Du Maurier had, of course, begun to write in his twenties with 'Recollections of an English Goldmine' and his first attempt at a story of the Latin Quarter, rejected by *The Cornhill* in 1862. Since then he had contributed a few poems and prose works to *Punch* and other magazines; 'The Rise and Fall of the Jack Spratts' was his most sustained attempt at continuous narrative. Thackeray's rejection of the embryonic *Trilby* had seriously discouraged him, and it was some years before he had the time or the confidence to think of attempting another serious work of fiction. During the 'eighties, the period of his great friendship with Henry James, he experienced a reawakening of his creative energies. His desire to be famous had always been there. It now seemed a possibility. He had no worries about the general outlines of the story, for his mind was always full of plots for novels, which he frequently recounted to Ainger or James; but he found it difficult to settle to work. Writing to Sir Henry Thompson to congratulate him on his first novel, Du Maurier remarked: 'I am always longing to write – I've got three stories at least, which have been festering in my head for the last 20 years! Your success encourages me'.[2] One of these three stories was *Trilby*, and, according to Charles Hoyer Millar, another was *Peter Ibbetson*:

> he used to talk to us from time to time about the couple very much in love, but separated by force of circumstances, who by 'dreaming true' were able to meet in dreams and carry on an ideal existence untrammelled by their ordinary mundane life. I think he had the idea so much in his thoughts that it became a kind of obsession that eventually took form in the shape of a book.[3]

A very definite distinction, however, still existed between these

2. 17 March 1886, University of Texas Library.
3. Hoyer Millar, p. 131.

plots and Du Maurier's own memories of his past, which he eventually incorporated into his novels. Canon Ainger and Henry James had not only been told the plots, but had received full accounts of several major incidents in Du Maurier's life. It was this theme of reminiscence, the wistful sadness of Du Maurier's backward gaze, which gave the novels their characteristic atmosphere. Almost every period of his youth was described in his novels; his childhood in Passy in *Peter Ibbetson*; his schooldays in *The Martian*; his student life in Paris in *Trilby*; his year in Antwerp and Malines in *The Martian*. Onto these themes of recollection, described with a sense of agonizing loss, Du Maurier insensitively imposed his melodramatic and often crude plots, which were his concession to the current demand for sensational novels. The first two parts of *Peter Ibbetson* are a superb account of childhood, as fine as that in Dickens' *David Copperfield* or Charlotte Brontë's *Jane Eyre*. Du Maurier's easy conversational style, modelled on Thackeray's, occasionally lapses into vulgar familiarity in his later novels, but is entirely appropriate in *Peter Ibbetson*. The Passy of Louis-Phillipe, with its large eighteenth-century houses, its gentle sleepy atmosphere, is recreated effortlessly. Everything that Du Maurier remembered of his own childhood with most pleasure is included, the shops in the rue de la Pompe, the long garden with the orchard-trees, the avenue through the park of La Muette, and the Bois de Boulogne itself. It is not just the important events, but the description of precise sensations, the smell of breakfast coffee and the taste of fresh French bread, which create the texture of his childhood so exactly and compellingly:

> And, once home, it was good, very good, to think how dark and lonesome and shivery it must be out there by the *mare*, as we squatted and chatted and roasted chestnuts by the wood fire in the schoolroom before the candles were lit . . . while Thérèse was laying the tea-things, and telling us the news, and cutting bread and butter; and my mother played the harp in the drawing-room above; till the last red streak died out of the wet west behind the swaying tree-tops, and the curtains were drawn, and there was light, and the appetites were let loose.[4]

Sounds are recalled, his mother playing the harp or the piano, the fine tenor voice of his father pealing through the house, the street-cries or the carriage wheels of Paris, and the curfew bell of the city, echoing malignantly across the quiet evening. There are few

4. p. 43.

127. The Big Drayman, *Peter Ibbetson*

literary parallels for the opening of *Peter Ibbetson*. Happy childhoods rarely find expression in literature, and Du Maurier was in no sense a mystic like William Blake or the metaphysical poets of childhood, Traherne and Vaughan. Nevertheless, it is Vaughan's line: 'Happy those early dayes! when I shin'd in my Angell-infancy', which best captures the quality of evocation in *Peter Ibbetson*, while Wordsworth's metaphor of growing up, 'Shades of the prison-house begin to close', sums up the whole theme of the novel.

The hero of the novel, Gogo Pasquier, later given the English name of Peter Ibbetson, is, of course, Du Maurier. Like many autobiographical heroes, he is strangely characterless, a vision of what Du Maurier wanted to be, rather than what he was. In the fight with the blacksmith, Boitard, which is purely fictional, Peter is resoundingly victorious, and he grows up to be six feet tall and amazingly strong. The description of the hero is a little larger than life, the daydreams of an adolescent who sees himself as a unique super-being. Taken with the minutely observed events of everyday life, the novel has a curiously intense and dream-like quality. Other changes subtly alter the outlines of Du Maurier's own past. Peter's family live in the house on the corner of the rue de la Pompe and rue de Passy, but they live in far greater comfort and security than the Du Mauriers ever did. Ellen Du Maurier becomes the 'tall' and 'beautiful' Madame Pasquier, while the infuriating and improvident Louis-Mathurin is described as the jovial 'beau Pasquier'. Du Maurier conveniently forgot his parents' disagreements and pictured for them a married life spent in perfect peace and concord. Although he dies in London on business, Pasquier is usually at home with his family, although the husband of the beautiful Madame Seraskier, next-door, is generally absent, like the real Louis-Mathurin. The Pasquiers die romantically early, M. Pasquier in an explosion caused by his patent lamp, his wife shortly afterwards of grief. Their death is a necessary step in the machinery of the story, but it also enabled Du Maurier to forget about the increasing tension of family life as he grew older. More significantly still, Du Maurier made Peter the only child, the adored darling of both his parents.

It never rains in the fictional Passy, although the passage quoted above deals with the pleasures of the fireside in Autumn. The summer day on which the story opens sets the mood for the first part of the novel: 'It was on a beautiful June morning in a charming French garden, where the warm, sweet atmosphere was laden with the scent of lilac and syringa, and gay with butterflies'.[5] This enchanted world is inhabited by suitably fairy-tale characters, Peter and his parents, the divine and statuesque Madame Seraskier, mother of Peter's charming friend, Mimsey. Major Duquenois, the supporter of Louis Napoleon, who is on parole at a house nearby, is all that an adult should be. He delights the children by telling them stories. Even the tradesmen of Passy become figures of an ideal world, kind and affectionate guardians of an established social order. When Peter, as an adult, returns to Passy in his dream-state, he sees with the eyes of experience, recalling the unpleasantness which had escaped him as a child, the threatening letters arriving from his uncle, Colonel Ibbetson, and the threat of penury to which they were subjected. The opening chapters of the novel, however, are written from the standpoint of the child, and no jarring incidents are allowed to disrupt the apparently perfect whole. Du Maurier found the writing of this entirely autobiographical section extraordinarily easy and

5. p. 8.

exhilarating; and he finished a quarter of it on the first night following his conversation with James. Walking along the small Bayswater garden, in the first light of dawn, Du Maurier saw a wheelbarrow, similar to the one he had just described, which Gogo pushes in the garden at Passy, and he interpreted it as a good omen. His decision to finish the novel was taken then. He wrote more slowly, however, as the demands of the 'plot' increased, and, paradoxically, more carelessly. Large sections of *Peter Ibbetson* and *Trilby* were written straight out of his head, which explains their extraordinary freshness, but also accounts for the many disastrous faults of style and construction. Nothing Du Maurier wrote surpassed his first night's work on *Peter Ibbetson*, when, relying on memories that were still vividly alive to him, he created an outstanding picture of a child's experience and development.

Once Du Maurier had written the early autobiographical chapters of *Peter Ibbetson*, which set the scene for the story, the problem of how to continue became an acute one. Du Maurier had no experience as a novelist, and no natural aptitude for sustained narrative. Peter's parents are dead, and he himself has been taken away from Passy and Mimsey by his wicked uncle, who is determined to bring him up as an Englishman. He changes the name of his nephew to his own, and has him educated at an English school, where Peter is wretchedly unhappy. After leaving home, because of his uncle's immorality, Peter enters the guards, and is then apprenticed to an architect in Pentonville. This part of the story, paralleling Du Maurier's own year in Pentonville, is a period of profound depression for the hero, as it was for the novelist. It ends with the appearance of the beautiful and unhappily married Duchess of Towers, whom Peter meets on an architectural commission, and who is, of course, his old flame, Mimsey. He worships her from afar, because she is both a married woman and his social superior, and does not therefore realize her identity. On a visit to Paris, Peter sees the Duchess driving through St Cloud in a carriage, but cannot approach her. On the last night of his stay in Paris, Peter begins to dream true, going back into the world of his Passy childhood as a detached observer, watching the events of the past unfolding without being able to interfere. Everything is exactly as it was, except for the appearance of the Duchess, who opens the way with which to return to the past. This 'dreaming true' becomes the central theme of the novel. Whenever Peter lies on his bed, with his arms behind his head and his legs crossed, and concentrates on Passy, he is able to return to the past.

At this point, Du Maurier failed to see how to keep the lovers apart, which was essential if the novel was not to degenerate into an ordinary love story. He even contemplated burning the manuscript. His eventual solution to the problem: 'I'll make the hero mad, . . . that will put everything right',[6] launched him into a series of melodramatic episodes which are artificial in conception, and implausibly handled. They were, however, essential to his 'plot'. Shortly after his return to England, Peter discovers that his uncle has been slandering his mother, Mme. Pasquier, and claiming that Peter is his own child, and not M. Pasquier's. Peter calls at his uncle's London house to force him to recant, and during his visit kills him in self-defence. This appalling mishap effectively divides him from the Duchess. Peter is found guilty of murder, and condemned to death. The fear and horror which he experiences on the eve of his execution, largely at the thought of leaving the Duchess, cause a complete mental breakdown from which he only partly recovers. In the description of Peter's mental processes, Du Maurier experimented with a crude form of the 'stream of consciousness' technique. Peter is unable to 'dream true' because of his mental excitement, until the night before his execution. In his dream, the Duchess appears and tells him that he has been granted a reprieve, and that she will send him a bunch of violets in the morning. She also explains that she is Mimsey Seraskier. Both of her prophecies prove true, and establish for Peter the reality of his dream. This is the turning point of the novel, for, although Peter is confined to a lunatic asylum for the rest of his life, his dream-world is securely established.

Peter and Mimsey, growing old in the flesh, meet again in their dreams permanently young. The Duchess separates from her worthless husband, and devotes herself to good works, returning every night to Peter, and the dream-world of Passy. Sometimes they watch themselves as children, sometimes they lead an adult life of their own. Their world is restricted by none of the ordinary human limitations. They are able to add whatever they wish from other buildings to their cottage, 'Magna sed Apta', an opera-box from La Scala, or the whole of the Louvre. They continue to experience the events of their common past, and also of their individual existences. The Duchess's life has been more exciting, and it is she who takes Peter to Venice, Russia, Rome and America, which he has never visited. This free movement in time and space becomes rather

6. Gilder J. L. and J. B., *Trilbyana* (New York, 1895), p. 12.

ludicrous when both are able to enjoy meals eaten by the other in real life, or to return to their common family past; their great-grandmothers were twin sisters. This last adventure into the world of their ancestors allowed Du Maurier to insert his own family-tree into the novel, tracing his descent from the noble family of Aubery. The later part of the book is chiefly concerned with the dream-world, and it only comes to an end when the Duchess is killed in the real world, saving a child from a railway-line. Peter temporarily becomes insane from grief, until he discovers that he is able to return to Passy alone, no longer a smart young architect, but an old and haggard convict, as he really is in the world outside. The Duchess briefly returns to tell him of the joys of eternal life, and the novel ends in a haze of unnecessary spiritual speculation and philosophical resignation. Peter dies, and rejoins the Duchess as what Rupert Brooke called 'a pulse in the eternal mind'.

Some of the novel's faults are evident even from this brief summary. Du Maurier constructed the story in fragments, beginning the early Passy chapters with no real idea of what was to follow. This lack of continuity between the first part and the rest of the novel gives the melodramatic episodes even less plausibility than they might otherwise have possessed. There is no preparation in the reader's mind for the extraordinary series of events which follow on the early and apparently realistic chapters. It was perhaps to overcome this basic fault, that Du Maurier added an introduction to the novel, purporting to have been written by Peter's cousin, Madge Plunket, whose name appears on the title page. She explains her position as the editor of Peter's memoir, and states the evidence for the story's veracity, the bunch of violets sent to the prisoner, for instance. This device of creating a fictional editor was in direct imitation of Thackeray's *The Newcomes*, and, to some extent, of *Henry Esmond*, which Du Maurier had illustrated in 1868. It is a piece of obvious narrative machinery, which is heavily handled and inappropriate. The other major flaw in the novel is the character of Colonel Ibbetson, the villain, whose entry into the story is prefaced by a long and unconvincing description of evil deeds and motives. He moves on a quite different plane from the lovers, a paste-board figure, who never comes to life. Du Maurier realized the weakness of his characterization, and before the novel was published in book form, he added further passages to his description of Colonel Ibbetson. Attempting to give a more substantial justification for Peter's hatred of his uncle he makes the latter out as a debauched womanizer and a bully. Increasing the catalogue of sins only succeeds in adding a touch of caricature to a poorly conceived character. Du Maurier's description of the Colonel is crude and bombastic:

> indeed this remote African strain still showed itself in Uncle Ibbetson's thick lips, wide-open nostrils, and big black eyes with yellow whites – and especially in his long, splay, lark-heeled feet, which gave both

128. Portrait Charmant, *Peter Ibbetson*

> himself and the best bootmaker in London a great deal of trouble.... He wore stays, and an excellent wig, for he was prematurely bald; and he carried his hat on one side, which (in my untutored eyes) made him look very much like a '*swell*', but not quite like a *gentleman*.[7]

The Colonel's letter to Mrs Deane, which leads to his death, is laboured and self-conscious:

7. p. 76.

Can you forgive me this 'entraînement de jeunesse'? I have repented in sackcloth and ashes, and make what reparation I could by adopting and giving my name to one who is a perpetual reminder to me of a moment's infatuation. He little knows, poor boy, and never will, I hope. 'Il n'a plus que moi au monde!'

'Burn this as soon as you have read it'.[8]

As in many autobiographical novels, the personality of Peter Ibbetson remains vague and inconclusive. We have no opportunity of judging him or seeing him from the angle of other characters. We hear that he is unhappy at school and mildly subordinate in the army, but neither of these two themes is exploited. When Du Maurier does try to investigate his character in depth, during the hero's gloomy year in Pentonville, he only succeeds in boring the reader with a series of philosophical doubts and speculations, worries about 'free-will and determinism, the whence and why and whither of man, the origin of evil, the immortality of the soul, the futility of life, etc'.[9] This passage of the novel becomes a platform for Du Maurier's own ideas, his agnosticism, his belief in natural selection and his conviction that cruelty is only real vice. These intellectual themes are unnecessary asides, which play no part in the development of the story.

Although *Peter Ibbetson* is far from satisfactory as a novel, the Passy scenes do have a strangely evocative mood, and an intensity which Du Maurier was unable to capture again. The supernatural theme was also comparatively original. It may owe something to Edgar Allen Poe, whose short-story, *Ligeia,* published in 1838, was also concerned with a dead woman who is able to return to her husband through the power of will and love. Rudyard Kipling used Du Maurier's theme in his short-story, *The Brushwood Boy*, where lovers meet in dreams of childhood. It is a powerful and romantic image.

Du Maurier's interest in telepathic communication was not purely scientific, for he longed to find some way of returning to his own golden past. There is no need to believe Luke Ionides' story that Du Maurier himself was in the habit of lying on his back, with his arms behind his head, and dreaming of Passy, like his fictional lovers. Two pieces of contemporary evidence contradict it. In the Autumn of 1889, William Allingham wrote about *Peter Ibbetson* in his diary: 'I cannot find that he himself has the least belief in the possibility, even the imaginative possibility, of the ground-motive of it.'[10] More

8. p. 24–5.
9. p. 110.
10. *A Diary*, edited by Helen Allingham and H. Radford (1907), p. 386.

interesting still is a letter from Du Maurier himself to a young admirer Miss Florence James Williams of Washington:

> In answer to your flattering letter, I can only say that *Peter Ibbetson* is entirely a work of fiction as far as the dream part is concerned – very much to my regret! I will go so far as to say I have frequently had, and have still, dreams of reminiscence, of going back to past times, and the keen pleasure of them is far beyond any waking pleasures I have ever felt – unfortunately the pleasure is so great that it wakens me; and then, on analysing the dream of such transcendant delight, I find that really everything was unlike the remembered scene, so that it was not a 'true dream', although the sensation has been just what a true dream would give. So that I have imagined and written what I *wished* were possible, what I venture to think *might* be possible. And that is the story of the genesis of *Peter Ibbetson*. Perhaps it *is* impossible, and perhaps there may be a way to it. Sometimes I can't help wishing and thinking so.[11]

Du Maurier was aware that a dream is often more satisfying than reality, corresponding, as Peter says, to the camera obscura on Ramsgate Pier, which gives every detail of the countryside a Pre-Raphaelite intensity: 'That clasp of the hands in the dream – how infinitely more it had conveyed of one to the other than even that sad farewell clasp at Cray!'.[12]

Du Maurier's passionate belief in the power and supreme value of beauty is implicit in the whole novel. Seen distantly through memory, Passy is purged of all its ugliness, and becomes a place of perfect beauty and peace. The lovers return there to escape the tedium and darkness of the real world. It is their Utopia. The adult world is the prison which threatens to close round, and overwhelm, them. The Duchess herself is an evocation of ideal beauty, and shares many of the characteristics of the heroines of the courtly love tradition. She unfolds to Peter the full possibilities of 'dreaming true'. Like him, she has little personality, and is characterized by her exceptional elegance, her neck like a classical column, and her perfectly set head:

> She was so tall that her eyes seemed almost on a level with mine, but she moved with the alert lightness and grace of a small person. Her thick, heavy hair was of a dark coppery brown; her complexion clear and pale, her eyebrows and eyelashes black, her eyes a light bluish-gray.

11. 16 Feb 1894, Pierpont Morgan Library.
12. p. 227.

Her nose was short and sharp and rather tilted at the tip, and her red mouth large and very mobile.[13]

The Duchess is hardly a woman of flesh and blood at all. She seems to have been deprived of all sexuality, and her relationship with Peter apparently remains ideal and platonic.

129. The Duchess of Towers, *Peter Ibbetson*

In contrast to the power of beauty, symbolized by the Duchess and by Passy, is the ugliness of Peter's every-day world, a spiritual prison even before he finds himself a real prisoner. It is exemplified by his vulgar companions in the architect's office, by the repulsive physical appearance and character of his uncle, but, most specifically, by the two hideous dwarves dancing in the streets of St Cloud, where they are put to flight by the arrival of the Duchess. They

13. pp. 156–7.

appear again in Peter's dream on the eve of his execution, where they
are seen as symbols of his incarceration. Once again, it is the radiantly
beautiful Duchess, like the good fairy of the pantomime, who comes
to rescue Peter from his tormentors. Like shadows before the dawn,
they disappear, leaving the prison walls to collapse like a pack of
cards.

The first version of *Peter Ibbetson* was finished during the summer of
1889: 'I took pains of course – most delightful pains – and now I see
that I should have taken more – It all came too easily – comme sur
des roulettes –'.[14] Not knowing how successful it would be, Du
Maurier read the novel to several friends, Ainger, Basil Champneys,
and, of course, Henry James, who all advised publication. The
saddest reading was that given to the poet, William Allingham, who
was dying at Lyndhurst Road in Hampstead. Allingham was
touched by Du Maurier's kindness, and wrote in his diary for 23
October 1889: 'He has nearly finished a story, one volume size. The
hero acquires a power of regulating and continuing his dreams . . . I
strongly advise him to intersperse plenty of sketches up and down
the pages, and to offer it first, tentatively, to Harper'.[15] In a letter, to
Du Maurier, Allingham offered one perceptive piece of advice: 'I
venture to add, be chary of supernatural business, it is terribly over-
worked: keep the circle of yr. experiences and thoughts'.[16] Allingham
died on 18 November, and never heard that the book had been
accepted by the very publishers he had suggested.

Peter Ibbetson was sent to Harpers in April 1890, at a time when
Du Maurier's worry about his eye sight was acute. He had long ago
promised to send any novel he might write to James Ripley Osgood,
London literary agent for Harpers. Osgood was in America when
Du Maurier finished the book, and the manuscript was sent on to
him there, with a covering letter, a strange mixture of shrewdness
and humility:

> I have no notion whether it is suited to a periodical or not – you will see;
> probably *not*, – but if it is I want to be well paid for it. . . . If Harper's
> doesn't see its way to it, I shall offer it elsewhere; and after that, I shall
> put it in the hands of an agent. And if I don't get what I think I ought to,
> I shall keep it and write another, as I have several good ideas, and
> writing this has taught me a lot. All of which sounds very cheeky and

14. To T. Armstrong, 6 Oct. 1891.   16. 19 Oct. 1889.
15. Allingham Diary, p. 386.

grand; but I am in no hurry to come before the public as a novelist before I'm ripe, and to ripen myself duly I am actually rewriting it in French, and you've no idea what a lesson *that* is![17]

Osgood liked the novel and accepted it, but, like Allingham, he suggested that Du Maurier should contribute illustrations. Possibly he thought that this would help the sales. It appeared in *Harper's Monthly* from June to December 1891, Du Maurier executing the drawings piece-meal for each separate instalment. He found the illustrations much more demanding than the writing. A book edition in two volumes was published in 1891 at ten shillings and sixpence, without the illustrations. A cheaper, one volume edition with illustrations, appeared in October 1891, published, not by Harper's, but by their subsidiary, Osgood McIlvaine. The letters between Osgood and Du Maurier which survive, show that Du Maurier was a difficult and demanding author to work with. Harper's reader, Mr Alden, had suggested two large cuts. Du Maurier grudgingly acceded to one of these: it 'might come out, if he wishes it', but the other passage, a description of Paris, 'had better be retained'.[18] The letters are full of remarks like: 'This is very important', 'When shall I have them? I hope there will be no mistake about this',[19] and, of the drawings, 'one or two look a little ragged in the printing, & some of them would have been more effective if they had been less reduced'.[20]

The magazine edition went smoothly enough, and Du Maurier was gratified to receive notes of congratulation from his friends, including James, Millais, Jusserand, and Ainger, and, more surprisingly, from Aglaia Coronio, who wrote to say that the book had recalled the old days at Tulse Hill. Another letter of congratulation came from Edward Burne-Jones, anxious to heal the breach between them which had existed for several years:

> I'm reading your story and have nearly finished it. I love you for having written it. Somehow I was trying to make up my mind to be content and not grumble at the ugly, squalid, vicious tales that people like nowadays. I thought the world was going all one way, and that I had better make peace while there is time and reconcile myself to it, and here comes your

17. *Trilbyana*, pp. 12–3.
18. 12 Jan. 1891. Pierpont Morgan Library.
19. 28 July 1891. Pierpont Morgan Library.
20. 24 April 1891. Pierpont Morgan Library.

book like a fresh wind – full of beauty, and beautiful people – so I want
to tell you how happy I am about it, and that I don't lightly say I love
you for having written it.[21]

Most of Du Maurier's close friends preferred *Peter Ibbetson* to his
other novels, but critical reception was luke-warm. Sales actually
increased after the *Trilby* boom in 1894 had made Du Maurier a
popular author.

130. Vignette from *Peter Ibbetson*

21. G. Burne-Jones, Memorials of Edward Burne-Jones (1904), II, 229.

Chapter 12

Trilby

DU MAURIER'S CARTOONS during the 1890s are mediocre, and express the weariness he felt in having to do them. He drew on an increasingly large scale to save his eyesight, and only drew outdoors occasionally, using thick blue smoked-glasses when he did so. The quality of his draughtsmanship had declined still further, and he made no attempt to develop new themes or ideas. He relied on familiar social situations, and the scenes of high life, which he understood so well. The outrageous developments in the art and literature of the period, which would in the past have aroused his intense interest and amusement, did not affect him. He has left no record of the decadent movement, of Bernard Shaw, or Ibsen, or the nascent socialist movement, or the entertainments of the Belle Epoque, of impressionism, or of the New English Art Club. He belonged to a generation that was already out of place, and ill at ease in a modern world.

Punch itself was going through a dull and reactionary period. Burnand was increasingly bored with the magazine, and he communicated his feelings to a dissatisfied staff. Du Maurier sent a tart telegram to Burnand, when he was criticized for contributing cartoons to *Harper's Monthly:* 'Man cannot live by *Punch* alone'.[1] Du Maurier's success as a novelist led to a further deterioration in their relationship. Burnand was bitterly jealous, writing a savage letter to Lucy on the subject:

> Had Thackeray had a bastard son in literature, and that bastard had had another bastard in literature, I think it possible that the last in this line might possibly have written 'Trilby'. The Deistic Little Billee sneering to his worthy confidant, a dog, at what he is utterly incapable of appreciating (I do not say of 'understanding' or 'comprehending') represents that tyrannical braggart school of French deism (absolute Atheism is impossible) which would, in the name of Liberty of thought, burn, behead and crucify all who might venture to differ from themselves.[2]

1. A. Bright, 'Mr Du Maurier at Home' *Idler* VIII (Dec. 1895), 417.
2. H. Lucy, *Sixty Years in the Wilderness* (1909), p. 393.

Although Du Maurier continued to moan about his financial position, he was earning more than he had ever done. Two of his children were already independent of him, and in March 1890 Sylvia became engaged to a young lawyer, Arthur Llewelyn Davies, the son of a clergyman. Davies was not well-off, and the engagement lasted for more than two years. Du Maurier liked the young man, and approved of the match: 'a barrister, with his own fortune to make; but young & clever & hardworking; and (but this is a detail) extremely good looking. And we are very happy in consequence'.[3] Emma was not as optimistic as her husband, sensing that Davies was dogmatic and obstinate, and, for once, she was right. Sylvia remained loyal and devoted, but the marriage was not an easy one; they both died tragically young, within a year or two of each other; their children were brought up by J. M. Barrie. Trixie had four sons, and Sylvia five, but the grand-daughters whom Du Maurier so much looked forward to did not materialize until after his death, with the birth of Gerald's three daughters.

After his return from India in the early 1890s, Guy was often at home. While stationed at Woolwich in 1892, he organised a performance of *The Forty Thieves* at the barracks, which ran for a week to packed houses. Guy was stage-manager, and both May and Gerald had parts. In spite of Du Maurier's affection for his children, and his growing affluence, he kept them on a very tight rein financially:

> During those years in England Guy had a pretty hard struggle to keep within the limits of his pay and the hundred a year allowed to him by his father, who thought that quite liberal and never grasped the fact that the requirements of a subaltern in a crack regiment were rather different to those of an artist in the Quartier Latin. But Guy never spoke of this to The Governor, as he always called his father. My father-in-law's attitude of mind to Guy was paralleled by his view that when his daughters were married their previous allowances for dress, etc., should come to an end. It never seemed to occur to him that every married woman likes to have a little, however little, money of her own and not to be dependent for everything on her husband.[4]

Du Maurier was overwhelmed with grief in the winter of 1890, when his sister, Isabel Scott, and then his brother, Eugène, died within three weeks of each other. Isabel, separated from her husband, had not had a happy life, and she often told her daughter that she

3. To J. E. Millais, 16 March 1890. Pierpont Morgan Library.
4. Hoyer Millar, p. 124.

wished she had married Tom Armstrong. Her death distressed Du Maurier profoundly, for they had always been devoted to each other. Eugène's illness upset him even more, for his brother refused to see him during the last four months of his life, though other members of the family were allowed to visit him in Torquay. The reasons for this refusal are not clear. Eugène's widow was left in depressed circumstances, and had to supplement the gifts of her brother-in-law with dress-making. Du Maurier's favourite niece was Dora Scott (now Mrs Footman), whom he often used as a model. One evening while Emma was away, she kept him company: 'I dined alone with little Dora & she read the papers after. She's a charming child'.[5]

For their summer holiday in 1889, the Du Mauriers deserted Whitby for Dieppe, a resort greatly patronised by the English, and famous for its casino. With the lawn-tennis tournaments, the pigeon-shooting and children's fancy-dress balls, the English residents and visitors must often have forgotten that they had ever left home. The Du Mauriers were a little more enterprising than most visitors, with their French cook and 'cuisine bourgeouise' which Du Maurier always demanded in France. Writing to Ainger, Du Maurier captured the atmosphere of the resort:

> There is a dance at the Casino two or three times a week – Hampstead could not produce anything duller or decorouser. C'est un monde de bourgeouis – in *beau*, in *laid!* As for the town and *plage*, nothing can be livelier or more picturesque; we never tire of the long High Street, in spite of many smells. . . . If one could only *draw* those odours, on wood! However, they would not be fit for *Punch*.[6]

The whole family spent much of their time in the casino, patronizing the less expensive amusements; May and Gerald had a winning run at a miniature horse-race, 'les petits chevaux'. Du Maurier was working harder than usual. Besides his regular *Punch* cartoons, and the first draft of *Peter Ibbetson*, which he was working on, he was writing two articles and a lecture on black-and-white art. The articles were published in *The Magazine of Art* for August and September 1890, under the title, 'The Illustrating of Books: from the serious artist's point of view'. Du Maurier was not concerned with his work as a *Punch* cartoonist, but with the art of illustration in general. His knowledge of the subject was considerable, and the articles were well-written, informative and intelligent, his style was conversational,

5. To Emma Du Maurier, 23 April 1892.
6. Sichel, p. 146.

but lucid. He began the subject with a discussion of the characters drawn by Hablôt Browne and Cruikshank, the two favourites of his childhood: 'solidified into imperishable concrete by these little etchings in that endless gallery, printed on those ever-welcome pages of thick yellow paper'.[7] Far more interesting is Du Maurier's retrospective attitude to the Moxon Tennyson, which he had parodied in *A Legend of Camelot*:

> I still adore the lovely, wild, irresponsible moonface of Oriana, with the gigantic mailed archer kneeling at her feet in the yew-wood, and stringing his fatal bow; the strange beautiful figure of the Lady of Shalott, when the curse comes over her, and her splendid hair is floating wide, like the magic web; the warm embrace of Amy and her cousin (when their spirits rushed together at the touching of the lips), and the dear little symmetrical wavelets beyond; the queen sucking the poison out of her husband's arm; the exquisite bride at the end of the Talking Oak; the sweet little picture of Emma Morland and Edward Grey, so natural and so modern, with the trousers treated in quite the proper spirit; the chaste Sir Galahad, slaking his thirst with holy water, amid all the mystic surroundings; and the delightfully incomprehensible pictures to the Palace of Art, that gave one a weird sense of comfort, like the word 'Mesopotamia', without one's knowing why.[8]

Du Maurier included almost all the famous illustrators of the '60s in his two articles, Leighton, Poynter, Millais, Hunt, Rossetti, and, above all, Fred Walker. The most surprising omission is Arthur Hughes; and Frederick Sandys, who had so decisively influenced Du Maurier's own style, is summarily dismissed. Later success was the chief yardstick of Du Maurier's critique. Leighton, whom Du Maurier had abused in his early letters as a hack, is praised for his illustrations to George Eliot's *Romola*. Among the younger generation, Du Maurier particularly singled out Randolph Caldecott, Walter Crane and Kate Greenaway.

The lecture was less interesting than the articles. It was prompted by the financial effort of setting Gerald up as a solicitor when he left Harrow: 'not from aptitude for it, but from want of aptitude for anything else (except play acting & music hall singing – which his mother won't hear of!'[9] Lecturers were in constant demand in provincial cities, and Du Maurier was encouraged by the example of Harry Furniss, who had just returned from a successful lecturing tour. Du Maurier decided that the *Punch* artists would be his

7. Illustration, p. 350.   9. To T. Armstrong, 6 Oct. 1891.
8. Illustration, p. 351.

subject, and he wanted particularly to talk about Leech and Keene; he had to add a few remarks on his own work at the end, on the instructions of his agents. Du Maurier not only had to write out the lecture in detail, but to memorize it, he was afraid of the consequences of an attack of migraine, from which he was now suffering periodically. His agents laid on a course of eighteen lectures in England and Scotland to be given during the winter of 1891–1892. The first was delivered for the Wolverhampton Literary and Scientific Society on 12 November 1891, and the poster advertising it informed the public that the lecture would begin at 7.30, preceded by an organ recital. Emma accompanied her husband on the train, and the pair arrived in Wolverhampton in a state of nervous excitement. They were inclined to agree with Gerald that 'un énorme succès de chats morts et d'oeufs pourris'[10] was to be expected:

> When we saw the hall & were told that it would be quite full, we both turned pale & dissembled – When we were told that the audience would thoroughly appreciate every *joke & hit* of a famous *Punch artist*, we reflected that there wasn't a single joke in the whole lecture, & dissembled again – When we traipsed up and down the street of the most unbeautiful town in an east wind & thought of what was before us, a deadly chill, a wave of terror swept over us both, & again we dissembled – & went back to the hotel to pretend to eat – and to dress.[11]

Du Maurier had his lecture printed in large type, so that he could read it easily. He also brought 18 slides with him, described by a reporter as 'limelight views', to illustrate his lecture. There was, as predicted, a large audience in the Agricultural Hall, but they were appreciative, rather than critical. After a time Du Maurier began to relax. He opened with some general comments on the subject:

> It is my purpose to speak of the craft to which I have devoted the best years of my life, the craft of portraying, by means of little pen-and-ink strokes, lines, and scratches, a small portion of the world in which we live.[12]

The major part of the lecture was devoted to the work of John Leech. Touching on his own friendship with the artist, Du Maurier went

10. To Henry James, 4 Nov. 1891. Houghton Library, Harvard.
11. To Henry James, 13 Nov. 1891. Houghton Library, Harvard.
12. S.P.S., p. 9.

on to describe the nostalgic pleasure he had always found in Leech's drawings for *Punch*:

> If ever there was a square English hole, and a square English peg to fit it, that hole was *Punch*, and that peg was John Leech. He was John Bull himself, but John Bull refined and civilised – John Bull polite, modest, gentle – full of self-respect and self-restraint, and with all the bully softened out of him; manly first and gentlemanly after, but very soon after.[13]

The seaside was not so amusing as it had been in Leech's day, girls were taller and more serious, beautiful, but no longer 'darlings', 'swells' had become 'mashers', 'snobs' had replaced 'aristocrats', and the time of the 'good pater-and-mater-familias who were actually looked up to and obeyed by their children',[14] seemed to have disappeared for ever. It was this nostalgic pleasure in Leech's cartoons, which led Du Maurier to place him above Keene in his order of preference; it was impossible to justify the choice on grounds of artistic excellence. Du Maurier's description of Keene is oddly ambivalent and unconvincing. While he recognized his great powers as a draughtsman, he found many of Keene's cartoon characters unsatisfactory, because they lacked any grace or reflective power. Nevertheless, he paid tribute to

> His costermongers and policemen, his omnibus drivers and conductors and cabbies, are inimitable studies; and as for his 'busses and cabs, I really cannot find words to express my admiration of them.[15]

His final judgement hinted at Keene's lack of perception as a social critic:

> But, somehow, one liked the man who drew these strange people, even without knowing him; when you knew him you loved him very much – so much that no room was left in you for envy of his unattainable mastery in his art. For of this there can be no doubt – no greater or more finished master in black and white has devoted his life to the illustration of the manners and humours of his time; and if Leech is even greater than he – and I for one am inclined to think he is – it is not as an artist, but as a student and observer of human nature, as a master of the light, humorous, superficial criticism of life.[16]

13. S.P.S., pp. 31–2.   15. S.P.S., p. 103.
14. S.P.S., p. 78.   16. S.P.S., p. 108.

Du Maurier had little to say about his own work. In a delightful aside, he recalled the classical basis of his training:

> On the mantelpiece in my studio at home there stands a certain lady. She is but lightly clad, and what simple garment she wears is not in the fashion of our day. How well I know her! Almost thoroughly by this time – for she has been the silent companion of my work for thirty years! She has lost both her arms and one of her feet, which I deplore; and also the tip of her nose, but that has been made good![17]

Du Maurier closed the lecture by looking forward to the great illustrator of the future:

> who, finding quite early in life that he can draw as easily as other men can spell, that he can express himself, and all that he hears and sees and feels, more easily, more completely, in that way than in any other, will devote himself heart and soul to that form of expression – as I and others have tried to do – but with advantages of nature, circumstances, and education that have been denied to us![18]

The lecture was well-received. After his ordeal, Du Maurier was at last able to eat, and the mutton chops at his hotel tasted more 'agreeable' than any dinner in the past. The Wolverhampton lecture was only a prelude. On 8 December 1891, he set out on a three-week tour, which took him as far as Glasgow, and in February he was on the road again: 'I was lecturing last night at Norwood & on Friday go to Anerley & next week I go touring again. Hull, Manchester and Kirkby Lonsdale & back just in time to be 58 at home'.[19] Like Dickens Du Maurier found the strain on his vitality was very considerable: 'It was a hard grind, coming on top of his other work. He permitted himself no luxuries, travelling, he told me, third-class, and putting up at second-rate hotels'.[20] His only consolation was Emma, who accompanied him faithfully on all his journeys.

After the lecture tours, Du Maurier and Emma spent three quiet weeks in Hampstead (there was no house in London this year), until news came that Beatrix was seriously ill at Shanklin in the Isle of Wight. Emma left at once, discovering that her daughter had gone down with typhoid, and then succumbing herself with blood-poisoning. She lay in the next room as her daughter's condition deteriorated, unable to help. Du Maurier and the children were

17. S.P.S., p. 133.   19. To T. Armstrong, February 1892.
18. S.P.S., p. 152.   20. H. Lucy, *The Diary of a Journalist* (1920), I, 90.

persuaded not to come to Shanklin for fear of infection, and they nervously waited for news. Du Maurier was very lonely without Emma: 'And now dearie, missing you awfully, I say à demain, j'espère – or else I mean to be ill myself. Suppose I'm found dead in my bed!'[21] At the end of April Trixie contracted influenza, and seemed to be dying, Du Maurier was desperately torn. He had to lecture at the Prince's Hall at the end of May, and he did not want to disappoint his sponsors or his audience. On the other hand, sitting at New Grove House was agonising: 'Trixie's sufferings & yours & your grief & anxiety haunt me day & night. I was never so miserable as last night'.[22] Emma was probably right to keep him away from the scene of illness, where he would only have added to her problems. Beatrix was slowly recovering, clinging to life with her usual tenacity. Sylvia was allowed to go down and help with the children in early May, and her father followed a few days later. He was appalled by Emma's condition, which she had been careful to disguise in her letters: 'she's rather deaf & can't yet put a foot to the ground'.[23] Beatrix was weak, but in good spirits, looking forward to moving to new lodgings, which she regarded as 'a great lark'.[24] Du Maurier was amused by the contrast between her two doctors; one was sober and thoughtful, and the other danced round her bed without a care in the world.

Du Maurier took Emma back with him to Hampstead on 12 May where she soon recovered. The lecture at the Prince's Hall took place as planned on 25 May 1892, with Lawrence Alma Tadema in the chair. Du Maurier resembled Tadema in looks, and was often mistaken for him by enthusiastic ladies. He told Anstey Guthrie that whenever such a lady rushed up to him, saying, 'Oh, Mr Tadema! I really *must* tell you! I do so adore your pictures! The wonderful way you represent marble! Oh, and roses – and everything! Too, *too* wonderful!',[25] Du Maurier would clasp her by the hands, and imitate Tadema's foreign accent, 'Gom to me on my Chewsdays'.[26] He often wondered whether they went. Among the audience at Prince's Hall was Henry James:

21. 1 April 1892.
22. To Emma Du Maurier, 26 April 1892.
23. To T. Armstrong, 14 May 1892.
24. To T. Armstrong, 14 May 1892.
25 and 26. 'Some Personal Recollections of Du Maurier', *Punch* CLXXXVI (7 March 1934).

I remember, one evening of the late spring, when London was distracted with engagements, sitting, uplifted and exposed, in the company of several of his distinguished friends, behind a not imperceptibly bored and even pathetic figure – a figure representing for the hour familiarly, sociably, quite in the manner of the books that had begun to come, though not yet to show what they could do, both one of the faculties as to which he had ever left us least in doubt and another that we might, later on, quite have felt foolish for not having, on that occasion, seen in the fullness of its reach.[27]

The lecturing programme stopped for the summer, and, after Sylvia's wedding in August, the family were able to get off to Whitby. They were there for five consecutive summers from 1890 to 1894. May and Gerald enjoyed themselves by taking part in concerts and theatricals in aid of the repair fund for St. Michael's Church, and the Whitby national schools. The programme for 2 September 1890, announced that Miss M. Du Maurier would sing 'Bonnie Wee Thing' and 'Venetian Boat Song', and would perform a 'Banjo Duet' with Mr E. Smalley, presumably G. W. Smalley's son, then a student at Harvard. May had performed at an earlier concert in 1887:

> Miss M. du Maurier . . . sang with charming effect a Tyrolese song, with pianoforte accompaniment by her father. The effort was received with loud and prolonged applause by the audience, which demonstration Miss du Maurier gracefully acknowledged by repeating one of the verses of the song. Master G. du Maurier gave 'The Whistling Coon', the ladies and gentlemen forming the chorus whistling the refrain. The young gentleman was vociferously applauded.[28]

Gerald's success in the amateur theatricals at Whitby turned his ideas to the professional stage. On 26 and 27 September 1892 Gerald and May appeared in an amateur performance of *Lady Clancarty*: 'I saw Gerald rehearsing yesterday in one of Charles Matthews' parts. He was really very good, to his mother's great distress'.[29]

Emma was ill again in Whitby, perhaps from the delayed effect of her blood poisoning in Shanklin, for she now suffered 'one of her sudden attacks of internal haemorrege [sic]'.[30] May gave her father a cold, and he and Emma spent most of 'our time . . . in nursing each other'.[31]

27. *Harper's New Monthly Magazine*, p. 603.
28. Undated cutting from *The Whitby Gazette*.
29. To T. Armstrong, 25 Sept. 1892.
30. To T. Armstrong, 25 Sept. 1892.
31. To T. Armstrong, 25 Sept. 1892.

They returned to Hampstead at the end of September, only to face another family crisis. Charles Hoyer Millar, who had gone off to the United States on a business trip, had himself contracted typhoid fever. He seemed to be recovering, but on 7 November Beatrix heard that he had suffered a relapse, and was in a critical condition. Beatrix wanted to join him but could not leave the children at New Grove House because May had chicken-pox, and so Hoyer Millar's brother went out instead. On arrival, he found that Hoyer Millar had been suffering from a combination of typhoid and brain fever for forty-six days, with the most indifferent medical care: 'It seems he is now so altered as to be unrecognisable. His legs are no thicker than his wrists'.[32] Henry James and Millais both wrote letters of relief to Du Maurier, when they heard that Millar was sufficiently recovered to travel home:

> Having a family may on the whole be a pleasure, but what a lot of care they bring on us. You say nothing of Sylvia. I hope she has not found matrimony a disappointment *yet* ?[33]

With this trouble over, Du Maurier had to prepare for another exhausting lecture tour in December and January:

> I am looking forward with very mixed feelings to my winter lectures a nice pair of cripples we are to go trapesing about from town to town . . . 'Ayez pitié d'un pauvre aveugle!' My only etching – of which you are the fortunate possessor, I believe – only, a magic lantern instead of a guitar.[34]

Writing to his agent Du Maurier agreed to lecture in Dumfries on the 30 January, in Belfast on the next day, and then in Dublin on 1 February. 'Are there', he asked, 'good boats from Stranraer & at a convenient time, so as to lecture at Belfast the evening after Dumfries'.[35]

Once the novelty of lecturing had worn off, Du Maurier found the process boring and exhausting:

32. To Henry James, 1 Dec. 1892. Houghton Library, Harvard.
33. From J. E. Millais, 9 Dec. 1892.
34. To T. Armstrong, 25 Sept. 1892.
35. 5 Aug. 1892. Henry E. Huntingdon Library.

I soon overcame my nervousness and am now a hardened lecturer without a blush or a stammer. . . . They seem to be approved both in Scotland and in England, but I shall never like lecturing even if I have to live by it.[36]

The strain on his health was severe. Near blindness forced him to give up his contributions to *Punch* from mid-December to mid-January 1891, during the most hectic period of his lecturing programme. When he began to draw again, in February, he was more handicapped than ever: 'About my drawings I draw very big & make studies beforehand, it takes me double the time & I'm very nervous – the spot though small is still there & I can't see the whole of the little face when I'm drawing it'.[37]

During this period of family ill-health, Du Maurier had begun work on his new novel, *Trilby*. It was similar to the story he had already related to James, of the servant girl with no musical talent, who becomes a famous singer under the mesmeric influence of a 'little foreign Jew'.[38] In place of the English girl and the setting of Pamphilon's and Newman Street, he substituted the grisette and the Quartier Latin. It is impossible to tell how much *Trilby* owed to the story Du Maurier had sent to the *Cornhill* in 1861, the 'natural antidotes to morbid Quartier-latin Romance',[39] the manuscript of which has disappeared. Writing about his story at the time to Armstrong, he commented: 'Lamont is there as the wise and facetious Jerry, you as the bullnecked & sagacious Tim; the street is our Lady of the Bohemians'.[40] How much there was of Trilby and her sensational story in that first effort at fiction is unknown. It was the combination of authentic student life in Paris, with a romantic and dramatic plot, which made the novel so enormously popular. Du Maurier was uncertain about the character of his heroine until the last moment: 'I had first thought of Trilby as a girl of very low birth – a servant, or something like that. Then it occurred to me that it would be much better to make her interesting – to create a person who would be liked by readers'.[41]

He began on the novel, in January or February 1892, during a

---

36. To J. E. Millais, 1892. Pierpont Morgan Library.
37. To T. Armstrong, Feb. 1892.
38. *The Notebooks of Henry James*, edited by F. O. Matthieson and K. B. Murdock – (1947), p. 97.
39. Letters, p. 92.
40. Letters, p. 92.
41. J. L. and J. B. Gilder, *Trilbyana* (New York, 1895), p. 11.

period of near-blindness when he had to stop working on his cartoons. He dictated the novel to his wife and children, writing to James on 6 February:

> J'ai commencé un autre roman – celui de la chanteuse magnétisée – ça m'amuse, énormément. J'ai beaucoup dévelloppé ça. Si la muse est prospère cela fera un volume de 50,000 mots à feu fier. L'amour y sera d'un brulant! Ça se passe à Paris dans le quartier latin d'il y a trente cinq ans – j'ai mieux cette vie là – 'nourri dans le sérail j'ai connu les détours'.[42]

On the envelope he added a further detail about his new work: 'Nouveau roman n'est pas pour les petites filles. Tour on coupe le pain au tartines. ... Th. Gautier'.[43]

More seriously worried about his sight than ever, Du Maurier had completed his novel early in November, 1892. Alfred Ainger remembered that the long and important scene, when Trilby renounces her lover, Little Billee, was written between dinner and bedtime on a winter evening. On 28 November Du Maurier dined with Henry Harper and 'le petit McIlvaine' to discuss the novel; Osgood had died in May 1892. The Harper's reader had greatly preferred *Trilby* to *Peter Ibbetson*:

> a decided advance upon Peter Ibbetson – & a beautiful piece of work, full of faults, but full also of that *illuminated* something that soars above criticism – it is so large, so human, so searching that it will appeal to a great multitude. The artist has wrought in a sad sincerity' & & &. But its too lively![44]

Harpers offered Du Maurier the same terms as before, £1,000, but he wrote and asked whether he should not be paid more for that 'illuminated something'. In the end, he settled for £2,000, without royalties, against the advice of friends. He was given a year in which to revise and illustrate the novel. Harpers objected to certain enthusiastic tirades in favour of nudity, and against the church, and Du Maurier promised to modify them. In a letter to Henry James he explained what he would like to do if given free rein: 'Illuminent en gros et en détail. Lampions anti clericaux. Spécialité d'éclairage moral. Nudité – chasteté &c &c voir "Trilby" '.[45]

---

42. Houghton Library, Harvard.
43. Houghton Library, Harvard.
44 and 45. To Henry James, 1 Dec. 1892. Houghton Library, Harvard.

The construction of *Trilby* is very similar to that of *Peter Ibbetson*. It begins with a long passage of autobiographical writing, and the novel then turns into a melodramatic story about a French grisette, and her hypnotist lover.

The plot is relatively simple. Three English art students, Taffy, the Laird, and Little Billee, are studying painting in Paris, and the opening chapters of the book describe the life and atmosphere of the Quartier Latin in some detail. The three young men meet the gorgeous Trilby, who models in the 'altogether' and is not entirely chaste, when she drops into their studio to see who they are. The priggish Little Billee falls desperately in love with her, and passion so overcomes his scruples that he asks her to marry him. Their engagement is destroyed by Little Billee's mother, who persuades Trilby that the marriage would be the ruin of her son. Trilby disappears, and Little Billee, after a severe mental breakdown, returns to London and success. Trilby is taken up by the sinister musician, Svengali, who realises that she has terrific potential as a singer, and releases her talent by means of hypnotism. Trilby becomes the toast of Europe as 'La Svengali', but she is entirely in the power of her cruel and loathsome lover. The three English friends hear of her fame, and come to Paris to attend one of her performances. They meet her in the Place de la Concorde, but she shows no sign of knowing them. The climax of the story comes in London, when Svengali recognizes Little Billee in the audience, and dies from a heart-attack in his box, thus releasing Trilby from her trance. She makes some attempt to sing her repertoire, but her voice was entirely the result of mesmerism, and she collapses. Now dying herself, she is surrounded by Little Billee and his friends during her last days, and the pathos of the story rises to a climax. Seeing a photograph of Svengali, she falls back under his influence once more and starts to sing Chopin's Impromptu in A Flat: 'She sang it just as she had sung it at the Salle des Bashibazoucks, only it sounded still more ineffably seductive, as she was using less voice – using the essence of her voice in fact – the pure spirit, the very cream of it'.[46] She dies immediately afterwards, and Little Billee soon follows her to the grave. It is Taffy, on his honeymoon in Paris with Little Billee's sister, who eventually discovers the truth about Trilby's voice, and her life with Svengali, and it is here that the story ends.

For the scenes of the Latin Quarter, Du Maurier relied heavily

46. p. 418.

131. Wistful and Sweet, *Trilby*

on his own memories, but not exclusively. There were many literary parallels and influences; the description of the students walking through Paris at sunset is clearly influenced by Zola's *L'Oeuvre* of 1886, which Du Maurier discussed at length with Henry James. But the most notable sources were the *Scènes de La Vie de Bohème* by Henri Murger, on which Puccini's famous opera was based, and *La Dame Aux Camélias* by Alexandre Dumas the younger. Murger's work, originally a series of fictional articles, linked by recurrent characters, and the background of the Quartier Latin, was first published in 1845. Murger made squalor romantic, imbued poverty with the status of an heroic resistance to bourgeois values, and established the philosophy of the gay, rootless, and amoral band of outcast writers and artists. Du Maurier, who told Luke Ionides that his novel owed 'so much to the *Scènes de la Vie de Bohème*, only the British public does not know that',[47] was well aware of the debt he owed to Murger. Both writers were describing the Quartier Latin of mid-nineteenth century Paris, when the city was the cultural capital of Europe, and an exciting place for a student to be. They both concentrated on a small group of student friends, who are all devoted to each other. In *Scènes de la Vie de Bohème*, the students are engaged in different arts; Rudolphe, the poet, Marcel, the painter, Colline, the philosopher, and the musician, Schaunard. Du Maurier's 'three musketeers of the brush', Taffy, the Laird and Little Billee are all painters. In both novels, the lovers, Du Maurier's Trilby and Little Billee, Murger's, Mimi and Rudolphe, are thrown into relief by their serio-comic friends. The Laird's incompetent scenes of Spanish life, or Taffy's inaccurate attempts at realism parallel Schaunard's absurd and unfinished symphony 'L'Influence du bleu dans les arts'. Both writers expressed a nostalgia for the spirit of masculine camaraderie, which is destroyed by the advent of women and love. Once Trilby and Little Billee have fallen in love, the group begins to disintegrate, and Trilby, like Mimi, moves to her inevitable end. Both heroines are grisettes, gay, courageous and amoral, who sacrifice themselves impulsively for love.

There are many points of comparison between the two books, but they only serve to accentuate the gulf that divided London in the 'nineties from Paris in the 'fifties. The delightful amorality which characterizes *Scènes de la Vie de Bohème*, where social conventions are

---

47. L. Ionides, *Memories* (Paris, 1925), p. 63.

only there to be broken, and marriage is the final defeat, becomes in *Trilby* the prudish mention of the 'altogether', Trilby's hesitating confession of past lovers, and Little Billee's refusal to accept her as a mistress. Neither novel is very realistic. The love-life of the characters in *Scènes de la Vie de Bohème* is always envisaged as idyllic and delightful, until it palls altogether; the absence of guilt or involvement gives the love relationships a two-dimensional and stylized quality. Little Billee's horror at seeing Trilby in the nude is more typical of the period, but his lack of sexual desire takes the sting out of his love for her. In Murger's world, to be in love naturally means a love-affair, in which resistance is seen only as an added incitement; in *Trilby* the whole idea of an affair, especially with a girl whom you 'respect', seems disgusting. Du Maurier's heroine, unlike his hero, may not be a virgin, but he implies that she should be.

The difference in the sexual atmosphere of the two books is paralleled by the contrast in the description of student life. *Trilby* is not, in any sense, written from a French point of view. Even Trilby, once she is drawn into the English group, is soon darning socks, and cooking, like a respectable housewife. It would be surprising that this very English novel, about Englishmen abroad, should have been written by someone brought up in France, if it were not clear how strongly Du Maurier was attracted to the English way of life, even as a student. *Scènes de la Vie de Bohème* is a simple book, romantic, impossible, and, like *Trilby*, frequently sentimental. In spite of its origin, as a series of short stories, it is more consistent than *Trilby* in atmosphere, and plot. Murger has no melodramatic Svengali, nor are the deaths of Jaques and Mimi raised to quite such heights of melodrama and pathos. Du Maurier was certainly familiar with Dumas' *La Dame aux Camélias*, first published in 1848, and performed as a play in 1852. The scene in *Trilby* where the heroine agrees to give up Little Billee, was evidently inspired by the passionate appeal of Armand Duval's father to Marguerite Gautier, asking her to give up his son, and save his family's reputation. Both Armand Duval and Little Billee suffer from brain fever when they are separated from the women they love. In outline, the story of both books is similar: the love of a man for a girl whose past has been promiscuous, and from whom he is separated until her deathbed. But the atmosphere of the two novels is very different. While *Trilby* is a tale of moral retribution, *La Dame aux Camélias* postulates no ethical standards. The tragedy is not a direct result of Marguerite Gautier's fall from virtue. Indeed, Dumas seems to agree with Armand

132. Cuisine bourgeouise en Bohème, *Trilby*

Duval that a beautiful courtesan, won from a host of rivals, is a much richer prize than a pure and simple country girl.

If these two French novels provided some of the material for Du Maurier's romantic setting and love story, the sources of his melodramatic theme of hypnotism were less distinguished. When Moscheles and Du Maurier were experimenting with mesmerism in Antwerp, in 1859, it was a fairly new phenomenon. It had, however, provided an exciting theme for several thriller stories of the period, two of which Du Maurier himself had illustrated in 1861 and 1862, for *Once A Week*, 'The Notting Hill Mystery', and 'The Poisoned Mind'. The latter, by A.G.G., appeared in Volume Five, on 21 December 1861, and was the story of a sinister foreigner, who, having lost the woman he loves to a scientist, hypnotises her so that she conducts experiments of which she is unaware. His aim is to separate her from her husband, who is desperately anxious to draw more information from her. Finally the husband kills her when he tries to make her explain what these experiments are. The hypnotist is therefore successful in his scheme for revenge. The theme is similar to that of *Trilby*, but the story itself is a crude sensation tale.

Most of the material for *Trilby*, however, came from Du Maurier's extraordinarily precise memories of his years in Paris. Thomas

Armstrong's 'Memoir' and Luke Ionides' *Memories* help to establish
the accuracy of *Trilby* as a straight autobiographical narrative. From
these, and from Val Prinsep's article on Gleyre's in the *Magazine of
Art*, it is clear that the scenes at Carrel's atelier closely parallel
Gleyre's, although the picture of student life is less brutal than the
reality. Armstrong remarked on the difference between the smart
young men of the illustrations to *Trilby*, and the real 'Paris Gang',
with their baggy trousers. There are many recollections of food in
Trilby. In the early sections of the novel it is simple French meals,
with Taffy dressing the salad, which set the atmosphere. Armstrong
remembered a restaurant 'kept by Trin', where the group used to
eat; Du Maurier referred to it by name in *Trilby*, and described the
menu: 'Good distending soups, omelets that were only too savoury,
lentils, red and white beans, meat so dressed and sauced and
seasoned that you didn't know whether it was beef or mutton –
flesh, fowl, or good red herring – or even bad, for that matter – nor
very greatly cared'.[48] Several other meals are described in detail;
the Laird cooks onions and beef with garlic, and Little Billee usually
buys cheese and salad, with new French bread. On a larger scale is
Little Billee's feast at Carrel's, rum punch and 'Babas, Madeleines,
and Savarins – three sous apiece, fourpence-halfpenny the set of
three'.[49] The climax of male camaraderie in *Trilby* is the Christmas
dinner, which was exactly based on the real dinner held in Lamont's
lodgings in 1856.

Du Maurier's love of Parisian food was closely related to his love of
Paris itself. The novel begins with a passage of description where
Little Billee is looking down

> at the old houses opposite, some of which were being pulled down, no
> doubt lest they should fall of their own sweet will. In the gaps between he
> would see discoloured, old, cracked, dingy walls, with mysterious
> windows and rusty iron balconies of great antiquity.[50]

Little Billee and his friends do not restrict themselves to the Quartier
Latin, but take long walks around the city, crossing the bridges and
looking into the shops:

> When they reached the Pont des Arts they would cross it, stopping in the

48. *Trilby*, p. 32.   50. p. 7.
49. pp. 80 and 82.

middle to look up the river towards the old Cité and Notre Dame, east-ward, and dream unutterable things, and try to utter them. Then, turning westward, they would gaze at the glowing sky and all it glowed upon – the corner of the Tuileries and the Louvre, the many bridges, the Chamber of Deputies, the golden river narrowing its perspective and broadening its bed as it went flowing and winding on its way between Passy and Grenelle to St Cloud, to Rouen, to the Havre, to England perhaps.[51]

The mood at the beginning of *Trilby* is nostalgic, but it is less poignant than that of *Peter Ibbetson*. The climax of the first section is the hilarious Christmas dinner, which is the last gathering of Little Billee and his friends. Little Billee's engagement to Trilby follows the dinner, and the novel now moves from the secure and successful ground of Du Maurier's own memories into the realms of fantasy. The melodramatic development of the story is prefaced by a sinister scene in which Svengali hypnotizes Trilby to cure a head-ache. No longer the gay and carefree frequenter of studios, Svengali is already assuming the characteristics of a classic villain. Even with Du Maurier's efforts to prepare the ground, the change from the innocent studio life of Paris to the highly elaborate story of hypno-tism and love is an abrupt one. Du Maurier was writing about a subject outside his own experience, and once away from the familiar Quartier Latin, his inadequacies as a novelist are strikingly evident. Little Billee's illness, and his subsequent career in London, are treated summarily and without conviction; the tone of these pas-sages is in marked contrast to the realism and intensity of the Paris scenes. The reaction of Little Billee and his two friends on redis-covering Trilby in Paris is stereotyped and banal: 'Yet the big Taffy was trembling all over; the Laird's jaw had all but fallen on to his chest; Little Billee was staring, staring his eyes almost out of his head'.[52]

The faults of the novel are, however, to some extent masked by the speed at which the narrative moves, until the death of Svengali in the opera-box. This is the second climax of the novel. Thereafter, Du Maurier laboriously works through two death-bed scenes, in which every opportunity for bathos is exploited to the full. The tradition of the English novel, inherited from Samuel Richardson, may partly have been responsible for these scenes, but they effectively destroy

51. p. 34.
52. p. 305.

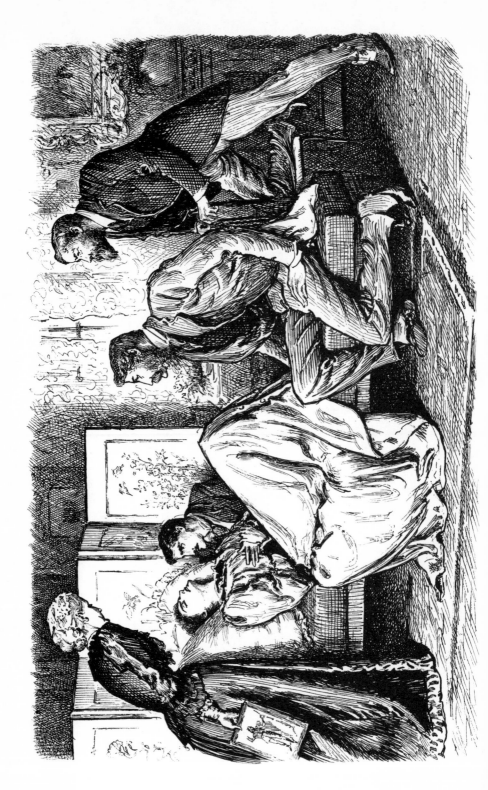

133. 'Svengali ... Svengali ... Svengali!', *Trilby*

the tension of the story. No sooner is Trilby dead, than we are once more launched into another death-bed drama, that of Little Billee. Du Maurier must have realized the monotony of the theme, for he suddenly breaks off his day-by-day description of Little Billee's decline, to describe the last events of his life retrospectively and summarily. Du Maurier had none of the technical powers necessary to sustain a long dramatic narrative, and the last third of the book is flat and uninteresting. The vitality of Trilby helps to keep the book alive, but even her spirit begins to weaken in the closing of her life. The early part of the book was easy enough to write, but Du Maurier's stratagems to develop the plot at the same pitch of intensity are crude and hopelessly inadequate. He did not understand the structural patterns which underlie a good novel, or he was unable to apply them to his own work. The last part of *Trilby* is the weakest passage in his fiction.

The presentation of character in *Trilby* is much more subtle and successful than in *Peter Ibbetson*. Trilby herself is a classic Victorian heroine, and she deserves to be. All attempts to identify her from among the girls Du Maurier knew in Paris have been inconclusive, but she comes closest to Carry, the tobacconist's assistant in Malines whom Du Maurier and Moscheles had tried to hypnotize. Gay, impulsive, generous, and enchantingly natural, Trilby's personality dominates the novel, and provides that combination of charm and exuberance, which the Victorian public found so irresistible. Like his readers, Du Maurier found it easy to defend her lapses from virtue with

> the shortest, best, and most beautiful plea I can think of. It was once used in extenuation and condonation of the frailities of another poor weak woman, presumably beautiful, and a far worse offender than Trilby, but who, like Trilby, repented of her ways, and was most justly forgiven – '*Quia multum amavit!*'.[53]

The other grisette of the novel, Mimi la Salope, is not treated so leniently, but she has none of Trilby's redeeming qualities. The theme of the fallen woman with a good heart was a common one in Victorian literature; *Tess of the D'Urbevilles* by Hardy appeared three years before *Trilby*, and Trollope's *The Vicar of Bullhampton* as early as 1869. The extenuating circumstances for Trilby's immorality are elucidated, her father's early death, her lax upbringing,

53. p. 49.

and the amoral atmosphere of the Quartier Latin; Du Maurier is careful to point out that her personal habits are clean and respectable.

There is something suggestive of the unfallen Eve when Trilby first appears, only seventeen, and unaware of the dark side of life. She does not conform to Du Maurier's ideal of beauty, with her freckles and broad chin, but this is immaterial. Her animal innocence is irresistible: 'Truly, she could be naked and unashamed'.[54] She is a superb model as a result, one painter describing her as 'a thing to melt Sir Galahad, yet sober Silenus, and chasten Jove himself'.[55] Her feet are her greatest physical glory:

> a true inspiration of shape and colour, all made up of delicate lengths and subtly-modulated curves and noble straightnesses and happy little dimpled arrangements in innocent young pink and white.[56]

Once Trilby comes into contact with the English students, she begins to lose her natural innocence, for they try to impose on her their own attitudes and values. The climax of this clash between English prudery and French promiscuity comes in the scene where Little Billee discovers her posing for another man in 'the altogether', and retreats in horror:

> Then she began to wonder in English – nice clean English of the studio in the Place St. Anatole des Arts – her father's English – and suddenly a quick thought pierced her through and through. . . . Could it possibly be that he was *shocked* at seeing her sitting there?[57]

For the first time in her life Trilby suffers from feeling of moral guilt. She confesses the facts of her past life to the Laird, and declares her intention of giving up modelling for ever. This victory for English respectability, an expression of Du Maurier's own life-story, is achieved at the cost of her innocence and her joy in living. The whole novel can be read as a clash between French and English traditions and temperaments. It was a subject which fascinated Du Maurier, and constituted one important strand in his friendship with Henry James. The ultimate victory of Trilby's English soul was symbolic of Du Maurier's choice of England as his home, and his submission to a conventional and moralistic way of life.

Du Maurier took the name of his hero from Thackeray's ballad,

54. p. 94.   56. p. 17.
55. p. 96.   57. p. 116.

'Little Billee', which he had often sung at after-dinner entertainments. Thackeray's hero, like Du Maurier's, is the third and youngest of a group of friends, but, unlike him, narrowly avoids being cannibalized by his fellows. It has often been suggested, by Henry James, Canon Ainger and John Millais, for instance, that Du Maurier's Little Billee was taken from Frederick Walker, the brilliant illustrator and painter, who had died tragically young in 1875. Little Billee's small stature, great talent and early death recall Walker, but Du Maurier himself denied the connection: 'Little Billee is not Fred Walker – whom I deliberately introduced in his own person, to avoid any misconception'.[58] A more interesting suggestion is that put forward by Whistler's lawyer, who wrote to say that Little Billee was thought to be Du Maurier himself. A very significant letter to Tom Armstrong, who had written to ask this very question, seems to confirm it: 'Tammy's the only portrait & blowed if I haven't turned him into an R.A. at the end! (and added 4 inches to his stature) – as for the others, if you'll swear I'm Little Billee I'll swear you're big Taffy!'[59] Little Billee is an unsympathetic character, a spoiled child of fortune and a prig. He looks down on Trilby for her moral failings, and discusses cultural topics with her which she is quite incapable of understanding. He is innocent, but in a tight-lipped way, and his discovery of vice does not arouse sympathy: 'It was as though a tarnishing breath had swept over the reminiscent mirror of his mind and left a little film behind it, so that no past thing he wished to see therein was reflected with quite the old pristine clearness'.[60] His mother's treatment of Trilby, and Trilby's departure, do lead to some understanding of her situation. Rounding on Taffy and the Laird, he screams: 'are you so precious immaculate, you two, that you should throw stones at poor Trilby! What a shame, what a hideous shame it is that there should be one law for the woman and another for the man!'[61] This outburst is a prelude to Little Billee's nervous breakdown, a graphic description of Du Maurier's own in 1862, but his compassion does not last. He is unable to feel warmth or affection for anyone, and coldly pursues his career. His greatness is described in terms that are wholly unconvincing, and his attempt to find consolation in a working man's club in the East End is self-conscious and adolescent. More tedious

58. A. Bright, 'Mr Du Maurier at Home',
Idler, VIII (Dec. 1895), p. 419.   60. p. 176.
59. 1 Jan. 1894.   61. pp. 196–7.

still are the lengthy descriptions of his spiritual doubts, which break up the narrative with unnecessary digressions. He never comes alive in the way that Trilby does, even when he is dying.

Du Maurier's characterization of the villain in *Trilby* is much more sophisticated than it had been in *Peter Ibbetson*. He attempted to incorporate Svengali closely into the pattern of the whole story, and his role is actively evil. Like Colonel Ibbetson, Svengali is a Jew, but, while Colonel Ibbetson is merely an Englishman with Jewish blood, Svengali has more sinister origins in Poland. He speaks German fluently, and is a rampant German nationalist. The Franco-Prussian war of 1870 had encouraged the novelist's hatred of the Germans. In his early days in London Du Maurier had been friendly with Abraham and Rebecca Solomon, and with the Levy family, and there were many Jews whom he admired. His castigation of Svengali as 'an Oriental Israelite Hebrew Jew'[62] must not be seen as the expression of an unthinking and general prejudice:

> He was very shabby and dirty, and wore a red *béret* and a large velveteen cloak, with a big metal clasp at the collar. His thick, heavy, languid, lustreless black hair fell down behind his ears on to his shoulders, in that musician-like way that is so offensive to the normal Englishman. He had bold, brilliant black eyes, with long heavy lids, a thin, sallow face, and a beard of burnt-up black, which grew almost from his under eyelids; and over it his moustache, a shade lighter, fell in two long spiral twists.[63]

Svengali's talent as a musician is given full value, and there is no attempt to pass him off as a charlatan. Trilby's singing is the outpouring of his soul, as Henry James was quick to realize: 'Svengali capers like a goat of poetry, and makes music like the great god Pan'.[64] It is the combination of evil and musical genius which makes Svengali such an original and sinister conception. Du Maurier's grotesque drawing of him as a spider with eight legs conveys more sharply than anything else his malevolent and divided nature.

Taffy seems to have been, like Trilby, a composite figure. With his huge stature and great physical strength, he resembled Val Prinsep, and perhaps Joseph Rowley, while his solid dependability recalled Thomas Armstrong. Taffy combines two of Du Maurier's ideals by being muscular, and a gentleman. His painting is evidently only a hobby, and he is still little more than an 'art student' at the end of the

62. p. 356.
63. p. 12.

64. H. James, 'George Du Maurier', *Harper's Weekly Magazine* XXXVIII (14 April 1894), p. 342.

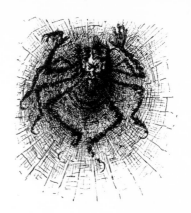

134. An Incubus,
Trilby

book. In his relation to hero and heroine, Taffy owes much to William Dobbin in *Vanity Fair*. As the reader realises early on, Taffy is himself in love with Trilby, and even proposes to her. The clash of loyalties to which he is subjected is never described, and what might have been an interesting psychological study is omitted. His love for Trilby excuses her past, but when he is asked about it by Mrs Bagot, his honour as an English gentleman forces him to tell the truth. He is the only person for whom the book ends happily. As Du Maurier wrote to Armstrong: 'They get so magnificent in the end that I have to kill off the little one before he's thirty – and make the big one paint very badly indeed. Otherwise they would be insupportable'.[65]

The character of the Laird, Sandy McAllister, was certainly taken from Du Maurier's friend, T. R. Lamont, but he does not emerge as a decisive character. He is similar enough to Taffy to become confused with him, and does little more than make up a trio of friends, of whom he is the least important. Like Lamont, the Laird paints Spanish pictures, and he is equally unsuccessful as an artist. His only positive quality is his kindness.

However accurate they may be as studies of the novelist's friends, many of the minor characters are not altogether successful in the context of the novel. The most effective are the studies of Du Maurier's own brother, Eugène, and his noble friend, the Prince de Ligne, who appear as Dodor and l'Zouzou. More famous, is Du Maurier's study of Whistler as Joe Sibley, 'the idle apprentice', while Poynter appears as Lorrimer, 'the industrious apprentice', and Alecco Ionides as 'the Greek'. Vincent, 'the Yankee Medical Student' and Carnegie from Balliol were obviously based on real people, but neither of them has been identified. Compared with

65. 1 Jan. 1894.

Miriam in *Sons and Lovers*, or Henry James' study of Lord Leighton
and Robert Browning, as Lord Mellifort and Clare Vawdrey
respectively, in 'The Private Life', Du Maurier's studies from life
lack the intensity and integration of characters who have passed
through a creative process, and taken a part in imaginative pattern.

They are introduced in passages of straightforward description,
accompanied, in most cases, with a compliments slip. Alecco Ionides
is no exception:

> Then there was the Greek, a boy of only sixteen, but six feet high, and
> looking ten years older than he was, and able to smoke even stronger
> tobacco than Taffy himself, and colour pipes divinely; he was a great
> favourite in the Place St Anatole, for his *bonhomie,* his niceness, his
> warm geniality.[66]

Du Maurier comments on his wealth and generosity, asks what he
was doing in the Latin Quarter (without providing an answer), and
finally gives an account of his subsequent career. This is typical of the
'thumb-nail' sketches. From then on, the Greek appears only in lists
of names; of people present at the Christmas dinner, or around
Trilby's bedside. He is never developed in depth, or integrated with
the story. The same is true of other characters; Carnegie is briefly
sketched as a 'swell', Vincent as an American in Paris, but the
account of their future lives is purely gratuitous. It was as if Du
Maurier felt compelled to follow through the lives of his friends to
the end, however irrelevant they are to the story; Vincent becomes a
world-famous oculist, Lorrimer is elected to the Royal Academy,
while Carnegie is only a rural dean, and l'Zouzou, married to an
ugly American millionairess, has no heir. Dodor has to give up his
aristocratic friend, go into trade, and marry his employer's daughter.

However unsuccessful the portraits of his friends are from a
literary point of view, they contain important biographical material.
Some of this has already been discussed in Chapter Two. The description of the later careers of his friends allowed Du Maurier to praise or
condemn, as he felt necessary. He takes the opportunity to congratulate Poynter, as he does Ionides, on the position which he has
reached: 'he is a graybeard, an Academician, an accomplished man
of the world'.[67] Whistler, on the contrary, is condemned as a play-
boy and malicious wit, who has achieved nothing admirable. Du

66. p. 135.
67. p. 141.

Maurier's sketch of Joe Sibley nearly led to a libel case, described in detail in the next chapter, and Whistler was able to demand its withdrawal from the book version.

A few of the minor characters are more essential to the plot, and are less obviously drawn from friends. In Mrs Bagot, Du Maurier presents a straightforward study of a conventional woman, her name significantly close to bigot. Mrs Bagot is an important character, for it is she, and not Svengali, who drives the young couple apart. Her hatred of Trilby, seen in terms of her possessiveness, is powerful and convincing. Her later conversion to Trilby is insipid and obvious, but inevitable in the context of the novel. Her clerical brother-in-law is a minor figure, whom Du Maurier used as a whipping post for his attacks on the Church.

Trilby was accepted by Harpers in 1893 for publication in the following year. The one hundred and twenty illustrations, however, kept Du Maurier busily at work, and prevented him from enjoying the rest and relaxation he so urgently needed. The strain of lecturing and a series of family illnesses had made him nervous and depressed. In May 1893 he went to Ramsgate with Emma and May, suffering from an unspecified illness, probably heart-strain:

> I am getting better, I think – altho' still very nervous about going out alone. It is a common enough ailment, I find; and doesn't interfere with my work – altho' they tell me that it's overwork that's brought it on.[68]

Back in Hampstead, Du Maurier relied on Ainger to cheer him up, but Ainger was not always there. As a Canon of Bristol Cathedral since 1887, Ainger had to spend several months there every year. In 1894, he was appointed Master of the Temple, and moved to the Master's lodgings, leaving Hampstead for ever.

The summer holiday in Whitby of 1893 was more successful than that of the previous year. The weather was good, and there were visits from the Hoyer Millars, the Llewellyn Davies and Gerald, who was now determined on a theatrical career. His parents had tried to dissuade him, but they were powerless, as Henry James had explained to them:

> that if Gerald really wanted to go on the stage he didn't see how they could prevent it. 'That's all very well, James; but what would you say if

---

68. To T. Armstrong, 2 June 1893.

you had a son who wanted to go into the Church?' Lifting both hands in horror Henry James replied, 'My dear du Maurier, a father's curse!'[69]

In November, the Du Mauriers took another Bayswater house for the winter, this time at No 3 Stanhope Terrace. They entertained Val Prinsep to dinner, 'though he had not crossed our threshold for more than twenty years! So much for living in Hampstead!'[70] Prinsep was present at an Arts Club dinner on 20 November 1893, in honour of Sir John Tenniel, where Du Maurier took the chair: 'What the deuce ever induced me to accept a thing so distressing? can't think! what an unfair thing is an application by word of mouth instead of by letter! Do you know Buzzard? He came & buzzed me into it, & when he'd gone I nearly had a fit'.[71] The dinner was a success, and Du Maurier was later to be grateful for Buzzard's support, when Whistler tried to have him removed from the Arts Club.

January 1894 was a significant month in the Du Maurier family calendar. On 6 January Gerald played his first professional role, Fritz the waiter, in John Hare's production of *An Old Jew*. Hare was an old friend of the Du Mauriers, and Gerald stayed with him for six months, before going on tour with Forbes Robertson in the autumn. January also witnessed the appearance of the first number of *Trilby* in *Harper's Monthly Magazine*. The immediate response from his friends was enthusiastic, James writing from Venice:

> Trilby goes on with a life and charm and loveability that gild the whole day one reads her. It's most delightfully and vividly talked! And then drawn! – no, it isn't fair.[72]

Ainger was more critical, and put his finger on the essential weaknesses of the book:

> You know how little I care for the supernatural in Fiction – so I don't mind betting you that I *love* the first half of your book, & don't care for the second – Up to the 'hypnotism' incidents, I think your story charming & beautifully true to nature & artistic – *after* that, as it seems to me, a pathetic and deeply interesting and credible story of real life degenerates into a Fairy-tale.
>
> I need not say that I don't care for your theological discussions, not

69. Hoyer Millar, p. 174.
70. Millais, II, 278.
71. To T. Armstrong, 18 Nov. 1893.

72. *Letters of Henry James*, edited by P. Lubbock (1920), I, 218–9.

because they are un-orthodox, but because they seem to me irrelevant.…

All through, save in one or two of the best passages, you are, in my judgement, too perpetually upon the 'humorous tiptoe'.[73]

From the start, *Trilby* was a major success, and as the *Trilby* 'boom' escalated, Du Maurier found himself the author of a popular best-seller. Such success, coming at the end of a lifetime of unrewarded effort and frustrated ambition, should have been a source of profound satisfaction. Ten or twenty years earlier it probably would have been, but Du Maurier was tired and nervous now, and his success overwhelmed him. Like a mole, searching for dark and familiar places, Du Maurier shied away from the limelight, and the public exposure to which he was subjected. The apparatus of publicity and public success, which had no note of jubilation for him, seemed to undermine his health and his confidence, to tear him from the secure and familiar patterns of his life. He was certainly suffering from fatty degeneration of the heart, but it is impossible to escape the conclusion that *Trilby*, to a very large extent, was the cause of his death.

It is always difficult for a later age to understand the reasons for the popularity of the best-sellers of an earlier era. Most modern critics would place *Peter Ibbetson* above *Trilby* on grounds of wholeness and intensity alone. What was Trilby's particular attraction for the readers of the 'nineties? Du Maurier's easy conversational style had a great deal to do with it:

> I do not know any writer whose printed words are more like his ordinary talk than some of the best passages in 'Peter Ibbetson' and 'Trilby' are to Kicky's after-dinner talk at the *Punch* table. In reading them, I can hear his pleasant voice with its musical intonation of every syllable, a gift that came to him with his French birth.[74]

Du Maurier most resembles Thackeray in this, who also writes as though he was recalling his life to a group of friends. In *Trilby*, Du Maurier assumes the role of narrator, introducing himself occasionally as the 'present scribe', as Thackeray had done in *Vanity Fair*. Thackeray also refers to his characters as if they were puppets to be manipulated and explained. When Becky Sharp makes her

73. 12 Sept. 1894.
74. H. Lucy, *Sixty Years in the Wilderness* (1909), p. 392.

famous statement 'I think I could be a good woman if I had five
thousand a year', Thackeray remarks:

> And who knows but Rebecca was right in her speculations – and that it
> was only a question of money and fortune which made the difference
> between her and an honest woman? If you take temptations into account,
> who is to say that he is better than his neighbour?

In a similar passage, Du Maurier defends Trilby:

> Whether it be an aggravation of her misdeeds or an extenuating circum-
> stance, no pressure of want, no temptations of greed or vanity, had ever
> been factors in urging Trilby on her downward career after her first false
> step in that direction – the result of ignorance, bad advice (from her
> mother, of all people in the world), and base betrayal.[75]

Thackeray's wit and incisiveness perhaps justify his intrusion into
the story, but Du Maurier's rambling style and clumsy parentheses
do not. Similar asides occur throughout Du Maurier's three novels,
awkwardly breaking into the narrative, and performing no function
but that of gratuitous comment. Du Maurier's assumption of an easy
familiarity with the reader leads to a colloquial and congenial style.
It does, however, frequently degenerate into slang and bathos, as
when Du Maurier describes the religions of the world in *Peter
Ibbetson*: 'ancient and modern, Hebrew, Pagan, Buddhist, Christian,
Agnostic, and what not'.[76] Such writing was likely to be popular
with the general public, as it was less serious and demanding than
the works of the High-Victorian giants, but fresher and more robust
than the sentimental novels of Miss Braddon or Mrs Henry Wood.

Ultimately, however, it was the subject-matter of *Trilby* which
accounted for its success. The Quartier Latin, with its exciting
bohemian characters and atmosphere, suitably bowdlerized for
public consumption, suggested an unfamiliar but intensely romantic
world. The interest in mesmerism, and the pathos of the love story,
combined to produce a novel that was new and daring, but not
outrageous. There were the inevitable protests from the moralists
and prudes, particularly in the United States, where the ethics of
Trilby were discussed in pulpits and in the press, but the public
found the book enthralling, and refused to be shocked. Enclosing to

75. pp. 49–50.
76. p. 120.

Du Maurier a letter from a belligerent American lady, who asked why he had not condemned the book in his review for *Harper's Weekly*, James wrote:

> Only see, my dear Kikaccio, to what my thick-and-thin espousal of your genius exposes me at the hands of an unknown American female. Guileless, stupid, muddled, distracted, well-meaning, but slightly hypocritical American female!... I trust fame and flattery and flowers flow in upon you with the revolving Harpers.[77]

On his return from Venice, James found his wish fulfilled, and wondered why:

> 'Let us', said Henry James, 'find a seat and sit down and endeavour – if it is in any way possible to arrive at a solution – to discover some reason for such a phenomenon as the success of *Trilby*.'[78]

135. Vignette from *Trilby*

Neither was able to do so.

Fan mail poured in on Du Maurier who was unable to cope with the effusions of adulation and uncritical praise: 'I trust that you will forgive my intrusion, as a perfect stranger in writing this letter to you', or (from the staff of a teacher's training college for ladies): 'We wonder at our boldness in adressing you'. They harassed Du Maurier, encouraging in him latent persecution mania: 'I have just finished reading "Trilby" – and I want to tell you what an immense amount of pleasure it has given me. It is, to me, an ideally perfect

77. James' Letters, I, p. 218–9.
78. Guthrie, p. 170.

book'. It was on Trilby herself that Du Maurier's correspondents lavished most of their sentiment. They informed him that they had actually imagined themselves in the Quartier Latin, and one lady expressed her surprise at hearing English outside her window, instead of French. At least three letters came from people who had searched the National Gallery for Little Billee's pictures. One enthusiast even sent a stamped and addressed postcard, requesting the name of the real Little Billee. Few clergymen wanted to defend themselves against Du Maurier's attacks on Christianity and the church, but a large number of evangelical ladies offered to convert him. Their letters suggest that Wilkie Collins' savage picture of an evangelical dragon in the character of Drusilla Clack was not a complete caricature. There were also the inevitable letters from autograph-hunters, and from people who wished to exploit the *Trilby* craze, besides the ordinary begging-letters. Requests to patent 'Trilby' songs, 'Trilby' shoes, and even a 'Trilby' kitchen range came by every post. One proud father informed Du Maurier that he had named his baby daughter Trilby Haidèe Moulder, was she, he wanted to know, the first Trilby? The fan mail had its comic side, but its quantity and persistence slowly wore Du Maurier down, and made him angry and resentful. He had started a landslide from which he could not escape, and he saw the exploitation of his literary creation with growing cynicism and distaste.

Chapter 13

'Joe Sibley'

136. Initial letter 'F' from *The Story of a Feather* by Douglas Jerrold (1867)

'TRILBY' WAS PARTLY A 'roman à clef', many of the characters being derived from Du Maurier's friends and acquaintances. This reflected the novelist's pleasure in writing for a double audience, as well as his limited powers of invention. *Trilby* enabled him to hand out a number of bouquets to those friends he admired, like Alecco Ionides, Poynter and Arthur Lewis. Unfortunately, the temptation to ridicule other old friends, in the same casual and light-hearted vein, was one which Du Maurier could not resist. Working quietly in Hampstead, such gentle banter seemed harmless and amusing enough. Only when the book appeared in *Harper's Magazine*, did it dawn on Du Maurier how angry some of his subjects would be.

The most famous of all the portraits, and the most vicious, was that of Whistler, who was introduced as Joe Sibley: 'the idle apprentice, the king of bohemia, *le roi des truands*, to whom everything was forgiven, as to François Villon, "à cause de ses gentillesses" '.[1] The illustrations to the novel, in particular 'The Two Apprentices', contained several portraits of Whistler, for those who were in any doubt about his identity from the satirical literary description:

Always in debt, like Svengali; like Svengali, vain, witty, and a most exquisite and original artist; and also eccentric in his attire (though clean), so that people would stare at him as he walked along – which he adored! But (unlike Svengali) he was genial, caressing, sympathetic, charming; the most irresistible friend in the world as long as his friendship lasted – but that was not for-ever!

1. *Harper's New Monthly Magazine*, LXXXVIII (March 1894), 577.

137. The Two
Apprentices, *Trilby*
(*Harper's Monthly
Magazine* version)

The moment his friendship left off, his enmity began at once. Sometimes this enmity would take the simple form and straightforward form
of trying to punch his ex-friend's head; and when the ex-friend was too
big, he would get some new friend to help him. And much bad blood
would be caused in this way – though very little was spilt. And all this
bad blood was not made better by the funny things he went on saying
through life about the unlucky one who had managed to offend him –
things that stuck forever! His bark was worse than his bite – he was
better with his tongue than with his fists – a dangerous joker! But when
he met another joker face to face, even an inferior joker – with a rougher
wit, a coarser thrust, a louder laugh, a tougher hide – he would just
collapse, like a pricked bladder![2]

This account of Whistler was not concerned with the period of his
friendship with Du Maurier, and it was not even first-hand. Du
Maurier was describing the events of 1867 when Whistler was twice
called before a Parisian magistrate, first for hitting a workman who
had dropped plaster on him, and then for pushing his brother-in-law,
Seymour Haden, through a plate-glass window. In the same year,
another of Whistler's estranged friends, Alphonse Legros, received a

2. Harper's, pp. 577–8.

violent blow in the face during a heated argument. But it was probably Du Maurier's scathing references to Whistler's present mode of life which most offended the painter:

> He is now perched on such a topping pinnacle (of fame and notoriety combined) that people can stare at him from two hemispheres at once; and so famous as a wit that when he jokes (and he is always joking) people laugh first, and then ask what it was he was joking about. And you can even make your own mild funniments raise a roar by merely prefacing them, 'As Joe Sibley once said'.
>   The present scribe has often done so.[3]

Du Maurier then proceeded to an unfortunate comparison between Whistler and Poynter, both of whom detested each other. At a musical party of Hamilton Aïdé's in 1881, the three members of the Paris group were all guests:

> He [Whistler] says I must take Trixy to him to be painted. Zut! He seems to have a great tooth against Poynter 'Look at him! Look at him, standing there!!' (Poynter *was* only standing there) – 'Et donc que nous avons connu ça!'[4]

Now Du Maurier got his own back, Poynter, as Lorrimer the industrious apprentice, was described as 'a pillar of the Royal Academy – probably, if he lives long enough, its future president – the duly knighted or baroneted Lord Mayor of "all the plastic arts" '.[5] In contrast to Lorrimer's passion for old masters, was Whistler's passion for himself:

> He was a monotheist, and had but one god, and was less tiresome in the expression of his worship. He is so still – and his god is still the same – no stodgy old master this divinity, but a modern of the moderns! For forty years the cosmopolite Joe has been singing his one god's praise in every tongue he knows and every country – and also his contempt for all rivals to this godhead – whether quite sincerely or not, who can say? Men's motives are so mixed! But so eloquently, so wittily, so prettily, that he almost persuades you to be a fellow-worshipper – *almost*, only! – for if he did *quite*, you (being a capitalist) would buy nothing but 'Sibleys' (which you don't). For Sibley was the god of Joe's worship, and none other! and you would hear of no other genius in the world![6]

3. Harper's, p. 578.
4. To T. Armstrong, 16 June 1881.
5. Harper's, p. 578.
6. Harper's, p. 578.

Du Maurier, perhaps realizing that he had gone too far, did try to camouflage his description, Sibley is described as having 'beautiful white hair like an Albino's, as soft and bright as floss silk', and being 'tall and slim and graceful . . . with pretty manners (and an unimpeachable moral tone)'.[7]

The whole passage on Joe Sibley appeared in the third part of *Trilby*, published in *Harper's Monthly* for March 1894. Exactly when and how Whistler first came across it is uncertain. He was living in Paris at the time, and was probably given a copy by a friend. His reaction was one of anger and grieved surprise – a stab in the back from an old friend, the sneer of the Victorian establishment (the 'idle apprentice' recalled the trial with Ruskin in 1878), the charge of cowardice and charlatanism. Whistler had grown more crabbed and sensitive as he grew older, and more dangerous. His immediate object was revenge. Of a pugnacious temperament, Whistler had substituted litigation for violence in his middle-age, and libel-cases had become his forte. His case appeared to be cast-iron, and he was determined to win it.

He opened fire with two letters, one to the *Pall Mall Gazette* and the other to the Beefsteak Club. The former, published on 15 May 1894 was savage and caustic:

Sir, – It would seem, notwithstanding my boastful declaration, that, after all, I had not, before leaving England, completely rid myself of that abomination – the 'friend'!

One solitary unheeded one – Mr George Dumaurier – still remained, hidden in Hampstead.

On that healthy Heath, he has been harbouring, for nearly half a life, every villainy of goodfellowship that could be perfected by the careless frequentation of our early intimacy and my unsuspecting camaraderie. Of this pent-up envy, malice and furtive intent, he never, at any moment during all that time allowed me, while affectionately grasping his honest Anglo-French fist, to detect the faintest indication.

Now that my back is turned, the old *marmite* of our *pot-au-feu* he fills with the picric acid of thirty years' spite, and, in an American Magazine, fires off his bomb of mendacious recollection and poisoned rancune.

The lie with which it is loaded, *à mon intention,* he proposes for my possible 'future biographer' – but I fancy it explodes, as is usual, in his own waistcoat, and he furnishes, in his present unseemly state, an excellent example of all those others who, like himself, have thought a foul friend a finer fellow than an open enemy.

Paris   J. McNEILL WHISTLER

7. Harper's, p. 578.

Reflection: The compagnon of the pétard we guillotine. Guineas are given to the popular companion who prepares his infernal machine for the distinguished associates in whose friendship he has successfully speculated.

He had already drawn up a draft letter on the same lines to be sent to Du Maurier, which was probably the reason for Du Maurier's refusal to offer an apology.

The second letter, dated 7 May 1894, went to the President of the Beefsteak Club, of which both men were members. Whistler drew the committee's attention to the club rules:

> As good faith and good fellowship are your essentials it becomes plain that Mr Du Maurier & I cannot both continue as members. Either I am a coward, or he is a liar – *That* is the issue.[8]

Whistler also demanded that a copy of his letter should be hung in the supper-room, a request which the committee refused. They pointed out that Du Maurier had already resigned from the club; it is not known if this was prompted by the trouble with Whistler, or had occurred earlier. Whistler's letter to the president, and the one which followed it, were shown to members of the club by Andrew Stuart Wortley, who sent Whistler a report: 'while most of them thought you did D.M. too much honour by taking any notice at all, the matter evoked expressions of sympathy & regard for you all round'.[9] The *Pall Mall Gazette* had meanwhile sent a reporter to New Grove House to interview Du Maurier. An account of the interview appeared on 19 May 1894. He began by refusing to answer questions: 'If a bargee insults one in the street, one can only pass on. One cannot stop and argue it out'. Then, seeking to justify himself, Du Maurier gave what was tantamount to an admission of guilt:

> Certainly, in the character of Joe Sibley, in my serial story, 'Trilby', I have drawn certain lines with Mr Whistler in my mind. I thought that the reference to these matters would have recalled some of the good times we used to have in Paris in the old days. I thought that both with Mr Whistler and with other acquaintances I have similarly treated, pleasurable recollections would have been awakened. But he has taken the matter so terribly seriously. It is so unlike him.

8. Whistler Collection, History of Fine Art Department, University of Glasgow.
9. 1 June 1894, Glasgow.

When the reporter asked a very leading question: 'I believe Mr. Whistler has himself said things which the objects of them have not particularly relished?', Du Maurier was tempted to declare that his original provocation had been his conversation with Whistler and Oscar Wilde, quoted in Whistler's *The Gentle Art of Making Enemies.*

> Mr Du Maurier and Mr Wilde happening to meet in the rooms where Mr Whistler was holding his first exhibition of Venice etchings, the latter brought the two face to face, and taking each by the arm, inquired:
>   'I say, which one of you two invented the other, eh?'[10]

This had appeared in 1890, its publication had clearly rankled with Du Maurier. He went out of his way to explain to the reporter exactly what the silly little joke had meant, and why he was so annoyed:

> The obvious retort to that on my part would have been that if he did not take care I would invent *him,* but he had slipped away before either of us could get a word out. This is really too small a matter to refer to; but the explanation of this bit of drollery of Mr Whistler's is that it suggested that I was unknown until I began to draw Postlethwaite, the aesthetic character out of whom I got some fun. Postlethwaite was said to be Mr Oscar Wilde. . . . As a matter of fact I had been drawing for *Punch* twenty years before the invention of Postlethwaite. However, that was Mr Whistler's little joke, and one would have thought that if he made jokes about me he might have expected me to play the same game upon him without anticipating that I should hurt his feelings.

This was Du Maurier's defence, and it was a good one. Whistler's own dedication to *The Gentle Art* might well be quoted in Du Maurier's favour: 'To All Good Comrades who like a fair field and no quarter these pages are peacefully inscribed'.

On the other side, it must be admitted that Whistler's attacks were usually witty and clever as well as cruel. The portrait of Joe Sibley lacks this redeeming quality, and was clearly prompted by envy and bitterness. Whistler would never have laid himself open in this way. Perhaps the most revealing part of Du Maurier's interview was his statement that:

> I am neither his friend nor his enemy. I am a great admirer of his genius and his wit, but I cannot say that I could call myself his friend, for thirty years past. We were intimate in the old days, but that is all. No,

10. Edited by Sheridan Ford (1890), p. 241.

his whole letter is incomprehensible to me. Of course he has been embittered through life, by reason of his genius not being recognized at its full value by the wide public, and it certainly has not. This circumstance, and possibly illness, may account for the leave he has taken of good manners. He talks of my pent-up envy and malice. I must ask you to believe that I am not such a beast as that. I have no occasion either for malice or for envy, and, as I say, I should never have written even what I have had I imagined it would give Mr Whistler pain.

In the matter of friendship, Du Maurier was more honest than Whistler. The latter may have informed the Pennells that he had always imagined it to be 'a genuine friendship',[11] but he must have been very blind and insensitive if he still imagined that this was the case in 1894. Whistler's biographers have dealt harshly and are in little sympathy with Du Maurier in this respect. Théodore Duret, for instance, wrote scathingly about Du Maurier's motives:

> The way in which Whistler was presented as Joe Sibley left no room for doubting the nature of the author's feelings. For a man so advanced in life as Du Maurier was to trace such a portrait of another man, his contemporary, he must have nursed an old rancour.
>
> Nevertheless there had never apparently been any cause of offence or conflict between them. They had known one another in Paris in the student days, and afterwards, established in London they had formed ties of friendship and maintained cordial relations. But one must have lived with artists to know what bitter sentiments are often hidden under the appearance of friendship. There is always the envy caused by those, who, having at first been unknown, eventually raise themselves above others by a real superiority of talent and invention. A real supremacy! Here is something which certain people can never accept or pardon.[12]

The *Pall Mall Gazette* interview gave Whistler his chance, and he decided to use it as an admission of guilt on Du Maurier's part. He wrote a letter about it in May to Harpers' agent, who replied that he 'did not understand the reference'.[13] Two more letters went to Poynter, and to Henry Stacy Marks, who had also been parodied in *Trilby*, and whom Whistler hoped would support him. The description of Marks was even more blatant than Whistler's:

11. Pennell, E. R. and J., *The Life of J. McNeill Whistler* (1909), I, 51.
12. *Whistler* (Paris, 1904). English translation by F. Rutter (1917), p. 122.
13. From Clarence McIlvaine, 21 May 1894, Glasgow.

And the Rabelaisian Macey Sparks (now most respectable of Royal Academicians), who sometimes, in his lucid intervals after supper and champagne, was given to thoughtful, acute, and sympathetic observation of his fellow-men, had remarked, in a hoarse, smoky, hiccuppy whisper to the Laird: 'Rather an enviable pair!'[14]

Marks was very much offended, though with less excuse than Whistler, and he promised to help. He wrote to the Arts Club, of which he and Du Maurier were members, asking for Du Maurier's resignation. A committee meeting was held at the Arts Club, of which Du Maurier was a founder member, and it was decided that he should be given the chance to defend himself. Buzzard, the chairman, telegraphed to Oxford Square, requesting Du Maurier to come to the club, and marking the summons 'urgent'. Du Maurier wrote to Tom Armstrong to tell him the sequel:

I have always been very fond of M. There had never been a cloud between us – and oddly enough I never felt more warmly towards him than when I was writing that unlucky par. about 'Macey Sparks' – I thought how he would laugh at this old reminiscence about him & be much amused! Mais pas du tout – He was *furious*; & I, in despair – so I went with Buzzard to Vere St & wired to New York to suppress the whole passage relating to him . . . I then went home & wrote all my sincere & heartfelt penitence to him, and he wrote me a very nice letter back – and I have since spent a whole day with him (& the R.A. Club) at Hatfield & St Albans, we sat with our arms round each others' necks. He hiccupped more than ever as we came home (& is very sensitive about it, I'm told.) We *mingled* our hiccups, in fact; and I'm fonder of him than ever, poor old chap![15]

Poynter, who disliked Whistler, was not so easily drawn as Marks. He wrote a cold and formal letter of reply:

My dear Whistler,
I have a general idea that Du Maurier has been making a story out of our old Paris life, but I have not read anything of it – partly because I wd. rather read a book when it is all out, than piecemeal in parts; – & partly because I generally dislike pictures of behind the scenes of an artist's life being put before the public.[16]

14. Harper's, June 1894, p. 840.   16. 23 May 1894, Glasgow.
15. 5 Aug. 1894.

Poynter then stated that he had not read the *Pall Mall Gazette* interview, and that he could scarcely believe that Du Maurier had written anything 'personally objectionable to any of us . . . I see very little of Du Maurier now, but we are always good friends'. Whistler was not so easily put off, and sent a full explanation of the whole matter, and copy of the *Pall Mall Gazette*. Poynter refused 'to quarrel with Du Maurier – altho' your letter is so seductive, that you almost persuade me to take a side. I know you will say this is just like me; but there is not time in this life to go into these things'.[17] When Whistler offered to send him the offensive passages in *Trilby*, Poynter replied briefly and acidly, saying that he would look them out at his club. His loyalty to Du Maurier remained firm, but he did not intend to defend him actively.

Du Maurier himself was slow to realize the implications of his position. He had informed the interviewer of the *Pall Mall Gazette* that he did not intend to offer Whistler an apology, after his rude letter, and that he was not sure whether he would withdraw Joe Sibley from the book edition of the novel. He made up his mind between 19 and 28 May, when he wrote to his publisher, McIlvaine:

> Is there still time do you think, to make a small alteration in parts 3 & 4 of Trilby for the American volume form? As I wish to replace the character of 'Joe Sibley' by another (& a better one), Joe Sibley as you may have seen, has given dire offence to J. Whistler, deeply to my regret.[18]

Du Maurier naïvely imagined that the removal of the offending pages would satisfy Whistler, and had no idea that legal proceedings for libel were already in motion. Whistler, galled by his failure to gain the support of Marks and Poynter, was preparing to inflict the maximum humiliation on his old friend, and to extract heavy damages for the slight cast upon his character. He wrote to the great lawyer of the day, Sir George Lewis, asking him to take on the case, but Lewis refused:

> Du Maurier is one of my oldest friends, and naturally it is impossible for me to act against him. I hope however that no proceedings will be taken. I know nothing of the article complained of.[19]

17. 27 May 1894, Glasgow.
18. Pierpont Morgan Library.

19. 21 May 1894, Glasgow.

As in the case of Poynter, when Whistler came up against a blank wall, he felt an overwhelming need to justify himself, and to extract the admission that he was in the right. In his reply to Lewis, Whistler once more catalogued the long and boring list of injuries he had suffered at the hands of Du Maurier, to 'make clear to you in its full light the infamous conduct of Du Maurier'.[20] Whistler was developing a monomania on the subject, and creating from the unfortunate characterization of Joe Sibley the illusion of a vast and sinister plot against himself. Lewis remained unimpressed, and Whistler had to turn to a firm of solicitors, the Webb brothers, then always found acting for him, an exciting but hazardous business. Joseph Pennell described William Webb as 'a little man, a thorough Englishman in big spectacles, with a curious sniff'.[21] The difficulties with which Webb had to contend are proved by the endless letters of advice and instruction that Whistler fired off to him, now at Glasgow University. Whistler told Webb that he wanted to sue Du Maurier or Harpers for damages, and that he expected a substantial sum. The lawyer suggested that his reputation as a painter was too strong to suffer much from *Trilby*, and that he could not expect any large compensation although he should receive a retraction and apology. Webb started the proceedings simply enough with a letter of 29 May 1894 to Harpers:

> Mr Whistler instructs us that proceedings will be commenced against you for an injunction unless you comply with the following requirements:–
>
> Mr Du Maurier's work containing the libel must be stopped.
>
> The March number of the Magazine must be destroyed and a satisfactory apology must be published wherever reasonably required, and an understanding not to repeat the libel when the work is published in book form.
>
> As to the damage done to Mr Whistler's reputation by the libel which has been circulated over the civilized world, this will have to be dealt with and provided for by you if proceedings are to be stayed.
>
> Be pleased to let us hear from you what you intend to do, in the course of a week, from this date, and if you are not willing to comply, please furnish us with the name of your Solicitors.
>
> Your obedient servants
> Geo & Wm Webb[22]

20. Undated, Glasgow.
21. E. R. and J. Pennell, *The Life of James McNeill Whistler* (5th revised edition, 1911), p. 314.
22. Copies of this document are in Glasgow and the Pierpont Morgan Library.

In his reply, McIlvaine informed Webb that he would have to have the consent of the New York Office of Harpers, and that in the meantime he had sent on his letter to the solicitors, Messrs Frere, Forster & Co. He also expressed regret for what had happened. Arthur Stirling, of Frere, Forster & Co, who took over the case for McIlvaine, immediately sent a telegram to Harpers in New York on his own initiative: 'Whistler threatens injunction March Trilby. Suggest deferring composition book'.[23] This was the first of the cryptic cables which caused such confusion on both sides of the Atlantic. Harpers were mystified, and sent a cable to McIlvaine, asking for an explanation. McIlvaine had meanwhile sought counsel's opinion, counsel argued that the description of Joe Sibley constituted a libel and suggested that the book should be altered, and a reasonable apology offered. McIlvaine therefore cabled to Harpers in New York: 'Advised March number libellous propose settling express regrets stop March circulation modify book cable sanction'.[24] Harpers replied: 'Cable proposed terms Trilby settlement',[25] and received another of McIlvaine's ambiguous answers: 'Fear Whistler will bring libel action after injunction. Propose acting as cabled Saturday to stop latter'.[26] Harpers were not sure what they were letting themselves in for: 'What do you mean by propose settling?'[27] McIlvaine answered more calmly: 'Counsel advises try stop injunction by apology stopping sale March number and promising book revision no money payment proposed'.[28] To this Harpers agreed: 'Terms suggested satisfactory. Du Maurier should make the apology'.[29] Harpers had meanwhile taken a legal opinion themselves, which confirmed the advice given to McIlvaine. The Joe Sibley and Macey Sparks passages, and several other sketches, might be considered libellous, if drawn from real people. McIlvaine therefore contacted Du Maurier, who was most unwilling to make the apology, particularly as he had already stated his intention of not doing so in the *Pall Mall Gazette*. He still hoped that the case would be put 'out of court'[30] by Whistler's abusive letter.

Whistler was still delighted by the progress of the case, writing to Webb 'so first round, first blood'.[31] He even had malicious hopes of stopping *Trilby* entirely. As the weeks went by, and Webb and Frere

23. 31 May 1894. P. Morgan Library.
24. 2 June 1894. P. Morgan Library.
25. 2 June 1894. P. Morgan Library.
26. 3–4 June 1894.
27. 3–4 June 1894.
28. 3–4 June 1894.
29. 5 June 1894. P. Morgan Library.
30. 7 June 1894. P. Morgan Library.
31. Undated, Glasgow.

continued to meet to make a settlement, Whistler became irritated
by the delay, and feared he might fail in his objective: 'They tell me
the Harpers are rather a hard lot to deal with, and of much experience'.[32] 'The letter of Messrs Harpers solicitors is satisfactory as
far as it goes, but of course it goes but a very little way'.[33] By 15 June
1894 it was clear that he had little hope of extracting money from
them for damages:

> But let us throw away nothing – If after what we exact from them in the
> way of amends we can still hold over their head the possibility of further
> action why not take it in some equivalent further *giving away* of Du
> Maurier in the very humble letter they are to publish for us?
>
> After all I suppose even when we have done with the Harpers we can
> still proceed against Du Maurier if we choose for damages – could we
> not? So that we might have this still kept open.[34]

Whistler did not merely want legal redress, he wanted to pursue his
vendetta against Du Maurier to the end; there was something
paranoic in his hatred.

Du Maurier undertook to replace Joe Sibley with a new character,
and sent two alternatives to Harpers in the first week of June. Mr
Kretsch, a Swiss Jew, resembles Joe Sibley in several respects, but
he has no connection with the arts: 'he is no less a person than
Kretsch & Co., the eminent soap boilers of Bermondsey, Cheapside,
and Bond Street – (his magnificent private residence is in Grosvenor
Place – a regular palace)'.[35] Harpers preferred the less provocative
character of Bald Anthony, partly based on Huniker, the Swiss
painter with whom Du Maurier had shared a studio in Dusseldorf, 'a
touching and beautiful character'.[36] The amended text was sent to
Whistler, who fortunately failed to see that he was being sent up:
'Compliments, and complete approval of the author's new and
obscure friend, bald Anthony – Whistler'.[37] With the question of the
text settled, wrangling now went on about the illustrations. Harpers
agreed to suppress 'The Two Apprentices', but they only altered the
features of Joe Sibley in the general sketch 'All as it used to be' in
some editions, and did nothing about the portrait of him in 'Taffy a
l'échelle'. They were anxious to start printing the book version, and
did not want long delays as new illustrations were prepared.

32. Undated, Glasgow.   35. P. Morgan Library.
33. 12 June 1894, Glasgow.   36. To C. McIlvaine, 7 June 1894. P. Morgan Library.
34. Glasgow.   37. *The Star*, 30 Oct. 1894.

Whistler had been told by counsel that his own conduct during the case had not been exemplary, and that he would be unwise to go to court. He was advised to press for a published apology, and he wrote Webb on the matter:

> [Harpers] don't understand me – and they don't dream that *I really don't care how much the March number* circulates *directly* the letter of apology and full explanation is published in all papers to accompany it!!!
>
> Indeed the more Mr Du Maurier's wretched stuff is read, the more *terribly* clear will his humiliation be to the whole people! The mind of the meanest capacity will be able to grasp the situation! for never was humble pie to such a sickening extent devoured as has been gobbled by the miserable Du Maurier!!! Fancy when it becomes known that he has had, not only to rewrite his manuscript, but to *submit it to me for approval!!* – And to think that he should have consented to do it!!! Why nothing so absolutely abject was ever heard of! And then *think* of the TELEGRAM!!![38]

Whistler was aware that the March issue had largely been sold out, and than it was impossible to stop it circulating. A public apology was a much more significant triumph.

The agreement drawn up between Harpers and Whistler in July 1894, stipulated that Harpers would stop the sale of the March number of the European edition of their magazine and any future sale, that they would publish a public letter of apology either in September or October, that they would alter the book version and remove the offending passages, and that they would pay Whistler's legal costs not exceeding ten guineas. Harpers nearly wrecked the agreement by publishing an illustration in the last serial number of the novel in August, which included an unmistakable likeness of Whistler as Joe Sibley in one of Trilby's death-bed scenes. Whistler was furious, and was only pacified by the assurance that the illustration would be altered (a beard was added in the book-version) and that no-one had realized it included a portrait of him. He was not able to shake Harpers' refusal to print any form of apology in the American edition of *Harper's Monthly*, or to stop the sale of the March number in America. Frere had warned Webb that Harpers were unwilling to humiliate themselves: 'They remind us that if you were to press Messrs Harper beyond the extent of their good-nature, you would have to sue them in New York, where, in an action for libel, no-one ever gets damages, as everybody is delighted to hear

---

38. Undated, Glasgow.

scandal'.[39] It was because of Whistler's remonstrance on this point, which he failed to win, that the agreement was not signed till September. His insinuation that Harper's had deliberately kept back the letter of apology till the October number of the European edition of *Harper's Monthly* was entirely without foundation, for Harpers signed the letter on 18 September, and published it two weeks later, back-dated by a month:

> The *book* has been hastened, and has been given a good two or three weeks start in its published form – while the 'letter' has been held back and *entirely kept secret,* so that the papers have not only had full time to establish the success of Trilby, – which we do not propose to contradict – but the occasion has been taken to refer in contemptuous terms to the thin skinned & apparently weak and ineffectual remonstrance we have made.[40]

Whistler's triumph had been minimised by the success of *Trilby,* and he was understandably annoyed. The official letter of apology, however, gave him no real grounds for complaint:

45, Albemarle St., London W.
Sept. 8th 1894

To J. McNeill Whistler, Esq.
Dear Sir, – Our attention has been called to the attack made upon you by Mr Du Maurier in the novel 'Trilby', which is now appearing in our Magazine. If we had any knowledge of personal reference to yourself being intended, we should not have permitted the publication of such passages as could be offensive to you. As it is, we have freely made such reparation as is in our power. We have agreed to stop future sales of the March number of the European Edition of Harper's Magazine, and we undertake that when the story appears in the form of a book the March number shall be so rewritten as to omit every mention of the offensive character. Moreover, we engage to print and insert in the European Edition of our Magazine for the month of October unless in amended form this letter of apology addressed to you.

   Assuring you again of our sincere regret that you should have sustained the slightest annoyance in any publication of ours.

We remain, dear Sir,
Yours faithfully,
HARPER & BROTHERS.

39. 22 June 1894, Glasgow.
40. 30 Sept. 1894. Glasgow.

This letter was published in slightly differing versions in various London newspapers and in *Harper's Monthly*, but it aroused little interest.

While Whistler was working himself into a frenzy in Paris, Du Maurier was passing a quiet summer in Whitby with Emma, May, Trixy and her family. His main worry was his health, which had not been good since March. His eye was causing trouble, and peripheral neuritis in his right hand made writing very difficult and drawing almost impossible. He continued work for *Punch* as best he could, now drawing on a scale three times as large as the published cartoons. He wrote sadly to Armstrong: 'on devient vieux – on a trop fumé de cigarettes, et trop bu de petit bleu – et voila'.[41] Trilby's success in *Harper's Magazine*, and particularly in America gave him some pleasure: 'She has cost Harper's Mag 30,000 old subscribers during her chequered life, & gained them 100,000 new ones. So that they've written to offer me fabulous wages to write for them any blessed thing I like not exceeding 7000 words a number, and illustrate the same'.[42]

The quarrel and settlement with Whistler caused Du Maurier little anxiety, for he was beginning to realise that he had written a best-seller. He was aware, however, that Whistler had been genuinely wounded by the affront:

> Joe Carr & Sargent, who saw him in Paris, say he was quite *furious* & stung beyond description – it seems he looked upon me as one of the faithful, & was hurt as well as angry – Hélas! . . . As soon as its all over with the lawyers & there are no more threats, I will write to him & make my amende honourable as well as I can – how he will take it, I don't know – but I am very sorry indeed about the whole unlucky business. I little thought he would have taken what I said in such bad part.[43]

A new friend, the painter Laurence Harrison, was staying in Whitby, and from him Du Maurier heard some of the details of Whistler's life in Paris. He told Armstrong, with malicious delight, that the Burne-Jones cult had put Whistler in the shade, and that Degas had managed to quell 'Jimmy & sits on him like anything – and the opinion is generally that J.W. est "un peu voyou, vous savez!" '[44]

Du Maurier made several attempts at his letter to Whistler. One

41. 5 Aug. 1894.
42. To T. Armstrong, 22 July 1894.
43. 5 Aug. 1894.
44. 5 Aug. 1894.

draft, addressed to Whistler's lawyers, was roughed out in a working-sketch-book, and was interspersed with the opening chapter of *The Martian*:

> had Mr W. only let me know by a line or a word that he wished it, & thus spared himself both trouble and expense.
>
> He was very angry – so angry that he even mispelt my poor name, which I have always spelt as my fathers & grandfathers spelt it before me. He wouldn't even give the devil his *du* if I may make such a jest on such a momentous occasion. A man's love of himself may be almost maternal in its ferocity of tenderness.

Another series of drafts are addressed to Whistler directly. Du Maurier reiterated his statement that Whistler had misrepresented him, but he did regret 'having written the unfortunate paragraphs that have given you so much offence, & of which I now see & admit the carelessness and indiscretion'. In answer to the charge of envy, which had clearly upset him, Du Maurier wrote: 'I hope it is no libel to say that I have never been envious of you'. This draft ended in further passages of self-justification: 'The whole thing has been to me a matter of much painful preoccupation, not indeed from any fear of what you & your lawyers might do – but that I should so needlessly and so deeply have offended you without ever wishing to do so'. It is not known if Du Maurier ever sent off a letter of apology to Whistler, or if he received a reply. That his regret was not entirely sincere is proved by a letter of his to Armstrong: 'I shall tell Jimmy in the most abjectly fulsome terms of adulation I can invent that he's the damned'st ass & squirt I ever met'.[45] Nevertheless, Du Maurier went to Whistler's next exhibition: 'in order to express his sorrow to him who had taken so savage a revenge for what was, after all, but a little fault not ill meant'.[45a]

One of the last episodes in the Joe Sibley affair occurred in Harry Furniss' new magazine, *Lika Joka*, which published a letter purporting to have been written by Whistler:

> My only regret was that too little was said about so charming a creation. I looked to see more of him in the published three volumes. But no! I found the addition of some thoughtful excuses by Mr Du Maurier upon nudity, agnosticism, and other hazardous subjects, which had, presumably, been judged too strong for the ice-watered, ice-creamed constitution of the American Philistine; but I looked in vain for the

45. 5 Aug. 1894.
45a. M. H. Spielmann, 'Death of Mr Du Maurier', *Daily Graphic*, 9 October 1896, p. 5.

delightful Joe Sibley. In his place I find a yellow-haired Switzer, one Antony, son of a respectable burgher of Lausanne, who is now tall, stout, strikingly handsome and rather bald, but who in his youth had all the characteristics of the lost Joseph Sibley – his idleness, his debts, his humor, his art, his eccentricity, his charm. I rushed to my eye-glass. Je me suis demandé pourquoi.

Whistler replied to *Lika Joka* in the *Westminster Budget* for 2 November 1894:

> there was no harm in the appearance of the article, but what caused my merriment, but not surprise, is that anyone would have thought for a moment that I had written it. But there, it was in England, and in England anything is possible.

Whistler's later comments on the Trilby case were crude and jubilant; writing characteristically to Heinemann in November 1894:

> I fancy I have wiped up Hampstead and manured the Heath with Du Maurier! . . . It will be time soon to begin preparations for a new edition [of *The Gentle Art of Making Enemies*].
>
> Meanwhile I think I must put together all the Du Maurier campaign and let you have it set up that we may see how it looks! – We can then get it into pretty shape.[46]

Whistler was still contemplating a new edition of his book in 1902, but it never appeared. Mrs Comyns Carr records a conversation with him at her sister's house in Paris, shortly before his death, but it may not be accurate:

> Whistler once more began the tale of his grievances against his erstwhile friend du Maurier. My husband interrupted him, saying firmly, 'I don't want to hear anything more about it, Jimmy. You know I've always said you were utterly in the wrong. You took offence where none was meant'.
>
> For a moment or two Whistler did not reply, and then slowly and painfully he remarked, 'Well, Joe, maybe there's something in what you say. Perhaps I have made a mess of things'.
>
> *It was very soon after this that the end came.*[47]

46. 9 Nov. 1894. Pierpont Morgan Library.
47. *Mrs J. Comyns Carr's Reminiscences*, ed. Eve Adam (1926), p. 109.

Chapter 14

Oxford Square

THERE WAS SOMETHING pathetic and ironic in Du Maurier's reactions to his succcess. In the character of Little Billee he had imagined himself as a great celebrity. Now that the dream had come true, he found the experience unnerving. It overwhelmed and oppressed him. A week with Beatrix at Boxmoor in May helped to revive his spirits, but he sank back into gloom and apathy on his return: 'I have been seedy & depressed these last weeks – holiday & rest mean désoeuvrement, & that means weldschmertz, or something like it, to be cured by alternations of iron & quinine'.[1] Henry Lucy noticed his increasing weariness:

> precisely the same simple-mannered, delightful companion as before (as he said) he 'struck ile'. Nevertheless, there was a palpable change in him, possibly the result of failing health. He felt that success had come too late, and was apt to fall into unwonted moods of depression. . . . There was in truth no sourness in his sunny nature. But he was growing very tired.[2]

There was more than false humility in Du Maurier's own reflection:

> Then 'Trilby' followed, and the 'boom' came, a 'boom' which surprised me immensely, for I never took myself *au sérieux* as a novelist. Indeed, this 'boom' rather distresses me when I reflect that Thackeray never had a 'boom'. And I hold that a 'boom' means nothing as a sign of literary excellence, nothing but money.[3]

Henry James was another friend who watched his decline with pain and compassion:

> The collapse of his strength seemed, at the last, sudden, and yet there

---

1. To Henry James, 7 May 1894. Houghton Library Harvard.
2. *Diary of a Journalist* (1920), I, 89–90.
3. Sherard, pp. 399–400.

had been signs enough, on looking back, of an ebbing tide. I have no kinder memory of the charming superseded Hampstead than, on the clear, cool nights, the gradual shrinkage, half tacit, half discussed, of his old friendly custom of seeing me down the hill. The hill, for our parting, was long enough to make a series of stages that became a sort of deprecated register of what he could do no more; and it was inveterate enough that I wanted to reascend with him rather than go my way and let him pass alone into the night. Each of us might have, I suppose, at the back of his head, a sense, in all this, of something symbolic and even vaguely ominous. Rather than let him pass alone into the night I would, assuredly, when the real time came, gladly have taken with him whatever other course might have been the equivalent of remounting the hill into the air of better days.[4]

138. Sketch, *Magazine of Art* (1890)

This tragic image of Du Maurier's lonely return to Hampstead, finds an echo in a letter to him from James, of July 1894: 'it's very good of you to have assuaged my anxiety. I had some after letting you turn up the long hill again, the other evening, in the lonely darkness'.[5]

Unable to cope with the burdens of being a successful and sought-after novelist, Du Maurier retired to Whitby in August 1894. Beatrix and her two sons joined him there, but the 'weldschmertz' did not lift. Writing to Armstrong, he remarked: 'I've been pretty

4. *Harper's New Monthly Magazine*, p. 608.
5. 22 July 1894. Houghton Library, Harvard.

bad for the last three months – but hope to improve a little – no more illustrating of my own immortal works for little d.m. It's easy to write but very difficult to draw – as I told dear Mrs Humphrey [sic] Ward, & sketched her!'[6] Armstrong's only son, Ambrose, had died in April 1894, after two years of illness. His death at the age of eleven shattered Armstrong, who never entirely recovered from the blow. Armstrong's monument to his son, in plaster-relief, still stands in Abbott's Langley Parish Church, Hertfordshire. Although they had grown apart in their later years, Du Maurier felt profound sympathy for his old friend, and could scarcely find words to express his grief in his first letter of condolence. He wrote again, shakily now, in August 1894: 'I should like to think that you and Mrs Armstrong are beginning to get over the acute stage of your trouble. Trixy & the Missus are both anxious to hear how she is'.[7] Another loss which upset Du Maurier was the death of Bill Henley in 1893. He had not seen Henley for many years, but the memory of old affection was still strong: 'One day I was drawing his (Taffy's) whiskers from poor Henley's Photo & that very moment I heard of H's death! I felt creepy all down the back . . . only 60, & such a healthy fellow, without any vices that I can remember'.[8] Du Maurier was also worried about John Millais, who had been in indifferent health for some time. He was suffering from a throat complaint, soon to declare itself as cancer.

Even so, the visit to Whitby was a success at first. The Smalleys and the Comyns Carrs were there, and Du Maurier made the acquaintance of the young impressionist painter, Laurence (Peter) Harrison, a founder member of the New English Art Club. Du Maurier flirted mildly with his wife, the singer and poet, Alma Stretell, who taught him Italian expressions with which to impress Henry James. She stayed on with her brother-in-law, 'Ginx' Harrison, when her husband returned to Paris to work. She was an engaging and intelligent companion, and an excellent substitute for Emma, who had been in bed since the middle of August, suffering from rheumatism. Du Maurier was sad when Alma Harrison left Whitby, but he had to stay on to look after Emma: 'Hélas! tout avait commencé si bien! (except the weather – the biggest liar I know is the public barometer at the corner of Skinner St & Flowergate & which has been pointing to "set fair" ever since we came'.[9] The Du

6. 22 July 1894.   8. To T. Armstrong, 18 Nov. 1893 and 1 Jan. 1894.
7. 5 Aug. 1894.   9. To Henry James, 11 Sept. 1894. Houghton Library, Harvard.

Mauriers spent ten weeks in Whitby as a result of Emma's illness, missing their holiday in Boxmoor with Beatrix, and the birth of Sylvia's second son, for which they had promised to return.

Du Maurier himself, however, came back to London feeling less tired and jaded, with the plan of a new novel already revolving in his mind. He wrote to Millais that he was 'trying hard to evolve another book. Sometimes I think it will come; sometimes I feel like giving it up and writing my reminiscences, which are very mild compared with yours'.[10] By December 1894, the novel was under way. 'I've got it on the brain',[11] Du Maurier told the American writer, Miss Sarah Orne Jewett, who had written to describe a performance of *An Evening with Trilby* in Boston. Robert Sherard visited him in the autumn of 1894, and saw a 'pile of thin copy-books, blue and red. "A fortnight's work on my new novel", said Du Maurier'.[12]

The Martian proved a more difficult task to write than *Trilby*, although it was more autobiographical. The fluency and creative enthusiasm which had characterized *Peter Ibbetson* were absent: 'I revise, very carefully now, for I am taking great pains'.[13] The novel, however, shows little sign of revision or careful construction. Du Maurier had never been a disciplined writer, or a technical craftsman, like Henry James, but he now threw all restraints overboard. *The Martian* is a novel of nostalgic reminiscence, a long and confused statement of personal emotion, rather than a work of literature. More than Du Maurier's other novels, it suffers.

The hero of the novel, Barty Josselin, is the last expression of Du Maurier's private mythology. The son of a beautiful French actress of humble origin and an English nobleman, Josselin's parentage recalls *The Princess Casamassima* and Mary-Anne Clarke's relationship with the Duke of York. Jocelyn was a Du Maurier family name (it was one of Ellen Clarke's names) and there is reason to believe that Du Maurier connected it with the great Rohan family, who lived at Castle Josselin in Brittany. Whether this is a clue to Ellen Clarke's parentage is unknown, but it is significant that in *The Martian*, Barty Josselin's grandfather, the Marquis of Whitby, lives at Castle Rohan, and has the crest of the real Rohan family, 'Roi je suis, prince ne daigne, Rohan suis'. Josselin is not Jocelyn, however, and Du Maurier may only have come across the Rohans fortuitously in his researches into the history of his own family.

10. Millais, II, 283.   12. Sherard, p. 392.
11. 2 Dec. 1894. Colby College Library.   13. Sherard, p. 400.

Two other characters in *The Martian* take their names from French castles, Bussy-Rabutin and Laferté. Barty Josselin combines the superb physical characteristics of his peasant birth (he is a brilliant swimmer, jumper and gymnast) with the refinements of a great aristocratic heritage. His beauty is almost feminine, but there is nothing effeminate in his character. He is illegitimate, like Hyacinthe Robinson in *The Princess Casamassima*, but this is a source of romantic mystery, not of squalid reality. Far more than Peter Ibbetson or Little Billee, Josselin is an expression of Du Maurier's myth-making about himself, an incredible figure who combines an impossible number of virtues. In a novel he is a disastrously inadequate and unreal character. His charm, laboriously described, is quite unconvincing, and so is the excessive admiration which he arouses in others. Du Maurier's opening description of his hero, 'it soon became evident that he was a most exceptional little person',[14] does not encourage the reader's sympathy. Barty Josselin's only failing is his weakness for women, which is excusable in one so generous and attractive.

The Martian has a similar structure to Du Maurier's earlier novels, with the early autobiographical chapters developing into a melodramatic plot. The extra-sensory theme, which had become such an essential ingredient of his novels, is here concerned with the possession of Barty Josselin's mind by a being from Mars, Martia, who is later reincarnated in one of his children, Marty, based on May Du Maurier. Under Martia's influence, Barty Josselin begins writing brilliant books which change the fate of the world. Martia's intention is to transmit to earth her profound knowledge of the universe.

The narrator of the story is Bob Maurice, Barty Josselin's closest friend. In the introduction, he seeks to establish the truth of the story, as Madge Plunket does in *Peter Ibbetson*, by taking Barty Josselin's fame for granted: 'When so great a man dies, it is generally found that a tangled growth of more or less contentious literature has already gathered round his name during his lifetime'.[15] Unfortunately, the reader is never convinced of Barty Josselin's greatness, nor is he told of what exactly it consists. The vagueness which surrounds his writings, and the reasons for his success, is never adequately resolved. His life has the quality of a fairy story.

The early part of the book is a straightforward account of Josselin's

14. p. 34.
15. p. 1.

life, narrated by Maurice, who is present at most of the scenes he describes. They both attend Pension Brossard, arriving there in the same year that Du Maurier had first gone to the Pension Froussard, 1847. The experiences of Barty and Maurice at school exactly parallel those of Du Maurier and Eugène. Maurice's middle-of-the-road career at the Pension Brossard may be a more accurate reflection of Du Maurier's own experience at school, but it is Josselin who fails the baccalauréat. The events of Du Maurier's own life are divided between his two characters after they leave school. Bob Maurice returns to London, and tries to become a scientist, as Du Maurier had done. Like Du Maurier, he enters University College in October 1851, and is set up by his father in his own laboratory two years later. Maurice also wastes his time there, and obtains few commissions.

Having told the story of his own dreary years in London through Maurice, Du Maurier is able to invent a suitably glamorous career for his hero without any qualms. Barty Josselin, six feet three or four inches in height, enters the Guards and becomes one of the most sought-after young men in London. Pursued by noble ladies, involved in love affairs and scandals, he always behaves like a perfect gentleman. Here, at last, Du Maurier was able to give shape to his dreams of the life he had always hoped to enjoy in London. Maurice, on the other hand, relinquishes his autobiographical connection with Du Maurier's life, entering the family business, and eventually becoming a Member of Parliament and a baronet. His is a straightforward success story. It is now Barty Josselin who follows in Du Maurier's footsteps, leaving art-school in Paris for Antwerp, where he too goes blind in one eye, and faces the dreadful doubt and gloom which had once attacked the novelist. The intervention of Martia is the first really fictional episode to occur in the novel. Josselin moves from Antwerp to Dusseldorf, and from there to London, where he starts to work as an illustrator. He marries Leah Gibson in Marylebone Church, where the Du Mauriers were married, and his first daughter is born on the same day as Beatrix Du Maurier, 1 January. Unlike Du Maurier, however, he rejects the daughter of a wealthy nobleman before deciding to marry the penniless Leah Gibson for love alone. The reappearance of Martia marks the end of long autobiographical introduction.

Martia dictates ideas and instructions to Barty Josselin in his sleep, which he then writes down and develops during the day. This extraordinary phenomenon, which is the basis for the second part of

139. A Little White Point of Interrogation, *The Martian*

the novel, is less credible than the 'dreaming true' of *Peter Ibbetson*, or the mesmerism of *Trilby*. It involves Du Maurier in a long explanation of the physical characteristics of life on Mars and of the creatures who live there. Speculation about life on other planets had been aroused in England with the publication of Sir David Brewster's book, *More Worlds than One*, which Du Maurier had read in 1867. Brewster's thesis is that the presence of an all-powerful God, proves, rather than refutes, the existence of life on other worlds. He also suggests that the inhabitants of other planets would conform to the conditions and climate there. Du Maurier was an inadequate writer of science fiction, and his description of Mars is banal and uninteresting.

Du Maurier never actually states that Martia exists, and, at times, he gives support to the idea that she is only a figment of Josselin's imagination. On one occasion, he asks her: 'Are you *me*?'[16] Her influence on his conduct does not amount to proof of her existence, for she is only able to effect it in his sleep. As she herself says, when she prevents Barty from committing suicide: 'I have managed to make you, in your sleep, throw away your poison'.[17] Josselin himself

16. p. 309.
17. p. 264.

considered the possibility that his 'brain in sleep had at last become so active, through the exhausting and depleting medical regime . . . that it actually was able to dictate its will to his body'.[18] Only at the end of the book, when Barty's daughter, Marty, calls out to him in Martia's voice, is any concrete evidence of her existence offered. Martia is less a character than a device in a contrived and artificial story, which Du Maurier was not experienced enough to handle with any conviction.

Josselin's weariness with success, his sense of being unworthy, if not a positive fraud, and his distaste for journalists, are obvious references to the *Trilby* boom. His books, however, are of a very different calibre: 'in two months *Sardonyx* was before the reading world, and the middle-aged reader will remember the wild enthusiasm and the storm it raised'.[19] 'He has robbed Death of nearly all its terrors . . . for to the most sceptical he (and only he) has restored that absolute conviction of an indestructible germ of Immortality within us'.[20] Such preposterous claims are impossible to justify, even had Du Maurier been a more imaginative writer. As it is, his literal attempt to explain a spiritual and philosophical revolution of the most profound kind is naïve and absurd. The titles of Barty Josselin's books, *The Infinitely Little, Interstellar Harmonics, The Footprints of Aurora, Étoiles Mortes, Gleams, La Quatrième Dimension,* and the extracts from his work, like the 'Song of the Seminarist', should not have been included:

> Twas April, and the sky was clear,
> An east wind blowing keenly;
> The sun gave out but little cheer,
> For all it shone serenely.[21]

Such examples reduce the novel to the level of comic farce. Du Maurier was not an intellectual, and he would have been wise to have abandoned such an inflated theme.

Josselin, like Du Maurier, idolises beauty. Every one of the major characters in *The Martian* has that nobility of stature so familiar to *Punch* readers from Du Maurier's cartoons. In his two earlier novels, Du Maurier had attempted to introduce an element of 'low life' with figures like Gecko and the Lintots. Such characterization did

18. p. 384.
19. p. 368.
20. p. 385.
21. p. 231.

not come easily to him, and it was probably only preconceived ideas about realism in the novel, which made him indulge in it. In *The Martian*, he entirely abandoned himself to upper-class beauty and manners. The narrator and the hero are both splendid physical specimens, and so are the other suitors for Leah Gibson's hand, Scatchard, and Captain Graham Reece, the future Lord Ironsides. Leah Gibson, and her rival, Julia Royce, later Lady Ironsides, are commanding females, with a classical purity of form and feature. They are representative, however, of contrasting ideals; Leah is the Rebecca, Julia the Rowena, of *Ivanhoe*. Leah has that Jewish beauty which Du Maurier so much admired, almost in spite of himself. With her dark good looks, and her flawless white skin, she is an idealization of Emma Wightwick, from whom she is obviously drawn. In Julia Royce, Du Maurier described a perfect type of English aristocratic beauty. She is immensely tall, nearly six feet, fair and blond, with elegance and nobility, a perfect grande dame. Most of the supporting characters in the novel are described in superlative terms.

Throughout his life Josselin, like his creator, unashamedly prefers beautiful people, and believes that only they should be allowed to procreate. He continually alludes to Maurice's physical defects, most notably his crooked nose, and Maurice is thankful that he has not been allowed to perpetuate his faults. Selective breeding was one of Du Maurier's favourite hobby horses. Barty Josselin's prejudices against the merchant classes are a reflection of those of his creator. He 'preferred the commonest artisan to M. Jourdain, the bourgeois gentilhomme'.[22] Nevertheless, he marries the daughter of a shop-keeper, as Du Maurier had done, and she dominates his home. Leah Gibson has none of Emma's stubbornness or strength. The sole occasion on which she shows any spirit, is her angry reaction to the description of herself in a newspaper, 'silent and cold and uncommunicative... good, motherly English wife'.[23]

Bob Maurice is much more convincing character than Barty Josselin or Leah Gibson. He is present at many of the important events of Josselin's life, and his apologetic apostrophes to the reader strike a note of truth: 'The reader will conclude that I was a kind of over-affectionate, pestering, dull dog, who made this brilliant youth's life a burden to him'.[24] Maurice's position in the book is that

22. p. 41.
23. p. 395.

24. p. 136.

140. Three Little
Maids from School,
The Martian

of a foil. He is in some ways representative of what Du Maurier
himself had achieved by 1896, success and standing, but not the
artistic greatness which he had once desired. Du Maurier's division
of himself into these two characters, Josselin and Maurice, is comparable to Henry James' representation of what was and what might
have been, in the hero of his partly-autobiographical short story, 'The
Jolly Corner', published in 1908. Maurice's later career is compressed
into short summaries. We are never told quite how he rose to the dizzy
heights of 'The Right Honourable Sir Robert Maurice, Bart., M.P.,
&c., &c., &c. That's me. I take up a whole line of manuscript. I
might be a noble lord if I chose, and take up two!'[25] Maurice, like
Du Maurier, enjoys giving the appearance of being a philistine:
'There I go again – digressing as usual, and quoting poetry, and
trying to be literary and all that!'[26] Although *The Martian* suffers
from a lack of coherence and convincing characterization, parts of
the book are surprisingly well written. If the early scenes have not the
effortless delight of those in *Peter Ibbetson*, they are vivid and entertaining:

25. p. 423.
26. p. 78.

141. I'm a Philistine and not Ashamed, *The Martian*

> [we] visited old historical castles and mediaeval ruins – Châteaudun and others – and fished in beautiful pellucid tributaries of the Loire – shot over 'des chiens anglais' – danced half the night with charming people – wandered in lovely parks and woods, and beautiful old formal gardens with fishponds, terraces, statues, marble fountains; charmilles, pelouses, quinconconces; and all the flowers and all the fruits of France.[27]

This contrasts well with Du Maurier's description of 'the pond of respite' in the forest, with its tragic history. Du Maurier's account of his days in Malines, with the threat of blindness hanging over

27. p. 82.

him, conveys a horror that was still vividly fresh in his memory. On any level, the book is very readable, and nothing in it approaches the banality of the last quarter of *Trilby*. With its anecdotal and rambling construction, and its embarrassing hero, it has none of the qualities, however, which give *Peter Ibbetson* a claim to be considered as a novel of distinction.

Du Maurier only finished *The Martian* shortly before his death in 1896. He corrected it meticulously at every stage, and it became his favourite book, and, as he believed, his best. He intended to follow it with another novel, set in Malines, which would be concerned with an ordinary middle-aged and middle-class couple, who suddenly discover that they can fly, and visit exotic countries all over the world. He never began work on this last book, and he might have been further discouraged by the harsh criticisms passed on *The Martian*, which he did not live to hear.

Writing *The Martian* helped Du Maurier to escape from some of his more urgent concerns. The dramatic version of *Trilby* adapted for the stage by the American dramatist, Paul Potter, was first performed in the United States in 1895, and further added to the popularity of the book. Du Maurier had no financial rights in the dramatic version, and was therefore not directly affected by the American performances. Early in 1895, however, Herbert Beerbohm Tree saw the play in New York, and realised that the part of Svengali was made for him. He bought the manuscript of the play, and returned to London to produce it in his own theatre. Du Maurier had, however, already sold the English rights for £75 to William Terriss. Terriss had no play, and he sold the rights to Tree for £100. Du Maurier was in Paris with the *Punch* staff while these negotiations were taking place, and he was bombarded with telegrams.

On his return from Paris, Du Maurier was plagued by Tree, who wanted his help in the search for an actress to play Trilby. It was Mrs William Playfair, who finally suggested Dorothea Baird, and it was she who played the part. Miss Baird was a professional actress, but she was little known and comparatively inexperienced. Du Maurier, who had seen her as a child on Hampstead Heath, was not sure if she was suitable for the role, until he saw her photograph: 'I said, "No acting will be wanted; for here *is* Trilby!" However, I was reckoning without Mr Tree. He listened, but was not convinced'.[28] Tree felt that Dorothea Baird was too much of a lady to be

28. A. Bright, 'Mr Du Maurier at Home', *Idler*, VIII (Dec. 1895), p. 421.

a good actress, and it took several auditions, and a flat refusal from Du Maurier to consider anyone else, before he was convinced.

Dorothea Baird was an excellent choice, for, although she was not a great performer, she had a natural gaiety and simplicity which suited the role, and charmed the audience. Tree, in contrast, was superbly histrionic:

> Tree's Svengali was the complete embodiment of the pictures and descriptions in the book: it was fantastic, weird and comical in turns, and rose to great heights of tragic intensity. His playing at the piano, his wild dancing at the studio supper-party, his delicious scene with the Rev. Thomas Bagot when he pulls down the model's skirt over her knee, and at last his failing strength, all combined to create a display of genius beyond all possible praise or commensuration. It was Tree's masterpiece of character-acting. [29]

Little Billee was originally played by another Hampstead actor, a draper's son called Evans, whom Du Maurier had discovered. He had used him as a model for his illustrations of Little Billee in the novel itself. Canon Ainger, who saw the play in Bristol, called it 'a ridiculous parody of the novel',[30] but he managed to enjoy the evening. All that was best in the book, the gentle writing, and the Parisian atmosphere, was sacrificed to melodrama. Everything leading up to Trilby's flight was compressed into the first two acts, and her reason for leaving Little Billee was disastrously changed. In the play Mrs Bagot's pleas do not persuade her, and Trilby and Little Billee are about to marry despite her. At the last minute Trilby is drawn away by Svengali's mesmeric pull. She is thus reduced to little more than a puppet, and her nobility in giving up her lover for the sake of his future is lost. The third act was taken up with the performance at which Svengali dies in his box, but another major, and not unjustifiable change was made in the fourth. Instead of dying slowly and drearily, Trilby recovers and agrees to marry Little Billee. Then a photograph of Svengali is brought in, she sings as in the opera-house, and then dies. In comparison with the book the play was over-dramatic, tasteless and often vulgar, making a good deal of Trilby's modelling and past love-affairs. However, it was very popular both in England and the United States.

The play was first performed in Manchester in October 1895,

29. Hoyer Millar, p. 154.
30. 4 Dec. 1895.

when Du Maurier was on holiday in Folkestone. After Emma's
illness in 1894, he had been wary of returning to Whitby: 'Tant va
la cruche à l'eau, qu' à la fin elle se brise!'[31] he told Sarah Orne
Jewett. James shared his doubts: 'You have gone there once too
often – give it up forever'.[32] In Folkestone, the weather was good,
but Du Maurier felt nervous and unwell. James became so worried
about his friend that he promised to come and visit him: 'we will
change all that: just wait till I get hold of you'.[33] James could
sympathise with Du Maurier's worries about the play, for his own
Guy Domville had failed the previous year. His arrival did something
to raise Du Maurier's spirits, who wrote to Armstrong: 'The place
suits me, I think & I am better in general health, and have "got the
hump" a little less severely than I had'.[34] During August, Du
Maurier paid what proved to be his last visit to France, and it was,
predictably, a sentimental journey:

> Last week we went to Boulogne & spent the night & visited my sainted
> grandmother's grave but couldn't find it – only my Aunt Mary's, on
> whose tombstone I deposited a little yellow wreath . . . Gerald won two
> pounds ten at petits chevaux, and the harbour stank all night & the food
> was good & the bedroom beastly – and the sea like a lake both ways –
> and Frenchman pleases me not, nor Frenchwoman either.[35]

Soon after their return from Boulogne Emma was ill again, and Du
Maurier, gloomy and depressed, decided not to go to Manchester
for the opening of the play. He sent Charles Hoyer Millar instead,
who returned in jubilation to report a huge success. Indeed, it was
the play which made *Trilby* popular in England.

Beerbohm Tree's production of *Trilby* opened at the Haymarket
Theatre in London on 30 October. The success in Manchester had
ensured a full house, which included the Prince and Princess of
Wales. The play was greeted with thunderous applause, and Du
Maurier was called to the Royal Box, presented and congratulated.
The Princess revealed that she had not read the book, by remarking
that she 'did not like Miss Baird having naked feet'.[36] The excitement of the occasion was bad for Du Maurier's nerves; he was left
more gloomy than ever. Dining with Lord and Lady Wolseley in the
late summer of 1895 he was asked the name of his new novel: 'I

31. 2 Dec. 1894. Colby College Library.
32. 12 Sept. 1894. Houghton Library, Harvard.
33. Aug. 1895. Houghton Library, Harvard.

34. 26 Aug. 1895.
35. 26 Aug. 1895.
36. Hoyer Millar, p. 156.

think', said Du Maurier, with a humorous smile, 'I'll call it "Soured by Success" '.[37]

The Du Mauriers finally gave up New Grove House in June 1895, and moved to 17 Oxford Square, near Hyde Park. In spite of his dissatisfaction with Hampstead, the decision to leave it was a surprising one. Du Maurier had a profound sense of place, and England for him was always associated with Hampstead and Whitby, as France was associated with Paris and Boulogne. Old, ill and depressed, he left his home and the familiar Heath, for a house and neighbourhood which had no associations for him. He only survived the move by a year, and he was consistently unhappy in Oxford Square. James described this time as 'a troubled, inconsequent year, in which the clock of his new period kept striking a different hour from the clock of his old spirit'.[38] Even James scarcely understood Du Maurier's motives for leaving Hampstead. He thought that it proceeded from a desire 'to simplify', to look again 'in a kind of resistant placidity, a stoicism of fidelity, at the things he had always loved, turning away more than ever from those he never had'.[39] James' last vision of Du Maurier was on the top of a London omnibus, looking down on the 'botherations' around him, as he had once looked down from Hampstead. Subtle as James' explanation is, it is not a wholly satisfactory one. Du Maurier was not only weary of Hampstead, but weary of life, and his move to central London should perhaps be seen as a recognition that he had only a short time to live. It was almost the expression of a death wish.

In February 1896, John Millais, who was dying of cancer of the throat succeeded Lord Leighton as President of the Royal Academy. Scarcely able to speak, and in great pain, Millais finally collapsed in May, and he lay in his room until his death on 13 August 1896. Writing to Miss Millais in June 1896, Du Maurier told her:

> I have often been to your door & read the bulletin, but did not like to ring – much as I should like to see you or Lady Millais. I wish you could manage to convey to him, if an opportunity should arise, how constantly he is in my thoughts, and what a trouble of my own all his trouble has been.[40]

As a result of this letter, Du Maurier was invited to visit Millais on

37. H. Lucy, *Sixty Years in the Wilderness* (1909), p. 394.
38. *Harper's New Monthly Magazine*, p. 608.
39. *Harper's New Monthly Magazine*, p. 608.
40. 3 June 1896. Pierpont Morgan Library.

7 June: 'the sight of him lying ill & weak was so great a grief to me that I forgot all the cheery things I meant to tell him. And yet he looked much better than I really thought he would'.[41] To his own family, Du Maurier expressed the horror he had felt in seeing the 'god' he had admired in 1862, 'always till then clean shaven, lying in bed with his face all disfigured by the unchecked growth of white hair on his face and chin'.[42]

In late July, Du Maurier set off for Whitby once more. Before leaving he attended his last *Punch* dinner: 'He looked curiously grey in the face, one sadly remembers, and, to begin with, was unusually quiet. But he brisked up when cigarette-time came, and stayed late in merriest mood'.[43] *The Martian* was finished, but only a few of the illustrations were ready. James interpreted this return to Whitby as 'half a cry of fondness and half a confession of despair . . . he found himself braving once too often, on a pious theory of its perfection, its interminable hills and its immitigable blasts'.[44] James did not visit him there that year, feeling too oppressed by memories of Lowell, but Canon Ainger joined the Du Mauriers, in August. The 'interminable hills' were wearing Du Maurier out, but he obstinately continued his rigorous programme of walks, until he became too ill to continue. 'It is only in going uphill that one realises how fast one is going downhill'.[45] He was by now almost blind, but with a supreme effort of will, he continued to execute his cartoons for *Punch*, inspired by what James later called 'the spark, burning still and intense, of his life-long, indefeasible passion for seeing his work through'.[46] The drawings became scratchier, but they still appeared. On 13 August, John Millais died and Du Maurier was asked to be a pall-bearer at the funeral in St Paul's Cathedral. In a pathetic and shakily written letter, he asked to be excused: 'This is to me a matter of profound regret, as I should have felt a deep satisfaction in paying this last act of homage to your dear father, as well as holding it a very great honour to myself. Indeed I had hoped to go up for the funeral anyhow, had I been better in health'.[47]

41. 7 June 1896. Pierpont Morgan Library.
42. Hoyer Millar, p. 182.
43. H. Lucy, *Sixty Years in the Wilderness* (1909), p. 395.
44. *Harper's New Monthly Magazine*, p. 602.
45. Sichel, p. 280.
46. *Harper's New Monthly Magazine*, p. 608.
47. 18 August 1896. Pierpont Morgan Library.

On this last visit to Whitby, Du Maurier must surely have remembered his first in 1864, when he had accompanied Leech on the
now familiar walks along the cliffs. John Leech, depressed and ill,
returned to London to die, as Du Maurier was now doing, and the
coincidence was a striking one. Du Maurier came back to London in
mid-September, and immediately saw his doctor. He was told that
he was suffering from heart-strain, brought on by his walks in hilly
country, and that he must rest in bed for the next three weeks, 'with
the alternative, which he did not use, of being carried back to his
bed room if he came down stairs'.[48] Instead of recovering, Du
Maurier's condition grew steadily worse. He had a gastric complaint
and swollen gums from a bad tooth, and he could only take nourish-
ment in liquid form. His eyesight grew weaker, and he began to
cough, apparently developing asthma.

When the three weeks were over it was clear that Du Maurier
was not well enough to get up. He was himself convinced that he
would never recover. James and Armstrong, those opposing forces
in his life, visited him together and found him 'talkative & apparently
not much depressed although he said it was "all over with him" '.[49]
Gerald came to visit his father on his way to join Beerbohm Tree in
the provincial tour of *Trilby*. As he left, Du Maurier smiled and
whispered, 'Si c'est la mort, ce n'est pas gai'.[50] He found it more
difficult to breathe, and he was not allowed visitors. Like many
hypochondriacs, he became calmer now that he was desperately ill,
and his composure raised the hopes of his family. On Wednesday
afternoon, 7 October, he asked Emma to read him some poems by
Mallarmé, and he talked with her for some time about the reading.
Armstrong was waiting downstairs, when a new specialist arrived
who confirmed that there was a dangerous accumulation of matter
around the heart and lungs. He gave Du Maurier an injection of
morphia to relieve the effects of asthma, and promised to call again
in the morning. At Bouverie Street the *Punch* staff, assembled for the
weekly dinner, waited anxiously for news. At nine o'clock, a telegram arrived, expressing a hope he might recover. Even his family
was more optimistic that evening. At three o'clock, however, the
doctor in attendance awakened Emma to tell her that her husband
was either dying or already dead. The post mortem revealed that he

48. T. Armstrong to John Chandler Bancroft, 11–12 Oct. 1896.
49. T. Armstrong to Bancroft, 11–12 Oct. 1896.
50. *Gerald*, p. 71.

had a 'mass of matter' in his heart 'from which it would have been impossible to extract it'.[51]

Du Maurier had always expressed a wish to be cremated, a rather unusual choice at the time, and one which attracted attention. Nothing else can explain or excuse the ghoulish account of the cremation in the *Hampstead and Highgate Express*. The body, in a plain coffin, was taken to Woking on Friday, 9 October, and the private mourners, Guy and Gerald, Charles Hoyer Millar, Llewelyn Davies and Tom Armstrong, followed on Saturday morning. Charles Hoyer Millar later described the occasion:

> being admitted into the furnace-room [we] saw – much to our horror though it was too late to go back – the swathed body lifted from the coffin and put on a steel cradle which was pushed into the furnace. At that time the process was a lengthy one; we had brought our lunch with us and stood in the damp, cold, autumn weather leaning against the neighbouring fir trees. We were all too miserable, mentally and physically, to talk, but Gerald, unable to restrain himself, burst out with, 'At all events we won't have to play rounders after lunch'.[52]

According to the reporter, who was probably accurate, the weather was brilliantly sunny; Hoyer Millar's account is another example of the 'pathetic fallacy'. After three quarters of an hour, the five mourners collected the urn containing the ashes, and took them back to Hampstead. Du Maurier's intentions in being cremated are clear. He hated the idea of corruption, but he did not apparently appreciate the practical difficulties.

The funeral, held in Hampstead Parish Church on Tuesday, 13 October, was a very different affair. Ainger had long ago decided that he would conduct the service, in spite of Du Maurier's declared agnosticism, and he was assisted by two local clergymen. Du Maurier's favourite pieces of music, Schumann's 'Der Nussbaum' and Schubert's 'Serenade' and 'Adieu', were played on the organ. Almost the entire *Punch* staff was present, only Burnand and Tenniel of Du Maurier's generation; his old Hampstead neighbours, Sir Walter Besant, Basil Champneys and Walter Field; Frederick Yeames and G. A. Storey of the St John's Wood Clique; and Tom Armstrong, Thomas Lamont and Edward Poynter of the old Paris

51. T. Armstrong to Bancroft, 11–12 Oct. 1896.
52. Hoyer Millar, p. 182.

group. Perhaps the saddest person present, apart from Emma, was Henry James, who was profoundly moved by the service.

The urn was carried to the new churchyard on the other side of Church Row. Ainger read the last words of the service over the grave, which is now marked by an unusual wooden memorial, a long panel parallel to the grave supported by two Celtic crosses at either end. It is almost identical to the gravestone of Ambrose Armstrong, and both may well have been the work of Tom Armstrong. Inscribed on the panel are the names of George Du Maurier, and Emma, who died in 1915; of Gerald and May, who died in 1924 and 1934; and of Guy, who was killed in France in 1915. Nearby is the grave of Sylvia and Arthur Llewelyn Davies. Beatrix, who died in 1913 of cancer, like all Du Maurier's children except Guy, preferred to be buried near her home at Bovingdon. The only other words on Du Maurier's grave are the last couplet of his translation of Léon Monte-Naken's 'Peu de chose':

> A little work, a little play
> To keep us going – and so, good-day!
>
> A little warmth, a little light
> Of love's bestowing – and so, good-night!
>
> A little fun, to match the sorrow
> Of each day's growing – and so, good-morrow!
>
> A little trust that when we die
> We reap our sowing! And so – good-bye!

142. Vignette from *Trilby*

Appendix

A. PUBLISHED WORKS BY GEORGE DU MAURIER

1861   'Recollections of an English Goldmine', *Once A Week*, V (21 September 1861), pp. 356–364.

1880   *English Society at Home: From the Collection of Mr Punch.*

1890   'The Illustration of Books from the Serious Artist's Point of View', *Magazine of Art* (August and September 1890), pp. 349–353 and 371–375.

1891   *Peter Ibbetson.* First published in *Harper's Monthly Magazine*, XXII (June to November 1891).

1894   *Trilby.* First published in *Harper's Monthly Magazine*, XXVII–XXVIII (January to July 1894).

1897   *The Martian.* First published in *Harper's Monthly Magazine*, XXXII–XXXIV (October 1896 to July 1897).

1898   *Social Pictorial Satire.* First published in *Harper's Monthly Magazine*, XXXVI (February to March 1898).

1898   *A Legend of Camelot: Pictures and Poems, etc.*

B. BOOKS AND ARTICLES DIRECTLY CONCERNED WITH GEORGE DU MAURIER

AINGER, ALFRED. 'George Du Maurier in Hampstead', *Hampstead Annual* (1897), pp. 12–19.

'George Du Maurier', *Dictionary of National Biography*, Supplement, II, pp. 161–166.

ARMSTRONG, THOMAS. 'Reminiscences of George Du Maurier', in *Thomas Armstrong C.B. A Memoir*, edited by L. M. Lamont, 1912.

BRIGHT, ADDISON. 'Mr Du Maurier at Home', *Idler*, VIII (December 1895), pp. 415–422.

DU MAURIER, DAPHNE. *Gerald – A Portrait.* 1934.

The Du Mauriers. 1937.

The Young George Du Maurier: A Selection of his Letters, 1860–1867, edited by D. Du Maurier, with a biographical index by D. P. Whiteley. 1951.

FEIPEL, L. N. 'The American Issues of Trilby', *Colophon*, II, No 4 (Autumn 1937), pp. 537–549.

GILDER, J. L. and J. B. *Trilbyana: The Rise and Progress of a Popular Novel.* New York, 1895.

GUTHRIE, T. A. 'Some Personal Recollections of Du Maurier', in 'George Du
    Maurier Centenary Number', *Punch*, CLXXXVI (7 March 1934),
    p. 2.
HOYER MILLAR, C. *George Du Maurier and Others.* 1937.
JAMES, HENRY. 'Du Maurier and London Society', *Century Magazine*, XXXVI
    (May 1883), 48–65. Reprinted in *Partial Portraits* (1888).
    Notes on Drawings by George Du Maurier. 1884. Catalogue of Fine Art
    Society Exhibition, 23 June 1884.
    'George Du Maurier', *Harper's Weekly Magazine*, XXXVIII (14 April
    1894), pp. 341–342.
    'George Du Maurier', *Harper's Monthly Magazine*, XXV (September
    1897), pp. 594–609.
LANOIRE, M. 'Un Anglo-Francais Georges Du Maurier', *Revue de Paris*
    (15 March 1940), pp. 236–281.
LUCAS, E. V. 'George Du Maurier at Thirty-Three', *Cornhill*, CL (October
    1934), pp. 385–410.
LUSK, L. 'The Artistic Position of George Du Maurier', *Art Journal* (Nov-
    ember 1900), pp. 337–340.
MOSCHELES, F. *In Bohemia with Du Maurier.* 1896. A shortened form appeared
    in an article with the same title in *The Century Magazine*, LII (May
    1896), pp. 105–119.
SCULL, W. DELAPAINE 'George Du Maurier, Romanticist', *Magazine of Art*
    (1892), pp. 229–231.
SHERARD, R. H. 'The Author of Trilby', *McClure's Magazine*, IV (October
    1895), pp. 391–400. Reprinted in the *Westminster Budget* (13 December
    1895), pp. 21–25.
STEVENSON, LIONEL 'George Du Maurier and the Romantic Novel', *Essays
    by Divers Hands* (1960), pp. 36–54.
WALLIS, A. F. 'George Du Maurier's Characters', *Fin de Siècle*, edited by
    N. Wallis, 1947, pp. 81–95.
WHITELEY, DEREK PEPYS *George Du Maurier.* 1948.
    'Du Maurier's Illustrations for "Once A Week"', Alphabet and
    Image, V (September 1947), pp. 17–29.
WINTERICH, J. T. 'George Du Maurier and Trilby' in *Books and the Man.*
    New York, 1929, pp. 102–122.
WOOD, T. M. *George Du Maurier – The Satirist of the Victorians : A Review of his
    Art and Personality.* 1913.

C. A SELECT BIBLIOGRAPHY OF OTHER WORKS
CONSULTED

BURNAND, F. *Records and Reminiscences.* 2 vols. 1904.
EDEL, LÉON. *Henry James : The Conquest of London. 1870–1883.* 1962.
    Henry James : The Middle Years. 1884–1894. 1963.
GUTHRIE, T. A. (FRED ANSTEY). *A Long Retrospect.* 1936.
HAMILTON, WALTER. *The Aesthetic Movement in England.* 1882.
IONIDES, LUKE. *Memories.* Privately printed, Paris. 1925.

JAMES, HENRY. *The Notebooks of Henry James*, edited F. O. Matthiessen and
    K. B. Murdock. New York, 1947.

LAYARD, G. S. *A Great Punch Editor: Being the Life, Letters and Diaries of
    Shirley Brooks.* 1907.

LUCY, SIR HENRY. *Sixty Years in the Wilderness.* 1909.
    The Diary of a Journalist. 1920.

MILLAIS, J. G. *The Life and Letters of Sir John Millais.* 2 vols. 1899.

PANTON, MRS (MISS FRITH). *Leaves from a Life.* 1908.

PENNELL, E. R. and J. *The Life of James McNeill Whistler.* 2 vols. 1909.

PRICE, R. G. G. *A History of Punch.* 1957.

PRINSEP, V. C. 'A Student's Life in Paris in 1859', *Magazine of Art* (February
    1904), pp. 167–172.

REID, FORREST. *Illustrators of the Sixties.* 1928.

SICHEL, EDITH. *The Life and Letters of Alfred Ainger.* 1906.

SILVER, HENRY. *Diary: 1858–1870.* Unpublished, in the *Punch* offices.

SPIELMANN, M. H. *The History of Punch.* 1895.

D. MAGAZINES ILLUSTRATED BY GEORGE DU MAURIER

Cornhill Magazine, 1863–1886.
English Illustrated Magazine, 1884 and 1887.
Good Words, 1861 and 1872.
Harper's Magazine, 1880–1897.
Illustrated London News, 1860.
Illustrated Times, 1862.
The Leisure Hour, 1864–1865.
London Society, 1862–1868.
Once A Week, 1860–1867.
Sunday Magazine, 1864.

Index

Abbey, Edwin Austin, 214
À Beckett, Arthur, 361, 366
Aberdeen, Lord and Lady, 381
Agnew family, 198
Agnew, art dealers, 209, 371
Agnew, Tom, 198, 199
Agnew, William, 366
Aïdé, Georgina, 188
Aïdé, Hamilton, 188, 198, 394, 465
Ainger, Canon Alfred, 216, 314, 325–6, 370, 371, 379, 380, 383, 389–91, 398, 417, 418, 428, 429, 433, 442, 453, 457, 458, 492, 495, 498
Airey, James Talbot, 208
Airlie, Lady, 381
Albert, Prince, 85
Alden, Mr, 429
Allingham, William, 187, 188, 212, 400–1, 425, 428, 429; *The music master*, 108
Alma-Tadema, Lawrence, 66, 102, 214, 219, 308, 381, 438
Alma-Tadema, Mrs, 381
Anderson, Mary, 381
Angelico, Fra, 264
Antwerp, academy of fine arts, 64, 65–68
Armstrong, Ambrose George, 383, 482, 498
Armstrong, Mary Alice, 232, 383, 482
Armstrong, Thomas; art student in Paris, 38, 44, 45, 46, 47, 48, 49, 50, 51, 53, 54, 57, 58, 59, 60, 63; on Whistler, 63; in Dusseldorf, 79, 80, 82, 83, 84; subsequent career, 38, 62, 232, 382–3; in *Trilby*, 53, 129, 441, 453, 454; *Memorials to his son*, 482, 498; *Reminiscences of Du Maurier*, 47, 56, 58, 448; other references, 89, 90, 93, 98, 118, 119, 121, 122, 126, 130, 132, 134, 140, 141, 142, 148, 155, 157, 158, 160, 164, 173–4, 196, 199, 200, 201, 207, 209, 210, 216, 228, 234, 254, 289, 371, 380, 396–7, 400, 433, 455, 470, 477, 478, 482, 496, 497, 498
Armstrong, Miss, 82
Arnold, Matthew, and Mrs, 219
Arrow, The, 161
Arts club, 153, 195, 458, 470
Ashton, 199
Aslin, Elizabeth, 287
Atelier system, 36–43
Aubery family, 1, 3
Austen, Jane; *Mansfield Park*, 340, 350

Baird, Dorothea, 491–2, 493
Balzac, Honoré de, 225
Bancroft, John Chandler, 79, 80, 98, 392–3, 496n, 497n
Barbizon school, 45, 46, 49, 54, 58
Barrie, James Matthew, 432
Baudelaire, Charles, 244, 245, 258, 289; *Les fleurs du mal*, 244–5
Bazille, Jean-Frédéric, 46
Beardsley, Aubrey, 184, 240, 243; *Morte d'Arthur*, 243
Bedford Park, Turnham Green, 251, 285, 287
Beefsteak club, 466, 467
Beerbohm, Max; *Seven men*, 251
Bell, Clara, 97, 152–3, 219
Bell, Courtenay, 152–3, 219
Bennett, Charles, H, 196
Bennett, Mrs, 196, 198
Benson, Edward Frederic; *As we were*, 258
Besant, Sir Walter, 31–2, 213, 497
Best, Henry, 79
Black, William; *Three feathers*, 370
Blackwoods, 88
Blake, William, 419
Blunt, Arthur, 196, 197, 199
Bodley, George Frederick, 208
Boileau, Nicolas, 213
Borgia, Lucrezia, 173
Botticelli, Sandro, 264–5
Boughton, George Henry, and Mrs, 381
Bowers, Georgina, 168

Bowker, R. R., 368–9, 370
Bowles, Alfred, 8, 13
Bowles, Charles, 8, 13, 112
Bowles, Mary Anne (née Clarke), 8, 13,
    143, 493
Bowman, 236
Bradbury and Evans, 162
Bradbury, William, 180, 181
Bradbury, William (the younger), 242,
    366, 367
Braddon, Mary Elizabeth, 460;
    Eleanor's victory, 145
Braquemond, Félix, 48, 289
Brassin, Louis, 74
Brett, Lady, 381
Brewster, Sir David; *More worlds than
    one*, 486
British Lion, The, 87
Brontë, Charlotte; *Jane Eyre*, 418
Brooke, Rupert, 423
Brooks, Charles William Shirley, 107,
    128, 158, 161, 163, 164, 165, 166, 168,
    169, 170, 181, 188, 191, 196, 198, 199,
    200, 201, 203, 225, 233, 236, 239, 240,
    241
Brooks, Mrs, 168, 188, 225, 233
Brown, Ford Madox, 175, 205, 284;
    An English autumn afternoon, 205
Browne, Hablôt Knight (Phiz), 88, 107,
    109, 125, 435
Browning, Elizabeth Barrett, 103, 327
Browning, Robert, 103, 213, 307, 380,
    456
Buchanan, Robert Williams; *The
    fleshly school of poetry*, 248
Burges, William, 97
Burnand, Francis, 145, 163, 164, 168,
    169, 170, 196, 197, 199, 203, 240, 241,
    278, 301, 307n, 361–2, 363, 364, 365,
    366, 381, 431, 497; *The Colonel*, 250
Burne-Jones, Edward, 99, 117, 118,
    130–1, 152–3, 173, 174, 178, 179, 209,
    210, 247, 258, 259, 261, 262, 280, 296,
    298–9, 308, 429, 477; *The flower of
    God*, 299; *The garden of the Hesperides*,
    210; *Heart of the rose tree*, 299; *Love
    among the ruins*, 210; *The prioress' tale*,
    299; *Sponsa de Libano*, 299; *The wine of
    Circe*, 209, 297
Burne-Jones, Georgiana, 130–1,
    152–3, 231, 430n
Burns, Robert, 213
Burton, Sir Frederic William, 239

Butler, Samuel, 14–15; *The way of all
    flesh*, 15
Butterfield, Harris, 44
Buzzard, Thomas, 458, 470
Byron, Lord, 19, 213, 245; *Sun of the
    sleepless, melancholy star*, 375

Caldecott, Randolph, 434
Calderon, Philip Hermogenes, 191,
    192, 194, 195
Calderon, Mrs, 191
Calverley, Charles Stuart, 31, 32
Cameron, Julia Margaret, 103, 225
Carlyle, Thomas, 161
Carolus-Duran, Émile Auguste, 37, 48
Carr, Jonathan, 285
Carr, Joseph Comyns, 219, 246, 251,
    396, 477, 479, 482
Carr, Mrs, 219, 246, 251, 273, 296n,
    298, 396, 479, 482
Carroll, Lewis, 88
'Carry' (Octavie L.), 70–72, 75, 76, 78,
    80, 81, 139, 451
Cassavetti, Mary (Mme Zambacco),
    117, 118
Century Magazine, The, 395, 399
Chalon brothers, Alfred and John, 192
Champneys, Basil, 208, 210, 212, 383,
    428, 497; *A quiet corner of England*, 212;
    Memoir of Coventry Patmore, 212
Chang, 220, 222, 228, 233, 369, 390,
    396, 397, 400, 410
Chang and Chung (giants), 191
Chapman, 129
Charles X, 244
Christie and son, 290
Churchill, Lady Randolph, 381
Cimabue, 251
Clarke, George, 7, 9, 11, 13, 24, 28, 30,
    33, 93, 123
Clarke, Georgina, 30, 121, 123–5, 140
Clarke, Joseph, 5
Clarke, Mary-Anne, 4–6, 7, 8, 9, 11, 12,
    28, 141, 143, 483, 493
Clarke, Robert (Bobby), 123, 124–5
Claxton, Florence; *The choice of Paris:
    an idyll*, 172
Clifford, William Kingdon, 235
Coates, Miss, 389
Coburn, Alvin Langdon, 399
Coleridge, Samuel Taylor, 161
Collins, Charles Allston; *Convent
    thoughts*, 178

Collins, William, 205
Collins, William Wilkie; *The moonstone*, 462; *The woman in white*, 205
Colvin, Sidney, 208
Constable, John, 204
Corneille, Pierre, 213
Cornhill Magazine, The, 88, 89, 107, 109, 129, 138, 143, 144, 148, 149, 150, 242, 370, 392, 393, 417, 441
Coronio, Aglaia (née Ionides), 99, 100–1, 102, 429
Courbet, Gustave, 45, 46, 47, 133
Cox and box, 106, 196–9
Crane, Walter, 259, 268, 295, 434
Crowhall, Joseph, 167
Cruikshank, George, 107, 434

Daily Telegraph, 119, 209
Dalrymple, Mrs John Warrender (née Pattle), 103
Dalziel brothers, 108
'Damask', 81, 124
Dante, 61
Darwin, Charles, 242, 327, 386; *On the origin of species*, 327
Darwin, Mrs George (Maud du Puy), 277
Daudet, Alphonse, 400, 406
Daudet, Léon, 406
David, Jacques-Louis, 38
Davies, Arthur Llewelyn, 432, 457, 497, 498
Day, Lewis F., 295
Defoe, Daniel; *Robinson Crusoe*, 19
Degas, Edgar, 477
Delacroix, Eugène, 38, 45, 63
Delaroche, Paul, 38, 40
Delatre, Auguste, 289
De Morgan, William, 93, 193, 280, 285, 291, 417; *Joseph Vance*, 417
Desoye, Mme, 289
Deutsch, Emanuel Oscar, 189–91
Dickens, Charles, 11, 14–15, 63, 88, 152, 168, 170, 196, 198, 326, 343, 349, 390, 437; *David Copperfield*, 15, 418
Disraeli, Benjamin, 15, 322, 363; *Coningsby*, 334–5
Don (terrier), 396
Dowson, Ernest, 327
Doyle, Richard, 107, 166, 362
Duff Gordon, Miss, 104
Du Maurier family, 1, 2, 3

Du Maurier, Adelaide, 4
Du Maurier, Angela, 432
Du Maurier, Beatrix Isabel ('Trixie', Mrs Charles Hoyer Millar), 153–5, 174, 222, 223, 224, 227, 370, 379, 380, 398, 408, 409, 432, 437–8, 440, 457, 465, 477, 480, 481, 482, 483, 485, 498
Du Maurier, Daphne (Lady Browning), 89, 125, 196, 370–1, 432; *The Du Mauriers*, 25
Du Maurier, Ellen (née Clarke), 4, 5, 6, 7, 8, 9, 10, 11, 12, 13, 14, 15, 16, 19, 20, 22, 23, 24, 25, 26, 27, 28, 30, 31, 32, 43, 64, 69, 72, 73, 74, 77, 78, 81–2, 83, 84, 86, 89, 90, 92, 94, 99, 107, 115, 118, 120, 121–2, 123, 124–5, 131, 132, 139, 143, 148, 153, 171, 173, 186, 198, 199, 201, 326, 420, 483
Du Maurier, Emma (née Wightwick), 2, 16, 19, 26, 27, 77, 82, 83, 84, 87, 92, 95, 103, 109, 111, 116, 117, 118, 119, 120–4, 125, 129, 130–1, 132, 139–41, 142–3, 152, 153, 154, 155–6, 157, 158–9, 185, 188, 189, 190, 191, 192, 198, 199, 200, 201, 203, 207, 210, 216, 219, 222, 225, 227, 233, 236, 237, 240, 365, 368, 371, 379, 381, 382, 387, 401, 412, 432, 433, 435, 437–8, 439, 440, 457, 477, 482, 488, 493, 496, 498
Du Maurier, Eugène, 9, 10, 11, 12, 13, 14, 16, 17, 19, 20, 22, 25, 27, 31, 79, 121, 124, 125, 139, 201, 381, 432–3; children of, 381
Du Maurier, George Palmella Busson; childhood, 7–19; at school, 20–24; at University College, 24–8; analytical chemist, 28–31; art student in Paris, 24–63; in Antwerp, 64–68; loss of eye, 67–8; in Malines, 69–78; in Dusseldorf, 79–83; early years in London, 84–141; draughtsmanship, 13, 27, 109–111, 128, 136–9, 143–8, 237, 368–70; and Whistler, 90–7, 133–5, 289–90, 463–79; and Millais, 140, 232–3, 383–7; marriage, 140–3; family life, 153–4, 219–24, 379–81; on *Punch*, 22, 160–84, 240, 361–3; love of music; 19, 27–8, 50; and Canon Ainger, 389–91; and Henry James, 392–407; in Whitby, 156–8, 409–13, 482–3, 495–6; as poet, 373, 375; lecturer, 434–9, 440–1; death, 496

Illustrations for magazines (other than *Punch*) and books: *The admiral's daughters*, 128; *Adventures of Harry Richmond*, 370, 371; *Carità*, 370; *The Cicilian pirates*, 143–4; *Eleanor's victory*, 145; *Faristan and Fatima*, 109; *The hand of Ethelberta*, 368, 370; *Hurlock chase*, 144, 145, 146; *A Laodicean*, 361, 368–9; *London Bridge*, 128; *Misunderstood*, 370, 372; *Non satis*, 111, 118, 120; *Notting Hill Mystery*, 137, 138, 148, 447; *On her death-bed*, 111, 112; *The poisoned mind*, 447; *Prudence*, 259, 367, 369; *Santa*, 135–7; *Sylvia's lovers*, 148, 156, 410; *Three feathers*, 370; *Washington Square*, 370, 392, 393, 394; *Wives and daughters*, 148, 149, 150, 204; *Zelda's fortune*, 370

Paintings etc.: *Canon Ainger*, 370, plate 12; *Apollinaris label*, 212–3; *Beatrix Du Maurier*, 370; *May Du Maurier*, 370, plate 15; *Sylvia Du Maurier*, 370; *New Grove House*, 370–1; *Osbaldistone and Di Vernon*, 54; *Miss Faudel Phillips*, 371; *Thumping legacy programme*, 101, 102; *Time's revenge*, 371; *Two thrones*, 371

Novels and other prose works: *The illustration of books*, 157, 433–4; *The Martian*, 19, 20, 21, 22, 24, 65, 66, 69, 80, 82, 116, 117, 129, 143, 156, 184, 186, 227, 375, 380, 409, 412, 418, 478, 483–91, 495; *Peter Ibbetson*, 2, 10, 14, 15, 16, 17, 19, 20, 22, 23, 25, 26, 33, 34, 35, 204, 212, 214, 373, 377, 379, 413–5, 416–30, 442, 443, 449, 451, 454, 459, 460, 483, 484, 486, 489, 491; *Recollections of an English gold mine*, 29, 128–9, 417; *Social pictorial satire*, 434–7; *Trilby*, 1, 23, 35, 39–40, 41, 42, 43, 44, 45, 50–53, 55, 56, 57, 58, 60, 61, 72, 75, 80, 81, 94, 100, 106, 113, 114, 117, 125, 129, 132, 135, 148, 184, 186, 237, 308, 314, 350, 367, 376, 404, 413, 414, 417, 418, 421, 430, 441–62, 463–79, 486, 487, 491, 498; play, 398, 491, 496

Poems: *Aux poètes de la France*, 213, 214, 373; *The chime*, 373; *A lost illusion*, 214, 373; *Music*, 50, 373–5; *Nocturne*, 375; *Peu de chose*, 498

Aesthetic *Punch* cartoons (with those containing related material) –

Characters: Sir Pompey Bedell, 256, 257, 283, 299, 317, 327; The Cimabue Browns, 257, 264, 288, 301, 367; Mrs Cimabue Brown, 251, 257, 259, 269, 271, 287, 298, 301, 304, 307, 317, 327; The Colonel, 253, 255, 257, 271; Grigsby, 256, 257, 299, 307, 317, 327, 331; Maudle, 250, 251, 252, 253, 254, 257, 260, 261, 271, 287, 304, 327; Postlethwaite, 250, 251–3, 254, 257, 260, 261, 271, 277, 287, 298, 299, 300, 304, 307, 327, 468; Prigsby, 254, 255, 257, 264–5, 304

Punch cartoons: *Acute chinamania*, 269, 291, 292, 293; *Aesthetic love in a cottage*, 287, 301; *Aesthetic with a vengeance*, 287; *An aesthetic midday meal*, 299, 300; *The appalling diffusion of taste*, 256, 257, 259, 283, 299; *Art and fashion*, 295; *Art in excelsis*, 293; *Artistic amenities*, 304; *A Bargain*, 285; *The Cimabue Browns*, 288; *Chronic chinamania*, 257, 269, 290–1; *A damper*, 265, 276, 277, 285; *The diffusion of aesthetic taste*, 262, 263; *A dilemma*, 295; *Dilletantism*, 285; *A discussion on women's rights*, 253; *A disenchantment*, 293; *Distinguished amateurs: the art critic*, 254, 255, 257, 273, 304; *A faithful guardian*, 269, 297; *Feline amenities*, 295; *Fleur des alpes*, 244, 254, 299–300, 304, 307; *Flippancy punished*, 257, 278; *Frustrated social ambition*, 257, 287, 299; *A happy man*, 268; *The height of aesthetic exclusiveness*, 301; *Hygienic excesses*, 274, 277; *An impartial statement in black and white*, 273, 275; *Incipient chinamania*, 290; *Induction*, 295; *Intellectual epicures*, 277, 283, 297; *The line of beauty*, 278; *A love agony*, 260, 261, 299, 305, 306; *Maudle on the choice of a profession*, 252, 253, 304; *Modern aesthetics* (10 Feb 1877), 257, 266, 304, 306; *Modern aesthetics* (Almanack 1878), 272, 273; *Music and aesthetics*, 285, 286, 297; *Nincompoopiana* (14 June 1879), 278; *Nincompoopiana* (20 Dec 1879), 304; *Nincompoopiana*: the mutual admiration society (14 Feb 1880), 253, 271, 273, 298, 304; *Nincompoopiana*

(24 April 1880), 261, 299;
Nincompoopiana (Almanack 1881),
264–5; *Oil and water*, 287; *Old times*,
284; *On a broken eggshell*, 305; *The
passion for old china*, 290, 291; *Pet and
hobby*, 283; *Picture Sunday*, 302; *A
pleasant prospect*, 284; *Reciprocity*, 262;
Refinements of modern speech (7 Feb
1874), 302, 304; *Refinements of
modern speech* (15 Jan 1876), 302;
Refinements of modern speech (14 June
1879), 281, 282, 287, 305;
Refinements of modern speech (26 March
1881), 302; *Rise and fall of the Jack
Spratts*, 259, 261, 262–4, 266–7, 269,
270, 277–8, 279, 283, 284, 285, 297,
301, 302, 305–6, 417; *A scare*, 301
The six mark tea pot, 253, 293, 294;
A smart youth, 295; *Too literal by half*,
274; *True aesthetic refinement*, 274;
Vers de société, 302, 303, 304, 306;
A vocation, 283; *What we may come to in
time*, 297; *Where ignorance is bliss*, 273;
Other contributions to *Punch*:
Cartoons, 109–10, 128, 145, 148,
164–5, 237, 308–60, 390–1, 431, 477,
495; titles of, 315, 317; Characters,
Mrs Lyon Hunter, 317, 333–4; Sir
Gorgius Midas, 248, 317, 327, 334,
336–8, 339; Lady Midas, 331, 338,
359, 360; Duchess of Stilton, 317, 331,
333, 341; Mrs Ponsonby de Tomkyns,
248, 295, 317, 327, 331, 333, 334, 353
Individual cartoons: *Aesthetics*,
388; *All the year round*, 344; *The artist's
studio*, 109, 110; *At her old tricks again*,
343; *At the R.A.*, 385; *Awkward
revelations*, 323; *Bad grammar but good
pluck*, 348; 349; *A ballad of blunders*,
172–3, 180–3, 306, 373; *The benefit of
the doubt*, 215; *Breaking the ice*, 354;
Catching a weasel asleep, 333; *A clincher*,
325; *A combination of disagreeables*, 378;
Cricketiana, 408; *Delicate consideration*,
223; *Distinguished amateurs: the
reciter*, 317, 320; *A dodge*, 81;
Drawing room minstrels, 342;
Egoism, 323, 325; *Elements of mischief in
hypocritical repose*, 218; *Emancipation*,
351; *Equality*, 349; *Est modus in rebus*,
310, 311; *A fact. – (free translation)*, 229;
Farewell to fair Normandy, 315, 318;
Fifty years hence, 356; *A forlorn hope*,

351–2; *Frustrated social ambition*, 334;
Lady Gatheremall at home, 332; *A goodbye
to jolly Whitby*, 411; *Sir Gorgius on the
continong*, 336; *Hard times*, 338; *The
height of magnificence*, 338; *A hint to the
younger sons of our aristocracy*, 341;
Hobson's choice, 237; *Humility in
splendour*, 336–8; *Jenkins' dreams*,
356–7; *A jubilee private view*, 339; *Kind
and considerate*, 226; *Knowing one's place*,
324; *A legend of Camelot*, 87, 107, 172–
81, 183, 201, 305, 373, 434; *A little
Christmas dream*, 18, 357; *A lost
illusion*, 214; *Love's labours lost*, 317,
319; *Missusism*, 344; *Mistress and
pupil*, 331, 359, 360; *Modern social
problems*, 342; *Mokeanna*, 145, 147;
The new craze, 340; *The new society
craze*, 352; *Noblesse oblige*, 341; *Not
fond of steering*, 315; *A nuisance*, 352;
Old Nickotin, 357, 358; *The old order
changeth*, 339; *One of Mrs Ponsonby de
Tomkyns' failures*, 333; *L'Onglay à
Paris*, 172; *The ornamental v the useful*,
346; *Out of town*, 346; *Outward bound*,
351; *A pathetic appeal*, 315, 316, 321;
Picture Sunday, 321, 322; *Pleasant*, 336;
*Probable results of the acclimatization
society*, 165; *Reading without tears*, 217;
Ready, aye ready, 333; *Realizing the ideal*,
354; *The reward of merit*, 341; *The
ruling passion*, 344–5; *Scenes of club life*,
195; *The school-room as it ought to be*,
350; *The secrets of literary composition*,
354; *Self-respect*, 344; *The social
position of the actor*, 340; *Souvenir de
Fontainebleau*, 364, 365; *The tables
turned*, 349; *Tempora mutantur*, 340;
*Terrible result of the higher education of
women*, 354, 355; *Those yellow sands*,
349; *Thought is free*, 353; *Time's
revenge*, 371; *Mr Titwillow in Paris*,
189–191; *To sufferers from nervous
depression*, 202; *True humility*, 97, 312,
313, 319; *Two thrones*, 371; *Two
victims of the turf*, 341, 342; *The
Viqueens of Whitby*, 315; *Waiting for the
express*, 338; *What a pity*, 352; *What
next indeed*, 349; *What we may look
forward to*, 339; *Where the shoe pinches*,
350; *Whitsuntide humours*, 346–8;
The wrong boy in the wrong place, 344;
Yankee exclusiveness, 352

Du Maurier, children of George, 117, 153–4, 189, 191, 199, 204, 216, 219, 222, 224, 368, 379, 382, 391, 396
Du Maurier, Gerald, 216, 223, 224, 227, 340, 380, 387, 432, 434, 439, 457–8, 493, 496, 497, 498
Du Maurier, Guillaume, 4
Du Maurier, Guy Louis, 159, 194, 201, 203, 222, 223, 224, 231, 380, 386, 409, 432, 497, 498
Du Maurier, Isabella Louise (Mrs Clement Scott), 11, 13, 14, 16, 17, 25, 26, 27, 33, 43, 64, 77, 78, 79, 81, 82, 83, 84, 89, 105, 113, 119, 120, 123, 124, 131, 132, 139, 140, 143, 148, 153, 155, 171, 198, 199, 200, 201, 381, 432–3
Du Maurier, Jacques, 3, 4, 27
Du Maurier, Mme Jacques, 27
Du Maurier, Jeanne, 432
Du Maurier, Louis-Mathurin, 3, 4, 6, 7, 8, 9, 10, 11, 12, 13, 14, 15, 16, 17, 19, 20, 23, 24, 25, 27, 28, 30, 32, 326, 420
Du Maurier, Louise (Mrs Godfrey Wallace), 3, 4, 7, 8, 9, 11, 24, 27, 82, 121, 190
Du Maurier, Marie (Mme Eugène Du Maurier), 201, 433
Du Maurier, Marie-Françoise (née Bruaire), 3, 4
Du Maurier, Marie-Louise ('May', Mrs E. H. Coles), 82, 203, 223, 224, 225, 370, 380–1, 387, 432, 439, 440, 457, 477, 484, 498
Du Maurier, Robert, 3, 4
Du Maurier, Robert Mathurin, 2, 3, 4, 8, 60, 367
Du Maurier, Sylvia Jocelyn (Mrs Arthur Llewelyn Davies), 148, 201, 223, 224, 370, 379, 387, 432, 437, 439, 457, 483, 498
Dumas, Alexandre, 19
Dumas, Alexandre (the younger); *La dame aux camélias*, 445, 446–7
Dürer, Albrecht, 108
Duret, Théodore, 469

Eastlake, Charles Lock, 92; *Hints on household taste*, 281
Eliot, George; 88, 212, 230, 234–5, 353, 417; *Romola*, 370, 434
Elmore, Alfred, 24
English Illustrated Magazine, 373, 375
Eugénie, Empress, 35

Evans, Frederick M. ('Pater'), 164
Evans (actor), 492
Exmouth, Lord, 225

Fantin-Latour, Henri de, 48, 94, 99, 134, 289
Farmer and Rogers, 290
Faulkner, Charles, 283
Field, Basil, 206, 212
Field, Edwin Wilkins, 212
Field, Emily, 212
Field, Walter, 212, 497
Fine Art Society, 254, 399
Fitzgerald, William, 6
Flaubert, Gustave, 400, 401
Forbes, James Staat, 364, 365
Forbes Robertson, Ian, 458
Fortescue, Mrs, 82, 224n, 239
Foster, John, 196, 197
Francillon, R. E. 299; *Zelda's fortune*, 370
Fraser's Magazine, 88, 161, 162
Frere, Foster & Co, 473–4
Freshfield, Douglas, and Mrs, 381
Frith, 'Sissie' (Mrs J. E. Panton), 102, 142n, 153–4, 160, 168, 187, 191–2, 194n, 224
Frith, Walter, 409, 410
Frith, William Powell, 85, 158, 191, 219, 224, 225, 240, 409, 413; *The private view of the Royal Academy 1881*, 307, 386
Frith, Mrs, 158, 191, 219, 224, 225, 240
Froussard, pension, 19, 20–4, 230
Fry, Samuel, 384
'Fumette', 48
Furniss, Harry, 213, 362–3, 364, 365, 366, 376, 434, 478; *Confessions of a caricaturist*, 376–7

Galsworthy, John; *The Forsyte saga*, 382
Gaskell, Elizabeth Cleghorn, 88, 148, 212, 409; *Sylvia's lovers*, 148, 156, 410; *Wives and daughters*, 148, 149, 150, 204
Gatty, Alfred Scott, 409, 410
Gatty, Mrs, 410
Gautier, Théophile, 244, 245, 442; *Mlle de Maupin*, 243–4
Gellens, 76
Gentleman's Magazine, 284
George III, 5
Germ, The, 298
Gérôme, Jean-Léon, 40
Gilbert, John, 107, 125, 145, 166
Gilbert, William Schwenck, 175, 274;

Patience, 249, 250, 258, 274, 277, 278, 299, 301

Gillies, Margaret, 212, 236, 389

Gladstone, William-Ewart, 307, 322, 363, 367

Glascock, Ellen, 12

Glascock, William Nugent, 12

Gleyre, Charles, 37, 38, 40, 46; atelier Gleyre, 35, 37, 38–43, 46, 47, 54, 60, 62, 63, 64, 66, 79, 95, 103

Godwin, Edward William; butterfly suite, 293

Goncourt, Edmond and Jules, 289

Good Words, 88, 126, 127

Gordigiani, Luigi, 104, 105, 193

Gosse, Edmund, 396, 397, 406

Gosse, Mrs, 396

Grafton, H. P., 371

Grant, Albert, 335

Graphic, The, 241

Gray, Thomas, 181

Greaves, Walter, 293

Green, Edward, 54

Greenaway, Kate, 214, 333, 416, 434

Greville, Colonel, 28

Gros, Baron, 38

Grosvenor Gallery, 246, 251, 259, 261, 376

Guthrie, Thomas Anstey ('Fred Anstey'). 188n, 314, 362, 366, 381n, 409, 410n, 461n; *Vice versa*, 362

Haberton, Lady, 267, 268

Haden, Annie, 92

Haden, Joanna, 92, 135

Haden, Seymour, 92; 132, 135, 464

Hamilton, Walter, 246, 249–50; *The aesthetic movement in England*, 246, 250–1, 262, 285, 287n, 296

Handel, George Frederick, 61

Hardy, Thomas, 213, 214, 361, 368–9; *The hand of Ethelberta*, 368, 370; *A Laodicean*, 361, 368–9; *Tess of the D'Urbevilles*, 451; *The woodlanders*, 370

Hardy, Mrs, 213, 369

Hare, John, 458

Harper, Henry, 361, 442

Harpers, 368, 369, 428, 457, 472–6; *Harper's Monthly*, 361, 368, 399, 416, 429, 431, 458, 463, 466, 472; *Harper's Weekly*, 399, 461

Harrison, Alma (née Strettell), 482

Harrison, Laurence Alexander ('Peter'), 477, 482

Harrison, Leonard Fred ('Ginx'), 482

Harte, Francis Bret, 214

Haweis, Mary Eliza; *The art of dress*, 267, 274

Hawthorne, Nathaniel; *The scarlet letter*, 222

Healthy and artistic dress union, 267; journal of, 268

Heath's book of beauty, 88

Heffernan, Joanna, 94, 133, 135

Heinemann, William, 479

Henley, Lionel Charles ('Bill'), 79, 80, 90, 93, 94, 96, 98, 99, 111, 112, 141, 148, 482

Hennessy and Mrs, 210

Henschel, George, 216

Heyermans, Jean, 66

Hichens, Andrew K., 226–7

Hiroshiga, 289

Hodgson, John Evan, 192, 194

Hokusai, 289

Holiday, Henry, 208, 264, 268

Holiday, Miss, 264

Holmes, Oliver Wendell, 214

Hook, Theodore Edward, 93

Household Words, 88

Howard, George James (Lord Carlisle), 224, 239

Hughes, Arthur, 108, 434; *The long engagement*, 133; *Silver and gold*, 301

Hugo, Victor, 19, 23, 213

Huniker, 79, 474

Hunt, William Holman, 35n, 36, 37–8, 87, 103, 106, 108, 172–3, 434; *The Ballad of Oriana*, 176, 434; *The lady of Shalott*, 176, 434

Huth, 289

Huxley, Thomas Henry, 307

Ibsen, Henrik, 431

Illustrated London News, 87

Illustrated Times, 136

Impressionist painters, 46, 246

Ionides, Alexander A. ('Alecco'), 52, 53, 57, 95, 98, 99, 101–2, 111, 455, 456, 463

Ionides, Alexander Constantine, 57, 98, 106

Ionides, Mrs, 100

Ionides, Constantine Alexander, 99

Ionides, Luke Alexander, 57, 101, 102, 109, 425, 445; *Memories*, 448

Ionides, family, 89, 98–9, 100–3, 117, 118, 133, 152, 155, 209, 295–6
Ingres, Jean Auguste Dominique, 38, 45, 48, 63
Irving, Henry, 307

Jacquemart, 289
James, Henry (Senior), 395
James, Henry, 12, 44, 155, 188, 213, 214, 219, 232, 233, 248–9, 308, 309, 312, 314, 349–50, 363, 366n, 370, 373, 377, 380, 381, 382, 383, 384, 386, 389, 390, 392–407, 409, 412, 413–4, 417, 418, 421, 428, 429, 435n, 438, 440, 441, 442, 445, 452, 453, 454, 457–8, 461, 480–1, 482, 483, 493, 494, 495, 496, 497, 498
   The American, 395; The awkward age, 350–1, 395; Daisy Miller, 394; The Europeans, 395; George Du Maurier (Harper's Weekly), 399; George Du Maurier (Harper's Monthly), 399; George Du Maurier and London society, 395, 399, 405; Guy Domville, 493; The jolly corner, 489; Notes on drawings by George Du Maurier, 399, 405; Partial portraits, 395, 405; Portrait of a lady, 395, 405; Portraits of places, 405; The Princess Casamassima, 395, 404, 405, 413, 483, 484; The private life, 456; The real thing, 413; The reverberator, 405; Roderick Hudson, 395; The sense of the past, 413; The spoils of Poynton, 395; Washington Square, 370, 386, 392, 393, 394; The wings of a dove, 395, 402
James, Major William, 386
James, William, 393, 400
James, Miss, 389
Jeaffreson, John Cordy, 167
Jealous, Samuel, 234
Jeckyll, Peter, 112
Jeckyll, Thomas, 31, 77, 96, 112, 122, 130, 141, 295
Jelu, Charles, 66
Jerdan, William, 161
Jerrold, Douglas William, 161
Jewett, Sarah Orne, 483, 493
Joe Miller, 161
Jonson, Ben, 317
Jusserand, Jules, 396, 406–7, 429; English wayfaring life, 406

Kang Hsi (Old Nanking), 289
Keats, John, 213, 245; La belle dame sans merci, 245; Endymion, 245; Eve of St Agnes, 245; Isabella, 245
Keene, Charles, 96, 98, 105, 106, 108, 122, 126, 129, 160, 164, 167, 169, 171, 181, 184, 195, 203, 312, 314, 322, 435, 436
Keyser, Nicaise de, 64
Kidd, Dr, 377
Kipling, Rudyard; The brushwood boy, 425

Lamont, Thomas Reynolds, 44, 47, 48, 49, 50, 51, 52, 53, 54, 56, 57, 58, 60, 77, 98, 109, 110, 122, 129, 148, 195, 232, 383, 441, 448, 455, 497
Landells, Ebenezer, 162
Landseer, Edwin, 85
Langtry, Lily, 307, 340, 386–7
Laver, James, 248, 277
Lawless, Matthew, 111
Lawrence, David Herbert; Sons and lovers, 456
Lee, Vernon (Violet Paget), 90; Miss Brown, 249, 251, 258, 264
Leech, John, 77, 82, 87, 89, 105, 106, 108, 109, 122, 157–8, 159–60, 161, 164, 165, 166, 171, 172, 196, 201, 233, 267, 311, 321, 328, 343, 349, 370, 387, 393, 435–6, 496; The great social evil, 158
Leech, Mrs, 157–8, 159, 160, 201
Leech, children, 158
Leeuwe, Hofrath de, 77, 78
Legros, Alphonse, 48, 94, 99, 134, 155, 464–5
Lehmann, Rudolf and Mrs, 219, 224
Leigh, Percival, 164, 168–9, 203, 240, 361
Leighton, Frederic, 89, 103, 106, 108, 114, 184, 192, 195, 308, 434, 456; Salomé, 151; Romola, 370, 434
Leisure Hour, The, 144, 145, 146, 151, 154
Lemon, Mark, 109, 110, 116, 128, 160, 161, 162, 163, 164, 165, 166, 167, 168, 169, 181, 196, 199, 239, 240
Leopold, king of the Belgians, 158
Léotard, 129
Leslie, George Dunlop, 192, 210
Leslie, Mrs, 210
Levy, Angelina, 118, 119, 141
Levy, Annie, 118, 119, 141

Levy, family, 371, 454
Levy, Helen (Nellie, later Lady Faudel
  Phillips), 118, 141, 371, 377
Levy, Joseph, 119, 141, 143
Levy, Miriam, 95
Levy Lawson, Edward (Lord
  Burnham), 119, 197, 381
Levy Lawson, Mrs, 381
Lewes, Charles Lee, 73, 212, 235–6
Lewes, George Henry, 212, 230, 234–5,
  239
Lewes, Gertrude, 212
Lewis, Arthur, 104, 105, 106–7, 126,
  160, 163, 194, 196–7, 463
Lewis, Sir George, 471–2
Lewis, John Frederick; *Lilium auratum*,
  298
Lewis, Louisa, 81, 82, 118, 124, 139
Lewis (father of Louisa), 81
Leyland, Frederick Richard, 105, 295
Liberty, Arthur Lazenby, 290, 295
Liberty's, 274
Ligne, Prince de, 125, 455
Lika Joka, 161, 478–9
Lillie, Lucy Cecil; *Prudence*, 259, 367,
  369
Lindsay, Sir Coutts, 259
Linell, John, 205
Locker Lampson, Frederick, 219, 235,
  239, 377
London Journal, 145
London Society, 88, 128, 136, 142, 145
Louis XV, 14
Louis-Philippe, King, 20, 23, 418
Lowell, James Russell, 380, 399, 407,
  409, 410, 412–3, 495
Lowell, Mrs, 409
Lucas, Samuel, 126
Lucy, Henry, 26, 56n, 116n, 167, 312,
  314, 362, 363, 366, 431, 437n, 459n,
  480, 494n, 495n

McClure's Magazine, 1
Macdonald, Alexander, 384
Macdonald of Kepplestone collection,
  384
McIlvaine, Clarence, 79n, 442, 469n,
  471, 473, 474n
Maclise, Daniel, 85, 107
Magazine of Art, 433
Maginn, William, 161
Maître, Abel, 54
Major, Rosa, 100

Major, sisters, 100
Mallarmé, Étienne, 496
Mallock, William Hurrell; *The new
  republic*, 249
Malory, Sir Thomas; *Morte d'Arthur*,
  174, Dent edition, 243
Man in the Moon, The, 161
Manet, Édouard, 46, 289
Marillier, Henry Currie, 285
Maris, Matthew, 66
Marks, Henry Stacy, 39, 96, 105, 106,
  107, 122, 192, 194, 469–70, 471
Marks, Murray, 289, 290
Marot, Clément, 21
Marsaudon, Virginie, 75
Martini, Gaetano de, 296
Matthews, Charles, 439
Maupassant, Guy de, 400, 401, 402,
  406; *La maison Tellier*, 402; *Mlle Fifi*,
  402, *Les soeurs Nordoli*, 402, *Une vie*, 402
Mayhew, Henry, 161, 162
Mayhew, Horace, 163–4, 168–9, 196,
  203, 241
Menken, Adah Isaacs, 170
Menzel, Adolf Friedrich Erdmann, 308;
  Life of Frederick the Great, 126
Meredith, George, 134, 327, 349; *The
  egoist*, 353; *Harry Richmond*, 370, 371
Michaelangelo, 61, 62
Middlecoat, Miss, 188
Millais, Effie Gray (Mrs William
  James), 386–7
Millais, Euphemia Chalmers, 140, 233,
  387
Millais, John Everett, 36, 37, 54, 87,
  88–9, 92, 103, 106, 108, 111, 114, 115,
  140, 145, 148, 160, 161, 165, 172, 173,
  180, 184, 214, 231, 232–3, 239, 323,
  328, 357, 370, 380, 382, 383–7, 429,
  432n, 434, 440, 441n, 453, 482, 483,
  494–5; *A dream of fair women*, 434;
  Portrait of George Du Maurier, 386;
  Edward Gray, 434; *Locksley Hall*, 434;
  The talking oak, 434
Millais, Mary Hunt, 494
Millais, children, 233
Millar, Charles, Hoyer, 142, 209n, 213,
  222, 224n, 371, 379–80, 381n, 387,
  391, 398, 406, 408, 409, 410, 412n,
  432n, 440, 457, 458n, 492n, 493, 495n,
  497
Millar, Geoffrey Hoyer, 440, 481
Millar, Guy Darracott, 398, 440, 481

Millet, Jean François, 46, 365
Millet, Mme, 365
Milliken, Edwin J, 241, 366
Milton, John, 213, 306
Molière, 407
Monet, Claude, 42, 46
Monte-Naken, Léon; *Peu de chose*, 498
Montgomery, Florence; *Misunderstood*,
  370, 372
Moore, Albert, 180, 259, 308
Moray minstrels, 105, 194, 197, 198
Morgan, Matthew, 141
Morris, Jane, 208, 209, 258
Morris, Jenny and May, 208
Morris, William, 152, 173, 174–5, 176,
  201, 208, 209, 247, 278, 280–1, 283–4,
  293, 373; *The earthly paradise*, 208, 284;
  Oxford Union murals, 296–7, 305
Morris & Co, 280–1, 283–4, 293, 295–6,
  330; *Bird*, 297; *Fruit* 283; *Peacock and
  dragon*, 301; *Sunflower*, 297
Morton, Madison, 196
Moscheles, Clara, 76, 77, 113
Moscheles, Felix, 64, 65–67, 69–72,
  74–77, 78, 80, 81, 112, 113, 114, 151,
  219, 447, 451; *In Bohemia with Du
  Maurier*, 42, 113
Moscheles, Ignaz, 76
Moxon, Edward; Illustrated Tennyson,
  87, 108, 109, 176, 178, 434
Murger, Henri; *Scènes de la vie de
  bohème*, 43, 445–6
Musset, Alfred de, 48, 213

Napoleon I, 363
Napoleon III, 16, 34, 190, 363, 420
National Gallery, 62, 231
Nerval, Gérard de, 245
New English Art Club, 431
New York Herald Tribune, 409
Norman Shaw, Richard, 208, 214, 285
North, John, 108

O'Connor, William H., 58, 92, 96
Offenbach, Jacques; *Les deux aveugles*,
  194, 196, 198
Oliphant, Margaret; *Carità*, 370; *Dress*,
  267
Once a week, 87, 100, 106, 107, 109,
  110–11, 112, 118, 120, 126, 128, 129,
  135, 136–7, 138, 145, 148, 392, 447
Orléans, Charles d', 21
Orrinsmith, Lucy, 283; *The drawing
  room*, 283, 285
Osgood, James Ripley, 369–70, 428–9,
  442
Osgood McIlvaine, 429
Oxenford, John; *A family failing*, 196,
  198
Oxford book of Victorian verse, 373

Pall Mall Gazette, 209, 252–3, 267n,
  273n, 466–8, 469, 471, 473
Palmella, Duke of, 7, 8, 9, 11, 14
Palmella, Duchess of, 7, 8, 9
Palmella, eldest son of, 7, 9
Palmerston, Lord, 85
Pamphilon's, 96, 97, 98, 113, 116, 122,
  129, 152, 167, 441
Parsons, Alfred, 381
Pater, Walter, 246, 247, 249; *The
  renaissance*, 246, 264
Patmore, Coventry, 212
Pearson, Hesketh; *Life of Oscar Wilde*,
  247
Pellew, 225
Pennell, Elizabeth Robins and Joseph,
  40, 41n, 54n, 62n, 102n, 289n, 293n,
  469, 472
Pergolesi, Giovanni Battista, 193
Perrot, Sam, 123, 199
Pevsner, Nikolaus, 212, 231
Phidias, 62, 308
Phillips, George Faudel, 371, 377
Phillips, daughter, 371
Picot, François Édouard, 39
Pinwell, George, 108, 209, 370
Plawd, 60
Playfair, Mrs William, 491
Poe, Edgar Allen, 258; *Ligeia*, 425
Poland, Sir Harry and Mrs, 224
Polly, 119
Pope, Alexander, 213
Pope, the, 14, 60, 213
Potter, Beatrix, 233
Potter, Paul, 491; play of *Trilby*, 398,
  491, 496
Power, Harold, 194, 196, 197
Power, Tyrone, 194
Poynter, Agnes, 231, 232
Poynter, Edward John; art student in
  Paris, 40, 44, 48, 52, 53, 54, 56, 60, 61,
  63, 66; in London, 90, 96, 97, 98, 99,
  103, 108, 116, 117, 122, 129–30, 140,
  141, 144, 148, 152–3, 155, 184; and
  Whistler, 48, 61, 62–3, 465, 469,

470–1, 472; subsequent career, 231, 232, 233, 308, 382, 434, 456, 497; in *Trilby*, 53, 61, 455, 456, 463, 465–6, 469, 470–1, *Ten lectures on art*, 54, 62; P.R.A., 62, 231; paintings, *A bunch of blue ribbons*, 97; *Dante's angel*, 97; *The day dream*, 97–8, *Waltham Abbey ceiling*, 97
Poynter, Miss, 153
Praxiteles, 46
Pre-Raphaelite Brotherhood, 36, 86, 87, 108, 111, 155, 172–3, 175, 176, 178–80, 183, 205, 243, 245, 246, 247, 248, 249, 266, 296, 298, 301, 335, 426
Primoli, Count Napoleon, 406
Prinsep, Florence (née Leyland), 105, 232
Prinsep, May (Mrs Andrew Hichens), 226–7
Prinsep, Sara Monckton (née Pattle), 103, 104, 114, 225
Prinsep, Valentine Cameron, 39, 40, 41, 47, 56, 103, 104–5, 122, 130, 151, 192, 225, 231, 232, 454, 458; *A student's life in Paris*, 448; *Whispering tongues can poison truth*, 151
Prinsep, family, 89, 103–5, 152, 225
Prout, Father Francis Sylvester Mahony, 161
Prudhomme, Sully; *L'agonie*, 50n, 375, 373; *Prière*, 375
Puccini, Giacomo; *La bohème*, 445
Punch, history of, 161–2; dinner, 22, 42, 128, 132, 152, 162–4, 165, 167, 168–9, 170–1, 180, 182, 186–7, 203, 233, 362–3, 495, 496

Quarterly Review, The, 88
Quilter, Harry, 371

Rabelais Club, 213–4, 368; *Recreations of the Rabelais Club*, 213, 354, 373
Racine, Jean, 213
Raffaelli, Jean François, 40
Ragan, 26
Raphael, 62, 308
Rational dress society, 267
Read, Samuel, 87
Reid, Forrest; *The illustrators of the sixties*, 370
Reid, James; *Hampstead Heath in 1860*, 206
Renoir, Auguste, 42, 46
Rethel, Alfred; *Death the friend*, 126

Richardson, Samuel, 449
Richmond, Sir William Blake and Lady, 381
Ridley, Matthew White, 155
Ritchie, Anne Thackeray, 114–5, 353, 381, 396
Ritchie, Sir Richmond, 381, 396
Romer, Louise, 168
Ronsard, Pierre de, 21
Rossetti, Christina Georgina, 152
Rossetti, Dante Gabriel, 36, 46, 47, 87, 99, 103, 108, 117, 134, 152, 155, 163, 170, 172, 173, 174, 175, 176, 178, 179–80, 209, 245, 247, 248, 249, 258–9, 261, 262, 264, 285, 289–90, 296, 298, 306, 434; *Ballade des dames du temps jadis*, 174; *The blessed damozel*, 298; *Ecce ancilla domini*, 298; *Girlhood of Mary Virgin*, 298; *Lady of Shalott*, 176; *Llandaff tryptych*, 301; *Oxford Union murals*, 174; *Palace of art*, 434; *Rosa Triplex*, 179–80; *Sir Galahad*, 176, 434
Rossetti, Elizabeth (née Siddal), 174
Rossetti, Maria, 152
Rossetti, William Michael, 152, 264
Rowley, Joseph, 54, 63, 454
Royal Academy, 62, 85, 86, 90, 92, 97, 105, 114, 133, 134, 148, 151, 185, 232, 263, 384, 456; Royal Academy schools, 36, 37, 46, 48
Rubens, Peter Paul, 64
Ruskin, John, 15, 140, 170, 214, 245, 261, 466; *The aesthetic and mathematical schools of art in Florence*, 264; *The art of England*, 360; *Praeterita*, 15

St John's Wood clique, 105, 192–4
Sambourne, Linley, 240, 366
Sandys, Frederick, 105, 108, 126, 127, 128, 134, 175, 184, 434
Sara, la petite, 43, 451
Sarasate, Pablo, 216
Sargent, G. E.; *Hurlock Chase*, 144, 145, 146
Sargent, John Singer, 37, 91, 477
Sartoris, Adelaide, 114
Scheffer, Ary, 37, 38, 47
Schubert, Franz, 105
Scott, Clement William, 200–1, 381, 382
Scott, Dora (Mrs Footman), 381, 432, 433
Scott, George Gilbert, 208, 210

Scott, Mrs George Gilbert, 210
Scott, Margaret, 382
Scott, Walter, 19; *Ivanhoe*, 488
Shakespeare, William, 213, 386, 401;
    As you like it, 188
Shannon, Charles Haslewood, 184
Shaw, Bernard, 431
Shelley, Percy Bysshe, 213, 245
Sherard, Robert Harborough, 1, 2, 3,
    4n, 10n, 19, 20, 24, 28n, 32n, 67, 68n,
    114n, 182n, 300n, 414n, 480n, 483
Sichel, Edith; *Life and letters of Alfred
    Ainger*, 389, 390, 391n, 409, 433n,
    495n
Signorelli, Luca, 266
Silver, Henry, 22, 42n, 82, 107n, 128,
    132n, 152n, 158n, 160, 162–3, 164,
    166, 169, 170, 172, 180n, 181, 182,
    183n, 186–7, 196, 200n, 201, 240,
    290n
Silver, Mrs, 201
Sisley, Alfred, 46
Sketching society, 192
Sketchley, R. F., 203
'Skittles', 225
Slade school of art, 54
Smalley, George Washburn, 381, 409,
    412, 439, 482
Smalley, E., 439
Smalley, Mrs, 381, 409, 412, 482
Smith, George, 198, 212, 213n, 219
Smith, Mrs George, 219
Smith, Sydney, 93
Smith, Dr William, 224
Smith, W. Frank, 143
Smith and Elder, 148, 212
Solomon, Abraham, 115, 454
Solomon, Rebecca, 454
Solomon, Simeon, 173, 175, 182
Solon, Marc Louis Emmanuel, 289
Somers, Earl of, 104
Somers, Countess of (née Virginia
    Pattle), 103, 104
Sotiri, 57
South Kensington school of art, 62, 231,
    382
Spartali, Christine (Countess de
    Cohen), 100, 155
Spartali, Marie (Mrs Stillman), 100,
    155
Sprenk, T. A. G., 66, 72
Squire, Dr, 377
Stanley, Arthur, 239

Stephen, Leslie, 389
Stevenson, Robert Louis, 212
Stillman, William James, 155
Stirling, Arthur, 473
Stone, Frank, 88
Stonor, Francis, 192
Storey, George Adolphus, 191–2, 194,
    497
Stuart-Wortley, Andrew, 467
Sue, Eugène, 19, 23
Suisse, Charles Louis, 43
Sullivan, Arthur, 175, 194, 196, 197
Sunday Magazine, 172
Sutherland, Duchess of, 92
Swain, Joseph, 108, 237
Swinburne, Algernon Charles, 134, 170,
    173, 174, 182, 183, 213, 245, 247, 248,
    306, 373; *Anactoria*, 182; *A ballad of
    burdens*, 182–3; *Chastelard*, 182;
    Dolores, 298; *Poems and ballads*, 182

Taylor, Tom, 128, 163, 164, 168, 169,
    196, 198, 203, 240–2, 243, 361, 362;
    A wolf in sheep's clothing, 196
Tenniel, John, 88, 108, 160, 163, 164,
    166–7, 171, 186, 189, 196, 203, 312,
    314, 322, 361, 363, 458, 497
Tennyson, Alfred, 87, 103, 108, 176,
    180, 183, 213, 227, 434; *The ballad of
    Oriana*, 434; *A dream of fair women*,
    434; *Edward Gray*, 434; *The lady of
    Shalott*, 175, 434; *Locksley Hall*, 434;
    Palace of art, 434; *Sir Galahad*, 176,
    434; *The talking oak*, 434
Terriss, William, 491
Terry, Ellen, 103, 152, 170, 196, 198,
    199, 307
Terry, Florence, 196, 199
Terry, Kate, 107, 196, 199
Thackeray, Harriet, 114
Thackeray, William Makepeace, 63, 88,
    103, 114, 115, 129, 143, 148, 153, 161,
    308, 349, 417, 431, 459–60;
    Adventures of Philip, 370; *Henry Esmond*,
    115, 423; *Little Billee*, 56, 452–3;
    The Newcomes, 423; *Vanity fair*, 117,
    328, 331, 333, 459–60
Thompson, Sir Henry, 158, 233, 289–
    90, 417; *Charley Kingston's Aunt*, 26
Thomson, James (B.V.); *Sunday afternoon
    on Hampstead Heath*, 205–6
Times, The, 241, 242
Tintoretto, 62

Tissot, James Jacques Joseph, 289
Titian, 62, 308
Tomahawk, The, 161
Traer, 132
Traherne, Thomas, 419
Tree, Herbert Beerbohm, 491–2, 493, 496
Trin, Père, 58, 448
Trollope, Anthony, 88, 219, 341; *Autobiography*, 416; *Barchester towers*, 317; *Framley parsonage*, 353, 370; *The small house at Allington*, 370; *The vicar of Bullhampton*, 451; *The way we live now*, 335–6, 338
Trollope, Mrs Anthony, 219
Trollope, Thomas and Mrs, 230
Turgenev, Ivan, 400
Twain, Mark, 240
Twiss, Quentin, 191, 196, 197
Twiss, Mrs, 191

Ukiyoye school, 289
University college, London, 24, 25, 26, 27, 28, 35, 44, 47, 63, 231, 485

Van Lerius, Jacob, 64, 68
Varley, John, 205
Vaughan, Henry, 14, 419
Veronese, Paul, 62
Victoria, Queen, 35, 297
Victoria and Albert museum, 99, 382
Victoria gold and copper mine company, 28, 29, 30
Villon, François, 21, 174, 463; *Ballade des dames du temps jadis*, 174
Vinot, M et Mme, 53, 190
Virgil, 21
Vivier, Eugène, 235

Wales, prince of, 85, 194, 493
Wales, princess of, 107, 493
Walker, Frederick, 105, 106, 108, 130, 138, 158, 165, 184, 192, 195, 209, 370, 434, 453
Wallace, Godfrey, 7
Wappers, Gustav, 64
Ward, Henrietta Mary Ada (Mrs E. M. Ward), 119
Ward, Mary Augusta (Mrs Humphry Ward), 482
Wardle, George, 382
Wardle, Mrs George (née Madeline Smith), 382

Wardle, Gwilym Lloyd, 5
Watts, George Frederic, 99, 103–4, 106, 152, 170, 225, 227, 239, 268, 308; *Portrait of Lady Somers*, 104
Watts, Isaac, 221
Webb, Philip, 295
Webb, William, 453, 472–5
Weekly Dispatch, 200
Welcome Guest, The, 87
Westminster Budget, 479
Whistler, Anna Matilda, 135
Whistler, James Abbott McNeill; as art student in Paris, 39–42, 47, 48, 49, 54, 56–7, 58, 60–1, 62–3; early years in London, 86, 89–96, 97, 98, 99, 100, 101, 102, 103, 105, 107, 109, 110, 111, 113, 116, 117, 122, 130, 132, 133–5, 148, 155; china collection, 163, 247, 290; Whistler v Ruskin, 63, 245, 247, 261, 466; in *Trilby*, 39, 51, 52, 53, 55, 60–1, 135, 455, 456–7, 463–79; *The gentle art of making enemies*, 253–4, 302, 468, 479; paintings and decorative works; *At the piano*, 92; *The balcony*, 293; *Butterfly suite*, 293; *The coast of Brittany*, 133; *The golden screen*, 293; *The lange lyzen of the six marks*, 293; *The last of old Westminster*, 133; *Nocturne in black and gold : the falling rocket*, 261, 262, 263; *Old Westminster Bridge*, 94; *Peacock room*, 295; *Princesse du pays de la porcelaine*, 155, 293, 295; *The Thames in ice*, 94; *Wapping*, 94; *The white girl*, 92, 133; other references, 219, 247, 248, 259, 261–2, 278, 280, 289, 293, 296, 302, 308, 384, 453
White, Gleeson; *English illustrators : the sixties*, 109
Whymper, Fred H., 126
Wightwick, Mrs, 77, 82, 83, 84, 92, 116, 117, 121, 125, 129, 131, 136, 140–1, 143, 198, 326
Wightwick, Mr, 92, 116, 117, 121, 125, 129, 136, 140, 326, 339
Wilde, Oscar, 243, 246, 247, 252–4, 267, 273, 296, 297, 298, 300–1, 302, 306, 307, 468; *The picture of Dorian Gray*, 302, 304; *An ideal husband*, 330; *A woman of no importance*, 352
Williams, Florence James, 426
Williamson, Dr, 24
Wolseley, Lord and Lady, 493

Wolverhampton literary and scientific society, 435–7
Wood, Mrs Henry, 460
Wood, T. Martin, 242n, 321, 367n
Woolner, Thomas, 214
Wordsworth, William, 14, 419
World, The, 197
Wynfield, David, 192
Wynford, Lord, 79
Wyss, Johan Rudolf; *The Swiss Family Robinson*, 19

Yates, Edmund, 169, 191
Yates, Mrs, 191
Yeames, William Frederick, 192, 497
Yellow book, 243
York, Frederick Duke of, 5, 6, 483

Zambacco, Dr, 117, 118
Zola, Émile, 400, 401; *L'assomoir*, 401; *Germinal*, 401; *La joie de vivre*, 401; *Nana*, 401; *L'oeuvre*, 401, 445; *Rougon-Maquart*, 401